Zinoviy Otenskiy and the Trinitarian Controversy in Sixteenth-Century Russia

Studies in Medieval and Reformation Traditions

Edited by

Christopher Ocker (*Melbourne and San Anselmo*)

In cooperation with

Founding Editor

Heiko A. Oberman †

VOLUME 239

Texts & Sources

Edited by

Falk Eisermann (*Berlin*)

VOLUME 13

The titles published in this series are listed at *brill.com/smrtts*

Zinoviy Otenskiy and the Trinitarian Controversy in Sixteenth-Century Russia

Introduction, Texts, and Translation

Edited by

Viacheslav V. Lytvynenko
Mikhail V. Shpakovskiy

BRILL

LEIDEN | BOSTON

Cover illustration: Zinoviy's autograph, housed in Moscow, Russian State Library, E.E. Egorov Collection, F. 98, no. 337, the year 1566, ff. 28^{v}–29^{r}.

The Library of Congress Cataloging-in-Publication Data is available online at http://catalog.loc.gov
LC record available at http://lccn.loc.gov/2023003147

Typeface for the Latin, Greek, and Cyrillic scripts: "Brill". See and download: brill.com/brill-typeface.

ISSN 1573-4188
ISBN 978-90-04-22210-6 (hardback)
ISBN 978-90-04-53805-4 (e-book)

This book is printed on acid-free paper and produced in a sustainable manner.

Printed by Printforce, United Kingdom

Viacheslav V. Lytvynenko dedicates this book to his senior colleagues—Irina M. Gritsevskaya, Anna A. Pichkhadze, Pirinka Penkova, and William R. Veder—with gratitude for their shaping influence

Mikhail V. Shpakovskiy dedicates this book to the memory of his teacher who inspired him to study Slavonic medieval theology and philosophy—Vladimir V. Milkov

Contents

Preface and Acknowledgements

This book is about Zinoviy Otenskiy (d. 1571/2) and the Trinitarian controversy in sixteenth-century Russia. It is the first work in English written on this subject, and for that reason, we considered it important to provide a substantial introduction for those who may not be familiar with the controversy and its context. In our introduction, we sought to cover the most relevant issues of history, theology, and the text, paying special attention to things that would help readers understand Zinoviy's thought and the circumstances in which he lived and wrote.

Zinoviy was a monk from Great Novgorod (northwest Russia) but came to be known especially as an eminent writer who defended the Christian faith against the teaching that denied the Trinity, as well as a number of other key points of traditional doctrine, such as the deity of Christ and his incarnation. As a result, we have from him what is arguably the best theological reflection from the time of medieval Russia, and this edition provides carefully selected texts in which Zinoviy discusses the issues of the Trinity, Christ, and salvation. The first and shorter writing is the *Panegyric to St. Hypatius of Gangra*—an example of high rhetoric and fine argumentation—and the second and much longer text is the *Demonstration of Truth*, in which we see a man of profound theological thinking and Biblical exegesis.

A brief remark is needed to explain the phrase "Trinitarian controversy" in the title of this book. Strictly speaking, the sixteenth-century controversy in Russia was neither "Trinitarian", nor a controversy in the classical sense. First, it was not "Trinitarian" because many other doctrines also received significant attention, such as Christology, salvation, icons, monasticism, and others. However, since Zinoviy and his contemporaries involved in the controversy (especially Iosif Volotskiy and Ermolay-Erasm, who will be mentioned in this book) regarded the doctrine of God and the Trinity as foundational and placed it in the first place in their discussions, we believe it is legitimate to call the controversy "Trinitarian".

Second, the word "controversy" needs some qualification, too. Scholars disagree as to how widely the anti-Trinitarian teaching was represented in Russia, suggesting that its adherents could have been as few as several individuals or groups of people, or as many as numerous monasteries and possibly lay people. But, again, since we see Zinoviy interacting with the new teaching in a way that looks very much like a normal theological dispute—with questions, answers, and arguments based on Scripture, natural theology, and reason—we propose that it be regarded as a controversy.

Finally, we owe a word of thanks to our colleagues and students from Charles University (Prague, Czech Republic), the Institute of Philosophy of the Russian Academy of Science (Moscow, Russian Federation), Gordon-Conwell Theological Seminary (USA), and the Evangelical Theological Faculty (Leuven, Belgium). Their contributions in our formal and informal talks about Zinoviy stimulated the progress of our research and helped to sharpen its relevance. We are especially grateful for the opportunity to share and hear feedback from the Czech Patristic Society conference and the seminar of the University Centre for the Study of Ancient and Medieval Thought (both of which took place at Charles University in the fall of 2020).

We are thankful to Andrew Funka and Bruce Barron for proofreading various parts of our book. Lytvynenko's wife, Oksana, created the Index of Names and Biblical Quotations, and was his partner in conversation during the whole project, for which he is deeply thankful! Lytvynenko's work was financially supported by the Charles University Research Centre program No. UNCE/HUM/016, which enabled him to have the time and focus needed for this project.

We are grateful to the State Historical Museum in Moscow for providing the manuscript of Zinoviy's *Panegyric to St. Hipatius of Gangra*; and we are equally thankful to the Russian State Library in Moscow for making available the copy of Zinoviy's autograph of the *Demonstration of Truth*.

Lytvynenko wrote the introduction, and Shpakovskiy contributed in various ways, most importantly by identifying several theological and philosophical parallels to Zinoviy's thought in sect. 3, as well as drawing up a table of Zinoviy's Trinitarian terms. Shpakovskiy prepared the Slavonic texts of this edition, and Lytvynenko doubled-checked and translated them into English. The book as a whole is an example of how authors from two different backgrounds (Lytvynenko is an Evangelical Protestant; Shpakovskiy is Eastern Orthodox) can do things together in service to others and for the glory of God!

Viacheslav V. Lytvynenko, Prague, Czech Republic
Mikhail V. Shpakovskiy, Moscow, Russia
September, 2022

Tables

Abbreviations

Miscellaneous Abbreviations

AHG	I. Schiro, ed., *Analecta Hymnica Graeca. Canones Martii*, vol. 7 (Roma: Università di Roma, 1971).
CA 1, 2, 3	*Oration against the Arians* 1, 2, 3 (see Table 1)
Chron. Ham.	*Chronicle* of George Hamartolos (see Table 1)
Chron. 1512	*Chronicle of the Year 1512* (see Table 1)
CPG	M. Geerard, *Clavis Patrum Graecorum: Qua Optimae Quaeque Scriptorum Patrum Graecorum Recensiones a Primaevis Saeculis Usque ad Octavum Commode Recluduntur* (Turnhout: Brepols 1974–1979).
Diss.	Dissertation
DT	*Demonstration of Truth*
edn.	Edition
Ep.	*Epistle to the Bishops of Egypt and Libya* (see Table 1)
esp.	Especially
F.	Manuscript repository
f., ff.	Folio
Gr.	Greek
Grig.	"Apocryphal" *Life of Hypatius* (see Table 1)
n.	Note
no.	Number
Min.	*Life of Hypatius* in the commemoration service composed by Iosif the Hymnographer (see Table 1)
MLSDV	Monumenta Linguae Slavicae Dialecti Veteris
MS, MSS	Manuscript(s)
MS 61	RGB, MDA F. 173/I, № 61, seventeenth century, published in *Истины показание къ вопросившимъ о новом учении. Сочинение инока Зиновия* [*Demonstration of Truth to Those Who Inquired about the New Teaching. The Book of Monk Zinoviy*] (Казань: Университетская типография, 1863).
PL	*Protracted Letter*
PG	J.P. Migne, ed., *Patrologiae Cursus Completus*, Series Graeca (Paris: Garnier & Migne, 1847–1866).
Prol.	*Prologue Version of the Life of Hypatius* (see Table 1)
Pros.	*Enlightener* of Iosif Volotskiy (*Prosvetitel'*) (see Table 1)
r	Recto = right hand side
repr.	Reprinted

sect.	Section
stlb.	Columns
Und.	"Canonical" *Life of Hypatius* (see Table 1)
v	Verso = left hand side
Vita Ath.	*Life of Athanasius* (non-Metaphrastic version) (see Table 1)
VMCh	*Velikie Minei Chetii* (*Great Menaia Reader*)
⟨⟩	Insertions from ***MS 61*** (RGB, MDA F. 173/I, № 61, seventeenth century) in the English translation of *DT*
[]	Emendations in the English translation of *DT*
()	Clarifications in the English translation of the *Panegyric* and *DT* that are not part of the Old Slavonic text
+	A mark of scribal corrections in the manuscript

Biblical Abbreviations

Gen.	Genesis
Ex.	Exodus
Lev.	Leviticus
Num.	Numbers
Deut.	Deuteronomy
Josh.	Joshua
Judg.	Judges
1 Sam.	1 Samuel
1–2 Kgs	1–2 Kings
1 Chron.	1 Chronicles
Job.	Job
Ps.	Psalms
Prov.	Proverbs
Is.	Isaiah
Jer.	Jeremiah
Ezek.	Ezekiel
Matt.	Matthew
Mk.	Mark
Lk.	Luke
Jn.	John
Acts	Acts
Rom.	Romans
1–2 Cor.	1–2 Corinthians
Gal.	Galatians

Eph.	Ephesians
Phil.	Philippians
Col.	Colossians
2 Thess.	2 Thessalonians
1–2 Tim.	1–2 Timothy
Tit.	Titus
Heb.	Hebrews
1 Pet.	1 Peter
1 Jn.	1 John
Rev.	Revelation

Libraries and Archives

GIM	State Historical Museum, Moscow (Государственный исторический музей)
ONNB	Odessa National Scientific Library, Odessa (Одеська національна наукова бібліотека)
RGB	Russian State Library, Moscow (Российская государственная библиотека)
RNB	Russian National Library, Saint Petersburg (Российская национальная библиотека)
RSAAD	Russian State Archive of Ancient Documents, Moscow (Российский государственный архив древних актов)

Manuscript Collections

Egor.	Collection of E.E. Egorov (RGB, Moscow)
Golub.	Collection of A.P. Golubtsova (RGB, Moscow)
Grig.	Collection of V.I. Grigorovich (Odessa, Ukraine)
Kiril.-Beloz.	Collection of Kirilo-Belozerskiy Monastery (RNB, Saint-Peterburg)
MDA	Collection of Moscow Spiritual Academy (RGB, Moscow)
Sin.	Collection of Sinodal Library (GIM, Moscow)
Sof.	Sofia Collection (RNB, Saint-Petersburg)
Tro.	Collection of St. Sergius Trinity Monastery (RGB, Moscow)
Und.	Collection of V.M. Undolskiy (RGB, Moscow)
Usp.	Collection of Uspenskie Manuscripts (GIM, Moscow)
Uva.	Collection of A.S. Uvarov (GIM, Moscow)
Volok.	Collection of Iosifo-Volokolamskiy Monastery (RGB, Moscow)

A Note on Slavic Names

In most cases, the Slavic names of people and places are given in transliteration. Thus, Iosifo-Volokolamskiy Monastery is used rather than Volokolamsk Monastery of St. Joseph, Afanasiy rather than Athanasius, Feodosiy rather than Theodosius, Maksim Grek rather than Maximus the Greek, Mikhail rather than Michael, Fyodor rather than Theodore, and so on. In the rare cases where we spelled names differently (such as St. Sergius rather than St. Sergey), we considered it reasonable to follow the standard spellings accepted in literature. The patronymics are normally omitted except when they served as helpful markers of kinship or were part of the translated text in Slavonic. The titles of all works in Slavic languages are translated in accordance with the guidelines of the Chicago Manual.

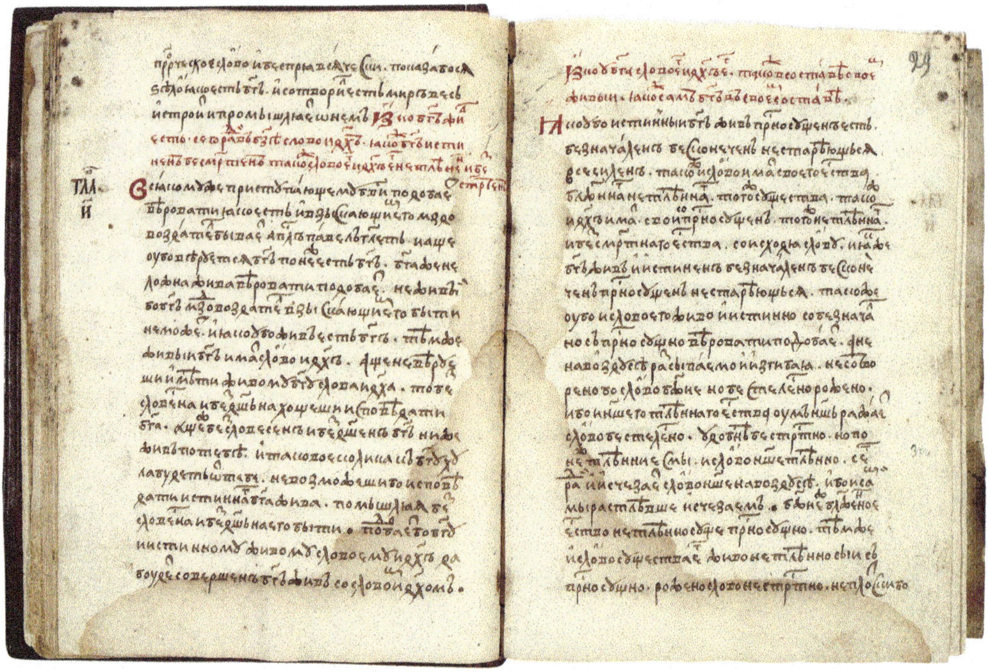

FIGURE 1 Zinoviy's autograph, housed in Moscow, Russian State Library, E.E. Egorov Collection, F. 98, no. 337, the year 1566, ff. 28ᵛ–29ʳ

FIGURE 2 An image of Zinoviy working on his book. Taken from the codex in Moscow, Russian State Library, V.M. Undol'skiy Collection, F. 310, no. 1190, the year 1708, ff. 8ᵛ–9ʳ

Introduction

1 Zinoviy Otenskiy and the Trinitarian Controversy

One day, most likely during the 1560s, a small group of Christians—two monks and one layman—visited the Otenskiy Monastery near Great Novgorod (northwest Russia), seeking answers concerning the recent teaching that (they claimed) had been spreading in the region since 1552.[1] In that monastery, they approached a monk by the name of Zinoviy Otenskiy, and after introducing themselves as kliros-chanters[2]—named Gerasim, Afanasiy, and Feodor—they ascribed that controversial teaching to a man named Feodosiy Kosoy.

In describing that teaching, they said, "It is commended and accepted by many, and many like this teaching and acknowledge it as being true, saying, 'No previous teacher has come to know the truth in this way, and no previous teaching has been such as this new teaching that appeared in the year 7060 [= 1551/52] since the creation of the world' ".[3] Around the same time, the so-called *Nikon Chronicle* recorded an entry under the year 1553, describing a teaching that had a striking similarity to the beliefs taught by Feodosiy Kosoy but that came from a different person:

> In the same year, a heresy emerged, causing agitation among people concerning an inappropriate way of describing God. Both the pious Tsar [Ivan the Terrible] and the Metropolitan Makariy made the investigation as to where that evil came from. And it was reported to the Tsar and the Metropolitan that Matyushka Semyonov, the son of Bashkin, together with his associates, Gregoriy and Ivan Timofeyevy, who were the sons of Borisov, as well as some others, belittle Christ, our Lord, thinking that the

1 DT 1.1. In this introduction, whenever we cite the *Demonstration of Truth* and the *Panegyric to St. Hypatius of Gangra* from the older editions, we indicate the Publisher (Kazan') for the former, and the editor's name (Koretskiy) for the latter. We also indicate the pages for any other Slavonic writings that lack numbered sections (books and chapters, as the case may be) in their editions.

2 Kliros is a special section in the Eastern Orthodox Church, in which the choir assembles to sing during the services.

3 DT (Kazan'), p. 15: "Множеми похваляемо и приемлемо, и любимо отъ многихъ, и познаваемо, яко истинно есть новое учение, и глаголютъ: никтоже отъ прежнихъ учителей тако истину позна, и не бысть иного учения такова преже, якоже новое учение, ныне явльшееся въ лете отъ создания 7060 [= 1551/52]". Russian Slavs used the Byzantine calendar, which placed the date of creation at the year 5508/9 before the incarnation of Christ.

 | DOI:10.1163/9789004538054_002

> Son of God does not exist, and [reject] the most glorious rites concerning the sacraments, and the liturgy, and the Eucharist, and the Church, and all the Orthodox who stand in the Christian faith. Both the Tsar and the Metropolitan ordered him to be seized and examined concerning that matter, even though he professed himself to be a Christian, hiding in himself the enemy's deceit, the heresy of Satan, for he assumed in his insanity to escape from the sight of the One who sees everything.[4]

Upon hearing about the new teaching from the kliros-chanters and not having previously been aware of its existence, Zinoviy accepted the challenge of taking their questions and answering them one by one over the course of ten meetings. The matter turned out to be more serious than he could have imagined, and one may want to remember that in the sixteenth century, "heresy" was much more than just novel thinking—it was illegal, punishable by severe state sanctions.

Taking the role of a Christian apologist seriously, Zinoviy discussed every single question posed by the kliros-chanters, and then put their conversations on paper, resulting in a massive volume (about a thousand pages of edited text),[5] completed in 1566 and entitled the *Demonstration of Truth*. Containing what most scholars consider the best theological reflections ever composed in medieval Russia, one half of this work discusses the practical issues of rites and worship in the Orthodox Church, such as icons, prayer, and monasticism. The other half of this writing (twenty-three of fifty-six chapters in the long version) is devoted to the doctrines of the Trinity, Christ, incarnation, and salvation, which were undermined by the new teaching.

---

4 *Полное собрание русских летописей: Летописный сборник, именуемый Патриаршей или Никоновской летописью* [*Complete Collection of Russian Chronicles: The Chronicle Miscellany Known as the Chronicle of Patriarch or Nikon Chronicle*], том 13 (Москва: Языки русской культуры, 2000), p. 232: "Того же лета прозябе ересь и явися шатание в людех в неудобных словес о Божестве. И царь благочестивый и Митрополит Макарий того посыскали, откуду сие зло изливается. И сказали царю и Митрополиту на Матюшку Семенова сына Башкина, что он с своими съветникы, з Григорием да с Ываном Тимофеевыми детми Борисова и с ыными, испражняют Владыку нашего Христа, непшуют Сына Божиа не быти, и преславная действа о Таиньстве и о Литоргии и о Причастии и о Церкви и о всех православных в вере крестьанской. И царь и митрополит велели его. изымав. истязати о сих; он же християна собя исповеда. скры въ собе вражию прелесть, сатанино еретичество, мняше бо безумьный от Всевидящаго Ока укрытися". All the Slavonic and Russian quotations are translated by Lytvynenko.

5 The entire text was published at Kazan' in 1863 and remains our only edition today: *Истины показание* [*Demonstration of Truth*].

Long before Zinoviy learned about that teaching from the kliros-chanters, he had already composed several other works, one of which was called the *Panegyric to St. Hypatius of Gangra* (probably written in 1551 or shortly thereafter), and about half of it offered refutations of those who rejected the Trinity and Christ's divine nature. In this much shorter treatise, Zinoviy treated the heretics as being active in Russia and described them as followers of Arius—a fourth-century priest from Alexandria, who was condemned at the First Council of Nicaea in A.D. 325 for denying the divine equality of God the Son with God the Father.

These are the two writings—the *Panegyric to St. Hypatius of Gangra* in its entirety, and parts of the *Demonstration of Truth*, comprising the Trinitarian and Christological chapters—that are offered in the present edition. Along with a handful of other texts and fragments, they represent the most significant surviving sources about the Trinitarian controversy in sixteenth-century Russia and also provide a unique window into the daily lives and thoughts of Christians at the time. Neither of the two texts has ever been made available in any translation, and their Slavonic editions (published in 1863[6] and 1965[7]) are clearly outdated according to modern standards. Therefore, the aim of this work is to provide a new edition and translation of these texts together with an introduction. In what follows, we will first outline the broader context in which Zinoviy lived and wrote (sec. 1), and then explore his two specific writings, focusing on the issues of authorship, dating, manuscript tradition, and Zinoviy's sources (sec. 2). After that, we will discuss his doctrine of the Trinity, Christ, and salvation, and explain the uniqueness and significance of Zinoviy's theology in that context (sec. 3).

We know very little about the author of our two texts from sources other than his own, and even that information is quite scant.[8] The date of Zinoviy's birth

---

6 *Истины показание* [*Demonstration of Truth*].

7 В.И. Корецкий, "Вновь найденное противоеретическое произведение Зиновия Отенского" [V.I. Koretskiy, "Newly Found Anti-Heretical Writing of Zinoviy Otenskiy"], in *Труды Отдела древнерусской литературы*, том 21 (Москва-Ленинград, 1965), pp. 166–182.

8 For some recent overviews of Zinoviy's life and work, see esp. Макарий, Архимандрит (Веретенников), "Зиновий" [Makariy, Archimandrite (Veretennikov), "Zinoviy"], in *Православная Энциклопедия*, том 20 (Москва: Церковно-научный центр "Православная энциклопедия", 2009), pp. 149–154, and his earlier article Макарий, Архимандрит (Веретенников), "Инок Зиновий Отенский—новгородский богослов XVI в." [Makariy, Archimandrite (Veretennikov), "Monk Zinoviy Otenskiy—Novgorodian Theologian of the XVI Century"], *Альфа и Омега* № 1/12 (1997): pp. 134–156; Золотухина, *Зиновий* [Zolotukhina, *Zinoviy*], esp. pp. 41–69.

is unknown, and our only information about him relates to his time as a monk at the Otenskiy Monastery (literally a "Monastery of the Fathers") in Great Novgorod.[9] Although the records of his death in the nineteenth-century inscription on his tomb at the Otenskiy Monastery are contradictory—giving dates of 1558 and 1571/2—most scholars agree that the later date is more likely one.[10] The fact that he was buried next to Iona (d. 1470)—the founder of the Otenskiy Monastery and the Archbishop of Great Novgorod—shows that Zinoviy was apparently a very well-respected man.

Beginning in the seventeenth century, several sources (such as some copies of his works)[11] depict Zinoviy as a disciple of a learned Greek monk from Mt. Athos by the name of Maksim Grek, born as Michael Trivolis (c. 1475–1556). In 1515, Maksim was sent to Moscow to do the work of translating and correcting the books, but found himself in trouble after introducing some linguistic innovations in the liturgical texts and taking a stand against the politics of the Grand Prince Vasiliy III and the religious party that supported him.[12] As a result, he was repeatedly found guilty and kept under arrest—first at the Iosifo-Volokolamskiy Monastery near Volokolamsk in 1525, and then at the Otroch-Uspenskiy Monastery at Tver' in 1531. Based on this, some argue that Zinoviy could have been consigned to the Otenskiy Monastery to share the fate of his teacher. Zinoviy does say that he had the occasion to visit Moscow early in his life,[13] but we do not have any direct evidence to prove that he was connected

9 On the origin and history of the Otenskiy Monastery, see Ф. Калугин, *Зиновий, инокъ Отенский, и его богословско-полемические и церковно-учительные произведения. Исследование* [F. Kalugin, *Zinoviy, the Monk of the Otenskiy Monastery, and his Theological-Polemical and Church-Didactic Writings. A Study*] (Санкт-Петербург: Типография А. Катанскаго, 1894), p. 86; Н.М. Золотухина, *Зиновий Отенский о власти, праве и правосудии* [N.M. Zolotukhina, *Zinoviy Otenskiy on Power, Law, and Administration of Justice*] (Москва: Норма Инфра-М, 2013), p. 43.

10 This is argued best by В.И. Корецкий, "Христологические споры в России (середина XVI в.)" [V.I. Koretskiy, "Christological Controversies in Russia (mid-XVI century)"], in *Вопросы истории религии и атеизма*, том 11 (Москва: Изд-во Академии наук СССР, 1963), pp. 334–335.

11 E.g., DT (Kazan'), p. 11: "This book belongs to a certain monk, *kyr* Zinoviy, who put [much] effort and work in composing it. He lived in the Russian land, at a monastery called Otenskaya Pustyn', which is in famous Great Novgorod, and he was a former disciple of the elder Maksim Grek" ("Сия книга счинена подвигомъ и трудами некоего черноризца киръ Зиновия, житие имуща въ российстей земли, славнаго и великаго Новаграда въ монастыре зовомомъ Отня пустыня, ученика бывшаго старца Максима Грека").

12 For a helpful description of Maksim Grek in the context of the Russian heresies, see И.Я. Фроянов, *Драма русской истории. На путях к опричнине* [I.Ya. Froyanov, *Drama of Russian History. On the Ways to Oprichnina*] (Москва: Парад, 2007), pp. 156–187.

13 DT (Kazan'), p. 938.

with Maksim there. Many scholars agree, though, that Zinoviy was significantly influenced by Maksim's works,[14] and some suggest the possibility that he could have even learned Greek from Maksim (based on some linguistic expositions that Zinoviy presents in his writings).[15] Those who do not believe that Zinoviy was Maksim's disciple note that the former often disputed certain ideas of the latter in his *Demonstration of Truth*, and they contend that Zinoviy's place in the Otenskiy Monastery does not need to be linked with Maksim's situation.[16]

Compared to the personal information about Zinoviy, our knowledge about him as a writer is more than sufficient to say that he was a man of encyclopedic mind and incredible erudition. One contemporary description praises Zinoviy as an extraordinary intellectual whose knowledge clearly surpassed most of the educated people of his time:

> Zinoviy easily applied Greek mythology (making references to the Greek deities such as Cronus, Zeus, Apollo, Artemis, Aphrodite, Poseidon, Hephaestus, Hera, and others), ancient literature (making mentions of Zenon, Plato, Menander, and others), and Byzantine history (showing that he knew the *Chronicles* of John Malalas and George Hamartolos). He constantly drew from the biblical texts (both Old and New Testaments) and the works of the Church Fathers (making appeals to Dionysius the Areopagite, Origen, Athanasius of Alexandria, Cyril of Jerusalem, Gregory the Theologian, Basil the Great, Gregory of Nyssa, John Chrysostom, Gennadius of Constantinople, Theodoret of Cyrus, John Climacus, John of Damascus, Symeon the New Theologian, Nikon of the Black Mountain, and others).[17]

---

14 E.g., А.И. Клибанов & В.И. Корецкий, "Послание Зиновия Отенскому дьяку Я.В. Шишкину" [A.I. Klibanov and V.I. Koretskiy, "Zinoviy's Letter to the Otenskiy Dyak Ya.V. Shishkin"], in *Труды Отдела древнерусской литературы*, том 17 (Москва–Ленинград: Академия наук СССР, 1961), pp. 209–210.

15 This view is held by such scholars as Л.Е. Морозова, *Сочинения Зиновия Отенского* [L.E. Morozova, *Works of Zinoviy Otenskiy*] (Москва: Институт истории СССР, 1990), p. 82; and Д.М. Буланин, "Зиновий Отенский" [D.M. Bulanin, "Zinoviy Otenskiy"], in *Словарь книжников и книжности Древней Руси*, выпуск 2 (вторая половина XIV–XVI в.), часть 1: А–К (Ленинград: Наука, 1988), p. 354. It is rejected by R.M. Mainka, *Zinovij von Oten'. Ein russischer Polemiker und Theologe der Mitte des 16. Jahrhunderts* (Roma: Pontificium Institutum Orientalium Studiorum, 1961), p. 17.

16 For the most developed argument, see Mainka, *Zinovij von Oten'*, pp. 11–28.

17 Золотухина, *Зиновий Отенский* [Zolotukhina, *Zinoviy Otenskiy*], pp. 50–51 (we modified the list of the Church Fathers to place them in chronological order). For similar evaluations, see Калугин, *Зиновий* [Kalugin, *Zinoviy*], I–III; and В.И. Корецкий, "Новые

Zinoviy's contribution for which he is most remembered has to do with his role in the history of the Trinitarian controversy in sixteenth-century Russia. Placing Zinoviy in this larger context leads us to another major precedent of denouncing the Trinity and Christ's divine nature in medieval Russia. That precedent is associated with the movement known in church terminology as a heresy of the "Judaizers" (in view of its connection with Judaism) that was spread in Great Novgorod and Moscow during 1470–1510.[18] While it could have developed from an earlier group known as "Strigolniki" (established in Pskov, Great Novgorod, and Tver' in the mid-fourteenth and early fifteenth centuries), the Judaizers' consistent rejection of the Trinity and Christ's divinity was a new feature with no parallel in previous times. To defend these two doctrines, the church leaders did two things (among others): they wrote polemical writings and copied anti-heretical books.

Most of the polemical works composed during that period came from the Archbishop of Great Novgorod, Gennadiy (1410–1505), and his younger contemporary, hegumen of the Iosifo-Volokolamskiy Monastery, Iosif Volotskiy (1439–1515). The five letters written by Gennadiy between 1487 and 1490,[19] and Iosif's main polemical work, the so-called *Enlightener* (*Prosvetitel'*, composed of sixteen Discourses in the long version and eleven Discourses in the short version)[20] are among the chief sources we have on the Judaizers today. Both

---

послания Зиновия Отенского" [V.I. Koretskiy, "New Letters of Zinoviy Otenskiy"], in *Труды Отдела древнерусской литературы*, том 25 (Москва–Ленинград: Академия наук СССР, 1970), p. 123.

18 Scholars disagree about the exact origin and nature of this movement. For a survey of the major views, see А.И. Алексеев, *Религиозные движения на Руси последней трети XIV–начала XVI в.: стригольники и жидовствующие* [A.I. Alekseyev, *Religious Movements in Rus' During the Last Third of the XIV–Early XVI Centuries: Strigolniki and Judaizers*] (Москва: Индрик, 2012), pp. 215–250.

19 The letters are published by Н.А. Казакова & Я.С. Лурье, *Антифеодальные еретические движения на Руси XIV–начала XVI века* [N.A. Kazakova & Ya. S. Lurie, *Anti-Feudal Heretical Movements in Rus'*] (Москва–Ленинград: Изд-во Академии наук СССР, 1955), pp. 305–382. For the best discussion of the letters, see Алексеев, *Религиозные движения* [Alekseyev, *Religious Movements*], pp. 251–269. Gennadiy's work is described by A. Pliguzov, "Archbishop Gennadii and the Heresy of the 'Judaizers'", *Harvard Ukrainian Studies* 16.3/4 (1992): pp. 269–288.

20 *Enlightener* is published in *Просветитель или обличение ереси жидовствующихъ. Творение преподобного Отца нашего Иосифа, Игумена Волоцкаго* [*Enlightener or Refutation of the Heresy of the Judaizers. The Writing of our Revered Father, Iosif, Hegumen of the Volotskiy Monastery*], изд. третье (Казань: Типо-литография Императорскаго Университета, 1896). For the best discussion of the *Enlightener*, see Алексеев, *Религиозные движения на Руси* [Alekseyev, *Religious Movements*], pp. 292–382. A short overview of Iosif's life and works is available in V.V. Lytvynenko, "Joseph von Wolokolamsk", in *Biographisch-*

writers treated the Russian heretics as "Judaizers" because of their focus on the Old Testament and contrasted them with Christians.[21] Whereas the primary concern in Gennadiy's letters was to combat the issue of iconoclasm, Iosif's *Enlightener* gave equal attention to all the major tenets denounced by that movement, beginning with the doctrine of the Trinity and Christology in the first and second Discourses. He continued that discussion in several other Discourses as well as his *Letter to the Archimandrite Vassian on the Holy Trinity*,[22] and in one of the Discourses he put special effort into showing that the three angels who visited Abraham at the Oak of Mamre (Gen. 18) were the three persons of the Trinity rather than God with two angels. This argument, along with others, inspired Zinoviy as he later built his own—much more elaborate—proofs of the Trinity in his *Demonstration of Truth* (more on this later).

Copying books was another way of refuting the Judaizers, and Gennadiy made it one of his primary tasks in Great Novgorod. He sent out letters to Russian monasteries inquiring about specific writings, and then had a team of scribes copy them in his scriptorium at the Church of St. Sophia. An often-quoted example is his letter (sent in the year 1489) to the former Archbishop of Rostov and Jaroslavl' Ioasaf (d. in 1514), in which Gennadiy asked him about the twelve specific titles needed to counter the new teaching:

> Do you happen to have these books in the Kirilov, or Ferapontov, or Kamenny Monasteries: *Roman Pope Sylvester, Athanasius of Alexandria, Oration of Cosmas the Priest Against the Newly Arisen Heresy of Bogomil, Epistle of Patriarch Photius to the Bulgarian Prince Boris, Prophets, Gene-*

---

bibliographische Kirchenlexikon, Band XL (Nordhausen: Verlag Traugott Bautz GmbH, 2019), pp. 3–5.

21 E.g., *Enlightener* 1, p. 32 uses the following expressions to describe the Judaizers: "they think in the Jewish way"; "they are Judaizers"; "they teach Jewish things"; "into the Jewish faith"; and "Judaizing" (жидовскаа мудръствующꙋ; жидове; наꙋчиша жидовствꙋ; в жидовскꙋю вѣрꙋ; жидовствовати). And it contrasts them with Christians: "those who think in the Christian way"; "Christians", and "Christianity" (хр҇тїаньскаа мꙋдрьствꙋющꙋ; хр҇тїане; хр҇тїанство), on pp. 31–32. It should be noted that the distinction involved no racial judgment and had to do only with the differences in faith.

22 On the relation between the *Enlightener* and the *Letter to the Archimandrite Vassian on the Holy Trinity*, see Алексеев, *Религиозные движения* [Alekseyev, *Religious Movements*], pp. 318–324. The letter is published by Казакова & Лурье, *Антифеодальные движения* [Kazakova & Lurie, *Anti-Feudal Movements*], pp. 305–309. For a brief survey of each Discourse, see А.И. Алексеев, *Сочинения Иосифа Волоцкого в контексте полемики 1480–1510* [A.I. Alekseyev, *The Writings of Iosif Volotskiy in the Context of the 1480–1510 Polemic*] (Санкт-Петербург: Российская национальная библиотека, 2010), pp. 52–55.

sis, *Kings*, *Proverbs*, *Menander*, *Joshua ben Sira*, *Logic*, and *Dionysius the Areopagite*? The heretics have all these books.[23]

For Gennadiy, the fact that the heretics had all those books made it all the more important that Christian apologists should have them as well. Clearly, the one book from Gennadiy's list that worked best for his purposes of defending the Trinity was Athanasius of Alexandria (c. A.D. 295–373), whose famous work, *Orations against the Arians*, was composed to rebut the heresy that depicted Christ and the Holy Spirit as lesser beings than God the Father.[24] Of the ten surviving copies of that work in the Slavonic translation, half of them date from the time of Gennadiy, and two make a direct reference to his name in the colophons.[25] One of such copies preserved a note written by Veniamin Timofeyev in 1489, reporting that the teaching of the Judaizers was promoted by both clergy and laypeople and seemed to have attacked the most fundamental Christian beliefs, specifically the doctrine of the Trinity:

> In that year, here in famous Novgorod, many priests and deacons—including those from simple folks—appeared to profane the pure faith. The town was overtaken by great trouble, and much darkness and suffering befell this place [and] the holy Orthodox faith, which the Holy Fathers set down at the seven Councils by preaching the Father and Son and Holy Spirit in the one divine inseparable Trinity … However, it did not take long for the holy Archbishop Gennadiy to expose the wickedness of their heretical teaching after he was filled with God's grace of the Holy Spirit.[26]

---

23 RGB, Tro. F.304, № 730, f. 252ᵛ: да е̑с ли ꙋ ва̑с в кириловѣ, или в фарофѡ̑нтовѣ, или на каменнѡ̑м, книги, селивестръ папа ри̑мскы̏, да афанасеи алексан̑дрѣискы̏, да слово ко̑змы прозвѵ̑тера, на новоꙗвльшꙋю̑с ересь на богꙋмилю. да посланїе фотѣꙗ патрїарха, ко кн҃зю борисꙋ болгарьскомꙋ. да п̑о̑ррчьства. да бы̑тиꙗ. да ц̑ср̑тва, да при̑тчи. да менандръ. да і҃соу сѵ̑рахов. да логика. да деѡнисеи арепаѡги̑т. зане̑ж тѣ книги, оу еретико̑вс е̑с. The letter is published with a brief introduction in Казакова & Лурье, *Антифеодальные движения* [Kazakova & Lurie, *Anti-Feudal Movements*], pp. 315–320 (the quoted passage is on p. 320). Since no answer from Ioasaf has survived, scholars dispute whether Gennadiy's letter was intended to request those twelve books from Ioasaf, or rather to provide them to him if he lacked any. For the most recent argument that supports the latter view, see V.V. Lytvynenko, *Athanasius of Alexandria, Oratio II contra Arianos: Old Slavonic Version* and *English Translation*, Patrologia Orientalis 248 (56.3) (Turnhout: Brepols, 2019), p. 18.

24 J. Behr, *The Nicene Faith: Formation of Christian Theology*, vol. 2, part 1 (New York: St. Vladimir's Seminary Press, 2004), pp. 207–249.

25 For an overview of the manuscripts, see Lytvynenko, *Oratio II contra Arianos*, pp. 23–28.

26 RGB, Volok. F. 113, № 437, the year 1489, f. 237ᵛ: в то лѣто здесе въ преимѣнитѡ̑м тꙋ неꙋполеѡс⟨е⟩ мнози с҃щенникы и дїакони; и ѿ просты̏х людїи дїаки ꙗвилисѧ сквернители на вѣрꙋ

Significantly, one of the copies of the *Orations against the Arians* came to serve as a principal resource to Zinoviy, and he used Athanasius to counter the Russian heretics throughout the first half of his *Panegyric to St. Hypatius of Gangra* (to be discussed later). Clearly, there is a sense in which Zinoviy is continuous with Gennadiy and Iosif when building on their works.

At the same time, scholars disagree about whether the heresy in Zinoviy's time was connected with the Judaizers, or influenced by the European Reformation, which reached Russia through the neighboring Grand Duchy of Lithuania and the Kingdom of Poland, or both.[27] If the first is true, then the heresy was of local origin. If the second or third is true, then to some extent, it was a Western product associated with the radical strand of Protestantism active in the region of the Polish-Lithuanian Commonwealth, which covered (after 1569) large portions of today's Lithuania, Poland, Latvia, Belarus, Ukraine, and Russia. Scholars also dispute whether the heresy was widespread.[28] They agree,

---

непорочнꙋю велика бѣда постигла гра҇ сеи и колика тма и тꙋга постиже мѣсто се ст҃ꙋю вѣрꙋ православїа что запечатлѣша ст҃їи ѿц҃и седмъ събѡр; проповѣдїю ѿц҃а и с҃на и ст҃го д҃ха въ тр҇ци едїно бж҇тво нераздѣлимо. Нъ҇ въскорѣ испълнися о б҃зѣ бл҃гти; д҃ха ст҃аго. прес҃щнны҇ архїеписко҇ генадїе; ѡбнажилъ й еретичества злодѣиство. This passage has been published multiple times, and most recently in Lytvynenko, *Oratio II contra Arianos*, p. 19.

27 The most recent overview of scholarly views on this issue is available in Золотухина, *Зиновий* [Zolotukhina, *Zinoviy*], pp. 26–35 and esp. 69–78. An especially elaborate example of describing the heresy as primarily evolving from the teaching of the Judaizers is Фроянов, *Драма русской истории* [Froyanov, *Drama of Russian History*], pp. 156–252. An example of seeing the heresy as significantly shaped under Western influences is M.B. Дмитриев, *Православие и Реформация: Реформационные движения в восточнославянских землях Речи Посполитой во второй половине XVI в.* [M.V. Dmitriev, *Orthodoxy and Reformation: Reformational Movements in the East-Slav Lands of the Polish-Lithuanian Commonwealth in the Second Half of the XVI Century*] (Москва: Изд-во Московского университета, 1990), pp. 67–97. An example of seeing both Russian and Western influences at work is Калугин, *Зиновий* [Kalugin, *Zinoviy*], pp. 44–80.

28 Most of the Russian scholars writing before 1917 suggested that the heresy was not significantly widespread, while most of the Soviet scholars writing between 1922 and 1991 argued that the heresy was widely popular among the people of the lower class and was an expression of the social protest against the exploitation of the poor by the rich. A good example of the former is И. Емельянов, "Учение Феодосия Косого" [I. Yemel'yanov, "The Teaching of Feodosiy Kosoy"], *Труды Киевской духовной академии* 6 (1862): pp. 212–213. Two classic examples of the latter are A.A. Зимин, *И.С. Пересветов и его современник. Очерки по истории русской общественно-политической мысли середины XVI века* [A.A. Zimin, *I.S. Peresvetov and his Contemporaries. Essays on the History of Russian Social and Political Thought in the mid-XVI Century*] (Москва: Изд-во Академии наук СССР, 1958), pp. 143–214; and A.И. Клибанов, *Реформационные движения в России в XIV–первой половине XVI вв.* [A.I. Klibanov, *Reformational Movements in Russia in the XIV–First Half of the XVI Centuries*] (Москва: Изд-во Академии наук, 1960), pp. 252–302.

however, that both before and during the time of Zinoviy, the heretical movements clearly denied the most fundamental doctrines of the Christian faith—the Trinity and Christ's divine nature.

When it comes to the main protagonist of the heresy, whom the kliros-chanters introduced to Zinoviy as Feodosiy Kosoy in the 1560s, scholars suggest that at least two other names came into play and could have possibly influenced what was viewed as his "new" teaching: Matvey Bashkin (d. second half of the sixteenth century) and Elder Artemiy (d. early 1570s). Before we come to learn anything of Kosoy in the surviving documents (of which the *Demonstration of Truth* is our leading source, and another is the so-called *Protracted Letter* to be discussed later), we first hear of Matvey Bashkin, who was found guilty of heretical teaching and consequently condemned by the Church Council at Moscow in December of 1553.[29] The *Nikon Chronicle*, cited in the opening paragraph of this introduction, claimed that he held erroneous beliefs about Christ, the sacraments (specifically the Eucharist), the liturgy, and the Church.[30] Among the conciliar charges, there was an accusation that "Matvey composed a prayer to the One Principle—he wrote of God the Father alone, leaving out the Son and the Holy Spirit",[31] which is all we know about his doctrine of God.

Bashkin acknowledged that he was influenced by two fellows from Lithuania, whom he identified as "Latins",[32] and we have no direct evidence that either he or the two people he followed had a direct link with Kosoy. The one person who did have such a link was Elder Artemiy, an esteemed monk from the Porfiriev Monastery in Beloozero (today's Belozersk, in northwest Russia). By that time, Beloozero and the entire Transvolga region (the territory to the east of the Volga River) were known as the leading center of a trend that promoted a somewhat liberal attitude towards a whole set of issues and was often viewed with suspicion by Moscow. This trend came to be known as a movement of the

---

29 For a helpful discussion of Bashkin's trial and accusations, see Фроянов, *Драма русской истории* [Froyanov, *Drama of Russian History*], pp. 195–197.

30 *Полное собрание русских летописей* [*Complete Collection of Russian Chronicles*], p. 232.

31 *Акты Археографической экспедиции* [*The Acts of the Archeographic Expedition*], том 1, № 239 (Санкт-Петербург: Императорская академия наук, 1836), p. 253: "написал Матфей молитву к единому началу, Бога Отца единого написал, а Сына и Святого Духа оставил". For a discussion of the accusations, see Фроянов, *Драма русской истории* [Froyanov, *Drama of Russian History*], pp. 195–198.

32 *Полное собрание русских летописей* [*Complete Collection of Russian Chronicles*], pp. 232–233: "He took his evil teaching from Lithuania: from the pharmacist Matyushka and Andryushka Choteyev, the Latins" ("злое учение принял от Литвы, Матюшки Обтекаря да Онъдрюшки Хотеева Латынников").

"non-possessors", or followers of Nil Sorskiy (ca. 1433–1508), and their stand on a number of issues differed from that of the "possessors", or followers of Iosif Volotskiy (1439–1515). The non-possessors normally maintained conservative views on all the fundamental tenets of the Christian faith but differed from the possessors on the question of whether it was appropriate for monasteries to own land, which they answered negatively. Some other differences included a focus on the inner spiritual life (also known as hesychasm—a mystical tradition of contemplative prayer) as opposed to a focus on the ritual aspects of faith, and a softer approach to punishing the heretics relative to the one taken by the possessors.[33]

Artemiy fell under suspicion after Bashkin identified him as a fellow propagator of heresy, which led to months of investigation. In the end, Artemiy was found guilty in matters that still remain murky for interpretation, being accused of such things as treating the Scriptures too freely, not holding a fast properly, objecting to the fairness of the punitive measures applied to the Judaizers in the previous times, and some others. He was not charged for denying the doctrine of the Trinity or Christ's divinity, and after being exiled to the Solovetskiy Monastery (on the Solovetskiy Islands in the White Sea in northern Russia), he managed to flee to Lithuania in 1554 or 1555.[34] According to one of his contemporaries, Zakhariya Kopystenskiy (second half of the sixteenth century—1627), Artemiy spent the rest of his life "leading numerous people out of the Arian and Lutheran heresies".[35]

From the surviving records,[36] we know that Kosoy was among the disciples of Elder Artemiy, and scholars assume that their relationship could have

---

33 On the history and ideology of these two movements, see А.Ю. Григоренко, "Иосифляне и нестяжатели—истоки противостояния" [A.Yu. Grigorenko, "The Josephites and the Non-Possessors"], *Вестник Русского христианского гуманитарного института* № 3 (2000): pp. 89–95. Zinoviy was the first one to use the term "non-possessors" ("нестяжатели") as he criticized the doctrine of Nil Sorskiy's followers. See А.И. Плигузов, *Полемика в Русской церкви первой трети XVI столетия* [*The Polemic in the Russian Church in the First Third of the Sixteenth Century*] (Москва: Квадрига, 2017), pp. 20–21.

34 For a helpful discussion of Artemiy's trial, accusations, and subsequent exile, see Фроянов, *Драма русской истории* [Froyanov, *Drama of Russian History*], pp. 212–221.

35 *Русская историческая библиотека издаваемая Археографическою комиссиею* [*Russian Historical Library Edited by the Archeographic Commission*], том 4 (Сакт-Петербург: Типография и Хромолитография А. Траншеля, 1878), p. 913: "от ереси Арианской и Лютеранской многих отвернул".

36 One such record is found in *Protracted Letter to Those Who Inquired about a Message of Godliness Against the Evil Beliefs of Kosoy and his Companion* (*Послание многословное к вопросившим о известии благочестия на зломудрие Косого и иже с ним*), published by А. Попов, *Послание многословное. Сочинение инока Зиновия по рукописи XVI века*

occurred between 1547 and 1551.[37] Whatever that meant for Kosoy, it seems that he came to shape too radical a worldview there. Before he met Artemiy, though, he lived in Moscow and was a slave of a certain noble man who served the Tsar, Ivan the Terrible (1530–1584).[38] In the year 1547, a great fire occurred in Moscow, displacing about 80,000 people and killing about 2,700 (or according to some estimates 3,700, not including children), and causing widespread poverty among the survivors.[39] It is possible that Kosoy used the momentum and fled together with two of his friends, Ignatius and Vassian, first to the region of Beloozero and then to Novoozero (about 45 km west of today's Belozersk).[40] Upon their arrival there, they became monks at the local monasteries[41] and consequently entered into the circle of Artemiy's intimate disciples.

Following the condemnation of Artemiy in January of 1554, the Church Council undertook an investigation of Kosoy, who had been arrested and brought to Moscow under the charge of teaching heresy.[42] But Kosoy managed to flee again—this time to Lithuania[43]—possibly around the year

(с приложением двух снимков) [A. Popov, *Protracted Letter. The Work of Monk Zinoviy according to the Sixteenth-Century Manuscript with Two Photographs in the Appendix*] (Москва: Издание Общества истории и древностей российских при Московском университете, 1880), hereafter *PL*. It states (on p. 1) that "Feodosiy, also known as Kosoy, and Ignatius, and Vassian [were] the disciples of Artemiy together with his circle" ("Феодосей, нарицаемый Косой, и Игнатей и Васиан, ученикы Артемиевы и инии с ними"). For other sources, see Зимин, *Пересветов* [Zimin, *Peresvetov*], p. 183, n. 313. The link between Kosoy and Artemiy is missing in the *Demonstration of Truth.*

37 This assumption takes into account the fact that by the year 1551, Artemiy was appointed a hegumen of the Trinity Lavra of St. Sergius near Moscow, and that therefore, his relations with Kosoy must have occurred before that appointment. See e.g., Клибанов, *Реформационные движения* [Klibanov, *Reformational Movements*], p. 270.

38 *DT* (Kazan'), pp. 24–25: "Kosoy is a Muscovite, a slave of a certain noble man who serves the Tsar" ("Косой москвитин есть, раб единаго от честных слуг царевых").

39 I. Madariaga, *Ivan the Terrible. First Tsar of Russia* (New Haven: Yale University Press, 2005), p. 62.

40 *PL*, p. 1: "Certain slaves fled from the city of Moscow to the region of Beloozero" ("Раби неции в граде Москве ... бежаша в пределы Белозерскиа"). The same text mentions Ignatius and Vassian as Kosoy's companion on p. 1.

41 *DT* (Kazan'), p. 26.

42 *PL*, p. 1: "And there was an investigation of that godless heresy [of Kosoy] by the Holy Council in Moscow" ("бысть же от святого собора, иже в Москве взыскание о безбожной сей ереси").

43 *DT* (Kazan'), p. 26: "At one point, Kosoy was detained at one of the monasteries in Moscow, but after winning the guard's disposition, he was able to have the restrictions relaxed and flee, departing to Lithuania" ("Ят же быв некогда Косой и блюдом во едином от монастырей московских. Приласкав же ся хранящим, прем пославление от них и бежав, в Литву отъиде").

1555.[44] It is said that he subsequently gave up his monastic vows and married a Jewish wife,[45] and some sources state that he spent the rest of his life actively promoting his beliefs from exile.[46]

What kind of beliefs were they? To mention the major ones briefly,[47] Kosoy distinguished people into those he called "internal", treating them as "sons of God", and those he called "external", labeling them as "slaves", who served earthly masters and followed human traditions. The "sons of God" were the ones who accepted the only true teaching, which was spread by Kosoy, allowing them to gain what he called the "spiritual mind" and thus, partake of a special revelation and be saved. He honored Christ as a mere man who had achieved the status of a great teacher worthy of imitation by others. God the Father, according to Kosoy, was the only true God, and he denounced the Trinity. He rejected the institution of the Church and its worship practices, treating them as dead rituals invented by the priests to control people. Kosoy also decidedly rejected monasticism and called for a return to the roots of the apostolic ideals. He relied primarily on the Old Testament (calling the Pentateuch the "foundational books"), and cited the New Testament only when it agreed with his beliefs. He did the same thing with a handful of the Church Fathers and contemporary authors, selecting only those bits and pieces that served his own purposes. One description of Kosoy's beliefs from the *Protracted Letter* (which is our second main source about Kosoy after the *Demonstration of Truth*) summarizes some of these points as follows:

44 Зимин, *Пересветов* [Zimin, *Peresvetov*], p. 186.

45 DT (Kazan'), p. 26.

46 For example, such information is reported by Kosoy's contemporary, Andrey Kurbskiy (1528–1583), who described him as a follower of Melanchthon and Luther in А.М. Курбский, "Послание пану Кодиаку Чаплину" ["Letter to Kodiak Chaplin"], in *Библиотека литературы Древней Руси*, том 11 (Санкт-Петербург: Наука, 2001), pp. 535–537; and by the seventeeth-century chronicler, Andrey Vengerskiy in Н. Костомаров, *Исторические монографии и исследования* [*Historical Monographs and Studies*], том 12 (Санкт-Петербург: Типография А. Траншеля, 1872), pp. 426–427.

47 We are able to reconstruct Kosoy's teaching based on two primary sources: the *Demonstration of Truth* and the anonymous *Protracted Letter* (for details on both of them, see the next section). For an overview of Kosoy's teaching from various perspectives (Orthodox, atheistic, and jurisprudential), cf. the following three authors: (1) Емельянов, "Учение Косого" [Yemel'yanov, "The Teaching Kosoy"], pp. 176–215 and И. Емельянов, "Полемика против учения Косого" [I. Yemel'yanov, "Polemic with the Teaching of Kosoy"], *Труды Киевской духовной академии* 9 (1862): pp. 88–120; (2) Клибанов, *Реформационные движения* [Klibanov, *Reformational Movements*], pp. 275–302; and (3) Золотухина, *Зиновий* [Zolotukhina, *Zinoviy*], pp. 89–107.

> And we are the children [of God] because we have come to know the truth, which is why we possess the spiritual mind. And he who has our mind is [our] spiritual brother and the child [of God] … But those who come to churches and follow human traditions are dogs and people of things "external". And while they do works of virtue, they cannot be saved, unless they accept our spiritual mind. There is no one else to whom the truth has been revealed in such a way as it was revealed to us.
>
> We should not obey authorities and priests, for it is written, "You should not be called teachers. Your only teacher is Christ" (Matt. 23:8). Likewise, you should not … call anyone father, for it is written, "Do not call [anyone] on earth 'father'; God is your only Father" (Matt. 23:9).
>
> And therefore, we are the sons of God, for nobody else has come to know the truth in such a way as we have. And those who do not have our mind are people of things "external" and are dogs.[48]

Although some of these things were also taught in some form by the Judaizers decades before Kosoy, one radical idea that belongs specifically to him is that humanity and the entire cosmos were not created by God but somehow came into existence by themselves.[49] Another peculiar feature of Kosoy's worldview is that his teaching had to be oral because he believed that it was against the Seventh Ecumenical Council to put anything in writing.[50] Additionally, Kosoy promoted pacifism and denied the state's right to levy taxes.[51] His followers appear to have included both simple folks and people of high status.[52] They were meeting secretly at night[53] and were called to share everything in com-

48 *PL*, pp. 144–145: "И чада мы есмы яко познахом истину. Зане же у нас разум духовный. И аще кто нашь разум имееть, то брат духовный и чадо есть … Тии же вси иже приходять к церквам и внимають человеческым преданием, пси суть и внешнии … и елико добродетели сътворяють не могуть спастися, аще не примуть нашего духовнаго разума. Никому так не открылася истина яко же нам открыся: не подобаеть же повиноватися властем и попом, понеже пишеть, не нарицайтеся наставницы, един есть вашь наставник Христос. Такоже не подобаеть … именовати отцев, пишеть бо не нарицайте себе отца на земли, един отец вашь бог, и посему мы сынове божии, яко истину никто же тако позна, яко же мы. Не имущии же нашего разума внешнии суть и пси".

49 *DT* (Kazan'), pp. 52–60.

50 *DT* (Kazan'), p. 929. To be sure, there is nothing to support this claim in the documents of that Council.

51 *PL*, p. 144.

52 For this argument, see Золотухина, *Зиновий* [Zolotukhina, *Zinoviy*], pp. 84–85.

53 *PL*, pp. 75, 80, 143, 285–286.

mon.[54] It is not clear how widely Kosoy's teaching was received, but in the mind of Zinoviy, "The entire East was deceived by Bakhmet, and the West by Martin of Germany, and Lithuania by Kosoy".[55]

The world in which Kosoy lived before fleeing to Lithuania was marked by all sorts of social evils, and some scholars suggest that such things as extreme poverty, mass exploitation, injustice, violence, and other crises in Russia could have led to the kind of reaction that we see in Kosoy's teaching.[56] Regardless, the second half of the sixteenth century in Russia was indeed a time of great unrest, and we see it reflected even in Zinoviy's writings, some of which sharply criticized the unjust practices of those in power and encouraged Christ-like service to society.[57]

Above all, it was the era of the first Russian Tsar, Ivan the Terrible, and his "Oprichnina" (1565–1572) that involved severe mass repression of the Russian aristocrats, public executions, confiscation of land and property, and the massacre in Great Novgorod (the home of Zinoviy) in 1570.[58] It was the time of the Russo-Turkish (1568–1570) and Livonian wars (1558–1583) with some of the most devastating losses ever known; the burning of Moscow by Tatars (1571), but also the conquest and annexation of large territories of the Khanate of

---

54 DT (Kazan'), p. 922.

55 DT (Kazan'), pp. 48–49: "и убо востокъ весь разврати Бахметомъ, западъ же Мартиномъ немчиномъ, Литву же Косымъ". The word "Bakhmet" (in various forms: "Бахмет", "Бохмит", and "Бохмет") was a corrupted name for the prophet Muhammad (571–632) in Slavonic, and it was used along with "Моамед" ("Muhammad"). Cf. М.А. Батунский, *Россия и ислам* [*Russia and Islam*], том 1 (Москва: Прогресс-Традиция, 2012), ch. 3, sect. 1. Martin of Germany refers to Martin Luther (1483–1546), who initiated the Protestant Reformation in Germany in the year 1517.

56 This is argued especially convincingly by Н.М. Золотухина, "Зиновий Отенский и Феодосий Косой: религиозно-философские, социальные и государственно-правовые воззрения" [N.M. Zolotukhina, "Zinoviy Otenskiy and Feodosiy Kosoy: Religious-Philosophical, Social, and State-Legal Beliefs"], *Историко-правовые проблемы: Новый ракурс* № 4/1 (2011): pp. 113–141.

57 A good example is Zinoviy's *Letter to the Otenskiy Dyak Ya.V. Shishkin*, in which he criticized Yakov Shishkin, a state official of Great Novgorod, for slowing down the court matters that involved the poor and called him to treat them more kindly and justly. For a discussion, see Л.Е. Морозова, "Тема праведного суда в сочинениях церковного публициста XVI в. Зиновия Отенского" [L.E. Morozova, "The Theme of Executing Justice in the Writings of Church Publicist of the XVI Century, Zinoviy Otenskiy"], *Палеоросия. Древняя Русь: во времени, в личностях, в идеях* № 2/10 (2018): pp. 180–184.

58 For a helpful description of the time of Ivan the Terrible with an emphasis on the religious situation, see А. Дворкин, *Иван Грозный как религиозный тип. Статьи и материалы* [A. Dvorkin, *Ivan Grozny as a Religious Type. Articles and Essays*] (Нижний Новгород: Изд-во братства во имя Св. Александра Невского, 2005).

Kazan (1552) and the Khanate of Astrakhan (1556). It was the time of the first government known as the "Chosen Council" (1549–1560) and its major reforms; the time of the expanded code of laws called "Sudebnik" of 1550; the time of the Stoglav Council of 1551 (a form of the first constitution of Russia) called to regulate the church and state life; and the time of the first Patriarch of Moscow and All Rus elected in 1589.[59]

It was also the time of canonizing an unprecedented number of Russian saints during the two local Councils in 1547 and 1549, which came to be known as the "era of the new miracle workers";[60] the time of the *Great Monthly Readings* or *Menology* (*Velikie Minei Chetii*)—the first Russian encyclopedia—which centralized the cult of the Russian saints and sought to collect all the major writings available in Slavonic under Metropolitan Makariy of Moscow (1482–1563);[61] and the time of the first book printing famous for its "Moscow Apostle" (Acts and Epistles of the Apostles), the first printed book of the Bible, published by Ivan Fyodorov in 1564.[62]

Finally, it was the time when Russia was rapidly gaining a geopolitical influence after the centuries of living under Tatars (1242–1480) and was now claiming that Moscow was a "Third Rome". According to that concept, shaped in the late fifteenth and mid-sixteenth centuries, the first Rome succumbed to the Trinitarian heresy of the *filioque*, and the second Rome fell to the infidel Turks. Moscow was now the new center of Christianity and would never fail to continue in that role.[63] It is important to keep this extremely charged Russian climate in mind when studying Zinoviy and the Trinitarian controversy of the mid-sixteenth century.

---

59 For more details on this background, see J. Martin, *Medieval Russia 980–1584*, sec. edn. (Cambridge: Cambridge University Press, 2007), pp. 364–415.

60 Е.В. Ткачев, "Канонизация" [E.V. Tkachov, "Canonization"], in *Православная Энциклопедия*, том 30 (Москва: Церковно-научный центр "Православная энциклопедия", 2012), pp. 269–259; P. Bushkovitch, *Religion and Society in Russia: The Sixteenth and Seventeenth Centuries* (New York–Oxford: Oxford University Press, 1992), pp. 80–87.

61 Н.К. Гаврюшин, "Первая русская энциклопедия" [N.K. Gavryushin, "First Russian Encyclopedia"], in *Памятники науки и техники* (Москва: Наука, 1982–1983), pp. 119–130.

62 Е.Л. Немировский, "Первопечатник Иван Фёдоров" [E.L. Nemirovskiy, "First Printer Ivan Fyodorov"], in *Острожская азбука Ивана Фёдорова. Исследование. Словоуказатель* (Москва: Книга, 1983), pp. 9–20.

63 О.Г. Ульянов, "О времени зарождения на Руси концепции 'Москва—Третий Рим' ('Donatio Constantini Magni' и 'Повесть о белом клобуке'")" [O.G. Ul'yanov, "On the Origin of the Concept of 'Moscow—Third Rome' in Rus ('Donatio Constantini Magni' and 'The Legend of the White Cowl'")], in *Терминология исторической науки. Историописание* (Москва: Институт всеобщей истории Российской академии наук, 2010), pp. 196–214.

2 Zinoviy's Writings

We have seven writings that are commonly acknowledged as belonging to Zinoviy, and there are several disputed texts.[64] The following list gives what is considered by contemporary scholars to be his authentic works:

	Zinoviy's works	Dates of composition
1.	***Zinoviy's Letter to the Otenskiy Dyak Shishkin.*** The manuscript title is *Посланная грамотка от старца Зеновия Отинскаго монастыря ис пустыни к государеву великаго князя диаку Якову Шишкину.* It is published by А.И. Клибанов и В.И. Корецкий, "Послание Зиновия Отенскому дьяку Я.В. Шишкину" [A.I. Klibanov & V.I. Koretskiy, "Zinoviy's Letter to the Otenskiy Dyak Ya.V. Shishkin"], in *Труды Отдела древнерусской литературы*, том 17 (Москва–Ленинград: Академия наук СССР, 1961), pp. 201–224 (the text is on pp. 219–224).	1534–1536
2.	***Letter of Encouragement to the Monks on Solovetskiy Island.*** The manuscript title is *Послание Зиновия, старца Отни пустыни, ко мнихом, бывшим в заточении в Соловецком острове, Гурию Заболоцкому, и Касияну и брату его Гурию Коровиным.* It is published by В.И. Корецкий, "Новые послания Зиновия Отенского" [V.I. Koretskiy, "New Letters of Zinoviy Otenskiy"], in *Труды Отдела древнерусской литературы*, том 25 (Москва–Ленинград: Академия наук СССР, 1970), pp. 120–134 (the text is on pp. 125–128).	1550/1
3.	***Letter to Those Who Inquired about Drinking.*** The manuscript title is *Послание Зиновия, старца Отни пустыни, к некоим, вопросившим его о питии.* It is published by В.И. Корецкий, "Новые послания Зиновия Отенского" [V.I. Koretskiy, "New Letters of Zinoviy Otenskiy"], in *Труды Отдела древнерусской литературы*, том 25 (Москва–Ленинград, 1970), pp. 120–134 (the text is on pp. 128–134).	1550/1

64 For an overview of Zinoviy's work in English, see N. Yanoshak, "A Fontological Analysis of the Major Works Attributed to Zinovii Otenskii", Ph.D. Diss. (Georgetown: Georgetown University, 1981).

(*cont.*)

	Zinoviy's works	Dates of composition
4.	***Panegyric to St. Hypatius of Gangra***. The manuscript title is Ȝиновїа черноризца. ѡ стѣмъ ипатїи гангрьсцѣмъ еппѣ, і чюдотворцы. First published (in modern Russian script) by В.И. Корецкий, "Вновь найденное противоеретическое произведение Зиновия Отенского" [V.I. Koretskiy, "Newly Discovered Anti-Heretical Writing of Zinoviy Otenskiy"], in *Труды Отдела древнерусской литературы*, том 21 (Москва–Ленинград, 1965), pp. 166–182 (the text is on pp. 173–182). The present book provides the newly edited text in the Slavonic script, and there are more details on the issues of authorship, manuscript tradition, and dating in the next section.	Dated differently between 1551 and early 1560s
5.	***Panegyric on the Discovery of Relics of Nikita***. The manuscript title is *О Божией благодати бывшей чудесы, явлением и прославлением священного телесе иже во святых отца нашего Никиты, епископа Великого Новеграда*. The text remains unpublished, and we have several manuscripts available (see Н.П. Барсуков, Источники русской агиографии [N.P. Barsukov, *Sources of Russian Hagiography*], том 81 (Санкт-Петербург: Типография М.М. Стасюлевича, 1882), p. 392). It is commonly dated from 1565, but sometimes incorrectly attributed to Ioasaf (hegumen of the Danilov Monastery in Great Novgorod), who wrote a work with a similar title *Panegyric on the Discovery of the Bodily Remains of Nikita* (*Слово об открытии телес Никиты*) in 1558. For more details about this, see М.В. Дмитриев, *Православие и Реформация: Реформационные движения в восточнославянских землях Речи Посполитой во второй половине XVI в.* [M.V. Dmitriev, *Orthodoxy and Reformation: Reformational Movements in the East-Slav Lands of the Polish-Lithuanian Commonwealth in the Second Half of the XVI Century*] (Москва: Изд-во Московского университета, 1990), p. 28.	1565
6.	***Demonstration of Truth***. It is known by a much longer title in the manuscripts and was first published in *Истины показание къ вопросившимъ о новом учении. Сочинение инока Зиновия* [*Demonstration of Truth to Those Who Inquired about the New Teaching. The Book of Monk Zinoviy*] (Казань: Университетская типография, 1863). The present book provides the autograph of this writing, and there are more details on the issues of authorship, manuscript tradition, and dating in the next section.	1566

(*cont.*)

	Zinoviy's works	Dates of composition
7.	***Panegyric on the Discovery of Relics of Iona.*** The manuscript title is *Того же о обретении мощемъ преподобнаго Ионы, архиепископа Великаго Новаграда, и о казнехъ, бывающихъ на насъ от Бога.* It is published by Ф. Калугин, *Зиновий, инокъ Отенский, и его богословско-полемические и церковно-учительные произведения. Исследование* [F. Kalugin, *Zinoviy, the Monk of the Otenskiy Monastery, and his Theological-Polemical and Church-Didactic Writings. A Study*] (Санкт-Петербург: Типография А. Катанскаго, 1894), pp. 17–26 (Appendix). The *Panegyric* ends with extensive excerpts from the *Demonstration of Truth* and is considered incomplete by some scholars, e.g., Д.М. Буланин, "Зиновий Отенский" [D.M. Bulanin, "Zinoviy Otenskiy"], in *Словарь книжников и книжности Древней Руси*, выпуск 2 (вторая половина XIV–XVI в.), часть 1: А–К (Ленинград: Наука, 1988), p. 354. Zinoviy's authorship of this work is rejected by Morozova, but accepted by most other scholars. For the points from Morozova, see Л.Е. Морозова, *Сочинения Зиновия Отенского* [L.E. Morozova, *Works of Zinoviy Otenskiy*] (Москва: Институт истории СССР, 1990), pp. 232–234. For the opposite view, see e.g., Макарий, Архимандрит (Веретенников), "Зиновий" [Makariy, Archimandrite (Veretennikov), "Zinoviy"], in *Православная Энциклопедия*, том 20 (Москва: Церковно-научный центр "Православная энциклопедия", 2009), p. 153.	Between 1566 and 1572

Among the disputed texts, the most important one is the *Protracted Letter*, which represents an extensive refutation of the doctrine of Kosoy. Written as a letter in the form of questions and answers to the Orthodox Christians in Lithuania who had inquired about Kosoy's teaching, and commonly dated after the year 1558[65] (and thus after Kosoy already fled to Lithuania), it gives additional information about the content of Kosoy's teaching beyond what we learn from the *Demonstration of Truth*. More than a half of this document is composed of a string of patristic and biblical quotations that follow the refutation of Kosoy's teaching. The text is preserved in a single manuscript (RNB, Kiril.-Beloz. 31/1108, sixteenth century) and was published by Popov in 1880.[66]

65 Зимин, *Пересветов* [Zimin, *Peresvetov*], p. 190.

66 А. Попов, *Послание многословное. Сочинение инока Зиновия по рукописи XVI века*

Zinoviy's name appears only in a copy of the manuscript made by monk Pavel from the Yuriev Monastery at Great Novgorod in 1836 (RNB, Sof. 1241). Although today most scholars do not accept it as authentic (based on observations of language, content, and codicology),[67] most of them use it to reconstruct the teaching of Kosoy.

Several other works attributed to Zinoviy at different times include two *Panegyrics* (one to Zosima and Savvatiy Solovetskie, and another to the martyrs of Chernigov, Mikhail and Fyodor); the *Life of Iosif Volotskiy*; the so-called *Azbukovnik*; and two theological treatises devoted to the topic of the Wisdom of God.[68] None of these works grew out of the mid-sixteenth-century Trinitarian controversy in Russia.

2.1 *Manuscript Tradition and the Issues of Authorship and Dating*

2.1.1 The *Panegyric to St. Hypatius of Gangra*

Of the two writings offered in this edition, the *Demonstration of Truth* (published in 1863) was known much earlier than the *Panegyric to St. Hypatius of Gangra* discovered by Koretskiy in 1965.[69] In this section, we will look briefly at the manuscript tradition and the issues of authorship and dating for these two writings, beginning with the *Panegyric to St. Hypatius of Gangra* (henceforth *Panegyric*) and then considering the *Demonstration of Truth* (henceforth *DT*).

The text of the *Panegyric* published by Koretskiy reproduces the oldest manuscript of the three that he knew at the time: (1) GIM, Uvar. № 349, end of the sixteenth century, ff. 1^r–25^r; (2) RGB, Egor. F. 98, № 1705, mid-seventeenth

---

(*с приложением двух снимков*) [A. Popov, *Protracted Letter. The Work of Monk Zinoviy according to the Sixteenth-Century Manuscript with Two Photographs in the Appendix*] (Москва: Издание Общества истории и древностей российских при Московском университете, 1880), pp. 1–305.

67 The authenticity of this text is most strongly disputed by Morozova in her two works from 1975 and 1990, Bulanin in 1982, and Yanoshak in 1991. See Л.Е. Морозова, "Вопросы атрибуции 'Послания многословного'", полемического произведения XVI в. [L.E. Morozova, "Issues of Attribution of the Protracted Letter, Sixteenth-Century Polemical Writing"], *История СССР* № 1 (1975): pp. 101–109; Морозова, *Сочинения Зиновия* [Morozova, *Works of Zinoviy*], pp. 150–163; Д.М. Буланин, "Кодикологические наблюдения над рукописью 'Послания многословного'" [D.M. Bulanin, "Codicological Observations Concerning the Manuscript with the 'Protracted Letter'"], in H.A. Rexheuser und K.H. Ruffmann, hrsg., *Festschrift für Fairy von Lilienfeld zum 65. Geburtstag* (Erlangen: Universität Erlangen–Nürnberg, 1982), pp. 153–164; N. Yanoshak, "The Author of *Poslanie Mnogoslovnoe*: A Fontological Inquiry", *Slavic Review*, vol. 50, no. 3 (1991): pp. 621–636.

68 For a discussion of these disputed works, see Макарий, "Зиновий" [Makariy, "Zinoviy"], p. 154.

69 Корецкий, "Вновь найденное произведение" [Koretskiy, "Newly Found Writing"], pp. 166–182.

century, ff. 70r–93r; (3) RBG, Und. F. 310, № 1190, the year 1708, ff. 9r–26r. All three manuscripts, according to him, descended from a common ancestor, and whenever the latter two copies differed from the base manuscript, Koretskiy gave their readings in the critical apparatus. To these three manuscripts, we should add another one that we found in RGB, Egor. F. 98, № 44, second quarter of the seventeenth century, ff. 698r–713v, containing the saints' lives for December–August.[70] According to our collations, in most of the variant readings where the two manuscripts differ from the base manuscript, the fourth manuscript follows the second and differs from the third.

The first and third manuscripts bear the name "Zinoviy" in their titles, and the third one states that Zinoviy was a disciple of Maksim Grek. Koretskiy made a convincing case for Zinoviy's authorship of the *Panegyric*, demonstrating close parallels between this text and Zinoviy's undisputed work of *DT*.[71] The issue of dating, however, remains unresolved. While Koretskiy dated the *Panegyric* from 1551, suggesting that it could have been written after a fire destroyed St. Hypatius Church on Rogataya Street in Great Novgorod, this has not convinced all scholars. Thus, some date it from the year 1553 after the appearance of the new heretical teaching in 1552 and the Councils that tried Bashkin and Kosoy in 1553–1554.[72] Still others date it much later, suggesting that it could have been written when the heretical movement experienced major growth during the 1560s.[73] Most scholars agree, though, that it was written before Zinoviy penned his main work of *DT* (rather than after), noting that there is no mention of Kosoy there.

In this edition, we follow Koretskiy and offer the text from the earliest manuscript, but we give it in the Slavonic script rather than modern Russian. We have also kept the text identical to how it appears in the manuscript.

2.1.2 The *Demonstration of Truth*

This writing is preserved in two versions—long and short—and it is commonly believed that the short version represents an improvement of the long one.[74]

---

70 The manuscript is described here: https://lib-fond.ru/lib-rgb/98/f-98-44/ (accessed on 10.2.2023).

71 Корецкий, "Вновь найденное произведение" [Koretskiy, "Newly Found Writing"], pp. 167–168.

72 Макарий, "Зиновий" [Makariy, "Zinoviy"], p. 150.

73 Дмитриев, *Православие и Реформация* [Dmitriev, *Orthodoxy and Reformation*], p. 29.

74 E.g., Калугин, *Зиновий* [Kalugin, *Zinoviy*], pp. 102–113; Т.В. Анисимова, "В поисках автографа Зиновия Отенского" [T.V. Anisimova, "In Search of the Autograph of Zinoviy Otenskiy"], *Обсерватория культуры*, том 13, № 6 (2016): pp. 743–744. A different view is suggested by Морозова, *Сочинения Зиновия* [Morozova, *Works of Zinoviy*], pp. 34, 42, who

We have four manuscripts of the long version and six of the short version, not counting the numerous documents, in which *DT* is quoted.[75] Both versions (the long version as the main text and the short version in the form of variant readings) were published in one volume based on two seventeenth-century manuscripts in 1863,[76] when the general picture of the manuscript tradition was still quite incomplete. Today, thanks to such scholars as Kalugin,[77] Zimin,[78] Morozova,[79] Rykov,[80] and especially Anisimova,[81] we can be confident that we possess the original of the long version (RNB, O.I.63), written at Zinoviy's request by an unknown calligrapher, and the autograph of the short version, which Zinoviy did not have time to finish, and thus, someone else completed it for him (RGB, Egor. F. 98, № 337). The autograph includes a later inscription on the back of the codex's front cover that relates Zinoviy to Maksim Grek, stating, "*Kyr* Zinoviy from the Otin Pustyn', the disciple of revered Maksim Grek".[82] Similar information is also contained in several other manuscripts dating from the seventeenth century.

The composition date of *DT* is the year 1566, as indicated by Zinoviy himself several times in the text.[83] By then, Zinoviy was already ageing and suffered from bad hearing and fatigue.[84] As mentioned in the opening paragraph of the introduction, the occasion for writing *DT* was the inquiry of three kliros-chanters from the neighboring monastery about the new teaching, and their

---

thinks that a short version is a distorted copy of the long. This is convincingly refuted by Анисимова, "В поисках автографа" [Anisimova, "In Search of the Autograph"], pp. 738–739.

75 See Калугин, *Зиновий* [Kalugin, *Zinoviy*], 91–100; Золотухина, *Зиновий* [Zolotukhina, *Zinoviy*], p. 61.

76 *Истины показание* [*Demonstration of Truth*]. For the description of the two manuscripts used in this edition, see pp. X–XII.

77 Калугин, *Зиновий* [Kalugin, *Zinoviy*], pp. 91–113.

78 Зимин, *Пересветов* [Zimin, *Peresvetov*], p. 194.

79 Морозова, *Сочинения Зиновия* [Morozova, *Works of Zinoviy*], pp. 35–40.

80 Ю.Д. Рыков, "Утраченный и вновь обретенный солодовниковский список 'Истины показания' Зиновия Отенского" (историко-археографические заметки) [Yu.D. Rykov, "The Lost and Newly Found Manuscript of Solodovnikov with the *Demonstration of Truth* by Zinoviy Otenskiy (Historical Archeographical Notes)"], in *От Средневековья к Новому времени. Сборник статей в честь Ольги Андреевны Белобровой* (Москва: Индрик, 2006), pp. 144–186.

81 Анисимова, "В поисках автографа" [Anisimova, "In Search of the Autograph"], pp. 736–745, who established Zinoviy's autograph of the short version.

82 "Киръ Зиновий отни пустини ученикъ прпдбнаго максима грека".

83 *DT* (Kazan'), pp. 56, 59.

84 These facts are especially stressed in Буланин, "Зиновий" [Bulanin, "Zinoviy"], p. 354, and Золотухина, *Зиновий* [Zolotukhina, *Zinoviy*], p. 47.

ten visits with Zinoviy exactly correspond to the ten conversations in his book (further sub-divided into fifty-six chapters).[85] Although *DT* provides headings and chapter numbers, Zinoviy has been criticized for lack of clear organization in the way he arranged his rubrics,[86] and according to Anisimova, he was planning to make improvements in the short version but died before he could do so.[87] It remains disputed whether this writing reflects the real conversations that took place between Zinoviy and the kliros-chanters, or if he chose to write in the form of a dialogue because that worked best for his literary purposes.[88]

As shown by Kalugin, the 1863 Kazan' edition of *DT* suffers from numerous mistakes and typographical errors.[89] In the present edition, we offer the diplomatic edition of Zinoviy's autograph[90]—the short or improved version of *DT*—and we give the long version only in the English translation (based on RGB, MDA F. 173/I, № 61, seventeenth century, from the 1863 edition). With the exception of dividing the words, this edition presents the text exactly as it appears in the manuscript, actually following Zinoviy's own instruction that called for making no changes in his texts, "And if you, a noble and wise scribe, set up to change [anything while copying my work]—words, or periods, or commas—these texts will then be neither yours nor of the one who put them down [in writing] … For that reason, I beg you to copy the words the way they are written down, including the periods and commas".[91]

The name of this work (Истины показание) has been translated into English in several different ways, most commonly as *Evidence of Truth* and *Testimony of Truth*. Although the term показание ("evidence", "testimony", or "demonstra-

85 The last conversation was joined by a certain Zakhariya Shyochkin, who directed it toward the discussion of the accepted rules for icon painting and church singing. In the longer version, the work is preceded by a brief outline of each of the fifty-six chapters and the corresponding folio numbers.

86 E.g., Калугин, *Зиновий* [Kalugin, *Zinoviy*], pp. 119–120. Kalugin went so far as to suggest his own structure for *DT* (see p. 120).

87 Анисимова, "В поисках автографа" [Anisimova, "In Search of the Autograph"], pp. 743–744.

88 For a discussion of this issue, see Золотухина, *Зиновий* [Zolotukhina, *Zinoviy*], pp. 58–59. She argues that the conversations were real rather than fictional.

89 Калугин, *Зиновий* [Kalugin, *Zinoviy*], pp. 104–113.

90 The manuscript is available today online at https://lib-fond.ru/lib-rgb/98/f-98-337/ (accessed on 10.2.2023).

91 *DT* (Kazan'), p. XI: "Ащели же учнешъ пременяти, ты добрый мудрый писарю, пословицы и точки и запятыя: будутъ убо книжицы сия ниже твоя, ниже предположившаго ихъ … Того ради молю тя преписовати тако, якоже лежатъ речи и точки и запятыя".

tion")[92] may have carried a juridical connotation at the time of Zinoviy, we chose to translate it as the *Demonstration of Truth* to convey the distinctly apologetic tone of this writing. Zinoviy himself uses the term several times in the text, and in each case, he clearly seeks to provide proofs and demonstrate the validity of certain claims, such as when he states, "[This is] a demonstration (Показание) of the fact that the Old Testament Law discloses the Trinity in specific details, and it also reveals that God's Son is the true God".[93]

2.2 *Zinoviy's Sources*

Zinoviy was a man of encyclopedic mind and incredible erudition, and his writings show that he used numerous sources. Some of them are directly cited, and others give credit to specific names (with or without references to their works), but most of the sources can be recognized only as paraphrases, elaborations, and allusions whose origins are not always clear. At the same time, identifying the exact sources of medieval authors is essential to understanding how they interacted with the ideas of other writers and developed their own. In this section, we will give a brief description of Zinoviy's sources in the *Panegyric* and DT, and additional details are offered in the tables.

2.2.1 Sources in the *Panegyric to St. Hypatius of Gangra*

To outline the sources in the *Panegyric*, we have developed two tables. In the first one, we have expanded the number of suggested sources from one to six for Zinoviy's description of the "Life of Hypatius", and from four to nine for "Arianism", compared with the previous study of this text by Koretskiy.[94] In the second table, we offer an outline of the *Panegyric* and a detailed analysis of how Zinoviy used his sources, indicating them as paraphrases, elaborations, allusions, and direct quotations. For all the details, we refer the readers to Table 1 and Table 2.

Overall, our analysis shows that Zinoviy relied primarily on two sources for the description of the "Life of Hypatius": (1) a text close to the so-called "Canonical" *Life of Hypatius*, and (2) the *Life of Hypatius* from the commemoration

---

92 The word показание has a wide range of meanings in Slavonic. See *Словарь русского языка XI–XVII вв.*, выпуск 16 (*Поднавесъ—Поманути*) [*Dictionary of Russian Language of the XI–XVII Centuries. Issue 16* (*Podnaves—Pomanuti*)] (Москва: Наука, 1990), p. 142.

93 *DT* 27: Показание ꙗко в ветхо̑ законѣ ꙗвлена есть тр̑ца тонцѣ и̑ ꙗвленъ е̑ сн҃ъ бж҃їи. ꙗко бг҃ъ истиненъ есть.

94 Корецкий, "Вновь найденное произведение" [Koretskiy, "Newly Found Writing"], pp. 166–182.

service composed by Iosif the Hymnogropher (ca. 816–886), whom Zinoviy mentions by name in the *Panegyric*. It also shows that his primary source for Arianism was the *Second Oration against the Arians*, written by Athanasius of Alexandria, while the order in which he used that writing was from back to front: (1) chs. 18–82; (2) chs. 11–18; and (3) chs. 1–11. Thus, instead of discussing Heb. 3:2, Acts 2:36, and Prov. 8:22 as Athanasius does, Zinoviy covers the three passages in the opposite order. It has been argued that the order in which Athanasius explored these passages had to do with his intention to begin with the least problematic texts of Scripture and use his points to explain the more challenging ones.[95] Zinoviy, on the other hand, begins with the most difficult passages and then discusses the least problematic ones.

His most preferred way of interacting with all these sources is either by paraphrasing them or by making elaborations. In doing that, he can take a small piece of something and make it larger (e.g., when he introduces certain points about Hypatius that are not found in his sources), or take a large text (such as the *Second Oration*) and make it smaller in his own re-telling. The cases of allusions are more difficult to pinpoint, but we did identify some. Zinoviy rarely quotes his sources directly, and even when he does, he tends to do two things: (1) change the original wording (e.g., cf. Zinoviy's phrase моvсеи бо ба҃ оугодни҃. хс҃ъ же поне҃ сн҃ъ with мѡѷси оубо слꙋга. а хс҃ сынъ in *CA* 2.10); or (2) change the order in which the words are found in the original (e.g., cf. Zinoviy's phrase на высотоv вѧыде дѡ҃родѣтелеи with на добро[д]телеи въсшелъ еси. высотоу in *Min.* f. 280ᵛ, *Sticheron* 2).[96] Table 2 provides an exhaustive list of all such cases, illustrating Zinoviy's interaction with the sources and providing the first study of this type available today.

Clearly, the source with which Zinoviy interacted most often for his Trinitarian arguments is Athanasius' *Orations*. We do not know whether Zinoviy could have used a surviving manuscript that contains this text. Still, it is worth noting that one specific copy (from around the same time as the *Panegyric* and likely made in Great Novgorod: GIM, Sin. Usp. VMCh 994, no later than 1552) preserved polemical glosses that speak against Luther and the *filioque*, and that also contain statements in defence of Christ's divinity, deification, and icons, reflecting the same concerns that Zinoviy addressed in his writings.[97] It

95 D. Fairbairn, "Context, Context, Context: Athanasius' Biblical Interpretation in *Contra Arianos*", *Perichoresis* 12/2 (2014): pp. 119–135.

96 The examples are taken from Table 2 (sect. 7.6 and 9.2).

97 V.V. Lytvynenko, "Athanasius' *Orations Against the Arians*: Theological Glosses in Two Slavonic Manuscripts", in Сборникът "Преславска книжовна школа", том 19 (Шумен: Научен център "Преславска книжовна школа", 2019), pp. 77–101.

is tempting to ask whether Zinoviy could have been the author of these glosses, but there is no direct evidence to support this assumption.[98]

2.2.2 Sources in the *Demonstration of Truth*

In contrast to the *Panegyric*, DT has a long history of research, and two major works have explored its sources. One was written by a Russian scholar, Kalugin,[99] in 1894 and remains our best resource to this day; another helpful study was done by a German researcher, Mainka, in 1961.[100]

Mainka does an especially good job of placing Zinoviy's DT in the larger context and tracing his ideas through the history of Christian thought. For example, in discussing Zinoviy's doctrine of creation, Mainka indicates parallels both with earlier thinkers, such as Tertullian (*De Testimonio Animae* and *Apologeticus*), Clement of Alexandria (*Stromata*), Athanasius of Alexandria (*Contra Gentes*), and Augustine, and with later writers, such as Photius (*Ad Amphilochium Quaestiones*), Gregory Palamas (*Capita Physica*), Mark of Ephesus (*Capita Syllogistica*), and Gennadius Scholarius (*Confessio Fidei Prior* and *Confessio Fidei Posterior*).[101]

Mainka fails, however, to make clear that such parallels between DT and other authors do not necessarily mean that Zinoviy relied on them. Thus, a parallel between Zinoviy, on the one hand, and Tertullian and Augustine, on the other, may tell more about the similarities between them than about the actual sources. To give a more specific example, Mainka's reference to *Contra Gentes* 27 and 36 of Athanasius of Alexandria[102] and Basil of Caesarea's *Hexaemeron*[103] does not recognize the fact that *Contra Gentes* was never translated into Slavonic,[104] whereas the *Hexaemeron* was not accessible to Zinoviy, as he himself admitted in DT 80.7.

A more thorough analysis of Kalugin provides evidence concerning both allusions and direct quotations, and he concludes that Zinoviy's most frequent

98 Our comparison of Zinoviy's handwriting in his autograph (the short version of DT) with the handwriting in the glosses showed some similarities, but the fragmentary nature of the glosses, and our doubts concerning some specific letters preclude definite conclusions.

99 Калугин, *Зиновий* [Kalugin, *Zinoviy*].

100 Mainka, *Zinovij von Oten'*.

101 Mainka, *Zinovij von Oten'*, p. 190.

102 Mainka, *Zinovij von Oten'*, p. 168.

103 Mainka, *Zinovij von Oten'*, p. 168, n. 129.

104 V.V. Lytvynenko & I.M. Gritsevskaya, "Athanasius in Slavonic", *Studia Patristica* (2021): pp. 68–69.

way of interacting with his sources in *DT* is by paraphrasing them and drawing his own observations rather than citing.[105] He also notes that this feature makes Zinoviy unique among his contemporaries (such as Iosif Volotskiy, 1439–1515, and Metropolitan Daniil, 1492–1547), who tended to quote large portions of texts with much less analysis and personal reflection than Zinoviy.[106] According to Kalugin, Zinoviy cited mostly three Church Fathers: Basil the Great (*Asceticon Magnum siue Quaestiones*), Gregory of Nazianzus (*Orationes*), and John Chrysostom (homilies from an old Russian miscellany called *Pearls*).[107] Kalugin also identified references to Athanasius of Alexandria (*Orationes Contra Arianos* and *Vita Antonii*), Cyril of Jerusalem (*Catecheses ad Illuminandos*), Gregory of Nyssa (*De Oratione Dominica*), Pseudo-Dionysius the Areopagite (*De Ecclesiastica Hierarchia*), Gennadius of Constantinople (*One Hundred Chapters on the Holy Faith*, no longer extant in Greek), and Nikon of the Black Mountain (*Pandectes*).[108]

Additionally, Kalugin showed that Zinoviy drew from hagiographical sources (more specifically, from the *Scala paradisi* of John Climacus, *Sermones Ascetici et Epistulae* of Isaac the Syrian, and *Orationes Ethicae* of Symeon the New Theologian), historical material (such as Flavius Josephus and various Slavonic chronicles), poetic gnomes of Menander, and the so-called *Palea* (an old Russian work, containing an exposition of Biblical history). Kalugin makes the important observation that Zinoviy significantly relied on the *Enlightener* of Iosif Volotskiy[109] and was apparently influenced by Maksim Grek.[110]

Our own research generally confirms Kalugin's observations. In the translated portions of *DT*, we found that Zinoviy makes direct references to five Church Fathers, naming at least nine writings of Basil the Great, and one or two of the other Fathers:

a. **Basil the Great:** (1) *Asceticon Magnum siue Quaestiones* (CPG 2875); (2) *Homiliae in Hexaemeron* (CPG 2835), with Zinoviy's indication that he had no access to this work; (3) *Homiliae* (CPG 2845–2869); (4) one of the following texts: *Contra Sabellianos et Arium et Anomaeos* (CPG 2869) or *Adversus Eunomium Libri* V (CPG 2837); (5) one or two of the three following texts: *Homilia in Martyrem Iulittam* (CPG 2849; BHG 972), *In Barlaam Martyrem* (CPG 2861; BHG 223), *In Gordium Martyrem* (CPG 2862;

105 Калугин, *Зиновий* [Kalugin, *Zinoviy*], p. 275.
106 Калугин, *Зиновий* [Kalugin, *Zinoviy*], p. 271.
107 Калугин, *Зиновий* [Kalugin, *Zinoviy*], pp. 216–230, 272–273.
108 Калугин, *Зиновий* [Kalugin, *Zinoviy*], pp. 273–274.
109 Калугин, *Зиновий* [Kalugin, *Zinoviy*], pp. 117, 153, 159–162, 274–275.
110 Калугин, *Зиновий* [Kalugin, *Zinoviy*], pp. 158–159, 182–183.

BHG 703), *In Mamantem Martyrem* (CPG 2868; BHG 1020), *In Martyres Omnes* (*dubia*; CPG 2941; BHG 1191m); (6) *Enarratio in Prophetam Isaiam* (CPG 2911); (7) *Homiliae in Psalmos* (CPG 2836); (8) *In Sanctam Christi Generationem* (CPG 2913; BHG 1922); (9) *In Quadraginta Martyres Sebastenses* (CPG 2863; BHG 1205).

b. **Gregory the Theologian:** *Orationes* (CPG 3010); *In Sanctum Pascha* II (CPG 3010 [45]).

c. **Cyril of Jerusalem:** *Catecheses ad Illuminandos* (CPG 3585).

d. **John Chrysostom:** *In Epistulam ad Hebraeos Argumentum et Homiliae* 1–34 (CPG 4440); *Pearls* (a name for an Old Russian miscellany containing a collection of Chrysostom's homilies).[111]

e. **Athanasius of Alexandria:** *Epistula Festalis* 39.15–21 (CPG 2102).

In addition, Zinoviy borrows several major themes from Athanasius' *Orations against the Arians* without naming him as a source: (1) the renewal of fallen humanity whose image and likeness were distorted by sin (e.g., *Second Oration* 6, 47, 65, 70, 73); (2) an anti-Arian argument: if there was a time when God was without the Word, then there was a time when God was not a Father (*First Oration* 9, 14–22); (3) the idea of seeing *an angel* sent from God versus seeing *God* who comes in the form of an angel (*Third Oration* 14); (4) the question of why Christ needed to become man (e.g., *Second Oration* 51–52); (5) the idea that Christ effected salvation of humanity within his own body (*Third Oration* 31, 38); (6) an illustration about the king and his painted image (*Third Oration* 5); (7) arguments for Christ's divine and human natures based on Athanasius' most discussed passages: Phil. 2:8–10, Heb. 3:2, and Acts 2:36 (*First Oration* 37–45; *Second Oration* 1–11 and 11–18); and (8) references to Arius and his inaccurate view of Christ.

By far the one source to which Zinoviy owes the most is the *Enlightener* of Iosif Volotskiy. He never mentions the author or his work in the selected texts of this edition (though he does so elsewhere), but draws from Iosif significantly. To show the extent of his dependence, we identified 36 significant themes that are clearly borrowed from Iosif and placed them in Table 3, where they are listed with specific references to the *Enlightener*. Our analysis shows that Zinoviy made the most use of the first five Discourses of the *Enlightener* (composed of sixteen Discourses in the long version and eleven Discourses in the short version), but especially the first and the fifth ones. Iosif wrote a lot

---

111 Е.Т. Казенина, "'Маргарит' и Историко-культурная ситуация на Руси XV–XVI в." [E.T. Kazenina, "'*The Pearl*' and the Historical-Cultural Situation in Rus' During the XV–XVI Centuries"], *Древняя Русь. Вопросы медиевистики* 4/10 (2002): pp. 57–66.

about the doctrines of the Trinity and incarnation in these first five Discourses, and it is not surprising that Zinoviy heavily relied on them for his own arguments.

Clearly, Zinoviy's principal source was the Bible. Since the new teaching of Kosoy was built primarily on the Old Testament and especially on the Pentateuch, Zinoviy spent most of his time exegeting the books of Genesis and Exodus. In doing so, he often began by citing some large portions of the Biblical text and then went through the individual verses, explaining how they prefigured the Trinity. When he used the New Testament, he quoted from the Gospel of John and Paul's Letter to the Romans most often, finding them especially helpful for demonstrating Christ's divinity. Zinoviy often charged Kosoy with misinterpreting the Scriptures by taking things out of context and cherry-picking. After learning that Kosoy rejected the Epistle to the Hebrews, he argued that it was accepted as canonical in the early church and that all the books of Holy Scripture are divinely inspired. For this edition, Lytvynenko identified all direct and indirect references to Scripture in Zinoviy and noted them in the text. Hopefully, this will encourage other researchers to study his treatment of the Bible as a topic that remains unexplored today.

3 Zinoviy's Doctrine of the Trinity, Christ, and Salvation

Zinoviy's concept of the Trinity, Christ, and salvation is best expressed in his two writings offered in this edition. Here, we will discuss the most significant aspects of his theological thought on these doctrines in the *Panegyric* and DT. Since the latter work is considerably longer and more elaborate than the *Panegyric*, we will give it considerably greater attention as well.

3.1 *The* Panegyric to St. Hypatius of Gangra

Of the two main sources on which Zinoviy relies in his *Panegyric* (see sect. 2.2.1.), Athanasius' *Second Oration against the Arians* provides the framework from and through which he develops much of his own thought about Christ and the Trinity. In this section, we will examine three significant aspects: Zinoviy's presentation of Arianism and the Russian heretics, his Trinitarian arguments, and the key points from biblical exegesis.

3.1.1 Arianism and the Russian Heretics

The particular circumstances that led Zinoviy to write his *Panegyric* had to do with the appearance of the anti-Trinitarian heretics in Russia. He identifies them as "Arian" because of their denial of the deity of Christ and calls them "croaking toads that crawl in the mire" (жа̑ в тинѣ пльѕающихъ квоктанїа)[112] for their life of depravity and their inability to deliver clear and accurate things. He also treats them as being "more senseless than pigs" (безсловеснѣиши свинеи соу̑)[113] in view of their lack of basic literacy, in contrast to Arius who "composed his heresy based on philosophy and gained many philosophers as followers in order to contend with the holy fathers".[114]

When describing their teaching, he calls it "more malicious than that of Arius" (злѣе арїа)[115] and links its origin to the Greek philosophical concept, in which gods were divided into "greater" and "smaller" deities (богы болшїа и боги ме̑шїа). According to Zinoviy—and beyond any explicit description of Arianism in Athanasius and any other surviving patristic document[116]—their predecessor, Arius, adopted this pagan concept from Greek philosophy,[117] believing that the Father was the "greater God", and the Son was the "smaller God". In drawing this comparison, he makes a statement that must have been borrowed from the ninth-century *Epistle to Boris-Mikhail of Bulgaria*, written by the Patriarch of Constantinople, Photius (810/20–893) and translated into Slavonic by Maksim Grek (the most notable parallels between the two are italicized below):[118]

112 *Panegyric* 4.1.

113 *Panegyric* 4.1.

114 *Panegyric* 4.1: поне̑ арїи свою ере̑ състави ѡпираѧса философїи. и мнгй философо̑ поборнико̑ по себѣ на прѣнїко стымъ ѿцемъ прїѡрѣте. This profile of Arius as a philosopher who led philosophically minded followers is not attested in the patristic texts, but there is a general consensus among scholars that Arius' thought (and that of some of his sympathizers, such as Asterius of Cappadocia) was indeed inspired by aspects of neo-Platonic and/or Stoic philosophy. See R. Williams, *Arius*, third edn. (London: SCM Press, 2005), esp. pp. 261–266; M. Wiles, *Archetypal Heresy: Arianism Through the Centuries*, repr. (Oxford: Oxford University Press, 2004), pp. 1–51; R.C. Gregg, D.E. Groh, *Early Arianism: A View of Salvation* (London: SCM Press, 1981), esp. pp. 1–42; R.P.C. Hanson, *The Search for the Christian Doctrine of God: The Arian Controversy 318–381* (Edinburgh: T&T Clark, 1993), pp. 32–41.

115 *Panegyric* 4.1.

116 For the most comprehensive treatment of the parallels between the Arian and Greek concepts of God, see Williams, *Arius*, pp. 181–229.

117 Elsewhere, Zinoviy's knowledge of philosophy is remarkable for this time period in Russia. A good example is his fifth proof for the existence of God, where he interacts with philosophers who debated about the movement of the starts and their relation to the earth. See *DT* (*Kazan'*), p. 68.

118 For the discussion of this epistle in the translation of Maksim Grek, see М.В. Корогодина, "Переводы с греческого языка в Кормчей Вассиана Патрикеева" [M.V. Korogodina, "Texts Translated from Greek in the *Nomokanon* of Vassian Patrikeyev"], *Древняя Русь. Вопросы медиевистики* № 1/75 (2019): pp. 161–166.

Photius' ***Epistle***	***Panegyric*** **3**
Where would the true sonship be, if the Father were of one essence and the Son of another? *How would this not cause the polytheism of Greek deception, if the deity were cut into a smaller* [*essence*] *and a greater essence*: the latter is defined as the first, creating, and oldest God, while the former is separated as the second God, who is both subserving and young.[119]	Infamous Arius, having learned from the Greek teaching, and exercising himself in vain concepts, *devised the greater deities and smaller deities, following the Greeks.* He waged war against piety by what in fact were the fables of the Greeks, for he spoke of the *greater God the Father and the smaller God the Son* ...[120]

3.1.2 Trinitarian Arguments

This description of Arianism goes hand in hand with a number of Trinitarian arguments, of which the most original is what we could call Zinoviy's analogy of "tools and products".[121] He quotes two key statements from Arius' work *Thalia* as found in Athanasius' *First Oration against the Arians* 1.5 (hereafter *CA*) ("there was once when the Son was not", and "the Son came into being so that through the Son, God could make the world")[122] and disputes them through this analogy, presented in two versions.

In the first version, he asserts that "material products" (вещи) are more significant or superior than the "tools" (ѡрѫдїѧ) that made them. To clarify this

119 гдѣ же бѹдеть истинное сн҃вьства. иномѹ оубо сѹщьствѹ ѡц҃ѹ сѹщѹ иномѹ же сн҃оу. какѡ не еллинскаго заблѹженїа възникне многобоство на меньшее и болшее сѹщьство пресѣцаемѹ бж҃твѹ. і ѡвомѹ оубо въ прьваго и съдѣтелнаго и старѣишаго б҃а предѣлаемѹ. ѡвомѹ же въ втора бг҃а разлѹчаемѹ и слѹжитела и юннаго. The text is from Т. Славова, *Славянският превод на посланието на патриарх Фотий до княз Борис-Михаил* [T. Slavova, *Slavonic Translation of Patriarch Photius' Epistle to Khagan Boris-Mikhail*] (София: Университетско издателство "Св. Климент Охридски", 2013), p. 168.

120 злоименитыи арїе, наоучивсѧ еллинскомоу оученїю. и сѫемоудраа по еллїнѡ, богы болшїа и боги мнешїа оумышлѧше. и бл҃гочтїе ратованїе бранемъ соименыи, еллинскими баснами. гл҃аше бо больша бг҃а ѡц҃а быти. и менша бг҃а сн҃а.

121 *Panegyric* 3.1–2.

122 Arius' *Thalia* is preserved in two sets of fragments, of which only one was translated into Slavonic. The first set is found in Athanasius' *De Synodis Arimini in Italia et Seleuciae in Isauria* 15 (CPG 2128), and the second (quoted by Zinoviy) is in *CA* 1.5–6. For the Slavonic text and translation of *Thalia*, see V.V. Lytvynenko, "Arius' *Thalia Fragments*: Old Slavonic Version of Athanasius' *Orations Against the Arians* 1:5–6", *Parresia. Revue pro vychodni krest'anstvi* 9–10 (2015–2016); the two quoted points in the *Panegyric* are on p. 48.

point, he refers to the production of "silk" (паволоⷦ) and "golden vessels" (златыа сосѫды), contending that they are more valuable in themselves than the tools that manufactured them.[123] In the second version, he adds a third element to create a more complete picture by introducing the idea of a "craftsman". Implying an identification of Christ with the "craftsman", he goes on to argue that since the Arians understood Christ to be a mere instrument necessary for creating the world, then Christ should be considered on the same level as "tools". And if so, then he must be lesser than creation, which is nonsense. In yet another illustration here, he refers to "scissors" and the "needle" (ножица и иглⷹ) for the description of the tools, and to the "royal dress" (црⷭ҇кїа багрѧница) for his description of the material product, ascribing to Arius both the illustration itself and the wrong logic about Christ to which it leads.[124]

Another major argument in which Zinoviy combats Arianism has to do with the question of how we should relate Christ, time, and creation. Explaining this in the *Panegyric* 3.4, he states:

> And since the ages and times and periods were made by the Son of God, how can these things that were made exist before their Maker? And how can the age or time or period be older than the Son of God, who made the ages and times and periods, and without whom "nothing was made that was made" (Jn. 1:3), including the time and period and age that were made, too?[125]

Based on this, Zinoviy contends that there was no time when the Son did not exist, for if the Son made time, he must precede it. To seal this point, he elaborates on Jn. 1:1–3 and concludes that the Son is eternal and "did not come into being" (а не быⷭ҇).[126] Anyone who has read Athanasius' *Orations* will immediately recognize that Zinoviy heavily draws from this writing to make his own argument here.[127]

---

123 *Panegyric* 3.1.

124 *Panegyric* 3.2.

125 і аще вѣки и времена и лѣта быша сн҃омъ бж҃їимъ. како сотворⷩенаа боудⷤ҇ преⷣже тволⷬца иⷯ. і како боудеⷮ вѣⷦ или врема или лѣта старѣе сн҃а бж҃їа, сътворшаⷢ вѣки и врема и лѣта. безъ него бо ничтоⷤ быⷭ҇ еже быⷭ҇. врема и лѣта и вѣⷦ бысть.

126 *Panegyric* 3.4. It is quite likely that this particular argument was meant to function as a syllogism with two premises and an inference: (1) time was created by the Son; (2) creation cannot exist before the Creator; (3) the Son existed before time. If this is correct, then Zinoviy could have borrowed this type of reasoning from John of Damascus' *Dialectic* ("Philosophical Chapters"), which contained a chapter on syllogism and was available to him in Slavonic.

127 It is likely that the source which inspired Zinoviy's syllogistic argument here (see the pre-

3.1.3 Christ in the Scriptures

In addition to this theological type of reasoning, Zinoviy makes important points from Scripture in the middle section of this work (*Panegyric* 7–8.1). He praises Hypatius for the way he "presented the words of sacred Scriptures" to "shut the blasphemer's mouth that uttered evil against God" because "Arius badly misinterpreted what was well written by the preachers of God".[128]

At the same time, most of Zinoviy's points from Scripture are clearly inspired by Athanasius' *Orations* rather than anything by Hypatius, since nothing survives from his own pen.[129] This includes Athanasius' key hermeneutical principle of the so-called twofold account of Scripture that sees Christ under two aspects: his eternal existence before the incarnation and his earthy life for the

---

vious note on syllogism in Zinoviy) is Athanasius *CA* 1.11–13, while a certain parallel to his points can be found in *Sanctam Christi Generationem* of Basil of Caesarea. For the specific reference, see *Великие Минеи Четии, собранные Всероссийским митрополитом Макарием. Декабрь 25–31* [*Great Minaia Reader, Collected by the Metropolitan of All Rus' Makariy. December 25–31*], выпуск 13 (Москва: Синодальная типография, 1912), stlb. 2290. Moreover, Zinoviy seems to work with the same distinction as Athanasius, who drew a contrast between two ontological modes of existence: (1) eternal being of God, which includes both the Father and the Son; and (2) becoming in time, which can be ascribed neither to the Father nor to the Son. Athanasius formulates this distinction by putting the Son together with the Father (first mode), and everything else below them (second mode). Linguistically, this distinction was expressed in early Slavonic literature by using different tenses of the verb "to be", e.g., "when speaking of God, it says that 'he has been' (бѣаше), but of man, it says that 'he came to be' (бы҃)" (ѡ бз҃ѣ гл҃а ре҃ бѣаше, ѡ чл҃цѣ же бы҃), quoted from Г.С. Баранкова, В.В. Мильков, *Шестоднев Иоанна экзарха болгарского. Памятники древнерусской мысли: Исследования и тексты* [G.S. Barankova & V.V. Milkov, *Hexameron of John the Exarch of Bulgaria. Documents of Old Russian Thought: Research and Texts*], выпуск 2 (Санкт-Петербург: Алетейя, 2001), p. 314. Given that this was a common point in the philosophical tradition of Slavia Orthodoxa, we may assume that Zinoviy could have been aware of it.

128 *Panegyric* 2.2, 3.3, 6.1: пр҃ѣлагаа словеса сщ҃ен҃а писанїа …; бг҃охꙋлникоу злѣ зїающаа оуста на бг҃а заградї …; поне҃ писа҃наа дѡ҃рѣ бг҃опропов҃ѣдники, арїи прїатъ злѣ.

129 On the surviving evidence concerning Hypatius, see А.Н. Крюкова, Е.Е. Макаров, Э.В. Шевченко, И.А. Орецкая, "Ипатий" [A.N. Kryukova, E.E. Makarov, E.V. Shevchenko, I.A. Oretskaya, "Hypatius"], in *Православная Энциклопедия*, том 26 (Москва: Церковно-научный центр "Православная энциклопедия", 2011), pp. 162–168. It is hard to know what exactly determined Zinoviy's selection of Athanasius in this part of the text, since neither of the two Slavonic versions of the *Life of Hypatius* that we studied mentions Athanasius alongside Hypatius. However, the Greek "Canonical" version of the *Life of Hypatius* does mention that Hypatius was elected as Athanasius' successor and oversaw the flock in peace, thus bringing the two men together; and if we assume that Zinoviy knew Greek (on this, see sect. 1) and had the chance to read the Greek *Life*, then we can also presume that it could have determined his focus on Athanasius here.

economy of salvation.[130] Equipped with this principle, Zinoviy goes on to rebut three major Arian prooftexts that were the subject of intense controversy in the fourth century: Prov. 8:22, Acts 2:36, and Heb. 3:2.[131]

Drawing from Athanasius, who discussed these passages in the reverse order in his *Second Oration*, Zinoviy distinguishes between the things that apply to the Son from eternity and those that apply to him in the incarnation. Using this Christological distinction, he refutes the claim that any of the three passages speak of Christ as a created being, arguing that a careful reading of them in their immediate and larger context shows that Christ is both divine and human.

To give a brief example of how Zinoviy does this, he quotes Heb. 1:1–3, which says that Christ was "*made* heir of all things" in verse 2, and insists that instead of taking the word "made" to mean that Christ was created, we should relate it to his time in the flesh, while recognizing his divinity from the verse that goes after this statement in verse 3, "Paul, the preacher of God, theologized and showed that Christ was the true and uncreated God (cf. Heb. 1:3), but when he recalls the economy of Christ (cf. Heb. 1:2), he relates it to his coming in the flesh according to the Father's good pleasure, speaking of him then as 'made'".[132]

To make his points in the *Panegyric*, Zinoviy uses technical theological terms (such as "consubstantial Trinity", "essence", "hypostasis", "subsistences", and others, to be discussed in the next section), cites parts of the Nicene Creed (*Panegyric* 2.1), and draws from both church tradition (*Panegyric* 6) and the Hellenistic *topoi* (*Panegyric* 1.1). He was not the first person in medieval Russia to write an anti-Arian work,[133] nor the first to relate Arianism to the anti-Trinitarian heretics or to use Athanasius for that purpose.[134] But his *Panegyric* is indeed

130 Cf. *CA* 1.54; 3.29. For an excellent discussion of this hermeneutical principle in Athanasius, see J. Behr, *The Nicene Faith, Formation of Christian Theology*, vol. 2, part 1 (New York, St. Vladimir's Seminary Press, 2004), pp. 208–215.

131 For the list of Arian prooftexts and their discussion, see Hanson, *The Search*, pp. 824–849.

132 *Panegyric* 7.5: Павⷧ҇е бг҃опроповѣдникъ бг҃словив, и показа х҃а б҃а истина несотворена. внегда же воспоминаа хв҃о и во плоти, ѿчаго бл҃говоленїа ѡ немъ нш҃е смотренїа смотренїе. тогда сотворенїе прїат.

133 The first anti-Arian work in medieval Russia belongs to Kirill Turovskiy (1130–1182) and is entitled the *Oration of the Sinful Monk, Kirill, on the Council of the 318 Holy Fathers* (*Кюрила грѣшнаго мниха слово на сбор святых отець 300 и 18*). The Slavonic text is available in И.П. Еремин, "Литературное наследие Кирилла Туровского" [I.P. Eremin, "Kirill Turovskiy's Literary Legacy"], *Труды Отдела древнерусской литературы*, том 15 (Москва–Ленинград, 1958), pp. 343–348. It appears that Kirill's main source about Arianism was the ninth-century *Chronicle* of George Hamartolos rather than Athanasius.

134 The first person in medieval Russia who used Athanasius in a polemical context to rebut

one of the most comprehensive Trinitarian responses composed in medieval Russia, and it is best appreciated when read together with his most foundational work, the *Demonstration of Truth.*

3.2 *The* Demonstration of Truth

3.2.1 The Structure of the Text

Zinoviy's discussion of God in this writing is shaped to a great extent by the specific questions he had to answer in his conversations with the kliros-chanters (see sect. 1). The latter's concern was to investigate whether the recent teaching spread by Feodosiy Kosoy (apparently representing the same strand of thought as the heresy critiqued in the *Panegyric*) was acceptable from the standpoint of Orthodoxy,[135] and Zinoviy deals with that question over the course of ten meetings. Before we see him addressing the doctrines of the Trinity, Christ, and salvation, Zinoviy spends chs. 5–7, raising doubts as to whether Kosoy actually believed in the existence of God and responding to his teaching that the universe came into existence by itself.[136] In the process, he articulates what amount to five proofs for the existence of God[137] and argues that everything was made by the divine power and providence.

---

the anti-Trinitarian doctrine was Iosif Volotskiy, who cited CA several times in his *Enlightener.* For more details, see V.V. Lytvynenko, "Anti-Arian Arguments in Iosif Volotskij's Polemic against the Judaizers", *Parresia. Revue pro východní křesťanství* 9–10 (2015): pp. 53–75.

135 In several places of DT, Zinoviy seems to suggest that the kliros-chanters may have been sympathizing with Kosoy's doctrines. E.g., DT 51.1: "This inquiry of yours exhibits Kosoy himself, and these words derive from his own doctrine" (вопрошение ваше сие показоуе҃ само косо҃. и ѿ оученїа є҃ бы҃ гл҃омъ симъ); DT 59.1: "Now, you are the kliros-chanters, as you profess yourselves, but the words you say do not befit the kliros-chanters, nor do these words have a Christian sense. Instead, these words of yours are entirely against the faith in Christ" (оубо крылошане есте ꙗко повѣдасте себе. гл҃ете гл҃ы и не сꙋ крылоша҃. ни хрїаньскиа гл҃ы. но по всемꙋ невѣрны во х҃а ваши гл҃ы); DT 76.8: "Therefore, do not have unbelief nor question how the Son of God came down from the heavens and became a partaker of humanity, or how it was possible for the flesh to take in God" (тѣмже да не невѣрꙋеши ни да ѡиыговае҃. како сниде сн҃ъ бж҃їи с нбс҃ѣ и примѣси чл҃чествꙋ. или како пло҃ возмо҃ бг҃а прїати).

136 According to Zinoviy, "Kosoy does not believe that God exists" ("не верует Косой, яко есть Богъ") and "reasons that life came by itself" ("самобытное мудрствующий") DT (*Kazan'*), pp. 51, 54.

137 Kalugin and Mainka examine Zinoviy's proofs for the existence of God in Калугин, *Зиновий* [Kalugin, *Zinoviy*], pp. 131–141 and Mainka, *Zinovij von Oten'*, pp. 142–170, but their assessments fail to take into account some important aspects of the historical and philosophical background behind Zinoviy's proofs. For an alternative analysis of this topic, see М.В. Шпаковский, "Естественная теология Зиновия Отенского в контексте древнерусской философской книжности" [M.V. Shpakovskiy, "Natural Theology of Zinovy Otensky in Light of the Philosophical Tradition of Medieval Russia"], *Вестник Православ-*

To help the reader follow Zinoviy's train of thought, we will begin this section by presenting nineteen major episodes that he discusses in his writing. For each of them, we will give the name of the episode and the most discussed passages of Scripture, as well as indicate where each episode is found. Different episodes may include repetitions and may address additional issues, but such division by episodes should help the reader follow the major turns of Zinoviy's thought and understand his logic. Since he makes his own (more nuanced) divisions into chapters and subchapters within his work, we have decided to offer our division into nineteen episodes only in the introduction to the edition.

Synopsis of the Main Episodes in DT

I. **The Trinity:**
  - **Episode 1:** Introductory reasoning for the Trinity and transition to the discussion of Scripture (*DT* 2–5.2)
  - **Episode 2:** "Creation" in Gen. 1:1–2:7 (*DT* 6–23.6)
  - **Episode 3:** "The Shema" in Deut. 6:4 (*DT* 24–26.6)
  - **Episode 4:** "The Tower of Babel" in Gen. 11:5–7 (*DT* 27–28.6)
  - **Episode 5:** "Three visitors appear to Abraham by the Oak of Mamre" in Gen. 18:1–5 (*DT* 29.1–13)
  - **Episode 6:** "Two Angels and Lot in Sodom and Gomorrah" in Gen. 18:20–23; 18:32–19:3; 19:12–26 (*DT* 30–31.1–10)
  - **Episode 7:** "The temptation of Abraham" in Gen. 22:1–3; 22:9–13 (*DT* 32–33.6)
  - **Episode 8:** "Jacob's ladder" and his "wrestling with God" in Gen. 28:10–19; 32:22–32 (quoted in *DT* 34.1–4; discussed in *DT* 35–37.4)
  - **Episode 9:** "The burning bush", "Moses and the glory of the Lord", and "Receiving the two Tablets on Mt. Sinai" in Ex. 3:1–8; 33:12–23; 34:4–11 (quoted in *DT* 34.5–9; discussed in *DT* 38–40.23)

II. **Christ**
  - **Episode 10:** Introductory points (*DT* 42–43.2)
  - **Episode 11:** Discussion of 1 Tim. 2:5 (*DT* 43.3–46.7)
  - **Episode 12:** Discussion of Acts 2:36 (*DT* 46.8–49.7)
  - **Episode 13:** Discussion of miscellaneous New Testament passages, and relating Christ to law, grace, and salvation (*DT* 49.8–10)

III. **Incarnation and Salvation**
  - **Episode 14:** Summaries of the earlier Trinitarian discussions (*DT* 50–51.6)

ного Свято-Тихоновского гуманитарного университета. Серия I: Богословие. Философия. Религоведение, том 92 (2020): pp. 35–56.

- **Episode 15:** Incarnation and God's renewal of his image in man (*DT* 52–54.7)
- **Episode 16:** *Cur Deus Homo*? (Question 1). Man's unique position of closeness with God (*DT* 54.8–57.7)
- **Episode 17:** *Cur Deus Homo*? (Question 2). Man's disobedience versus the obedience of Christ (*DT* 57.8–60.2)
- **Episode 18:** *Cur Deus Homo*? (Question 3). Incarnation and salvation as the work of the entire Trinity (*DT* 60.3–80.6)
- **Episode 19:** Christ and salvation in the patristic tradition and Paul's Letter to the Hebrews (*DT* 80.7–81.5)

In the rest of our discussion, we will examine Zinoviy's major points, following his own structure—Trinity, Christ, incarnation, and salvation—as outlined above. However, before we go into details of his theological thought, we will first make several observations about Zinoviy as an interpreter of Scripture, since exegesis is the principal thing that occupies his attention in this work.

3.2.2 Zinoviy as an Interpreter of Scripture

While Scripture is clearly Zinoviy's primary source of theology, he claims that he builds his arguments on three main sources—natural logic, church tradition, and Scripture[138]—and he masterfully uses all of them throughout *DT*. At the same time, he charges his opponent, Kosoy—who focused only on the books of the Old Testament[139] and a meager selection of church fathers[140]—with distorting the sense of Scripture[141] and ignoring important details in his interpretation of the Old Testament,[142] and actually basing his thoughts on human traditions.[143]

---

138 *DT* 24.5: "We have sought to tell you that God truly exists, offering arguments based on the natural logic and on the tradition, as well as on the holy book of Genesis" (и восприѩхомъ сказовати вамъ. ѩко во истиноу есть бг҃ъ. приводѩщи ѿ ѥ҆ствена разоума и ѿ ѡбычаа. таже и ѿ ст҃ыѧ бытескїа книгы).

139 *DT* 61.1: "Now, you claimed that we must read only the books of the Old Testament, and you call them foundational" (рекосте ѹбо ѩко кни ветхиѧ пѡбае прочита точию. их҃ъ и стопoвыми нарицаете).

140 *DT* 49.18.

141 *DT* 49.14: "[He] lies against divine Scripture, and badly distorts it" (бественое писание лжѹща и ѕлѣ равращающа. и бг҃а хѹлѩща безмѣрно).

142 *DT* 10.1–3.

143 *DT* 48.5–6.

In his treatment of Scripture, Zinoviy may occasionally take a pause to pray for God's help in understanding certain Biblical passages or specific questions, of which the following statement is typical:

> Therefore, even though answering them goes beyond our ability and is very difficult, still, if the truth itself genuinely helps us, it will supply our incompetence with the grace of the supremely holy and good Spirit of God. For it once allowed even Balaam, an unworthy man, to prophesy the truth (Num. 22:24). And placing my trust in the power of the life-giving Spirit, through faith in Christ, I venture to answer you beyond our ability, being determined from the very beginning to be concerned only with the truth, and not with what is deceitful.[144]

Related to this, Zinoviy makes traditional statements of negative theology and calls for silence and worship when he reflects about God, "And concerning this blessed nature of God that is beyond all beings, it befits us, who are endowed with minds, to simply believe and worship rather than to inspect, and also to learn from the Scriptures".[145] While believing, worshipping, and learning from the Scriptures are all parts of the necessary activity of the Christian interpreter according to Zinoviy, his biblical exegesis is guided by the same hermeneutical principle of Christological reading of the Bible that he stated in the *Panegyric*, although this time, he develops it in two significant respects.

First, Zinoviy insists that proper Christological reading of Scripture should go together with the Trinitarian reading, "And we must recognize that wherever there is a sign of the incarnation of God's Son in the divinely-inspired Scripture, there we also have the revelation and manifestation of the Holy Trinity".[146] And second, he urges the reader to pay attention to the context[147] and spends a great deal of time demonstrating the unity of Scriptures, especially between

144 *DT* 51.2: тѣм же и а҃. аще и выше наⷭ҇ еже ѡ сеⷨ вѣщати. и тажко ѕило. ѡбаче аще сама истинна посоⷠствꙋеⷢ поистиннѣ. подасть и нш҃емꙋ неможению. всесⷭ҇го бл҃гаго бг҃а. дх҃а блⷣгть. даде бо иногда и валамовѣ истинꙋ вѣщаⷮ и не достоинꙋ сꙋщю емꙋ. оуповающеⷤ на силꙋ живоⷮворащаго дх҃а вѣрою хⷭ҇вою и выше нш҃еа немощи дерьзнꙋвъ ѿвѣщаю ваⷨ. ꙗко истиⷩною единою пещиⷭ҇ проꙋставивше сами в себѣ в началѣ. се и нн҃ѣ точию.

145 *DT* 26.5: ѡ бжⷭ҇твенеⷨ же пресꙋщественеⷨ блаженнеⷨ ѡномъ ⷭ҇ествѣ вѣровати точию и покланꙗтиⷭ҇ оумъ имꙋщимъ а не ѡпытовати. и наоучатиса ѿ писанїа. Cf. *DT* 49.14; 74.1.

146 *DT* 71.2: Видѣтиⷤ е҃ въ бг҃одх҃новенноⷨ писанїи. идѣже аще е҃ воѡбражение воплощение сн҃а бжїа. тꙋ и ст҃ыа трⷪ҇ца ѿкровение и ꙗвление е҃.

147 *DT* 43.2: "So, let us read the words of the Apostle, taking into account the overall context in order to understand them better" (прочтемⷤ҇ оубо свыше апⷭ҇лово писание. да разꙋмнѣе боудеⷮ).

the Old and New Testaments[148] as well as between the different books of the New Testament.[149]

Based on his belief about the unity of Scripture, Zinoviy calls the reader to recognize the "prefiguration" (прѡбражение)[150] of Christ and the Trinity in the Old Testament and interprets numerous passages "allegorically" (сѣнно).[151] A typical example is his interpretation of Gen. 3:8–9:

> Now, what do you envision when Scripture says, "And they heard the voice of the Lord God walking in the garden in the afternoon; and both Adam and his wife hid in the midst of trees of the garden. And the Lord God called Adam" (Gen. 3:8–9)? Now, is this not a prefiguring of the descent of God's Son from the heavens in order to seek man, who strayed away from the true God into false polytheism, and to call him to salvation through the second birth?[152]

Among the other major examples, Zinoviy contends that God's visit with Abraham in the tent (Gen. 18:1–5) prefigured the dwelling of Christ in a human body, whereas God's solution for Sarah's inability to bear children due to her old age (Gen. 18:10) was a sign of Christ's miraculous conception.[153] Sarah's doubt that she would bear a child (Gen. 18:12–15) points to the unbelief of the Jews and the heretics in the incarnation of Christ;[154] the indwelling presence of God in the burning bush (Ex. 3:1–8) prefigures the coming of God's Son to dwell in the flesh;[155] God's descent to wrestle with Jacob (Gen. 32:22–32) prefigures the incarnation of the Son to save the world from the violence of the devil, and just as Jacob was freed from Esau (Gen. 32:1–21), so would Christ deliver everyone

---

148 *DT* 49.19: "All the writings of the Old Testament have already been completed and fulfilled by Christ's advent" (всемꙋ писанию ветхомꙋ скончаннꙋ оуⷤ сꙋщꙋ. и съвершившꙋсѧ хⷭвыⷨ пришествиⷨе).

149 *DT* 46.4: "For the Apostle's Epistle to Timothy belongs to the same Apostle who wrote these words in Romans" (ꙗкоⷤ бо к тимоѳѣю апⷭ҇лово послание ѡно. такоⷤ тогоⷤ апⷭ҇ла и к римлꙗноⷨ сїе писание).

150 *DT* 68.1.

151 *DT* 78.1.

152 *DT* 68.1: чтоⷤ оубо мнитсѧ ваⷨ писанию гл҃ющꙋ. И слышаста глаⷭ гⷭа бг҃а ходѧща в раюⷡ полꙋдне. и скрыстасѧ посредѣ древа раискаго адамⷤъ и жена его. и призва гⷭь бг҃ъ адама. Нⷭѣ ли оубо се прѡбражение сшествиѧ сн҃ꙋ бж҃ию съ нбⷭе. на взыскание чл҃ка заблꙋжьшаⷢ ѿ бг҃а истиннаго. во многобж҃ие ложное. и призвавшаⷢ в пакибытие спⷭенїа.

153 *DT* 70.

154 *DT* 71.

155 *DT* 76.

from the devil's deceit.[156] These examples are only a handful of what we find in *DT*, and they form an important part of Zinoviy's method of theologizing, rooted in his understanding of the unity of Scripture.

At the same time, Zinoviy makes important philological observations (such as whether a certain pronoun has a singular, plural, or dual number when it talks about the divine and non-divine subjects),[157] creating his own distinctions (such as between the downward and upward movements of God and the angels in the book of Genesis),[158] and showing the importance of treating the Scriptures chronologically (as in the first nine episodes and in some of his own remarks).[159]

We will now turn to the actual thought of Zinoviy, beginning with the doctrine of the Trinity.

3.2.3 The Trinity

Of the nineteen episodes that we outlined above, the doctrine of the Trinity clearly receives the greatest attention. While the first nine episodes, in which Zinoviy directly talks about the Trinity, contain numerous valuable points, we have chosen to focus on several significant concepts that will help to paint the bigger picture of his thought. In one of the many statements where Zinoviy articulates his doctrine of the Trinity, he says:

> The sacred Scripture truly shows … the holy and all pure and single divinity and lordship of the supreme Trinity. In its supreme wisdom, it averts men from the deities of the Greeks that are oligarchic, evil, false, and dead. In many of its words, it reveals the true living God with his Son, who is proper to him, and his Holy Spirit. It declares the monarchy, the common lordship, the common desire, the common will of the one divinity of the Father and the Son and the Holy Spirit [who exist] in supreme perfection, supreme peace, supreme inseparability, supreme eternality. It shows the

---

156 *DT* 79.

157 *DT* 31.5–6, 9.

158 *DT* 39.1–2; 68.2. When introducing a certain distinction, Zinoviy may state something like this: "You see how in this passage, too, Scripture distinguishes between the description of the ministering angels and their Lord" (Видитє писаниє и всє. како разлꙋчає бесѣдою слꙋжебны аггла ѿ гā и). The passage is found in *DT* 39.1.

159 E.g., *DT* 30.1: "Let us then proceed by going to the very beginning, and in love of the truth, read everything in an orderly fashion, so that we may truly understand the truth, instead of wandering around according to the falsehood of Kosoy's godlessness" (Ходитє оубо поидємъ в любви истинны. на прєписанїа. пачє по радꙋ прочитающє. да познаємъ истиннꙋ воистиннꙋ. а нє по косо прєсти бєбжїа влающєса).

> Lord to be the only-begotten Son, the Word of God, doing the wonderful works of the Lord, God the Father.[160]

So, what exactly is the logic behind this Trinitarian statement? To answer this question, it is important to remember that Zinoviy's opponent, Kosoy, acknowledged only the Father and rejected the Son and the Holy Spirit. To counter this unitarian view of God, Zinoviy goes to great lengths to demonstrate the existence of the Trinity and the unity between the divine persons on two levels—ontological and functional.

Describing the ontological unity of the persons, Zinoviy presents the Father as the source of divinity and perfections for the other two persons by identifying him with the divine essence, "The supremely blessed divine essence is simultaneously God and Father".[161] The fact that the Son and the Holy Spirit share all the divine attributes of the Father/divine essence (among which Zinoviy likes to give long lists, such as immortality, goodness, love, glory, power, honor, life, and others), shows the former two "to be equal" (равныⷯ быти) and "consubstantial" (единосꙋщныⷨ) with the latter.[162]

To express this idea on the technical level, Zinoviy develops three sets of terms that stress the commonality of attributes shared in the Trinity, using the prefixes "common" (едино), "equally" (равно), and "co-" (со). A few examples based on these three prefixes illustrate how different Trinitarian terms are designed to express the triune oneness of God under three categories:

The first category of attributes with the prefix "common" (едино):
- "Sharing *common* honor" (единочⷭ҇тные)
- "Sharing *common* glory" (единославные)
- "Sharing *common* headship" (единоначальные)

The second category of attributes with the prefix "equally" (равно):
- "Possessing *equal* power" (равномощные)
- "Possessing *equal* honor" (равночестные)
- "Possessing *equal* throne" (равнопрестⷪ҇ные)

160 *DT* 40.20: истинно показа сщ҃нное писание ... ст҃го прчⷭ҇таго. единоⷪ҇ бжⷭ҇тва и гⷭ҇ьства. единоначаⷧ҇нꙋю трⷪ҇цꙋ. премⷬ҇ѣ ѿводѧ чл҃ки ѿ мнⷪ҇начаⷭ҇ственыⷯ скверныⷯ и ложныⷯ мрⷮ҇выⷯ бг҃овъ. ѿкрываа неложнаⷢ҇ живаⷢ҇ бг҃а со прⷭ҇ныⷨ сн҃омъ его и дх҃омъ его ст҃ыⷨ. Многими гл҃ы. и извѣстꙋа единачаⷭ҇твеное. единогⷭ҇ьственое. единохотѣнное. единовⷪ҇ное. единоⷢ҇ бжⷭ҇тва. ѿц҃а и сн҃а и ст҃го дх҃а. всесъвершено всемирно. все нераздѣлно всепрⷭ҇нено. ꙗко гⷭ҇ь единорⷪ҇ный сн҃ъ слово бж҃ие. сотворѧеⷮ҇ бж҃їа ѿч҃а гн҃а дѣлеса чюⷣнаа.

161 *DT* 22.6: преблж҃енное. бжⷭ҇твеное сꙋщество. вкꙋпѣ бг҃ъ вкꙋпѣ ѿц҃ъ.

162 *DT* 27.7; 49.4.

The third category of attributes with the prefix "co-" (со):

– "*Co*-ruling" (совладычествоующие)
– "*Co*-directing" (соповелительные)
– "*Co*-eternal" (соприсносоущие)

He has a remarkably rich Trinitarian vocabulary, and one could probably say that he constructs far more neologisms than we find in most other Slavic writings from medieval Russia.[163]

According to Zinoviy, "The perfection of the eternal nature does not become inferior or more complete",[164] and therefore, all three persons of the Trinity are equally divine and perfect, as they share the same set of attributes.

The unity of divine persons does not contradict the distinctions in the Trinity, and Zinoviy demonstrates this through his famous analogy of the mind, word, and breath. Believing that "by looking at the image of God in man, one can recognize the true God, rational and intelligent, existing in the Trinity",[165] he uses this analogy to describe the relations of "fatherhood", "sonship", and "procession" as distinct properties of the Trinitarian persons:

> For the mind generates the word that becomes revealed through the breath, and then, by means of the breath that comes from the mouth, we can recognize the paternity of the mind and the generation of the word in man. It is the same with the Godhead itself: by means of the divine Spirit, believers can genuinely recognize the fatherhood of God and the sonship of his Word that is likewise without beginning. And the Godhead is neither divided into three nor merged into one—out of God and his Word and the Spirit—nor is it a pre-existing oneness, nor is it a godhead to which the other two are added afterward. For the Word and the Spirit are eternally co-existing with the Father. And thus, the Father and the Son and the Holy Spirit are recognized and believed to be in one Godhead, neither merged nor separated. For, in man, too, who is the image and likeness of the Godhead, the mind and the word and the breath in his soul are neither separated nor merged.[166]

---

163 See the list of the most significant terms and specific references to them in *DT* Table 4, prepared by Shpakovskiy.

164 *DT* 22.5: прⷭ҇носꙋщагѡⷤ ес҃тва совершение. беⷥ ѡскꙋдѣнїа есть и бес прибыванїа.

165 *DT* 21.1: ѿ ѡбраза бж҃їа чл҃ка дш҃и оумны и словеⷭ҇ны. бг҃ъ истинныи в трⷪ҇цы познаваетсѧ.

166 *DT* 22.2–4: оуⷨ слово ражаетъ дх҃мъ ꙗвлꙗемо и дх҃омъ из оꙋстъ исходꙗщемъ. познаваемо ꙋма ѿч҃ество. и слова рожение въ чл҃цѣ. – Акоⷤ и в самоⷨ бжⷭ҇твѣ дх҃мъ бж҃їимъ познаваетсѧ право вѣрꙋющимъ бг҃а ѿч҃ьство и слова ⷭ҇е собезначаⷧ҇ное сн҃овьство. не раздѣлано бжⷭ҇тво на три. ни слито

At one point, Zinoviy refutes the idea that man was made according to the angelic image rather than that of the Trinity and argues that if this were true, then man would have possessed the distinct features of the angels, such as multiple eyes, wings, and fiery appearances.[167] He also refutes the idea that any physical part of the human body can render any analogical insights worthy of the Trinity.[168] Parts of the body are found in man just as they are in the non-rational animals, but the triad of the mind, word, and breath is the only aspect that proves the Trinity and exhibits that man is "the icon of the Godhead" (икона бжтва члкъ).[169] In fact, the very words "Let us make man in our image and likeness" (Gen. 1:26), according to Zinoviy, confirm that creation was the work of the entire Trinity, as it follows from the way its members counseled or conversed with each other by using the plural pronouns "us" and "our" when referring to the creation of man.[170] It shows that the Father spoke to those who

---

въ едино. в бзѣ и словѣ и дсѣ его. ни пре бытно едино. ни послѣди прибытно два дрѹгаа бжтвоу. Сопрносѹщны бо бгоу слово и дхъ. познавается и вѣрѹется Ѿцъ и снъ и стыи дхъ. во едино бжтвѣ. не слитно ни раздѣлно. поне и въ чцѣ и wбра и подобие бжтва не раздѣляются. ни сливаются в дши оумъ слово ї дыхание. For similar reflections and analogies from this time period, see the *Explanatory Paleya*, and the works of Iosif Volotskiy, Dosifey Toporkov, and Ermolay-Erasm: *Палея толковая* [*Explanatory Paleya*] (Москва: Согласие, 2002), pp. 71–87; *Enlightener* 1, pp. 62–66, 88–93; *Полное собрание русских летописей. Русский хронограф редакции 1512 года* [*Complete Collection of Russian Chronicles. Russian Chronicle of the Year 1512*], том 22, часть 1 (Санкт-Петербург: Типография М.А. Александрова, 1911), pp. 14–15; *Библиографические материалы, собранные Андреем Поповым. VIII. Книга Еразма о Святой Троице* [*Bibliographic Materials Collected by A. Popov. Erasm's Book on the Holy Trinity*] (Москва: Издание Общества истории и древностей российских при Московском университете, 1880), pp. 2–3.

167 For similar reflections during this time period, see a text penned by Metropolitan Makariy in his debate with Dyak Viskovaty in О. Бодянский, *Розыск или список о богохульных строках и сумнении святых честных икон диака Ивана Михайлова Висковатого в лето 7062* [O. Bodyanskiy, *Investigation or Material of Dyak Ivan Mikhaylovich Viskovaty on the Blasphemous Lines and Doubts Regarding the Holy Honorable Icons in the Year 7062*] (Москва: Издание Общества истории и древностей российских при Московском университете, 1858), pp. 17–18. Cf. also Мильков В. *Древнерусские апокрифы* [V. Milkov, *The Old Russian Apocrypha*] (Санкт-Петербург: Изд-во РХГИ, 1999), pp. 504–516.

168 It is possible that behind this argument is Zinoviy's reaction against the excessively material analogies of his contemporary, Ermolay-Erasm. See, e.g., *Библиографические материалы* [*Bibliographic Materials*], p. 63.

169 *DT* 21.

170 *DT* 12.1–5. This interpretation of Gen. 1:26 is representative of Christian exegesis that originates in the early church and appears very early in the Slavonic writings. Cf. e.g., *Hexameron of John the Exarch of Bulgaria* in Баранкова, Мильков, *Шестоднев* [Barankova & Milkov, *Hexameron*], p. 624.

existed “closely with him”—the Son and the Spirit—and that there was “nothing mediating between them”.[171]

Related to this point, Zinoviy argues that the ontological unity of divine persons presupposes the functional unity of the Trinity, and he explains it in several ways. First, there is a functional submission of the Son and the Holy Spirit to the Father based on love:

> And it is not because of force nor of necessity that the Son and the Holy Spirit obey God the Father, but the Son and the Holy Spirit submit to God the Father, rather, out of love. They do it according to the common desire and according to the common will, as those who have equal power and share the same throne with God the Father on account of the consubstantial divinity and dominion.[172]

Again, all three persons of the Trinity are equal because they share the same divine attributes or possess the same nature, so there is no “greater” or “lesser” God, as Zinoviy emphasizes later.[173] Yet each member of the Trinity is personally and functionally distinct, operating in three different roles, even though their will and activity are still one. Thus, the second way in which Zinoviy depicts the functional unity of the Trinity is their common (yet distinct) economy in the world. And here, Zinoviy spends considerable time, showing that both creation and redemption are the work of the whole Trinity, while each person plays his own role. At one place, he articulates this point by picturing a conversation within the Trinity, where the Father says, “Now that this ‘image and likeness’ of ours [that is, man] that we created has grown weak and become broken, it remains for you, Son, then, to renew it through the incarnation, and it remains for you, Holy Spirit, to descend and advance my illuminating power”.[174]

---

171 *DT* 15.1: бл҃и бг҃а; *DT* 14.3: имѣющее посрⷣство межоу бг҃а.

172 *DT* 36.5: но едина волѧ едино хотѣние тремъ ѿц҃ꙋ и сн҃ꙋ и ст҃мꙋ дх҃ꙋ. и не по насилию ни не волею послꙋшающимъ сн҃ꙋ и дх҃ꙋ ст҃мꙋ бг҃а ѿц҃а. Но волею повинꙋющеⷭ҇ бг҃оу ѿц҃ꙋ сн҃ъ и дх҃ъ ст҃ыи. по единомꙋ хотѣнию и по единои воли. равносⷭ҇ины и единопрⷭ҇тльны бг҃ꙋ ѿцꙋ сꙋща. за единосꙋщество бжⷭ҇тва и вⷧ҇чества.

173 *DT* 40.13: “For the divinity of the Father is named no differently than the divinity of the Son, with no distinction between a ‘greater ⟨God⟩’ and a ‘lesser God’ ” (нⷭ҇ѣ бо ино имѧ бжⷭ҇тва ѿц҃ꙋ. и ино имѧ бжⷭ҇тва сн҃оу жⷷ҇е быти бⷧ҇ошемꙋ и меншемꙋ бг҃ꙋ. но едино бжⷭ҇тво ѿц҃ꙋ и сн҃ꙋ). Cf. *Panegyric* 3 and sect. 3.1.1.

174 *DT* 53.5: озидаемꙋ ѡбразꙋ семꙋ нш҃емꙋ и пⷣобию. внегда емꙋ ѡветшавшꙋ съкрꙋшитⷭ҇и. тогда тебѣ сн҃оу поновити его воплоцениемъ своимъ. и тебѣ дх҃ꙋ нашествиемъ содѣистоваⷮ҇. моеи силѣ ѡсѣнающи.

Zinoviy likes to contrast the perfect unity and distinction in the Trinity with the confusion and chaos of the Olympian gods, "There is no contradiction within the Trinity, between the Father and the Son and the Holy Spirit; neither is there any disagreement nor competition, like the contradiction and disagreement and competition among the many false Hellenistic deities. Instead, the three—Father, and Son, and Holy Spirit—have one will and one desire".[175] And when asked why God chose not to reveal himself as the Trinity plainly in the Old Testament—instead, having done it gradually—Zinoviy makes a similar point:

> We have to account for the fact that Scripture was given to the people who lived among the polytheistic nations that used to hear of many emerging deities and deities of deities [known] for killing each other and fighting among themselves, such as when Zeus murdered his own father Cronus, and also killed others for the sake of gaining wives ... The book of Genesis taught them about the one God in a very wise, true way so that the Jews, who did not hear of God the Father, and of his Word, the Son, and of his Holy Spirit from the very beginning, and who were not able to recognize the incorporeal, divine, entirely perfect being, would not come to think that Moses was speaking of many gods. For the Jews in their insanity were always inclined toward polytheism, just as we now saw this man, Kosoy, in his insanity being prone to godlessness.[176]

In fact, much of what Zinoviy writes in the episodes that cover the Trinity is primarily his demonstration of the proofs that God revealed himself in that way from the very first pages of Scripture. Perhaps, the two dominant passages, to which he gives considerable attention, are the "Creation of man" in Gen. 1:26

---

175 *DT* 36.4: ꙗко нѣсть сѹпротивїа въ тр҃цы ко ѿц҃ѹ сн҃а и дх҃а ст҃го ни распра ни рати. ꙗкоже во лживыхъ еллиньскихъ многыхъ бг҃овъ. сѹпротивие и распра и рати. но едина волꙗ едино хотѣние тремъ ѿц҃ѹ и сн҃ѹ и ст҃мѹ дх҃ѹ.

176 *DT* 28.1–2: понеже прелагает сꙗ книга. чл҃комъ живший посредѣ ꙗзыка многобожна. и навыкшим слышати многи бг҃и бывающаа. и боги боговъ оубивающа и ратѹюще сꙗ межи себе. ꙗкоже зевесъ крона ѿца своего оуби. и ины женъ ради побивающихъ сꙗ ... наоучаетъ книга бытеискаа. да не ѿ начатка слышавше иоудѣа бг҃а ѿца и слова его сн҃а. и дх҃а его ст҃го. познати не возмогѹть. бесплотное бж҃твеное всесъвершеное сѹщество. и вознмнꙗть пакы многы богы быти сказоующа имъ и моисѣа. понеже присно ко многобж҃ию июдѣомъ неистовство належит. ꙗкоже нн҃ѣ видимъ косого се. неистовѣ к безбж҃ию належаща. Cf. *DT* 36.4; 40.3–4, 12, 20. For a similar point, see *Enlightener* 1, p. 60. The patristic source (in the Slavonic translation) that makes this point and could inspire medieval theologians in Russia is the *Hexameron of John the Exarch of Bulgaria* in Баранкова, Мильков, *Шестоднев* [Barankova & Milkov, *Hexameron*], p. 624.

(episode 2) and the story about the "Three visitors who appear to Abraham by the Oak of Mamre" in Gen. 18:1–5 (episode 5). Using the early classical argument based on the plural pronouns "us" and "ours" in the phrase, "Let us make man in our image and likeness" (a point which he reiterates again and again in various parts of *DT*), he argues that the whole Trinity participated in the creation of man. And interpreting the three angels who appeared to Abraham as the three persons of the Godhead, he portrays the one who stayed with Abraham as the Father (Gen. 18:22), and the other two who went to Sodom as the Son and the Holy Spirit (Gen. 19:1). These and other places where Zinoviy discerns the Trinity in the Old Testament are examples of outstanding theological reflections of the time.

3.2.4 Christ

Zinoviy's discussion of Christ is found in the middle (and shortest) part of his writing (episodes 10–13), where he is primarily concerned with the refutation of his opponent's belief that Christ was a mere human being. Just as in the *Panegyric*, where he identified the Russian heretics as Arians, so here, too, he draws a direct parallel between Arius and Kosoy:

> And in his perverse mind, just like the heretic Arius, he treats the Word lightly and reasons in an evil way when making reference to Peter's statement that says, "God made this Jesus" (Acts 2:36). And to this, he also adds Paul's words that "there is one God, and there is one mediator between God and men, the man Jesus Christ" (1 Tim. 2:5). With these statements, Kosoy says that Christ is both "made" and a "mere man", and that Christ is not God.[177]

Having made this statement, Zinoviy spends the rest of the episodes, dealing with Acts 2:36 (also discussed in *Panegyric* 7.4), 1 Tim. 2:5, and some other passages to show that they "proclaim Christ as being simultaneously God and man".[178] In the process, he makes several major arguments. First, he restates his hermeneutical principle of the twofold account of Scripture that sees Christ under two aspects—his eternal existence before the incarnation and his earthly life in the world—and argues that "the Apostles applied the name

177 *DT* 43.1: и по раⷥвращенномꙋ своемꙋ оумꙋ. ꙗкоⷤ и арїи еретикъ. наго приеⷨ слово и раⷥсꙋжаеⷮ ѕлѣ. глⷮе бо апⷭ҇ла петра гл҃юща. ꙗко сотвори сеⷢ҇ ї҃са бг҃ъ. к томꙋ҃ приводѧ и павлово ѡноⷤ е҇ единъ есть бг҃ъ и единъ ходатаи бг҃ꙋ и чл҃комъ чл҃къ ї҃съ хⷭ҇ъ. сими гл҃ы и сотворена хⷭ҇а и чл҃ка еⷢ҇ проста глⷮе его косои а не бг҃а хⷭ҇а.

178 *DT* 43.2: проповѣдаеⷮ хⷭ҇а. бг҃а кꙋпно и чл҃ка.

'Christ' to his divinity, and the name 'Jesus' to his humanity".[179] In light of this principle, he urges the reader to pay careful attention to the Biblical context and interprets Acts 2:36 as an example where doing so helps us gain a proper understanding of the phrase, "God *made* him both Lord and Christ, this Jesus", which Kosoy misinterpreted as an indication of Christ's created nature:

> After he [Peter] had clearly expressed the exalted divinity of Christ, through what he had already preached concerning his resurrection, and after he had shown the ultimate greatness of the uncreated divinity, due to his ascension to the heavens and his seating at the right hand of God and his sending of the Holy Spirit to them, he went on to speak of his humiliation through the cross and death, that he suffered because he assumed our flesh when "God *made* him both Lord and Christ, this Jesus" (Acts 2:36).[180]

Second, Zinoviy realizes that his insistence on understanding Christ as both divine and human requires an explanation of how the two natures were related in him. In one of his statements concerning this issue, we can recognize that Zinoviy's points were firmly grounded in the patristic Christology of Chalcedon that proclaimed Christ "in two natures without confusion, without change, without division, without separation":[181]

> And you should believe that Jesus Christ is a single person, divine and human. The divinity did not mingle with the flesh into a fusion [of the two], but both natures were intact: the divinity and humanity in one person, Jesus Christ, without confusion. In him, divinity did not turn into flesh, nor did the flesh turn into divinity.[182]

---

179 *DT* 44.2: еⷭ҇ оубо хⷭ҇во имꙗ на бжⷭ҇тво приемлемо апⷭ҇лы. і҃сово҇ имѧ на чл҃чество. Cf. *DT* 46.3: "Depending on what he speaks about, he assigns the [appropriate] name, proclaiming him in all to be God incarnate and the one who delivered all men" (по послѣдованию слова. и имꙗ емꙋ примаа во всеⷨ проповѣдаеⷮ его бг҃а вочл҃чьшаⷭ҇. и томꙋ единомꙋ избавити всѣⷯ).

180 *DT* 49.7: внегдаⷤ воскрⷭ҇нїа раⷣ высотꙋ бжⷭ҇тва хⷭ҇ва. преⷤ проповѣдаⷤ оуⷤ ꙗвиⷡ вознесенїа раⷣ его на нбⷭ҇са. и сидѣниеⷨ его ѡдеснꙋю ѿц҃а. и посланїа раⷣ дх҃а ст҃го к ниⷨ. еⷤ краинее величества бжⷭ҇тва не сотворенна҇ показа. тогда и смиреное кртⷭ҇а раⷣ и смр҃ти реⷭ҇. за сꙋщее еⷬ҇ приатие плоти нш҃еа. ꙗко і гаⷭ҇ и хаⷭ҇ сотвори бг҃ъ сеⷭ҇ і҃са.

181 The quotation is from A. Grillmeier, *Christ in Christian Tradition*: *From the Apostolic Age to Chalcedon* (*451*), vol. 1 (Atlanta: John Knox Press, 1975), p. 544. See the same book for a discussion of Chalcedonian Christology on pp. 543–550.

182 *DT* 80.2: и вѣрꙋеши ꙗко единъ і҃съ хⷭ҇. бг҃ъ и чл҃къ еⷭ҇. и не смѣшаⷭ҇ бжⷭ҇тво с плотию слитиеⷨ. но ѡба еⷭ҇ства бжⷭ҇тво и чл҃чество цѣла. въ единоⷨ составѣ не слитно і҃съ хⷭ҇вѣ. ни бжⷭ҇твꙋ на плоⷮ преложившꙋⷭ҇. в немъ. ни плоⷮ на бжⷭ҇тво.

Based on this, Zinoviy contends that Christ's "divinity did not change because of his taking on flesh"[183] and that both Paul and Peter (in the disputed passages of Acts 2:36 and 1 Tim. 2:5) "preached that Christ truly became human, and not that he was made man simply in thought or as an illusion (не мниниеⷨ ни привидѣниеⷨ)".[184] Having established the fact of the genuine incarnation of Christ, Zinoviy goes on to elaborate on the meaning of the incarnation and its significance for the history of salvation in the final set of the episodes.

3.2.5 Incarnation and Salvation

Before moving directly into the discussion of the incarnation and salvation in this part of his writing (episodes 14–19), Zinoviy actually touches on some of their aspects in the earlier episodes, and especially in episode 13, where he explores miscellaneous passages from the New Testament and relates Christ to law, grace, and salvation.[185] In fact, it is there that he first begins to ponder the question of why an incarnation was needed, and he goes on to unpack it more fully here.[186] In this section, we will organize our discussion of Zinoviy's treatment of the incarnation and salvation around the "Anselmian" type of question—*Cur Deus Homo?* (Why did God become a man?)[187]—which the kliros-chanters explicitly or implicitly ask him three times: in episodes 16, 17, and 18. His thorough treatment of this question is unprecedented in the Slavonic medieval tradition.

---

183 DT 49.3: не премениⷭ҇ бжⷭ҇твоⷨ ѿ приѧтїа плоти. Cf. DT 49.6: "Therefore, the only-begotten Son of God did not impair the glory of the Godhead, even after becoming flesh. Instead, he (retained) in the flesh the glory of his deity that he eternally possessed. For the Son of God is the only-begotten, as he himself said, 'I and the Father are one' (Jn. 10:30)" (посемꙋ не поврєдⷭ҇а славою единородⷩ҇ыи сн҃ъ бж҃їи бывъ плоть. но и во плоти тꙋюⷤ҇ славꙋ бжⷭ҇тва прнⷭ҇ѣ имаⷮ. понеⷤ҇ единородⷩ҇ыи сн҃ъ бж҃їи сыи. ꙗкоⷤ҇ и саⷨ рече. азъ и ѡ҃ц҃ъ едино есвѣ).

184 DT 46.8: истиⷩ҇ною въчл҃чение ⷭ҇е проповѣдаша. а не мниниеⷨ ни привидѣниеⷨ чл҃ка бывша. Cf. DT 49.3.

185 For this discussion, see DT 49.8–10.

186 Thus, explaining the reasons behind the incarnation in one of the previous episodes, he claims, "For it is impossible for a mere man to deliver all from sin and from death ... Jesus Christ alone, being without guilt, was able to deliver all men through himself" (невозможно бо чл҃кꙋ простꙋ дати себе во избавꙋ за всѣхъ. всѧⷦ҇ бо чл҃къ ложь по прⷪ҇ркꙋ. едиⷩ҇ неповиненъ гⷭ҇ь іⷭ҇съ хⷭ҇ъ. могїи избавити всѣⷯ собою даⷡ҇ себе за всѣхъ. беⷥ҇грѣшенъ сыи, DT 43.6). Adding slightly later, he says, "since it is impossible for God to undergo suffering, it was also impossible for the divine Son of God to suffer other than by clothing himself in the flesh" (истиⷩ҇ною въчл҃чение ⷭ҇е проповѣдаша. а не мниниеⷨ ни привидѣниеⷨ чл҃ка бывша, DT 46.8). Cf. DT 49.3.

187 *Cur Deus Homo?* is the Latin name of the work written by Anselm of Canterbury in 1094–1098, which became famous for his satisfaction view of the atonement. The first theologian to raise and explore this question was Athanasius of Alexandria in his writing *De Incarnatione Verbi* (CPG 2091).

But before we reach the place where this question is explicitly asked, Zinoviy reflects on whether the Old Testament foretells anything about the incarnation of God's Son and foreshadows his grace to humankind. There, he summarizes his earlier thoughts from the Trinitarian episodes to answer this question and—most importantly for our purposes—reflects on humanity before and after the fall in order to explain how Christ solved the problem of sin (episodes 14–15). More specifically, he discusses the ontological and legal consequences of the fall, depicting the first in terms of death, corruption, mortality, and broken image, and explaining the second in terms of transgression of the law, guilt, and curse. The coming of Christ had to deal with both aspects by "liberating [man] from transgression and mending his image and likeness"[188] to restore humanity to its original state.

Zinoviy spends more time exploring the ontological aspect than the legal one in episode 15, because he had been challenged to discuss the latter in episode 13, disputing Kosoy's claim "that salvation depends on keeping the Law".[189] In his response, Zinoviy argued that "Jesus Christ has come in the flesh and fulfilled [the Law] with his advent",[190] whereas Kosoy's attempt to live according to the Law was actually breaking it because "he does not fast, and does not do the rituals of purification, and does not offer sacrifices, and does not circumcise, and does not keep the Passover according to the Law".[191] To solve the legal problem of sin there is no other way but through the incarnation, "because it is impossible for a mere man to deliver all from sin and from death. For all men are under sin and guilty (Rom. 3:19, 23). Jesus Christ alone, who came in the flesh, 'committed no sin'" (1 Pet. 2:22).[192] Thus, by the time Zinoviy is ready to focus on the ontological aspect of the fall and salvation he has made it clear that the substitutional sacrifice of Christ brought humanity what it needed from the legal standpoint: forgiveness of sins, reconciliation, freedom from guilt, and deliverance.[193]

---

188 *DT* 54.1: свободити ѿ престꙋпленїѧ. и исправи свои ѡбра и повие.

189 *DT* 49.14: оуча законо спсати.

190 *DT* 49.16: хꙋ ісꙋ во плоти пришешꙋ и скончa того своимъ пришествие.

191 *DT* 49.17: не постиса бо. и не ѡчищается. ни жртвы жре ни ѡбрѣзꙋется. ни пасхꙋ законнꙋю твори.

192 *DT* 43.6: ибо невозможно простꙋ члкꙋ избави всѣхъ ѿ грѣ ха и ѿ смрти. всѣ бо по грѣхо бѣша и повинни. единъ ісъ хсъ пришедыи во плоти тои бо грѣха не сотвори.

193 For these motifs, see especially *DT* 49.9: "In speaking of the Son, or more specifically, 'in whom we have deliverance', he [Paul] implied that the Father offered the sacrifice, while the Son dealt with the main problem [of men]—bringing about the 'forgiveness of sins' 'through his blood' (Col. 1:14). For if the sins had not been forgiven, we would not have been transferred to the 'kingdom' of the 'beloved Son' of God" (Col. 1:13) (ѡ нем же ре снꙋ. рекше ѡ

When reflecting on the ontological aspect, Zinoviy concentrates primarily on the problem of the broken image in man and the way Christ restored it through the incarnation. His thoughts here grow directly from the way he defines humanity as a "rational" (оумна) and "self-governing being" (самовластенъ), brought into existence "out of non-being" (ѿ небытиѧ):[194] "For man to be in the image of God means to have an intelligent and rational soul; and it means that man is self-governing. In view of this, while all the works have the need to move according to their nature, man alone has the will to choose in what direction he wants to move—toward the good things or toward the evil things".[195] Choosing to move in the wrong direction because of "his desire to become equal with the Creator"[196] and "using his self-governing ability to demolish the prototype and corrupt the likeness of God in himself",[197] man found that his "image and likeness were weakened and became broken".[198]

To heal this aspect of human nature, Christ became man, and Zinoviy stresses that the reason why he assumed a human body rather than that of celestial things or angels[199] was that the rational, living soul of man could be

---

нем же имамы избавление. ıа ѿцъ оубо прѣложи. снъ дасть винꙋ кровию е ѡставление грѣхо содѣлавъ. аще бо быша грѣси не ѡставлени. не быхо преставлени были въ цртвие сна бжиа возлюблена); *DT* 49.12–13: "But give heed to the words of those statements that said, 'making peace' and 'through him, he reconciled' us. These words that I am quoting are not about his command, but about his acting according to the flesh. They are not about anything done purely for him, but about his doing it [for others]: his shedding blood, becoming a sacrifice, establishing a reconciliation by dying a shameful death through the crucifixion, while knowing of his divine nature" (вижь же ренны извѣщение примири ре и смирина имъ. е есть не глю повелѣвъ но плоски дѣиствовавъ. не просто его ра но крове его ра излианныѧ. закланиѧ поносныѧ ради смрти распатие. ѡбра примиренїа полагаа. вѣды бжтвеное е сꙋщество).

194 *DT* 57.5.

195 *DT* 54.10: по ѡбразꙋ оубо бжию члкъ. ıако дшꙋ имѣа оумнꙋ словенꙋ. и ıако самовластенъ е члкъ. поне вса тварь по ествꙋ своемꙋ нꙋжею движение има. единъ члкъ волю има. избрати е хоще. или к добры двизати или къ злымъ. Cf. *DT* 54.12–13, where Zinoviy describes man as a "king" over creation and explains how his self-governing ability was designed to make him imitate God. In another place, Zinoviy contrasts rational human beings with non-rational animals and argues that man's ability to talk and sing is one of the most evident features of his special position in the world as the one who was made in the image of God (see *DT* 18.1–2). On the idea of man being created with the ability to make moral judgements in terms of controlling his direction or behavior, cf. Athanasius, *Contra Gentes* 32–33 [CPG 2090] and *De Incarnatione Vebi* 17.

196 вравнити к создателю восхотѣста. Cf. *DT* 20.1–2; 21.1; 59.2.

197 *DT* 53.3: хоташе члкъ ѿ самовластиѧ свое сокрꙋшити и истлѣти поѡбразное и подобное бжие в себѣ.

198 *DT* 53.5: ѡбразꙋ … и пдбию … ѡбетшавшꙋ съкрꙋшити.

199 *DT* 53:6: "And the Word, the Son of God, took neither a heavenly body nor that of the

restored only by someone who himself was rational and living:[200] "For that reason, God was willing to send the One who was rational and living in order to save the perishing man, to renew in him his image that was corrupted … And there was no other way to accomplish this renewal other than by means of the very flesh into which the Word of God clothed himself".[201] In this context, Zinoviy calls Christ the new Adam and explains that his coming was to renew the old Adam, and thus, bring the fallen creation back to life.[202] To accomplish this, the new Adam had to be God in order to do what humans could not do on their own, and Zinoviy formulates it as a soteriological principle, "For that which is inferior is saved by that which is superior, and that which is better cannot be saved by that which is worse".[203] He never loses the motif of God's common work in salvation and insists that all three persons of the Trinity were engaged in a special way during Christ's incarnation.[204]

Although Zinoviy has already touched on various aspects of why God became man, episode 16 is the first place where we see the kliros-chanters explicitly asking the *Cur Deus Homo?* type of question, "And if God really wanted to prepare help for man, then why should his Son become incarnate rather than having God send someone else to help human weakness?"[205] To answer this

---

angels. Instead, the Word of God assumed the human flesh through the Holy Spirit in order to renew his image and likeness [in man]" (ꙗко не прıати словꙋ сн҃ꙋ бж҃ию нбн҃ыѧ пло҃ти агг҃льскиѧ. но прıати чл҃чю пло҃ словꙋ бж҃ию дх҃омъ ст҃ымъ. зан҃е поновит҃ ѡбра҃ свои и по҃бие).

200 Cf. *DT* 3.1–2, where Zinoviy makes a similar point with regard to the Trinity, explaining why God must be rational and living as opposed to being non-rational and lifeless.

201 *DT* 53:3: и ꙗко словесное живое сего ра҃ хоташе посла҃ бг҃ъ въ е҃ сп҃ти погибша҃ чл҃ка. ѡбновити в не҃ престꙋпление҃ и истлѣвшїи свои ѡбра҃ и подобное назда҃ паки и҃ сокрꙋшившееса прегрѣшенми. не инако҃ сего поновити есть аще тою҃ плотию не ѡдѣетса.

202 *DT* 57.6: "And therefore, after Adam died, and the corruption of sin consumed his flesh, the Word of God was incarnated and became the new Adam, to renew through his coming the old Adam, corrupted because of sin" (и по семꙋ внегда ѹмершꙋ адамꙋ и истлѣвшꙋ. и грѣ҃ его в не҃ истлѣ҃е. и истлѣвшꙋ грѣхꙋ его с плотию его. слово бж҃ие воплоти҃ новыи ада҃ бы҃. ѡбнови пришꙋ҃ истлѣвша҃ древнаго адама грѣха ра҃).

203 *DT* 56.1: ѿ бо҃шаго҃ меншее сп҃саетса. ѿ хꙋжшаго же бо҃шемꙋ невозможно сп҃сатиса. He makes similar statements in describing the legal aspects of salvation: e.g., *DT* 57: "One can deliver someone with a lower status from the heavy guilt only if one possesses an equal position of honor" (равночт҃ныи точию возможе҃ избавити ме҃ша҃ ѿ вины тажки).

204 *DT* 54.7: "In saying, 'Let us make man in our image and likeness', [he implied] that his only-begotten Son would become incarnate and bring the dead man back to life through himself, while the Holy Spirit would work together in all of this" (сотвори҃ ре҃ чл҃ка по ѡбразꙋ нш҃емꙋ и по по҃бию. ꙗко сн҃ꙋ его единоро҃но мꙋ воплотити҃. и собою воскр҃ти ѹмръшвена҃ чл҃ка. ст҃мꙋ дх҃ꙋ его содѣиствꙋющꙋ всиа).

205 *DT* 54.8: бꙋ҃ ѹбо ꙗко и восхотѣ бг҃ъ чл҃кꙋ. помощь изготова҃. да чесо ꙋбо ра҃ сн҃ꙋ его воплотити҃. а не посла҃ бг҃ꙋ иного ко҃ на помо҃ хꙋдости чл҃чи.

question, Zinoviy introduces another aspect of the fall and salvation—the relational one. He remarks that "we can view man as being exceptionally close to God above all other works, by virtue of how man was actually fashioned",[206] and explains it by noting the fact that man was the only being whom God made by taking counsel as he fashioned him to give humanity a special status of honor and dignity in creation.[207]

In describing man as "close" to God, Zinoviy uses two specific terms—близъ ("close", "near") and присвоенъ ("made one's own" or "part of one's possession")—but reserves the first one (близъ) exclusively for expressing the "closeness" of the persons of the Trinity to each other.[208] This unique position of man relative to God is further manifested in the fact that God created him by taking the dust of the ground, whereas he made all other things by simply speaking them into existence. Quoting Ps. 119:73 that says, "Your hands made me and formed me", Zinoviy suggests that "God formed man with his own hand"[209] and makes two points. First, he ties this verse to the fact that the incarnation was the work of God's own hand:

---

206 *DT* 54.13: и посемѹ видѣти чл҃ка ѕѣло присвоена бг҃ѹ. па҃ всеа твари в самѡ҃ зданїи чл҃чи. He makes this point even stronger when he says, "For neither the heavens and the earth and everything that is in them, nor the angels and archangels and the thrones are made in the image and likeness of God. Only man alone is in the image and likeness of God, and from the beginning of creation man is set close to the Godhead through the image and likeness" (аще бо нб҃са и земля и все ж҃е в ни҃. аще аг҃гли и арханг҃гили. и пр҃тли. ничт҃о по ѡбразѹ бж҃ию и по пд҃бию. токмо единъ чл҃къ по ѡбразѹ бж҃ию и по пд҃бию. и е҃ из начала сотворения присвоенъ чл҃къ бж҃твѹ ѡбразѡ҃ и подобие҃). In fact, Zinoviy's favorite formula for describing man's relationship with God is by saying that he is a creature that is "closest to God and most beloved by him" (ближаишѹ и любезнѣишю бв҃и чл҃ка), *DT* 60.2; cf. 55.3, 5.

207 Zinoviy reflects on this point throughout the entire work, but one of the passages that expresses the main idea most concisely is *DT* 8.1–4.

208 E.g., *DT* 14.1: "Considering that God said, 'Let us make man in our image', this phrase reveals those who truly shared God's image, and existed closely with God, and were worthy of participating in God's counsel and his work" (яко ре҃ бг҃ъ сотворимъ чл҃ка по ѡбразоу нш҃емѹ. сие слово показоуе҃ по истиннѣ соѡбразны҃ бг҃оу. и бли҃ бг҃а соущи҃. и достоины҃ бж҃иа и совѣта и дѣиствиа с ни҃). *DT* 14.3: "This phrase was directed at those who existed closely with him; (more specifically), not at those who were far away or apart from him, but at those who existed with God and had nothing mediating between them" (и къ бли҃ его сѹщимъ речение. а не ѿ далеча пребывающи҃ и стоящи҃. но и҃ оу бг҃а сѹщи҃ бес посре҃ства.). For the definition of the terms близъ ("close", "near") and присвоенъ ("made one's own" or "part of one's possession"), see *Словарь русского языка XI–XVIII вв.* [*Dictionary of the Russian Language of the XI–XVII centuries*], выпуск 1 (А–В) (Москва: Издательства Наука, 1975), p. 240; *Словарь русского языка XI–XVIII вв.* [*Dictionary of the Russian Language of the XI–XVII centuries*], выпуск 20 (Присвоение–Прочнутися) (Москва: Наука, 1995), pp. 9–10.

209 *DT* 55.2: тѣмже рѹкою своею бг҃ъ созда чл҃ка.

> There is no one else who is able to help humankind. And therefore, just as God himself wished to form man by his own hand in the beginning, so also later, when humanity—the work of his own hand, and the image and likeness of his Godhead—became corrupted, God the Word himself, in his goodness and through his flesh, was willing to mend and renew the work of his own hand and his image and likeness [in man].[210]

Second, he explains that the incarnation was needed to restore the lost closeness of man to God:

> And who else is able to mend the work of God's hand and renew his image and likeness, if not a certain mediator? And the mediator for man must be in such a relation to God that he is closer to God than man and more honorable compared to man's image and likeness. But the sacred Scripture showed no other work that had a position closer to God than man, nor did it show any work more greatly loved by God that it could mediate on behalf of humankind before God and save man.[211]

Thus, the incarnation of Christ became the means of mediation, "drawing man—the closest to him of all the works—to his own divinity."[212] In other places, he expresses the same point by emphasizing that God's economy of salvation was "to unite and deify man through his descent"[213] and thus, reconnect men with God,[214] because from the very beginning they "were close to the one who made them on account of his love and were tied to him on account of their image and likeness."[215]

---

210 *DT* 57.1: И по семꙋ точию бг҃ꙋ самомꙋ своєю рꙋкꙋ созданныи ѡбраⷥ свои и поⷣобие спⷭ҇ти. иномꙋⷤ никомꙋ нⷭ҇ѣ возможно чл҃чествꙋ помощи. сего раⷣ ꙗкоⷤ и в началѣ самъ бг҃ъ своєю рꙋкою изволи создати чл҃ка. такоⷤ и послⷣѣ истлѣвшее чл҃чество создание рꙋкꙋ его сꙋще и ѡбраⷥ и поⷣобие бжⷭ҇тва его. бл҃говоли паⷦ сⷨа бг҃ъ слово. исправиⷮ плотию рꙋкꙋ свою соⷥдание. и ѡбраⷥ свои и поⷣобие ѡбно-вити.

211 *DT* 55.4: комꙋ иномꙋ возмощи аще не ходатаеⷨ нѣкиⷨ. ходатаюⷤ подобаеⷮ быти ѡ чл҃цѣ к бг҃ꙋ таковомꙋ. иⷤ бꙋдеⷮ ближаиши чл҃ка къ бг҃ꙋ. и мнⷭ҇очⷭ҇тнѣиши чл҃ка ѡбраза бж҃иа и поⷣобиа. сщ҃нноеⷤ писание не показа приближнѣиши присвоениеⷨ чл҃ка къ бжⷭ҇твꙋ. ни единои ѿ твари иныа ниⷤ возлюбленѣиши бжⷭ҇твꙋ кою тварь инꙋю показа. да возможеⷮ ходатаиствоваⷮ къ бг҃ꙋ ѡ ѡ (*sic*) чл҃чествѣ. и спⷭ҇ти чл҃ка.

212 *DT* 54.13: єлма приближнѣиши всеа твари присвоити къ своемꙋ бжⷭ҇твꙋ чл҃ка.

213 *DT* 55.2: ꙗко соединити и ѡбж҃ити чл҃ка своимъ съшествиеⷨ.

214 *DT* 68.4: "In order to reconnect them to the mind of God through the incarnation of the Word" (ради иⷯ совокꙋпити паки в бг҃оразꙋмие. воплощениеⷨ слова).

215 *DT* 57.5: бывшиⷯ блⷥиⷯ сотворшаго иⷯ возлюбленїа раⷣ. и оусвоеныⷯ к немꙋ ѡбраза раⷣ и подобиа.

When asking the second *Cur Deus Homo?* question, the kliros-chanters build it on Zinoviy's previous points, "Why, then, does he himself need to come in the flesh? For he could have renewed his image and likeness [in man] by his own hand, without being incarnated".[216] Responding to this question, Zinoviy explains that God's forming of man by his own hand was important to bring humanity from non-being into existence, but now that humanity already existed, it was necessary to fix what was *already* there. The only way to do that was to have the Son assume the broken image and restore it "within his own human body".[217] To explain this point further, Zinoviy says:

> For that reason, God himself comes [to renew] his image and assumes the entirety of created man and likeness into himself. He clothed himself with humanity—his image and likeness—and in that way, through his own person, he himself, mended his fallen creation by renewing his own image and likeness, [since] that had grown weak [in man]. And it befitted the good God to use his hand as a means of mercy and generosity toward his creation; but when the image and likeness of his Godhead [that was in man] fell, he came down to him in mercy, and by having clothed himself with [humanity], he mended and saved him in his generosity.[218]

Behind this saving work of Christ lay God's intention to redirect humanity to himself. The disobedience of the first man[219] led all the subsequent generations of people "to fall from the knowledge of God"[220] and caused them to begin making their own idols. As a result, humans became enslaved by the devil and found themselves in need of the restoration that would deal with the epistemological problem,[221] or to put it in Zinoviy's own words, a divine intervention was

216 *DT* 57.8: почто ѹбо саⷨ приходить въ плⷮо. можаше бо рѹкою своєю и паки поновиⷮ ѡбраⷥ свои и пⷣⷪбие. и не воплотивсѧ.

217 *DT* 60.1: на своⷨе чл҃ческомъ составѣ. Zinoviy's response to the second question is formulated most succinctly in *DT* 58.1. For a similar point, cf. Athanasius, *De Incarnatione Verbi* 6.

218 *DT* 58.2: того раⷣ самъ бг҃ъ прихоⷣиⷮ. на своⷨ ѡбраⷥ. и всеⷢ чл҃ка создание и подобие на сѧ восприеⷨ. ѡблексѧ чл҃чествоⷨ. ѡбразоⷨ своиⷨ и пⷣⷪбиемъ. и тако саⷨ собою исправи пⷣашее создание свое. поно-вивъ ѡбетшавшїи ѡбраⷥ свои и пⷣⷪбие. ⷤе и достоино бл҃гомѹ бг҃ѹ. помиловати и ѹщедриⷮ рѹкѹ своєю создание пⷣаше сѹще. ѡбразъⷤ и пⷣⷪбие бж҃ⷭтва ⷭе. и помиловаⷡ снити на нⷢе. и оущⷣерити. и ѡбⷣокъсѧ в него ѹдобриⷮ его и сп҃ти.

219 Zinoviy considers human disobedience and the way Christ dealt with it in *DT* 59.1–7.

220 *DT* 57.5: низъ пⷣашихъ ѿ разѹма бж҃їа.

221 Zinoviy understands the human capacity to know things as a feature of his special closeness with God. See especially *DT* 57.2–6.

needed "to reconnect them to the mind of God through the incarnation of the Word".[222] He expands this explanation as follows:

> Humankind also forgot its Maker and departed from the Lord God, its Savior. Man fashioned idols for himself and worshiped the work of his own hands. And he called idols his gods in place of the true God, and made sacrifices to his old enemy. And his children, made in the image and likeness of God, he offered as burnt offerings. Having trusted the deceiver of men, he departed from his Creator. Since then, the old enemy has held men in his possession and pushed them into all kinds of sin. And being unable to frame his own creation, the old enemy, the devil, came to possess God's work, humanity, [although] he did not make it. And humankind honored the murderer instead of its Savior.[223]

The incarnation and resurrection of Christ snatched humanity out of the devil's control, rectified the old disobedience of Adam, restored the fallen nature of man, and put him back to where he could know, honor, and worship the true God.

Finally, the kliros-chanters pose the *Cur Deus Homo?* question once more (DT 60.4), although this time they express it as a statement, after which the "why" question comes up in various forms as the conversation progresses. The attention now switches to the issue of the impassibility of the incarnated Christ, "The kliros-chanters said, 'It is strange and difficult to hear that God dwelled in such an impure place as the womb, and anyone would think that it was impure for God to go through the female passages' ".[224] In response, Zinoviy goes into a long discussion of instances in the Scripture, where God interacted with various people without being impacted by them in any way.

In particular, Zinoviy reasons that if God created Adam and Eve, then he also formed all parts of their body, and since he did it with his own hand, then it passed through their entire physical being. Therefore, why should it be a prob-

---

222 DT 68.4: ради и҆ совокꙋпити паки в бг҃оразꙋмие. воплоцение҆ слова.

223 DT 59.6: и забы чл҃чество сотворшаго его. и ѿстꙋпи ѿ г҃а бг҃а сп҃са свое҃. содѣла са҆ собѣ идолы. и поклони҃ свой рꙋкъ дѣлесемъ. и наре҃ идолы боги собѣ. вмѣсто бг҃а истинна҃. и жрътвы сотвори старомꙋ врагꙋ~~мꙋ~~ своемꙋ. и дѣти своа томꙋ закла. вѣровавъ прелестникꙋ чл҃къ ѿстꙋпи ѿ создателꙗ свое҃. поне мꙋ҆ древнїи врагъ ѡблада чл҃ки. и во всꙗко согрѣшение поринꙋ и҆. и старыи врагъ дьаво҃ не могїи сотвори҆ свое҃ зданїа. бж҃їимъ здание҆ чл҃чество҆ совладе его҆ не сотвори. и чл҃чество гꙋбителꙗ вмѣсто сп҃са свое҃ почте. For a similar point, cf. Athanasius, *De Incarnatione Verbi* 11.

224 DT 60.6: Рѣша҆ крылошане. странно и тажко слышати. ꙗко бг҃ъ вмѣсте ка҃не пребысть во чревѣ. и проходы женьскими проити бг҃ꙋ. нечисто ѿ всѣ҆ непщꙋемо.

lem for the Son to go through the womb of the Virgin? Similarly, though in a different way, if God was able to come and dwell in such an impure place as Sodom and Gomorrah, then why should it be difficult for him to live in the world? But just as God made everything very good in creation and made his holiness prevail over the uncleanness of the Sodomites, so does the incarnated Christ purify all the places that he touches.[225] Summarizing this point, Zinoviy writes:

> And that is how much he was willing to stoop down in his love for the sake of his image and likeness [in man] from the beginning. And would he not be willing to assume the parts and members [of the body] that are the same as those through which he had passed, so that he might afterward renew his image and likeness [in man]? His hands and fingers had passed through them before with no effect on his divinity, just as the angels were not affected when they entered the impure Sodom and stayed the night in it.[226]

Additionally, Zinoviy spends some time explaining how different parts of Genesis foreshadowed the birth of Jesus Christ, and he pays a special attention to explaining how Sarah's inability to bear children due to her old age was a sign of the future immaculate conception.[227] His arguments here connect with his earlier points about the tri-partite nature of man (with mind, word, and breath), where he argued that the incorporeal manner of interaction between the three elements is the proof of God's impassibility. For just as there is no corporeal involvement of male and female elements in the way the human mind, word, and breath function, so is there no passion or suffering in the way the Father incorporeally begets the Son and spirates the Holy Spirit.[228]

---

225 For these and other examples, see *DT* 61–67.2.

226 *DT* 67.3: и селико спⷣобиса любвѣ раⷣ ѡбраза своⷢ҇ и поⷣбиа преклонитиⷭ҇ прⷤе. и послⷤѣ ѡбновиⷮ ѡбраⷥ свои и поⷣбие. не споⷣбит ли са тыⷤа оудовы и члѣны восприıавъ тѣмиⷤ проити. ихⷤъ прⷤе рѹцы и перъсты еⷢ҇ прохожаста. и не повредивъ своⷢ҇ бжⷭтва. елма и аггли не возмогоша стⷭости своеа повредити. вшⷣеше в нечистыи содоⷨ и ѡбнощьствовавше в неⷨ.

227 *DT* 70.1–8.

228 *DT* 4.6–7: "Let those profane men feel ashamed for blaspheming God's incorporeal generation and wishing to present God with a wife for the Word's begetting, not realizing that their own minds generate words without wives. They are extremely irrational and insane to search out a wife for God's incorporeal, and incorruptible, and blessed nature so that God may beget the immaterial, incorruptible Word. And if they cannot deny the fact that our incorporeal minds in the fleshly essence of our corrupted nature do not need a wife to generate our words, then [why do they] try to deny that the incorruptible nature of God begets the Word without a wife? What insanity for these godless men to think in such a

Toward the end of his treatment of the third *Cur Deus Homo?* question, Zinoviy comes back to his constant motif of the common activity of the triune God in salvation[229]—this time, emphasizing that Christ was in no way estranged from the other two persons[230]—and talks about how the work of the Trinity was prefigured in the Old Testament.[231] He also points to the Epistle to the Hebrews[232] (which was rejected by Kosoy as non-Pauline and inauthentic), where the fulfilled prophecies about Christ are made especially clear, and he directs the kliros-chanters to specific names and writings from the patristic tradition that can teach them further truths about this.

---

profane way"! (да стыдятса скверногловцы хꙋлящїи бжтвꙋ рж҇тво бесплотное. и хотяще бг҇ꙋ привводити женꙋ на рожение словꙋ. не хотяще разоумѣти оума свего ражающа слово бе҇ жены. безоу҇ствꙋю ѕѣло бе҇словеснѣ. бесплотномꙋ и нетлѣнномꙋ бл҇женномꙋ е҇ствꙋ бж҇ию. жены взыскающе на рожение бесплотна҇ нетлѣнна҇ слова бг҇ꙋ. И аще тлѣнное е҇ство нш҇е во плотнѣ соуществѣ бесплотна҇ оума нш҇его не могꙋще во҇бранити. бе҇ жены не ражати слово свое. бжт҇веномꙋ же нетлѣнномꙋ е҇ствꙋ бе҇ жены ро҇ти слово во҇бранити тщатса. коликаго безꙋмиа есть таковое скверновие бе҇бж҇ьны). Cf. *DT* 26.4. "With God the Father being incorporeal, the Word, who is the Son, is begotten from him incorporeally, too, and the Spirit, who proceeds from God the Father, is perfect. The perfect God the Father begets his Son without having suffered any exhaustion, for our minds do not become exhausted either when they generate words in our souls" (бесплотныи бг҇ъ ѿц҇ъ. бесплотно ро҇са и слово ѿ него сн҇ъ. и дх҇ъ изыде совершенъ ѿ бг҇а ѿца. не пострада истощенїа совершеныи бг҇ъ ѿц҇ъ родивъ сн҇а. ибо и нш҇ь оумъ не истощевается родивъ слово нш҇еа дш҇а). Zinoviy's argument here can be related to his third proof for the existence of God in *DT* (Kazan'), pp. 60–62.

229 *DT* 70.7–8.

230 *DT* 70.7–8: "The Son, who is the Word, was not estranged from God the Father when he came down in the incarnation ... Christ suffered not unwillingly, but out of obedience to the Father, willingly enduring everything, as man, and for man's sake. And the Holy Spirit co-worked with him" (не ѿстꙋпльшꙋ бо словꙋ сн҇ꙋ ѿ ѡца бг҇а сниде воплоти҇са. но волею бг҇а ѿц҇а сниде сн҇ъ ... но послꙋшание ко ѿц҇ꙋ исполнаia. волею претерпѣ вса iако чл҇къ чл҇ка ра҇. и дх҇ъ ст҇ыи содѣиствова).

231 *DT* 68–79.8.

232 *DT* 80.7–81.5.

A Note on Translation

In rendering Zinoviy into English, the translator (Lytvynenko) has tried to stay faithful to his style and render him as literally as possible while letting him speak for himself as best as he could in a modern language. Readers should be aware that Zinoviy's writings are distinguished by several features that seem unusual to us today. One such feature is Zinoviy's manner of repeating his own arguments multiple times, which has been noted and sometimes criticized by others.[1] However, Zinoviy's over-repetitiveness could have been his way of caring for his readers. Specifically, his repetitions perhaps were governed by his motivation to help his audience comprehend very complex theological issues.

The second unusual feature is his use of a technique called "word-weaving", which means that Zinoviy stylized the text to make it more persuasive.[2] During his time period, the most common methods of word-weaving involved the use of high metaphors, wordy language, and repetitions. A good example from DT is the following statement: "And how did the angels, who came to the dwelling place of *unclean* people—those who became *unclean* by subjecting their nature to the *unclean* ways of every *impure uncleanness*—not become *unclean* themselves?"[3] Zinoviy's use of the italicized words is a typical way of word-weaving. To a modern reader, it appears quite redundant, but for people of his time, such word-weaving functioned as a kind of highlighter, intended to draw attention to a particular theme or generate a certain emotion, and this is exactly what Zinoviy seems to be doing in some places.[4]

Finally, Zinoviy tends to mix his verb tenses—both in his own discussions and in quoting the Biblical texts—and he often speaks in the past tense, which may appear incorrect to a modern reader. For him, however, this was an essen-

1 See esp. Калугин, *Зиновий* [Kalugin, *Zinoviy*], pp. 150–151.

2 For the phenomenon of stylization in the Slavonic medieval literature originating with the literary reforms of the Patriarch Euthymius in the fourteenth century in Tarnovo, see e.g., В.Д. Петрова, "Проблемы исихазма и древнеславянского 'плетение словес' в современной филологии" [V.D. Petrova, "Problems of Hesychasm and Old Slavonic 'Word-weaving' in Contemporary Philology"], *Вестник Чувашского университета* 1 (2011): pp. 251–257.

3 *DT* 67.1: и како в жилищє скверны҃ людеи. и҃ чре҃ єство скверна҃щийса. скверною скверненшею всакиа нечистоты. прїидоша агг҃ли и не шскверневахꙋса.

4 On the issue of word-weaving in Zinoviy, see М.В. Каравашкина, *Сочинения Зиновия Отенского в истории русского литературного языка XVI века* [M.V. Karavashkina, *The Writings of Zinoviy Otenskiy in the History of Russian Literary Language of the Sixteenth Century*], Диссертация (Москва: Московский педагогический государственный университет, 2000), pp. 234–248.

 DOI:10.1163/9789004538054_003

tial feature of the literary style,[5] and I sought to reflect it in the English translation. Scholars note that Zinoviy lived at a time when the Slavonic language was going through some significant changes, transitioning from one form into two: a literary language and a colloquial language. Zinoviy clearly recognized the challenges of that transformation.[6] He primarily applied the high literary style in his writings, but at times, he also used everyday speech and drew from daily life and experience. Reading Zinoviy with these points in mind gives a unique window into the Russia of his time and helps us appreciate his theological and exegetical discourses in that context.

The translation includes over a thousand variant readings from the long version of this treatise. They come from the seventeenth-century manuscript RGB, MDA F. 173/I, № 61, published in the 1863 edition. Unfortunately, circumstances prevented us from accessing the original manuscript (RNB, O.I.63). All these readings are placed in the footnotes and are designed to give an idea of how Zinoviy went about improving his writing. Some of them were also important for reconstructing a few problematic places in Zinoviy's autograph, and we marked them in the translation with triangle brackets ⟨⟩.

5 See Каравашкина, *Сочинения Зиновия* [Karavashkina, *Writings of Zinoviy*], pp. 79–109.
6 This issue received the most attention in the work of Каравашкина, *Сочинения Зиновия* [Karavashkina, *Writings of Zinoviy*].

Tables

Lytvynenko has developed two tables that describe the structure of the *Panegyric* and its sources. In the first table, he has expanded the number of suggested sources from one to six for the "Life of Hypatius", and from four to nine for "Arianism", compared with the previous edition of this text by Koretskiy.[1] In the second table, he has provided an outline of the *Panegyric* and a detailed analysis of how Zinoviy used his sources by making paraphrases, elaborations, allusions, and direct quotations.

TABLE 1 Suggested sources for the *Panegyric*

	Suggested sources for the *Life of Hypatius*
Grig.	**"Apocryphal"** ***Life of Hypatius.*** ONNB, Grig. 1/112, 2nd half of the fifteenth century, ff. 16–19 (Serbian origin). Quoted from the edition of Н.С. Тихонравов, *Памятники отреченной русской литературы* [N.S. Tikhonravov, *Historical Texts of Recantation in Russian Literature*], том 2 (Москва: Типография товарищества "Общественная польза", 1863), pp. 121–145.
Min.	***Life of Hypatius*** **in the commemoration service composed by Iosif the Hymnographer** (AHG, vol. 7, pp. 338–350). RGB, Tro. F. 304, № 541, Liturgical Menaion, March 31, the 30s of the fourteenth century, f. 280ᵛ (Russian origin). Quoted from the edition of M.V. Zhivova, "La ricezione del culto dei pontefici romani nella tradizione liturgico-letteraria medievale della Slavia Orthodoxa", Ph.D. Diss. (Pisa: Università di Pisa, 2016), pp. 193–201.
Prol.	***Prologue*** **version of the** ***Life of Hypatius.*** RSAAD, Sin. № 164, November 14, Longer *Prologue*, early fourteenth century, stlb. 133г–4б (Russian origin). Quoted from the edition of Л.В. Прокопенко, *Славяно-русский Пролог по древнейшим рукописям. Тесты, источники, комментарии* [*The Slavonic Prologue of Russian Origin According to the Oldest Manuscripts*], 2016–2020. The text of ***Prol.*** is identical to that of ***MVCh.*** (http://prolog-manuscript.org/content_pr.php?page=t133d).

1 Корецкий, "Вновь найденное произведение" [Koretskiy, "Newly Found Writing"], pp. 166–182.

TABLE 1 Suggested sources for the *Panegyric* (*cont.*)

VMCh	***Menaia* version of the *Life of Hypatius*.** *Великие Минеи Четии, собранные Всероссийским митрополитом Макарием. Ноябрь 13–15* [*Great Menaia Reader, Collected by the Metropolitan of All Rus' Makariy. November 13–15*], выпуск 8 (Москва: Синодальная типография, 1899), stlb. 1991–1992.
Und.	**"Canonical" *Life of Hypatius*.** RGB, Und. F. 310, № 1190, eighteenth century, ff. 106r–109r (Russian origin). Greek text is in GIM, Gr. 183, ff. 158v–162v. Suggested as a source by Корецкий, "Вновь найденное произведение" [Koretskiy, "Newly Found Writing"], p. 169.
ShV	***Panegyric to St. Hypatius* (short version).** RGB, Golub. F. 596, № 28, nineteenth century, first two folios (not numbered). For the description, see С.А. Морозов, *Описание собрания рукописей А.П. Голубцова (Ф. 596). Единица Хранения 46. XVII–XIX вв.* [S.A. Morozov, *Description of the Manuscript Collection of A.P. Golubtsov* (*F. 596*). *Shelf Number 46. XVII–XIX Centuries*]. (Москва: Государственная Библиотека им. В.И. Ленина, 1974), (typeset description), p. 13. More research is needed on whether there might be earlier copies of this text. Until then, this source must be treated with reservations.
	Suggested sources for arianism
CA 1	***First Oration against the Arians*.** A. Vaillant, *Discours contre les Ariens de Saint Athanase. Version slave et traduction en français* (Sofia: Académie des sciences de Bulgarie, 1954). Greek text (CPG 2093) in K. Metzler, K. Savvidis, *Orationes I et II contra Arianos*, Athanasius Werke, Die dogmatischen schriften, Band II, Teil 1, Lieferung 2 (Berlin–New York: De Gryuter, 1998). Suggested as a source by Корецкий, "Вновь найденное произведение" [Koretskiy, "Newly Found Writing"], p. 168.
CA 2	***Second Oration against the Arians*.** V.V. Lytvynenko, *Athanasius of Alexandria. Oratio II contra Arianos: Old Slavonic Version and English Translation*, Patrologia Orientalis, 248 (56.3) (Turnhout: Brepols, 2019). See the above edition for the Greek text. Suggested as a source by Корецкий, "Вновь найденное произведение" [Koretskiy, "Newly Found Writing"], p. 168.

TABLE 1 Suggested sources for the *Panegyric* (*cont.*)

CA 3	***Third Oration against the Arians.*** П. Пенкова, *Св. Атанасий Александрийский. Трето Слово против арианите* [P. Penkova, *Athanasius of Alexandria. Third Oration against the Arians*], том 2 (София: Изд-во "Валентин Траянов", 2016). Greek text (CPG 2093) is in K. Metzler, K. Savvidis, *Orationes III contra Arianos*. Athanasius Werke. Die dogmatischen schriften, Band I, Teil 3, Lieferung 2 (Berlin–New York: De Gryuter, 2000). Suggested as a source by Корецкий, "Вновь найденное произведение" [Koretskiy, "Newly Found Writing"], p. 168.
Ep.	***Epistle to the Bishops of Egypt and Libya.*** E. Weiher, & al., *Die Grossen Lesemenäen des Metropoliten Makarij: Uspenskij spisok*, Mai, Band 1: 1.–8. Mai, MLSDV 51 (Freiburg i. Br.: Weiher, 2007), pp. 288–303. Greek text (CPG 2093) is in K. Metzler, K. Savvidis, *Epistula ad episcopos Aegypti et Libyae*, Athanasius Werke, Die dogmatischen schriften, Band I, Fascicle 1 (Berlin–New York: De Gryuter, 1996). Suggested as a source by Корецкий, "Вновь найденное произведение" [Koretskiy, "Newly Found Writing"], p. 168.
Vita Ath.	***Life of Athanasius* (non-Metaphrastic version).** Weiher, et al., *Die Grossen Lesemenäen*. Compiled from two Greek sources: John Moschus, *Pratum spirituale* ch. 197 (PG 87, 3084–3085) and ***Chron.*** pp. 344–351.
Chron. Ham.	***Chronicle* of George Hamartolos** (late ninth century). В.М. Истрин, *Хроника Георгия Амартола в древнем славянском переводе. Текст, исследование и словарь. Текст* [V.M. Istrin, *Chronicle of George Hamartolos in Old Slavonic Translation. Text, Analysis, and Glossary*], том 1 (Slavonic Text) & том 2 (Greek text) (Петроград: Российская Государственная Академическая Типография, 1920).
Chron. 1512	***Chronicle of the Year 1512.*** *Полное собрание русских летописей. Русский хронограф редакции 1512 года* [*Complete Collection of Russian Chronicles. Russian Chronicle of the Year 1512*], том 22, часть 1 (Санкт-Петербург: Типография М.А. Александрова, 1911).
Pros.	***Enlightener* of Iosif Volotskiy (*Prosvetitel'*).**
Phot.	*Epistle to Boris-Mikhail of Bulgaria*. Т. Славова, *Славянският превод на посланието на патриарх Фотий до княз Борис-Михаил* [T. Slavova, *Slavonic Translation of Patriarch Photius' Epistle to Khagan Boris-Mikhail*] (София: Университетско издателство "Св. Климент Охридски", 2013). This source was identified by Shpakovskiy.

TABLE 2 Main episodes and sources in the *Panegyric*

Episodes	Sources
1. A call to praise Hypatius for our personal sanctification.	
1.1. A brief mention of his pursuit of spiritual labor and good deeds for the sake of the imperishable crown.	
1.2. A brief mention of his martyrdom and pastoral ministry of shepherding Christ's flock.	Much of this sect. is an elaboration of ***Min.*** f. 280ᵛ, *Canon* 7 ([Б]деи вере ереси. ꙗко зверїе. ѡ[ч] ѿгнавъ и невре[д]нꙋ соблю[л] еси. ѿ гр[д]оу. твоего. стада ꙗко пастырь пр[ѣ]чю[д]ныи. ѡц҃).
2. Hypatius' participation at Nicaea and the Council's deposition of Arius.	Cf. ***Und.*** f. 106ʳ: єдин҇ бѣ ѿ триста и ѡсмь҇десати ст҃ыхъ оц҃ь. на пер- вомъ вселенскѡмъ соборѣ, въ цр҇ство великагѡ константїна в никеи собраннѡм. на немъ же с прочими ст҃ыми оц҃ы побораа по бл҃гочестїи, исполненъ д҃ха ст҃агѡ. арїа ѡ ереси ѡбличилъ. и анафемѣ тогѡ пре- даде; ***VMCh*** stlb. 1991 & ***Prol.*** f. 133г: Тъ бѣ єдинъ ѿ трии сотъ и· ӣı· ст҃хъ оц҃ь· иже в никеи сшедшихъса на арыꙗ суꙗмъıслнаго· въ цр҇тво костантина великаго (with no mention of Arius' deposition). ***Grig.*** p. 126 only mentions Arius by name.
2.1. The creedal statement affirmed by Hypatius and the rest of the fathers.	Cf. ***Min.*** f. 280ᵛ, *Kathisma* (Повеленїе веры оудержавъ прп[д]бне. оц҃). ***Grig.*** p. 130 contains a much shorter creedal statement with no relation to Nicaea and Arianism.
2.2. Hypatius' exposure of Arius' heresy from the Scriptures.	Cf. ***Min.*** f. 280ᵛ, *Sticheron* 2 (ариевы ѕїници. омрачилъ еси), *Canon* 3 (Оуста загра[д]лъ еси Злочестивы[х] м[д]рыми словесы твоими ѿ писанїи х[с]вы[х]), *Kathisma* (посрамилъ еси. ариевъ зломысле- ныи разоумъ), *Canon* 5 (избавїлъ еси ѡ[ч] ѿ еритїчески[х] зверей), *Canon* 7 ([Б]деи вере ереси. ꙗко зверїе. ѡ[ч] ѿгнавъ).

TABLE 2 Main episodes and sources in the *Panegyric* (*cont.*)

Episodes	Sources
3. Arius based his Christology on the Greek idea of greater and smaller deities.	For the closest parallel where the Arian doctrine of God is compared to that of the Greeks who taught an unequal triad, cf. the text злоименитыи арїє, наоучивсѧ єлли҃ском҄оу оучєнїю. и сѫемоудраа по єллїно҃, богы болшїѧ и боги мє҃шїѧ оумышлѧ҃ше. и бл҃гоч҃тїє ратованїє бранємъ соимє҃ныи, єлли҃скими баснами. гл҃аше бо больша҃ бг҃а ѿц҃а быти. и менша҃ бг҃а сн҃а. with the text гдѣ же бꙋдеть истинноє сн҃вьства. иномꙋ оубо сꙋщьствꙋ ѡц҃ꙋ сꙋщꙋ иномꙋ же сн҃оу. како҃ не єл'линскаго заблꙋженїа възникнє҃ многобо҃ство на меньшєє и болшєє сꙋщьство пресѣцаємꙋ бж҃твꙋ. і ѡвомꙋ оубо въ прьваго и съдѣтелнаго и старѣишаго б҃а предѣлаємꙋ. ѡвомꙋ же въ в'тора҃ бг҃а разлꙋчаємꙋ и слꙋжитела и юннаго. in **Phot.** p. 168 (this parallel was identified by Shpakovskiy). For other parallels with the Arian doctrine of God, cf. *CA* 1.18 [pp. 80–82]: Нъ никтоже ѡтъ крьстиянъ не сътръпить таковыⅹ еретикъ. свое бо Єллиномъ се на приснѣ, еже рожденѫ вънносити троицѫ и съ рождьныими тъчиѫ ѭ творити рождьныиⅹъ бо есть недостаткы и прилаганиѧ приимати. On the Arian idea of the Father's superiority over the Son, cf. *CA* 3.7 [p. 247]: Нъ понеже нечьстивїи, и си приносѧште, хѫлѧть же г҃а. поносѧть же намъ глаголѭште. есе єдинъ и цѣлъ и пръвъ глаголеть сѧ б҃ъ. каковы глаголете христоса б҃ъ сѫшта. For several other themes in the passage, cf. allusions to *CA* 3.9 [p. 257] (єллиньскыиⅹъ баснїи), and *CA* 1.5 [p. 30] (єште же въсхотѣвъ насъ сътворити, тъгда сътворилъ есть нѣкого и именовалъ его … Сына …, да насъ имъ сътворить).
3.1. First Christological analogy (silk and golden vessels).	Cf. Arius' key statements in *CA* 1.5 [p. 30], *CA* 1.18 [pp. 80–82], and *CA* 3.7 [p. 247], quoted in sect. 3. Cf. an allusion to *CA* 3.10 [p. 257] (баснословесными глаголѭште).
3.2. Quotes from Arius' *Thalia* and second Christological analogy (scissors, needle, and royal dress).	Cf. Zinoviy's version of Arius' formula from *Thalia* with *CA* 1.5 [p. 30] (бѣ нѣкогда егда не бѣ), and *CA* 1.5 [p. 30] (сътворилъ есть … Сына … да насъ имъ сътворить); ***Chron. Ham.*** p. 341 (б҃ы нѣкогда, єгда же не б҃ы), and (тѣмь и всѧ и того створи б҃ъ); ***Vita Ath.*** 79c17 [p. 158] (б҃ы нѣкогда. егда бысть). Cf. an allusion to *CA* 1.13 [p. 62] (богъратьници).

TABLE 2 Main episodes and sources in the *Panegyric* (*cont.*)

Episodes	Sources
3.3. Hypatius' preaching of the creedal statement against Arius.	Cf. ***Min.*** f. 280ᵛ, *Sticheron* 3 (цр҃ѧ хⷭ҇а. его[ж] ꙗсно проповѣда[л] еси, ѡц҃ю единосоущнꙋ), *Kathisma* (е[д]носоущна слова проповедалъ е[с]).
3.4. Hypatius' refutation of Arius' *Thalia* statements based on Jn. 1:1–2.	For the argument against "there was when he was not" based on Jn. 1.1, see ***CA*** 1.13 [p. 62]. Cf. Zinoviy's often-used phrase in this passage вѣки и времена и лѣта with въ врѣмена и въ дьни и въ лѣта in ***CA*** 2.27 [p. 178].
4. A call to remember Hypatius and be in agreement with his teaching.	Cf. ***Min.*** f. 280ᵛ, *Sticheron* 2 (сщ҃енноую память твою. чтⷨ҇ъ и блⷤ҇имъ), and *Canon* 5 (всебложеннеи памети. бж҃имъ пїщомы[м] смысломъ). Cf. Zinoviy's phrase ꙗⷦ҇ в раю напитоватиса, къ оутѣше нїю и к наоученїю нашемѫ with ***Min.*** f. 280ᵛ, *Canon* 6 (имеѧ желанїе. раю бе[з]вещественого добротою. ослажааса).
4.1. Arius is said to have had many philosophers as his followers, and the newly emerging heretics are compared to Arius in a derogatory way.	Cf. ***Chron. 1512*** 119 [p. 270], where Arius is twice called a "philosopher": "прящагося по Аріи философа", and "Рече же философъ [i.e., Arius] к другомъ своимъ". ***CA*** 1.32 [p. 136], where Астер философ (the Sophist Asterius) is said to be the follower of Arianism. Cf. ***Chron. Ham.*** p. 342 that mentions "философи и ритори" among those who defended Arius at Nicaea. Cf. Zinoviy's phrase for the heretics поⷤ҇е безсловеснѣиши свинеи соⷮ҇у with ꙗко свиниа in ***CA*** 2.1 [p. 72]. Zinoviy's reference to Achillas has a parallel in ***Chron. 1512*** 119 [p. 270].
5. Bringing delight to Hypatius by remembering his fight against Arius, miracles, and martyrdom.	
5.1. Hypatius inspires Christians to proclaim the Trinity and condemn Arius and the newly emerging heretics.	Cf. Zinoviy's phrase трїедїно, и едино три with едино въ троици божьство in ***CA*** 3.15 [p. 277].

TABLE 2 Main episodes and sources in the *Panegyric* (*cont.*)

Episodes	Sources
6. Arius' misinterpretation of Scriptures resulted in his own destruction.	Cf. Zinoviy's phrase ꙑаꙁсѣданїє юдино пострада with ***Pros.*** 15 [p. 525] (і абїє разсѣдеся Арїє), ***Ep.*** 19 [150c34–36, p. 300] (спадеⷭ҇ и … живота абїє лишеⷩ҇ бⷭ҇ы), and ***Chron. 1512*** 121 [p. 274] ("вънезапу разседеся ему чрево и проходомъ излиася внутрьнея его").
6.1. Arius used the distorted interpretation of the New Testament to contend with Hypatius and the fathers.	Cf. Zinoviy's phrase писаⷩ҇наа дѿбре … арїи прїатъ злѣ with ихъже они ѕлѣ размышлаѭть. правъ имоуща разоумъ in CA 3.35 [p. 345].
7. Exposition of Arius' Christology founded on Prov. 8:22, Acts 2:36, and Heb. 3:2.	Cf. Arius' key statements in CA 1.5 [p. 30], CA 1.18 [pp. 80–82], and CA 3.7 [p. 247], quoted in sect. 3. Cf. CA 2.18b–82 [pp. 140–390] for the discussion of Prov. 8:22; CA 2.11a–18a [pp. 112–140] of Acts 2:36; and CA 2.1–11a [pp. 72–114] of Heb. 3:2.
7.1. Hypatius (together with Athanasius) provided the accurate teaching of the Wisdom in Prov. 8:22.	Cf. Zinoviy's phrase премⷣрость съставнаа with начрътаниа съставна in CA 2.32 [p. 196]; and приєвⷣти вса ꙗзыки в поꙁнанїє бг҃а ѿц҃а with отьць … хотя всѣми познанъ быти in CA 2.14 [p. 124]. Cf. CA 2.18b–82 [pp. 140–390] for the discussion of Prov. 8:22.
7.2. Scriptural evidence clarifying the meaning of the phrases "the beginning", "his ways", and "for his works" in Prov. 8:22.	Cf. CA 2.23 [p. 160] for the Christological argument based on Matt. 3:17, and CA 2.53 [p. 278] based on Phil. 2:8. Cf. Zinoviy's phrase соⷣза ма в наⷱ҇тѿⷦ поутїи. свой в дѣла своа. єⷤ҇ чисто показоует бл҃говоленїє бж҃їє with еже зъдалъ есть. не начатъкъ естованїа его, нъ строение бывъшее о дѣлѣⷯ оуказаеть in CA 2.53 [p. 276].
7.3. Explanation of the phrases "he created me" and "he begot me" in relation to Christ in Prov. 8:22, 25.	Cf. CA 2.53, 56, 82 [pp. 276, 288, 388] for the Christological argument based on Prov. 8:30. For the discussion of "he created me" (Prov. 8:22) versus "he begot me" (Prov. 8:25), cf. esp. CA 2.60 [pp. 304–306]. For the idea that the incarnation creates the Church, cf. CA 2.67 [p. 330] (глаголетьса плътьскы ꙗко зиждетьса. да съкончавъ ꙗ и цѣла сътвориⷡ҇ прѣдъставить отцеви цр҃ькви).

TABLE 2 Main episodes and sources in the *Panegyric* (*cont.*)

Episodes	Sources
7.4. Explanation of the true meaning of Peter's statements about Christ in the Book of Acts.	The initial part of this passage that mentions Peter and his statement in Acts 2:31 is a paraphrase of *CA* 2.16a [p. 130]. For the Christological arguments based on Acts 2:35 and Acts 2:36, cf. *CA* 2.13, 14, 16 [pp. 120, 128, 130], and *CA* 2.1, 11–12, 14, 17 [pp. 74, 114, 116–120, 126, 132–138, 139]. Zinoviy's illustration with the king and his succeeding son, and further reference to Solomon as first being a son of David and Bathsheba and only then becoming king, is an elaboration of *CA* 2.79 [p. 378] (ѩкоже се нѣкоторъи сынъ цѣсаревъ), *CA* 2.27 [p. 176] (по сй не единъ, нъ мнѡѕи цѣсаре), and *CA* 2.3 [pp. 82–84] (версавее же ѧ и мати сѫшти сынъ нарицааше раба … бѣ бо сѫтьствомъ сынъ давыдовъ). Cf. Zinoviy's phrase петръ не начало бытїѧ хв҃а сказоу гл҃тъ. with ѩко не естьства божиѩ сътворена сѫшта глаголааше петръ in *CA* 2.12a [p. 116].
7.5. Explanation of the true meaning of Paul's statements about Christ in Heb. 1:1–3.	For the Christological argument concerning Christ's divine pre-existence and economy, cf. esp. *CA* 2.6b, 9a, 11a [pp. 96, 106, 112]. Cf. Zinoviy's phrase ѿчаго бл҃говоленїа ѡ немъ нш҃е смотренїа with строениемъ же бл҃говолениемъ отьчемъ in *CA* 2.11 [p. 112]; не ѿ внѵ with не из вноу in *CA* 2.3 [p. 80]; единосоущна сн҃а ѿц҃ѹ with отцѫ же … единомѹ сѫштоу сыноу in *CA* 2.39 [p. 222]; сѫшта слово съ отьцемъ in *CA* 2.38 [p. 220]; прноcоущнe ѿцѫ сн҃ъ, with сынъ … присносѫштьно сы съ отьцемь in *CA* 2.40 [p. 224]; нѣ бо слава никогдаже бее сїанїа with къгда бо кто видѣлъ есть свѣтъ бес [с]иѩниа *CA* 2.32 [p. 196]; не бѣ сїанїа слнце with аште коли слънце без сиѩниѩ in *CA* 2.33 [p. 202].
7.6. Points about the economy of the Son and the explanation of the meaning of the "High Priest", "made", and "was faithful" in Heb. 3:1–2.	For the discussion of Heb. 2:16–17, Ps. 145:13 and Heb. 3:1–2, cf. *CA* 2.8b–9a [pp. 104–106], *CA* 2.6 [p. 94], and *CA* 2.1–11a [pp. 72–114]. Zinoviy's reference to Moses' ministry of being "faithful in all his house" is a paraphrase of *CA* 2.10 [pp. 110–112]. For the explanation of "made" and "High Priest" in terms of Christ's economy, cf. esp. *CA* 2.8a [pp. 100–102]. For the reference to Moses leading the Israelites out of Egypt, cf. *CA* 2.27a, 68 [pp. 174, 334]. Cf. Zinoviy's phrase моѵсеи бо ѩ оугодни. хс҃ъ же поне сн҃ъ with мѡѵси оубо слѹга. а хс҃ сынъ in *CA* 2.10 [p. 110].

TABLE 2 Main episodes and sources in the *Panegyric* (*cont.*)

Episodes	Sources
8. Hypatius and the fathers deposed Arius and proclaimed Christ as equal with the Father.	
8.1. Biblical evidence on the consubstantial nature of the Father-Son relationship.	For the biblical references in this passage, cf. e.g., *CA* 2.22, 41 [pp. 158, 228] (for Matt. 11:27); *CA* 2.17, 22 [pp. 138, 156] (for Jn. 14:9); *CA* 2.33, 54 [pp. 202, 278] (for Jn. 10:30); *CA* 2.1, 7 [pp. 74, 100] (for Jn. 1:1); *CA* 2.14, 53 [pp. 126, 278] (for Phil. 2:6–7).
9. Hypatius glorified God in his words and deeds.	Cf. ***Min.*** f. 280v, *Canon* 7 (про[с]вети[л] еси. миръ деѧние[м]. слово[м]. научи[л]).
9.1. He also glorified God with his spiritual labor	
9.2. He carried out a ministry of social care.	Cf. ***Min.*** f. 280v, *Canon* 7 ([С]ироты застоупаа. и в[д]овица. бг҃амы[с]лено. ѡ[ч] ипатие. и елле по[до]ваеши. ѹбг҃имъ бгатно поа). Cf. Zinoviy's phrase на высотоѵ вꙁыде дѿродѣтелеи with на добро[д]телеи въсшелъ еси. высотоу in ***Min.*** f. 280v, *Sticheron* 2.
9.3. God glorified Hypatius by allowing him to perform miracles.	Cf. ***Und.*** f. 106r (Идѣже велїю ѿ б҃а чѹдотворенїа силѹ); ***VMCh*** stlb. 1991 & ***Prol.*** f. 133г (створї же чюдеса многа); ***Min.*** f. 280v, *Canon* 5 (Чю[д]действѹ[ѧ]. и тобою жи[з]нодавець. х҃с. бг҃ъ), and *Canon* 6 (Чю[д]са преестественны[х] храмина ави[с] ипатїе. примъ ѿ бг҃а блг҃ода[т]); ***Grig.*** p. 122 (знаменїа же и чюдеса многа. дамь тебѣ сътворити).
10. Hypatius performs a miracle by turning bitter water into sweet.	Cf. ***Und.*** f. 106v (В нѣкоей веси воды горкїа ѿ горъ текѹщыѧ в сладость преложи); ***Min.*** f. 280v, *Canon* 6 (Єоупа[т]е, сла[д]ко чю[д]сы горкїе. со[д]ваеши … Це[л]бамъ источни[к] бы[л] еси. ѡби[л]но проливаеши. всемъ певание). Cf. Zinoviy's phrase ипатїе ѩко же и моѵсе with Мѡѵсеи проѡброзоуѧ еси in ***Min.*** f. 280v, *Canon* 9.

TABLE 2 Main episodes and sources in the *Panegyric* (*cont.*)

Episodes	Sources
11. Hypatius' close relationship with God made him a partaker of the divine light.	Cf. ***Min.*** f. 280^{v}, *Canon* 1 (Свѣто[м] тр[о]ичны[м]. озаренъ), and (бо[ж]ственою и троическою светлостїю. всю вселенноую про[с]вети[л] еси), *Canon* 4 (Дховное сїанїе. ѡ[ч] в тѧ бг҃атно вселивъше[с]. светоно[с]ного. сто[л]па покоза. озарѧющимъ ми[р]. бо[ж]ствеными повеленїи), *Kontakion* (Оучите[л] и свети[л]никъ. бг҃оза[р]ны[м]и ло[у]чам[и]).
11.1. God illumined the path where Hypatius walked at night by sending him light from water.	Cf. ***Und.*** f. 106^{v}: (Хо[д]ѧщꙋ же емꙋ в темнѣй нощи нѣгдѣ близъ рѣки. Свѣщи горѧщыѧ ѿ воды ꙗвлѧхꙋсѧ. пꙋть емꙋ ѡсвѣщающыѧ. да не поползнетсѧ. и в водныѧ да не впадетъ стрꙋй); ***Min.*** f. 280^{v}, *Canon* 6 (напоꙗниемъ стрꙋѧ. света сщн[н]о. м[ч]нче ипатие. въжегъречноую нощью преше[д]шемоу ти. и стезю покоза. проꙗвлѧꙗ всемъ дш҃а тво[е]ѧ светлость).
11.2. God repeatedly sent him light whenever he was carrying out his charitable deeds at night.	
12. Hypatius performs a miracle by causing dry land to spring forth with hot water in order to bring warmth and physical healing to the villagers.	Cf. ***Und.*** f. 106^{v} (и на иномъ мѣстѣ источникъ теплы̆ водъ в цѣлбꙋ чл҃кѡмъ м҃лтвою изыде); ***Min.*** f. 280^{v}, *Canon* 6 (це[л]бам. сокровище водоу покоза. мл҃твами твоими), *Sticheron* 3 (тепълы[х] излиѧнїи. твоими мл҃тв[а]ми. воды изведе на вра[ч]боу стр[ас]теи изве). Cf. Zinoviy's phrase чюдѐ зарѧми сїѧꙗ with чю[д]съ лоуча во[з]сїа in ***Min.*** f. 280^{v}, *Sticheron* 1.
13. The miraculous deeds of Hypatius transcend human understanding.	Cf. ***Min.*** f. 280^{v}, *Canon* 7 (Неи[з]ре[ч]ны[х] чюде[с] самодете[л]. ст҃лю ѿ хр҃а бывъ).

TABLE 2 Main episodes and sources in the *Panegyric* (*cont.*)

Episodes	Sources
14. The story about the serpent that crawled into Emperor Constantius' treasury.	This sect. is a close paraphrase of ***Und.*** f. 106^{v}. ***Grig.*** pp. 128–133 offers a different version of the story starting as follows: ѱѧкѡлю-бивь б҃ъ. иже въси на ползꙋ строе. повѣле змїю страшнꙋ. из мора изыти и вънити въ полатуꙋ ц҃ревꙋ идеже бѣше злато и ср҃ѣбро и въсе именїе его. Cf. ***VMCh*** stlb. 1991–1992 & ***Prol.*** ff. 133г–4а: змиеви велику въ хранилищ҃и ц҃рьскаго имѣньꙗ вползавшю· ї не дадущю никомуже въ двери полатнъıꙗ внити.
14.1. Hypatius is summoned by the Emperor to chase away the serpent.	Cf. ***Und.*** f. 106^{v}; ***VMCh*** stlb. 1991–1992 & ***Prol.*** ff. 133г–4а: ѿ нихъже єдино б҃ы се· призванъ б҃ы ц҃ремь в костантинь градъ· сеꙗ ради ви нъı; ***Grig.*** p. 130.
14.2. Hypatius gives instructions to prepare an oven in the center of the hippodrome.	This sect. is a close paraphrase of ***Und.*** f. 107^{r}. Cf. ***Grig.*** p. 131 (гл҃а емꙋ ст҃ы принеси ми. г҃. свѣщь и кадилницꙋ).
14.3. Hypatius overcomes the serpent by using his staff and destroying it in the burning oven. Everyone is petrified.	This sect. is a close paraphrase of ***Und.*** f. 107^{r}–107^{v}. Cf. ***VMCh*** stlb. 1992 & ***Prol.*** f. 134а: створи же молитву ст҃ъıи єоупа тии· ї оукроти змиꙗ· и повелѣ на торгу възгнѣтити ѡгнь и ѿ полатъı изведе змиꙗ въгръıзнувъша зубъı въ краи жезла єго· и въ слѣдъ єго идаше· и въ съжьже и· ꙗкоже чю дитиса всѣмъ; ***Min.*** f. 280^{v}, *Sticheron* 3 (змиа оубивъ), and *Canon* 9 (же[з]ломъ твоимъ. о[у]ронаеми змиа. бл҃годерзновенно. ꙗко о[у]дицею извлекъ. ѡ[ч] ѿ клитеи цр҃скии[х] огнемъ изнꙋри[л] еси); ***Grig.*** p. 132 (простерь жезль свои, и оудари его въ главꙋ и гл҃а ѡ имени іс҃ х҃вь. тебѣ гл҃ю изиди из гра҃ сего прѣже даже те злѣ не погꙋбе … простерь жезль свои, и оудари его въ главꙋ и гл҃а ѡ имени іс҃ х҃вь. тебѣ гл҃ю изиди из гра҃ сего прѣже даже те злѣ не погꙋбе. извлече его до врать. Вьземь вѣригы железни свѣза его за вїю и влечаахꙋ мꙋжїе ,гтс и влекоше его из гра҃ сьжегоше его тоу).
14.4. The Emperor gives honor and gifts to Hypatius for his victory over the serpent.	This sect. is a close paraphrase of ***Und.*** ff. 107^{v}–108^{r}. Cf. ***Grig.*** pp. 132–133: да҃ же ц҃рь ипатїю дарꙋванїа многа злато и ср҃ѣбро и сьсꙋди златы. и сребрьни воины избранны. и пославь его кь своемꙋ гра҃у ра҃ующесе.

TABLE 2 Main episodes and sources in the *Panegyric* (*cont.*)

Episodes	**Sources**
14.5. The emperor orders the placement of Hypataius' image above the doors of the royal chambers. The serpent signifies the wickedness of Arius' heresy that enticed Constantius and Valens.	Cf. ***Und.*** ff. 107^{v}–108^{r}; ***VMCh*** stlb. 1992 & ***Prol.*** f. 134a: тѣ мже и въ дверехъ ложница своеѩ ц҃рь написати ѡбразъ ст҃го повелѣ. On Constantius holding to the Arian heresy and using his royal authority to protect the Arian followers, cf. ***Chron. Ham.*** p. 348 and *CA* 1.10 [p. 48]. On the persecution of Christians by Valens, cf. ***Chron. Ham.*** p. 349. For a reference to Eusebius of Nicomedia as a promoter of Arianism, cf. e.g., *CA* 2.24 [p. 168]. For Constantius, see ***Chron. 1512*** 120 [p. 273].
15. Hypatius uses the gifts to help the poor and build the churches in Gangra.	
16. Hypatius' way of life: self-control, guidance by the Holy Spirit, virtues, contemplation, and vision.	Cf. Zinoviy's phrase в преславноую высотѫ взыде сн҃ны дѡ҇родѣтелеи with на преславноую добро[д]телеи въсшелъ еси. высотоу in ***Min.*** f. 280^{v}, *Sticheron* 1; and his phrase простреса к видѣнїю таиномꙋ with воспростирааса. к ви[д]нию таиномоу in ***Min.*** f. 280^{v}, *Sticheron* 1. Cf. also Zinoviy's description of self-control with *Canon* 1 (ѡбоу[з]да[л] еси пло[т]скїа стр[с]ти. осиавъ дш҃о[у] твою. бе[з]стр[с]тїемъ све[р]шенны[м]), and the Holy Spirit's guidance with *Canon* 3 (Домъ бо[ж]ственого дх҃а бы[л] еси).
16.1. Hypatius shone with light to all in Gangra and faithfully carried out his ministry of pastor, interpreter, and preacher of true doctrine against heresy.	The initial part of this sect. is a paraphrase of ***Min.*** f. 280^{v}, *Sticheron* 1 (его[ж] сїании оумоу. и светлости озари въ. и всемъ во[з] блиста[л] еси. ѵю[дъсъныа зара), and *Canon* 1 (ѡблїставъ житїемъ. све[т]лымъ ꙗко сл҃нц[е] все. ст҃лю хр҃оу про[с]вети[л] еси. ѡ[ѵ] цр҃квь лоуѵамї). Cf. ***VMCh*** stlb. 1992 & ***Prol.*** f. 134a: възъ вращь же са въ свою цр҃квь пасаше стадо х҃во.
16.2. Hypatius dispelled the darkness of heresies with divine light and fulfilled fruitful service to the Orthodox faith.	Cf. ***Min.*** f. 280^{v}, *Canon* 7 ([Б]деи вере ереси. ꙗко зверїе. ѡ[ѵ] ѿгнавъ).

TABLE 2 Main episodes and sources in the *Panegyric* (*cont.*)

Episodes	Sources
17. The end of Hypatius' life: he can be compared to the Apostles and Prophets.	
17.1. In addition to many rewards, it remained for Hypatius to endure the crown of martyrdom.	Cf. ***Min.*** f. 280ᵛ, *Canon* 8 (венець приѧтъ сꙋгоубь сщ҃нном[ч]нїче), and *Kathisma* (вѣнченосець).
17.2. Even though Constantine the Great had stopped the persecution, Hypatius' life was still to end in martyrdom.	
17.3. The Novatianists attacked Hypatius from an ambush, throwing him down from the cliff and showering him with rocks; Hypatius prayed that their sins would not be counted against them.	This sect. is a close paraphrase of ***Und.*** f. 108ʳ. Cf. ***Min.*** f. 280ᵛ, *Canon* 9 (Побивае[м] камение[м]. за х[с]а. ѿ скв[ѣ]рны[х] оубїицъ ипатїе), and (Въ истинꙋ неправе[д]но тѧ хв҃а ст҃лѧ каме-ниемъ побивъши). Cf. Hypatius' prayer for his murderers with ***Min.*** f. 280ᵛ, *Canon* 9 (о[у]мираа молаще[с]. ты о оубинце[х] пол[оу]чити. прощение блж҃не. Єупа[т]е).
17.4. A woman who held to the Arian heresy hurled a rock at Hypatius' head and killed him.	This sect. is a close paraphrase of ***Und.*** f. 108ʳ–108ᵛ. Cf. ***VMCh*** stlb. 1992 & ***Prol.*** f. 134a: идущю же юму нѣкаꙗ жена арьєвъı єреси· верже съ полатъı камень на главꙋ ст҃го· и тѣмь оуби єго.
17.5. Hypatius' body hidden in a barn is found by a farmer after he hears the praise of the heavenly powers singing over it.	This sect. is a close paraphrase of ***Und.*** f. 108ᵛ.

TABLE 2 Main episodes and sources in the *Panegyric* (*cont.*)

Episodes	Sources
17.6. Miracles following the death of Hypatius: the murderers are punished by demon possession, and the woman begins to beat her breast.	This sect. is a close paraphrase of ***Und.*** f. 108^{v}. Cf. ***Min.*** f. 280^{v}, *Canon* 9 (моуҹащ[є]моу предаєши. демонꙋ. своими же рꙋкама. каменїемъ стрꙋжешї ѧзвы и терпїши. во[з]данїи бо[ж]ствены[х]. ѡжидающи[х]).
17.7. The mourning people of Gangra bring the body back to the city.	This sect. is a close paraphrase of ***Und.*** ff. 108^{v}–109^{r}.
17.8. Hypatius' body brings healing to the woman who killed him and to all others.	This sect. is a close paraphrase of ***Und.*** f. 109^{r}. Cf. ***Min.*** f. 280^{v}, *Canon* 6 (Ҹю[д]са преестественны[х]. храмина яви[с]).
18. A call to communal praise of Hypatius.	Cf. Zinoviy's phrase ипатї҃ ... хвалитє ... ст҃ѣноу нєзыблємоу with ты бо стєна in ***Min.*** f. 280^{v}, *Theotokion*. Cf. ***ShV.***
18.1. Prayer to Hypatius.	Cf. ***Min.*** f. 280^{v}, *Kontakion* & *Exapostilarion.*

In table 3, Lytvynenko has outlined thirty-six significant themes that Zinoviy drew from the *Enlightener* of Iosif Volotskiy and on which he elaborated in his *Demonstration of Truth*. For each of them, Lytvynenko has indicated the number of the Discourses where it is found in the *Enlightener* and has specified the pages—first in the Slavonic edition and then in the Russian translation, in the square brackets.

The Russian translation of the *Enlightener* is available in Преподобный Иосиф Волоцкий, *Просветитель* [Revered Iosif Volotskiy, *Enlightener*] (Москва: Институт русской цивилизации Родная страна, 2016). The Slavonic edition is found in *Просветитель или обличение ереси жидовствующихъ. Творение преподобного Отца нашего Иосифа, Игумена Волоцкаго* [*Enlightener or Refutation of the Heresy of the Judaizers. The Writing of our Revered Father, Iosif, Hegumen of the Volotskiy Monastery*], изд. третье (Казань: Типо-литография Императорскаго Университета, 1896).

TABLE 3 Significant themes in the *Demonstration of Truth* borrowed from the *Enlightener* of Iosif Volotskiy

1. **A list of common features shared by the persons of the Trinity: one nature, one will, one action, one grace, one power, one wisdom or mind, one throne, one life, one glory, and one honor:** *Enlightener* 1, pp. 57 [43]; 59 [45]; 60 [45]; 62 [47]; 91–92 [68–69]; 92 [70]; *Enlightener* 5, pp. 174 [130]; 180 [134]; 184 [136].
2. **God is one (without confusion and division) but distinguished as Father, Son, and Holy Spirit:** *Enlightener* 1, pp. 43 [57]; 91–92 [69].
3. **The persons of the Trinity are consubstantial with one another, co-unbegun, living, and true:** *Enlightener* 1, pp. 59 [45]; 60 [45]; 81 [61]; 91 [68]; *Enlightener* 5, pp. 179 [133]; 182–183 [135–136].
4. **The reason why God did not explicitly reveal himself as the Trinity in the Old Testament is that the Jews were inclined to the polytheism of the neighboring nations and were not prepared to understand the Trinity yet:** *Enlightener* 1, pp. 60–61 [45–46].
5. **The Trinity is shown in the fact that God did not say, "Let me make man" (in the singular), but "Let us make man" (in the plural):** *Enlightener* 1, pp. 62 [47]; 62–63 [47]; 66 [50].
6. **Before creating man, God said, "Let it be", and "it was so", whereas in making man, he conversed and counseled with the other persons of the Trinity, which can be deduced from the phrase, "Let us make man":** *Enlightener* 1, pp. 63 [48]; 63 [48]; 65 [49]; *Enlightener* 5, pp. 184 [136].
7. **In saying "Let us make man", God did not refer to the angels:** *Enlightener* 1, pp. 65 [49]
8. **The angels are not made in the image and likeness of God, and they are not divine either:** *Enlightener* 1, pp. 65 [49]; *Enlightener* 5, pp. 174 [130]; 179 [133].
9. **The phrase "Come, and having gone down, let us confuse them" (Gen. 11:5–7) indicates the fact that God the Father spoke to his Son and the Holy Spirit:** *Enlightener* 1, pp. 66 [50]; *Enlightener* 5, pp. 184 [136].
10. **The three men who visited Abraham in Gen. 18 were the three persons of the Trinity:** *Enlightener* 1, pp. 66–67 [50–51]; *Enlightener* 5, pp. 172 [129]; 180–181 [134]; 205–206 [150–151]; 208 [152]; 211 [154]; 216 [158].
11. **In the past, God appeared not once but often: e.g., to Noah, Abraham, Moses, and Jacob:** *Enlightener* 5, pp. 173 [129–130].
12. **The two men who went to Sodom were the Son and the Holy Spirit, and when Scripture says that the "Lord rained down fire" on Sodom "from the Lord" (Gen. 19:23), it indicates that one person of the Trinity was co-acting with another:** *Enlightener* 1, pp. 66 [51]; *Enlightener* 5, pp. 182–183 [135–136].
13. **Ex. 34:4–6, where the "Lord called upon the Lord", indicates the Trinity:** *Enlightener* 1, pp. 66 [51].
14. **The Trinity is indicated in the phrase, "The Lord said to my Lord, 'Sit at my right hand'" (Ps. 110:1; Acts 2:35):** *Enlightener* 1, pp. 69 [53]; *Enlightener* 5, pp. 177 [132].

TABLE 3 Significant themes in the *Demonstration of Truth* (cont.)

15. **There are instances in the Scriptures where God is called an angel, and Gen. 22:11–12 is one of them:** *Enlightener* 5, pp. 207–208 [152].
16. **Jacob wrestled with God and saw him face to face:** *Enlightener* 5, pp. 209 [153].
17. **We can compare our rational soul/mind to the Father, our word (generated by the soul/mind) to the Son (begotten from the Father), and our breath (which proceeds from the mouth) to the Holy Spirit (who proceeds from the Father):** *Enlightener* 1, pp. 90 [68].
18. **Greek deities are contrasted with the true God:** *Enlightener* 1, pp. 92 [70]; *Enlightener* 4, pp. 167 [126].
19. **Christ's divinity is indicated in the phrase, "You are a priest forever, in the order of Melchizedek" (Ps. 110:4):** *Enlightener* 1, pp. 69 [53]; *Enlightener* 5, pp. 176 [131].
20. **1 Tim. 3:16 shows Christ to be God:** *Enlightener* 2, pp. 95 [71].
21. **Christ is not a mere man but God:** *Enlightener* 2, pp. 96 [72].
22. **Christological arguments drawn from Heb. 1:2–3 and Phil. 2:7:** *Enlightener* 4, pp. 140 [105].
23. **The birth of Isaac (Gen. 18:9–10) is a prefiguring of Christ born without male sperm:** *Enlightener* 5, pp. 181–182 [134–135].
24. **Dealing with the question of why God had to become man:** *Enlightener* 4, pp. 145–146 [108–109]; 154–155 [116].
25. **The incarnation was necessary to renew the human image:** *Enlightener* 4, pp. 143 [107].
26. **Christ was conceived without male sperm:** *Enlightener* 4, pp. 155 [116]; *Enlightener* 5, pp. 181 [134].
27. **The Law foreshadowed the grace of Christ to humankind (Heb. 10:1):** *Enlightener* 3, pp. 121 [91]; *Enlightener* 4, pp. 153 [115].
28. **The Law has been fulfilled, and there is no need to make sacrifices, celebrate the Jewish Passover, or circumcise:** *Enlightener* 3, pp. 123 [93]; 129–130 [97].
29. **A great nation will come from Abraham (Gen. 18:18):** *Enlightener* 5, pp. 182–183 [135].
30. **Human words vanish in the air once they are spoken, but the Word of God is eternal:** *Enlightener* 1, pp. 81 [62]; 88–89 [66–67].
31. **Humans are small and weak:** *Enlightener* 1, pp. 65 [49].
32. **Man is a self-governing being:** *Enlightener* 1, pp. 90 [68].
33. **The human mind cannot comprehend divine things or define them:** *Enlightener* 4, pp. 140 [105].
34. **God made everything out of nothing:** *Enlightener* 4, pp. 151 [113].
35. **A reference to a king and his painted image:** *Enlightener* 1, pp. 9 [67].
36. **A reference to Greek philosophers:** *Enlightener* 4, pp. 167 [126].

Zinoviy develops a remarkably rich Trinitarian vocabulary and constructs far more neologisms than we find in any other Slavonic writing from medieval Russia. In this table, Shpakovskiy provides a list of the most significant Trinitarian terms in the *Demonstration of Truth*. The list is not exhaustive but is fairly representative of Zinoviy's theological vocabulary. The spelling of terms is standardized according to the most frequent form used by Zinoviy, and the terms are divided into six different categories.

TABLE 4 Zinoviy's Trinitarian terminology in the *Demonstration of Truth*

No.	Terms	Translation	Place in the manuscript: the first numbers mark the folios; the second numbers in the square brackets mark the corresponding sections in the English translation
	General/common		
1.	соущество	Nature, essence, substance	29^{r} [4.1, 4.3], 45^{r} [22.6], 48^{r} [24.6], 53^{r} [28.2], 104^{r} [49.13]
1.1.	єдиносоущныи	Consubstantial	30^{v} [4.8], 43^{r} [21.2], 45^{v} [23.2], 49^{v} [26.2], 50^{r} [26.2], 59^{r} [31.2], 59^{v} [31.2], 71^{v} [36.5], 103^{r} [49.9], 106^{v} [51.4], 127^{v} [71.2], 143^{r} [79.9], 146^{v} [80.11]
1.2.	єдиносоущество	Consubstantiality	59^{v} [31.4], 64^{v} [33.6], 71^{v} [36.4]
2.	єстество	Essence, nature, substance	29^{r} [4.1], 30^{r} [4.6], 30^{v} [4.7, 4.8], 45^{r} [22.5], 50^{r} [26.3], 50^{v} [26.5]
2.1.	соєстественыи	Co-essential	30^{v} [4.8]
3.	ѡбразъ	Image	See below
3.1.	єдиноѡбразныи	Sharing the same image	37^{v} [14], 40^{r} [16.3], 40^{v} [17.2] 47^{v} [24.5], 59^{r} [31.2], 64^{v} [33.6]
3.2.	соѡбразныє	Possessing a common image	37^{v} [13, 13.1, 14.1], 38^{r} [14.2], 39^{r} [14.7], 39^{v} [16.2], 40^{v} [17.2], 43^{r} [21.2], 43^{v} [21.2] 45^{v} [23.1, 23.2], 52^{r} [27.4], 54^{r} [28.6], 59^{r} [31.2], 64^{v} [33.6]
3.3.	тожеобразныє	Having an identical image	38^{r} [14.4, 14.5], 38^{v} [14.5], 40^{r} [17.1]

TABLE 4 Zinoviy's Trinitarian terminology in the *Demonstration of Truth* (*cont.*)

No.	Terms	Translation	Place in the manuscript: the first numbers mark the folios; the second numbers in the square brackets mark the corresponding sections in the English translation
	Personal/distinct		
4.	составъ	Subsistence	29^{r} [4], 46^{r} [23.4], 51^{v} [27.4], 52^{r} [27.4], 55^{v} [29.4], 61^{v} [31.9], 64^{v} [34.1], 126^{r} [70.5]
4.1.	живосоставныи	Living being	29^{v} [4.4]
5.	ипостась	Hypostasis	43^{v} [21.3], 45^{v} [23.2, 23.3], 52^{v} [28.1], 53^{v} [28.5], 59^{r} [31.1], 73^{r} [37.3, 37.4], 76^{v} [40.2], 82^{r} [40.22] 106^{v} [51.3, 51.4], 107^{v} [52.1]
6.	лицо	Person	43^{v} [21.3], 44^{r} [22.2], 52^{r} [27.4], 54^{r} [28.5], 55^{v} [29.4], 57^{v} [29.12], 61^{r} [31.9], 72^{v} [37.3], 106^{v} [51.3, 51.4]
	Divine attributes		
7.	безначаленъ	Without a beginning	29^{r} [4.1], 57^{v} [29.12], 123^{v} [68.3]
8.	безсмертныи	Immortal	28^{v} [3], 29^{r} [4.1], 29^{v} [4.3]
9.	гⷭ҇ьствие	Dominion, lordship	52^{v} [27.7], 55^{v} [29.4], 56^{v} [29.9], 57^{v} [29.12], 61^{r} [31.9], 61^{v} [31.9], 71^{v} [36.5]
10.	истинныи	True	28^{v} [3.2], 29^{r} [4.1], 30^{v} [4.8], 43^{r} [21.1], 53^{r} [28.2], 64^{r} [33.5], 82^{r} [40.22], 107^{v} [52.1]
11.	живыи	Alive	28^{v} [3, 3.1, 3.2], 29^{r} [4.1, 4.3], 29^{v} [4.3], 30^{v} [4.8], 42^{v} [20.1], 43^{r} [21.2, 21.3], 45^{v} [23.2], 46^{v} [24.1], 81^{v} [40.22]
12.	нестарѣющьсѧ	Ageless	29^{r} [4.1]
13.	присносоущенъ	Eternal	29^{r} [4.1, 4.2, 4.3], 29^{v} [4.4], 30^{v} [4.8], 45^{r} [22.5], 45^{v} [23.2]
	Common divine attributes (едино)		
14.	единогⷭ҇ьствоующие	Sharing the same lordship	52^{v} [28.1], 63^{r} [33.3], 63^{v} [33.3], 77^{r} [40.4], 81^{v} [40.20], 106^{v} [51.4], 143^{r} [79.9]

TABLE 4 Zinoviy's Trinitarian terminology in the *Demonstration of Truth* (*cont.*)

No.	Terms	Translation	Place in the manuscript: the first numbers mark the folios; the second numbers in the square brackets mark the corresponding sections in the English translation
15.	єдинославныє	Sharing the same glory	36^{r} [12], 52^{v} [27.7, 28.1], 56^{r} [29.6], 63^{r} [33.3], 143^{r} [79.9]
16.	єдинопрестольныє	Sharing the same throne (cf. 22, 26)	40^{v} [17.1], 52^{v} [28.1], 54^{r} [28.6], 71^{v} [36.5], 106^{v} [51.3], 143^{r} [79.9]
17.	єдиночестныє	Sharing the same honor (cf. 27)	38^{r} [14.2], 52^{v} [27.7, 28.1], 63^{r} [33.3], 64^{v} [33.6], 106^{v} [51.4], 143^{r} [79.9]
18.	єдиносилныє	Sharing the same power (cf. 29)	77^{r} [40.4], 143^{r} [79.9]
19.	єдиноначальство	Sharing the same headship (cf. 21)	72^{v} [37.3], 81^{v} [40.20]
	Common divine attributes (со)		
20.	соприсносоущныє	Co-eternal (cf. 13)	29^{r} [4.1], 30^{v} [4.8], 43^{r} [21.1, 21.2], 42^{v} [20.1], 43^{r} [21.1, 21.2], 44^{r} [22.3], 46^{r} [23.5], 49^{v} [26.2]
21.	собезначалныє	Equally without a beginning (cf. 19)	29^{r} [4.1], 30^{v} [4.8], 43^{r} [21.1], 44^{r} [22.3], 44^{v} [22.5], 52^{r} [27.5], 111^{v} [54.13]
22.	сопрестольныє	Sharing the same throne (cf. 16, 26)	40^{v} [17.1, 17.2], 43^{r} [21.2], 47^{v} [24.5], 51^{v} [27.3] 64^{v} [33.6]
23.	соцарствоующиє	Co-ruling	40^{v} [17.1]
24.	соповелительныє	Co-directing	56^{r} [29.8]
25.	совладычествоуют	Having the same lordship	40^{r} [17.1], 40^{v} [17.1]
	Common divine attributes (равно)		
26.	равнопрестѻ̑ство	Sharing the same throne (cf. 16, 22)	51^{v} [27.3]
27.	равночестныє	Having equal honor (cf. 17)	37^{v} [14], 55^{v} [29.6], 56^{r} [29.6], 56^{v} [29.9], 59^{r} [31]
28.	равномощныє	Having equal might	37^{v} [14], 40^{r} [17.1], 40^{v} [17.2]

TABLE 4 Zinoviy's Trinitarian terminology in the *Demonstration of Truth* (*cont.*)

No.	Terms	Translation	Place in the manuscript: the first numbers mark the folios; the second numbers in the square brackets mark the corresponding sections in the English translation
29.	равносильные	Having equal power (cf. 18)	38^r [14.2], 40^r [17.1], 40^v [17.2, 17.3], 45^v [23.1], 47^v [24.5], 51^v [27.3], 54^r [28.6], 59^r [31], 71^v [36.5], 106^v [51.3], 127^v [71.2]
	Common divine activity		
30.	единосодействоующие	Sharing in the same work	38^r [14.3]
31.	сосодетельствоующие	Doing the same work together	39^r [14.7, 15.1], 39^v [16.2], 40^r [17.1], 40^v [17.2], 43^r [21.2], 43^v [21.2], 50^r [26.2]
32.	сосотворительные	Making the same work together	39^v [16.2], 40^v [17.2]

The *Panegyric to St. Hypatius of Gangra*

Introduction to the *Panegyric to St. Hypatius of Gangra*

The *Panegyric to St. Hypatius of Gangra* is considered one of Zinoviy's earliest writings, composed between 1551 and the early 1560s. It is an example of high rhetoric and fine argumentation, in which one part is devoted to the Trinitarian controversy and the other to Hypatius of Gangra, one of the participants at the First Council of Nicaea, who died as a martyr in around A.D. 326. The text is reproduced according to the earliest manuscript housed in Moscow, GIM, Uvar. № 349, end of the sixteenth century, ff. 1–25.

The Slavonic text was prepared by Shpakovskiy and verified by Lytvynenko. The English translation, text divisions, and Biblical references are the work of Lytvynenko. The headings are introduced to help the reader follow the text, but they are not present in the original. For the sake of convenience, the translation includes page references to the previous edition in В.И. Корецкий, "Вновь найденное противоеретическое произведение Зиновия Отенского" [V.I. Koretskiy, "Newly Found Anti-Heretical Writing of Zinoviy Otenskiy"], in *Труды отдела древнерусской литературы*, том 21 (Москва–Ленинград: Академия наук СССР, 1965), 166–182.

Readers should keep in mind the distinguishing features of Zinoviy's writing discussed in sect. 4 of the introduction ("A Note on Translation"), such as repetition of arguments, word-weaving, mixing of verb tenses, and speaking in the past tense.

 | DOI:10.1163/9789004538054_005

Text and Translation of the *Panegyric to St. Hypatius of Gangra*

1r/173 Зиновїа чернори̑ца. ѡ ст҃ѣмъ ипа
тїи гангрьсцѣмъ еп҃пѣ, і чю̑ⷮворцы,[1]
Прїиде намъ дн҃ь. и̑ дⷪⷭбрыхъ виновны̏
и вѣнечниⷦ҇ свѣтлыи. ст҃ль и м҃нкъ и
патїе. е҇ⷤ бы пⷪ҇ⷣ стоанїю похвалити
моужа. сеи не наша гроубаа словеса
точїю превъсходитъ но и мнⷪ҇ⷢгоучеⷩ҇ны̏
м҃рецъ могїи превыти словеса. намⷤ҇
како боуде̑ⷮ пⷪ҇ⷣ стоанїю похвалити его.
но токмо воспоминанїемъ ипатїа о
ст҃итиса. есть бо ост҃итиса намъ
паматїю ст҃го пⷪ҇ⷣвиги е҇ⷢ почитающи.
не ѿ прилжчающиⷯ҇ бо са пⷪ҇ⷣвижникоⷡ҇ едиⷩ҇
ипатїе пришедыи к наⷨ҇ дн҃ь. ниⷤ҇ иже дре
вле по еллиноⷯ҇ бывающиⷯ҇ пⷪ҇ⷣвижникоⷡ҇ и
менοуемыⷯ҇ олиⷨ҇бїискыⷯ҇. ниⷤ҇ в колесницаⷯ҇
1v/174 тичющиⷯ҇ оуправленїе. ниⷤ҇ иныⷯ҇ таковыⷯ҇
пⷪ҇ⷣвижникоⷡ҇. і еллиⷩ҇стїи оубо пⷪ҇ⷣвижн̏
цы, ѡ цветныⷯ҇ троудовоⷯ҇ истлѣненъ
вѣнецъ ѿ смⷬ҇тнаⷢ҇ пⷪ҇ⷣвигоположникаⷣ҇
прїемлюⷮ҇. ~ Nо чюдимыи нами ипⷮ҇
тїе. подвигоⷨ҇ оубо пⷪ҇ⷣвиеаса дⷪ҇ⷠрымъ,
наставльса ѿ павла ап҃ла, верⷤ҇ съ
бл҃ю, теченїе скоⷩ҇ча. прочее щадимы̏
томоу правдѣ вѣнецъ воспрїемла.
не ѿ смⷬ҇тнаⷢ҇ подвигоположника рⷤ҇кї
оусваноувшиⷯ҇ цвѣтецъ вѣнеⷰ҇ по еллин
скыⷯ҇ ѡтрⷪ҇ⷦ боренїю, но ѿ рⷤ҇кї цр҃а
цр҃емъ, и г҃а гд҃емъ едїнаⷢ҇ безсмⷬ҇тна
вѣнецъ нетлⷩ҇ѣныи съпр҃носоущныⷨ҇ жи
вотоⷨ҇ прїемла о дⷪ҇ⷠрыхъ свои̑ⷯ троудо
воⷯ҇, чтⷭ҇аⷢ҇ ст҃льства, и бжⷭ҇твенаⷢ҇ испо

1 *In the margin*: слоⷡ҇. ҂ѳ҃.

© KONINKLIJKE BRILL NV, LEIDEN, 2023 | DOI:10.1163/9789004538054_006

On St. Hypatius, the Bishop of Gangra and Wonderworker, by Monk Zinoviy 1r/173

A Call to Praise Hypatius and Descriptions of His Spiritual Achievements, Martyrdom, and Pastoral Ministry

1. Today, Hypatius has come to us, the saint and martyr, the one who is the source of (goodness) for the virtuous and who bears the bright crown, so that we may give him the praise that he deserves. His [words] not only surpass our coarse words but are also able to exceed the words of the wise men of erudition. How else, then, will we give him the praise that he deserves, if not by remembering Hypatius for our own sanctification? For the way for us to become holy is to honor the saint by remembering his feats.

1.1. For Hypatius, who has come to us today, is not one of the short-lived heroes, nor of the heroes whom the Greeks call Olympians from the old times,
nor of those who drive | the chariots, nor of any other such heroes. Indeed, the 1v/174
Greek heroes receive the "perishable crown" in vain labor from the mortal judge (1 Cor. 9:25). But our admired Hypatius pursued the good of spiritual labor by taking the admonition from the Apostle Paul, "He kept the faith, finished the race", and received the "crown of righteousness that was already in store" for him (2 Tim. 4:8). And this is not from the hand of the mortal judge, who awards with the crown of fading flowers, in accordance with the (rules) of competing Greek youth (cf. 1 Cor. 9:25), but from the hand of the "King of kings and Lord of lords" (Rev. 19:16), the only one who is "immortal" (1 Tim. 1:17), that he received the "imperishable crown" of everlasting life (1 Cor. 9:25). It came from his good
works of genuine holiness and his marvelous labor for his godly testimony. | 2r/174

2r/174 вѣданїа, дивныⷯ потовъ еⷢ҇, с симиⷤ
и мчнⷱ҇ства почестеи наслажⷣенїе.
мⷭ҇ческы бо жизнь ипатїеви совршⷭ҇иⷯ.
стⷧ҇ьство сщⷩ҇но прⷤ҇е исправиⷡ҇. стадо по
рчⷩ҇еное томоу хⷭ҇ртоименитое, ꙗⷦ҇ исти
нныи пастыⷬ҇ оупасъ, пастыремъ наⷭ҇
лникоу хⷭ҇ви всесоврьшⷩ҇ено прⷭ҇естави. па
гоⷠ҇ныа волкы ѿгнавъ хотащаа погоⷢ҇
бити хⷭ҇ртово стадо. ереси погибⷭ҇ены
wбличиⷡ҇ потреби. И тои бо посредѣ
трїесотъ и йⷢ҇і. тиⷯ бгⷪ҇носныⷯ стыⷯ ѿць
съпровозгїа стекшиⷯса оуꙗснити прⷭ҇
вославноую вѣрж въ едїносоущнѹю пре
пѣтоую трⷭ҇цоу ѿца і сна и стго дха. в пⷷ҇
рвоⷨ вселеⷩ҇скоⷨ соборѣ. и ꙗжⷣа арїа прокⷧ҇
нши, возмоутившаⷢ҇ злыⷨ своиⷨ оученїе
2v/174 стоую соборноую і апⷭ҇льскоую црⷭ҇квь хⷭ҇ртвⷹ.
спроповѣда ѿцемъ во вселеⷩ҇стѣⷨ соборѣ
ипатїе сеи, гдⷭ҇а нⷭ҇шго їса хⷭ҇рта сна бжїⷭ҇
единороⷣна соуща, ѿ бга ѿца рожⷣена
преже всѣⷯ вѣкоⷡ҇. ꙗⷦ҇ свѣта ѿ свѣта,
тако бга истинна ѿ бга истинна, рожⷣе
на а не сътворена, едїнасоущна ѿцж.
имжⷤ вса быша. аще вѣцы аще нбса
аще земла і ꙗже в ниⷯ, аще каа видї
маа, аще каа невидимаа, вса тѣⷨ
быша, і без неⷢ ничтоⷤ быⷭ еже бысть.
насⷤ же ради въ члкоⷯ, и нашеⷢ ради спⷭ҇нїа
съшⷣеша с нбсъ, і въплощьшаⷭ ѿ дха стⷣ .
і мрїа двы вчлчьшаⷭ, и распата ꙁа ныⷩ
сⷮрадавша и погребена, и воскрⷭ҇ша три
дневно. и въсшⷣеша на нбса, и сѣдащⷣ
3r/174 одеснжю ѿца, і паки градѹща соудити
живыⷨ и мртвыⷨ, и црьствѹюща бес коⷩ
ца. тако ипатїе проповѣда ха ба, сⷮра
шнаⷢ его таинства смотренїе, с препо
лнымъ того бжⷭ҇твомъ. бга ѿца блго
воленїемъ. безоумнагоⷤ арїа новаго
іждоу, на единосоущное бжⷭ҇тво хоула
щa. посредѣ собора ипатїе всестго дхⷯ

1.2. With these, there was also the delight of the martyr's honor, for Hypatius' life ended in martyrdom. Before that, as a true shepherd, he first accomplished the vocation of the holy priesthood, "shepherding" Christ's "flock" that was entrusted to him (cf. 1Pet. 5:1–4). Presenting himself to Christ the "Chief Shepherd" (1Pet. 5.4), he drove away the "fierce wolves" that wanted to destroy Christ's "flock" (cf. Acts 20:29), and exposed and crushed the destructive heresies.

Hypatius' Participation at Nicaea, His Creedal Statement, and Exposure of Arius' Heresy from Scripture

2. For he shone with the three hundred and eighteen God-bearing holy fathers who gathered together to explain the Orthodox faith in the consubstantial glorious Trinity—the Father and Son and Holy Spirit—at the First Ecumenical Council, and to condemn estranged Arius, who troubled the Holy Catholic and Apostolic Church of Christ with his evil teaching. | 2v/174

2.1. At the Ecumenical Council, this man Hypatius preached the Father together with our Lord Jesus Christ, the only-begotten Son of God, begotten of God the Father before all ages, as Light of Light, so also true God of true God, begotten, not made, consubstantial with the Father; by him all things were made, whether times, or heaven, or earth, or all the things that are in them, both visible and invisible, "all things were made by him, and without him, nothing was made that is made" (Jn. 1:3); who for us men, and for our salvation, came down from heaven, and became incarnate by the Holy Spirit and of the Virgin Mary, and was made man; he was crucified for us, suffered, and was buried, and on the third day he rose again, and ascended into heaven, and sat | at the 3r/174
right hand of the Father, and will come again to judge the living and the dead, and will rule without end. This was how Hypatius preached Christ as God and the economy of his awesome mystery that overflowed with his divinity and the good pleasure of God the Father.

2.2. And as for insane Arius, the new Judas, who blasphemed the consubstantial Godhead at the Council, Hypatius reproached him with the power of the

силою, бг҃одх҃новеⷩны писанїеⷨ обличаа
посрамлаше. прелагаа словеса сщ҃енаⷢ
писанїа ветхаⷢ и новаго. наипаче бж҃їа
словеса еѵⷢлїа гн҃а, и бж҃твены апл҃ъ.
злоименитыи арїе, наоучивса еллиⷩ
скомоу оученїю. и сжемоудраа по еллї
нⷯо, богы болшїа и боги мⷩешїа оумышлⷩа
ше. и благочⷭтїе ратованїе бранемъ со
3v/174 имⷩеныи, еллискими баснами. гл҃аше
бо болшаⷢ бг҃а ѿц҃а быти. и меншаⷢ бг҃а
сн҃а. сътворена на здⷣанїе твари, да
сн҃омъ твⷭа зижетъ бг҃ъ. ѡ безоумїⷣ
зра предо оочима вынꙋ, орждїа имиⷤ
в нⷭа сотворяютса вещи. хꙋⷣжьши соⷮу
ѿ вещи. ѡроудїа бо содѣловающаа па
волоки. и колико хѫⷣжьши соуть ѡрꙋ
дїа паволоⷦ. такоⷤ и содѣловающаа
златыа сосѫды. колико хѫⷣжьши соⷮу
ѡрѫдїа сосоудоⷡ златыⷯ сотворенⷩыⷯ ими
и многа таковаа ѿрацоⷠу. колико ѡбⷷ
зоумствоваса арїе гл҃а. величати е
моу бг҃а ѿц҃а тⷨе, имжⷤ сн҃а е сътворенⷩа
нарецⷮе. еллискїи оубо басногланⷩи, бг҃оу
величїе сътворити глаⷢше. да сн҃а е
4r/175 хоуⷣжьша здⷣанїа нарецⷮе. зинжв бо бгⷪра
тнⷭискаа оуста скверныⷨ азыкоⷨ своиⷨ
изблева арїи, баше гл҃а нѣкогдⷣа времⷩа
егда не баше сн҃а. и бысть сн҃ъ да сн҃оⷨ
бг҃ъ сотворитъ миⷬ. колико оубо нече
стїе е таковое арїево. і како премꙋⷣра
ѧса безоумїе, не могїи поне сеⷢ разоумѣ
ти. ножица швецы имоⷮу да краѧт
цр҃кїа багряница. и оубо ножица и иглⷹ
сътворяютъ да ножицами кроѧтъ
багряницѫ. иглоⷤу сотворяюⷮ, да сши
ваютъ цр҃коую багряницѫ. і кто не
вѣсть колика хѫдость ѿ багряница
ножица и иглы. арїе оупоⷣдоблаеⷮ тварь
багряницы. сотворшагоⷤ тварь хⷭа
оуподоблаетъ ножицаⷨ, и иглы.

supreme Holy Spirit, exposing (his heresy) from the divinely inspired Scripture. He presented the words of the sacred Scriptures of the Old and New Testaments, especially the divine words of the Lord's Gospel and the divine "Apostle" (i.e., Acts).

A Description of Arian Beliefs with Roots in Greek Polytheism, and Zinoviy's Refutation of Arius' Statements in *Thalia* with Christological Analogies

3. Infamous Arius, having learned from Greek teaching, and exercising himself in vain concepts, devised the greater deities and smaller deities according to the Greeks. He waged war against piety | by what in fact were the fables of the 3v/174 Greeks, for he spoke of the greater God the Father and the smaller God the Son (who was) made for the sake of creation so that by means of the Son, God could fashion the creation.

3.1. Oh, madness! Every time we direct our eyes to the tools by which things are produced for us, we see that they are of lesser value than the things produced. For (if we consider) the tools that produce silk, how less valuable are the tools compared to the silk? Likewise, (if we take) the production of the golden vessels, how less valuable are the tools that produce the golden vessels as compared to the golden vessels themselves? And many other such things can be found (to show) how insane it was for Arius to glorify God the Father while saying that the Son was made by him. Indeed, the Greek fable-tellers say that they give glory to God, yet they treat the Son | as being lesser than creation. 4r/175

3.2. For Arius opened his mouth to fight God with his evil tongue and vomited the words that said, "There was once when the Son was not", and "The Son came into being so that through the Son, God could make the world". What impiety, then, for Arius (to say) such things, and how can he not understand in his utterly insane "wisdom" that scissors are used by the tailor to cut out the royal dress? And indeed, the scissors and needle are made so that the scissors can be used to cut out the dress, and the needle is made so that it may be used to sew the royal dress. And who does not know how less valuable the scissors and the needle are as compared to the dress? Yet Arius likens creation to the dress and likens Christ, who made the creation, to the scissors and the needle.

4ᵛ/175 ипатїⷤе чюдныи своиⷨ исповѣданїеⷨ
и свѣтлостїю бжⷭ҇твены правыⷯ велѣ
нїи апⷭ҇лькыⷯ і еⷢ҇льскиⷯ, бг҃охѫлникоу
злѣ зїающаа оуста на бг҃а заградї.
і обличиⷡ҇ того посрами. и конечномѫ
проклатїю врага ст҃ѣи собѡⷬнѣи і апⷭ҇
ст҃ѣи црк҃ви предⷣаⷷ. свѣтло съ ѿц҃ы
бг҃оносными всест҃ѹю трⷪ҇цѫ единосоу
щнѫ православно проповѣда. безнаⷱлн
бг҃а ѿц҃а, ѿ негⷪ҇ събезнаⷱлна сн҃а едино
рѡдна, бг҃а истиⷩна ѿ бг҃а истиⷩна г҃а нⷭ҇
шеⷢ҇ іс҃а х҃а. и всест҃го дх҃а г҃а и бг҃а, ѿ бг҃
ѿц҃а исходащаⷢ҇, съ ѿц҃емъ и с сн҃омъ,
покланаема и славима. трⷪ҇цѫ безнаⷱ
лноую единосоущнѫю въ треⷯ составѣ
единаⷢ҇ бг҃а блг҃о, сътвѡшаⷢ҇ нб҃о и зе
5ʳ/175 млю. и вса иⷤ҇ в ниⷯ видимаа и невиди
маа. по бг҃ословїю верховнаⷢ҇ бг҃ословⷡц
і еⷢ҇листа. исповѣда бо бг҃а ѿц҃а безн
чална, бг҃а сн҃а единорѡⷣнаⷢ҇ собезнаⷱлн
ѿц҃оу. не баше времени никогда же
егда не бѣ сн҃а. но в наⷱлѣ бѣ слово съ
ѿц҃емъ. и слово бѣ оу ѿц҃а прⷭ҇но искони.
и вса тⷨѣ быша, и без сн҃а ничтоⷤ ~~не~~ быⷭ҇.
еже бысть. і аще нб҃са и землѧ види
маа и невидимаа. і аще времена, і а
ще вѣкы, всаческаа тъ сн҃ъ бж҃їи едї
норѡⷣныи сътвори. і аще вѣки и вре
мена и лѣта быша сн҃омъ бж҃їимъ.
како сотвореⷩнаа боудѫ преⷤе твⷪца
ⷯи. і како боудеⷮ вⷦѣ или времѧ или лѣ
та старѣе сн҃а бж҃їа, сътворшаⷢ вѣ
5ᵛ/175 ки и времѧ и лѣта. без него бо ничтоⷤ
быⷭ҇ еже быⷭ҇. времѧ и лѣта и вⷦѣ бысть.
сн҃ъ бж҃їи едїнорѡⷣны всегда прⷭ҇но еⷭ҇ а не быⷭ҇.
ꙗко сын баше всегⷣа. и не баше никогⷣа
же егда не баше. но всегⷣа баше сын
оу ѿц҃а бг҃а сн҃ъ единорѡⷣныи, и съ ст҃ыⷨ
дх҃омъ. единославеⷩ, съпрⷭ҇толеⷩ, съвлⷣ
дычествоуа равеⷩ рождьшемоу еⷭ҇ ѿц҃ѫ,

3.3. | But Hypatius, with his marvelous confession and the brightness of $4^{v}/175$
his divine true apostolic commands from the Gospels, shuts the blasphemer's
mouth that uttered evil against God and exposed him to reproach. Having
subjected the enemy of the Holy Catholic and Apostolic Church to the ulti-
mate condemnation, he splendidly preached together with the God-bearing
fathers the Orthodox faith in the supremely holy consubstantial Trinity: God
the Father without beginning, and the Son who is from him and equally with-
out beginning, only-begotten, true God of true God, our Lord Jesus Christ and
the supreme Holy Spirit, Lord and God, who proceeds from God the Father,
who with the Father and the Son is worshipped and glorified; the consubstan-
tial Trinity without beginning in three subsistences; the only good God, Maker
of heaven and earth, | and of all things in them, visible and invisible, according $5^{r}/175$
to the pre-eminent theologian and evangelist, for he professed God the Father
without beginning, (and with him) God the Son, the only-begotten, without
beginning the same as the Father.

3.4. There was never a time when the Son was not, but "in the beginning
was the Word" with the Father, "and the Word was" with the Father always and
from "the beginning"; and "through him, all things were made", and "without"
the Son "nothing was made that was made" (Jn. 1:1–3). And whether heaven or
earth, visible or invisible, whether times or ages, all things were made by him,
the only-begotten Son of God. And since the ages and times and periods were
made by the Son of God, how can these things that were made, exist before
their Maker? And how can the age or time or period be older than the Son of
God, who made the ages | and times and periods, and without whom "noth- $5^{v}/175$
ing was made that was made" (Jn. 1:2), including the time and period and age
that were made, too? But the Son of God, the only-begotten, exists always and
eternally, and did not come into being. As the Son, he has always been, and
there was never when he was not. Instead, the Son "was" always "with God" the
Father (Jn. 1:1). Together with the Holy Spirit, the only-begotten Son is glorified
and shares the same throne and power, being equal and consubstantial with
the Father who begot him.

і единосоущенъ. ~ Подобно бы̏ нам
в памати ст҃го сѐ мнка и ст҃ла іпатіа
въ единых бгословных его оученій, іако
в раю напитоватиса, къ оутѣше
нію и к наоученію нашемѫ, и воспо
минанію многих его чюдес. и мнческаг
скончанія є. возвеселившиса тръже
ствовати. но никтож ми порцы, и
6r/175 теплѣ любащих ст҃го. хотащѹ ми прѣд
ложити и ѿ словес бывших во ст҃омъ,
и великом вселенском соборѣ. понеж слышах
и ннѣ нѣкых жаб в тинѣ плъгающихъ
квоктанія. по ѡномоуж арію безоумных
ересь. рѣх же оубо и жабы в тинѣ плъ
гающих ѿ арїа і еще. понеж арии свою ерес
състави ѡпираиса философіи. и мно
гих философов поборников по себѣ на прѣнїе
ко ст҃ымъ ѿцемъ прїѡбрѣте. еще же
и житїемъ нерастлѣнным, ни пїаным
живаше арїи. протопопъ бо ѿ патрїа
рха ахыллы александрѣистеи црк҃ви
поставлен бы̏. иже і ѡбраз житїа по
казоваше прельщаемым ѿ негъ къ своеи
емоу ереси. сїи же еретицы ѡ нихж
6v/175 ннѣ слышах. ихъ и жабы нарекох по
семоу. понеж безсловеснѣиши свинеи
соут, токмо змїино шептанїе имѹт.
не токмо грамотических не вѣдахоу сло
вес, неж и поборников мѫжеи философов.
но нижи народных грамот вѣдат, или оумѣ
ютъ прочитати. токмо в пїанствѣ
и въ ѡбъадении, и в нечистотах всегда, а
ки жабы в тинѣ жироутю. таковым
гробъ отвръстъ грътани ихъ, квокчют.
зловонїе арїевож. пачеж и злѣе арїа во
лжи и хоулы̏ на бг҃а. ~ Не мнюж и семоу
сїе ст҃моу ипатїю несладостно быти.
еж произведохса в памат ед прѣложити.
іаже ст҃їи на ѡбличенїе арїю изложиша.
пачеж и оусладитиса емоу ѡ семъ болма

A Call to Remember Hypatius and His Teaching, and a Comparison of Arius and Russian Heretics

4. In memory of this martyr and saint Hypatius, it befits us to be one with his doctrinal teaching, and to nourish ourselves with it as in paradise for our own consolation and admonition and to remember his numerous miracles and how his life ended in martyrdom so as to celebrate it joyfully. But let no one who | 6ʳ/175
dearly loves the saint reproach me for my desire to also present the words that were (proclaimed) at the holy and great Ecumenical Council.

4.1. For I heard that even now there is a croaking of some "toads" that crawl in the mire, (promoting) the insane heresy of Arius. And the reason I speak of them as toads that crawl in the mire in comparison with Arius is that Arius composed his heresy based on philosophy and gained many philosophers as followers in order to contend with the holy fathers. Besides, he lived a life that was neither depraved nor spent in drunkenness—for he was ordained as a presbyter by the patriarch of the Alexandrian Church, Achillas—and this way of life he displayed before those whom he enticed into his own heresy. But as for these heretics, of whom | I have now heard and thus called them toads, they are more 6ᵛ/175
senseless than pigs, and the only thing they are able to do is to make sounds of snakes hissing, (for) not only do they have no knowledge of literary grammar to represent the men who are philosophers, but they also have no basic literacy and do not know how to read. They (spend their lives) in constant drunkenness and in gluttony and in impurity, like the toads which fatten themselves in the mire. Such men have the grave set open for them; their throats rage with Arian stench. In fact, they are even more malicious than Arius in their lies and blasphemy against God.

Hypatius' Fight against Arius, Miracles, and Martyrdom as an Inspiration to Teach the Trinity and Battle the Newly Emerging Heretics

5. Neither do I think that it will bring no delight to saint Hypatius to recount in his memory what the saints expounded (in their effort) to reproach Arius; and I suppose, there would be even more delight for him (to know) | that Christ, 7ʳ/176

7r/176 непщѹю. єлма в на҃с х҃с прославлѧеⷮ сѧ
нн҃ѣ, єдїносоѵщ҃еⷩ бг҃ꙗ ѿц҃оу. ѡ немъⷤ
ст҃моу ипатїю ве҃с пѡ҃вигⷢ бы҃с с бг҃оносны҃мⷨ
ѿц҃ы во ст҃омъ великомъ соборѣ пръ
вомъ. ѡ немъⷤ пѡ҃визаса дѡⷠрѣ, і все
времѧ живота своеⷢ. ѡ немъⷤ и бл҃жеⷩ
ноую коⷩчинꙗ прїѧтъ повїенїемъ.
по исповѣданїи єдиносоущныѧ трⷪцⷣ
бж҃твенѣи. смр҃ть стр҃тїю претръ
пѣ, како же ли не оусладитса и нн҃ѣ
ст҃ль ипатїе. намъ болшїи пѡⷣвигъ
его єⷤ ѡ православной вѣре гл҃ющимъ
и славащиⷨ с нимъ и намъ препѣтоⷰ
пр҃стоую трⷪцꙗ єдиносоущнꙗ. трїєдї
но, и єдино три, бг҃а єдинаⷢ во треⷯ съ
ставѣ, ѿц҃а і сн҃а и ст҃го дх҃а живоⷮво
7v/176 рѧща. і арїи проклинаетса ѿ право
вѣрныⷯ. с нимъⷤ и новыѧ жабы ныра
ющїи в тинѣ злобѣсїа стр҃теи.
Понеⷤ чюжїи арїи скврьными оусты
своими, ѿ сщ҃енныⷯ слове҃с, злѣ на пре
пиранїе игношаше къ ѿц҃емъ. первⷣа
бг҃опроповѣдникоⷡ бг҃одх҃новеⷩнаа оу
ста. ꙗже въ плоти смотренїа ѿч҃иⷨ
бл҃говоленїемъ єдинорѡⷣнаⷢ сн҃а бж҃їа
г҃а бг҃а нш҃го і҃са х҃а, претыкати҃с арїеви
возпепщеваса къ своеи емоу погибели.
иже и надомса разоума помыслъ своⷯі.
разсѣданїе юдино пострада. тако
во бо что бг҃опроповѣдниⷦ паве҃ⷣ, писа
в посланїи кориⷩфоⷨ. ꙗко хж҃ бл҃гооуха
нїе есмы бг҃ви, во сп҃нныⷯ и погибеⷣныⷯ
8r/176 овѣмъ оубо вона ѿ смр҃ти в смр҃ть.
ѡвѣмъⷤ вона ѿ живота в животъ.
єⷤ слоучиса чюжемоу арїю вона погы
бели. понеⷤ писаⷩнаа дѡⷠрѣ бг҃опропоⷡѣ
дники, арїи прїатъ злѣ. соⷠрав бѡ
словеса ч҃та ꙗже ѿ еѵ҃глїа і ѿ ап҃ла, пре҃д
лагааше к препиранїю ѿц҃емъ, в ниⷯⷤ
и чюдотворивыи сеи ѿц҃ъ ипатїе. гл҃а

who is consubstantial with God the Father, is still being glorified among us now. It was for his sake that Hypatius, together with the God-bearing fathers, ventured all his endeavors at the holy great First Council. For his sake, too, he pursued good things during the entire time of his life, and for his sake, he also accepted the blessed end by being stoned. After having professed the divine consubstantial Trinity, he suffered the agony of death. How will saint Hypatius not be delighted still now?

5.1. He (inspires) us toward greater deeds—to join him in the proclamation of the Orthodox faith and the praising of the glorious supremely holy consubstantial Trinity: three in one and one in three, one God in three subsistences, Father and Son and Holy Spirit, the Life-giver. | And together with Arius, who 7v/176
is condemned by the Orthodox faithful, the new toads, who drift in the mire of passions (inflamed) by the evil spirits, are also (condemned).

Arius' Misinterpretation of Scripture

6. Since estranged Arius proclaimed evil things with his impure mouth, (misinterpreting) the sacred words (of Scripture) in order to dispute with the fathers, who were the first ones to preach about God with their divinely inspired mouths, and stumbled over the bodily economy of the only-begotten Son of God, our Lord Jesus Christ, who accomplished it by the good pleasure of the Father, it resulted in his own destruction when he became arrogant in the thinking of his mind and suffered the gushing out (of his bowels) like Judas (cf. Acts 1:18). For that is what Paul, the preacher of God, described in the Epistle to the Corinthians, writing that "we are the fragrance of Christ to God among those who are being saved and among those who are perishing. | To the one we are 8r/176
the fragrance of death leading to death, and to the other the fragrance of life leading to life" (2 Cor. 2:15–16). And it occurred that for estranged Arius, the fragrance led to death.

6.1. For Arius badly misinterpreted what was well written by the preachers of God. Having collected the genuine words that are found in the Gospels and in the "Apostle" (i.e., Acts), he put them forth to contend with the fathers among whom was also this father Hypatius the Wonderworker.

шеⷤ арїи х҃с нѥсть роженъ ѿ соущⷭ҇тва ѿ
ч҃а бж҃їа. но созанъ преⷤ всѣⷯ, и тѣмъ
сътвори бг҃ъ всю твⷬ҇. писано бо есть
ꙗⷦ гл҃етъ премⷣрость. г҃ь созⷣа мѧ в нⷱ҇а
тⷦ҇ѡ поутїи свойⷯ, в дѣла своа. и петр
в дѣанїйⷯ гл҃етъ, ꙗко бг҃ъ сътворилъ
еⷭ҇ и г҃а і х҃а сего іс҃а. и павеⷧ къ евреомъ
пишеⷮ, вѣрна реⷱ҇ сотворшемꙋⷢ еⷭ҇. сїа сⷩ҇
8v/176 ныа гл҃ы арїе злѣ на хꙋленїе, единород
номоу сн҃ꙋ бжїю гⷭ҇оу и бг҃оу нашемоу іс҃ꙋ
хⷭ҇оу прелⷪ҇жи. ~ Бжⷭ҇твеный ипатїе
съ ст҃ымъ афонасїеⷨ дⷭ҇ѡбрѣ наоучишⷶ
нⷭ҇а. сїа сщ҃енныа гл҃ы прїемше на смо
тренїе еⷭ҇ⷤ на сп҃нїе нⷶ҇ єдїнорⷣѡнⷶ҇ сн҃а бжїⷶ
ꙗкоⷤ истинⷩ҇а во ст҃омъ писанїи еⷭ҇. и гл҃а
ше и проповѣдаше. ꙗⷦ есть премⷣрость
съставнаа г҃ь нш҃ь іс҃ х҃с. и гл҃тъ ѡ себⷷ
воплотивса в чл҃чтво, ꙗко г҃ь созⷣа мⷪ҇
в нⷱ҇атⷦ҇ѡ поутїи свойⷯ в дѣла своа сїа, еⷤ
въчл҃читиса и распатиⷭ҇, и пострада
ти і оумрети за всаскаа. и съжи
вити всаскаа въскрⷭ҇нїеⷨ свойⷨ. и привⷶ҇
ти вса ꙗзыки в познанїе бг҃а ѡ҃ца, и ѡ
правдати вса. ꙗкоже самое сїе писа
9r/176 нїе показꙋетъ. не твⷶ҇ бо созидатї
премⷣрость созⷣа г҃ь, но в нⷱ҇атⷦ҇ѡ поутїи
свойⷯ в дѣла своа созⷣа г҃ь премⷣрость. Ре
кше искоупити нӹ своєю кровїю бг҃ви
ѡ҃цꙋ. а не еⷤ арїи злослови хоулаⷮ, гл҃а
в дѣла своа созⷣа бг҃ъ премⷣрость во тво
ренїе твари. но в дѣла своа въ ѡна г҃ь
созⷣа премⷣрость. ꙗⷦ и въ еѵ҃лїи с нб҃си свї
дѣтльствова гл҃а. сеи еⷭ҇ сн҃ъ мои во
злюблⷩ҇ный ѡ немъ блгⷭ҇оволиⷯ. еⷤ и павеⷧ
пишетъ, прежеⷦ вѣⷦ таина сокровенⷩ҇а
ѿ родовъ. ꙗвльшиже нн҃ѣⷭ писанїи прⷪ҇
роческыми. Понеⷤ созⷣа бг҃ъ дх҃омъ
ст҃ымъ въ оутробѣ дв҃ыа, плоть пре
мⷣрости своеи единорⷣѡномꙋ сн҃оу своеⷨⷹ

Refutation of Arius' Interpretation of Proverbs 8:22, Acts 2:36, and Hebrews 3:2

7. And Arius said, "Christ was not begotten of the divine essence of the Father but created before all other things, and by means of him, God made the entire creation". For it is written that the Wisdom says, "The Lord created me in the beginning of his ways for his works" (Prov. 8:22). And Peter says in the Acts that "God has made this Jesus both Lord and Christ" (Acts 2:36). And Paul writes to the Hebrews, "It is said, 'he was faithful to the one who made him'" (Heb. 3:2). Arius put forth these sacred statements | in a distorted way in order to blas- 8v/176
pheme the only-begotten Son of God, our Lord and God, Jesus Christ.

7.1. But godly Hypatius, together with holy Athanasius, gave us the accurate teaching of these sacred expressions by relating them to the economy of the only-begotten Son of God who was set for our salvation. They stated and preached that truth is found in the sacred Scripture and that there exists a hypostatic Wisdom, our Lord Jesus Christ, who said of himself that he became incarnate as man in the words, "The Lord created me in the beginning of his ways for his works" (Prov. 8:22). This means that he had to become incarnate, and be crucified, and suffer, and die for all men, and bring to life everyone by his resurrection, and summon all nations to the knowledge of God the Father, and justify all men, just as the Scripture itself | shows. For the Lord created the Wis- 9r/176
dom not to fashion the creation, but instead, the Lord created the Wisdom to be "the beginning of his ways for his works" (Prov. 8:22). This means to redeem us with his blood to God the Father, and not what Arius blasphemously said with the evil words that God created the Wisdom "for his works" in order to frame the creation, as opposed to (saying) that the Lord created the Wisdom for exactly these works of his.

7.2. This is also declared from the heavens in the Gospel that says, "This is my beloved Son, whom I have chosen" (Matt. 3:17). And likewise, Paul writes, "the mystery hidden for ages" is "now made manifest" according to the prophetic Scriptures (Col. 1:26; cf. Eph. 3:9–12). That is why God created the flesh of his Wisdom for his only-begotten Son by the Holy Spirit in the womb of the Virgin

в на҇тѡⷦ поутїи свойⷯ. рⷦеше поутїи, и
9v/177 миⷤ да спⷭ҇етъ вⷭ҇ѣⷯ. в дѣла своа, в ниⷯⷤ
быⷭ҇ хⷭ҇ послѫшливъ до смⷬ҇ти ѿц҃ѫ
своемоу. смⷬ҇тиⷯ крⷭ҇тнѣи ꙗкоⷭ҇ павеⷧ
пишеⷮ. нⷭ҇ѣ бо повѣдано писанїемъ во
творенїе твари, похоженїа бжⷭ҇їа в пꙋ
теⷯ нї единоа твари. но реⷱ҇ бгъ и быⷭ҇ тваⷬ҇
здⷤѣ глⷮ҇ъ, гь созⷣа ма в натѡⷦ поутїи.
свойⷯ в дѣла своа. еⷤ чисто показоует
блгⷭ҇оволенїе бжїе. натѡⷦ поутеи бжїи
и дⷭ҇ѣ еⷢ, спнⷭ҇їе члⷱ҇твоу въплощенїемъ
единорⷪ҇днаго еⷢ сна. понⷤ҇е внегаⷣ созанїⷷ
твари глⷮ҇ъ, тамо о себѣ премдⷬ҇ость
рече. бⷯѣ емоу пѡвⷪ҇на, а не реⷱ҇ созⷣана
бⷯѣ. агъ бⷯѣ ѡ неи же радовашеⷭ҇ рече, со
безналⷱ҇ное показоуⷮе. і ꙗко не внегаⷣ
созⷣатиса плотїю, натѡⷦ быⷭ҇ премдⷬ҇о
10r/177 сти бжїи. но преⷤ вⷭ҇ѣ хоⷧмъ ражает ма
реⷱ҇. і егда готовлаше нбо и всю тварь,
бⷯѣ емѫ пѡдоⷠна. прежⷣе даже созатиⷭ҇
плотїю в члⷱ҇ествѣ, тамо не глⷮ҇ъ гь
созⷣа ма, но глⷮ҇ъ ражает ма. и внегⷣ
созидати емоу тваⷣ и тогⷣа бⷯѣ емоу
пѡвⷪ҇на рече. а не реⷱ҇ созⷣана бⷯѣ, но рече
тогⷣа бⷯѣ емоу пѡдоⷠна. тѣмⷤъ самаⷣ
словеса показѫютъ соуцⷭ҇ее в плоти
созⷣанїе въчлⷱ҇ченїе сна бжїа. в натѡⷦ
поутїи блгоⷭ҇волενїа бжїа ѡ немъ, в дⷭ҇ѣ
ла своа имⷤи созⷣа црⷭ҇квь срадаⷩми кре
ⷭ҇томъ и воскрⷭ҇нїемъ. еⷤ самыи въ евⷢа
лїи глаⷭ҇съ съ, разорите реⷱ҇ црⷭ҇квь сїю, и
треми днⷭ҇ьми возⷣвигноу ю. ~ Такоⷤ
и бгⷭ҇опроповѣднⷦи петръ бгⷭ҇словⷡи преⷤ
10v/177 ѡ хⷭ҇ѣ. показа еⷢ бга соуцⷭ҇а. і внегда же
въспрїати гнⷭ҇е еже плотїю распатїⷷ.
тогⷣа и сотворенїе воспоманѫ. глⷭ҇ет бо
поманоуⷡ прⷪрⷷчтво двдⷭ҇во ѡ воскрⷭ҇нїи хⷭ҇вⷡ.
ꙗко не ѡстависа дшⷭ҇а еⷢ въ адѣ, ни пло
ть еⷢ видѣ истлѣнїа. и рече сего ісⷭ҇а въ
скрⷭ҇си бгъ. емⷤѫ мы есми вси свидѣтⷭ҇е
таже прⷭ҇носоуцⷭ҇ное еⷢ бжⷭ҇тво проповѣдаⷣ

as “the beginning of his ways” (Prov. 8:22). In other words, “the ways” | means 9^{v}/177
that he would save all men, and “for his ways” means that Christ was “obedient”
to his Father “unto death—even death on a cross” (Phil. 2:8), just as Paul writes.
For Scripture does not tell us that there was any creature in the way God origi-
nally framed the creation. Instead, God spoke, and the creation came into being
(cf. Gen. 1; Jn. 1:1–3). But here, it says, “The Lord created me in the beginning of
his ways for his works” (Prov. 8:22), which clearly shows God’s good pleasure.
“The beginning” of God’s “ways” and “his works” is the salvation of humankind
through the incarnation of his only-begotten Son.

7.3. For this reason, when the Wisdom speaks there of herself in relation to
the framing of creatures, it says, “I was like him” (Prov. 8:30), instead of say-
ing, “I was created”. It says, “I was the one in whom he had delight” (Prov. 8:30),
showing that there was no beginning and that God’s Wisdom did not come into
being with the creation of bodily beginning, | but as it is said, “Before all the 10^{r}/177
hills he begets me” (Prov. 8:25), and when the heavens and the entire creation
was being established, “I was like him” (Prov. 8:30) before I was actually created
according to the human flesh. The Lord does not say there, “He created me”
(Prov. 8:22), but says “He begot me” (Prov. 8:25), and when it comes to the way
he frames the creation, it says there, too, “I was like him” (Prov. 8:30). Instead of
saying, “He created me” (Prov. 8:22), it says in that case, “I was like him” (Prov.
8:30). The same words show the creation of the flesh for the purpose of the
incarnation of God’s Son: “in the beginning” (Prov. 8:22) (points to) God’s good
pleasure (that was manifested) in him, and “for his ways” (Prov. 8:22) is what
creates the Church through the suffering, cross, and resurrection, of which the
Gospel resounds, “Destroy this temple”, it is said, “and in three days I will raise
it up” (Jn. 2:19).

7.4. In the same way, also, the preacher of God Peter first theologized | about 10^{v}/177
Christ in the manner that shows him to be God, and after reaching the fact that
the Lord was crucified in the flesh, then he mentions creation, for he states
recalling David’s prophecy on the resurrection of Christ that “his soul was not
left in hell, neither did his flesh see corruption” (Acts 2:31; Ps. 16:10; cf. Acts
2:27). And he said, “This Jesus has God raised up, of which we are all witnesses”
(Acts 2:32). Likewise, preaching about his eternal divinity, he said, “Being, there-

рече. десницею оубо бж҃їею възнесъса
обѣтованїе же ст҃го дх҃а прїемъ ѿ оцⷣ҇.
излїа се ѥⷤ вы̏ нн҃ѣ видите и слышиⷮ҇.
не бо дв҃ⷣъ възыде на нбса. гл҃тъ бо сам
реⷱ҇ гь гв҇ⷭи моемоу сѣди ѡдеснꙋю мене.
доноⷤде положоу врагы̏ твоа пѡⷣножїе
ногама твоима. таⷤ проповѣдает
паки крⷭтъ. и соущаⷢ҇ оуже сотворенїⷣ҇
11ʳ/177 гл҃тъ. а не ѿ небытїа сътворенїе его
гл҃а. твердо оубо да разоумѣетъ веⷭ҇
домъ иил҃евъ. ꙗко и г҃а и хⷭ҇а его бг҃ъ съⷮво
рилъ ѥⷭ҇ сего іс҃а его же вы̏ распасте. ꙗ
коⷤ и цр҃ь сн҃а своⷢе сътворитъ цр҃а. не не
сѫщаго ниⷤ не рожеⷩнаго сн҃а своего цр҃ь
сотворяетъ цр҃а. но оуже преже рожеⷩ
наⷢ и всеⷣга съ ѿцемъ црⷭтвꙋющаго, и но
во прославлаа того рожеⷩнаго древле.
сн҃а своⷢе и сѫщаⷢ сътворяет ѥⷢ цр҃а.
ꙗкоⷤ двд҃ъ соломана сотвори цр҃а роже
ннаⷢ оуже и соущаⷢ. соломанъ҃ не тоⷣга
бытїю своемѫ наⷱ҇ло прїатъ, внеⷣга
дв҃ⷣъ сотвори ѥⷢ цр҃а. но преⷤ сотворенїⷣ
црмъ рожеⷩ двⷣомъ, соломаⷩ ѿ вирⷭ҇савїа.
сїе и петръ не начало бытїа хв҃ⷭа сказоуⷣ
гл҃тъ.
11ᵛ/177 ꙗко и гаⷭ҇ и хв҃а ѥⷢ бг҃ъ сътворилъ есть іс҃а.
но соущаⷢ оуже тѡⷢ егоⷤ вы̏ распасте реⷱ҇. аще
и распасте іс҃а реⷱ҇. не мнитеⷭ҇ оуже ꙗⷦ҇ и оу
бисте ѥⷢ и смр҃тїю истлѣти емоу. но бг҃
сътворилъ ѥⷭ҇ ѿ распатїа и г҃а хв҃а, сего
іс҃а его же вы̏ распасте рече. ~ Такоже
и Павеⷧ бг҃опроповѣдниⷦ бг҃ословиⷡ, и пока
за хв҃а б҃а истиⷩна несотвореⷩна. внегдаⷤ
воспоминаа хв҃ⷭо иⷤ во плоти, ѿчаго бл҃го
воленїа ѡ немъ нш҃ⷢе смотренїа смотре
нїе. тоⷣга сотворенїе прїаⷮ, гл҃тъ бо.
мноⷢчастнѣ и мноⷢѡⷠразнѣ древле гл҃а
бг҃ъ, ѿцемъ пр҃ⷪрки. впослѣдоⷦ днїи сиⷯ
гл҃а намъ сн҃ⷨѡ. егоⷤ положи наслⷣѣникⷶ
всеⷨ имъⷤ и вѣки сотвори. иⷤ сыи сїанїⷷ

fore, exalted at the right hand of God, and having received from the Father the promise of the Holy Spirit, he poured out this which you now see and hear. For David did not ascend into the heavens, but he himself says, 'The Lord said to my Lord, 'Sit at my right hand, until I make your enemies your footstool''" (Acts 2:33–35; Cf. Ps. 110:1). Similarly, again, when he preaches about the cross, he also speaks | about the reality of creation, and not about his creation from non- 11r/177
being, saying, "Therefore, let all the house of Israel know firmly that God has made him both Lord and Christ, this Jesus whom you crucified" (Acts 2:36). It is like a king who "makes" his own son the king (after him): the son who is "made" king by the king (father) is not unborn but already born and has always been ruling with the father, and now by having his son extolled as the one who had already been born in the past, he "makes" him king. It is like when David "made" Solomon, who had already been born, to be king (1 Kgs 2:12). For Solomon did not begin to exist when David "made" him king. Rather, before Solomon was "made" king, he had been born from David and Bathsheba (1 Chron. 3:5). And it is the same with Peter's statement: he does not say | that Christ began to exist 11v/177
when "God made Jesus to be both Lord and Christ", but he says that the one who already existed, him "you crucified" (Acts 2:36). And he says that even though "you crucified" Jesus, do not think that you "killed" him and he would "decay" in "death" (Acts 2.23–24, 27). Instead, he says, through the crucifixion, "God has made him both Lord and Christ, this Jesus whom you crucified" (Acts 2:36).

7.5. In the same way, Paul, the preacher of God, theologized and showed that Christ was the true and uncreated God. But when he recalls the economy of Christ, he relates it to his coming in the flesh according to the Father's good pleasure, speaking of him then as "made", (saying) "In the past God spoke to our fathers through the Prophets at many times and in various ways, but in these last days he has spoken to us by his Son, whom he made heir of all things, and through whom, also, he made the ages; who being the radiance of his glory,

славы и ѿбразъ состава є. носа же вса
12r/178 ческаа глѡм силы своеа, собою очищен(і)е
сътвори грѣхо наши. сѣде ѡдеснѫю
пртла велиствїа на высоки. аще сїа
нїе славы бжїа хс, тѣмь нѣсть сово
ренъ снъ, но роженъ. сїанїе бо ѿ сѫще
ства само славы є, а не ѿ вноу прибли
жаѧса сїанїе славы. но само соуцтво
славы сїаетъ. и посемоу ѕѣло еди
носоущна сна ѿцу паве проповѣда.
и съсоущна сна ѿцж соуща, а не послѣ
снъ ѿца, ни бы егда не бѣ. но прносоу
ще ѿцж снъ, поне славы сїанїе нѣ посл
же. ни бѣ слава егда не бѣ сїанїе, нѣ
бо слава никогда без сїанїа. но прносу
соущно сїанїе славѣ. ни може же сла
ва без сїанїа ꙗвитиса. и в слнцы бо
12v/178 слава никогда без сїанїа. аще кога и
застоупи землею ѿ сїанїа слнечнаго,
или лоуна пѡпадъ слнцоу. но слнчна
слава единаче сїаетъ. а не бе сїанїа
слнце, иже и краевѣ слнчна тѣла ꙗ
влаютъ внега ѿ лоуна кржга ѿстоу
пати начинаютъ. ~ По семъ гла
паве ꙗко плоть прїатъ гь ѿ сѣмени
авраамла. и оуподоби по всемоу бра
тїи, рекше чл꙯къ совршен быть. та
рече, и мти боуде и вѣре прьвосщни
ꙗже к бгоу е ѡцыстити грѣхы людеⁱ.
еже и двдъ гтъ, вѣре гь во всѣ слове
сѣ свой, и прпвен во всѣ дѣле свой, и т
ко гтъ паве. братїа стаа єванїю бжї
пристницы, разоумѣте посланикъ
13r/178 апла і стла исповѣданїю нш҃му їса ха,
вѣна соуща сотворшемоу є и прире гла.
ꙗко моусѣи вѣре во все домоу своемъ.
и помалѣ, множаишеи бо славѣ па мо
усеа сыи спвби. ꙗко еликоу множаи
шю честь има сотворивыи є. всак бо
храмъ созидаетса ѿ нѣкое, а сотво

and the image of his subsistence, upholding all good things | by the word of his power, when he had by himself purged our sins, sat down at the right hand of the majesty on high" (Heb. 1:1–3). If Christ is the radiance of God's glory, then he is not a Son by creation, but the one who is born. For the radiance comes from the very essence of the glory, and not from without, as if only approximating the radiance of glory. Rather, it radiates from the essence of the glory itself. And therefore, Paul proclaims very well that the Son is consubstantial with the Father, and that the Son is of the same essence with the Father, and the Son is not "after" the Father, nor "was there when he was not", but the Son exists with the Father eternally. Indeed, the radiance of glory is not "after", nor "was there when" the radiance "was not", for the glory is never without radiance, but rather, the radiance exists with the glory all the time. The glory cannot appear without the radiance, just as also the glory of the sun | never exists without its light— even when the earth blocks sunlight or the moon overshadows the sun. Even then, the glory of the sun continues to radiate, and the sun is not deprived of the light when only the edges of the solar body appear as the disc of the moon begins to depart. 12r/178 12v/178

7.6. After this, Paul says that the Lord "took on him the seed of Abraham" (Heb. 2:16) and "became like his brothers in every way" (Heb. 2:17), that is, he became a perfect man. And the same one, he says, will be God's merciful and faithful High Priest to cleanse the sins of the people (cf. Heb. 2:17). Just as David says, too, "The Lord is faithful in all his words and gracious in all his works" (Ps. 145:13). And Paul makes the following statement, "Holy brothers, partakers of the heavenly calling, consider the appointed | Apostle and High Priest of our profession, Christ Jesus, who was faithful to the one who made him" (Heb. 3:1–2), adding a further statement, "just as Moses also was faithful in all his house. For the Son was found worthy of more glory than Moses, by just so much as the builder of the house has more honor than (the house). For every house is built by some man, but he who built all things is God" (Heb. 3:2–4). And thus, 13r/178 ривыи вс҃акаа бг҃ъ. и моисеи же оу бо вѣрⷩ҇ во всемъ домоу своⷨ҇, ꙗⷦ҇ оугоⷣниⷦ҇ во свидѣтльство гл҃анныимъ. хс҃ⷤъ ꙗко сн҃ъ в домоу своⷨ҇. И павⷧ҇ не искоⷩ҇ное бытїе хв҃о гл҃тъ, вѣна соуща сътвоⷬшемоу еⷢ҇, реⷦше апл҃а и стл҃а вѣна сѫща, сътвоⷬшемоу еⷢ҇ стл҃еⷨ и апл҃ѡⷨ, еⷤ҇ въ плоти смореⷮнїе гл҃тъ, сътвореⷩ҇ стл҃ь хс҃ъ. соущїи оуⷤ сътвореⷩ҇ стль, а не бытїю хв҃оу, на҃ло

13v/178 сътворенїе гл҃тъ павⷧ҇, но стльствоу сотворенїе и посланїе соущее во плоти. имⷤъ и моусеа прⷣестави сотвореⷩна на избавленїе иил҃ю ѿ егупта. и понеⷤ рече моисеи. прⷪрка ваⷨ воставиⷮ гь бгъ ѿ братїа вашеа ꙗко мене тѡⷢ послоушаите во всемъ, и показоуⷮе имъ павⷧ҇. ꙗко хс паⷭ҇ еⷭ҇ моусеа, а не ꙗⷦ и мⷪсеи. аще и прире ꙗко и моусеи вѣрⷩ҇ во всеⷨ домоу своемъ. хс҃ъ вѣреⷩ сътворшемоу еⷢ стл҃еⷨ и послаⷩникоⷨ. толико разлⷱ҇ино хвⷭ҇о ѿ моусеа положи. елико сътворивыи домъ. рекше ꙗковоуⷤ честь влⷣка наⷣ рабы имаⷮ. моусеи бо ꙗⷦ оугодниⷦ. хс҃ъ же понеⷤ сн҃ъ в домоу своеⷨ. Тако ипатїе с бг҃оносныⷨ ѿцы арїа низложиша, похоулиша сн҃а

14r/178 бж҃їа. и нѣмы сотвориша оуста еⷢ гл҃ющаа на бг҃а неправдоу. га же і бг҃а нш҃ іса ха сн҃а бж҃їа, едїнородна единосоущна бг҃оу ѿцѫ проповѣдаша, бг҃а истинна ѿ бг҃а истинна. рожена а не сотворена. преⷤ всѣⷯ вѣкѡⷡ, имⷤъ быша вса. сам бо гь и бгъ и спситеⷧ нш҃ь рече іс҃ъ хс҃. никтоⷤ знаетъ сн҃а токмо ѿць. ни ѿц҃а кто знаеⷮ токмо сн҃ъ. і емоуⷤ аще волиⷮ сн҃ъ ѿкрыти. и видѣвыи мене видѣ еⷭ ѿц҃а. і азъ і ѿць едино есвѣ. и бгопроповѣдницы бгословцеⷨ врьхъ гл҃тъ. въ начⷶлѣ бѣ слово. и слово бѣ к бг҃оу, и бг бѣ слово. и ѡно еⷤ не восхыщенїемъ непщева равеⷩ быти бг҃оу. но себе излїⷶ

Moses' ministry of being "faithful in all his house" (Heb. 3:2) fulfilled the witness spoken of Christ—that he would be Son in his own house. And Paul is not speaking of Christ's eternal existence when he says, "he was faithful to the one who made him", but instead implies that he was "made" into the faithful "Apostle and High Priest", indicating by "Apostle and High Priest" the economy of the flesh, and asserting that he was "made" the "High Priest" (Heb. 3.1–2). Paul is speaking about the fact that the pre-existing Christ is now "made" the "High Priest", and not that the origin of Christ's being was "made" to exist. | 13^{v}/178
What is "made", instead, is the ministry of High Priest and his earthly mission. And Moses, too, is described to them as being "made" to bring about the deliverance of Israel from Egypt, "For Moses said, 'The Lord God will raise up for you a Prophet like me from your brothers. You must listen to him in everything'" (Deut. 18:15). And Paul shows that Christ is greater than Moses rather than being like Moses, and adds further that just like Moses "was faithful in all his house", so Christ "was faithful to the one who made him" the "High Priest" and the "Apostle" (Heb. 3:1–2). He makes Christ and Moses so different from one another that they are like a "builder" and a "house" (Heb. 3:4), indicating the honor that the sovereign has over his subjects. For Moses is like a servant, whereas Christ is the Son in his own house.

Hypatius' Proclamation of Christ's Divinity and Biblical Evidence on the Consubstantial Nature of the Father-Son Relation

8. Thus, Hypatius, together with the God-bearing fathers, deposed Arius, who blasphemed the Son | of God; and his mouth that spoke lies against God, they 14^{r}/178
made dumb. And they preached our Lord and God, Jesus Christ, as the only-begotten Son of God, consubstantial with God the Father, true God of true God, begotten, and not made, pre-existing before all ages, by whom everything was made.

8.1. For our Lord and God and Savior, Jesus Christ, himself said, "No one knows the Son except the Father; nor does anyone know the Father except the Son, and anyone to whom the Son wills to reveal him" (Matt. 11:27), and "Whoever has seen me has seen the Father" (Jn. 14:9), and "I and the Father are one" (Jn. 10:30). And the preachers of God who tower above all theologians say, "In the beginning was the Word, and the Word was with God, and the Word was God" (Jn. 1:1), and the same (Word) "did not count equality with God a thing

зраⷦ҇ раба прїемъ. и множаишими же
14v/179 бг҃одх҃новеⷩ҇ными писаньми, трⷪ҇цоу едї
носоущнѫ правослаⷡ҇но проповѣдаша
ꙗсно. ~ Бл҃жеⷩ҇ныиⷤ҇ ипатїе силеⷩ҇ оубо слⷪ҇
весӹ бг҃одх҃новеⷩ҇ныⷯ писанїиⷯ. и елма же
и в чюдесныⷯ творенїиⷯ ст҃ль велиⷦ҇ бж҃їи
апⷭ҇лькыми дарованїи свѣтаса. понеⷤ҇
прослави бг҃а ипатїе дѣлы бл҃гими.
и дѣꙗⷩ҇ми бг҃оугодными, и гласомъ
рⷢ҇ътани, прослави ѕѣло въ трⷪ҇цы едї
наⷢ҇ бг҃а. оустнамиⷤ҇ и ꙗзыкоⷨ҇ възвѣ
сти правоⷣу бж҃їю вⷨсѣ. еⷤ҇ краинаа радї
мⷭ҇ти к намъ сшествїе единоⷣрⷭѡнаⷢ҇
сн҃а бж҃їа. и преславно намъ сп҃нїе съ
дѣлавша вочлⷱ҇енїеⷨ҇ своиⷨ҇, и крⷭ҇тоⷨ҇ и во
скрⷭ҇нїемъ. Такоⷤ҇ и троудӹ своими
сщⷩ҇ныи ипатїе прослави бг҃а. в млтваⷯ
15r/179 непрестаⷩ҇ныⷯ к бг҃ѫ поⷣжаваа. і въ бдѣ
нїиⷯ всенощныⷯ претрьпѣваа, постъ
съ воздрьжанїеⷨ҇ желаⷩ҇но стажа. слеⷥ҇ныⷣ
истоⷱ҇ники проливаа, очⷭ҇ти срⷣ҇це свое
и оумъ на высотоу бж҃їа лⷠюве вознеⷭ҇.
нищаа прїѡⷠрѣте. вдовыа и сиротꙑ
не имоущиⷯ снабдителеи, взыскаⷡ҇ оу
щⷣери и снабдѣ. алчныа напита. и сⷮра
нным прїимате̑ бываа, и нагыⷯ не
презⷡрѣ. велми оубо пⷣѡвизаꙗⷭ҇ на вы
сотоу взыде дⷠѡродѣтелеи. Тако бо ѡ
немъ предастъ прⷣпдобныи іосиⷴ҇, иⷤ҇ ѡ неⷨ҇
извѣстно вѣдаше. И понеⷤ҇ про
слави бг҃а вⸯ телеси своеⷨ҇ ипатїе и в дс҃ѣ
своеⷨ҇, мнⷢѡ и бг҃ъ ипатїа прослави. сла
вщаа ма реⷱ҇ г҃ь прославлю. тѣмъже
15v/179 и дары бжⷭ҇твеныа подастъ бг҃ъ ипа
тїю. источити поучиноу сⷲноⷠѡра
зныⷯ чюдеⷭ҇. и ісцѣленїеⷨ҇ потокы излїа
ти. болныⷨ҇ бо мноⷨѕѣ, іпатїе ⷣзравїе по
дастъ млтвами своими. иⷤ҇ молащї
мса емѫ болащимъ, недоуги ѿ ниⷯ ѿгнаⷣ
и бѣсныа приводимыа к немоу ѡчищаⷣ

to be grasped, but emptied himself, by taking the form of a servant" (Phil. 2:6–7). And with many (other) | divinely inspired words of Scripture, they preached 14v/179
the consubstantial Trinity with clarity and faithfulness.

A Description of how Hypatius Glorified God through his Spiritual Achievements and Ministry of Social Care, and how God Glorified him Through Miracles

9. And blessed Hypatius shone as a man strong in the words of the inspired Scriptures, and no less (did he shine) with the apostolic gift of performing wondrous miracles in his great and divine ministry of a priest. Indeed, Hypatius glorified God through his good works and God-pleasing actions, and with the voice of his throat he greatly glorified the Trinity in one Godhead; with his mouth and tongue He declared to all the truth of God that out of his uttermost mercy and for our sake, the only-begotten Son of God descended to us and gloriously brought about salvation through his incarnation, and cross, and resurrection.

9.1. And holy Hypatius also glorified God with his spiritual labor. Patiently waiting in his constant prayers | to God and enduring fasts during the night vig- 15r/179
ils, he persevered with eagerness and self-control. Shedding streams of tears, he purified his heart and mind, ascending to the summit of God's love.

9.2. He aided the poor, (especially) seeking widows and orphans who had no provision, and offered charity and supply. He fed the hungry and received the strangers, and did not despise the naked. Thus, undertaking so much effort, he ascended to the summit of virtue, as was recounted by revered Iosif, who had a lot of knowledge about him.

9.3. And since Hypatius glorified God in his own body and spirit, God glorified him as much, as it is said, "Those who glorify me I will glorify" (1Sam. 1:30).
Thus, | God, too, gave the divine gifts to Hypatius—to pour out the boundless 15v/179
sea of sacred miracles and let the streams of healing flow. For Hypatius restored health to many sick people through his prayers. By praying over the sick, he expelled their illnesses, and whenever the demon-possessed were brought to him, he cleansed them and drove out the evil spirits.

прогона лꙋкавыа доухы. Сїи апл҃ь
скїи мѫжь нѣвкоеи веси хода, потре
бѣ приноудивши лю҆стѣи. и тамоо[2]
воды текоуцаа из горы гръки соуцⷭ҇
и сла҇кы вѡ҇ веси не имоуца. молим
оу бо тамошними жители ипатїе, і
жалацїⷨи гръкы ради непла҇ны вѡд.
ипатїеⷤ ꙗкоже и моусе преложи на сл
дость. нагнамена҇ текоуцїа воды
16r/179 токмо гнаменїеⷨ кр҇та. и по елисѣю
пр҇ркѫ бл҇женыи ипатїе горькїа воды
цѣлбоносны сотвори. ~ И понеⷤ при
ближиса бг҇ви сн҇ныи ипатїе. млтв
ми сц҇ныими і оума чтотою, прїемни
ца бы бж҇твенаго просцѣнїа ѿ прибли
жающагоса бж҇тва, приближающиⷨи
мса[3] къ бж҇твоу. ѡсвѣтивса пресв
тлооумными лоучами. тѣмⷤ и в но
щи темнѣи шествоующꙋ прп҇бномꙋ
семѫ ст҇лю. потреба бѣ ѡсвѣтит
поути бли҇ воды идоуцѫ. да не попо
зши нога водамъ ходацаго подаст.
и порѣꙗнїеⷨ оутопити впаша в воды.
не имоуцѫⷤ блж҇нномоу ипатїю свѣ
тила. оумныма оочима взимаше.
16v/179 къ пр҇носоуцномоу свѣтѫ иⷤ люба все
гда осїавати не захѡмы свѣтомъ
тѣмⷤ абїе и свѣща многи горац
ѿ воды вьсїаша емоу, многоу свѣло
подающа пр҇бномѫ, внега по поути
емоу шествовати. Иногда такоⷤ
творенїа ради бг҇оугоны дѣ ходацꙋ
ноцїю ипатїю. и гн҇ю заповѣдь дѣ
лающѫ глющꙋю, да не оувѣ шꙋица
твоа еже твори десница твоа. ѡбхо

2 тамоо (*sic*).

3 приближающиⷨмса (*sic*).

Hypatius' Miracle of Turning Bitter Water into Sweet

10. (Once) this apostolic man went to a certain village, forced by the need of the local people who had (only) bitter water streaming there from the mount, and there was no sweet water in the village. Hypatius was entreated by the villagers and felt sorry that they had (only) bitter water that was no good. And Hypatius, just like Moses (Ex. 15:22–25), turned the running waters | into sweet 16r/179
after merely making the sign of the cross over it. And in imitation of the Prophet Elisha (2 Kgs 2:19–22), Hypatius made the bitter water capable of bringing healing.

Hypatius' Relationship with God and Miracles of Light

11. And because holy Hypatius drew near to God through (his) holy prayers and purity of mind, he became a partaker of divine enlightenment that stemmed from the approaching Godhead and was enlightened by the rays of the supreme rational light adjacent to the Godhead.

11.1. And thus, also, when this revered priest walked along the river in the dark night, he needed light to illumine his path so that he could keep his slipping feet from throwing him into the water and drowning him if he were to fall into that river. Having no light with him, blessed Hypatius lifted his rational eyes | to the eternal Light, for he was fond of drawing enlightenment from the 16v/179
unsetting Light, and at once there appeared many glaring flames, glowing in the water and giving him plenty of light all the way as he walked (there).

11.2. Also, at times, Hypatius was doing charitable works at night, keeping the Lord's command that says, "Do not let your left hand know what your right

посѣщаше вдовы̏ и сирыꙗ и нищаꙗ
и бѣдныꙗ воⷤ҇е спомогати иⷨ҇. постига
етъⷤ ипатїа и паки вѣⷣчнїи глаⷭ҇ глющїи
не можеⷮ граⷣ оукрытиⷭ҇ врьхꙋ горы стоꙗ
и свѣтило на свѣщницѣ да свѣтиⷮ
всѣⷨ. и тако да просвѣтитсѧ свѣт
17r/179 вашъ преⷣ чл҇ки, ꙗⷦ да видаⷮ ваша и дѡⷠраⷣ
дѣла, и прославаⷣ ѿца ваше҇ нбнагѡ
сеⷢ раⷣ ѡбїавиша ипатїа ꙗвльшисѧ
и паки ѿ воды̏ свѣща горащаа, ѡза
рающа ипатїа внегда емоу оучрежа
ющоу оубогїа нощїю. Бысть нѣкоⷢ҇а
и в нѣкоеи веси своеи чюⷣныи сеи ипатїⷷ.
пѡⷣ стѫдены̏ⷨ возоуⷯ҇ и влажны̏ⷨ соуще
мѣсту томоу. и жителеⷨ веси тоꙗ.
ѿ недѫⷢ возоушныꙗ стоуⷷни сражоуⷮ
щиⷨ изнемогати. къ оутишенїю не
доугоⷡ бань не имоущиⷨ имъ. видѣ сїⷶ
иⷤ всѣⷨ срцемъ ко истоⷱ҇никоу дѡⷠрымъ
хоⷭ҇ вмѣстивый. ѿ негоⷤ богаⷮно чюдеⷭ҇
зарами сїаꙗ. млⷭ҇рдоваⷡ ѡ ниⷯ ѕѣло.
млⷭ҇тивомꙋ хоⷭ҇ послѣдовате҇ ипатїⷷ.
17v/180 и походиⷡ на мѣстѣ страⷩ оуⷯгоны к баⷩно
моу оустроенїю. на ниⷯъⷤ млⷭ҇твами
натолико себе простре к бгоу, доньдеⷤ
соухїа боки земныꙗ происпѫстиⷲ
истоⷱ҇никы. непрестаⷩно текоущїа ⷮ
плы̏ⷯ водъ. подающа всакиⷨ недоугѡⷨ
исцѣленїа. Что же ми оубо исчиⷶ
ти содѣⷩанаа чюⷣ҇ⷪдѣвиствены̏ⷨ ипатїеⷨ
како же ли и хощꙋ исчитати, иⷤ прево
сходиⷮ оума достиженїе ѥ блгⷭ҇ти, и ꙗ
зы̏ⷦ изрещи не возможеⷮ ипатїевыⷯ.
чюⷣⷷсъ безмѣⷭ҇рноую пѫчиноу. едино оу

hand is doing" (Matt. 6:3). As he went about visiting widows, and orphans, and the poor in order to help them, Hypatius heard the Lord's voice another time, saying, "A city set on a hill cannot be hidden", and "a lamp on a stand" should give "light to all" so that your light | may shine before men and "they may see 17r/179
your good works and give glory to your heavenly Father" (Matt. 5:14–16). This explains why Hypatius repeatedly had glowing flames appear to him like those from the water and providing Hypatius with light every time he made distributions of goods to the poor at night.

Hypatius' Miracle of Causing Dry Land to Spring Forth with Hot Water

12. One time, this marvelous Hypatius was in a certain village (where people) suffered from dealing with cold winds and dampness in their area. The people of that village were afflicted with sicknesses that they suffered from the cold winds, and they had no steam house that could ease their afflictions. After seeing that, Hypatius, who with all his heart was attached to Christ as the source of all goodness and who was shining with the light of many miracles, became sorry for them and earnestly prayed to the merciful Christ whom he followed. | 17v/180
And he went around to the parts of that land that were good for placing steam houses and prostrated himself before God, praying at those places so intensely that dry spots of land began to spring forth with endless streams of hot water, giving healing from any kind of diseases.

The Miraculous Deeds Performed by Hypatius Transcend Human Understanding

13. But what would it do if I were to count all that was done by Hypatius the Wonderworker? If I wanted to count his good works, how would I do that if they transcend the mind's ability to comprehend them and the tongue's capability of expressing the immeasurable sea of Hypatius' miracles?

бо ѿ всⷯѣ чюдⷭ҇е прⷣѣложоу чⷣюⷪ ст҃го, слово
съкращю. Призваⷩ быⷭ҇ бл҃жⷩеный сеи
цр҃мъ коⷩстаⷩтїеⷨ с҃номъ великаⷢ коⷩста
нтина. змїю бо привеликоу ѿ нѣкоⷡ
18r/180 дѫ припоⷣзшю. і въ хранилище цⷭ҇рскаго
имѣнїа вплъзшю. идⷤѣ все злато и
богаⷮство лежитъ. змїеви оубо ѿⷠемⷲ
хранилище имѣнїа, и главꙋ свою к во
сходѫ приложшоу. и не дадꙋщѫ ни
комоуⷤ в двери полатныа внити. и
цр҃ю коⷩстаⷩтїю ѡ сеⷨ в велицѣ пеⷱ҇ли бышⷡ.
и многїа сⷳ҇ныа моужи ѡ сеⷨ мл҃твоваⷮ
поноуди да ѿженⷮѫ змїа. послѣдⷤи
и бл҃жⷩенаго іпатїа привеⷣ. моли оубо
цр҃ь ипатїа да мл҃твою прожеⷮне змїа.
речеⷤ да не без соблюⷣенїа звѣрю прⷠилижі
тсѧ лютоу емꙋ соущѫ. показашаⷤ ипа
тїю змїа иⷣзалеча. бл҃жⷩеныⷤй ипатїе
паⷣ на земли, помолⷭ҇и чаⷭ҇ доволеⷩ. и востаⷡ
ѿ мл҃твы гл҃а цр҃ю. на мѣсте идⷤѣ ест
18v/180 ѿⷠразъ ѿц҃а твоеⷢ повели посреⷣѣ пороⷣⷨ
велицѣи скрадѣ ѡгненѣи быти, реⷦ
ше ѡгницꙋ или роуⷢда дроⷡ а не сковраⷣ
но скрада. и тоу вжеⷢше да жⷣоутъ тⷣ
мо донеⷤлѣ азъ доидоу. и цр҃ю повелѣ
вшꙋ тако сотворити. бл҃жⷩеныⷤй ипа
тїе врата хранилищꙋ црⷭ҇кⷯи имѣнїи ѿ
врⷥъ. и звѣра жезлоⷨ своⷨи оудараше.
не оуспѣвашеⷤ ничтоⷤ и дн҃ю преклона
юшоⷭ҇у. всиⷤ издалеча позоржюще баⷯ
и боахоуса ѿ звѣри оумрети ст҃мѫ.
тои же оочи на н҃бо возвеⷣ, и г҃а призвав.
жезлъ свои во оуста звѣрю вложи,
и реⷱ, во има г҃а і҃са моеⷢ послѣⷣствꙋи мі.
змїиⷤ ѕоубы своими краи жезла емⷭ
и послѣдоваше ст҃омоу. бл҃жⷩеныи же
19r/180 извеⷣ его ѿ полаты и веⷭ пⷣѿроⷨ прошедъ
даⷤ и до тръга жезлъ по земли влекїи.
иⷤ и все позорище видѣвше змїа за кра
жезла дрьжащаⷭ и влекома. оужаса

The Story about the Serpent (a Symbol of Arius' Heresy) that Crawled into Emperor Constantius' Treasury and How Hypatius Helped to Destroyed it

14. To make the account short, then, I will offer only one miracle out of all
the miracles (performed) by the saint. This blessed man was summoned by
Emperor Constantius, the son of the great Constantine, on account of an
immense serpent that managed to crawl from nowhere | into the imperial trea- 18^{r}/180
sury, where all the gold and riches were stored. Then, the serpent seized the
treasury and lay his head near the entrance, allowing no one to come in through
the chamber doors. And Emperor Constantius fell into great sorrow over that
(situation) and appointed many holy men to pray about it and chase away the
serpent.

14.1. After all of that, he also brought blessed Hypatius. Then, the Emperor begged Hypatius to chase the serpent away through his prayer, and having instructed him to be careful and not approach the horrible serpent, he showed the serpent to Hypatius from afar.

14.2. And blessed Hypatius prostrated himself on the ground and spent some
time praying. Having risen from prayer, he said to the Emperor, "Command
them to set a big fiery oven"—which signifies a bonfire or a pile of firewood; not
a 'pan' (*skovrada*), but an 'oven' (*skrada*)—"in the center of the hippodrome,
where there is | a statue of your father, and kindle it. And after kindling it, let 18^{v}/180
them wait there until I reach them".

14.3. And the Emperor commanded them to do that, while blessed Hypatius
opened the door of the imperial treasury and beat the serpent with his staff
without stopping. Everyone looked on from a distance as the day was ending,
fearing that the saint had been killed by the beast. But he lifted his eyes to the
heavens, and after calling upon the Lord, he put his staff into the beast's mouth
and said, "In the name of my Lord, Jesus Christ, follow me"! And the serpent
seized the edge of the staff (with his teeth) and followed the saint. And blessed
(Hypatius) | brought him out of the chamber, walking across the entire hip- 19^{r}/180
podrome as far as the marketplace and dragging the immense serpent on the
ground as it held onto the edge of the staff in front of the entire petrified crowd

хоуса вси. баше бо ѕмїи велиⷦ ѕѣло и сⷮра
шеⷩ взороⷨ. и приближиⷭ҇ ипатїе къ ѡⷢне
нѣи скрадѣ реⷱ҇ къ ѕмїю. во има хⷭ҇во егоⷤ
и аⷥ меⷩшїи проповѣдаю. повелѣваю
тебѣ внити посредѣ ѡгна. сⷮраш
ныиⷤ ѡнъ ѕмїи нагръбиⷡ себе. ввержеⷭ҇
средї и скрадыⷯ ѡⷢненыа преⷣ всѣми, и і
згорѣ. тоⷣга коⷩстантїе цр҃ь ѕѣло блⷣ
годариⷡ аки и своеⷢ ѿца блаженаⷣ ипатїа
и многиⷨ имѣнїеⷨ почте еⷢ. и ѡⷠразъ ли
ца еⷢ на сцⷣѣ възѡⷠразити повелѣ. и семꙋ
бывшоу в цр҃стѣи полатѣ наⷣ двеⷬми
19v/180 вѕложити повелѣ. мнюⷤ оубо нечи
стомоу семоу звѣрю внити в цр҃кїа
клѣти. прознаменати нечⷭ҇таⷣ бѣсо
ванїа, арїева. коⷩстаⷩтїе бо цр҃ь ѿ евсеⷡ
вїа еп҃па никомидїискаⷢ прецⷣеⷩ бы, по
плъѕеⷭ҇ во арїевоу ересь. тажеⷦ быⷭ҇ право
вѣрныⷨ. последиⷤ его таⷤчаишї и еⷢ оуа
лѣⷩтъ. тогоⷤ злочестїа арїева, правосⷣ
выⷨ досади по многоⷹ. Блаженыиⷤ ипа
тїе богатствоⷨ ѡбогащеⷩныⷨ емоу ѿ цр҃а
града своеⷢ гангра нищаа оудовоⷨ. і ꙗко
дш҃ю свою и срц҃е цр҃квь трⷪ҇цы сотвори
ипатїе. реⷱ҇ бо г҃ь люба и ма вѕлюⷠлеⷩ боуⷣ
деⷮ ѿцеⷨ моиⷨ. и прїидевѣ к немоу і оби
теⷣ оу неⷢ сотворивѣ. и во прⷪ҇рцѣ реⷱ҇, ꙗко
вселюса в на и похожⷪоу и боудоу имъ бⷢъ.
20r/181 тѣмъ и сщ҃еныа цр҃кви ипатїе многи
созⷣа на славоу хⷭ҇оу бг҃оу. Сице ипатїе
пожиⷮ, плⷮоскїа стр҃ти возⷣрьжанїемъ
оумр҃твиⷡ прежⷣе. иⷤ наⷭ҇ ради оумр҃ьшаⷢ
на кр҃тѣ хр҃а истиⷩныи живоⷮ стажа. тⷡ
мⷤъ и вса шествїа ипатїева в дш҃ѣ стѣⷨ
к себѣ направлающа. і ꙗко дѡⷠрѣ восп
тавса возⷣрьжанїемъ. в преславноую
высотѫ вѕыде снⷭ҇ныⷯ дѡⷠродѣтелеи.
оумоⷨ простреса к видѣнїю таиномоу
дѡⷠротоу хвѫ созеⷬцати. ѿ негоⷤ сїанїа

that observed it, for the serpent was very big and had a frightening appearance. And Hypatius approached the burning oven and said to the serpent, "In the name of Christ, whom I, the littlest one, preach, I command you to go into the midst of the flames"! And the serpent, as terrifying as he was, curled himself up and leaped into the midst of the fiery oven in front of all and was burned.

14.4. Then, Emperor Constantius thanked him greatly, honoring blessed Hypatius as his own father and with numerous gifts. He ordered the image of his face to be made on a wooden board and placed | it above the doors of the 19v/180
royal chambers.

14.5. I assume, then, that this nasty beast that crept into the Emperor's chambers signifies the wickedness of Arius' demonic (heresy). For Constantius was enticed into the Arian heresy by Eusebius, the bishop of Nicomedia, who was hard on the Orthodox. After that, and far more severe than (Eusebius/Constantius), was Valens, whose impious Arianism did much harm to the Orthodox.

Hypatius' Use of the Emperor's Gifts to Help the Poor and Build Churches in Gangra

15. And having received many riches from the Emperor, blessed Hypatius helped to satisfy (the needs) of the poor in his city, Gangra. And Hypatius also built the Church of the Trinity, (cherishing it) as his own heart and soul, for the Lord said, "He who loves me will be loved by my Father" (Jn. 14:21), and "We will come to him and make our abode with him" (Jn. 14:23). And in the "Prophets", he said, "I will rejoice over them", and "walk" (among them), "and be their God" (Jer. 32:38, 41; 2 Cor. 6:16). | And thus, Hypatius built many sacred churches for 20r/181
the glory of the divine Christ.

A Descriptions of Hypatius' Godly Life, his Pastoral Ministry, and Fights with Heresies

16. Such was the way of life of Hypatius, in which above all, he put to death the passions of the flesh by self-control in order to attain the true life of Christ who died for us on the cross, and thus, in all his paths, Hypatius was directed by the Holy Spirit. And having exercised proper self-control, he ascended to the glorious summit of sacred virtues, stretching his mind toward the mysterious vision of contemplating the goodness of Christ.

оумⷨо и мыслїю ѡзаривсѧ. бⷭ҇ы вⷭ҇е свѣ
товидеⷩ ст҃ль. достоиⷩ бⷡы пр҃тлоу га
нгрьскїа цр҃кви. и вⷨсѣ иⷤ с вѣрою прихо
дащиⷨ к немоу вⷥосїаваше лоуча чюⷣⷷсныⷶ
ст҃льствⷤаваⷤ[4] прⷣпбнои праведно. бж҃е
20v/181 ствеными законы оⷢражⷣаѧⷭ҇ слово б҃іⷷ
не корчемствова. но истиⷩно съдрь
жа и ⷣзраво и цѣло совршеⷩнѣ. и оуче
нїе нескврьно ѿ еллиⷩскаⷢ и ѿ еретиⷩскаⷢ
самосмыⷲленїа собⷣлюⷷ. правaа велѣнїⷶ
апⷭ҇льскаа възгласи. и глⷭ҇а бо бл҃жеⷩнаⷢ
ипатїа свѣтоⷨ смѣшеⷩ баше, поⷤнеⷩ осїаⷩ
бжⷭ҇твеными свѣтлостьми. и тмⷹ
ересеⷨ разори. восїаⷡ аки сл҃нце, направї
ⷣлю къ дн҃и православїа, имѣа краснѣ
ишїи ѧзыⷦ, ѧко трость ѧвлⷭ҇ь скоро
писца книжника. написа премⷣро ѕакоⷩ
иже в блⷢти новыи, поглаⷡди иже на ⷣскⷯ
ветхаⷢ закона ѡⷠразы стѣневныѧ. про
чее въ глоубокоую старость достиже
во сщ҃еⷩны троуⷯдѣ не изнемⷢо. подоⷣб
21r/181 етⷤъ емоу къ ѿцемъ преити. ничтоⷤ
ми возбранаⷮе рещи, ѧко пѡⷣⷪбаⷮе ипⷣ
тїю патрїархоу к патрїархоⷨ преложи
тⷭ҇и, и істиⷩнѣ проповѣдникоу іпатїⷻ.
къ бг҃опроповѣдникоⷨ апⷭ҇лоⷨ и к прⷪркомⷺ
востещи. и послѣди иⷯ ѧко с ними же
пⷣѡвизасѧ и поты многы покаѕа, во
истиⷩнѣмъ словеси исправленїи. и ко
еретикоⷨ кръчемствоующиⷨ слово бж҃їе.
и къ еⷧлиноⷨ пагоуⷠныⷨ волкомъ, хапающїⷨ
злѣишими зоубы раѕногласїеⷨ и зло
вѣрїеⷨ хⷭ҇ва стада ѡвеⷰ. премⷣраюшиⷨсѧ
соуими помышлеⷩми, и тщими словⷷ
сы раѕливающимиⷭ҇ на воⷣзоухъ. препі
ратⷭ҇и точїю вѣдащими, и ничтоже
пⷧозоующими. иⷤ мрътвыѧ богы прі
21v/181 вводащиⷨⷺ в миⷬ. слѣпыа и глоухыа

4 ст҃льствⷤаваⷤ (*sic*).

16.1. And having his mind and thought illumined by him (Christ), the priest
appeared as entirely shining with light, worthy of the (episcopal) throne of the
Gangran churches. To all who were coming to him with faith, he shone with
wondrous rays of light. The revered (father) was righteously fulfilling his min-
istry of a priest: he guarded himself with the divine | commandments, he did 20^{v}/181
not distort the Word of God but kept it entirely true and sound and whole, and
protecting the purity of doctrine from the Greek and heretical concepts, he pro-
claimed the true apostolic commands.

16.2. And the voice of blessed Hypatius was fused with light in virtue of him
being illumined with the light of God, and he dispelled the darkness of here-
sies by shining forth like the sun that guides people throughout the day. He had
an eloquent tongue in the service of Orthodoxy and appeared as a quill pen of
the well-read energetic scribe, writing down in supreme wisdom the Law that
by grace took the place of what was recorded on the stone tablets of the Old
Testament as shadowy images of the things to come (cf. Heb. 10:1). In the end,
he reached a very old age, and it befitted | him to depart to the fathers as one 21^{r}/181
who did not become weary in sacred work.

Hypatius' Martyrdom and Miracles Following his Death

17. And nothing prevents me from saying that Hypatius died as a patriarch
departing to the patriarchs, and as a preacher of truth, he ascended to the
preachers of God—the Apostles and the Prophets. Though living after them,
he was like them in pursuing spiritual labor and shedding much sweat in order
to correct through the Word of truth both the heretics who distorted the Word
of God, and the Greeks—the fierce wolves that were snatching the sheep of
Christ's flock with their most destructive teeth through discord and impiety—
who argued with each other by throwing worthless concepts and useless words
into the air, possessing only head knowledge but bringing no fruit, for their
dead deities, | whom they themselves brought into the world, (and who) were 21^{v}/181

и нѣмыꙗ идолы. ипатїемъⷤ҇ испо
вѣдаемыи єдиⷩ҇ бг҃ъ въ тⷪ҇рцы, иже нⷶ҇
нб҃си и на ꙁемли вса єлика восхотѣ
и сотвори, и нб҃о самое и ꙁемлю и море
и вса ꙗⷤ҇ в ниⷯ҇. єлма ипатїеви востещ
пѡⷣбⷪаеⷮ҇, къ бг҃опроповⷣѣникоⷨ апⷭ҇лом
и къ прⷪ҇ркомъ. ꙗко приⷭ҇тниⷦ҇ потовъ
и троудоⷡ҇ ихъ. пѡⷣбⷪаетъⷤ҇ ємоу еще и
болѣзнемъ иⷯ҇ приⷭ҇тити. ⷷ҇ краиⷨ҇не
пѡⷣвигоу совершенїе крови своеа за хⷭ҇
изліати. хоуⷭ҇ бо свою прⷭ҇тжю кровь
за ны излїавшюⷪ҇ на крⷭ҇тѣ. и ипатїⷷ҇
ви многыⷯ҇ потоⷡ҇ его и троудоⷡ҇ ѡ блг҃очⷭ҇тї
многїа вⷩ҇ѣца щадимы соⷮ҇ в соⷬ҇кови
щаⷯ҇ безсмр҃ьтїа. в нѣдроⷯ҇ нбⷭ҇наⷢ҇ црⷭ҇вїⷮ҇ⷶ҇
препѣтыа трⷪ҇ца. и иⷤ҇ сего вⷩ҇ѣца еже о
22r/181 мⷭ҇нчествѣ ѡстаⷮ҇е ипатїе, да и с мⷭ҇ні
кы хⷭ҇выⷣ҇ вⷣ҇оворитса. но тогⷣ҇а оубо хⷭ҇
мⷭ҇лтїю своею миⷬ҇ глоубⷦ҇ѡ стѣ҃и своеи
црк҃ви подаⷣⷷ҇. потребиⷡ҇ гонителеи и мⷹ҇
чителеи ѿ неа, поржчиⷡ҇ земное црⷭ҇тво
кроткомоу коⷩ҇стантиноу, ꙗкоже и
двдⷣ҇оу воꙁлюблⷷ҇еномоу ѿ неⷢ҇. ипатїе
виⷤ҇ ѿ иноудоу вⷩ҇ѣца мⷭ҇нчества изгото
ваютса. не пѡⷣбⷪает бо емоу ѡстааⷮ҇
мⷭ҇нческїа дⷠ҇ѡроты. иⷤ҇ хⷭ҇а исповѣда и і
патїе ꙗкоⷤ҇ и мчн҃ики. и троудиⷭ҇ и по
ты пролїа ꙗкоⷤ҇ ст҃ии апⷭ҇ли и прⷪ҇рцы, и
чюдесы ꙁемлю оꙁари. да мⷭ҇ническї и
скоⷩ҇чавса ипатїе, ꙗко мчн҃къ к мⷭ҇никоⷨ҇
приложитса. и ꙗко исповѣдниⷦ҇ со и
22v/182 сповѣдники вчинеⷩ҇ боудеⷮ҇. и ꙗко исти
нномоу словеси правыи исправитеⷶ҇.
к бг҃опроповѣдникоⷨ҇ прⷪ҇рком і апⷭ҇ломъ
вселитса. таковоеⷤ҇ на трижненїе
ипатїеви слоучаетса сице. Єрети
цы наватова мⷣ҇ръствоующеи ꙁави
стїю многою распаливⷭ҇шее на блж҃енаⷩ҇ⷢ҇
ипатїа. и ідѣже ѡбычаи имѣашⷷ҇,
ст҃ыи шествовати сквоѕѣ тѣснаⷣ҇

blind and deaf and dumb idols. But the God confessed by Hypatius was the one of the Trinity, who created all things in heaven and on earth—indeed, the very skies, and land, and sea, and everything that is in them—as he was willing. Considering this, it befits Hypatius to ascend to the preachers of God—the Apostles and Prophets—as a partaker of their sweat and labor.

17.1. And it also befits him to partake of their affliction, to shed his blood as a heroic act of ultimate accomplishment for Christ's sake, for Christ shed his pure blood for us on the cross. And for so much sweat and labor of piety, many crowns are stored for Hypatius in the treasuries of immortality, in the depths of the heavenly kingdom | of the glorious Trinity, and there remained for him 22r/181
only to endure that crown of martyrdom so that he could triumphantly join the martyrs of Christ.

17.2. Now, at that time, though, Christ in his mercy brought great peace to his holy Church by destroying its persecutors and tyrants after entrusting the earthly kingdom to humble Constantine, as he once did to his beloved David. And the crowns of martyrdom, prepared for Hypatius, were not of this world, and since it did not befit him to leave behind the honor of martyrdom, Hypatius confessed Christ as other martyrs did. And just as he imitated the holy Apostles and Prophets in laboring and shedding much sweat, as well as illumining the earth with his miracles, so also Hypatius was to end his life in martyrdom in order to join the martyrs; and as a confessor, | to be numbered among the 22v/182
confessors; and as the one who faithfully used the true Word to correct (what was not true), to dwell with the preachers of God—the Apostles and Prophets. Such was the reward given to Hypatius on account of that!

17.3. The heretics who held the doctrine of Novatian were burning with great jealousy toward blessed Hypatius, and when the saint walked, as was his habit,

и бреговитаа мѣста. засѣдше та
мо стрежахоу. и бл҃жⷩеномоу ипатїю
идѹщѫ напрасно, ꙗко звѣрїе востаⷡшⷷ
нань оустремившаⷭ҇, и нⷥи с высоты̏ бре
га тⷢѿ свⷬ҇егоша, многи раны на нⷷ во
зложиша. и каменїе ꙗкоⷤ нѣкоⷣга ю
дее на прьвомⷱ҇нка стефана посыпаⷲ
23r/182 ст҃ⷤыи в рекоу ввержеⷩ бⷭ҇ы еле жⷡи. роуцѣ
мало простеⷬ҇, и очи на нб҃о возвеⷣ, г҃и не
постави имъ грѣха сеⷢ҇ гл҃аше. і еще емⷹ
молашѫсѧ жена нѣкаа арїевы ереси.
камеⷩ велїи въземши, въ главоу ст҃го
оудари. и тако мⷱ҇ническїи конⷰе воспрїаⷮ
ипатїе. венецъ емоу камеⷩнаа меⷮ
нїа свыше быша. и къ нбⷭ҇нѣи высотѣ
степени и лѣствица. по неи же восшеⷣ
бг҃ви присвоиса ближаише. тѣло же
ст҃го оубїицы в плѣвницу скрывше
ѿидоша. дѣлатеⷤль его же бѣаше плⷺ
вница, прїиде плѣвы̏ взати своемⷹ
скотоу. слыша нбⷭ҇ны сиⷯ славословⷷі
наⷣ телесеⷨ блжⷢ҇нна ипатїа. и вѣстнⷦи
быⷡ всѣⷨ о прⷣпбнⷨѣ. не оукоснѣвши же
23v/182 блⷣгть на ипатїи чюⷣеⷭа содѣвающа.
бѣсоⷨ бо горкиⷨ предашаⷭ҇ грько иⷤ зезбо
жно оуморившїи ипатїа. злокозⷷнⷩ
наⷤѧ ѡна жена оубившїа ст҃го злыⷨ
дѹхомъ ѡдрьжима. оубїиствены̏
камеⷩ въземши, своа прьси непрестаⷩ
но бїаше. такоⷤ і обѣщницы тако
вомѫ оубїиствоу, нечистыми дѹ
хы казнахоуса вси. Оувѣдавшеⷤ
жителїе гангрьстии сїе. собрашаⷭ҇
тамо и мноⷢ рыдахоу. вземше ст҃ое
тѣло еⷢ ѿнесоша во свои граⷣ. и поло
жиша на мѣсте нарочите. женаⷤ
ѡна послѣдѹющи по нⷯи, и бїющи се
бе каменеⷨ имⷤъ ст҃го оубила баше.
исповѣдающⷭ҇и. и по еже положити

through a narrow pass and by the steep places, they made an ambush, lying in wait for him there. And when blessed Hypatius was passing by, they suddenly rose up and rushed at him like animals. And having thrown him down from the top of that cliff, they inflicted many wounds upon him, and then showered him with stones as the Jews once did (by stoning) the first martyr Stephen. | 23^{r}/182
And having been cast into the river, the saint was barely alive. Raising his arms a little bit and lifting his eyes to the heavens, he said, "Lord, do not hold this sin against them" (Acts 7:60), and he prayed for a few more moments.

17.4. A certain woman who adhered to the Arian heresy took a big rock and hurled it at the saint's head. And that was the way Hypatius received the crown, ending (his life) in martyrdom from the rock that struck him from above and made him step on the upward ladder to the heavens. By climbing it, he drew near to God.

17.5. And after hiding the saint's body in a barn, the murderers withdrew. When the workman, whose barn it was, came to get some straw for his cattle, he heard the praise of the heavenly powers singing over the body of blessed Hypatius, and he spread the news about the revered (father) to all.

17.6. And the grace that rested on Hypatius did not cease | from making mir- 23^{v}/182
acles. For those who godlessly killed Hypatius were made to suffer bad tortures from malicious demons. And that evil woman who murdered the saint, being overcome by an evil spirit, took the rock by which she killed (Hypatius) and began to beat her breast without stopping. In the same way, all those who participated in that killing were also punished by unclean spirits.

17.7. And having learned about it, the people of Gangra gathered together there and wept greatly. Taking the body of the saint, they brought him to their city and placed him at a special place. And that same woman followed them, hitting herself with the rock by which she had killed the saint and confessing (what she had done).

24r/182 ст҃ое тѣло ипатїево абїе исцѣлѣ жеⷩ҇
и вси иже оубїиствоу прⷭ҇тившеи.
и такою моукою истаıавша вси исцⷹ
лѣша. быша же и ина множаиша
исцѣленїа, в дн҃ь положенїа бл҃женаⷢ
телесѣ. непрестанно же рака его
истѣкаше исцѣленїа. и бл҃госло
венїе же честныа его прьсти прїе
млющимъ извѣстно, ıако прахъ
истнѣваетъ всакїа страсти.
Прїидѣте оубо вси любащїи ипатїⷶ.
и ѡ мнѣ ставше вѣнценосца со мною
хвалите. бжⷭ҇твеⷩа стрⷭ҇трьпца
пастыра добраго. црковно оутвⷷ
ржение, ереси ѡмрачившаго, беⷥ
конныхъ соборища бжⷭ҇твеною силоⷪ
24v/182 потребившаго, и чюдесными за
рами вса просвѣщающаго. стоⷣп
бжⷭ҇твенаго к высотѣ нбнⷭ҇ѣи взимⷨ
емаго. правовѣрїю стѣноу незы
блемоу, ст҃лемъ степень. мнⷭ҇къ
касноую лѣпотоу. И сїа оубо
тебѣ ѿ наⷭ҇ ѡ бжественаа и сⷮнаⷣ
главо. аще и скоудна. и твоеа
доброты много ѡстающа. но на
шеа силы не мⷩ҇еше. ѡбаче и бг҃ви
еже по силѣ неѿметно.
Ты же насъ свыше назираи. и
жизнь нашоⷪ҇ на лоучшее ıаводи.
и моучитеⷭ҇тво оукроти. и не
мощноующимъ силоу, и возвы
шенїе, хрⷭ҇тїанскомꙋ рогоу и црь

17.8. And once the holy body of Hypatius was laid to rest, | the woman was 24r/182
immediately healed, and everyone else who had participated in the killing and who had been overwhelmed with such torture—all were healed. And there were many other healings on the day of burying the blessed body, and his grave was a permanent source of healing. And those who received the blessing from his sacred relics know how his remains destroy all kinds of passions.

A Call to Communal Praise of Hypatius

18. Come, then, all of you who love Hypatius, and standing next to me, praise with me this crown-holder, divine passion bearer, good shepherd, who together with the whole Church prevented the heresy from growing strong, who de-
stroyed the lawless assemblies with the divine power | and illumined every- 24v/182
thing with his wondrous rays of light, the pillar of God that elevates (others) to the height of the heavens, the indestructible wall of Orthodoxy, the priest of ascent (to the heavens), the gorgeous beauty of martyrs.

18.1. And even though our (praise) to you, oh godly and holy leader, is meager and surely fails to measure up to your goodness, we do what we can in our small effort, and this effort is not to be rejected by God. Watch over us from above and direct our lives to what is best, and keep us from martyrdom, and grant strength to the weak and expansion of the advancement of Christians

25r/182 кви миръ и согласїе дароуи. ѡ са
момъ хⷭ҇ѣ истиннѣмъ бѕ҃ѣ нашⷨ҇е
емоѵ же слава и дрьжава честь
и поклананїе. со безнⷶ
чалнымъ его ѿц҃ем.
и с прⷭ҇тымъ блⷶ
гимъ и жи
вотвѡ
рѧщїї
мъ
его дхⷪ҇мъ. нн҃ѣ и прⷭ҇но
і въ вѣки вѣкоⷨ҇ъ
ами
нь.~

and peace and harmony to the Church, | (and all) this in Christ himself, our true 25r/182
God! To him be the glory and might and honor and worship, together with his Father without beginning, and with his supremely good and life-giving Spirit, now and forever and to the ages of ages. Amen.

The *Demonstration of Truth*

Introduction to the *Demonstration of Truth*

The *Demonstration of Truth* was written by Zinoviy in the year 1566, according to his own statement (see Introduction), and it shows us a man of profound theological thinking and Biblical exegesis. Scholars consider this treatise the best theological reflection ever written in medieval Russia, and the present edition provides carefully selected texts in which Zinoviy discusses the doctrines of the Trinity, Christ, incarnation, and salvation. These texts are reproduced in the form of a diplomatic edition from Zinoviy's autograph housed in Moscow, RGB, Egor. F. 98, № 337, which preserves the short and improved version of this work.

The English translation includes over a thousand variant readings from the long version of this treatise. They come from the manuscript RGB, MDA F. 173/I, № 61, seventeenth century, published in the 1863 edition. Unfortunately, circumstances prevented us from accessing the original manuscript (RNB, O.I.63). All of these readings are placed in the footnotes and are designed to give an idea of how Zinoviy went about improving his writing. Some of them were also important for reconstructing a few problematic places in Zinoviy's autograph, and we marked them in the translation with triangle brackets ⟨⟩.

The Slavonic text was prepared by Shpakovskiy and verified by Lytvynenko. The English translation, text divisions, Biblical references, and footnotes are the work of Lytvynenko. For the sake of convenience, the translation includes page references to the previous edition in *Истины показание къ вопросившимъ о новом учении. Сочинение инока Зиновия* [*Demonstration of Truth to Those Who Inquired about the New Teaching. The Book of Monk Zinoviy*] (Казань: Университетская типография, 1863).

Readers should keep in mind the distinguishing features of Zinoviy's writing discussed in sect. 4 of the introduction ("A Note on Translation"), such as repetition of arguments, word-weaving, mixing of verb tenses, and speaking in the past tense.

 | DOI:10.1163/9789004538054_007

Text and Translation of the *Demonstration of Truth*

1r/11 Истины показание к вопросившиⷨ ѡ новоⷨ ꙋче
нии. и прерочно паки вопросившиⷨ ѡ правоⷨ мⷣро
вании. и ѡⷣвою заповⷣѣ̈ вторӧ и пⷬ҇вои, иⷤ на
б҃гописаныⷯ скрижалеⷯ, и ѡ бжⷭ҇твенё славѣ иⷤ
в книзѣ бытиѧ і иⷤ в нё ѡ проѡбраженіи грѧдꙋ
щиⷨ. і ѡ аⷭ҇пльскиⷯ гл҃ехъ нѣкиⷯ, і ѡ оправданиⷯ иже
хрⷭ҇тїаньство имаⷮ. і ѡ чл҃ческоⷨ предании еⷤ писа
василё кесарӥ і ѡ здравё вѣре и бл҃гочⷭ҇тивё сла
вѣ иⷤ в посныⷯ его, и ѡ иныⷯ свидѣниⷯ иⷤ в хрⷭ҇ти
ꙗньствѣ. ~

Прїидоша в манастырь. идѣⷤ живꙗⷯ. трие моуⷤ̈
два в ниⷯ мниха и единъ мирꙗниⷩ. иже ѡбрѣтше
мѧ во ст҃ѣи цр҃кви ст҃ыхъ великиⷯ триё ст҃леи. ва
силиѧ великого. григориѧ бг҃ослова. їѡанна зла
тaꙋстаго. и в конецъ п҃ѣнїа приступивше ко
мнѣ единъ ѿ нихъ иже преⷤ пришедыи. сотвори̂
млⷭ҇твꙋ гл҃ꙗ. гⷭ҇и іⷭ҇се хⷭ҇е сн҃е бж҃їи помилоуи наⷭ҇. мнѣⷤ
ѿвѣщавшꙋ аминь. і ꙗкоⷤ ѡбычӓ есть поклонение
сотворшиⷨ. вопросихⷤъ ихъ азъ. кто и ѿкꙋдꙋ соуⷮ.
ѡниⷤ рѣша крылошане еⷭ҇мы. сп҃сова манасты
рѧ ѿ старыѧ рꙋсы. вопросихⷤъ именъ ихъ. како
1v/12 нарицаютсѧ. и ѡба мниха повѣдастасѧ. едиⷩ
ею нарицаетсѧ герасимъ иже первие прїиде.
вторыи нарицашесѧ аѳанасие. мирѧнинⷤъ по
вѣда себе ѳеѡдороⷨ зовома і иконописецъ хꙋдоⷤ
ствоⷨ. абие же сотвори три метаниѧ гера
сиⷨ ко мнѣ. молꙗ съ заклинаниеⷨ гл҃ꙗ. бг҃а ради
не ѿрини ѿ себе не скрӹ ползы како спастисѧ.
мнѣ же ѡ сеⷨ оудивльшоусѧ ѕѣло. и рѣⷯ к нимъ.
повѣдаете себе ꙗко крылошане есте. оубо
прⷭ҇но почитаете сщ҃еннаѧ писанїа. повѣ
дꙋющаѧ како спастисѧ хотѧщемꙋ. ѡни же
рѣша книги писаны закрыто. рѣхⷤъ к нимъ
ѿкрыто ꙋбо ѕѣло бжⷭ҇твеное еⷢ҇алїе. и ѡч҃ь

 | DOI:10.1163/9789004538054_008

1. To those who inquired about the new teaching and then raised contentious questions about the right way of thinking, and about the two commandments—the first and the second—which are written on the divine tablets, and about the glory of God from the book of Genesis, as well as about that which is prefigured there as things to take place in the future, and about certain statements made by the Apostles, and about the regulations found in Christianity, and about the human traditions of which Basil of Caesarea wrote as well as about the sound faith and godly glory that are found in his *Book on Fasting*,[1] and about other subjects related to Christianity. 1r/11

1.1. Three men—two monks and one layman—came to the monastery where I lived and found me at the Holy Church of the Three Great and Holy Bishops, Basil of Caesarea, Gregory the Theologian, and John Chrysostom.[2] And at the end of the chanting, one of them—who had already visited (this place) before—approached me as he was saying the prayer, "Lord, Jesus Christ, Son of God, have mercy on us". And I responded[3] with "Amen", and according to the tradition, I bowed before them and asked who they were and where they were from. And they said, "We are the kliros-chanters from the Monastery of the Savior in Staraya Russa".[4] And after I asked which | names they went by, 1v/12
the two monks told me that one of them was called Gerasim—who had visited (this place) before—and the other one was named Afanasiy. And the layman said that he was called Feodor and was an icon-painter by profession.

1.2. And immediately afterwards, Gerasim made three bows toward me and pleaded with me, saying, "For God's sake, do not turn us down or withhold your help. ⟨Tell us⟩, how can we be saved"? This took me by complete surprise,[5] and I said to them, "You introduced yourselves as kliros-chanters, and you do constantly read the sacred Scriptures, which explain[6] how one can be saved". But they said, "The Scriptures are written in a concealed way". And I said to them, "The divine Gospel and the words of the fathers are completely open

1 *This is a reference to* Asceticon Magnum siue Quaestiones (CPG 2875).

2 at the Holy Church of the Three Great and Holy Bishops, Basil of Caesarea, Gregory the Theologian, and John Chrysostom.] at the Church of the Three Holy Bishops

3 responded] responded to them

4 in Staraya Russa] *omitted*

5 complete surprise,] surprise,

6 explain] explain to everyone

скаа словеса. и всакомꙋ хотащемꙋ готово ра
зоумѣти есть. ѡниж ѿвѣщаша просвѣщеным
оубо ѿкрыто писание. не просвѣщенымж
и ѕѣло закрыто. рекохж и паки имъ ꙗко вса
комꙋ и неоученꙋ соущꙋ комꙋ книгам. оудоб разꙋ
мно бжтвеное евгаліе. и ѡчьскаа словеса.
ѡниж глаша ми естьннѣ оучение. и ннѣшнее
оучение похвалꙗют мнози. понеж ѿкрыто.
а ѿчьское оучение закрыто. и тго ради ѿчь
2r/13 ское оучение прочитат не полезно. глеть же
ннѣшнее оучение. ꙗко во ѿчьскомъ оученни
есть и члчьскаа предания. и василие вели
кїи въ своеи книзѣ члчьскомꙋ преданию по
слѣдовати возбранꙗет. молимса рцы намъ
ты истиннꙋ. а не ѿрини нас бга рад. ѿвѣщав
же рекох к ним. ѿческое оучение вѣмъ добрѣ.
и бжтвенꙋ василиа книгꙋ постническоую знаю.
а ннѣшнег оученїа егож глете не вѣмъ ниже слы
шах его. ѡниж прилѣжнее молꙗхꙋ ма глюще.
бга ради скажи нам истиннꙋ. ннѣшнее оученние
како ты мниши. есть ли бжтвено и ѿ бга ли.
добро бо ꙋчение ннѣшнее. понеж возбранꙗет
послѣдовати члчьским преданием. и пове
левает послѣдовати писанию стлповым
книгамъ. бга ради скажи нам истиннꙋ.
аз же ѡ семъ новомъ и неѡбычном вопрошенїи их
во мнозѣ оудивленїи бывъ. ѿвѣщавъ рекох
к нимъ. сїа ꙗже вы глете. нѣсть моеа мѣ
ры. но црковное есть дѣло се. ѡниж и паки
неѡслабно принꙋжахꙋ ма ѡ семъ. азж не
возмогох ѿрещиса имъ сего рад. понеже
2v/13 бжие има преступит нѣсть без бѣды.
ѡбѣщах са имъ по ѡбѣде снитиса с ними
на расмотрение вопрошенїа их. ~
…

to everyone who wants to understand them". But they replied, "The Scriptures
are indeed open to those who are enlightened, yet they are entirely concealed
to those who are not enlightened". And I said to them, again, that the divine
Gospel and the words of the fathers are easily comprehensible even to those
who are not learned in books. But they said to me,[7] "There is a teaching that
many find praise-worthy because this new teaching is open, whereas the teach-
ing of the fathers is concealed, and therefore, | it does no good to read the 2^{r}/13
teaching of the fathers. But the new teaching says that the teaching of the
fathers contains human traditions, and Basil the Great in his writing prohibits
the following of human traditions. We beg you, tell us the truth, and do not
turn us down, for God's sake"! And in response, I said to them,[8] "I am quite
familiar with the teaching of the fathers and I know the *Book on Fasting*[9] by
godly Basil,[10] but I do not know the new teaching of which you are speaking,
nor have I heard about it". Yet they begged me even harder, saying, "For God's
sake, tell us the truth! Do you think the new teaching is godly, and[11] is it from
God? For the new teaching is good in that it prohibits following human tradi-
tions, and it commands[12] following the Scripture, its foundational books. Tell
us the truth, for God's sake"! But I was very surprised to hear them asking their
unusual question again, and in response, I said to them, "What you say is some-
thing I cannot deal with and is a matter to be addressed by the church". Yet they
did not stop pressing me about that matter, again,[13] and in view of that, I could
not turn them down, for | to go against the name of God is not without trou- 2^{v}/13
ble.[14] For that reason, I promised to meet with them after dinner and consider
their inquiries.

7 to me,] *omitted*
8 And in response, I said to them,] I replied to them,
9 *This is a reference to* Asceticon Magnum siue Quaestiones (CPG 2875).
10 godly Basil] Basil of Caesarea
11 and] or
12 commands] teaches
13 again,] *omitted*
14 for to go against the name of God is not without trouble.] for had I happened to go against the name of God, it would have simply not been without trouble.

28v/70 … Ꙗко бг҃ъ жиⷡ҇ есть. сего раⷣ҇ въ бз҃ѣ слово и дх҃ъ. ꙗкоⷤ бг҃ъ истиненъ бесмр҃тенъ такоⷤ слово еⷭ҇ дх҃ъ еⷭ҇ нетлѣнеⷩ҇ и беⷥст҃ртенъ.[15]

Всꙗкомꙋ же пристꙋпающемꙋ бв҃и подобаеⷮ вѣровати ꙗко есть и взыскающиⷨ его мздо воздатеⷧ҇ бываеⷮ апⷭ҇лъ павелъ гл҃еть. и аще оубо вѣрꙋетсѧ бг҃ъ понеⷤ есть бг҃ъ. бг҃а же не ложна жива вѣровати подобаеⷮ. не живы бо бг҃ъ мⷣзовоздатеⷧ҇ взыскающиⷨ его быти не можеⷮ. и ꙗко ꙋбо живъ есть бг҃ъ. тѣмже живыи бг҃ъ имаⷮ слово и дх҃ъ. аще не вѣрꙋеши имѣти живомꙋ бг҃ꙋ слова и дх҃а. то беⷥсловеⷭ҇на и беⷥдш҃ьна хощеши исповѣдати бг҃а. ащеⷤ беⷥсловесенъ и беⷥдш҃енъ бг҃ъ ниже живъ по тебѣ. и таковое колика къ бг҃ꙋ хꙋла будеть ѿ тебе. не возможеши бо исповѣдати истиннаⷢ҇ бг҃а жива. помышлꙗа беⷥсловеⷭ҇на и беⷥдш҃ьна его быти. поⷣⷪбаеⷮ бо бг҃ꙋ и истинномꙋ живомꙋ слово емꙋ и дх҃ъ да боудеⷮ совершенъ бг҃ъ живъ со словоⷨ и дх҃омъ.

---

15 *In the margin*: глаⷡ҇ и҃.

2. [FIRST VISIT OF THE KLIROS-CHANTERS]

3. Showing that God is alive, from which it follows that God has the Word and Spirit. Just as God is truly immortal, so are his Word and his Spirit incorporeal and immortal as well. CHAPTER 8.[16] 28v/70

3.1. "Everyone who comes to God must believe that he exists and that he rewards those who seek him", says the Apostle Paul (Heb. 11:6). And if it is believed that God exists—for he does exist[17]—one must truly believe that he is alive, because if he were not alive, he would not be able to reward those who seek him.[18] And now, given the fact that God is alive, the living God must have the Word and Spirit. But if you do not believe that the living God has the Word and Spirit, then you need to declare God to be irrational and lifeless. And if God is irrational and lifeless, he is not alive either, according to you.

3.2. And with such things, what great blasphemy there will come from you against God![19] For you cannot profess the true God to be alive if you consider him to be irrational and lifeless. Therefore,[20] it is proper for the true living God to have the Word and Spirit so that God may be perfect and alive together with the Word and Spirit.[21] | 29r/71

16 **Showing that God is alive, from which it follows that God has the Word and Spirit. Just as God is truly immortal, so are his Word and his Spirit incorporeal and immortal as well. CHAPTER 8.] Investigation as to whether the one who holds possession over living things must, likewise, be alive, and as to whether the Word and Spirit are somehow like the one who is the living providential sustainer of living things. CHAPTER 8.**

17 for he does exist] *omitted*

18 *MS 61 adds*: **Showing that since God is alive, God must have the Word and Spirit; and just as God is immortal by nature, so are the Word of God and God's Spirit immortal by nature as well.**

19 he is not alive either, according to you. And with such things, what great blasphemy there will come from you against God!] he will not be alive either, according to you. But with such impiety that you have, what great blasphemy, then, comes from you against God!

20 Therefore,] indeed,

21 it is proper for the true living God to have the Word and Spirit so that God may be perfect and alive together with the Word and Spirit.] We must believe, then, that it is proper for the true living God to have the Word and Spirit so that the true God may be perfect and alive together with the Word and Spirit.

29r/71 ꙗко ꙋ бг҃а слово еⷢ҇ и дх҃ъ еⷢ҇. такоⷤ в составѣ своеⷨ
живыи. ꙗкоⷤ самъ бг҃ъ въ своеⷨ составѣ.
ꙗко ꙋбо истинныи бг҃ъ живъ прⷭ҇носꙋщенъ есть.
безначаленъ бесконеченъ не старѣющьсѧ.
всесиленъ. такоⷤ и слово имаⷮ своего еⷭ҇тва.
бл҃жнаⷢ҇ нетлѣннаⷢ҇. тогоⷤ сꙋщества. такоⷤ
и дх҃ъ имаⷮ. своиⷭⷪ прⷭ҇носꙋщенъ. тогоⷤ нетлѣннаⷢ҇.
и беⷥсмр҃тнаго еⷭ҇тва. со исходѧ словꙋ. и ꙗⷦ҇же
бг҃ъ живъ и истиненъ безначаленъ бесконе
ченъ прⷭ҇носꙋщенъ не старѣющьсѧ. тако же
оубо и слово его живо и истинно собезначаⷧ҇
но съпрⷭ҇носꙋщно вѣровати подобаⷮ. а не
на воздꙋсѣ раⷥсыпаемо и изгибаѧ. не сотво
рено бо слово бж҃ие но бестелеⷭ҇но рожено.
ибо и нш҃его тлѣннаго еⷭ҇тва оумъ нш҃ь ражаеⷮ
слово бестелеⷭ҇но. ꙋдобнѣ бестрⷭ҇тно. но по
неⷤ тлѣнни есмы. и слово нш҃е тлѣнно. сеⷢ҇
рⷣа и исчезаеⷮ слово нш҃е на воздꙋсѣ. ибо и саⷨ
мы растлѣвше исчезаемъ. бж҃иеⷤ бл҃женⷩ҇ое
еⷭ҇тво нетлѣнно сꙋще прⷭ҇носꙋщно. тѣмже
и слово сꙋщества еⷢ҇ живо нетлѣнно сыи съ
прⷭ҇носꙋщно. рожено слово нестрⷭ҇тно. не плⷮоски бо
29v/72 ражаемо. понеⷤ бг҃ъ бесплотеⷩ҇ не плⷮоски слово
свое рⷣо. и слово живо беⷥстрⷭ҇тно беⷥсмр҃тно
ражаѧⷭ҇. ѿ беⷥсмр҃тнаⷢ҇ и беⷥстрⷭ҇тнаⷢ҇ бг҃а. ибо
и мы стрⷭ҇тнѣ и смр҃тни сꙋще. оумъⷤ има
мы бесплотенъ. беⷥстрⷭ҇тно слово прⷭ҇но ра

4. Showing that God has his Word and his Spirit existing in their respective subsistences, just as God himself exists in his own subsistence.[22]

4.1. Now, just as the true God is eternally alive, without beginning, infinite, ageless, omnipotent, so the Word must be that way, too, as being proper to the same[23] blessed, incorruptible nature and essence; and likewise, the Spirit must be co-eternal, as being proper to the same incorruptible and immortal nature, from which he proceeds together with the Son.[24] And just as God is alive and true,[25] without beginning, infinite, eternal, ageless,[26] so we must believe that his own Word is alive, true, equally without beginning, co-eternal,[27] and it does not disintegrate and vanish in the air. For[28] the Word of God is not made, but immaterially begotten.

4.2. For (when it is compared with) our minds, which belong to our corrupted nature, they easily generate words in an immaterial and passionless way, too, but because we[29] are corrupted, our words are corrupted as well. For that reason,[30] our words disintegrate in the air, because we ourselves disintegrate, too, when we decay.[31] But the blessed nature of God is incorruptible and eternal.

4.3. Therefore, the Word that belongs to his being is also alive, incorruptible, and co-eternal. The manner of the Word's begetting is without passion because he[32] is not begotten by the flesh. | For since God is immaterial, he also begets his 29^{v}/72
Word in an immaterial way. And being begotten by the immortal and passionless God, the Word is alive, passionless, and immortal. For we, too, even being enslaved to passions and mortality, nevertheless, have immaterial minds, which always generate words in a way that is without passion.

---

22 **Showing that God has his Word and his Spirit existing in their respective subsistences, just as God himself exists in his own subsistence.**] *omitted*

23 the same] *omitted*

24 incorruptible and immortal nature, from which he proceeds together with the Son.] blessed and incorruptible nature.

25 And just as God is alive and true, without beginning,] Just as it is believed that the true living God is without beginning,

26 ageless] *omitted*

27 equally without beginning, co-eternal,] co-eternal, equally without beginning,

28 For] Indeed,

29 we] we ourselves

30 *MS 337 adds in the margin*: Note!

31 For that reason, our words disintegrate in the air because we ourselves disintegrate, too, when we decay.] For that reason, our words disintegrate in the air and vanish.

32 he] Word

жаеⷮ. ты не можеши домыслитисѧ како в тебѣ созданнѣмъ тлѣннеⷨ еⷭ҇твѣ бесплотныи оуⷨ твои слово тебѣ ражаеⷮ. како же тлѣненъ ты хощеши мысльми тлѣнными бесплотное нетлѣнное рⷭ҇жтво бж҃ие. словꙋ его живомꙋ испытати. но точию вѣроваⷮ подобаеⷮ. ꙗко бг҃ъ не беⷥсловесенъ. слово же бг҃а живаго по бл҃женномꙋ его еⷭ҇твꙋ. живо составно прⷭ҇носꙋщно нетлѣнно бесплотно дѣиствено рожено а не сотворено. и в нш҃еⷨ бо тлѣнномъ плⷮоскомъ сꙋществѣ слово ꙋма нашеⷢ҇ не сотворѧемо но ражаемо бесплⷮонымъ оумоⷨ нш҃имъ. не имаⷮ бо ꙋмъ нш҃ь рꙋкꙋтворити слово бесплотенъ сыи. ниⷤ требоуеⷮ жеⷩ҇ска полꙋ оумъ нш҃ь на зачатие словесѣ своемꙋ. но беⷥ зачатїа ражаеⷮ оумъ нш҃ь слово нш҃е. беⷥ мѣшканїа и беⷥ предѣла вкꙋпѣ оумꙋ 30r/73 слово нш҃е съпребываѧ. и внезапꙋ ражаетсѧ слово нш҃е ѿ оума нш҃его. да стыдѧтсѧ сквернословцы хꙋлѧщїи бжⷭ҇твꙋ рⷭ҇жтво бесплотное. и хотѧще бгꙋ привводити женꙋ на рожение словꙋ. не хотѧще разоумѣти оума своего ражающа слово беⷥ жены. безоуⷨствꙋюⷮ ѕѣло беⷥсловеснѣ. бесплотномꙋ и нетлѣнномꙋ блж҃енномꙋ еⷭ҇твꙋ бжию. жены взыскающе на рожение бесплотнаⷢ҇ нетлѣннаⷢ҇ слова бгꙋ.

И аще тлѣнное еⷭ҇тво нш҃е во плотнѣ соуществѣ бесплотнаⷢ҇ оума нш҃его не могꙋще воⷥбранити. беⷥ жены не ражати слово свое. бжⷭ҇твеномꙋ же нетлѣнномꙋ еⷭ҇твꙋ беⷥ жены рⷣоти слово воⷥбранити тщатсѧ. коликаго безꙋмиѧ есть таковое скверновие беⷥбжⷯьны. коликїа хꙋлы бжⷭ҇твꙋ прилагаюⷮ. и не оустрашаютсѧ ѕлѣ неистⷭ҇ствꙋюще. бжию дⷣготерпѣнию чюⷣтисѧ есть ѕѣло. ꙗко в толикыхъ скверноглⷢ҇ны хꙋлаⷯ. на божественое ωно еⷭ҇тво рⷥсѣданїа и трѣсновенїа не стражꙋть. всѧко всѣмъ хотѧи сⷭ҇птисѧ и в разоуⷨ истинныи прїити. сего

4.4. You cannot comprehend the way your immaterial mind generates a word for you[33] in your created corrupted nature. And, being corrupted (by nature), how do you wish to inquire into the immaterial, incorruptible divine generation of his living Word with your corrupted thoughts? Instead, we must simply believe that God is rational ⟨and that God has his Word with him⟩.[34] According to the blessed nature (of the Godhead), the Word of the living God is a living being, eternal, incorruptible, incorporeal, active, begotten, and not made.

4.5. And (to use the same illustration), the words of our minds in our corrupted fleshly essence are not made, but generated from our immaterial minds. For being incorporeal, our minds do not need to create words by hands, nor do our minds require a female partner in order to conceive their words. Instead, our minds generate our words without conception, without waiting, and without limit. Our words co-exist together with | our minds, and our words are 30r/73
generated from our minds in an instant of time.

4.6. Let those profane men feel ashamed for blaspheming God's incorporeal generation and wishing[35] to present God with a wife for the Word's begetting, not realizing that their own minds generate words without wives. They are extremely irrational and insane to search out a wife for God's incorporeal, and incorruptible, and blessed nature so that God may beget the immaterial, incorruptible[36] Word. And[37] if they cannot deny the fact that, in the fleshly essence of our corrupted nature, our incorporeal minds do not need a wife to generate our words, then (why do they) try to deny that the incorruptible nature of God begets the Word without a wife?

4.7. What insanity for these godless men to think in such a profane way! They put forth so much blasphemy against God[38] and have no fear about such insane evil thoughts! And we must be greatly astonished at God's long patience, that those who say such profane and blasphemous things against this blessed nature do not suffer destruction and collapse. He always "desires all men to be saved and come to the knowledge of the truth" (1 Tim. 2:4), and for that reason, | God's 30v/74

33 generates a word for you.] generates for you a word that is without passion.

34 *MS 61 adds:* **Showing that it belongs to God to have his Word and his Spirit as eternally existing and alive in their own subsistences, just as God himself exists eternally.**

35 wishing] seeking

36 incorruptible] *omitted*

37 And] *omitted*

38 God] the supremely pure Godhead

30v/74 рⷣи и пожидаше бж҃ие до҇готерпѣние. скверⷬ҇но словцевъ хꙋлꙗщыⷯ прчⷭ҇тое его и блж҃нное еⷭ҇ство. По возможномꙋ оубо наⷨ показа слово. вѣроваⷮ҇ бг҃а со словомъ своиⷨ. прⷭ҇носꙋщна сꙋща. бес прꙗⷤ оубо и дх҃ъ бж҃ии собезначаленъ. сопрⷭ҇носꙋщеⷩ҇ бв҃и. и единосꙋщенъ живъ. и истиненъ. то ꙗⷤ силы словꙋ бж҃ию. по прⷭ҇носꙋществꙋ бж҃иꙗ еⷭ҇ства. соеⷭ҇твенꙋ и дх҃ꙋ сꙋщꙋ. ꙗковоⷤ бж҃ие еⷭ҇ство. тогоⷤ еⷭ҇ства бесплотнаⷢ҇ нетлѣннаⷢ҇ вѣровати и дх҃а бж҃иꙗ ꙗкоⷤ и слова. вѣдиⷨ бо и в нашеⷨ плотноⷨ тлѣнномъ еⷭ҇твѣ. слово по рожении своеⷨ ѿ оума нш҃его дх҃омъ ѿ ꙋстъ нш҃ихъ происходиⷮ. беⷥ дх҃а же нш҃его ѿ оустъ нш҃ихъ слово не происходиⷮ. но рожено слово нш҃е ѿ оума нш҃его. в срⷣцы нашеⷨ лежить неꙗвленно. аще не дх҃омъ оустъ нш҃ихъ происшеⷣ слово показано бꙋдеть. Ꙗко пⷪ҇баеть по писаⷩ҇ю вѣроваⷮ҇ бг҃ꙋ Рекоⷯ ꙋбо преже ꙗко еⷭ҇ствоⷨ всꙗка дш҃а любить слꙋжити бг҃ꙋ. вѣрꙋюци ꙗко есть бг҃ъ. аще правѣ кто разꙋмѣвъ или неправѣ разоумѣвъ. и ѿ того разоумѣние готово есть. ꙗко чл҃къ бж҃ие создание есть. бг҃аⷤ 31r/75 плотныма ѡчима вѣдѣти невозможно. точию мысленыма ѡчима разоумѣти есть бг҃а long patience bears with these profane men, who blaspheme his supremely holy and blessed nature.

4.8. Thus, whenever it was possible, he revealed this to us in the Word (of Scripture) so that we may come to believe in God and his own Word, who eternally exists with him. Without a doubt, then, God's Spirit, too, is equally without beginning, co-eternal, consubstantial with God, living, true, and has the same power that belongs to the Word of God. According to the everlasting nature of God, the Spirit is co-essential. Since the divine nature is incorporeal and incorruptible, we must believe that the Spirit of God, in terms of nature, is that way, too, just like the Son.[39]

4.9. For we can observe (by analogy) that after being generated by our minds in our fleshly, corrupted nature, our words come out of our mouths through breathing. And no word comes out of our mouths without being breathed out. Rather, after being generated within our minds, our words lie hidden in our hearts until they are revealed through the breath of our mouths, from which our words come.[40]

5. Showing that we must believe in God according to the Scripture.[41]

5.1. Indeed, as I said before, every soul by its nature loves to serve God, trusting that God exists, regardless of whether one has a correct understanding, or an erroneous understanding about it. And this being the case, one is predisposed to understand that man is God's creation. But it is impossible to see God | with 31r/75
the eyes of the flesh; we must comprehend God only with our rational eyes.

39 equally without beginning, co-eternal, consubstantial with God, living, true, and has the same power that belongs to the Word of God. According to the everlasting nature of God, the Spirit is co-essential. Since the divine nature is incorporeal and incorruptible, we must believe that the Spirit of God, in terms of nature, is that way, too, just like the Son.] co-eternal, living, true, and has the same power that belongs to the Word of God according to the everlasting nature of God that is incorporeal and incorruptible. Since he comes from the essence of God, we must believe the same things about God's Spirit as we do about the Word of God.

40 *MS 61. adds*: One of their three laymen said, "Is it really true that Kosoy teaches bad doctrine in saying that there is one God, just as it is written in Genesis that one 'God made the heavens and the earth' (Gen. 1:1), and in the Law, it is commanded, 'Hear, O Israel: The Lord your God, the Lord is one' (Deut. 6:4), and God himself says, 'I am God, and besides me there is no other God' (Is. 45:5)? And how do you say that Kosoy is a godless man, considering that Kosoy teaches that God is one according to Genesis"? And I gave them (the following) answer.

41 **Scripture.] Scripture, rather than thinking of God in a different way, according to our own wisdom.**

попадающижй стрстемъ и тли члсчтвꙋ бга забыва оудобно есть. се ради бжиею волею. дадеса писание на помощь во ежe не забывати бга. се мꙋ же слꙋжителꙗ бывша вѣдѣти есть впервых моисѣа. тѣмже видимй оубо самыꙗ моисѣовы книги. да не растлѣни бꙋдем косо безоумие. но разгнꙋвше книги прочтемъ чсто.
Искони сотвори бгъ нбо и землю. землꙗж бѣ не[42] видима и неоукрашена и тма верхꙋ безны. и дхъ бжїи ношашесе верхоу воды. и рече бгъ да бꙋдет свѣт. и бысть свѣтъ. и вѣдѣ бгъ свѣтъ ꙗко добро. и разлꙋчи бгъ межю свѣтомъ и межꙋ тмою. и нарече бгъ свѣт днь. а тмꙋ нарече нощь и бысть ꙋтро и бысть вечеръ днь единъ. и рече бгъ да боудет твердь посредѣ воды. и да бꙋдеть разлꙋчаа посреди воды и воды. и бысть тако. и сотвори бгъ твердь. и разлꙋчи бгъ межю водою ꙗж бѣ под твердию. и посредѣ воды ꙗж бѣ над твердию. и нарече бгъ твердь нбо. и вѣдѣ бгъ ꙗко добро. и бысть вечеръ. и быс
31v/76 оутро днь вторыи. и рече бгъ да соберетса вода ꙗже под нбсемъ в совокꙋпление едино. и да ꙗвитса сꙋша. и бысть тако. и собрасa вода ꙗж под нбсемъ в сонмы своа и ꙗвиса сꙋша. и нарече бгъ сꙋшꙋ землю. а составы водныꙗ нарече море. и вѣдѣ бгъ ꙗко добро. и рече бгъ да прорастит землꙗ былие травное. сѣюще сѣмꙗ по родꙋ и по подобию. и древо пловито творꙗщее плод. емꙋж сѣмꙗ его в нем по родꙋ на земли и бысть тако. и изнесе землꙗ былие травное. сѣюще сѣме по родꙋ и по подобию на земли. и древо пловито творащее плод емоуж сѣмꙗ его в немъ по родꙋ на земли. и вѣдѣ бгъ ꙗко добро. и бысть вечеръ. и бысть оутро днь третии. и рече бгъ да бꙋдꙋть свѣтила на твердѣ нбснѣи. ѡсвѣщати землю. и разлꙋчити межоу днем и межꙋ нощию. и да боудꙋть въ знаме

42 *In the margin*: глава д

5.2. And it is easy for humankind, which is subjected to passions and corruption to forget God. This is why, by the will of God, we were given the Scripture in order to help us not to forget God. And, as we can see, it all begins with the servant, Moses. Therefore, consider now the books of Moses so that you may not fall victim to Kosoy's insanity but, having opened the Scriptures, you may read them clearly.

6. CHAPTER 9.[43]

6.1. "In the beginning, God made the heaven and the earth. The earth was without form and without order, and darkness was over the face of the deep. And the Spirit of God was hovering over the waters. And God said, 'Let there be light', and there was light. And God saw that the light was good. And God separated the light from the darkness. And God called the light 'day', and the darkness he called 'night'. And there was evening and there was morning, the first day.

6.2. And God said, 'Let there be a vault in the midst of the waters and let it separate the waters from the waters'. And it was so. And God made the vault, and God separated the waters that were under the vault from the waters that were above the vault. And God called the vault heaven. And God saw that it was good. And there was evening and there was | morning, the second day. 31v/76

6.3. And God said, 'Let the waters under the heavens be gathered to one place, and let the dry land appear'. And it was so. And the waters under the heavens were gathered to their own places, and the dry land appeared. And God called the dry land 'earth', and the gathering of waters he called 'seas'. And God saw that it was good. And God said, 'Let the earth sprout green plants that yield seed each according to its kind and likeness, and fruit trees bearing fruit in which is their seed, each according to its kind, on the earth'. And it was so. And the earth brought forth green plants yielding seed according to their own kind and likeness, on the earth, and trees bearing fruit in which is their seed, each according to its kind, on the earth. And God saw that it was good. And there was evening and there was morning, the third day.

6.4. And God said, 'Let there be lights in the heavenly vault to give light upon the earth and separate the day from the night. And let them be for signs and sea-

43 CHAPTER 9.] **Investigation, according to the holy book of Genesis, as to whether the primal and eternal God is single. More specifically, is he alone and has he no other co-eternal being, or does he somehow have more than himself? And is this many or few? CHAPTER 9. Showing that every statement of God is entirely true, and that even when something small is spoken, its significance is still immense. Genesis.** Now, this book opens with the first chapter that begins as follows:

нїа и времена. и во дни и в лѣта. да бꙋдеть
в просвѣщение на твердѣ нбⷭнѣи. ꙗко свѣ
тити по земли и бысть тако. И сотвори
бг҃ъ двѣ свѣтили велицѣи свѣтило великое
32r/77 в начатⷦо дни. и свѣтило мⷩшее в начатокъ
нощи. и звѣѕды. и постави иⷯ бг҃ъ на твердѣ
нбⷭсѣи. ꙗко свѣтиⷮ по земли. владѣти днеⷨ
и нощию. и разлꙋчи межи свѣтомъ и межꙋ
тмою. и вѣдѣ бг҃ъ ꙗко добро. и бысть вечеⷬ
и бысть оутро дн҃ь четвертыи. И реⷱ бг҃ъ
да изведꙋть воды гады дш҃ь живыхъ. и пти
ца летающе на земли по тверди нбⷭнѣи и
бысть тако. и сотвори бг҃ъ киты великїа.
и всакꙋ дш҃оу животныⷯ гаⷣ ꙗже изведоша
воды. по родꙋ ихъ. и всакꙋ птицꙋ пернатꙋ
по родꙋ ихъ. и вѣдѣ бг҃ъ ꙗко добро. и блⷭви ꙗ
бг҃ъ гл҃ꙗ. раститеса и множитеса и на
полните воды ꙗⷤ в мореⷯ. и птица да оумно
жатса на земли. и бысть вечеръ и бысть
оутро дн҃ь патыи. и реⷱ бг҃ъ да изведеть зе
млꙗ дш҃ꙋ живꙋ по родꙋ четвероногa. и гады
и звѣра земныа. и скоты и вса гады земли
по родꙋ и бысть тако. и сотвори бг҃ъ звѣра
по родꙋ ихъ. и вса гады земли по родꙋ ихъ. и вѣ
ди бг҃ъ ꙗко добро. И реⷱ бг҃ъ сотвориⷨ чл҃ка
по ѡбразоу нш҃емꙋ и по поⷪбию. и да ѡбладаеⷮ
32v/78 рыбами морьскими и птицаⷨ нбⷭными. и звѣ
рми и скоты и всею землею. и всѣми гады
пресмыкающимиⷭ по земли. И сотвори бг҃ъ
чл҃ка по ѡбразоу бж҃ию сотвори его. мꙋжа
и женоу сотвори иⷯ. и блⷭви иⷯ бг҃ъ гл҃ꙗ. расти
теса и множитеса и напⷧните землю и
ѡбладаите ею. и ѡбладаите рыбами моⷬ
скими и птицами нбⷭными. и всѣ скоты
и всею землею. и всѣми гады пресмыкаю
щимиса по земли. И реⷱ бг҃ъ се даⷯ вамъ вса
кꙋ травꙋ сѣменнꙋ. сѣюще сѣмꙗ еⷤ есть ве
рхоу землꙗ всеа. и всако древо еⷤ имать
в себѣ плоⷣ сѣмене сѣменна. вамъ боудеⷮ
въ сн҃ѣ и всѣмъ звѣремъ земнымъ. и всѣⷨ

sons, and for days and years. Let them be lights in the vault of the heavens to give light upon the earth'. And it was so. And God made the two great lights—
the greater light | to commence the day and the lesser light to commence the 32r/77
night—and the stars. And God set them in the vault of the heavens to give light on the earth, to govern the day and the night, and to separate the light from the darkness. And God saw that it was good. And there was evening and there was morning, the fourth day.

6.5. And God said, 'Let the waters teem with living creatures, and let birds fly above the earth across the vault of the heavens'. And it was so. And God created the big fish and every living creature that creeps, with which the waters teem, according to their kinds, and all the winged birds according to their kinds. And God saw that it was good. And God blessed them, saying, 'Be fruitful, and multiply, and fill the waters in the seas, and let birds multiply on the earth'. And there was evening and there was morning, the fifth day.

6.6. And God said, 'Let the earth bring forth living creatures according to their kinds—four-footed creatures, and creeping things, and beasts of the earth, and livestock, and all the reptiles, according to their kinds'. And it was so. And God made the beasts according to their kinds and all the creeping things according to their kinds. And God saw that it was good.

6.7. And God said, 'Let us make man in our image and likeness. And let him
subdue | the fish of the sea, and the birds of the heavens, and the beasts, and the 32v/78
livestock, and all the earth, and every creeping thing that creeps on the earth'. And God made man, in the image of God he made him; male and female he made them. And God blessed them, saying, 'Be fruitful, and multiply, and fill the earth, and subdue it; and subdue the fish of the sea, and the birds of the heavens, and all the livestock, and all the earth, and every creeping thing that creeps on the earth'. And God said, 'Behold, I gave you every seed-bearing plant yielding seed that is on the face of all the earth and every seed-bearing tree with seed in its fruit. You will have them for food. And to every beast of the earth, and

птицаⷨ нбⷭнымъ. и всакомꙋ гадꙋ пресмыка
ющемоуса по земли. еⷤ имаⷮ в себѣ дшꙋ҃ живо
тнꙋ. и всакꙋ травꙋ зеленꙋ в сн҃ѣ. и бысть
тако. и вѣдѣ бгъ҃ вса елико сотвори. и се до
бра ѕило и бысть вечеръ. и бысть оутро днь҃
шестыи. И совершишаса нбо҃ и землꙗ. и
все оукрашение ихъ. и соверши бгъ҃ в днь҃ ше
стыи дѣла своꙗ ꙗⷤ сотвори. и препочи бгъ҃
33r/79 в днь҃ се҃мыи. ѿ всѣⷯ дѣлъ своиⷯ их же сотвори. и
блⷭви бгъ҃ днь҃ се҃мыи и ѡсти҃ его. ꙗко в тои по
чи ѿ всѣхъ дѣⷧ своихъ. ихⷤъ нача бгъ҃ творити.
сїа книга бытию нбси҃ и земли. егда бысть
в онⷤь днь҃ сотвори бгъ҃ нбо҃ и землю. и всꙗкъ
злакъ сⷧ҃ныи. прⷤе даже быти на земли. и всꙗ
коу травꙋ селноу. прⷤе даже прозꙗбнꙋти.
ни бо ѡдожди бгъ҃ на землю. и члкъ҃ не бѣꙗше
дѣлатию. источникⷤъ исхожаше иⷥ землꙗ
и напаꙗше все лице земли. и созда бгъ҃ члка҃
перьсть вземъ ѿ землꙗ. и вдꙋноу в лице его
дыхание жизни. и бысть члкъ҃ в дшꙋ҃ живоу.
Ꙗко всꙗкъ гль҃ бжїи истиненъ ѕѣло. аще
в малѣ речеⷩ боудеⷮ мноⷢ превеликъ есть.
Здѣ всꙗкъ кто взыскоуꙗи истинꙋ. да смо
триⷮ разоумѣти. речено бысть в книзѣ ꙗⷦ
рече бгъ҃ да боудеⷮ свѣⷮ и бысть. и реⷱ бгъ҃ да боу
деⷮ твердь. и реⷱ бгъ҃ да соберетса вода в сонь
мы своа и да ꙗвитса сꙋша. и прочаа всꙗ
творенїа. реⷱ бгъ҃ и бысть тако. смотри и
внемли всꙗ оубо великаа дѣла. оудивлꙗюща
и оустрашающа всꙗкъ оумъ. реⷱ бгъ҃ просто
33v/79 и быша. помысли многїа животоⷡ роды в водаⷯ
и на земли. великаа и малаꙗ. беⷭчисленаа
животнаа. и самыꙗ мора раздѣли ѿ сꙋши.
и соушꙋ толикоу ѿ воⷣ разлꙋчи. и в неи изведе
беⷭпрестани текꙋщїа рѣки. и источники

to every bird of the heavens, and to everything that creeps on the earth, (everything) that has the breath of life, I gave every green plant for food'. And it was so. And God saw everything that he had made, and behold, it was very good. And there was evening and there was morning, the sixth day.

6.8. Thus, the heavens and the earth were finished, and all that was arrayed in them. And on the sixth day, God finished his works that he had done, and God rested | on the seventh day from all his work that he had done. And God 33r/79
blessed the seventh day[44] and made it holy because on it, he rested from all his work that God began to do.

6.9. This is the book of Genesis of the heavens and the earth when they came into being, in that day, God made the earth and the heaven. And no plant of the field was yet in the land and no bush of the field had yet sprung up, for God had not caused it to rain on the land, and there was no man to work on it, but a stream was coming up from the land and was watering the whole face of the ground. And God created the man, by taking the dust from the ground and breathing into his face the breath of life, and the man became a living being" (Gen. 1:1–2:7).

7. Showing that every word of God is absolutely true, and that even when something small is stated, it has incredible significance.[45]

7.1. Let everyone who seeks the truth, see and understand this here! It is stated in the Scripture[46] that God said, "Let there be light, and it was so";[47] and God said, "Let there be a vault";[48] and God said, "Let the waters be gathered to their own places, and let the dry land appear and all the other creatures; and God said, and it was so" (Gen. 1:3, 6, 9). See and recognize that indeed all the great works that amuse and appall the mind were brought into being after God simply spoke a word.[49] | 33v/79

7.2. Consider the numerous kinds of animals in the water and on the earth—the infinite number of big and small living creatures—and (how God) separated the seas from the dry land, and (how) he made the dry land completely separate from the waters and caused the streams of unceasing rivers and the

44 And God blessed the seventh day] *omitted*

45 **Showing that every word of God is absolutely true, and that even when something small is stated, it has incredible significance.**] *omitted*

46 Scripture] divine Scripture

47 and it was so";] and there was light";

48 "Let there be a vault";] "Let there be a vault, and it was so";

49 after God simply spoke a word.] soon after God simply spoke a word and they immediately (appeared).

бесчислены. древаж и былїа. и самѹю твердь. и долѣносн҃ѹю водѹ возведе верхѹ на тверди. вса та рѐс бг҃ъ и бысть тако. Ѩко бг҃ъ созда чл҃ка чтс҃а пас всеи твари бж҃їи сотворенои прѐж чл҃ка Внегдаж малъ живот создати чл҃ка восхотѣ. тогда совѣта потребова бг҃ъ а не просто рече и бысть чл҃къ. ꙗкож великаа и страшнаа и дивнаа дѣла вса. просто рѐс да боудѐт и быша. и нѝж со земными животы вкѹпѣ бысть чл҃къ. а имас живот сѹщи. но насобно ѿ всакого животнаг. и ѡсобно ѿ всеа твари ѕижѐт чл҃ка. вне мли и се не просто ѕижѐт. ꙗкож свѣтъ и твѐрдь. и сады и животы и прочаа великаа. рѐс бо просто вѐз совѣта и быша. чл҃ка же ѕижа преже совѣтоват восприят. рекоша бо книги. и рѐс бг҃ъ сотворѝм чл҃ка по ѡбразѹ нш҃емѹ и по подобию. и тогда ѕижѐт чл҃ка. и не тако ꙗкоже

34r/80 прочаа животы. и птица и рыбы. и киты великїа. и гады и звѣри и скоты. и елефант. но взѐм персть ѿ землꙗ бг҃ъ. и сотвори чл҃ка гл҃ют книгы. чтож оубо се есть ѡ толикы дивных страшных дѣлех не совѣтѹꙗ твораше бг҃ъ. ꙗково ѹбо нб҃сное величество. коликаж широта и глѹбина земли. коликож и морю простран ство. и вса ꙗж в нихъ бесчисленаа. и ѕвѣздных ликовъ чины лоуны красотѹ. и сл҃нца безмѣрнѹю славѹ. и самыа тыа прдестоꙗщїа славы бжс҃тва его. ст҃ых аггл҃ъ тмы тмами и тысаща тысащами. бвоши пас сл҃нчныа славы блистающих. и незаходимо сїающих. сотворꙗа бг҃ъ infinite number of springs to flow in it, and (how he made) the trees along with the plants, and (how he made) the vault itself, and (how) he raised to the vault the water that flowed below. God spoke a word concerning all those things, and it was so.

8. Showing that God created man far more honorable than any other creature that God made before man.[50]

8.1. And when he wished to create a small human life, then God needed to take counsel instead of causing the man's being by simply speaking a word, as was the case with all the other great, marvelous, and awesome things that he did, when he simply said, "Let it be", and it was so.[51] Nor did man come into being together with the other living creatures of the earth, but however small his life was, God formed man separately from all the animals and apart from all the creatures.

8.2. Consider also this, that he does not simply form (man),[52] as he did the light, and the vault, and the gardens, and the living creatures, and the rest of the great things, for he spoke them into existence without taking counsel. But when he formed man, he first takes counsel, for the Scriptures state, "And God said, 'Let us make man in our image and likeness'", and henceforth he forms man, which is not what he did | with the rest of the living beings—the birds and the 34^{r}/80
fish, including the big ones, and the reptiles, and the beasts, and the livestock, and the elephants[53]—but God took the dust of the ground and made man, as the Scriptures say.[54]

8.3. Why is it, then, that God did not take counsel concerning such amusing and awesome works that he did? Indeed, how mighty are the heavens! How wide and deep is the earth! How vast is the space of the seas with all the infinite number of things in them, and of the hosts of the stars assembled together! (And consider) the beauty of the moon, and the never-ending glory of the sun, and the holy angels themselves that stand in the glory of his divinity, "numbering myriads of myriads and thousands of thousands" (Rev. 5:11), who shine and glow with the never-fading light that greatly transcends the glory of the sun!

---

50 **Showing that God created man far more honorable than any other creature that God made before man.**] *omitted*

51 when he simply said, "Let it be", and it was so.] when he simply spoke and had them immediately come into being.

52 Consider also this, that he does not simply form (man)] *omitted*

53 and the livestock, and the elephants] and the elephants, and the livestock

54 as the Scriptures say.] *omitted. MS 61 adds*: **Showing that he created man far more honorable than any other creature that he made before man.**

вса сїа. не рекоша книги. ꙗко реⷱ бг҃ъ ѡ нихъ
сотвориⷨ сие и ѡно. коликоⷤ ꙋмаление ѿ всѣⷯ
ѿ тѣхъ чл҃къ. не ꙗкоⷤ ли ничтоже сꙋщи чл҃къ.
в тацѣи мнозѣи и велицѣи твари. и ѡ чл҃цѣ
гл҃еть бг҃ъ сотворимъ чл҃ка рекоша книги. ~
Ꙗко побаⷮе прилѣжнѣ вниⷨма всакꙋ гл҃ꙋ во
ст҃омъ писанїи. Не оубо мимохоⷣ словесъ про
читаа книгоу ст҃оу. что раⷣ рече бг҃ъ сотво
риⷨ чл҃ка. не гл҃авъ таковаго совѣта преже
34v/82 ни ѡ единои твари. ни ѡ чи҃номъ агг҃льскомъ
бесчислїи. здѣⷤ ѡ единоⷨ чл҃цы гл҃еть бг҃ъ совѣ
тꙋа сотвориⷨ чл҃ка. и аще не бы всѣⷯ твареи
лоучши и вышьши бы҃ чл҃къ. не гл҃алъ бы бг҃ъ
совѣтꙋа сотворимъ чл҃ка. и аще бы точеⷩ
бы҃ чл҃къ твари всеи бывшеи преⷤ его. не бы
взѧ҃ самъ бг҃ъ перьсть ѿ землѧ и созда҃ чл҃ка.
таковою чⷭ҇тию на҃ всею тварию бг҃ъ почте
чл҃ка. ꙗко рꙋкою своею взѧти перьсть ѿ
землѧ и создати чл҃ка. и преⷤ созданїа воспри
ꙗти совѣⷮ и гл҃ати сотворимъ чл҃ка. ѿселеⷤ
оубо даетса разоумѣти ꙗко тваⷬ чл҃ка ради
бысть. аще землѧ аще мора. аще тверⷣь
аще и вса ꙗⷤ в ниⷯ. вса та чл҃ка раⷣ сотворилъ еⷭ҇
бг҃ъ. вѣдѣⷤ и ѿ сего внеⷢа гл҃ють книгы. ꙗкоⷤ
реⷱ бг҃ъ да владѣⷮе всею землею. и ѡбладаⷮе ры
бами и птицами и скоты. Чтоⷤ ради в та
цѣи велицеи чести чл҃къ. да совѣтꙋетъ бг҃ъ
ѡ неⷨ преⷤ и гл҃еть сотвориⷨ чл҃ка. таⷤ ѕижеⷮ его
взеⷤ перьсть ѿ землѧ. не велиѧ҃ оубо нбⷭ҇а.
и не оукрашено ли многою лѣпотою. не мно
гою҃ славою сл҃нце намъ ѡзарꙗше. земли же
35r/82 широта и морю простраⷩство. не многою ли
добротою оутворена. и не гл҃еть тамо бг҃ъ
сотвориⷨ нбⷭ҇о и землю и прочаа. послѣⷣнююⷤ
тварь здати хота гл҃еть сотвориⷨ чл҃ка.
не простоⷤ реⷱ бг҃ъ сотвориⷨ чл҃ка и оумоⷧ҇ча. но при
ложиⷧ есть к семꙋ еще и сие. сотвориⷨ чл҃ка реⷱ

8.4. When God was making all this, the Scriptures do not say that God spoke of them, "Let us make this and that", ⟨but that he simply said, and it came to be in the way he commanded⟩. How insignificant is man compared to all those things! Isn't man nothing in comparison with such great and numerous creatures? And it is concerning him, that God says, "Let us make man", as it was asserted in the Scriptures (Gen. 1:26).

9. Showing that we must pay careful attention to every word in the sacred Scripture.[55]

9.1. Now, do not ignore (specific) words when you read the sacred Scripture. Why did God say, "Let us make man" (Gen. 1:26), while taking no such counsel when he previously spoke of | other creatures, not even of the wonderful 34v/82
angelic host? But here, only when speaking of man, God takes counsel, "Let us make man". God would not have taken counsel about man (with the words) "Let us make man", had man not been better than and superior to all the creatures. And God would not have taken the dust of the ground to form man, had man not been of greater worth than all the other creatures that were before him. For God honored man over the rest of creation so greatly, that he took the dust of the earth with his own hand and formed man. And before creating him, he took counsel and said, "Let us make man".

9.2. From this, then, we are to understand that the entire creation, whether the earth, or the seas, or the vault, or anything that is in them, was made for the sake of man; God has made them all for the sake of man. And we also see it from the fact that the Scriptures assert that God said, "Let him rule over the entire earth and subdue the fish, and the birds, and the livestock" (Gen. 1:28).

9.3. What is so great about man's honor, that God takes counsel about him before creating and says, "Let us make man", and also forms him by taking the dust of the ground? Indeed, are the heavens not mighty, and are they not arrayed with much beauty, and does the sun not shine on it with great glory? And are the breadth of the earth | and the expanse of the sea not framed with 35r/82
such great goodness? And yet, God does not say concerning them, "Let us make the heaven and the earth, and other things". But when he wished to form the very last creature, he said, "Let us make man". And God did not simply say, "Let us make man", and then become quiet, but also added to the words, "Let us

55 **Showing that we must pay careful attention to every word in the sacred Scripture.] Showing that God's words are not in vain, and that for that reason, we must receive them with great fear, far more so than the words of a king.**

по ѡбразоу нш҃емꙋ и по подобию. и здѣ пакы рекъ сотвори̑ чл҃ка по ѡбразоу нш҃емꙋ. и не а бие оумо̑ча. да приложилъ есть и по по̑бию. Ꙗко не празны бж҃їа гл҃ы сего ра̑ подоба̑е вни мати е̑ со многы̑ страхо̑ мно̑ па̑. нежели црв҃а гл҃а. Не оудоволилъ есть создати чл҃ка по ѡбразоу точию но и по по̑бию гл҃еть. что ꙋбо есть сие. с ꙋе оубо гл҃ати в бж҃їихъ книга̑ невозможно есть. егда̑ самъ гл҃еть в кни га̑. празно̑ ли хощеши положити бж҃ие ре чение. и кто боуде̑ тако безоуменъ. да бж҃ие речение празно̑ во̑мнить быти. аще гл҃ъ црв҃ъ ꙗковъ же боуде̑ не лѣпо мнѣ̑ праздѣ̑. не оубо̑ и по̑ба̑е что црви празно̑ гл҃ати. аще̑ и цр҃ь ѡба̑ ничи̑ же оуньши чл҃ка. поне̑ чл҃къ есть и цр҃ь. ꙗкови̑ вси чл҃цы. такова̑ чл҃ка сꙋща. 35v/83 точию цр҃твїа достоꙗние имꙋща. гл҃юща что любо не празно̑ прочи̑ чл҃комъ мнѣти лѣпо. и са момꙋ томꙋ цр҃ю чл҃коу сꙋщꙋ. не подоба̑е что пра̑но гл҃ати. колико̑ бг҃ъ разньствꙋе̑ ѿ цр҃а. то бж҃ие ли речение празно хощеши положити. и бг҃а само̑ мниши празно̑ гл҃ати. да которыа м҃ти достои̑ боудеши сїа помышлꙗа. не хо щеши бг҃ꙋ дати достои̑ства. чл҃коу цр҃ю по даеши достои̑ство. не просто ꙋбо восхощи мимохо̑ти бж҃ие речение. но прочитаа при make man", the phrase, "in our image and likeness". And here, again, he said, "Let us make man in our image", and did not become quiet immediately after that, but instead added, "and in our likeness".[56]

10. Showing that God's words are not in vain, and that for that reason, we must receive them with great fear, much more so than the words of a king.[57]

10.1. He has not been satisfied with saying only "in our image", but also says "and likeness". What is this, then? It is in no way possible[58] that God's Scriptures would say anything in vain. And since it is God himself who speaks in the Scriptures, do you really want to treat the words of God as useless? And who would be so insane as to imagine the words of God to be useless?

10.2. Take the words of a king! How foolish would it be to think of them as useless, for it does not befit the king to say any useless thing! And even if we take the king, he is no better than any other person, for though he is a king, he is also a human. He is a man like all other people, | with the only difference 35v/83
that he possesses an honor of (ruling) a kingdom and saying what is pleasing to him.[59] It is better for other people not to take his words as useless, and for the king himself, who is a human (like all others), it does not befit him to say anything that is useless. But how greatly different is God from a human king!

10.3. So, do you want to treat the words of God as useless and to think that God himself spoke useless things? What mercy, if any, are you worthy of with this kind of thinking? Do you not wish to give[60] God as much honor as you give to a human king? Instead of simply ignoring the words of God, then, read them

56 But when he wished to form the very last creature, he said, "Let us make man". And God did not simply say, "Let us make man", and then become quiet, but also added to the words, "Let us make man", the phrase, "in our image and likeness". And here, again, he said, "Let us make man in our image", and did not become quiet immediately after that, but instead added, "and in our likeness".] But when he wished to form the very last creature, he did not simply say, "Let us make man", and become quiet, but also added to the words, "Let us make man", the phrase, "in our image". Nor did he become quiet there, but added further, "and likeness".

57 **Showing that God's words are not empty, and for that reason, we must receive them with great fear, far more so than the words of a king.**] *omitted*

58 It is in no way possible] For it is impossible

59 And even if we take the king, he is no better than any other person, for though he is a king, he is also a human. He is a man like all other people, with the only difference being that he possesses the honor of (ruling) a kingdom and saying what is pleasing to him.] And the king is a human like all other people, with the only difference being that he possesses the honor of (ruling) a kingdom and saying what is pleasing to him.

60 to give] *omitted*

лѣжнѣ разоумѣваи. ре҃ бг҃ъ сотвори҃ чл҃ка по wбразоу н҃шемꙋ и по по҃бию. Бг҃мъ[61] реченнаа сотвори҃ чл҃ка по wбразꙋ нашемꙋ и по по҃бию разоумѣти. помолимса самомꙋ томꙋ бг҃ви рекшемꙋ. сотвори҃ чл҃ка по wбразоу н҃шемꙋ и по подобию. да дасть и намъ хꙋдымъ ст҃ое его речение разоумѣти. бе҃ его бо бл҃гти разоумѣти ꙗко҃ подобае҃ ст҃ое его речение невозможно. и оубо по wбразоу и по по҃бию соблюде҃ послѣди гл҃ати. нн҃ѣ помолимса разоумѣ҃ что есть речено. еже есть по wбразоу н҃ше моу. а не по wбразоу моемꙋ. сотвори҃ ре ре҃ 36r/85 бг҃ъ чл҃ка по wбразоу н҃шемꙋ. а не по wбразоу моемꙋ сотворю чл҃ка. Ꙗко по ст҃мꙋ писанию единъ е҃ бг҃ъ. показоуеть гл҃ъ бж҃їи и единославны҃ емꙋ нѣкой равны҃ Рѣша книги. и ре҃ бг҃ъ сотвори҃ чл҃ка по wбразоу н҃шемꙋ. а не ре҃ бг҃ъ сотворю чл҃ка по wбразꙋ моемꙋ. здѣ видитса. ꙗко и спомощниковъ бг҃ъ приемле҃ дѣлоу. а не едино токмо совѣтꙋе҃. сотвори҃ бо ре҃ чл҃ка по wбразоу н҃шемꙋ. егда бг҃ъ н҃бо и землю и вса ꙗ҃ в ни҃ сотвори в шесть днеи точию. не воспрїатъ спомагающи҃ емꙋ. ни совѣтꙋющи҃. на сотворение н҃беси и земли. и всѣ҃ иже в ни҃. внегда҃ чл҃ка единого создати совѣтоуе҃ бг҃ъ. и аки спомагающи҃ приемле҃. сотвори҃ бо ре҃ чл҃ка. а не ре҃ да боуде҃ чл҃къ. чи оубо множае н҃беси чл҃къ. или колицѣмъ

61 *In the margin*: гл҃ ві.

carefully and think of them diligently:[62] God[63] said, "Let us make man in our image and likeness" (Gen. 1:26).

11. CHAPTER 10.[64]

11.1. To understand the phrase spoken by God, "Let us make man in our image and likeness", let us pray to the very God who said, "Let us make man in our image and likeness" (Gen. 1:26), so that he may allow us, too, poor men, to grasp his holy words. It is impossible to understand his holy words in the way that we should, apart from his grace.

11.2. Now, we will discuss the expression "in our image and likeness" later, but at this point, we will pray to understand the phrase that says, "Let us make man in *our* image", and not "in *my* image". For God said, "Let us make | man in *our* 36r/85
image", and not "I will make man in *my* image".

12. Showing that although there is one God according to the sacred Scripture, the words of God nevertheless indicate some, who possess the same glory and are equal with God.[65]

12.1. Now, the Scriptures asserted, "And God said, 'Let us make man in *our* image'" (Gen. 1:26), and they did not state, "God said, 'I will make man in *my* image'". Here, we can see that God not only takes counsel, but that he also calls upon the helpmates to share in his work, for he said, "Let us make man in our image".[66] When God was making the heaven and the earth and everything that was in them, he made them in just six days, without calling upon any helpmates or counselors to create the heaven and the earth and everything that was in them. And it is only when God formed man, that he took counsel and, so to speak, invited the helpmates, for he said, "Let us make man", instead of saying, "Let there be man".

---

62 think of them diligently.] consider them diligently with your mind.

63 God] thus, God

64 CHAPTER 10.] **On the fact that the divinely inspired Scriptures of the book of Genesis reveal some, who are co-eternal with God, and proper to him in their being, and have equal power with him. CHAPTER 10.**

65 **Showing that although there is one God according to the sacred Scripture, the words of God nevertheless indicate some, who possess the same glory and are equal with God.**] *omitted*

66 counsel, but that he also calls upon the helpmates to share in his work, for he said, "Let us make man in our image".] counsel, when he says, "Let us make", but that God also calls upon the helpmates to share in his work, for he said, "Let us make man in (our) image".

пространнѣе землꙗ чл҃къ. и коликаа вноу
трь творенїа въ чл҃цы множаиша паче ꙗже
въ нб҃си и земли. да спомощники прїимеⷮ сотво
рити чл҃ка. или малѣиши чл҃ка нб҃са и землꙗ
и ꙗⷤ соуⷮ в ниⷯ. ꙗко не потребова ѡ ниⷯ совѣтоваⷮ
бг҃ъ. ни спомагающиⷯ емꙋ приꙗⷮ тогда. внегⷣа
твораше нб҃о и землю. и вса сꙋщаа в ниⷯ. понеⷤ
36v/86 егда чл҃ка сотвориⷮ. тогда совѣтоваⷮ изволи.
и спомагающиⷯ потребова. не реⷱ бо сотворю
чл҃ка по ѡбразоу моемꙋ. но сотвориⷨ реⷱ бг҃ъ чл҃ка
по ѡбразоу нш҃емꙋ. И пакы инако недооумѣ
тено слово въ средꙋ вниде. рѣша ꙋбо книгы
в началѣ. ꙗко искони сотвори бг҃ъ нб҃о и землю.
здѣ сказоуеⷮ ꙗко ѿ верхоу творити начаⷮ бг҃ъ.
сотвори бо реⷱ иⷡскони бг҃ъ нб҃о и землю. нб҃о преⷤ.
потоⷨ землю сотвори. не ѿ долꙋ начень тво
рити ꙗкоⷤ мы. мы бо егда что сотворꙗемъ
ѿ долꙋ начинаеⷨ творити. бг҃ъⷤ не тако но ѿ
верхоу начаⷮ творити. и по творению бы на
шемꙋ. подобало бы ѕѣло внегда твориⷮ нб҃са.
и совѣта и спомагающиⷯ. понеже ѿ верхоу
нб҃о сотвори. ѿ долꙋ несꙋщи еще земли. да тре
бѣ совѣта. како ꙋтвердити кровъ ѡснова
нию не сꙋщꙋ. требѣ спомагающиⷯ въ творе
нїи нб҃съ. воⷤе поⷣдержати творимое. понеⷤ
не имѣющꙋ ѡснованїа. на нем же оутве
рдитиⷭ кровꙋ. и к такомꙋ величествꙋ нбⷭ҇но
мꙋ. бг҃ъ не требова совѣта на творение еⷢ.
и таковаⷢ величества нбⷭ҇наго толицеи та
37r/86–87 гости. ѿ верхоу сотворꙗемѣ. не призва спо
магающиⷯ или споⷣдержавающиⷯ. донелѣ же
ѡснование оутвердитса землꙗ. на неиⷤ
поставлено боудеⷮ нб҃о. малѣишееⷤ творение
чл҃ка созидати. восприꙗⷮ совѣтоваⷮ бг҃ъ гл҃ꙗ.
сотвориⷨ чл҃ка по ѡбразоу нш҃емꙋ и по подобию.
и сие малѣишее здание. не ѿ верхоу начина
емо видитса но ѿ долꙋ. рѣша бо книгы ꙗко
созда бг҃ъ чл҃ка взеⷨ персть ѿ землꙗ. зиже
мо еже ѿ долꙋ ѕижетса на ѡснованїи. и заⷣ

12.2. In what way, then, is man greater than the heavens? Or in what way is man vaster than the earth? And how many created things are there in man in comparison with the far more numerous things in the heaven and the earth, that he[67] was urged to call upon the helpmates ⟨exclusively⟩ for the creation of man? Or are the heavens and the earth and everything that is in them smaller than man, that God did not need to take counsel about them, nor to call upon the helpmates at the moment when he was making the heaven and the earth and everything that was in them? For | when he was making man, at that very 36^{v}/86
moment, he chose to take counsel and began to need the helpmates. For God did not say, "I will make man in *my* image", but said, "Let us make man in *our* image".

12.3. In the midst of this, there comes another perplexing message here. Thus, in the opening words of the book, it is said that "in the beginning, God made the heaven and the earth" (Gen. 1:1), which is an indication here that God began to create from the top. For it is said that "In the beginning, God made the heaven and the earth". He first made the heaven, and then he made the earth.[68] He did not begin to create (what is) underneath as we do it—when we make something, we begin to do it from below. But God did not do it in that way; instead, he began to create from the top. And after making us, it would have been especially fitting for him to require counsel and helpmates in order to make the heavens.

12.4. Since he ⟨began⟩ to create the heaven from the top, when the earth below did not yet come into being, he needed counsel on how to establish a shelter without having a foundation for it. In creating the heavens, he needed helpmates to support what was being made, for there was no foundation on which to establish the shelter. And yet God did not (deem it) necessary to take counsel in order to make such majestic heavens, and in creating such a great weight | of these majestic heavens in the upper realm, he did not call upon the 37^{r}/
helpmates or supporting companions (to assist him) until after the earth had 86–87
been established, and the heavens had been set on it.

12.5. However, God did take counsel in forming man, the smallest creation, saying, "Let us make man in our image and likeness" (Gen. 1:26). And as we can see, he began to make this smallest creation not from above, but from below, for the Scriptures stated that God created man by taking "the dust of the ground" (Gen. 2:7). And that which was formed from below, was formed on the exist-

---

67 he] God

68 He first made the heaven, and then, he made the earth.] He made heaven before the earth, and the earth he made afterward.

ти се҇ начинаа совѣтꙋа ре҇ бг҃ъ сотворимъ чл҃ка по ѡбразоу нш҃емꙋ и по пⷪ҇биию. акы многа тагота и безмѣрно величество чл҃къ хотѧаше быти. или многосꙋгоубно величаиши и тѧжчаиши нб҃си и землѧ. чл҃ч҃а тва҇ хоташе быти. но ѡ семъ слово во времѧ е҇ речетса. нн҃ѣⷤ ѡно смотрѣти подобаетъ. ѩко книгы рѣша бг҃а едино҇ быти. бг҃ъⷤ рече сотвориⷨ чл҃ка по ѡбразоу нш҃емꙋ и по подобию. а не ре҇ сотворю чл҃ка по ѡбразоу своеⷨꙋ. ~

Ѩко по бж҃ию гл҃ꙋ имаⷮ бг҃ъ пⷪ҇бныⷯ емꙋ и соѡбразныⷯ емꙋ сꙋщиⷯ.

37ᵛ/87 Аще бг҃ъ ре҇ ѩкоⷤ книги гл҃ють. сотвориⷨ чл҃ка по ѡбразоу нш҃емꙋ а не по ѡбразоу моемꙋ сотворю. показоуⷮе здѣ книга ѩко не к себѣ самомꙋ бг҃ъ ре҇ но ко иⷤ ту с ниⷨ соущимъ. сотворимъ чл҃ка по ѡбразоу нш҃емꙋ и по пⷪ҇биию. не къ прилꙋчившиⷨ же са просто к коимъ тꙋ ре҇ бг҃ъ. сотвориⷨ чл҃ка по ѡбразоу нш҃емꙋ. но к соѡбразныⷨ емоу видитса речение. понеⷤ единъ ѡбраⷥ зижеⷮ бг҃ъ. ѩкоⷤ по своемꙋ ѡбразоу. такоⷤ и по ѡбразоу сꙋщиⷯ с нимъ к нимъⷤ гл҃а зижеть чл҃ка. сотвориⷨ бо ре҇ чл҃ка по ѡбразоу нш҃емоу. ~

ing foundation,[69] and in starting to form it, God took counsel and said, "Let us make man in our image and likeness", as if he wanted man to be of immeasurable majesty and of great weight, or even (wished) the human creature to be many times more majestic and weightier than the heavens and the earth. But we will discuss this at its own time.[70]

12.6. And now, we must look at what the Scriptures said about the unity of God, (considering that) God said, "Let us make man in *our* image and likeness" (Gen. 1:26), and did not say, "I will make man in *my* own image".

13. Showing that according to the divine words (of Scripture), God has those who are like him and share a common image with him.[71] | 37ᵛ/87

13.1. Since God said, as the Scriptures state, "Let us make man in *our* image", and not, "In *my* image I will make him", this fact in the Scripture[72] shows here that God was not speaking to himself, but to those who existed with him, ⟨and to them, God said⟩, "Let us make man in our image". As we can see, God spoke the words, "Let us make man in our image" not to those who just happened to be there, but to those who share a common image with him. For while God forms one single image (in man) after himself, he also does that after the image of those who are with him, and it is to them, that he speaks when he forms man.[73] For he said, "Let us make man in our image".[74]

---

69 And that which was formed underneath, was formed on the existing foundation,] And that which was formed on the foundation, was formed underneath,

70 *MS 61 adds*: **Showing that according to the divine words (of Scripture), God has those who are like him and share a common image with him.**

71 **Showing that according to the divine words (of Scripture), God has those who are like him and share a common image with him.**] *omitted*

72 Scripture] divinely inspired Scripture

73 For while God forms one single image (in man) after himself, he also does that after the image of those who are with him, and it is to them, that he speaks when he forms man.] For while God forms one single image (in man), he also bestows on him a mind, because in addition to forming man after himself, he also forms him after the image of those who are with him, and it is to them, that he speaks when he makes man.

74 image".] image", and did not say, "I will make man in my image".

Ꙗко единоѡбразницы бг҃ꙋ равночⷭ҇тни емꙋ соуⷮ.
по гл҃ꙋ его и творцы твари вкꙋпѣ сꙋ҃ з бг҃омъ
равномоцни емꙋ сꙋще Показоуⷮе оубо книга симъ бж҃їи
мъ речениемъ. нѣкоиⷯ соущиⷯ съ бг҃мъ соѡбра
знымъ быти тогда. ѩко рⷱ҇е бг҃ъ сотворимъ
чл҃ка по ѡбразоу нш҃емꙋ. сие слово показоуⷮе
по истиннѣ соѡбразныⷯ бг҃оу. и блⷥиⷯ бг҃а соущиⷯ.
и достоиныⷯ бж҃иа и совѣта и дѣиствиа с ниⷨ.
поⷤне рече по ѡбразоу нш҃емꙋ чл҃ка сотворимъ.
ѩвлѩющꙋ словоу ѩко не к меⷩшимъ ниⷤ къ слоу
жащимъ речено. не повелѣваа бо рⷱ҇е да сотво
38r/89 рите чл҃ка по ѡбразоу моемꙋ. или сотворите чл҃ка
по ѡбразоу вашемꙋ. но совѣтꙋюще речение есть.
и прїимание соⷠ҇разныⷯ себѣ. равносилныⷯ еди
ночⷭ҇тныⷯ емꙋ. рече бо сотворимъ чл҃ка по ѡⷠ҇ра
зоу нш҃емꙋ. къ единосодѣиствꙋющымъ емоу.
совѣщатеⷧ҇ство есть. и тоⷤ дѣиствꙋющимъ ра
вно бг҃оу. прїимание къ сотворению знаменꙋⷮе
книга. и къ блⷥи его сꙋщимъ речение. а не ѿ далеча
пребывающиⷯ и стоѩщиⷯ. но иⷤ оу бг҃а сꙋщиⷯ бес по
срⷣ҇ства. не рⷱ҇е бо бг҃ъ прїидѣте и сотворимъ
чл҃ка. еⷤ бы назнаменало ѿ далеча призывание.
еⷤ рецы прїидѣте ѿ иного мѣста звати есть.
имѣющее посрⷣ҇ство межоу бг҃а и призывае
мыми иⷨ. поⷤне идꙋще прїидꙋⷮ к бг҃оу. нн҃ѣⷤ по
емлеⷮ бж҃ие речение к сотворению чл҃ка. сꙋщыⷯ
оу бг҃а бес посрⷣ҇ства пребывающиⷯ. рече бо сотво
римъ чл҃ка. показоуⷮе не приходѩщиⷯ къ бг҃ꙋ. но иⷤ
съ бг҃мъ сꙋщихъ и оу бг҃а сꙋщиⷨ тꙋ. рⷱ҇е сотвориⷨ чл҃ка

14. Showing that those who possess the same image as God are also equal in honor to him, according to his words, and being the co-makers in creation, they possess equal power together with him.[75]

14.1. By these words of God, then, the Scripture reveals[76] certain beings, who existed with God at the moment (of creation) and shared a common image with him. Considering that God said, "Let us make man in our image", this phrase reveals those who truly shared God's image, and existed closely with God, and were worthy of participating in God's counsel and his work. Therefore, he said, "Let us make man in our image".[77]

14.2. And this statement reveals that these words are not directed at those who are lower or have a status of slaves, for he did not say it as a command, "You, make | man in my image!", or "You, make man in your image"! Instead, 38r/89
these words were spoken when he took counsel with and called upon those who shared a common image with him, who were equal in power, and who had the same honor as him.[78]

14.3. For (by the phrase in which) he said to them, "Let us make man in our image", the Scripture indicates the "counsel" he took with those who shared the same work with him, and the "call" for those who, being equal with God, were to do the identical work of creation. This phrase was directed to those who existed closely with him; (more specifically), not to those who were far away or apart from him, but to those who existed with God and had nothing mediating between them. For God did not say, "Come, and let us make man", which would indicate a call from afar. And if he were to say, "Come", it would imply a call from a different place and the presence of a mediating thing between God and those whom he called, and it would be by means of (that mediating thing), that the latter were to come to God.

14.4. But the phrase is said at this point to reveal those who existed with God at the creation of man, without being (separated from him) by a certain mediating thing. For God said, "Let us make man", showing not those who came to God, but those who existed with God, and it was to them who were with God,

---

75 **Showing that those who possess the same image as God are also equal in honor to him, according to his words, and being the co-makers in creation, they possess equal power together with him.**] *omitted*

76 By these words of God, then, the Scripture reveals] By this, then, the truly authentic Scripture reveals

77 *MS 61 adds*: **Showing that those who possess the same image as God are also equal in honor to him, according to his words, and being the co-makers in creation, they possess equal power with him.**

78 him.] him, who were equal in power, and who had the same dignity as him.

показоуеⷮ ꙗко къ единоѡбразнымъ и тоⷤѡбразнымъ бв҃и таковое реченїе есть. Аще не бы единоѡбразны были бг҃ꙋ. и не тоⷤѡбразны бв҃и. к нимⷤ рече бг҃ъ сотвориⷨ члк҃а по ѡбразоу нш҃емꙋ.
38ᵛ/90 оубо мноⷢѡбразеⷩ бы члк҃ъ бы҃. и разназраченъ. и ꙗко бы се было во единоⷨ животноⷨ мноⷢѡбразно и разнозрачно составленїе. видиⷨ оубо ꙗко члк҃ъ единоѡбразенъ. едиⷩ составъ члкꙋ. и едиⷩ зракъ имаⷮ члк҃ъ. и по семꙋ бл҃горазоумно ѕѣло. ꙗⷦ соѡбраⷥни сꙋще и тоⷤѡбразни тїи бг҃ꙋ. к нимⷤ бг҃ъ реⷱ сотвориⷨ члк҃а по ѡбразоу нш҃емꙋ. и ꙗко к соущиⷨ оу бг҃а бес посреⷣства реⷱ бг҃ъ сотвориⷨ члк҃а. понеⷤ не реⷱ бг҃ъ призываа еⷤ прїидѣте сотворимъ члк҃а. но реⷱ сотвориⷨ члк҃а. еⷤ есть с нимъ сꙋщимъ реⷱ бг҃ъ. а ꙗко не к себѣ самомꙋ се реⷱ бг҃ъ ѡ члц҃ы сотворити его. но к сꙋщимъ оу неⷢ рече. понеⷤ не реⷱ бг҃ъ сотворю члк҃а по ѡбразоу своемꙋ но реⷱ бг҃ъ сотворимъ члк҃а по ѡбразоу нш҃емꙋ. по семоуⷤ ꙋбо разоумѣти ꙗкоⷤ дѣтеⷩни сꙋще и тїи. к ним же рече бг҃ъ сотворимъ члк҃а. по семꙋ словеси ꙗⷤ бг҃ъ твораше вкꙋпѣ съ бг҃оⷨ творꙗхꙋ и сами тїи. к нимⷤ рече бг҃ъ. вкоу потворитеⷩно бо совѣтованїе бж҃ие со ѡнѣми. к нимⷤ рече бг҃ъ сотворити члк҃а. не рече бо к ниⷨ ꙗко сотворю члк҃а по своемꙋ ѡбразоу. но ѡⷠщитеⷩѣ. и равнодѣиственѣ соприемлꙗ
39ʳ/91 соѡⷠразныⷯ себѣ к сотворенїю. реⷱ бг҃ъ сотвориⷨ члк҃а по ѡбразоу нш҃емꙋ. И сїа оубо бл҃горазоумна соуⷮ. ꙗко бг҃ъ совѣтова сꙋщиⷨ оу неⷢ бес посреⷣства емоу. и соѡбразнымъ емꙋ. и сосодѣтеⷩствꙋющиⷨ емꙋ. и тоⷤ творащимъ вкоупѣ съ бг҃мъ ꙗⷤ бг҃ъ сотвори. ꙗко реⷱ бг҃ъ сотворимъ члк҃а по ѡбразоу нш҃емоу. Рѣшаⷤ ми крилошане не сказа моисѣи разоумно к комꙋ реⷱ бг҃ъ сотвориⷨ члк҃а. точию сказа ꙗко реⷱ бг҃ъ сотвориⷨ члк҃а.

that he[79] said, "Let us make man". This shows[80] that the phrase was directed to those who possessed the same and identical image as God.

14.5. If they had not possessed the identical image of God, and if that image had not been the same as God's, then the phrase which God spoke to them, "Let us make man in our image", | would have implied that man had to possess mul- 38^{v}/90
tiple images and multiple appearances. And how would multiple images and appearances fit in the constitution of one living animal? Now,[81] we see that man possesses the same image, and man's being is composed of the same thing, and the same man has one general appearance. And it especially makes sense, then, that those concerning whom God said, "Let us make man in our image", would also possess the same and identical image as God.

14.6. And (it is also reasonable) that God was speaking to those who were with him, and this—without any mediation, when he said, "Let us make man". For God spoke not by calling, "Come, let us make man", but rather saying, "Let us make", which indicates that God spoke to those who were with him. And (again), in making man, God did not speak to himself. Instead, he spoke to those who were with him because God did not say, "I will make man in my own image", but said, "Let us make man in our image". And so, we can understand, then,[82] that those beings did the identical work, and it was to them, that he said, "Let us make man".

14.7. According to these words, by which God was creating, God spoke to those who themselves were doing the identical work together with God. For the counseling of God with these assumes a common work, and it is to them, that he said, "Let us make man". For[83] instead of saying to them, "I will make man in *my* image", | God said, "Let us make man in *our* image",[84] inviting those 39^{r}/91
who shared a common image with him to participate in the common and equal work of creation. And it is reasonable, then, that God took counsel with those who were with him—for "God said, 'Let us make man in our image'"—and this without mediation between him and those who shared a common image with him and were doing the identical work of creation together with God, the Maker of all those things.

14.8. But the kliros-chanters said to me, "Moses did not state it intelligibly, to whom exactly God said, 'Let us make man'. He only mentioned that God said, 'Let us make man'".

79 he] God
80 This shows] And the fact that God said, "in our image we will make man", shows
81 Now,] But
82 And so, we can understand, then,] From this, we can also understand
83 For] Indeed,
84 God said, "Let us make man in our image",] he said, "Let us make man",

Взыскание х комꙋ рⷱ҇е бг҃ъ сотворⷨи чл҃ка по w бразꙋ нш҃емꙋ и по [подобию] Азъ ѿвѣщавъ рекⷪ҇ к нимъ. прочее помолимсѧ бл҃гомꙋ гв҃и бг҃ꙋ да дасть намъ разоумѣти правѣ и се. к которымъ таковымъ рⷱ҇е бг҃ъ. сотворимъ чл҃ка по wбра зоу нш҃емꙋ. кои оубо блⷥи бг҃а бес посрⷣества сowбразни емꙋ и сосодѣтⷩ҇ени твари. понⷤ҇е не писа моусѣи ꙗвленно. к комꙋ рече бг҃ъ со творⷨи чл҃ка по wбразоу нш҃емꙋ. Ꙗко аггл҃и и херꙋвими не сowбразни бг҃ꙋ. нⷤ҇и совѣтники емꙋ нѣсть бо побⷪ҇ни бг҃ꙋ властию но слꙋги сꙋⷮ бж҃їа аггл҃и.

Повѣдаюⷮ оубо книгы. аггл҃и и херꙋвими сотворꙗа[85] бг҃ъ тогⷣа к сⷨи рече. къ агглⷨо или к херꙋвимⷨо
39v/92
сотворⷨи чл҃ка по wбразоу нш҃емꙋ. аще сowбраⷥны. бг҃ꙋ аггл҃и и херꙋвими. да к нⷨи рече бг҃ъ сотворимъ чл҃ка по wбразоу нш҃емоу. и како чл҃къ не пламⷩ҇ено зраченъ по wбразоу аггл҃а. какⷤ҇о и не пернⷮа по wбра зоу херꙋвⷨискоу чл҃къ. почтⷤ҇о и глꙗдаⷮе чл҃къ двѣма wчима точию. а не имⷮа многⷯы wчесъ ꙗкоже и херꙋвимъ. и по семꙋ мощно разоумѣти. ꙗко не ко аггломъ нⷤ҇и к херꙋвимⷨо рⷱ҇е бг҃ъ сотворимъ чл҃ка по wбразоу нш҃емꙋ. понⷤ҇е чл҃къ нѣсть w гнезрачⷩ҇е ꙗкⷤ҇о и аггл҃и. нⷤ҇и пернⷮа и многоѻчⷮи чл҃къ ꙗкⷤ҇о и херꙋвими. познаваⷮе же сѧ ѿ пи санїа. ꙗко и не сowбразны бг҃оу аггл҃и и херꙋ

85 *In the margin*: глⷡ҇а аı҃.

15. Investigation as to whom God said, "Let us make man in our image and likeness" (Gen. 1:26).[86]

15.1. And in response, I said to them: Regarding all the other issues, let us pray to the good Lord God that he may grant us correct understanding about this as well, namely, about who it was to whom God said, "Let us make man in our image", taking into consideration that they were close to God—and this without mediation—and that they shared the same image and did the same work of creation. For Moses did not write clearly as to who it was to whom God said, "Let us make man in our image".

16. Showing that the angels and the cherubim do not share God's image, nor are they his counselors, for they are not like God in power, but instead, the angels are God's servants. CHAPTER 11.[87]

16.1. The Scripture will tell us, then, whether it was after the creation of the angels and the cherubim, and whether it was to the angels or the cherubim that he spoke, when he said, | "Let us make man in our image".[88] If the angels and 39v/92
the cherubim share God's image so that God could say to them, "Let us make man in our image", then how is it that man does not appear with flames according to the angelic image? And how is it that man is without wings according to the image of the cherubim?[89] And why is it that man sees things with only two eyes, instead of having many eyes like the cherubim? In view of this, we can learn that[90] God did not speak to the angels or to the cherubim (when he said),

---

86 **Investigation as to whom God said, "Let us make man in our image and likeness" (Gen. 1:26).**] *omitted*

87 **Showing that the angels and the cherubim do no share God's image nor are they his counselors, for they are not like God in power, but instead, the angels are God's servants. CHAPTER 11.**] **Investigation, according to the holy book of Genesis, as to whom God said, "Let us make man in our image and likeness" (Gen. 1:26). CHAPTER 11.**

88 The Scripture will tell us, then, whether it was after the creation of the angels and the cherubim, and whether it was to the angels or the cherubim that he spoke, when he said, "Let us make man in our image".] The Scripture will tell us, then, whether it was to the angels and the cherubim that he spoke, when God said, "Let us make man in our image". **Showing that the angels and the cherubim do not share God's image, nor are they God's counselors, for they are not like God in power, but instead, the angels are God's servants.**

89 image of the cherubim?] image of the angels and the cherubim?

90 In view of this, we can learn that] This prepares us to understand that

вими. тѣмже не ко аг҃гломъ ниⷤ к херꙋвимоⷨ реⷱ҇ бг҃ъ сотворимъ чл҃ка по ѡбразоу нш҃емоу. не к тѣⷨ рече бг҃ъ иⷯ емꙋ соѡбразны и сосодѣтеⷧ҇ни твари. и сосотворителни зданию. и по семоу разоумно ꙗко не ко аг҃гломъ реⷱ҇ бг҃ъ сотвориⷨ чл҃ка понеⷤ аг҃гли не соуⷮ равномощни бг҃ꙋ. гл҃юⷮ бо книгы ꙗко слꙋгы аг҃гли бв҃и. ꙗкоⷤ и самое имꙗ иⷯ сказоуⷮе. аг҃гли бо взываютсѧ. еⷤ слꙋжбы иⷯ имꙗ нарицаемо есть. Пакыⷤ иⷮ[91] сюдꙋ ѕѣло разоумѣвается. ꙗко не ко аг҃гломъ
40r/93 реⷱ҇ бг҃ъ сотвориⷨ чл҃ка. понеⷤ рече бг҃ъ сотвориⷨ чл҃ка по ѡбразоу нш҃емꙋ и по подобию. и не оубо просто по ѡбразоу реⷱ҇ бг҃ъ токмо. но и по поⷣбию иⷯ сотворити чл҃ка. ꙗвлꙗюⷮ книгы. ꙗко не къ слꙋгаⷨ реⷱ҇ бг҃ъ сотвориⷨ чл҃ка по ѡбразоу нш҃емоу и по поⷣбию. приложениⷨе бо реченїа еⷤ и по подобию. оуказоуⷮе ꙗко к подобнымъ бг҃ꙋ. а не токмо къ единоѡбразныⷨ бг҃ꙋ. реⷱ҇ сотворимъ чл҃ка по ѡбразоу нш҃емꙋ и по подобию. слꙋгы оубо аг҃глиⷤ и херꙋвими не соуⷮ подобни бг҃ꙋ. не црьствоуюⷮ бо аг҃гли и херꙋвими. ниже совлⷣчествꙋюⷮ бв҃и. не равносиⷧ҇ни бо сꙋть бг҃ꙋ.

---

91 *Read:* и ѡⷮ.

"Let us make man in our image", because man does not appear like fire or with wings as the angels do, nor is man with many eyes as the cherubim.[92]

16.2. And we learn from the Scriptures that the cherubim and the angels do not share God's image. Therefore, it was not the angels nor the cherubim, to whom God said, "Let us make man in our image". Instead, God said it to those who shared his image, and who did the same work of creation and the same things as he did. And from this, it reasonably follows that God did not speak to the angels and the cherubim (when he said), "Let us make man", because the angels do not possess equal power with God, for the Scriptures say that the angels are God's servants[93] (cf. er 1:14), which is clear from their name, because the angels are called with this name according to the service (they carry).

16.3. Furthermore, given the fact that God said, "Let us make man in our image and likeness", we can understand very well that it was not the angels, | to 40r/93
whom God said, "Let us make man". For God did not simply say, "in the image", without anything else, but also (added) that he created man in his likeness. With this added phrase, "and likeness", the Scriptures show that God did not speak to the servants (when he said), "Let us make man in our image and likeness". (Instead), they indicate that God was speaking to those who had the same likeness, and not only possessed the same image with God (when he said), "Let us make man in our image and likeness".[94] Thus, being servants, the angels and the cherubim are not like God. For the angels and the cherubim do not co-rule with God, nor do they share the same dominion with God. For they do not pos-

92 like fire or with wings as the angels do, nor is man with many eyes as the cherubim.] like fire, nor with wings, nor with many eyes, as the cherubim and angels.

93 the angels are] the angels and the cherubim are

94 Furthermore, based on the fact that God said, "Let us make man in our image and likeness", we can understand very well that it was not the angels to whom God said, "Let us make man". For God did not simply say, "in the image", without anything else, but also (added) that he created man in his likeness. With this added phrase, "and likeness", the Scriptures show that God did not speak to the servants (when he said), "Let us make man in our image and likeness". (Instead), they indicate that God was speaking to those who had the same likeness, and not only possessed the same image with God (when he said), "Let us make man in our image and likeness".] Furthermore, it is also quite plausible (to draw) from this that another reason that God did not speak to the angels (when he said), "Let us make man in our image and likeness", is indicated by the fact that God was speaking to those who had the same likeness, and not only possessed the same image, (based on the words), "Let us make man in our image and likeness".

ıакоⷤ ıавлıаеⷮ наречение иⷯ. понеⷤ агг҃ли иментуютса. Iако разоумѣти равныⷯ бг҃у кто суⷮ во ѡбразѣ бж҃іи. понеⷤ сотвори бг҃ъ ѡбраⷥ по подоⷣбию своеⷢ бж҃е ства чл҃ка И оубо показаша книгы. ıако соѡбразніи и единоѡбразніи соуⷮ нѣкои подоⷣбни бг҃у есть. и равномощни емꙋ к содѣтеⷭствоу твари. совлⷣчествꙋюще и съцр҃ьствоую ще бв҃и прⷭно понеⷤ подобни бг҃у соуще. тѣмже и равносиⷭлни емꙋ. тоⷤ твораще еⷤ бг҃ъ твориⷮ. и аще сосодѣтеⷭни твари бв҃и ѡни.

40v/94 оубо и съцрⷭтвꙋюⷮ бв҃и. совлⷣчествꙋюще емоу. единопрⷭтльни въ твари сотвореннои ими понеⷤ подобни сꙋть бг҃у и ѡни. рече бо к ниⷨ бг҃ъ сотвориⷨ чл҃ка по ѡбразоу н҃шемꙋ и по подоⷣбию. ктоⷤ сіи иⷤ единоѡбразни. и соѡбразни и подобни бг҃у. съсотворающе и съсодѣтеⷭствꙋюще емꙋ тваⷬ. и сопрⷭтльствоующе емꙋ гⷭьствоⷨ. и мощию. книгы насⷠно не ꙋбо ıавиша сихъ. ѿкꙋдꙋ разꙋмѣемъ равномощныⷯ бг҃у сопрⷭтль sess equal power with God, as it is revealed by their name, because they are called "angels".[95]

17. Showing that we can understand who it is that is equal with God (by looking) into God's image, for God made man in the image and likeness of his own Godhead.[96]

17.1. And thus, the Scriptures showed that those who possess the same and identical image, also possess God's likeness, and they have equal power with him and do the common work of creation. They share eternal rule and government with God.[97] Since they are like God, they also have equal power with him and do the identical work that God does. And if they make the same things as God does, | then they also co-rule with God, governing with him in creation and 40v/94
sharing the same throne.[98] And it is because they, too, are like God, that God said to them, "Let us make man in our image and likeness".[99]

17.2. But when it comes to the question of who it is that shares and possesses the same and common image and likeness with God, and participates together with him in the same activity and work in regards to creation, and shares the same throne and government and might, the Scriptures[100] do not specifically reveal this. But where else can we know of those who have equal power with

---

95 Thus, being servants, the angels and the cherubim are not like God. For the angels and the cherubim do not co-rule with God, nor do they share the same dominion with God. For they do not possess equal power with God, as it is revealed by their name, because they are called "angels".] The angels and the cherubim are thus servants, and therefore, not like God. For the angels and the cherubim do not co-rule with God, nor do they possess equal power, as is revealed by their name, which is "angels".

96 **Showing that we can understand who it is that is equal with God (by looking) into God's image, for God made man in the image and likeness of his own Godhead.**] *omitted*

97 the same and identical image, also possess God's likeness, and they have equal power with him and do the common work of creation. They share eternal rule and government with God.] the same image, also possess God's likeness, and they eternally rule with God.

98 governing with him in creation and sharing the same throne.] governing in creation made by them.

99 *MS 61 adds*: **Showing that we can understand who it is that is like God (by looking) into God's icon, the man, for God made man in his image and likeness, according to what he said, which means that he created the icon of his own Godhead.**

100 shares and possesses the same and common image and likeness with God, and participates together with him in the same activity and work in regards to creation, and shares the same throne and government and might, the Scriptures] shares the same image and likeness with God, and participates in the same work of creation together with him—which makes it clear that they also share the same throne of dominion and power—the Scriptures.

ныⷯ емꙋ. ꙗко во агглоⷯ и херꙋвимеⷯ не ѡбрѣтохомъ. понеⷤ аггли и херꙋвими слꙋгы сꙋть. и не соуⷮ подоⷠни бгꙋ. и ниⷤ соѡбразни емꙋ. ѿкоудꙋ оубо ѿ инꙋдꙋ хощеⷨ познатї иⷯ. аще не точию ѿ ѡбраза и подобиа иⷯ. сотворена ⷩⷢ имиⷯ. Ѡбразъⷤ и подобие иⷯ сотворенныⷯ ими есть члкъ. реⷱ бо бгъ сотворимъ члка по ѡбразоу ншемꙋ и по поⷣобию. и книгы реⷱ ша. и сотвори бгъ члка по ѡбразоу бжию сотвори его. тѣмже ѿ ѡбраза бжїа члка. поⷣобныⷯ бгꙋ и равносилныⷯ емꙋ познаемъ. Члкъ живоⷮ ѿ прочиⷯ животоⷡ познаваемъ[101] ꙗко словесеⷩ есть. ни едино бо животное. [41r/95] во всеⷨ мирѣ гливо. точию едиⷩ члкъ глеть. есть бо ї ины члчию тварию животи и в мори и на сꙋши. но не глють ꙗкоⷤ и члкъ. ни аще кїи члкъ прїимы и которыи живоⷮ. возмоⷤ же наꙋчити глати. не сотворено бо имъ ѿ бга глати. аще и кои праⷥни приемше птиⷲ мнатса наꙋчати нѣкїа глы вѣщати. и по наꙋчению пѣваа птица маⷧ нѣкїи глъ

101 *In the margin*: глаⷡ вı.

God and share with him the same throne? For this is not found in the angels and the cherubim, because the angels and the cherubim are God's servants and are not like God, nor do they share the same image.

17.3. How, then, are we going to learn about them at all, if not precisely from the image and likeness that was made by them?[102] And their image and likeness is man whom they made, for God said, "Let us make man in our image and likeness".[103] And since the Scriptures say, "And God made man, in the image of God he made him" (Gen. 1:27),[104] it is from the icon of God, namely, man, that we learn the evidence about those who are like God and have equal power with him.[105]

18. CHAPTER 12.[106]

18.1. Man is a living animal, and the way in which he is recognized as being different from the rest of the living beings is that he is able to speak. For no other animal (made) by God[107] | in the entire world can speak, only man has 41r/95
the speaking ability. Indeed, besides man there are also other animals in creation, both in the sea and on the dry land, but none of them speaks as man.[108] Nor can any man who adopts a certain living being be able to train it to speak, for God did not design it with the speaking ability.

18.2. And this also applies to those who take birds and vainly think that they can train them to reproduce certain words. And even in the case of a songbird that can be trained to reproduce a few small sounds of speech, it forgets these

102 to learn about them at all, if not precisely from the image and likeness that was made by them?] and learn about those who are like God, who share the same image and have equal power with him, if not precisely from their icon, namely, from the image and likeness, that was made by them?

103 likeness is man whom they made, for God said, "Let us make man in our image and likeness".] likeness, namely, the icon of the Godhead, is man whom they made, for God said, "Let us make man in our image and likeness", which is the icon of the Godhead.

104 And since the Scriptures say, "And God made man, in the image of God he made him"] For the same reason, the Scripture says, "And God made man, in the image of God he made him", that is, he made man into an icon of God.

105 it is from the icon of God, namely, man, that we learn the evidence about] it is from the image of God in man, that we learn about

106 CHAPTER 12.] **Consideration, according to the divinely inspired Scripture, that man is made after God's image and after his likeness, and of the difference between man and other animals, and of the fact that among the animals only man is able to speak. CHAPTER 12.**

107 by God] *omitted*

108 but none of them speaks as man] but none of them speaks the way man speaks.

провѣщавши. забываеⷮ и пакы гл҃ъ. и по томⷨ его не вѣщаеⷮ. понеⷤ не разоумѣетъ словеси птицъ. но точию по гласꙋ гл҃ъ нѣкїи пѣваеⷮ. и не ѿимаеⷮ естⷭва гл҃ива. ни можеⷮ быти словеⷭна. единъ чл҃къ гл҃ивъ живоⷡ. ꙗко ѡбраⷥ бж҃їи есть иⷡ подобие. чⷣл҃къ. ~

Ꙗко ѡбраⷥ бж҃їи есть чл҃къ или поⷣбие. разꙋмѣвается икона поⷣбиа бж҃їа. в чл҃цѣ Какоⷤ ꙋбо разꙋмѣемъ чл҃ка. в чесомъ ѡбразъ бж҃їи и подобие чл҃къ. по семоу ли ꙋбо. имⷤ чл҃къ главꙋ имаⷮ. и ѻчи и оуши. и ноздри. и оуста и гортаⷩ. и рꙋцѣ. и чрево и нозѣ. и како по симъ оудесемъ можеⷮ быти чл҃къ ѡбраⷥ и подобие бг҃оу. понеⷤ и скоти. и прочїи животи. тыꙗже
41v/97 оудовы имоуⷮ. главꙋ и ѻчи и оуши. и ноздри и оуста и гортань. чрево и ногѣ. но рꙋкꙋ ли не имоуⷮ инїи животи. и почемꙋ ли чл҃къ боудеⷮ ѡбраⷥ бж҃їи ꙗко рꙋцѣ имаⷮ. аще и мнози не имоуⷮ рꙋкꙋ животнаа. но соуⷮ и рыбы нѣкои в мори рꙋцѣ имоуⷮ. и чл҃чию тварию сꙋть. и ѡбеⷥꙗньскїи роⷣ такоⷤ. ї инїи животи. иⷤ не часто во вселеⷩнꙋю приходꙗще. чл҃чиюⷤ тварию зримы соуⷮ. и видимъ оубо ꙗко ничим же различьствꙋеⷮ чл҃къ ѿ иныⷯ животныⷯ. и что имѣꙗ чл҃къ излише во ꙋдесеⷯ свойⷯ паⷱ прочиⷯ животъ. тыꙗⷤ бо иⷡмаⷮ оуⷣды чл҃къ в телесѣ своемъ. ꙗⷤ и ѡбеⷥꙗна оуды в телесѣ имаⷮ. ї аще чл҃къ по телеснымъ оудесемъ бꙋдеⷮ ѡбразъ бж҃їи и подобие. ꙋбо и прочаа животнаа ѡбрази и подобие бж҃ие боудꙋть. но нѣсть всꙗкое животное ѡбразъ

sounds in time and then, it cannot repeat those things again.[109] Since the bird does not understand words, it can only be trained to sing some words (by imitating) the vibration of the voice.[110] And it does not gain the nature that would make it capable of speaking,[111] nor is it able to speak by itself. Man is the only kind of being who is able to speak, for man is God's image and likeness.

19. Showing that the meaning of man's image, or likeness, must be understood from the likeness of God's icon in man.[112]

19.1. And how, then, do we understand man? What is God's image and likeness in man? Now, is it something by virtue of which man has a head, and eyes, and ears, and nostrils, and mouth, and throat, and hands, and belly, and legs? But how can man be the image and likeness by virtue of these parts of the body? For the livestock and other animals have the same | parts of the body—a head, 41ᵛ/97
and eyes, and ears, and nostrils, and mouth, and throat, and belly, and legs.

19.2. Is it rather because other animals do not have hands, that man is the image of God, since he does have hands? Yet even though many animals do not have hands, some of them, such as certain types of fish in the sea, do have hands and their bodies look similar to man's; and the species of monkeys have hands, too. And there are other animals that have human-like bodies, though they do not come into this world often.

19.3. And we see, then, that man is no different from other animals, and among his parts of the body, man has nothing that other animals do not have. Thus, man has the same things in his body as the monkey has in its body. If man is to be God's image and likeness based on his having certain bodily parts, then other animals, too, will be God's image and likeness. But no animal is the

---

109 it forgets these sounds in time and then, it cannot repeat those things again.] it forgets in time what it was trained to say and then, it cannot repeat those things again.

110 Since the bird does not understand words, it can only be trained to sing some words (by imitating) the vibration of the voice.] When this kind of bird is kept by man and taught to say (certain things), it forgets its own sound. But when it becomes free and joins other birds, it begins to reproduce its own sound again and forgets the things that man trained it to say. And henceforth, (the bird) no longer knows how to say it, because the bird does not understand words; it can only be trained to say some words (by imitating) the vibration of the voice.

111 And it does not gain the nature that would make it capable of speaking,] For it does not possess the nature that would make it capable of speaking,

112 **Showing that the meaning of man's image, or likeness, must be understood from the likeness of God's icon in man.] On the question of how and in what way we should understand the icon and likeness of the Godhead in man, and in what way man is different from the rest of the animals.**

бж҃їи и поⷣобие. единъ есть чл҃къ ѡбраⷥ бж҃їи и по
добие. понеже ѡ всѣⷯ животныⷯ. рече бг҃ъ да
изведеⷮ вода. да изведеть землѧ. ї изыдоша
вса животнаа. ѡ единоⷨ чл҃цы точию совѣ
тꙋа реⷱ҇ бг҃ъ. сотворимъ чл҃ка по ѡбразоу нш҃е
мꙋ и по поⷣобию. и ѿ сего разоумѣваетсѧ. ꙗⷦ҇
42r/98 нѣсть чл҃къ ѡбраⷥ бж҃їи по семꙋ. еⷤ имѣти чл҃кꙋ
главꙋ и прочаа оуды в телесѣ своеⷨ. понеже
и всѧко животно главꙋ и прочаа оуды имꙋⷮ
ꙗкоⷤ и чл҃къ. тѣмже не сие ѡбраⷥ бж҃їи и подо
бие чл҃къ. еⷤ имаⷮ в телесѣ своемъ оудовы. но
ино есть ѡбраⷥ бж҃їи чл҃кꙋ. еⷤ прочїи животи не
имꙋⷮ. еⷤ имаⷮ чл҃къ. да поистиннѣ единъ чл҃къ
боудеⷮ ѡбраⷥ бж҃їи. аще ли едина точию таа
имаⷮ чл҃къ, ꙗⷦ҇ и вса животнаа имоуⷮ. главꙋ
гл҃ю и прочаа в телесѣ оуды. боудꙋть оубо по
семꙋ всакое животное ѡбраⷥ бж҃їи. понеⷤ
всакомꙋ животномꙋ. такоⷤ главꙋ и прочаа
оуды имꙋщꙋ. ꙗкоⷤ и чл҃кꙋ тыⷤ имꙋщꙋ оуды.
и не боудеⷮ чл҃къ едⷣинъ ѡбраⷥ бж҃їи. но мнози бꙋⷣ
дꙋ ѡбрази бж҃їи ꙗкоⷤ и преⷤ реⷱ҇. книгы сказꙋюⷮ
единоⷨ точию чл҃ка ѡбраⷥ бж҃їи. ꙗко ѡ единоⷨ
точию чл҃цѣ реⷱ҇ бг҃ъ. сотвориⷨ чл҃ка по ѡбразꙋ
нш҃емꙋ и по подобию. инаꙗⷤ животнаа
вса преⷤ чл҃ка сотворена быша. и не рѣша
книгы ꙗко всѧ животнаа по ѡбразꙋ бж҃їю
сотворена. но ꙗко просто реⷱ҇ бг҃ъ. да изведеⷮ
землѧ и вода животнаа. и бысть тако.
42v/99 абие бо быша всѧ животнаа имꙋщи вса

image and likeness of God; only man is the image and likeness of God.[113] For with regard to all the animals, God said, "Let the water appear, let the earth appear, and there appeared all the animals", and only with regard to man, God took counsel and said, "Let us make man in our image and likeness".[114]

19.4. From this, we can understand that | man is not God's image in virtue of 42r/98
having a head and other things in his being, for every animal has a head and other parts of the body that man has.[115] Hence, man is the image and likeness of God not by virtue of having such things in his body.[116] Instead, the image of God in man is something else—it is that which man has, but other animals do not have, making man alone the true image of God. And had the man had just the things that all other animals have, I mean, a head[117] and other things that are found in his body, then every animal should have been God's image based on this logic. For every animal, too, has a head and other parts of the body, just as man has such parts of the body. And man would have no longer been the only image of God. Instead, there would have been many images of God, as I already said earlier.[118]

19.5. The Scriptures declare that only man alone is God's image. It is only of man alone, that God claims that he will make him in his image and likeness. And all other animals were made before man,[119] and the Scriptures do not say that all the animals were made in God's image. Instead, God simply said, "Let the water and the earth teem with living creatures", and it was so.[120] | For all the 42v/99

113 But no animal is the image and likeness of God; only man is the image and likeness of God.] But this is not so. Instead, man is God's image and likeness.

114 likeness".] likeness", whereas concerning other animals, he simply said, and there they were.

115 in virtue of having a head and other things in his body, for every animal has a head and other parts of the body that man has.] by virtue of having a head and other parts of the body in his being, for every animal has a head and other parts of the body that man has, yet (animals) are not God's image.

116 such things in his body.] such things in his body as a head and other parts.

117 a head] a head and hands

118 For every animal, too, has a head and other parts of the body, just as man has such parts of the body. And man would have no longer been the only image of God. Instead, there would have been many images of God, as I already said earlier.] But as I said earlier, this would have made many images of God, for every animal has the same parts of the body—a head and other things—as man does. **Showing that the image of the Godhead in man is the intelligent and rational soul, which man received afterward as a greater possession than what the animals have.**

119 before man,] earlier,

120 Instead, God simply said, "Let the water and the earth teem with living creatures", and it was so.] Instead, the Scriptures state that God simply said, "Let the water and also the earth teem with animals", and it was so.

оуды. главѹ имѣющѹю ѡчи и оуши и нозⷣри и оуста и прочаа оудовы в телесѣ. ничѣⷨ же скоⷮнѣе чл҃ка по ѹдесеⷨ и по ниⷯ создаⷩ бысть чл҃къ. таковаⷤ чюⷡства во ѹдехъ имѣꙗ. ꙗкоⷤ и прежнꙗа животнаа. и ничтоⷤ излишнее во ѹдесеⷯ имѣа паⷱ прочиⷯ животныⷯ. и ѡ неⷨ рѣша книгы. ꙗко сотвори бг҃ъ чл҃ка. по ѡбразоу бж҃ию сотвори еⷢ. и вдѹнѹ на лице еⷢ дыхание жизни. и бысть чл҃къ в дш҃ѹ живѹ. сего ѡ иныⷯ животныⷯ не сказаша книгы ꙗко быті имъ в дш҃ѹ живѹ. ꙗкоⷤ ѡ чл҃цѣ сказаша. ⷤе вдѹнѹ бг҃ъ чл҃кѹ дыхание жизни. и бысть чл҃къ в дш҃ѹ живоу. Ꙗко ѡбраⷥ бжⷭтва в чл҃цѣ. дш҃а ѹмна словеⷭна Посемѹ оубо познавается чл҃къ. им же есть по ѡбразоу бж҃ию. понеже бысть чл҃къ в дш҃ѹ живѹ. дш҃аⷤ живаа оумна и словеⷭна сѹщи. и оубо бг҃ъ живъ. слово имаⷮ и дх҃ъ. по немоуⷤ и ѡбраⷥ бж҃іи. дш҃а жива. оумна словеⷭна. бг҃ъ роⷣ слово сопрⷭносѹщно себѣ. и дх҃ъ соисходеⷩ. и ѡбраⷥ бж҃іи оумъ ражаетъ. слово и дыхание жизни ѿ дш҃а исходиⷮ. понеⷤ
43r/100 вдѹнѹ бг҃ъ на лице чл҃кѹ дыхание жизни. и бысть чл҃къ в дш҃ѹ живѹ. И вѣдиⷨ ѡбраⷥ бж҃іи извѣстеⷩ чл҃ка. имѣа дыхание жизни. быⷡ в дш҃ѹ живѹ оумнѹ и словеⷭнѹ. Ꙗко икона бжⷭтва чл҃къ имаⷮ в себѣ тр҃цоу по ѡⷠразѹ бжⷭтва. оуⷨ слово дх҃ъ. Бг҃ъ бо ѿц҃ъ. и слово сн҃ъ. и дх҃ъ ст҃ыи сотвориша чл҃ка по ѡбразоу своемѹ и по поⷣбию. в дш҃ѹ

animals received the parts of their body all at once. They had a head—which had eyes, ears, nostrils, mouth—and all the other things in the body. This made them in no way more deficient than man in terms of things of the body; and man was made after they were created, with the same senses in his parts of the body as those animals that were previously (made), and there was nothing extra in his parts of the body that the rest of the animals did not have.

19.6. And the Scriptures say about him that "God made man, in his image he made him", and "he breathed into his face the breath of life, and the man became a living soul" (Gen. 1:27; 2:7). The Scriptures did not say this of other animals that they "became a living soul", whereas of man, they did say that God "breathed into" man "the breath of life, and man became a living soul".

20. Showing that the image of the Godhead in man is the intelligent and rational soul.[121]

20.1. This is how we can recognize, then, that man is made in the image of God, for "man became a living soul", and the living soul is intelligent and rational. Since God is a living being who has the Word and Spirit, then the image of God—the soul—is also living, intelligent, and rational. God begets the Word that is co-eternal with him, and he has the Spirit who proceeds from him at the same time.

20.2. It is the same with the image of God—the mind generates the word, and from the soul there comes the "breath of life". Since | God "breathed into" 43r/100
man's face "the breath of life, and man became a living soul", from this we see that God's image in man is recognized by the presence of the soul. Having received the "breath of life", "man became a living soul", intelligent and rational.

21. Showing that the icon of the Godhead—man—has a triad in his soul in accordance with the image of the Godhead: the mind, the word, and the breath.[122]

21.1. For God, and the Word, who is the Son, and the Holy Spirit made man in their image and likeness, (forming) him into a living, intelligent, and rational

121 **Showing that the image of the Godhead in man is the intelligent and rational soul.**] *omitted*

122 **Showing that the icon of the Godhead—man—has a triad in his soul in accordance with the image of the Godhead: the mind, the word, and the breath.**] *omitted*

живꙋ оумнꙋ и словеⷭнꙋ. бг҃ъ ѿц҃ъ. ѿ негоⷤ родиⷭ слово и ст҃ыи и дх҃ъ нераздѣлныи изыде. ѿ ѡбраза бж҃їа чл҃ка дш҃и оумны и словеⷭны. бг҃ъ и стинныи в троⷪ҇цы познаваетсѧ. ꙗко бг҃ъ сопрноⷭсꙋщна троⷪ҇ца. бг҃ъ и слово еⷭ. и ст҃ыи дх҃ъ его. понеⷤ ѡбраⷥ бж҃їи чл҃къ бысть. в дш҃ꙋ живꙋ оумнꙋ. ꙗко приаⷮ дыханиє жизни. и оуⷨ чл҃ка ражаеⷮ слово. и дх҃омъ исхоⷣномъ ѿ оустъ познаваемо. ѿсюдꙋ извѣстно вѣрꙋетсѧ. бг҃оу истинномꙋ имѣти слово рожено. имѣтиⷤ бг҃оу и ст҃го дх҃а исходѧща. живы събезначаⷧны бг҃оу и сопрноⷭсꙋщны. со прⷭ҇тльствꙋюще емꙋ. и сосодѣтеⷧствꙋюще емꙋ тваⷬ всю. к ниⷨ же и реⷱ бг҃ъ ꙗко соѡбразныⷨ и к поⷣоⷠнымъ. и прⷭ҇нымъ единосꙋщныⷨ. 43v/101 и съсодѣтеⷧныⷨ емꙋ. сотвориⷨ чл҃ка по ѡбразоу нш҃емꙋ и по поⷣоⷠбию. им же подоⷠни бг҃оу и соѡбразни. слово бж҃ие роженое. и ст҃ыи дх҃ъ исходѧщїи. бг҃ъ ѿц҃ъ гл҃а словꙋ сн҃ꙋ своемоу живомꙋ. и къ ст҃мꙋ дх҃ꙋ своемꙋ живомоу. сотвориⷨ чл҃ка по ѡбразоу нш҃емꙋ и по поⷣоⷠбию. познаваетсѧ оубо не мнее треⷯ живыхъ soul.[123] By looking at the image of God in man, we can recognize the true God, rational and intelligent, existing in the Trinity, for God eternally exists as Trinity: God, and his Word, and his Holy Spirit. He is God the Father, from whom the Son is begotten, and the Holy Spirit proceeds indivisibly.[124] Since the image of God—man—"became a living soul" on account of receiving the breath of life,[125] and since the mind generates the word, while the latter is recognized by being breathed out of the mouth, we can accurately believe from this that the true God has the begotten Word and that God also has the proceeding Holy Spirit.

21.2. They are living, equally without beginning, and co-eternal with God, sharing with him the same throne;[126] and they share in the same work of making the entire creation, and it is to them—who have the common image and likeness and character, who are consubstantial | and share the same work with 43v/101
him—that he said, "Let us make man in our image and likeness" (Gen. 1:26). And they are like God and share a common image:[127] the Word of God is begotten from him, and the Holy Spirit proceeds from him.

21.3. Thus, it was to the living Word, his Son, and to his living Holy Spirit, that God the Father said, "Let us make man in our image and likeness".[128] And thus,

123 For God, and the Word, who is the Son, and the Holy Spirit made man in their image and likeness, (forming) him into a living, intelligent, and rational soul.] For God, and his Word, and his Holy Spirit are recognized by the fact that they made man in their image and likeness, (forming) him into a living, intelligent, and rational soul.

124 By looking at the image of God in man, we can recognize the true God, rational and intelligent, existing in the Trinity, for God eternally exists as Trinity: God, and his Word, and his Holy Spirit. He is God the Father, from who the Son is begotten, and the Holy Spirit proceeds indivisibly.] And by looking at the image of God, namely man, we can recognize in his soul the presence of the true God, intelligent and rational, in three hypostases, the co-eternal God, and his Word and his Holy Spirit. **Showing that the icon of the Godhead, namely, the image of God—man—has three things in his soul in accordance with the image of the Godhead: the mind, the word, and the breath. This is what other animals do not have—neither the soul, nor the word, nor the mind.**

125 on account of receiving the breath of life,] and since the soul of man is intelligent,

126 sharing with him the same throne;] co-sovereign with him;

127 And they are like God and share a common image:] Since their being comes from his essence, therefore, they also share a common image and likeness with him:

128 Thus, it was to the living Word, his Son, and to his living Holy Spirit, that God the Father said, "Let us make man in our image and likeness".] Thus, it is evident that it was to them—to his living Word and to his Holy Spirit—that God said, "Let us make man in our image and likeness". **Showing that in man—the icon of the Godhead—and in accordance with God's likeness, the mind generates the word, while the breath reveals in man the paternity of the mind and the sonship of the word.**

лицъ. нⷤи множае трⷯе ипостасеи. в бжествѣ единⷨо. ꙗкⷤо видⷨи самыи бжⷭ҇тва ѡбраⷥ чл҃ка создана по подобию бжⷭ҇тва. Ꙗко по пⷣобию бж҃ию оумъ ражаⷮе слово. дⷯом же показоуемо бываⷮе ~~сн҃овьство~~ ѿчество оума и сн҃овьство слова.

Ꙗко во ѡбразѣ бжⷭ҇тва въ чл҃цѣ, есть подобие бжⷭ҇тва. дш҃а оумна в неⷤи слово дⷯомъ ꙗвлꙗемо. сїа бо три точию въ чл҃цѣ паⷭ҇ прочиⷯ животнⷯы. вси бо животи имоⷮу главоу в неⷤи зрїние. ѡбонание слоⷯу. оуста и прочаа оуды гортаⷩ зѹбы. а рѹкъ не имоⷮу ногы вмѣсто рѹкъ напоⷩнꙗю. ѡвїиⷤ крила вмѣсто сиⷯ имѹⷮ. чревⷤо и срⷣце и проходы. и ногы ꙗкⷤо и чл҃къ имаⷮ. оумаⷤ и слова и живы дш҃а
44r/103
не имѹⷮ прочаа животнаа. ⷤе чл҃къ паⷭ҇ прочихъ животнⷯы имаⷮ бжⷭ҇тва икона сѹщи. по ѡбразоу и по пⷪобию бг҃а и слова ⷢе и дх҃а ⷢе. ни множае трⷯе в бжⷭ҇твѣ нⷤи мнее лицъ. таковаⷤ и икона бжⷭ҇тва чл҃къ. по ѡбразоу бж҃ию и по подобию имѣюци. оумъ слово и дыхание. нⷤи паⷭ҇ сего нⷤи скоⷮунѣе в чл҃цы паⷭ҇ животнⷯы. оуⷨ слово ражаетъ дхⷤмъ ꙗвлꙗемо и дⷯомъ из оѹстъ исходꙗщемъ. познаваемо ѹма ѿчество. и слова рожение въ чл҃цѣ. ~

[Several lines of blank space]

Ꙗкⷤо и в самⷨо бжⷭ҇твѣ дⷯмъ бжїимъ познаваетсꙗ право вѣрѹющимъ бг҃а ѿчьство и слова ⷢе собезначаⷩлное сн҃овьство. не раздѣ in one Godhead, we can recognize three living persons,[129] or three hypostases, neither fewer nor more, as we can see from the very image of the Godhead, man, who is created in the likeness of the Godhead.[130]

22. Showing that in accordance with God's likeness, the mind generates the word, while the breath reveals in man the paternity of the mind and the sonship of the word.[131]

22.1. Man, as the image of the Godhead, has the likeness of the Godhead—his intelligent mind, from which there comes the word, revealed by the breath.[132] For in comparison with the other animals, these three things are found only in man. For all animals have heads—with their eyesight, the sense of smell and hearing, and the mouth—and all other parts of the body. They have a throat and teeth,[133] and even though they do not have hands, they can compensate for them with their legs, and some have wings instead of hands. And they have a heart, and intestinal tracts, and legs, just as the man has them.

22.2. But these other animals do not have the word and the living soul, | 44ʳ/103
which man has, in comparison with the other animals. He is the icon of the Godhead, (made) in the image and in the likeness of God, and his Word, and the Holy Spirit. There are three persons within the Godhead, neither more nor fewer. Such is also the icon of the Godhead, man, who, in accordance with God's image and likeness, has the mind, the word, and the breath.[134] There is neither more nor fewer than this in man when compared with the animals. For the mind generates the word that becomes revealed through the breath, and then, by means of the breath that comes from the mouth,[135] we can recognize the paternity of the mind and the generation of the word in man.[136]

22.3. It is the same with the Godhead itself: by means of the divine Spirit, believers can genuinely recognize the fatherhood of God and the sonship of

129 three living persons] three persons

130 Godhead.] Godhead, as the Scriptures said.

131 **Showing that in accordance with**] **Showing that in man—the icon of the Godhead—and in accordance with**

132 mind, from which comes the word, revealed by the breath.] mind, which generates the word that is revealed by the breath.

133 teeth,] hands,

134 has the mind, the word, and the breath.] has the living soul, intelligent and rational.

135 mouth,] man's mouth,

136 *Here* MS *337 has a blank space for a missing heading.* generation of the word in man.] generation of the word.

лно бжⷭтво на три. ни слито въ едино. в бз҃ѣ и словѣ и дс҃ѣ его. ни прⷤе бытно едино. нⷤи последи прибытно два дрꙋгаа бжⷭтвоу. Сопрⷭносꙋщны бо бг҃оу слово и дх҃ъ. познаваетса и вѣрꙋетса ѿц҃ъ и сн҃ъ и ст҃ыи дх҃ъ. во единⷨо бжⷭтвѣ. не слитно ни раздѣлно. 44v/104 понⷤе и въ чл҃цѣ иⷤ ѡбраⷥ и подобие бжⷭтва не раздѣлꙗютса. нⷤи сливаютса в дш҃и оумъ слово ї дыхание. ибо видⷨи въ чл҃цы во ѡбразѣ бж҃їи и подобии. в дш҃и оумъ есть и родⷡи слово ꙋмъ не ѡхꙋдѣваеть ни погыбаⷮе. но пребываⷮе оумъ цѣⷧ҇. и слово рожено оумⷨо пребываⷮе слово. и не бываⷮе слово пакы оумомъ превращаꙗса. и дыхание бываⷮе дыхание. и не превращаетса пакы въ слово и въ оумъ. и видѣти есть во ѡбразѣ бжⷭтва въ чл҃цѣ. вкꙋпѣ оумъ. вкꙋпѣ во ꙋмѣ слово. ни слово без оума. нⷤи оумъ беⷥ слова есть. нⷤи без дыханїа мощи познати оума ни слышати слова. сопрⷭнена сꙋщи оуⷨ и слово и дх҃ъ. въ чл҃цѣ во ѡбразѣ бжⷭтва и в подобїи. и понⷤе бг҃ꙋ ѿцꙋ слово сн҃ъ собезначалⷩе со ст҃ымъ дх҃мъ. ни бѣꙗше никогдаⷤ бг҃ъ беⷥ слова. тѣмже не бѣꙗше никогдаⷤ бг҃ъ не ѿц҃ъ. не прⷤе именоваса бг҃ъ ни последи бысть ѿц҃ъ his Word that is likewise without beginning.[137] And the Godhead is[138] neither divided into three[139] nor merged into one—out of God and his Word and the Spirit—nor is it a pre-existing oneness, nor is it a godhead to which the other two are added afterward. For the Word and the Spirit are[140] eternally co-existing with the Father. And thus, the Father and the Son and the Holy Spirit are recognized and believed to be in one Godhead, neither merged nor separated.[141] | 44ᵛ/104

22.4. For, in man, too, who is the image and likeness of the Godhead, the mind and the word and the breath in his soul are neither separated nor merged. For in man—God's image and likeness—we can see that the soul has the mind, and after generating the word, the mind does not become lesser nor does it perish, but remains whole; and the word, after being generated by the mind, keeps on being the word, and this word does not turn back into the mind again;[142] and the breath keeps on being the breath and does not turn into the word and into the mind again.[143] And by looking at the mind in the image of God—the man—we can see a concurrent existence of the word in the mind. There is neither word without mind, nor mind without word, nor is it possible to hear a word without a breath ⟨nor to understand the mind⟩. In man—God's image and likeness—the mind, and the word, and the spirit always exist together.

22.5. And since the Word, who is the Son, together with the Holy Spirit, are without beginning along with God the Father—and there was never a time when God was without the Word—therefore, there was never a time when God was not a Father, nor was he first called God and afterward, became a Father.[144]

---

137 likewise without beginning] co-eternal

138 Godhead is] Godhead must be seen

139 three] three essences

140 are] are understood as

141 And thus, the Father and the Son and the Holy Spirit are recognized and believed to be in one Godhead, neither merged nor separated.] And thus, in human terms, the Father and the Word and the Holy Spirit are recognized and believed to be in one Godhead—neither merged nor separated—from the (evidence of) the image and likeness, which the Father established in creating the living soul, intelligent and rational.

142 again] *omitted*

143 and does not turn into the word and into the mind again.] does not turn back into the word and into the mind.

144 the Word, who is the Son, together with the Holy Spirit, are without beginning along with God the Father—and there was never a time when God was without the Word—therefore, there was never a time when God was not a Father, nor was he first called God and afterward, became a Father.] Word, together with the Holy Spirit, are equally without beginning along with God—and there was never a time when God was without the Word, and the Word was begotten from God—therefore, there was never a time when God was not a Father, nor was he first called God and afterward, became a Father, as it is understood.

бг҃ъ аще совершенъ ꙗко и есть совершенъ. поне нѣсть бг҃ꙋ оумалꙗтиса или преисполнꙗтиса. оумалꙗтиса бо и преисполнатиса, не стоꙗщаг есства несвершение есть. [45r/105] присносꙋщаго есства совершение. бе ѡскꙋдѣнїа есть и бес прибыванїа. тѣмже преблженное. бжс҃веное сꙋщество. вкꙋпѣ бг҃ъ вкꙋпѣ ѿц҃ъ. а не ѡскꙋдѣваасꙗ бжс҃тво пре кромѣ ѿчьства. и послѣди исполнꙗꙗса ѿчествомъ. е оумалению исполнение и скꙋдости свершение знаменае. нѣсть подобно бжс҃твꙋ быти скоуднꙋ и послѣди исполнꙗти. хꙋла бо многа на бжс҃тво е гл҃ати бг҃а оумалена. и послѣди совершиша. прибываниемъ ѿчества. аще ли гл҃ати ѿца мнее ѿ бжс҃тва. пакы болшаа хꙋла на бе ство. гл҃ати бг҃а ѿ совершенїа оумалшаса. и ѡхꙋдѣвша нишествие ко ѿчествꙋ. бывающа бг҃а послѣди того прибывающа ѿ ѿца. поне оубо совершено есть бжс҃тво. тѣмже не пре бг҃ъ послѣ прибысть ѿц҃ъ. присно бо ѿц҃ъ а не послѣди бысть ѿц҃ъ бг҃ъ. по свершенномꙋ преблженномꙋ своемꙋ есствоу. бг҃ъ ѿц҃ъ. ѿц҃ъ есть сн҃оу. нѣсть бо ѿцꙋ быти не поровшꙋ пороженїа свое. Ꙗко бг҃ъ ѿц҃ъ гл҃а

Thus, if God is perfect, as he is perfect indeed—and a perfect thing does not become either inferior or more complete, and God has perfection within his own being and is perfect—therefore, it does not befit God to become inferior or more complete. For to become inferior or more complete is a feature of imperfection that belongs to an unstable nature. | But as for the eternal nature, its 45^{r}/105
perfection does not become inferior or more complete.

22.6. Therefore, the supremely blessed divine essence is simultaneously God and Father. And the Godhead was not at one point less, lacking fatherhood, and afterward, becoming complete when it gained fatherhood. This happens when an inferior thing becomes perfected and when a thing that lacks something becomes more complete. But it is not like that in the case of the Godhead—to lack something and then become complete. For it is a great blasphemy against the Godhead to say that God was inferior, and afterward, became perfected by gaining fatherhood. And if we say that becoming a Father makes the Godhead inferior, this, again, is a great blasphemy against the Godhead—to say that God's perfection became diminished or reduced by his descent to the level of fatherhood, that he first was God, and afterward, and in addition to that, the same God became a Father.

22.7. Since the Godhead is perfect, it is not true, then, that first there was God, and afterward, there came a Father. Instead, we understand him to be always God the Father—according to his perfect supremely blessed nature—and not that he came to be a Father later. And in being a Father, God is a Father to the Son, for the Father cannot be without his offspring, whom he begot.[145]

---

145 *MS 61 adds*: Instead, once he begets, he becomes a Father, and without begetting, whose Father will he be? Therefore, it is because he begot his Word, that God is a Father, by whom the Word was begotten. As a living being, God has never been without his Word, which is why God is always a Father, on account of the generation of the Word. And the Word, begotten from the Father, is called the Son, on account of the generation. And since the Word was begotten from God the Father, the Word is, therefore, the Son to God the Father, just as God, in virtue of begetting the Word, who is the Son, is God the Father to his Son, who is the Word. Therefore, God is a Father, and his Word is his Son.

к пⷣоⷪбнꙑⷨ себѣ бжⷭтвомъ и силою и влⷣчествомъ къ словꙋ҃ е рⷣжьшемꙋⷭ ѿ него и къ дх҃ꙋ ст҃мꙋ҃ е исходѧщемъ ѿ него.

45ᵛ/106 Показаⷭ оубо вѣрне по книгаⷨ къ комꙋ реⷱ бг҃ъ[146] сотвориⷨ чл҃ка по ѡбразоу нш҃емꙋ и по подобию. ꙗко к подобнꙑⷨ себѣ реⷱ бг҃ъ сотвориⷨ по ѡбразоу и по пⷣоⷪбию чл҃ка. и к соѡбразнꙑⷨ себѣ и к равномощнымъ на прⷭнѣ а не к рабоⷨ ѿ далеча стоꙗщиⷨ. реⷱ бг҃ъ сотвориⷨ чл҃ка по ѡбразоу нашемꙋ и по пⷣоⷪбию. пⷣоⷪбныхⷤъ и соѡбразныхъ и равносⷧнныхъ бг҃ꙋ. познаваеⷨ ѿ ѡбраза и подобиа бжⷭтва сотвореннаⷢ ѿ самѣⷯ ихъ съ бг҃омъ по ѡбразоу иⷯ и по пⷣоⷪбию. ѿ чл҃ка иже в неⷨ живыа дш҃а оумныа и словесныа дыхатеⷧнныа. без дыханиа бо жити чл҃къ не можеⷮ. и ꙗко единосꙋщны бг҃ꙋ слово и дх҃ъ. живы въ свойⷯ ипостасеⷯ. совершены бжⷭтвоⷨ. подоⷠни бг҃ꙋ равеⷩствомъ в силѣ и творенїи. и влⷣчествѣ и въ прⷭносꙋщїи. к ним же рече

146 *In the margin*: глаⷡ гї.

23. Showing that God the Father spoke to those who were like him in terms of divinity and power and dominion, to his Word, begotten from him, and to his Holy Spirit, who proceeds from him. CHAPTER 13.[147] | 45v/106

23.1. Thus, in faithful keeping with the Scriptures, it has been shown to whom God said, "Let us make man in our image and likeness", (demonstrating) that God spoke to those who were like him, when he (called upon them) to make man in the image and in the likeness of those who always shared a common image and equal power. It was not to the servants, who stood afar from God, that he said, "Let us make man in our image and likeness".[148]

23.2. The way we recognize those who are like God and share with him a common image and power is (by looking at) the Godhead's image and likeness, made by the very beings who were with God,[149] according to their image and likeness. ⟨We do that by looking at⟩ man, the living soul: intelligent and rational and capable of breathing, for man[150] cannot live without breathing. And the Word and the Spirit are consubstantial, alive in their own hypostases, perfect in divinity, alike to God in equal power, and in the way they create, and in dominion, and in their state of eternality; and to them, God said,[151] "Let us make man in our image and likeness".

---

147 **Showing that God the Father spoke to those who were like him in terms of divinity and power and dominion, to his Word, begotten from him, and to his Holy Spirit, who proceeds from him. CHAPTER 13.] Examining the statement in the divinely inspired Scripture, where God said to them, "Let us make man in our image and likeness", and whether such words of God have any special sense. CHAPTER 13.**

148 *MS 61 adds*: **Showing that God spoke to those who shared a common image, who were like him in terms of divinity and power and dominion, to his Word, begotten from him, and to his Holy Spirit, who proceeds from him. (To them, he spoke) when making man in the image and in the likeness of the Godhead.**

149 made by the very beings who were with God] made by those who were with God

150 living soul: intelligent and rational and capable of breathing, for man cannot live without breathing.] living soul that is found in him, and the mind that is in it, and the word and the breath that come from it, for man cannot live without breathing. And by means of the mind that is found in the soul and which generates the word, we recognize God the Father, who begets his Word. And by means of the word that is found in the soul and which is generated by the mind, we recognize the Word of God, begotten from God the Father. And by analogy of the breath that comes from the soul and from which the word, generated by the mind, becomes revealed, we receive the Holy Spirit, who proceeds from the Father. They teach our mind to believe that God is the Father of the Word and that he is God of the Son, who is the Word;

151 alike to God in equal power, and in the way they create, and in dominion, and in their state of eternality; and to them, God said,] alike to God in their state of eternality, share a common image and are equal in power, and in the way they create, and in dominion, according to the divine words that God said to them,

бг҃ъ сотворимъ чл҃ка по ѡбразоу нш҃емꙋ и по подобию. по немоуⷤ истинное слово въ книгаⷯ. гⷭь бг҃ъ гⷭь единъ есть. бг҃ъ ѿц҃ъ родивъ слово сн҃а. и дх҃ъ исходѧщь. гдⷭьство едино в треⷯ сꙋщи ипостасеⷯ. посемꙋ гл҃еть. гⷭь бг҃ъ гⷭь единъ есть. бг҃ъ ѿц҃ъ. и слово роженное ѿ ѿца. и дх҃ъ 46r/108 бж҃їи исходѧщь. к ним же реⷱ҇ бг҃ъ сотворимъ чл҃ка по ѡбразоу нш҃емꙋ и по пⷣоⷪбию. по ѡбразꙋ оубо ꙗко во единоⷨ бжⷭтвѣ три состава. ѿц҃ъ и сн҃ъ и дх҃ъ. посемоуⷤ во единоⷨ чл҃цѣ три состоѧщиса. дш҃а жива оумна и словесна. по пⷣоⷪбиюⷤ оубо ꙗко въ бз҃ѣ единоⷨ слово и дх҃ъ. бг҃ъ родивъ слово. ржⷭтва раⷣ ѿц҃ъ. и слово рожениѧ раⷣ сн҃ъ. понеже ѿ ѿца родиса. и дх҃ъ ст҃ыи исхожениѧ раⷣ дх҃ъ. понеже ѿ бга изыде единого. посемꙋ и дш҃а чл҃коу по пⷣоⷪбию бжⷭтва оумна словⷭена. оумъ ражаеⷮ слово беⷥ зачатїа и кромѣ жⷩества. бес предѣла и кромѣ времене. беⷥ мешканїа ниⷤ послѣди. нѣсть бо ꙋмъ беⷥ слова когда. но кꙋпно ꙋмъ ~~ко~~ кꙋпно во ꙋмѣ и слово. дхмⷤ҃ъ оустъ оума порожение сꙋщее слова показоуемо по пⷣоⷪбию бжⷭтва. ꙗко

23.3. ⟨It is clear that God spoke to his Son, the Word, begotten from him, and his Holy Spirit⟩, through whom come the words of truth in the Scriptures,[152] "The Lord your God, the Lord is one"[153] (Deut. 6:4). God the Father[154]—who begets the Son, who is the Word, and from whom the Holy Spirit proceeds—has one lordship shared by three hypostases, which is why it is said, "The Lord God, the Lord is one" (Deut. 6:4), God the Father, and the Word, begotten from the Father,[155] and the Spirit | of God, who comes by proceeding. And to them, 46r/108
God said, "Let us make man in our image and likeness".

23.4. Now, the phrase "in the image" implies three subsistences[156] in one Godhead—the Father, and the Son, and the Holy Spirit.[157] And hence, one man, the living soul, intelligent and rational, consists of three elements.[158] And so, the phrase "in the likeness" implies that the Word and the Spirit are in one God:[159] God begets the Word, and on account of the generation, God is the Father, and the Word, on account of the generation, is the Son, for he is begotten from God the Father; and the Holy Spirit,[160] on account of the procession, is the Spirit,[161] because he comes from the one God.

23.5. Hence, the soul of man is intelligent and rational, according to the likeness of the Godhead. The mind generates the word without conception, without requiring a female partner, without end, without time, without waiting.[162] Nor does the word appear only afterward, for the mind is never without the word. Instead, the mind is there all along, the mind and the word existing together. And the breath of the mouth[163] reveals the word as an offspring of

152 through whom come the words of truth in the Scriptures,] through whom we understand the words of truth recorded in the Scriptures,

153 one"] one". For it is from his own being, that God begets the Son who is the Word, and from his own being, too, the Holy Spirit proceeds.

154 God the Father] Father

155 Father] God

156 subsistences] hypostases

157 The Father, and Son, and Holy Spirit.] God the Father, and the Word, who is the Son, and God's Spirit.

158 And hence, one man, the living soul, intelligent and rational, consists of three elements.] And hence, the one soul of man, too, consists of three elements: the mind, and word, and breath, which make up the image of God.

159 the Word and the Spirit are in one God:] *omitted*

160 Holy Spirit] Spirit of God

161 Spirit,] Holy Spirit,

162 without conception, without requiring a female partner, without end, without time, without waiting.] without conception, without waiting, without requiring a female partner, without end, and without time.

163 breath of the mouth] breath

бг҃оу ѿцꙋ рожено слово ⷢ҇е. сопрⷭ҇носꙋщно бес пре
дѣла преже всакоⷢ҇ времени и лѣта. и ст҃ымⷨ
дх҃мъ ѿ бг҃а исшⷣ҇ешимъ. ꙗвлено ѿч҃ество
бж҃ие сн҃оу ⷢ҇е словꙋ. и сн҃овъство ѿ ѿц҃а слова
бж҃їа. и дх҃мⷤъ ст҃ымъ ѿкровено бысть. ~
Пакы рѣша мнѣ крылошане. сїа оубо ты гл҃еши
46v/ 109–110 писаниⷤе гл҃еть. гⷭ҇ь бг҃ъ твои гⷭ҇ь ~~единъ~~ единъ есть.
Ꙗко косои книги прочитаⷮе на раⷥвращение. а не
вѣрꙋⷢе писанию ст҃ⷨо. Ѿвѣщавⷤъ азъ рѣⷯ к нимъ. поⷤне
наоучаюⷮ насъ книги добрѣ. слыши їил҃ю гⷭ҇ь бг҃ъ
твои гⷭ҇ь единъ есть. косогоⷤ безоуⷨствие моци
познавати. всакомꙋ хотꙗщемꙋ разоумѣ
ти правѣ. носить косои книгы в рꙋкꙋ и раⷥгы
баⷮе принꙋжаа прочитаⷮ но поⷤне имаⷮ косои
сокровеⷩ҇ въ срⷣ҇цѣ его гл҃ъ безаⷥконїа ѿстꙋпиⷮ
ѿ бг҃а жива. кореⷩ҇ жеⷧ҇чи и горесть прозабаа
выспрь. ꙗкоⷤ и преⷤ рѣхъ. бѣглецъ косои. в чю
жю землю раⷠ҇ лꙋкавъ гладоⷨ таа. оумысли но
вꙋ ересь ꙋчити. раⷥвращаꙗ ст҃ыа книгы. пи
саннаа в ниⷯ добрѣ. гл҃еть ѕлѣ. да сеⷢ҇ раⷣ приꙗⷮ
бывъ. беⷥ боꙗзни сотвориⷮ всакое безаⷥкоⷩе.
возносꙗⷭ҇ на всакоⷢ҇ гл҃емаго бг҃а или чтилища.

the mind, according to the likeness of the Godhead, because by virtue of being begotten from God the Father, the Word co-exists eternally with him, without a limit, before any time and years; and the Holy Spirit, by proceeding from God, discloses the fatherhood of God to his Son, the Word, and it is by the Spirit, that the sonship from the Father becomes revealed to the Word of God.[164]

23.6. Again,[165] the kliros-chanters said to me: "Now, while you are saying these things, | the Scripture states,[166] 'The Lord your God, the Lord is one'" 46ᵛ/
(Deut. 6:4).[167] 109–110

24. Showing that Kosoy reads the Scriptures in order to distort them instead of believing the Holy Bible.[168]

24.1. And in response, I said to them: The Scriptures surely teach us well when they say,[169] "Hear, O Israel: The Lord your God, the Lord is one" (Deut. 6:4). And Kosoy's insanity[170] can be recognized by everyone, who wishes to have the right understanding. Kosoy[171] carries the Scriptures in his hand, and when he discloses them, he urges (men) to read them. However, the reason he does that is that Kosoy is latched on to the words of iniquity that are hidden in his heart in order to depart from the living God, spreading the root of bitterness and trouble,[172] as I already said before.

24.2. Kosoy, the cunning slave that he is, fled to the foreign land, concealing his greed and intending to teach the new heresy by distorting the sacred Scriptures through his misinterpretation of things that are written well. And because he was welcomed there, he engaged in all kinds of iniquity without fear, acting in arrogance with respect to everything that was named "divine" or was a sub-

164 and it is by the Spirit, that the sonship of the Father becomes revealed to the Word of God.] and reveals the sonship of the Father to the Word of God.

165 Again,] And

166 Scripture states,] Scripture speaks of one God,

167 one'" (Deut. 6:4).] one' (Deut. 6:4), just as Kosoy asserts, and others, too".

168 **Showing that Kosoy reads the Scriptures in order to distort them instead of believing the Holy Bible.**] *omitted*

169 Scriptures surely teach us well when they say,] Scripture teaches us well when it says,

170 insanity] vain wisdom

171 Kosoy] You say that Kosoy

172 However, the reason he does that is that Kosoy is latched on to the words of iniquity that are hidden in his heart in order to depart from the living God, spreading the root of bitterness and trouble,] It is not because Kosoy believes the sacred Scripture, that he urges (men) to read it, but because Kosoy is latched on to the words of iniquity that are hidden in his heart in order to depart from the living God, bringing forth the root of bitterness for trouble,

понеⷤ гл҃еть въ срⷣцѣ своеⷨ нѣсть бг҃а. и послоу
шающаа е҃ в тоⷤ свое безбж҃ие введеⷮ. хота
хⷭ҇а проста чл҃ка именовати а не бг҃а. да ѿ
вратиⷮ послꙋшателеи своиⷯ ѿ хⷭ҇а бг҃а. сего
раⷣ гл҃еть ѕлѣ иⷤ добрѣ писаннаа. гⷭ҇ь бг҃ъ тво
гⷭ҇ь едиⷩ҇ есть. и развѣ его нѣсть. привводꙗⷤ ѕлѣ
47r/111 и петра и павла писавшиⷯ добрѣ. ꙗко и гⷭ҇а
и хⷭ҇а его бг҃ъ сотвори сеⷢ҇ іⷭ҇са. и едиⷩ҇ ходатаи
бг҃ꙋ и чл҃комъ чл҃къ іⷭ҇ъ хⷭ҇ъ. да егда прⷧ҇стиⷮ
послꙋшателꙗ своꙗ. вѣровати хⷭ҇а чл҃ка
быти а не бг҃а. бг҃аⷤ единого бг҃а а не в трⷪ҇цы.
тогда и самонаоученно ѿстꙋпꙗть ѿ бг҃а.
навыкше преⷤ ѿстꙋпити ѿ цр҃кви. и ѿ
цр҃ковныⷯ оучителеи. оукарꙗюще еⷭ҇пкпоⷡ
и попоⷡ преⷤ. потоⷨ прⷭ҇бныхъ мꙋжеи по
стникоⷡ и дѣвъствꙋющиⷯ. потоⷨ и ст҃ыⷯ
ѿцъ. и ст҃ыⷯ седми соборовъ. потоⷨ чⷭ҇тныꙗ
ѡбразы. и ст҃ыⷯ мчⷩ҇къ мощи. потоⷨ всѣⷯ
ст҃ыⷯ. и бг҃ородицꙋ. и крⷭ҇тъ хв҃ъ. потоⷨ
апⷭ҇ловъ и прⷭ҇тчю. таⷣ и самого хⷭ҇а сн҃а бж҃їа
и бг҃а. тꙋ боудеⷮ готово иⷤ оукориⷮ и самоⷢ҇
бг҃а ѿстꙋпити ѿ него. Сего раⷣ мы.
ваⷨ принꙋжающиⷨ насъ ѡ косого ꙋченїи
новомъ сказати. потщахомсꙗ преⷤ
вамъ ѿкрыти. косоⷢ съкровенныи гл҃ъ
беⷥаконїа сꙋщїи въ срⷣцѣ его. еⷤ ѡ немъ
прⷪ҇ркъ повѣда гл҃ꙗ. реⷱ законопрестꙋ
пныи согрѣшати в себѣ. нѣсть страха бж҃їа
47v/ преⷣ ѡчима еⷢ҇. ꙗко ꙋльсти преⷣ нимъ ѡбрѣ
111–112 сти беⷥаконие свое. и возненавидѣти
гл҃ы оустъ его беⷥаконие и лесть. не во
схотѣ разоумѣти да оублажить. беза
коние помысли на ложи своемъ. прⷣ҇ста
всꙗкомꙋ поути не бл҃гꙋ. и реⷱ безоуменъ
въ срⷣцѣ своемъ нѣсть бг҃а. растлѣша и
ѡмразиша в начинанїихъ. тѣмже и во
сприꙗхомъ сказовати вамъ. ꙗко во исти
ноу есть бг҃ъ. приводꙗщи ѿ еⷭ҇твена ра
зоума и ѿ ѡбычаа. таже и ѿ ст҃ыꙗ быте
скїа книгы. юⷤ косои разгибаа прⷧ҇щаеⷮ грꙋ
быꙗ. сказахомъ по писанию ꙗко бг҃ъ имаⷮ

ject of reverence—for he said in his heart, "There is no God" (Cf. Ps. 14:1)—so that he may introduce his listeners to the same godlessness. He wanted to treat Christ as a mere man, rather than God, so that he may also lead his listeners away from Christ and from God. That is why he misinterprets what is written well, "The Lord your God, the Lord is one" (Deut. 6:4).

24.3. And as if (God) did not exist, | he introduced evil things to what is well 47r/111
written both by holy Peter and Paul—"God has made him both Lord and Christ, this Jesus" (Acts 2:36), and "there is one mediator between God and men, the man Christ Jesus" (1Tim. 2:5)—so that he may entice his listeners into believing that Christ is man, and not God, and that God is single, and not triune. Then, they would depart from God, driven by their own doctrine and being first instructed by his teaching to depart from the Church and from the ecclesiastical teachers, subjecting to criticism first the bishops and priests, and then the saints and the ascetics and the virgins, and then the holy fathers and the holy seven Councils, and then the honorable icons,[173] and the relics of the holy martyrs, with all the other saints, too, and the Mother of God, and the cross of Christ, then the Apostles and (John) the Forerunner, along with Christ himself, the Son of God who is himself God. This being the case, they are ready to assail God himself and depart from him.

24.4. For this reason, being asked by you to tell you of Kosoy's new teaching, we first tried to expose for you the words of iniquity that Kosoy hid in his heart. Concerning him, the Prophet spoke, saying, "The transgressor, that he
may sin, said within himself, 'There is no fear of God | before his eyes', for he 47v/
dealt craftily before him, to discover his iniquity and hate it. The words of his 111–112
mouth are lawlessness and deceit: he does not want to understand how to do what is pleasing. He devises iniquity on his bed, he gives himself to every evil way" (Ps. 36:1–4); and "The fool said in his heart, 'There is no God'. They became corrupt and abominable in their first ways" (Ps. 14:1).

24.5. Therefore, we have sought to tell you that God truly exists, offering arguments based on natural logic and on tradition, as well as on the holy book of Genesis, which Kosoy opens in order to entice the simple.[174] And we spoke according to the Scripture,[175] (showing) that God has those who possess the

173 and then the holy fathers and the holy seven Councils, and then the honorable icons,] as well as the holy fathers, and holy seven Councils, and honorable icons,

174 opens in order to entice the simple.] opens and reads in a distorted way in order to entice the simple.

175 Scripture,] divinely inspired Scripture,

единоѡбразныⷯ и поⷣ҇бныⷯ себѣ. равносилныⷯ
же и сопрⷭ҇тльствꙋщиⷯ. на прⷭ҇нѣ емꙋ соу
щиⷯ. и содѣиствꙋющиⷯ с нимъ. и ꙗко сїи по
знаваеми ѿ ѡбраза и поⷣ҇биꙗ иⷯ. сотворе
наⷭ҇ ими чл҃ка. и вѣрꙋем и воистиннꙋ. ꙗко
слово бж҃ие есть. и дх҃ъ ст҃ыи бж҃їи вынꙋ
съ бг҃мъ. и к ниⷨ рече бг҃ъ сотвориⷨ чл҃ка по ѡ
бразоу нⷲ҇емꙋ и по поⷣ҇бию. посемꙋ бг҃ъ въ
троⷪ҇цы есть едиⷩ҇. единоⷢ҇ сꙋщества и бжⷭ҇тва
раⷣ҇.
48r/113 ѿц҃ъ и сн҃ъ. и дх҃ъ ст҃ыи. Ꙗко во второⷨ законѣ
заповѣⷣ бг҃а в троⷪ҇цы показа гл҃ѧ. гⷭ҇ь бг҃ъ твои гⷭ҇ь едиⷩ҇ есть.[176]
Ꙗкоⷤ и самаа бж҃їа книга заповѣдываа наⷨ
чаⷮе гл҃ѧ. слыши їил҃ю гⷭ҇ь бг҃ъ твои гⷭ҇ь едиⷩ҇ есть.
почто ꙋбо ꙋтроиваа единъ гл҃ъ реⷱ҇. гⷭ҇ь бг҃ъ
гⷭ҇ь единъ. довлѣющꙋ наꙋчити единымъ
гл҃омъ и рещи. слыши їил҃ю бг҃ъ твои единъ
есть. или рещи слыши їил҃ю гⷭ҇ь твои единъ
есть. ⷤе бы твердѣе и разоумнѣе единоⷢ҇
бг҃а навыкнꙋти. ⷤе гл҃ати писанию бг҃ъ
твои единъ есть. или гⷭ҇ь твои единъ есть.
бж҃їа же заповѣⷣ в законѣ не тако. но пи

176 *In the margin*: глⷡ҇ дı҃.

same image and are like him, who share equal power and the same throne, who eternally exist with him and participate in the same acts with him; and that they are recognized from their image and likeness found in man whom they made.

24.6. And we truly believe that the Word of God and the divine Holy Spirit exist with God, and it is to them, that God said, "Let us make man in our image and likeness" (Gen. 1:26).[177] Therefore, in virtue of having one being and divinity, God exists as one in the Trinity |—the Father, and the Son,[178] and the Holy Spirit. 48r/113

25. Showing that in Deuteronomy, the commandment of God reveals him as existing in the Trinity, when it says, "The Lord your God, the Lord is one" (Deut. 6:4). CHAPTER 14.[179]

25.1. The divine Scripture itself teaches (this), when it proclaims the commandment, "Hear, O Israel: The Lord your God, the Lord is one" (Deut. 6:4).[180] Now, why does it[181] use a triplet (when it refers to God) in the statement that says, "The Lord your God, the Lord", when it[182] had to teach the listeners to say one thing, "Hear, O Israel, 'Your God is one'", or to say "Hear, O Israel, 'Your Lord is one'", in order to have them learn of one God more firmly and with a better understanding? Would it not make more sense for God to say in the Scripture,[183] "Your God is one" or "Your Lord is one"? Yet this is not what we find in

---

177 exist with God, and it is to them, that God said,] are always alive in their own hypostases and eternally exist with God, and it is to them, those who are proper to him, that God said,

178 the Father, and the Son,] God, and his Word,

179 **Showing that in Deuteronomy, the commandment of God reveals him as existing in the Trinity when it says, "The Lord your God, the Lord is one" (Deut. 6:4). CHAPTER 14.**] *omitted*

180 *MS 61 adds*: **Consideration of the command found in Deuteronomy (6:4), "Hear, O Israel: The Lord your God, the Lord is one", as to whether it refers to one person or signifies more than one person. CHAPTER 14.** Take heed of the commands of God, not according to the vain wisdom of Kosoy, but according to the way God's commands are recorded in the words (of the Bible). And think correctly, according to the Scripture, instead of becoming corrupt from your personal ideas that are foreign to the divine Scripture. Think well of what is well written in the divinely inspired Scriptures. When something is written in a certain way, take it exactly that way. Now, the command is written as follows, "Hear, O Israel: The Lord your God, the Lord is one" (Deut. 6:4). **Showing that in Deuteronomy, too, God's commandment reveals God existing in the Trinity when it says, "The Lord your God, the Lord is one" (Deut. 6:4).**

181 it] sacred Scripture

182 it] Scripture

183 for God to say in the Scripture,] for the Scripture to say,

саше трⷪ҇цоу. слыши ї҇илю г҇ь бг҇ъ твои г҇ь едиⷩ
есть. видѣтⷤи есть в началѣ книгы еди
нⷪ҇ бг҇а разоумѣвати велꙗше. гл҇еть бо.
искони сотвори бг҇ъ нбо и землю. и рⷱ҇е бг҇ъ
да боудⷮе свѣтъ. и разлꙋчи бг҇ъ межю свѣ
тⷨо и межю тмою. и всюдꙋ бг҇а единого
именоваше тамо. г҇а же не прилагаше.
в законⷤѣ заповѣдꙋа трⷪ҇цоу разоумѣвати
оуча гл҇ꙗ. слыши ї҇илю г҇ь бг҇ъ твои г҇ь едиⷩ
есть.

48v/115 А ꙗко бг҇ъ и г҇ь едино есть имꙗ. и тⷪⷤ еже бг҇ъ се и г҇ь.
иⷤе г҇ь се и бг҇ъ. тⷪⷤ и моисѣи ꙗвлꙗеⷮ в начало книгы.
бг҇а гл҇ꙗ бес приложенїа г҇а. сотвори бг҇ъ. и рⷱ҇е
бг҇ъ се и ѡно. тⷤа единⷪ҇ г҇а именоваше. бес при
ложенїа бг҇а гл҇ꙗ. принесе каиⷩ ѿ плодⷪⷡ земли
жⷬ҇твꙋ г҇ви. и призрѣ г҇ь на авелꙗ. и рече
г҇ь каинꙋ. что ѡскорбленъ бысть. здѣ не при
ложи бг҇а ко г҇оу. но едино имꙗ гⷭ҇а именова
точию. ꙗкⷪⷤ и в начало книгы едино имꙗ бг҇а
точию именова. сотвори бг҇ъ и рⷱ҇е бг҇ъ. и
прочаа. такⷪⷤ и послѣди едино имꙗ имено
ваше точию г҇а. призрѣ г҇ь и рⷱ҇е г҇ь. и прочаа.
В законѣ же писаше заповⷣѣ. три име
ны тыꙗⷤ именꙋꙗ во едино. слыши ї҇илю г҇ь
бг҇ъ твои г҇ь единъ есть. не ꙗве ли трⷪ҇ца
едиⷩство писаше законъ гл҇ꙗ. г҇ь бг҇ъ твоⷵ
г҇ь единъ есть. ащⷤе не трⷪ҇цы единьство
бжⷭ҇тва показоваше писание. чесо раⷣ
трикраты рⷱ҇е едино имꙗ гл҇ꙗ. слыши
ї҇илю бг҇ъ бг҇ъ твои бг҇ъ единъ. едино бо и
тⷪⷤ имꙗ бг҇ъ или г҇ь. показано ꙋже ѿ пи
санїа. и како трикраты оубо именова
49r/116 тⷪⷤ имꙗ. г҇ь г҇ь твои г҇ь единъ есть. ащⷷ҇е мни

the divine commandment of the Law.[184] Instead, it describes the Trinity, ⟨when it says⟩, "Hear, O Israel: The Lord your God, the Lord is one" (Deut. 6:4).

25.2. And we must see that in the beginning, the Scriptures instruct us to recognize one God, for they say, "In the beginning, God made the heaven and the earth", and "God said, 'Let there be light'", and "God separated the light from the darkness" (Gen. 1:1, 3–4). And in all other places, the reference is only to "God", and there is no addition of "Lord". And in the Law, the commandment is teaching us to recognize the Trinity, when it says, "Hear, O Israel: The Lord your God, the Lord is one" (Deut. 6:4).[185] | And the fact that "God" and "Lord" 48v/115 are one name—and whenever we have "God", there is also "Lord", and whenever we have "Lord", there is also "God"—is revealed by the same Moses, who speaks of "God" in the beginning of Scripture without adding "Lord", (when he states), "God made", and "God said" this and that.

25.3. Similarly, when he refers to the "Lord", he does so without adding "God", saying, "Cain brought of the fruits of the earth a sacrifice to the Lord" (Gen. 4:3), and "The Lord looked with favor on Abel" (Gen. 4:4), and "The Lord said to Cain, 'why have you become sorrowful'?" (Gen. 4:6). Here, he did not supplement "Lord" with "God", but referred only to one name, "Lord". And just as in the beginning of the Scripture, he refers only to one name, "God"—"God made", and "God said", and so forth—so also afterward, he refers only to the name, "Lord"—"the Lord looked with favor", and "the Lord said", and so forth. But in the Law, when recording the commandment, he refers to the same names three times in one statement, ⟨saying⟩, "Hear, O Israel: The Lord your God, the Lord is one".

25.4. Is the Trinity united in one Godhead not evident when he writes in the Law, saying, "The Lord your God, the Lord is one"?[186] And if the Scripture did not intend to show the Trinity united in one Godhead, then why did it refer to (God) three times, saying, "Hear, O Israel: The Lord your God, the Lord is one"? For it has already been shown from the Scripture that the names "God" and "Lord" are the same, and (if so), how is it that he refers to (God) three times, | 49r/116 "The Lord your God, the Lord is one"? And if, according to your thinking, the

184 Yet this is not what we find in the divine commandment of the Law.] Yet this is not the way the commandment of God in the Law is written.

185 *MS 61 adds*: **Showing that the names "God" and "Lord" are equally honorable, and there is no difference between them, as if one name was greater, and the other name was lesser.**

186 Is the Trinity united in one Godhead not evident when he writes in the Law, saying, "The Lord your God, the Lord is one"?] *omitted*

ши бж҃їе имѧ гⷭ҇нѧ чⷭ҇тнѣиши. рⷱ҇ено бы в писа
нїи бг҃ъ гⷭ҇ь твои бг҃ъ едⷩ҇и. ащⷤ҇е ѕлѣ развращае
ши писаное добрѣ трⷪ҇ца едⷩ҇иство гⷭ҇ь бг҃ъ твӧ
гⷭ҇ь едⷩ҇и есть. и речеши ꙗко се именование
единьствꙋ лежⷮ҇и а не трⷪ҇цы. и аще бы тако пи
саное было по твоемꙋ разоумѣнию. къ единь
ствꙋ а не къ трⷪ҇цы. было бы писано гⷭ҇ь бг҃ъ твӧ
бг҃ъ единъ есть. но писано гⷭ҇ь бг҃ъ твои гⷭ҇ь едⷩ҇и
есть. ⷤ҇е чⷭ҇то троичное единьство ꙗвлꙗеⷮ҇.
не рⷱ҇е бо писание бг҃ъ твои единъ есть. или гⷭ҇ь
бг҃ъ твои единъ есть. но гⷭ҇ь бг҃ъ твои гⷭ҇ь единъ
есть. да познаеши едино гⷭ҇ьство трⷪ҇цы.
и да не вознепщꙋеши слова сн҃а и ст҃го дх҃а.
не тогⷤ҇о гⷭ҇ьства быти ѿ бг҃а ѿц҃а. того рⷣ҇ӓ
в начало заповѣди писаше. гⷭ҇ь единъ есть.
а не писа бг҃ъ единъ есть. да навыкнеши еди
номꙋ гⷭ҇ьствꙋ быти ѿц҃а и сн҃а и ст҃го дх҃а. гⷭ҇а
бг҃а гⷭ҇а единⷢ҇о слыша. да разоумѣеши слыша
писанное. к комꙋ рⷱ҇е бг҃ъ сотворⷨ҇и чл҃ка по ѡбра
зоу нш҃емоу и по пⷣⷪ҇бию. ꙗко къ сн҃оу и ст҃омꙋ
дх҃оу своемꙋ. рⷱ҇е бг҃ъ сотворⷨ҇и чл҃ка. понⷤ҇е едино
49v/117 гⷭ҇ьство бжⷭ҇тва во ѿц҃ѣ и сн҃ѣ и ст҃емъ дс҃ѣ. а
ще ли хощеши въ бз҃ѣ и въ словѣ его и въ дс҃ѣ еⷭ҇.
семꙋ наоучаеⷮ҇ писанное. гⷭ҇ь бг҃ъ твои гⷭ҇ь единъ
есть. писанⷤ҇о рече бг҃ъ сотворⷨ҇и чл҃ка по ѡбразꙋ
нш҃емꙋ и по пⷣⷪ҇бию. да навыкнеши трⷪ҇цꙋ по
знати. а не едⷩ҇ство ни двоицꙋ. не рече бг҃ъ
сотворю чл҃ка по ѡбразоу моемꙋ[187] да бꙋдеⷮ҇ еди
ница. нⷩ҇и рече бг҃ъ сотворивѣ чл҃ка по ѡбразꙋ
наю. да боудеⷮ҇ двоица. но рⷱ҇е бг҃ъ сотворⷨ҇и чл҃ка
по ѡбразоу нш҃емꙋ и по пⷣⷪ҇бию. и есть трⷪ҇ца.

187 *Scribal correction in the margin*: сво

name "God" were more honorable than the name "Lord", it would say in the Scripture, "God your Lord is one".[188]

25.5. And if you are distorting the fine statement about the oneness of the Trinity—"The Lord your God, the Lord is one"—and saying that it refers to the oneness rather than the Trinity, (then recognize that) had it been written that way, according to your understanding, in reference to the oneness rather than the Trinity, then it would have been recorded, "The Lord your God, God is one".[189] Instead, it is written, "The Lord your God, the Lord is one", which surely reveals the triune oneness. For the Scripture did not say, "Your God is one", or "The Lord, your God, is one". Instead, (it said), "The Lord your God, the Lord is one"[190] to have you recognize the one lordship of the Trinity and not to assume that the Word, who is the Son, and Holy Spirit[191] do not possess the same lordship as God the Father.

25.6. That is why he wrote in the beginning of the commandment, "the Lord is one", instead of writing, "God is one", so that we may learn of the one lordship of the Father, and the Son, and the Holy Spirit.[192] And upon hearing, "The Lord God" and "The Lord is one", you must listen to what is said and recognize to whom God said, "Let us make man in our image and likeness"; that God did not direct the phrase "Let us make" to his Son and his Holy Spirit. The fact that there is one | lordship of the Godhead in the Father, and the Son, and the Holy 49^{v}/117
Spirit—or if you wish, in God, and his Word, and his Spirit[193]—is taught from what is written, "The Lord your God, the Lord is one".[194]

25.7. And it is written, "God said, 'Let us make man in our image and likeness'", so that we may recognize the Trinity,[195] not the monad nor the dyad. He did not say, "I will make man in my image", to mean the monad. Nor did God say, "(The two of us) will make man in our image", to mean the dyad. Instead, God said, "Let us make man in our image and likeness", which indicates the Triad.

188 one".] one". Instead, it is written, "The Lord your God, the Lord is one".

189 "The Lord your God, God is one".] "The Lord, your God, is one".

190 Instead, (it said), "The Lord your God, the Lord is one"] *omitted*

191 Holy Spirit] God's Spirit

192 Holy Spirit.] God's Spirit.

193 his Spirit] the Spirit of God

194 *MS 61 adds*: **Showing that we must discern the way in which oneness, and dyad, and triad are treated in the Scripture, and from this, we must recognize the triune Godhead.**

195 Trinity] Trinity in the Godhead

Ꙗко бесплотенъ бг҃ъ бесплотно и ржⷭ҇тво его сло
вꙋ. бесплотно и исхожение дх҃ꙋ. по пⷣоⷪбию иконы
бжⷭ҇тва. ѿ оума слово раждаемо въ дс҃ѣ исхⷣнѣ.
Зрⷤ҇ꙗ ты сⷨ҇а себе. ꙗко ѡбраⷥ бж҃їи еси. имѣꙗ дш҃ꙋ оумнꙋ
словеⷭ҇нꙋ. да разоумѣеши ѿ ѡбраза первоѡбра
зное. бг҃а ѿца. и слова сн҃а. и дх҃а ст҃го внимаꙗ
своⷢ҇е оума. ꙗко беⷥстⷭ҇ртно беⷥ женьства беⷥ зача
тїа раждающа слово твое. и дх҃мъ оустъ тво
иⷯ износимо и слышимо. ѿ сего да познаеши
первопⷣоⷪбие. бг҃а ѿца роⷣ҇вша беⷥстⷭ҇рно беⷥ жеⷩ҇
ства. беⷥ зачатїа. слово свое сн҃а сопрⷭ҇носꙋщна
и дх҃а ст҃го исходѧща. нѣсть бо во агг҃леⷯ и херꙋ
50r/119 вимеⷯ. подобныⷯ бг҃ꙋ бжⷭ҇твомъ. ниⷤ҇ дрꙋгыⷯ бг҃овъ
нѣкоиⷯ. сосоⷣ҇тⷭ҇ствꙋющиⷯ емоу показаша кни
ги. тоⷪ҇чию едины единосꙋщныꙗ бг҃ꙋ показаша

26. Showing that God is incorporeal, and that the generation of his Word is also incorporeal, along with the procession of the Spirit, which is incorporeal, too. It goes in accordance with the likeness of God's icon: the word is generated by the mind and comes out by means of the breath.[196]

26.1. And examine yourself—the fact that you are the image of God and have an intelligent and rational soul.[197] You must understand the prototype—God the Father, and the Word, who is the Son, and the Holy Spirit—from the image, by examining your own mind: that it is without passion, without a female partner, that it generates your word without conception, and that (this word) is pronounced and heard by means of your mouth.[198]

26.2. From this, you ought to understand the original likeness, God the Father, who begot his consubstantial Word, the Son—without passion, without a female partner, without conception—and from whom the Holy Spirit proceeds.[199] For there is no one among the angels and the cherubim | that are like 50r/119
God in divinity, nor do the Scriptures show us any deities that participate in the acts of God. The Scriptures show that only those who are one with him are

---

196 **Showing that God is incorporeal, and also incorporeal is the generation of his Word along with the procession of the Spirit, which is incorporeal, too. It goes in accordance with the likeness of God's icon: the word is generated by the mind and comes out by means of the breath.**] *omitted*

197 examine yourself—the fact that you are the image of God and have an intelligent and rational soul.] observe yourself, that you are the image of God—you are created by God, according to God's image—and you have an intelligent and rational soul. **Showing that God is incorporeal, and that the way he generates his Word is also incorporeal, and the procession of God's Spirit, too, must be understood as incorporeal. This, then, is in accordance with the likeness of God's icon, that is, man, in whom the word is immaterially generated by the mind and is glorified by means of the breath through which it comes out.**

198 that it is without passion, without a female partner, it generates your word without conception, and (this word) is pronounced and heard by means of your mouth.] that it is incorporeal and generates the incorporeal word, and that the way the mind generates (the word) is also incorporeal. With the mind being incorporeal, it also generates the word incorporeally, without passion, without a female partner, without conception; and it is through the breath of your mouth, that the things generated by your mind are heard and recognized.

199 God the Father, who begot his consubstantial Word, the Son—without passion, without a female partner, without conception—and from whom the Holy Spirit proceeds.] God the Father, that he is incorporeal and also begets his incorporeal Word in a way that is incorporeal. (Understand also) the passionless generation—that God begets the eternal Son—and the procession of God's Spirit.

книгы. к нимⷨ же и реⷱ бг҃ъ сотвориⷨ чл҃ка по ѡбразоу нш҃емоу и по пⷣобию. ктоⷤ соуⷮ единосоущнїи бг҃оу. по знашаⷭ во ѡбразѣ иⷯ и пⷣобїи въ чл҃цѣ. ꙗко трⷪцы ѡбраⷥ. оумъ и слово и дх҃ъ. и по пⷣобию бжⷭтвеныа трⷪца. оумъ нш҃ь ражаеⷮ слово беⷥстрⷭтно беⷥ женьства. и слово ражаꙗⷭ не младо но съвершено. и дх҃мъ ѿ оустъ нш҃иⷯ исходꙗ. показоваше роженное слово оумъ. и оума родившаⷢ слово показоваше дх҃ъ. слова раⷣ не ѡхоудѣваꙗ оумъ родиⷡ слово по пⷣобию бг҃а ѿца. понеⷤ бг҃ъ не ѡхоудѣ родивъ слово сн҃ъ. но пребысть беⷥ стрⷭти. не плоⷮ бо бг҃ъ. не плоⷮскиⷤ и роди сн҃а слова. но по бжⷭтвеномоу дховномоу своемоу еⷭствоу роⷣ. бг҃ъ совершеⷩ сыи. совершена сн҃а слова роⷣ а не млада. бесплотныи бг҃ъ ѿцъ. бесплотно роⷣса и слово ѿ него сн҃ъ. и дх҃ъ изыде совершенъ ѿ бг҃а ѿца. не пострада истощенїа совершеныи бг҃ъ ѿцъ родивъ сн҃а. ибо и нш҃ь оумъ не истоцеваетса родивъ слово нш҃еꙗ дш҃а.

consubstantial.[200] And[201] it is to them, that God said, "Let us make man in our image and likeness", and in man, who is their image and likeness, that they are recognized as being consubstantial with God.[202]

26.3. The image of the Trinity is the mind, word, and breath, and in accordance with the divine Trinity, our minds generate words without passion, without a female partner; and when a word is generated, it is already perfect, and not infantile, and it proceeds with the breath of our mouths.[203] The mind reveals the generated word, and this word generated from the mind is then revealed through the breath.[204] With respect to the word, the mind generates the word without becoming diminished, after the likeness of God the Father, for God[205] did not become diminished when he begot the Word, who is the Son, remaining without passion. For God is not flesh nor does he beget his Son, the Word, corporeally. Instead, he begets him according to his divine spiritual nature. Being perfect, God also begets the Word, who is the Son, as perfect, and not infantile.

26.4. With God the Father being incorporeal, the Word, who is the Son, is begotten from him incorporeally, too,[206] and the Spirit, who proceeds from God the Father, is perfect. The perfect God the Father begot his Son without having suffered any exhaustion, for our minds do not become exhausted either when

---

200 consubstantial.] consubstantial, eternal, alike, and share with God a common image.

201 And] *omitted*

202 and in man, who is their image and likeness, that they are recognized as being consubstantial with God.] and they are accurately recognized and understood in man, who is their image and likeness.

203 The image of the Trinity is the mind, word and breath, and in accordance with the divine Trinity, our minds generate words without passion, without a female partner, and when a word is generated, it is already perfect, and not infantile, and it proceeds with the breath our mouths.] The image of the Trinity is the intelligent and rational soul, and in accordance with the divine Trinity, our incorporeal minds generate our incorporeal words in a way that is incorporeal, without passion, without a female partner, without conception, without being infantile and then becoming older in age after some time. Instead, the mind generates a perfect word that proceeds with the breath of our mouths.

204 The mind reveals the generated word, and this word generated from the mind is then revealed through the breath.] (The breath) reveals the word generated by the mind, simultaneously revealing the word of the mind that generated it.

205 With respect to the word, the mind generates the word without becoming diminished, after the likeness of God the Father, for God] The mind generates the word without becoming diminished, just as God

206 With God the Father being incorporeal, the Word, who is the Son, is begotten from him incorporeally, too,] Being himself incorporeal, God the Father begets the perfect Word, who is the Son, incorporeally, too,

ниⷤ возмоⷦ҇но разоумѣти ни самѣⷨ намъ. оума
50v/120 нш҃его како слово нш҃е ражаеⷮ в насъ. нѣсть бо оумꙋ
жены. ни имаⷮ потребы оумъ временѣ ниже
часца на зачатие словесѣ. ниⷤ на оусырение
и ботѣние. ꙗкоⷤ плоⷮ во ꙋтробѣ питаеⷮ. ни оуⷨ
беⷥ слова никогдаⷤ. ни слово беⷥ оума. но вкꙋпѣ
оумъ вкоупѣ слово во ꙋмѣ. и аще невозможно
разоумѣти ржⷭ҇тва своеⷢ҇ оума словꙋ нш҃емꙋ.
како любопритсѧ кто бг҃оу воⷥбранити
беⷥ женьства не роⷣт̏и сн҃а. да воⷥбраниⷮ преⷤ
аще можеⷮ своемꙋ оумꙋ беⷥ женьства не ража
ти слова. ащеⷤ и сие смѣшное возможно бы
было ⷤе оумꙋ воⷥбранити. беⷥ женьства не ра
жати слова. и тако невозможно нашими
земными мысльми пренбⷭ҇ное бжⷭ҇твеное
еⷭ҇ство мечтати. колико посреⷣство ѿ тлѣ
нного еⷭ҇ства. нетлѣнное еⷭ҇ство. ѡ бжⷭ҇тве
неⷨ же пресꙋщественеⷨ блж҃еннеⷨ ѡномъ
еⷭ҇ствѣ вѣровати точию и покланꙗтиⷭ҇
оумъ имꙋщимъ а не ѡпытовати. и на
оучатисѧ ѿ писанїа. ꙗко реⷱ҇ бг҃ъ сотвориⷨ
чл҃ка по ѡбразоу нш҃емꙋ и по поⷣоⷪбию. и разꙋ
мѣвати. ꙗкоⷤ во ѡбразѣ трⷪ҇ца дш҃а оумна
51r/121 словеⷭ҇на. и в поⷣоⷪбїи ꙗко бесплотно оумъ слово
ражаеⷮ и дх҃ъ исходить. а не мечтатисѧ
мысльми ѡ бз҃ѣ всꙋе. но по ѡбразоу и по подо

they generate words in our souls.[207] Nor is it possible for us ourselves to grasp the way our minds | generate our words in us, for our minds[208] do not have 50v/120 wives, nor do the minds require time, not even an hour, for conceiving a word or "curdling it like cheese" (Job 10:10), or for allowing it to be shaped into a growing form, similar to the way the flesh is fed from within the womb. The mind is never without the word, nor is the word without the mind.[209] Instead, the mind is coterminous, and the word is present in the mind in a coterminous way, too.

26.5. And if it is impossible to grasp the way our minds generate our words, then, how can anyone argue and oppose God in his begetting of the Son without a female partner?[210] Let him first, if he can, oppose the fact that his own mind generates the word without a female partner.[211] And even if this ridiculous idea had been possible—to oppose the fact that the mind generates the word without a female partner—it would still be impossible to envision the heavenly nature of God through our earthly speculations. How[212] greatly distant is the incorruptible nature from the corrupted nature? And concerning this blessed nature of God that is beyond all beings, it befits us, who are endowed with minds, to simply believe and worship, as opposed to inspecting, and also to learn from the Scriptures, where God said, "Let us make man in our image and likeness".

26.6. We[213] must recognize that the "image" of the Trinity is the intelligent and | rational soul, and that "in the likeness" indicates the incorporeal gener- 51r/121 ation of the word by the mind and the proceeding out of breath. And instead of conceptualizing God with vain ideas, we are to draw from God's image and

207 his Son without having suffered any exhaustion, for our minds do not become exhausted either when they generate words in our souls.] his perfect Son without having suffered any exhaustion, just as the way the human mind in the soul does not become exhausted in generating the perfect word.

208 our minds] they

209 The mind is never without the word, nor is the word without the mind.] The perfect God is never without his perfect Word. In the same way, the mind is never without the word, nor is the word without the mind.

210 argue and oppose God in his begetting of the Son without a female partner?] oppose the begetting of God, irrationally seeking a female partner in the incorporeal beings for the immaterial begetting?

211 partner.] partner, and then oppose the divine begetting! But it is surely impossible to oppose the fact that the mind generates the incorporeal word.

212 How] And how

213 We] And from this, we

бию бжⷭ҇тва в трⷪ҇цы познаваⷮ. а не неможе ние бжⷭ҇твоу притыкати и хоулити. при емлѧи бо имѧ гⷭ҇а бгⷭ҇а своⷭ҇е на сꙋ҃е да оумрⷮе. и да потребитсѧ дш҃а ѡна ѿ людїи еѩ. бж҃иа великаѩ заповⷣѣ повелѣваⷮе.

Показание ѩко в ветхⷨо законѣ ѩвлена есть трⷪ҇ца тонцѣ иⷤ ѩвленъ еⷭ҇ сн҃ъ бж҃їи. ѩко бг҃ъ истиненъ есть.[214]

По многоуⷤ ѡбрѩщемъ аще восхощемъ во свѧ щеннⷨе книзѣ бытеистѣи. тонко нѣка ко сн҃а бж҃їа. показоваема бг҃а сꙋща. естⷤь пакы и трⷪ҇ца ѿкрываема. ѩкⷤо при стⷪ҇лпо творенїи познаваетсѧ. внегда писано. сниде гⷭ҇ь бг҃ъ видѣти града и стⷪ҇лпа. и рⷱе гⷭ҇ь се рⷣо единъ и ѩзыкъ единъ всѣмъ. и се начаша творити. прїидѣте сшⷣеше смⷨѣ симъ и. оубо аггⷭлы ли призываⷮе бг҃ъ. прї идѣте сшⷣеше смѣсⷨи и. едаⷧ҇ на помощь себѣ призываⷮе. аки не могїи дѣтели сеѩ сотворити единоѩ. иⷤ сотворивыи

51v/122 нб҃о и землю и всѧ ѩⷤ в нⷯи. рⷱе и быша всѧ. повелѣ и создашаⷭ҇. ко единоⷤи ли малѣи дѣтели помощникы потребова. ⷤе размѣ сити мꙋⷨжⷭе ѩзыки. и се не бесчислены. на сⷣемъ десѧⷮ бо и два ѩзыка повѣдаетсѧ. всѩко равнопрестⷪ҇лство и равносилное слова и дх҃а бж҃їа книгы повѣдаюⷮ. аггⷭлиⷤ нѣсть пⷪ҇бни бгꙋ. не сопрⷭ҇тльствꙋють бо. но слоужаⷮ бв҃и. тѣмже не к нимъ речение бж҃їе ѡно есть. ⷤе прїидѣте низъ шⷣеше размѣсⷨи ѩ. но к сопрⷭ҇тльствꙋющⷨи емꙋ. и к пⷪ҇бнымъ себѣ глⷮеть бг҃ъ. прїидѣ

214 *In the margin*: глаⷡ еі҃.

likeness[215] and to recognize the Godhead of the Trinity[216] rather than assigning a deficiency to the Godhead and blaspheming it. For anyone who treats the name of the Lord God profanely "is to be put to death" (Lev. 24:16), and his soul "must be cut off from" its "people" (Lev. 17:4), as the great commandment of God enjoins.

27. A demonstration of the fact that the Old Testament Law discloses the Trinity in specific details, and it also reveals that God's Son is the true God. CHAPTER 15.[217]

27.1. If we wish, we can find many instances in the holy book of Genesis, where God's Son is shown to be God in certain details, and there are also instances where the Trinity is revealed. And this is also recognized in the building of the Tower of Babel, when it states, "And the Lord came down to see the city and the tower, and the Lord said, 'Behold, there is one race, and one tongue for all of them, and they have begun to do this. Come, and having gone down, let us confuse them'" (Gen. 11:5–7).

27.2. Now, is God calling upon the angels, (when he says), "Come, and having gone down, let us confuse them"? Is he really calling for help, as if he were not capable of doing that one thing by himself; he who "made | the heaven and the 51v/122
earth" (Gen. 1:1) and everything that is in them; who "spoke, and all things came into being, commanded, and they were created" (Ps. 33:9)? Did he really need helpers to do this one small thing by means of such great creatures in order to confuse the human tongues, and this, not into the infinite number (of tongues), for the account talks of seventy-two languages?

27.3. The Scriptures tell us everything related to the fact that the Word and God's Spirit[218] share the same throne and equal power. And[219] the angels are not like God, nor do they share the same throne with him. Instead, they serve God. Therefore, the statement of God, "Come, and having gone down, let us confuse them", is not directed at them, but at those who share with him the same throne and are like him. It is to them, that the Lord[220] says, "Come, and having

215 likeness] his likeness

216 to recognize the Godhead of the Trinity] to believe that one Godhead exists in the Trinity

217 **A demonstration of the fact that the Old Testament Law discloses the Trinity in specific details, and it also reveals that God's Son is the true God. CHAPTER 15.] Investigation in the holy book of Genesis as to how we are to receive the divine, and concerning the passage where the Prophet Moses put a veil over his face. CHAPTER 15.**

218 God's Spirit] Sprit

219 And] For

220 Lord] God

те нⷥишеⷣше размѣсимъ ꙗ. готовоⷤ разоу
мѣти ꙗко къ сн҃ꙋ своемꙋ и дх҃ꙋ реⷱ҇ бг҃ъ прїи
дѣте нⷥишеⷣше размѣсиⷨ ꙗ. здѣ пакы трⷪ҇цꙋ
ѝꙗвиша книги при размѣшенїи, ꙗкоⷤ
и первие внеⷢ҇а создати чл҃ка. трⷪ҇цꙋ кни
гы показаша. заⷤе гл҃ати тамо. рече бг҃ъ
сотворимъ чл҃ка по ѡбразоу нш҃емꙋ и по
подобию. кто не по чю̈тсꙗ премⷬ҇рости
и свѣтлости сщ҃еннѣи книѕѣ бытё
ст҃ѣи. сказоующи бг҃а единоⷢ҇ в трехъⷤ со
ставоⷯ
52r/123 гаⷭ҇ единоⷢ҇ в треⷯ лицеⷯ. понеⷨ҇ начахоⷨ прочитати
книгꙋ сию. прочтохомъ оубо писаное. реⷱ҇ бг҃ъ
сотвориⷨ чл҃ка по ѡбразоу нш҃емꙋ и по подобию.
и разоумѣхоⷨ к комꙋ реⷱ҇ бг҃ъ. ꙗко к соѡбразныⷨ
емꙋ и к подобнымъ емꙋ величествоⷨ и силою и
вл҃ⷣчество. и познахомъ ѿ ѡбраза сотворе
наⷢ҇ ими чл҃ка. бжⷭ҇тво въ треⷯ составо. бг҃а
ѿца ровша сн҃а слово. и дх҃а исходꙗща ст҃го.
и рожеⷩ҇ое слово сн҃ъ ѿчии. събезначаленъ
ѿцꙋ. и дхъ ст҃ыи и исходꙗи ѿ бг҃а. ни смѣсно
ни раздѣлно. ꙗкоⷤ и подобие иⷯ во ѡбраѕѣ
въ чл҃цѣ. оумъ ражаеⷮ слово беⷥсмⷭ҇ртно беⷥ за
чатїа. и дхъ ѿ оустъ исходꙗ. показоуеⷮ
оума ѿца словꙋ. и слово показоуеⷮ сн҃а оумꙋ
по подобию съвершеннаⷢ҇. беⷥсмⷭ҇ртнаго бе
сплотнаⷢ҇ бжⷭ҇тва. во плотꙗнѣ и тлѣннѣ
чл҃цѣ оумъ и слово дхомъ познаваемо. ибо
и бжⷭ҇тва невозможно познати аще не дхоⷨ
ст҃ымъ. плотны ибо дховныⷯ не можеⷮ по
знати в разоумѣ. понеже ѿ плоти воѡ
бразоуеⷮ тлю. и смыслиⷮ земнаа истлѣю
щаа в погибеⷧ. дховнымⷤ дховнаа прилага
ютсꙗ.

gone down, let us confuse them". And this should make us ready to understand that it is to his Son and Spirit,[221] that God said, "Come, and having gone down, let us confuse them".

27.4. Here, again, the Scriptures reveal the Trinity at the event of confusing the tongues, just as earlier, at the creation of man, the Scriptures also showed the Trinity because it says there, "God said, 'Let us make man in our image and likeness'".[222] Who would not be amazed at the supreme wisdom and brightness of the holy book of Genesis that depicts one God in three subsistences, | 52r/123
one Lord in three persons?[223] For as we began to read this Scripture,[224] we read the statement that "God said, 'Let us make man in our image and likeness'", and we recognized who it was to whom God spoke—to those who possessed a common image and were like him in might and power and dominion. And we learned from their image—the man whom they made—that the Godhead exists in three subsistences: God the Father, the begotten Son, who is the Word, and the proceeding Holy Spirit.[225]

27.5. And the begotten Word, the Father's Son, is the same as the Father, without beginning, and the divine Spirit proceeds from God, neither merged nor separated. Their likeness, reflected in man as their image, (is seen) from the way the mind generates the word without passion, without conception,[226] and when the breath comes out of the mouth, it reveals the mind, the "father" of the word, whereas the word shows itself as the mind's "son", according to the likeness of the perfect, passionless, incorruptible, incorporeal Godhead.

27.6. In man, who is enslaved to flesh and corruption,[227] the mind and word are recognized by means of the breath, for[228] it is impossible to recognize the eternal Godhead either, except by the Holy Spirit. For the man of flesh cannot understand[229] the things of the Spirit by his mind, because he uses flesh to imagine what is bound to corruption and to think of the earthly things that perish in decay. But as for spiritual men, the things of the Spirit lead them | to 52v/124

221 Son and Spirit,] Son, the Word, and to his Holy Spirit,

222 *MS 61 adds*: **Showing that in the Old Testament Law, the Trinity is revealed with great wisdom, and certain details are also indicated with respect to the Son of God.**

223 subsistences, one Lord in three persons?] subsistences, indicating them to be equal in activity and equal in power?

224 this Scripture,] this sacred Scripture,

225 Holy Spirit.] divine Holy Spirit.

226 without conception,] without conception, incorporeally,

227 to flesh and corruption,] to flesh and passion and corruption,

228 for] just as

229 understand] accept

52v/124 в жизнь неистлѣннꙋ и въ славꙋ бж҃ию. по ѡ
бразномꙋ и по поⷣбномꙋ. такоⷤ прочтохоⷨ
и разоумѣхоⷨ пакы. ꙗкоⷤ еⷭ бг҃ъ сие и гⷭ҇ь. и еже
гⷭ҇ь тоⷤ и бг҃ъ. ї ꙗко бжⷭ҇тво и гⷭ҇ьство бг҃ꙋ ѿцꙋ
и словꙋ сн҃оу и дх҃оу ст҃мꙋ едино еⷭ. такоже
прочтохоⷨ и при размѣшенїи. и разꙋмѣхоⷨ
ꙗко не ко аггломъ реⷱ бг҃ъ. сшⷣеше смѣсиⷨ и.
ниⷤ самъ к себѣ сие реⷱ бг҃ъ. но къ единочⷭ҇тныⷨ
себѣ. и единославнымъ реⷱ бг҃ъ. сшⷣеше смѣ
сиⷨ и. само трⷪ҇чное едиⷩство бжⷭ҇тва по
малꙋ показаша книгы. И рѣша ми трие
ѡни ѡба мниха и мирꙗнинъ. чесо раⷣ не
писа моисѣи. ѿкровенно. оу бг҃а сн҃а бж҃їа
и дх҃а ст҃го равныⷯ емꙋ быти. и тацѣхъⷤ
бжⷭ҇твомъ. Ꙗко моисеи жидовоⷨ безꙋмїа
иⷯ раⷣ не писа в трⷪ҇цы бг҃а насоⷠно. писаниемъⷤ
ꙗвленнѣ множицею ѿкры трⷪ҇цꙋ бг҃а.
Ѿвѣщаⷯ оубо имъ гл҃ꙗ. и ѕѣло книгы сщ҃енныꙗ
добрѣ ѿкрыша единоⷢ бг҃а в трехъⷤ ипоста
сеⷯ. бг҃а ѿца и сн҃а бж҃їа. бг҃а ѿца и дх҃а ст҃го
бг҃а. единочⷭ҇тныⷯ. единославныⷯ. едино
прⷭ҇тльныⷯ. единогⷭ҇ьствꙋющиⷯ. смотритеⷤ
53r/125 оубо здѣ истинны писанїа. понеⷤ прⷣелагает сꙗ
книга. чл҃комъ живщиⷨ посредѣ ꙗзыка много
божна. и навыкшиⷨ слышатⷺ многи бг҃и бываю
щаꙗ. и боги боговъ оубивающа и ратꙋюще сꙗⷺ

life free of corruption and to the glory of God, in keeping with the image and likeness.[230]

27.7. Similarly, we read and recognized again that whenever we had "God", there was also "Lord", and whenever we had "Lord", there was also "God"; that there is one deity and lordship of God the Father, and Word the Son, and Holy Spirit.[231] Likewise, we read about the confusion of tongues and understood[232] that it was not to the angels, that God said, "having gone down, let us confuse them", nor did God say it to himself, but to those who have the same honor and glory as him. To them, God said, "Having gone down, let us confuse them". The Scriptures offer a gradual self-revelation of the Godhead's triune oneness.

27.8. And those three—two monks and the layman—asked me, "But why[233] didn't Moses openly write that the Son and Holy Spirit are equal with God, and that they are such in terms of divinity, too"?

28. Showing that Moses did not directly describe the Trinity for the Jews because of their senselessness, and that the Scripture clearly reveals the triune God in numerous ways.[234]

28.1. Then, in response, I said to them: The sacred Scriptures have revealed one God in three hypostases very well. God the Father, and the Son of God, ⟨and the divine Holy Spirit are clearly from God⟩, sharing the same honor, the same glory, the same throne, the same lordship.[235] And see, | then, the truth of Scrip- 53ʳ/125
ture here! We have to account for the fact that Scripture was given to people who lived among the polytheistic nations that used to hear of many emerging deities[236] and deities of deities (known) for killing each other and fighting

230 image and likeness.] prototype and likeness.

231 "God"; that there is one deity and lordship of God the Father, and Word the Son, and Holy Spirit.] "God". The reference is legitimate and indicates equal honor, that there is one deity and lordship of God the Father, and Word and Son, and Holy Spirit.

232 and understood] and after some reflection, we understood

233 "But why] "And if it were the way you say, then why

234 **Showing that Moses did not directly describe the Trinity for the Jews because of their senselessness, and that the Scripture clearly reveals the triune God in numerous ways.**] *omitted*

235 from God⟩, sharing the same honor, the same glory, the same throne, the same lordship.] from God, possessing the same power, the same honor, the same glory, the same lordship, and consubstantiality.

236 many emerging deities] many deities

себе. ꙗкоⷤ зевесъ крона ѿца своеⷢ҇ оуби. и ины
женъ раⷣ побивающиⷯ сꙗ. наоучаꙗ таковыꙗ
чл҃ки книга сїа. ѿвращатиса многобж҃їа
ложнаⷢ҇. познатиⷤ истиннаⷢ҇ бг҃а. сотворшаⷢ҇
нб҃о и землю. и создавшаго чл҃ка. премⷣрѣ ѕѣло
и истиннѣ. единоⷢ҇ бг҃а знати наоучаеⷮ кни
га бытеискаа. да не ѿ начаⷮка слышавше
иоудѣа бг҃а ѿца и слова еⷢ҇ сн҃а. и дх҃а еⷢ҇ ст҃го. по
знати не возмогѹть. беспоⷧ҇тное бж҃тве
ное всесъвершеное сѹщество. и воⷥмнꙗть
пакы многы богы быти сказоующа имъ
и моисѣа. понеⷤ прⷭ҇но ко многобж҃ию июдѣѡⷨ
неистоⷡ҇ство належиⷮ. ꙗкоⷤ нн҃ѣ видиⷨ косоⷢ҇ сеⷢ҇.
неистовѣ к безбж҃ию належаща. таковыⷯ
и евреи неистовыⷯ ко многобж҃ию належа
щиⷯ видѣⷮ есть. вчера бо и днеⷭ҇ ѿ работы тꙗ
жкїа и ѡзлобленїа моукъ лютыⷯ египеⷮ
скиⷯ. свободиⷡ҇ чюдесы страшными бг҃ъ.
53v/127 ведꙗше иⷥ моисѣемъ. и стоⷧ҇пома ѡблачныⷨ
и ѡгненыⷨ. в землю ѡбѣтованнѹю. скво
ѕѣ море по сѹхѹ. и в пѹстыни манною. и
крастеⷣ питаа. оужасное видѣние бж҃їе
в горѣ показа. в нейⷤ моисѣи бг҃ѹ пⷬ҇естоꙗ
ше. страⷯ велїи ѕлыꙗ пагоубы. ѿ прико
сновенїа горы належащъ зрꙗще. манноу
во ѹстѣⷯ имоуще. абие вса сїа забывше.
и ꙗко ничтоⷤ положше. единою оупившеⷭ҇
неистовъствоⷨ многобж҃їа. ноудꙗхѹ аа
рона сотвори наⷨ бг҃и гл҃юще. и видѣвше
единъ телецъ вопиꙗхѹ. сїи б҃зи твои
ї҃илю извеⷣшїи тꙗ иⷥ египта. како ѹбо к та
ковымъ неистовымъ людемъ безоумь
ствѹющиⷨ вынѹ. мечтаниеⷨ многобж҃иа.

among themselves, such as when Zeus murdered his own father Cronus, and also killed others[237] for the sake of gaining wives.[238]

28.2. This Scripture taught[239] those men to stay away from false polytheism and to acknowledge the true God, who made the heaven and the earth and who created man. The book of Genesis taught them about the one God in a very wise, true way so that the Jews, who did not hear of God the Father, and of his Word, the Son, and of his[240] Holy Spirit from the very beginning, and who were not able to recognize the incorporeal, divine, entirely perfect being, would not come to think that Moses was speaking of many gods. For the Jews in their insanity were always inclined toward polytheism, just as we now saw this man, Kosoy, in his insanity being prone toward godlessness. That is the way we should see the Jews as being inclined in their insanity to polytheism.

28.3. For while they were experiencing the hardship of daily work and anger about the terrible tortures of the Egyptians, God delivered them through awesome miracles (Ex. 7:1–11:10). | He led them into the promised land through 53ᵛ/127
Moses and by means of the pillar of cloud by day and of fire by night (Ex. 13:21–22) had them cross the sea by walking on dry ground (Ex. 13:17–14:29), fed them with manna and quail in the desert (Ex. 16), showed them a petrifying vision of God on the mountain (Ex. 19). And at that place, Moses stood before God, while they were in great fear about the possibility of terrible destruction from touching the mountain (Ex. 19:12–13). And even with manna still in their mouths, they forgot all those things very soon, as if they did not endure anything (Ps. 106:21).

28.4. Being driven purely by their insanity of polytheism,[241] they urged Aaron, saying, "Make us gods" (Ex. 32:23), and when they saw *one* calf, they exclaimed, "These are your gods, O Israel, who brought you out of Egypt" (Ex. 32:4). ⟨And given that they called upon many gods after seeing *one* calf, what would they do, if they were to hear of the Trinity?⟩ How would Moses openly write about God the Father, and his Son, the Word, and his Holy Spirit as

237 others] other gods

238 *MS 61 adds*: **Showing that it was because of the Jews' longing for idols, that Moses did not directly reveal to them God in the Trinity, and yet he opened their mind for understanding by describing God as Trinity in numerous wise ways.**

239 This Scripture taught] With these books, Moses taught

240 his] *omitted*

241 polytheism] idol-worship

ѿкровенно написати моисѣю. съ б҃гомъ ѿцемъ сопрⷭ҇тльствꙋющиⷯ емꙋ слова его с҃на и дх҃а его ст҃го. сеⷢ҇ ради много премⷣро и ѕѣло истинно писаше сщ҃еннꙋю книгꙋ моисѣи. ѿводѧ евреѧ ѿ многобж҃иа. наоучаа единоⷢ҇ б҃га вѣдати. и помалѣ в треⷯ ипостасеⷯ. едино бжⷭ҇тво ѿкрываа. 54r/128 тогоⷤ г҃а в треⷯ лицеⷯ. гл҃авъ преⷤ ꙗко сотвори б҃гъ н҃бо и землю. и реⷱ б҃гъ да боудеⷮ свѣⷮ. и реⷱ б҃гъ да боудеⷮ твердь. и реⷱ б҃гъ да соберетсѧ вода и да ꙗвитсѧ сꙋша. и сотвори б҃гъ свѣтила. и реⷱ б҃гъ да прорастиⷮ землѧ. и реⷱ б҃гъ да изведꙋть воды животнаа по родꙋ. и реⷱ б҃гъ да изведеⷮ землѧ четвероногаа. пришеⷣ же къ единомꙋ животномꙋ. и реⷱ б҃гъ сотвориⷨ чл҃ка по ѡбразоу нш҃емꙋ и по подⷪ҇бию. понеⷤ всѧ тварь беⷥдшьна смыслити не можеⷮ пѣти и покланѧтисѧ творцꙋ своемꙋ единомꙋ б҃гꙋ в трⷪ҇цы. беⷥсловеⷭна бо тваⷬ всѧ. точию добротою своею и величествоⷨ исповѣдоваюⷮ славоу бж҃ию и творение еⷢ҇. сего раⷣ тамо в творении твари не ѿкрываеⷮ славоу трⷪ҇цы во единоⷨ бжⷭ҇твѣ. но единьство бж҃ие. чл҃ка ѡ дш҃евлена и словесна пѣвца и поклонника своемꙋ бжⷭ҇твꙋ создати прїиде. тꙋ показа тогда и подобныⷯ б҃гꙋ. соѡбразныⷯ равносилныⷯ. еⷣ sharing the same throne, to those insane people, who were madly dreaming about polytheism all the time?[242]

28.5. For that reason, Moses wrote the holy book (Pentateuch) with great wisdom and absolute truth, leading the Jew away from polytheism and teaching him to know the one God. And gradually, he revealed the one Godhead in three hypostases, | one and the same Lord in three persons, when he said ear- 54ʳ/128
lier that "God made the heaven and the earth" (Gen. 1:1),[243] and "God said, 'Let there be light'" (Gen. 1:3), and "God said, 'Let there be a vault'" (Gen. 1:6), and "God said, 'Let the water be gathered up, and let the dry land appear'" (Gen. 1:9), and "God made (two) great lights" (Gen. 1:14), and "God said, 'Let the earth sprout (green plants)'" (Gen. 1:11),[244] and "God said, 'Let the earth bring forth the four-footed creatures'" (Gen. 1:24). And when the time came to (create) one (specific) animal, God said, "Let us make man in our image and likeness" (Gen. 1:27).

28.6. For no created things that are considered to be soulless can sing and worship their Creator, the one God in the Trinity, because all the other works are irrational. They can only confess God's glory and his creation by means of their goodness and majesty. That is why he does not reveal the glory of the Trinity in one Godhead at this point of the world's creation, and instead, (he shows) the oneness of God. And when the time came (for God) to create man, the living and rational singer and worshiper of his Godhead, then he also revealed here those who were like God, who possessed a common image, who had equal

242 time?] time? Nevertheless, I think that Moses gave the Israelites a sign in the following way: since the Israelites were not yet able to grasp the true glory of the triune Godhead at that point, for that reason, he put a veil over his face. For they could not see his face because of how it shone, and that glorious radiation was caused by the hand of God (Ex. 34:29:35). For the same reason, I think, Moses himself was allowed to see God's "back" (Ex. 33:23), rather than having been allowed to see the face of God, namely, God in the Trinity: the Father, and Son, and Holy Spirit. It was for that reason, that God also covered him with his hand to not let him see the face of God, I think (Ex. 33:22–23). And it is to cover the glory of the triune God, that this is said. For the "back" of God at that point, in my view, had to do with the fact that they were still limited in knowledge of the only one God on account of the idols of pagan polytheism. And to see the face of God, namely, the glory of the Godhead in the Trinity, will become appropriate when the light of God appears in the flesh on the earth. Just as it happened at that time with Moses' face on the mountain, so will the glory of God in the Trinity shine forth over the surface of the entire earth, that is, the whole humankind, when the light of God comes upon the earth and the pagan deities, the work of men's hands, will hide from the terrifying face of the Lord, who will come in the flesh.

243 earth" (Gen. 1:1),] earth" (Gen. 1:1), and "God said, 'Let there be light'" (Gen. 1:3),

244 plants)'" (Gen. 1:11),] plants)'" (Gen. 1:11), and "God said, 'Let the water bring forth the living creatures according to their kinds'" (Gen. 1:20–21),

нопрⷭ҇тльныⷯ совѣта раⷣ҇. сотвориⷨ бо рⷱ҇е члⷭ҇ка
по ѡбразоу нⷲ҇емꙋ и по пⷣ҇обию. рⷱ҇е бг҇ъ. понеже
члⷭ҇коу воспѣваⷮ҇ и славиⷮ҇ бг҇а в трⷪ҇цы. словеⷭ҇нꙋ
54v/129 и ѡдⷲ҇евленꙋ животꙋ соущꙋ. а не мⷧ҇ъчанием
славиⷮ҇ бг҇а. ꙗкоⷤ҇ бездⷲ҇ьнои и беⷥ҇словеⷭ҇нои тваⷬ҇.

[Several lines of blank space]

Авраамоуⷤ҇ велико ѿкровенно трⷪ҇цоу бжⷭ҇твенꙋ еди[245]
но сⷭ҇ъщественꙋ. книгы сказаша гл҇юще сице.
Авижеⷭ҇ авраамꙋ бг҇ъ. оу дꙋба мамріа сѣдꙗщꙋ емꙋ.
прⷣ҇е двѣми храмꙋ еⷢ҇ полꙋдн҇е. возрⷠ҇ѣ же ѡчима
своима и видѣ. сеⷤ҇ трие мꙋжи стоꙗхꙋ верхоу еⷢ҇.
и видѣвъ притече въ срⷮ҇ѣтение имъ. ѿ двере
храмꙋ его. и поклониса до землꙗ. и рⷱ҇е. гиⷭ҇. аще
есмь ѡбрⷮ҇ѣ прⷣ҇е тобою блⷢ҇ть. не мини раба сво
еⷢ҇. да са принесеⷮ҇ вода. да сꙗ ѡмыюⷮ҇ ногы
ваша. и простꙋдитеⷭ҇ пⷣ҇о дꙋбомъ. и принесоу
хлѣбы да ꙗсте. и по сеⷨ҇ минете на поуⷮ҇ свои.
с негоⷤ҇ совратистеⷭ҇ сѣмо к рабоу своемꙋ. и рⷱ҇ѣ
ша емꙋ тако сотвори ꙗкоⷤ҇ гл҇а. Смотри
те пⷡ҇исаніа оуⷣ҇бо. и не мимохоⷣ҇те гл҇ъ. нⷺ҇ѣ
сть бо в книгаⷯ҇ празⷣ҇на словеси. глⷮ҇еть писаⷩ҇е.
ꙗвиⷭ҇ авраамꙋ бг҇ъ. таⷤ҇ наводиⷮ҇ писание ꙗко
полꙋдне ꙗвиⷭ҇ авраамꙋ бг҇ъ. да не помыслиши
вечера. понеⷤ҇ множицею в сꙋмрацѣⷯ҇ чистꙋ
55r/131 нбⷭ҇и егда бывающꙋ. призорѣ ѡчима блазнь бы
ваеⷮ҇. и в малѣ многа видѣти. и великое мало
и малое велико зрѣти. но полꙋдне рⷱ҇е ꙗвися
бг҇а авраамꙋ. внегда ѡчи зрꙗⷮ҇ всꙗко чтⷭ҇о. беⷥ҇

245 *In the margin*: глⷡ҇а ѕ҇і.

power and shared the same throne with him. For it was in view of his taking counsel, that he said, "Let us make man in our image and likeness". That is why man, being a rational | and living[246] animal, sings and glorifies the triune God, 54v/129
rather than glorifying God in silence, like the creatures who have no soul and are irrational.

29. CHAPTER 16.[247]

29.1. But as for great Abraham, he was given a revelation about the divine and co-ruling Trinity, which is taught by the following passage[248] that says in the Scriptures,[249] "And God appeared to him by the oak of Mamre, as he sat by the door of his tent at noon. And he lifted up his eyes and looked, and behold, three men stood in front of him; and having seen them, he ran to meet them from the door of his tent and bowed himself to the ground. And he said, 'Lord, if I have found grace in your sight, do not pass by your servant. Let water be brought, and let them wash your feet, and refresh yourselves under the oak. And I will bring bread, that you may eat, and afterward, you may continue going[250] on your journey, from which you turned aside here[251] to your servant'. And they said, 'Do as you said'" (Gen. 18:1–5).

29.2. Now, observe the Scriptures and do not pass by any words, for no words in the Scriptures are (written) in vain. The Scripture says, "God appeared to Abraham", and it also indicates the fact that God appeared to Abraham at noon so that we may not think of evening, for it often happens that in the twilight of the sunset, | even when the skies are clear, the eyes are led by illusion and see 55r/131
small things as big and big things as small.[252] But it is said that God appeared to Abraham at noon, when the eyes see everything clearly and without any

246 rational and living] living and rational

247 *Here MS 337 has a blank space for a missing heading. MS 61 adds:* **On the brightest revelation of the true divine glory in the holy book of Genesis, and on how to understand the appearance of God to great Abraham that took place at noon, which is when (God) also visited him in his tent.** CHAPTER 16. At the creation of man, male and female, the Scripture shows us God in the Trinity in a latent way. For in creating the woman, God said, "It is not good for the man to be alone, let us make for him a helper suitable to him" (Gen. 2:18), and at the Tower of Babel, (the Trinity) is also latent.

248 by the following passage] *omitted*

249 *MS 61. adds:* **Showing that in the case of Abraham, Moses showed God, the Trinity, clearly, and not latently nor figuratively.**

250 you may continue going] you may depart

251 here] *omitted*

252 see small things as big and big things as small.] see small things as big

всꙗкого соблазна. возрѣвъж видѣвъ. се трие
мѹжие стоꙗхѹ верхѹ его. глт҇е оубо ꙗко ꙗвис
бгъ авраамѹ. возрѣвъж авраамъ видѣ ѡчи
ма своима трие мѹжи. ꙗвно ѿкрываетъ пи
сание трцы славѹ. рѣ бо писание ꙗвитис
бгоу авраамѹ. возрѣвъж видѣти авраамѹ
трих а не единог. и притеч авраамъ въ стрѣ
тение имъ. а не емѹ. ꙗвѣ ꙗко трием а не едино
мѹ. тажъ глеть писание. и поклонисѧ до землꙗ.
и рѣч гис. бгаꙗвитис оубо рѣч. триехъж зрить.
и срѣтаетъ ихъ авраам. тажъ глеть гис. ꙗко ѡбрѣтох
благть прѣд тобою. единомѹ здѣ глеть гис. три
ехъж оусрѣтив. что ѹбо есть се. егда ѡблазни
тис правдивомѹ. видѣвшѹ ѡчима три. и при
шед единого ѡбрѣсти. к немоуж бы и рещи точию гис
двоюж бы емѹ тѹ не ѡбрѣсти. к нимъж и не рѣч
гдис и влки. но прѣжд ꙗви писание ꙗко полѹ
дне ꙗвис бгъ авраамѹ. триех же видѣти емѹ.
55v/132 и въ срѣтение теч имъ. глетьж оубо единомѹ гис.
аще ѡбрѣтох блгть прѣд тобою. не соблазнивсѧ
оубо видѣнием авраам. ꙗко полѹдне ꙗвисѧ емоу
бгъ. и авраамѹ чисто видѣти три мѹжи. и къ е
диномѹ глати. гис аще ѡбрѣтох блгть прѣд тобою.
не мини раба своег. нѣсть ли оубо се бга единог.
в трех же составох книги бжїа исповѣдаша.
имже трием лицемъ едино гсьство авраам про
повѣда. ѿкровено ѕѣло здѣ при авраамѣ кни
ги сказаша трцю бга гса единог. Аще кто глт
бга единог быти ѿ трием мѹжеи. да сег ради та
ко рѣч авраам. гис аще ѡбрѣтох блгть прѣд тобою.
понеж идоста в содом два аггла. авраам же стоа
прѣд гмъс ї еще. но здѣ книги не даютъ мѣста
таковым помышлением быти. понеж внегда
глати авраамѹ. гис аще ѡбрѣтох блгть прѣд
тобою. не мини раба своег. абие тѹ навед рѣч

delusion. "And he lifted up his eyes and looked, and behold, three men stood in front of him" (Gen. 1:2).

29.3. Now, in saying that God appeared to Abraham, and Abraham saw three men with his own eyes, the Scripture clearly reveals the glory of the Trinity. For the Scripture said that God appeared to Abraham, and when he looked up, Abraham saw "three men", and not "one". And Abraham ran to meet "them", not "him". It is evident that there are three, and not one. And the Scripture also says that "he bowed himself to the ground" and said, "Lord", mentioning this in order to reveal God. And Abraham sees three men, and them he meets, and to them, he says, "Lord, if I have found grace in your sight". Having met the three, he speaks here to one. What does that mean? Did the righteous man make a mistake—after seeing three men with his own eyes, he came and found one, and precisely to him he also said, "Lord", for he did not find two men there,[253] and on that account, did not say to them collectively, "Lords" or "Masters"? But the Scripture showed first that God appeared to Abraham at noon, and the latter saw three men, | and them[254] he ran to meet, but then, he said to only one, 55v/132
"Lord, if I have found grace in your sight".

29.4. Now, it was not the case that Abraham failed to see things accurately, for God appeared to him at noon, and Abraham clearly saw three men and spoke to only one,[255] "Lord, if I have found grace in your sight, do not pass by your servant". Now, is this not where the divine Scriptures confessed God, one in three subsistences, and whom Abraham proclaimed, three persons who have one lordship?[256]

29.5. And if someone speaks of one God with reference to those three men based on the words of Abraham, "Lord, if I have found grace in your sight", is it because the other two angels went to Sodom while Abraham still stood before the Lord?[257] (Gen. 19:1). But the Scriptures do not allow such thoughts here, because when Abraham said, "Lord, if I have found grace in your sight, do not pass by your servant", he immediately added there (in the plural), saying,

---

253 men there] men with him there

254 them] those three

255 spoke to only one] to all of them together he said,

256 confessed God, one in three subsistences, and whom Abraham proclaimed, three persons who have one lordship?] confessed the common lordship of God and where Abraham proclaimed him? **Showing that those who are like God can be recognized from the fact that they possess equal honor and unity of mind; and that there are three in one Godhead on account of their common glory and equal power.**

257 angels went to Sodom while Abraham still stood before the Lord?] angels from those three (left) when Abraham still stood before the Lord, for the Scriptures say that "the two angels arrived at Sodom" (Gen. 19:1)?

да ѡмыютса ноги ваша. и простꙋдитеⷭ поⷣ дꙋбомъ. и принесꙋ хлѣбы да ꙗсте. и рѣ ша тако сотвори ꙗкоⷤ гл҃а. посемꙋ триехъ равночⷭтие. и единоⷭгьствие книги сказоуⷮю. заⷤе гл҃ати вкꙋпѣ къ триеⷨ. и рещи да ѡмы ютса ноги ваша. и да ꙗсте. а не прⷣепочитаⷮ единоⷢ ѿ прочиⷯ двоиⷯ. и рещи. да ѡмы[258]

56r/134 ютса ноги твоа. и да ꙗси. наипачеⷤ здѣ триеⷯ единославное и равночⷭтное. и вкꙋпомыслѣное. познаваетса. внегда показаⷮ книгаⷨ гл҃ющи. и рѣша тако сотвори. ꙗвѣ ꙗко вкꙋпѣ ѿвѣ щаша авраамꙋ трие ѡни мꙋжи. и рѣша та ко сотвори ꙗкоⷤ гл҃а. не рѣша бо книги и реⷱ гⷭь та ко сотвори. но гл҃еⷮ писание и рѣшаⷣ ꙗко сотво ри ꙗкоⷤ гл҃а. ⷤе ѕѣло показоуеⷮ писание. триеⷯ достоинство равночⷭтїа и вкꙋпомыслїа. заⷤе показаⷮ ꙗко вкꙋпѣ трие мꙋжи рѣша авра амꙋ. тако сотвори ꙗкоⷤ гл҃а. аще бо бы два агг҃ла были два ѡни мꙋжи с третїимъ мꙋ жеⷨ съ гдⷭемъ. не бы сопрⷭтльни были бв҃и. ниⷤ сповелитеⷧни съ бгмъ во едино. и не гл҃али бы вкꙋпѣ съ бгмъ авраамꙋ тако сотвори ꙗкоⷤ гл҃а. сице бо реⷱ писание. ꙗко вкꙋпѣ рѣша а враамꙋ тако сотвори ꙗкоⷤ гл҃а. аще бы слꙋ жебнїи агг҃ли были. то прⷣестоꙗли бы прⷣе бгмъ. и не быша сопрⷭтльствоваⷮ емꙋ сидѣ ниеⷨ. ниⷤ бы дерзнꙋли сповелѣваⷮ съ бгмъ.

258 *Lines 6–7 are added by the scribe in the margin.*

"let them wash your feet and refresh yourselves under the oak. And I will bring bread, that you may eat. And they said, 'Do as you said'" (Gen. 18:3–5).[259]

29.6. Therefore, the Scriptures describe[260] equal honor and common lordship of the three, because Abraham speaks to the three collectively, saying, "Let them wash your feet"[261] and "that you may eat" (Gen. 18:4–5), instead of preferring one over the other two and saying (in the singular form), "Let them wash | 56r/134
your feet", and "that you may eat".[262] But above all, we learn here of common glory, and equal honor, and one mind that the three share when the Scriptures show and state how they said to Abraham, "Do as you said".[263]

29.7. It is evident that all three of those men answered to Abraham[264] collectively, "Do as you said". For the Scriptures do not state (in the singular), "And the Lord said, 'Do as you said'". Instead, the Scripture states (in the plural), "And they said, 'do as you said'".[265] The Scripture does a good job of showing the one dignity of the three that share equal honor and collective thought, because it[266] shows that all three men together said to Abraham, "Do as you said".

29.8. For if the two men along with the third one, who were with the Lord, had been two angels, they would not have shared the same throne with God, nor would they have ruled in union with God, nor would they have said to Abraham together with God, "Do as you said".[267] For that is what the Scripture stated, that they said to Abraham collectively, "Do as you said". If they had been the ministering angels, they would have stood before God and would not have shared the same seat with him on the throne, nor would they have dared to

---

259 *MS 61 adds*: **Showing that the angels are not worthy to co-rule with God nor remain next to him, as the royal counselors do—however great additional titles lend them support, they will be far less significant with respect to the king.**

260 describe] show

261 feet"] feet", and "refresh yourselves under the oak"

262 eat".] eat", from which we would recognize the one God in relation to "three". But Abraham pays equal honor worthy to all three of them together, saying, "Let them wash your feet", and other such things that describe common honor.

263 common glory, and equal honor, and one mind that the three share, when the Scriptures show and state how they said to Abraham, "Do as you said".] lordship that the three share in common glory, and equal honor, and one mind, when the Scriptures show how they spoke to Abraham, "And they said, 'Do as you said'".

264 answered to Abraham] spoke to Abraham

265 as you said'".] *omitted*

266 It] Scripture

267 For if the two men along with the third one, who were with the Lord, had been two angels, they] And if the ones who were with the Lord had been the angels—two men along with the third one—they

но паⷣ молчаниⷨ бж҃ие повелѣние прⷣепочитали бы. да боудеⷮ познаваемⷨ вл҃ка наⷣ рабы. 56v/135 бг҃ъ наⷣ агг҃лы своими. нн҃ѣ сщ҃енное писание показа. не сꙋмнѣте҃ное двоиⷯ ко еⷣномꙋ. не различноеⷤ ни раздвоеное меншиⷯ ѿ бо҃шаго. но еⷣно гс҃ьство триеⷯ показа. и равночт҃ное вл҃чество бж҃тва. внегда гл҃ати триеⷨ вкꙋпѣ сие. еⷤ тако сотвори ꙗкоⷤ гл҃а. аще были бы ша меншїи два прⷣестоꙗли бы ѡба единомꙋ. и продерзоваⷮ не быша смѣли прⷣе вл҃кою. вкꙋпѣ повелѣвати авраамꙋ и рещи емꙋ с нимъ. сотвори ꙗкоⷤ гл҃а. ꙗкоⷤ и прⷣе рѣхъ. мо҃чанием бы паⷣ бж҃їа велѣнїа прⷣепочитаⷯ. не быша восхищали бж҃їа сана на са. прⷣе самѣмъ сꙋщи бг҃мъ. ни бо сигклити прⷣе цр҃мъ повелѣвати могоуⷮ. такомꙋ соущꙋ чл҃кꙋ црю. ꙗкоⷤ и сигклити. точию санⷨо вл҃чества преимѣющꙋ иⷯ. и сеⷢ ради з боꙗзнию и мо҃чаниеⷨ слово еⷢ прⷣепочитаюⷮ. велие оубо и мноⷢ и се единоеⷤ точию агг҃ломъ прⷣестоꙗти бв҃и. прⷣе лицеⷨ его. а еⷤ вкꙋпѣ гл҃ати. и вкꙋпѣ повелѣвати съ бг҃мъ. тоⷢ бж҃тва точию достоиⷩство есть се. Чесоⷤ раⷣди оубо агг҃лоⷡ слꙋжебныⷯ поꙗти бг҃ꙋ ко авраамꙋ. еда чт҃и 57r/136 раⷣ бж҃тва своеⷢ вожаше съ собою два агг҃ла. ꙗвлꙗꙗса бг҃ъ авраамꙋ. и како се боудеⷮ. имѣꙗ тмы тмами. и тысꙗща тысꙗⷲⷨи агг҃лъ. два точию поемлеⷮ с собою бг҃ъ ко авраамꙋ. еда велїа боудеⷮ чт҃ь бж҃твꙋ вселицѣ. ѿ толикыⷯ бесчисленыⷯ нб҃ныхъ агг҃лъ два точию водити. и се не по ~~воли~~ себѣ. но с собою равночт҃ны творꙗ и сопр҃тльны приемлꙗ. и сповелѣваⷮ себѣ даꙗ иⷨ. како ꙋбо возможно быти единославныⷨ рабоⷨ вл҃цѣ. како ли смѣти сосѣдѣти рабоⷨ вл҃цѣ на единоⷨ пр҃тлѣ. или кто попꙋсти в толикꙋ дерзость произыти рабоⷨ ꙗко сповелѣвати вл҃цѣ. едаⷤ пакы сего раⷣ поꙗⷮ бг҃ъ два точию co-rule with God. Instead, they would have preferred to take God's command in silence[268] to help us recognize the master over the servants—| God over his angels. 56v/135

29.9. But the sacred Scripture is showing now that the other two are undoubtedly[269] no different nor divided into two—smaller ones and a greater one. Rather, it shows one lordship of the three and equal honor of the Godhead's dominion, when all three collectively say this, "Do as you said". If the two were smaller than the third one, both of them would have stood before the latter one,[270] and would not have dared to be so audacious as to make commands to Abraham in the presence of, and together with, their master, and say to him,[271] "Do as you said". As I said before,[272] they would have rather preferred to take God's commands in silence and would not have put divine status on themselves in the presence of God himself. For neither can royal counselors make commands in the presence of a king. As king, such a man surpasses the royal counselors precisely in virtue of his ruling status, which is why they take his word in fear and silence.

29.10. Indeed, it is a great and immense privilege for the angels to do that one thing—to constantly stand in the presence of God, before his face. But for one to speak together with God and to make commands together with him, one should be[273] of exactly the same divine dignity. And why, then, would God need to take two angels with him (to visit) Abraham? Did it have to do with the Godhead's honor, | that he had two angels accompany him when God[274] 57r/136
appeared to Abraham? And how is it that he who has "myriads of myriads and thousands of thousands" of angels (Rev. 5:11), took only two angels with him (to see) Abraham? Was it not of much less honor for the Godhead to have a company of only two (beings) out of such an infinite myriad of heavenly angels, and in addition to that, to have them share equal honor—those who did not have it in themselves—and to accept them as sharing the same throne, and to let them co-rule with him? How is it possible, then, for the one who shares the same glory with his master to be a slave to him? How can the slave dare to stand next to his master? Or who would let the slave reach the point of such audacity as to co-rule with his master?

---

268 in silence] in silence and would not have been seated with God,
269 undoubtedly] *omitted*
270 one,] one, as I alerted you in what I said,
271 say to him,] say together with him,
272 before] *omitted*
273 one should be] one should clearly be
274 God] he

ѾⷮѾ бесчисленыⷯ аг҃глъ. понеⷤ хотяше ясти оу авраама дрꙋга своеⷢ. да не тщетꙋ емоу содѣлаеⷮ имѣнию. множествоⷨ прѣⷣтекꙋщий и послѣⷣствꙋющий емꙋ аг҃глъ. всѣмъ имъ имꙋщийⷨ ясти ꙋ авраама. и како се боуⷮде. даяи пищꙋ всяко плоти. насыщаа всяко животно бл҃говоленїа. то или. ѡⷠ оубожаеⷮ авраама. во мноⷤствѣ ядыи у неⷢ. празⷣны оубо таковыя бесѣды. не даⷭ бо 57v/137 таковыⷯ гл҃ъ писание гл҃ати. но чтоⷭ ѿкрываеⷮ едино ⷭгьство единоⷢ бжⷭтва безначаⷧныя трⷪца. понеⷤ гл҃юⷮ книги явися бг҃ъ авраамꙋ. авраⷨ же возрѣвъ видѣ три мꙋжи. и срѣте иⷯ. рече гиⷭ. аще ѡбрѣтоⷯ бл҃гть прⷣе тобою. пакы реⷱ да ѡмыются ногы ваша и да ясте. и ѿ ѿвѣщанїи самⷯѣ трие мꙋжеи. яко рѣша аврааⷯ мꙋ вкꙋпѣ. сотвори якоⷤ гл҃а. во всеⷨ семъ показаша книгы сими бесѣдами. яко бг҃ъ едиⷩ есть в треⷯ лицеⷯ единыⷨ гⷭьствоⷨ. не оубо бы смѣли слꙋжебнїи аг҃гли. толикꙋ дерзость содѣяти. еже ⷣенослӓвныⷨ бг҃ꙋ и равночⷭтнымъ быти. и сосѣдѣти иⷨ бв҃и на единоⷨ прⷭтлѣ. и вкꙋпѣ бг҃оу споველѣвати. единоⷢ бо гⷭьства таковое. слꙋгиⷤ аще ко влⷣцѣ таковаа начинаюⷮ явленно сопротивление ко влⷣцѣ и раⷮ на ⷭга своеⷢ воздвизають. Раⷥсмоⷮрение во стⷭеи бытеистеи книзѣ. бг҃ословⷪному в неи писанию. внегда оⷮхоⷤдаше гдь оⷮ авраама і ꙋклониⷭ к содоме лицъ.+[275]
Ходите оубо поидемъ в любви истинны. на[276] прѣⷣписанїа. пачеⷤ по радꙋ прочитающе. да познаемъ истиннꙋ воистиннꙋ. а не по косоⷢ прѣⷧсти беⷥбжїа влающеся. гл҃еⷮ оубо

275 *In the margin*: + о еже како тамо о бжїи славѣ, приⷨелетса.

276 *In the margin*: гл҃аⷧ ꙁі.

29.11. And again, did the reason why God took only two angels out of an infinite myriad, when he wanted to eat with his friend Abraham, have to do with the fact that the latter's estate would suffer loss, if all of them were to eat with Abraham? And how would it look when the one "who gives food to every flesh" (Ps. 146:25) and "feeds every living thing with good pleasure" (Ps. 145:16) would rob Abraham by eating with him with this many (visitors)?

29.12. These are worthless talks, then, for | the Scripture does not allow us 57v/137
to speak in such terms. Instead, it clearly reveals the common lordship of the one Godhead of the Trinity without beginning. For the Scriptures say, "God appeared" to Abraham, and "Abraham lifted up his eyes and saw three men", and when he met them, "he said, 'Lord, if I have found grace in your sight' ", and again, he said,[277] "let them wash your feet", and "that you may eat"; and also based on the response of the three men themselves, when they said to Abraham collectively, "Do as you said", in all of these words,[278] the Scriptures showed that God is one in three persons, sharing common lordship (cf. Gen. 18:1–5).

29.13. Indeed, the ministering angels would not have been so audacious as to share[279] the same glory with God and equal honor with him, and sit with God on the same throne,[280] and co-rule together with God. For such lordship belongs to the One, and if the servants begin to usurp it from their master and go to war[281] against their Lord, their confrontation toward the master becomes evident.

30. Investigation of the theological account in the holy book of Genesis,[282] where the Lord departed from Abraham and turned his face toward Sodom, and of how we should understand the glory of God there. CHAPTER 17.

30.1. Let us then proceed by going to the very beginning, and in love of the truth, read everything in an orderly fashion, so that we may truly understand the truth, instead of wandering around according to the falsehood of Kosoy's godlessness.

---

277 again, he said,] again,

278 in all of these words,] according to all these words,

279 as to share] as to assume the position of sharing

280 sit with God on the same throne] sit next to God

281 war] their war

282 **Investigation of the theological account in the holy book of Genesis,] Investigation of the holy book of Genesis and the theological account found there,**

58r/138 писание. Въставшⷤ҇ моужи ѿ тѹдѣ. оуклониша҃ к содомѣ лицъ. авраамъⷤ идꙗше с нимⷨ҇ проводꙗа. речеⷤ гⷭ҇ь. не потаю аⷥ ѿ авраама раба моеⷢ҇. еже аⷥ творю. тⷨа по сеⷮ глⷭе. реⷱ҇ гⷭ҇ь. вопль содомескъ и гомореескъ оумножиса. и грѣси иⷯ велици ѕѣло сшеⷭ҇ оубо да вижѹ. аⷷ҇ по воплю иⷯ приходꙗщѹ ко мнѣ скончаютса. аще҃ то разоумѣю. и ѡбративше҃ мѹжи ѿ тѹдѣ. прїидоша в содомъ. авраамъ же бѣꙗше еще стоꙗ преⷣ гⷭ҇демъ бгⷭ҇мъ. и присту пивъ авраⷨа рече. не погѹби правⷣнаго с не чⷭ҇тивыми и прочее. даⷤ не погѹблю десꙗти раⷣ҇. ѿиде҃ⷤ гⷭ҇ь. ꙗко скончa глⷭ҇ꙗ ко авраамоу. авраⷨа ѡбратиⷭ҇ на мѣсто свое. прїидостаⷤ два аггла в содоⷨ вечеръ. лотъⷤ сѣдꙗше преⷣ враты содоⷨскими. видѣвъⷤ лотъ воста. и срѣте и поклониⷭ҇ лицеⷨ до земли. и реⷱ҇ се гⷭ҇на ѡбратитаⷭ҇ в домъ раба ваю. да почиета. и ѡмыета нозѣ. и ѡсвѣтша изыдѣта на поуⷮ свои с негоⷤ совратистаⷭ҇ к рабѹ своемѹ. рѣстаⷤ ни. оубо на стогнаⷯ почиевѣ. и ноу жаше еа. и совратистаⷭ҇ в доⷨ его. и сотвори

58v/139 има пиръ. тⷤа на преⷣ глⷭе. ꙗкоже оутро бысть тщахѹса аггли лота глⷭюще. воставъ поими си женѹ. и дщери ꙗⷤ имаши изыди. да не и ты погыбнеши в беззаконїи града сеⷢ. и воⷥтщаса имша аггла за рѹкѹ. и за рѹкѹ женѹ его. и за рѹ кѹ дщери его. понеⷤ пощадї и гⷭ҇ь бгъ. и бысть егда изведоста и вонъ. и рѣста емѹ спⷭ҇аа спⷭ҇и дⷲю твою. не ѡзираиса въспаⷮ. ни по стои во всеⷨ предѣле семъ. в горѣ спⷭ҇ешиса. еда когда та ѡбыдеⷮ. реⷱ҇ лотъ к нима мо лю та гⷭ҇и. елмаⷤ рабъ твои ѡбрѣте блⷢ҇ть преⷣ тобою. и оувеличи правдѹ твою до мене. да живеⷮ дⷲа моꙗ. азъⷤ не могѹ оуцѣлити до горы. егда постигнеⷮ ѕло и оумрѹ. сего раⷣ҇ вонъⷤ граⷣ оубѣгаю сиⷤ есть малъ. в томъ спⷭ҇ѹса. нѣсть маⷧ но живеⷮ дⷲа моꙗ тебе раⷣ҇. и реⷱ҇ емѹ се чⷭ҇тюхса лицѹ твоемѹ и словѹ семѹ. да не погибнеⷮ граⷣ ѡ нем же глⷭ҇еши.

30.2. Now, the Scripture says, | "And having risen up from there, the men turned their face toward Sodom.[283] And Abraham went with them to see them off. And the Lord said, 'I will not hide from Abraham, my servant, the things I will do'" (Gen. 18:16–17). And after this, it says,[284] "The Lord said, 'The outcry of Sodom and Gomorrah has increased, and their sins are enormously great. I will, therefore, go down to see if they correspond with the outcry that comes to me, and if not, that I may know'. And the men, having departed from there, came to Sodom; and Abraham was still standing before the Lord God. And Abraham drew near and said, 'Do not destroy the righteous with the wicked men'" (Gen. 18:20–23). 58r/138

30.3. ⟨And he made more pleas until⟩ (the Lord said), "'I will not destroy it for the sake of ten'. And the Lord departed when he stopped speaking to Abraham, and Abraham returned to his place. And the two angels came to Sodom at evening. And Lot sat by the gate of Sodom, and Lot having seen them, rose up and met them, and he worshiped with his face to the ground, and said, 'Behold, lords, turn in to the house of your servant, so that you may rest, and wash your feet, and having risen early in the morning, you may depart on your journey, from which you turned aside to your servant'. And they said, 'No, we will lodge in the street'. And he constrained them, and they turned aside to his house, and he made | a feast for them" (Gen. 18:32–19:3). 58v/139

30.4. And also, further,[285] "But when it was morning, the angels hurried Lot, saying, 'Rise up, take your wife and the daughters that you have, and go forth, lest you also be destroyed with the iniquities of this city'. And when he hesitated, the angels took ⟨his⟩ hand, and the hand of his wife, and the hands of his daughters, for the Lord God spared him. And it came to pass when they brought him out, and they said to him, 'Save your own soul by all means; do not look back, nor stay in this entire valley, escape to the mountain, lest you be swept away'. And Lot said to them, 'I pray, Lord, your servant has indeed found grace before you, and you magnified your righteousness toward me so that my soul may live, but I cannot escape to the mountain, lest the evil overtake me, and I die. Therefore, let me escape to this city,[286] which is a little one, and there I will be rescued, is it not a little one? But my soul will live because of you'. And he said to him, 'Behold, I found your face and word delightful to not destroy the

283 Sodom] Sodom and Gomorrah.
284 And after this, it says,] Somewhat later, it also says,
285 And also, further,] And a little bit further,
286 city,] city that is near,

потщиⷭ҇ оубо да сѧ сп҃сеши тꙋ. не могꙋ со
творити дѣтеⷭ҇. дондеже внидеши тамо.
сеⷢ҇ ради прозва имѧ градꙋ томꙋ сигоръ.
взыдеⷤ слн҃це на землю. лотъⷤ вниде в сигоръ.
59r/140 гⷭ҇ьⷤ надожди в содоⷨ и гоморъ камыки горющими
и ѡгнь ѿ гⷭ҇а посла. и раⷥсыпа грады. Ꙗко в содоⷨ
идоста два равночⷭ҇тнаа бг҃ꙋ и равносⷭ҇инаа еюⷤ мꙋжа
и аг҃гла реⷱ҇ писание. послѣдиⷤ ѿкры ѡ ниⷯ ꙗко гⷭ҇а еста сїа два
Видите истиннꙋ писанїа. преⷤ гл҃аше сотвори
бг҃ъ. и реⷱ҇ бг҃ъ да боудеⷮ. таⷤ и реⷱ҇ бг҃ъ ~~да боудеⷮ~~. сотво
риⷨ чл҃ка по ѡбразꙋ нш҃емꙋ и по поⷪ҇бию. по сеⷨ при
идѣте реⷱ҇ сшⷣеше смѣсиⷨ и. тамо ꙋбо совѣта раⷣ
показаша книги бг҃а ѿца и слова еⷢ҇ сн҃а. и дх҃а еⷢ҇
ст҃го. здѣⷤ оу авраама самоличнѣ в треⷯ ипоста
сеⷯ бг҃а показꙋють книги. ꙗвиⷯ рече бг҃ъ авра
амꙋ оу дꙋба. и возрѣⷭ҇ аврааⷨ видѣ верхꙋ его три
мꙋжи стоꙗща. и авраамꙋ мꙋжи рѣша. сотво
ри ꙗкоⷤ гл҃а. И понеⷤ реⷱ҇ гⷭ҇ь. вопль содомескъ и го
морескъ оумножиⷭ҇. и грѣси иⷯ велицы ѕѣло. глеⷮ
же сшеⷣ оубо да вижю. тамо ꙋбо гл҃еть писание.
сотвориⷨ чл҃ка. и придѣте сшⷣеше смѣсиⷨ. здѣⷤ
три гл҃еть писание. а не реⷱ҇ сшⷣеше оубо да видиⷨ.
но реⷱ҇ сшеⷣ оубо да вижю. нѣсть ли се. ꙗко та
мо гл҃юща бг҃а показоуюⷮ книгы. к соѡбразныⷨ
и к поⷪ҇бныⷨ емꙋ. сотвориⷨ чл҃ка по ѡбразоу нш҃е
мꙋ и по поⷪ҇бию. и къ единосꙋщныⷨ своимъ рече.
59v/141 придѣте сшⷣеше смѣсимъ. здѣⷤ не к поⷪ҇бнымъ

city you speak of. Hurry, therefore, to get rescued there, for I cannot do anything
until you enter there'. Therefore, he called that city with the name Sigor. And
the sun had risen over the earth when Lot entered into Sigor. | And the Lord 59r/140
rained down burning sulfur on Sodom and Gomorrah and sent fire—from the
Lord, and he overthrew the cities" (Gen. 19:15–26).

31. Showing that the two who went to Sodom shared equal honor and equal power with God, and of them, the Scripture spoke as "men" and "angels", but afterward, revealed concerning them that the two were the Lord.[287]

31.1. See the truth of Scripture! First, it said, "God made", and "God said, 'Let there be'", and also, "God said, 'Let us make man in our image and likeness'". Afterward, it said,[288] "Having gone down, let us confuse him" (Gen. 11:5–7). Now, in those places, the Scriptures revealed God the Father, and his Word, who is the Son, and his Holy Spirit on account of the counsel. But here, in the case of Abraham, the Scriptures show God in three hypostases in the most personal way, (for) it is said, "God appeared to Abraham by the oak", and "having lifted up his eyes, Abraham saw three men, who stood in front of him", and "the men said to Abraham, 'Do as you said'" (cf. Gen. 18:1–5). For[289] "the Lord said, 'The outcry of Sodom and Gomorrah has increased, and their sins are enormously great'", and it says, "I will, therefore, go down to see" (Gen. 18:20–21).

31.2. Thus, in the former case, the Scripture says, "Let us make man", and
"Come, and having gone down, let us bring confusion",[290] but here the Scrip-
ture speaks of "three", and instead of saying, "*We* will therefore go down to see",
it says, "*I* will, therefore, go down to see".[291] Is it not (evident) that in those places
the Scriptures show God as speaking to those who share the same image and
are like him, "Let us make man in our image and likeness", and that he said[292] to
those who were consubstantial with him, | "Come, and having gone down, let 59v/141

287 Showing that the two who went to Sodom shared equal honor and equal power with God, and of them, the Scripture spoke as "men" and "angels", but afterward, revealed concerning them that the two were the Lord.] On the question of who it was, that entered Sodom "from the Lord", the two who destroyed Sodom and Gomorrah.

288 it said] *omitted*

289 For] And here

290 bring confusion",] confuse him",

291 *MS 61 adds*: **Showing that there is a difference between the way the same words describe the common lordship of those who have equal power and (the way they describe) the servants.**

292 he said] *omitted*

ни къ единосꙋщнꙑⷨ себѣ рⷬе. сошⷣе оубо да вижю. но к рабꙋ своемꙋ авраамꙋ чл҃кꙋ сꙋщю. сⷢе раⷣ тогда гл҃ⷮе сотворимъ чл҃ка. и придѣте сошⷣе ше смѣсимъ. понⷤе не к рабоⷨ бесѣдоваше бг҃ъ. но к поⷣоⷨбнꙑⷨ себѣ бжⷭтвомъ и силою. нн҃ⷤѣ к ра боу бесѣдоваше бг҃ъ. сⷢе ради гл҃ⷮе сшⷣе оубо да вижю. ѡ сеⷨ чисто ꙗвлꙗеⷮ писание гл҃ꙗ. и ѡбратившⷭе мꙋжи и ѿ тꙋдѣ. прїидоша в со домъ. авраамⷤъ еще стоꙗше прⷣе гдⷭмъ бг҃оⷨ. ꙗко сего раⷣ не рⷬе гⷭь сшⷣеше да видиⷨ. понⷤе слово еⷢ и дх҃ъ еⷢ ѡбратившⷭе ѿ тꙋдѣ прїидоша в со домъ. ихⷤъ мꙋжи нарⷬе писание. и ꙗко авраⷣⷨ стоꙗше прⷣе гдⷭмъ бг҃мъ. к немⷤꙋ не ꙗко к поⷣⷪ бнꙑⷨ себѣ но ꙗко къ чл҃кꙋ сꙋщꙋ бесѣдꙋꙗ рече бг҃ъ. сшⷣе оубо да вижю. ꙗвно показа гл҃омъ симъ единосꙋщества раⷣ снити бг҃ꙋ въ словѣ сн҃ѣ еⷢ. и в дꙋсѣ ст҃емъ его в содоⷨ. понⷤе два снидо ста в содоⷨ а не три. и не рѣша книги ꙗко бг҃ъ сниде в содоⷨ. но два мꙋжа. гл҃юще и ѡбрати вшⷭе мꙋжи ѿ тꙋдѣ прїидоша в содомъ. бг҃ⷤъ рⷬе сшⷣе оубо да вижю. нѣсть ли се гл҃ъ бж҃їи.
60^{r}/143 ꙗко сн҃омъ словоⷨ своиⷨ и дх҃омъ ст҃ымъ своиⷨ сниде в со доⷨ. таⷤ чистѣе писание ѿкрываеⷮ гл҃ꙗ. прии доста два агг҃ла в содоⷨ вечеръ. видѣв же лотъ

us bring confusion"?[293] But here, the Lord spoke to those who were neither like (him) nor consubstantial with him, "I will, therefore, go down to see". Instead, (he spoke) to his human servant Abraham. That is why in those places, he says, "Let us make man", and "Come, and having gone down, let us bring confusion", for God spoke not to the servants, but to those who were like him in divinity and power.

31.3. But this time, God speaks to the servant, which is why he says, "I will, therefore, go down to see".[294] The Scripture makes this crystal clear, saying, "And the men, having departed from there, came to Sodom; and Abraham was still standing before the Lord God" (Gen. 18:22). And in view of this, the Lord did not say, "*We* will go down to see", for his Word and his Spirit—whom the Scripture called "men"[295] (cf. Gen. 18:2)—departed from there, going to Sodom. Rather, when "Abraham was still standing before the Lord God", God said, "I will go down to see", speaking with him not as if (Abraham) was like him, but as with someone who was human.

31.4. In this passage, he clearly displayed the consubstantiality (of the three persons) when descending onto Sodom with his Word, the Son, and with his Holy Spirit. For while God said, "I will go down to see", there were two others who went to Sodom. Of these two—and not three—the Scripture spoke of two men, and instead of saying that God went down to Sodom, it said, "And the men, having departed from there, came to Sodom" (Gen. 18:22).[296] Isn't God saying in this passage | that he came down to Sodom with his Son, who is the Word, 60r/143
and his Holy Spirit?

31.5. The Scripture reveals the same thing even more clearly when it says, "And the two angels came to Sodom at evening. And Lot having seen them,

293 bring confusion"?] confuse him"?

294 *MS 61 adds*: **Showing that those who went to Sodom shared equal honor and equal power with God, and of them, the Scripture speaks as "men" and "angels", but afterward, reveals concerning them that these two are the Lord.**

295 "men",] "men", according to that passage, where Abraham saw three men that stood in front of him (cf. Gen. 18:2).

296 For while God said, "I will go down to see", there were two others who went to Sodom. Of these two—and not three—the Scripture spoke as two men, and instead of saying that God went down to Sodom, it said, "And the men, having departed from there, came to Sodom" (Gen. 18:22).] And the Scriptures did not say that God went down to Sodom, but rather, God said to Abraham, "I will go down to see", and there were two who went. Indeed, the Scripture spoke of all of them as "men", who "departed from there and came to Sodom", and then, it spoke of the "Lord" when Abraham was still speaking in that place. And God said, "I will go down to see", but he did not actually go.

воста и срѣте и. Смотрите гл҃а. не реⷭ восрѣтение имъ. ꙗкоⷤ к тремъ авраⷨ. но срѣте и. еⷤ двою показание. таⷤ и реⷭ се гнⷭа ѡбратитаса в доⷨ раба ваю да почиета. и ѡмыета ноѕи. ѡсвѣтша изыдѣта на поⷮ свои с негоⷤ совратистаⷭ. во всеⷨ двою здѣ глⷭе а не еⷣного ни треⷯ. не реⷭ гдⷭие или гⷭи. или ѡбратиⷭ или ѡбратитеⷭ. ꙗкоⷤ единомꙋ или триемъ. но реⷭ гнⷭа и ѡбратитаⷭ. и не реⷭ почиите. и ѡмыите ноѕи ваши. и изыдете на поⷮ. но реⷭ почиета и ѡмыета ноѕи. и изыдѣта на поⷮ с негоⷤ совратистаⷭ. еⷤ двою ꙗвлꙗеⷮ писание. тамоⷤ не реⷭ сотворивѣ чл҃ка. но сотворимъ реⷭ. и по ѡбразоу не реⷭ наю. но нашемꙋ реⷭ. и не реⷭ прїидѣта смѣсивѣ. но придѣте реⷭ сшеⷣше смѣсимъ. еⷤ не двою но тройⷤ книгы показоуⷮю. и здѣ еще понеⷤ авраⷨ преⷣ гмⷭъ. два же прїидоста в содоⷨ. ихⷤъ реⷭ два агг҃ла. на прежⷣе идыи писание. не к томꙋ два агг҃ла. но гаⷭ показоуⷮю книги. и гаⷭ бг҃а тⷤꙋю двою агг҃лꙋ пришеⷣшую.

60v/144 в содоⷨ гл҃е. внегда писанию рещи. и воⷥтщаса имша агг҃ла за рꙋкоу и женꙋ и дщерꙗ еⷢ. таⷤ на веде. понеⷤ пощадї и гь бг҃ъ. и пакы ѡ ниⷯ гл҃еть. и реⷭ лотъ к нима молю та гⷭи. елмаⷤ ѡбрѣте раⷠ твои блгⷣть преⷣ тобою. видите како ѿкрываеⷮ писание ѡ двою агг҃лꙋ. ꙗко гь есть и бг҃ъ rose up and met them" (Gen. 19:1).[297] Notice that he did not say these words (in the plural), "met them", as Abraham did with respect to the three, but (in the dual) "met them", showing that there were two. Likewise, he also said, "Behold, lords, turn in to the house of your servant so that you may rest, and wash your feet, and having risen early in the morning, you may depart on your journey, from which you turned aside" (Gen. 19:2), speaking here of the two, and not of one nor of three. He did not say "lords" or "Lord", nor "turn in" (in the singular) or "turn in" (in the plural), as if addressing either "one" or "three".[298] Instead, he said (in the dual form): "lords" and "turn in". And he did not say (in the plural), "that you may rest, and wash your feet, and may depart on your journey", but he said (in the dual) "that you may rest, and wash your feet, and may depart on your journey, from which you turned aside", because the Scripture shows the "two".

31.6. And in the earlier instances, he did not say (in the dual), "Let us make man", but said (in the plural), "Let us make man". And with respect to the phrase "in the image", he did not say "our" (in the dual), but rather, he said, "our"[299] (in the plural). And he did not say (in the dual), "Come, let us bring confusion", but (in the plural), "Come", he said, "and having gone down, let us bring confusion", because the Scriptures show not one or two, but three. And while it ⟨says⟩ in one place, "And Abraham was still standing before the Lord God", (it also says in another that) "the two angels came to Sodom". The Scriptures first called them "two angels", who came (to Sodom), yet afterward, they did not ⟨show⟩ the "two angels". Instead, the Scriptures showed the "Lord". And the same two angels are said to be the Lord God[300] on their coming | to Sodom, when the Scriptures 60ᵛ/144
say, "And when he hesitated, the angels took his hand, together with his wife and daughters"[301] (Gen. 19:16). It is also added, "for the Lord God spared him", and then it is said of them, "And Lot said to them, 'I pray, Lord, your servant has indeed found grace before you'" (Gen. 19:16, 19). You see how[302] the Scripture

297 *MS 61 adds*: **Showing that the dyad and the triad, as well as the monad, are recognized from the difference in the names.**

298 He did not say "lords" or "Lord", nor "turn in" (in the singular) or "turn in" (in the plural), as if addressing either "one" or "three".] For he did not say, "Lord", or "turn in" as if addressing a singular subject, nor did he say (in the plural), "lords" or "turn in" as if addressing three subjects.

299 "our",] "in our image",

300 the Lord God] both "Lord" and "God"

301 together with his wife and daughters"] and the hand of his wife, and the hands of his daughters"

302 how] that

есть. ꙗже преже мужа и агг҃ла нарече писание. про исходяже показа єю и г҃а и б҃га. а ꙗко г҃лаша кни ги. в содомѣх при лотѣ г҃а б҃га. не то преже нимъ єще стоꙗща авраама книги рекоша. но пришедшаа два мужа ѿ треего мужа. ихже авраам преже видѣвъ. г҃лет бо писание. воста вшии мужи ѿтудѣ. оуклонишася к содомѣ лиц. авраам же идꙗше с ними проводꙗа. рече г҃ь. не потаю азъ ѿ авраама раба моег. таже г҃леть и ѡбративше мужи и ѿтудѣ прїидоста в со домъ. авраамже бѣꙗше єще стоꙗ пред г҃дмъ б҃гмъ. таже г҃лет ꙗко сꙗгша мужа рукама вдернуста лота въ храмину. и паки рѣста мужа к лоту. есть ли кто здѣ. или зꙗт. или с҃нове. или кто во градѣ. изведи ꙗ ѿ мѣста сег. ꙗко погубляем мѣсто се. поне возвы сися

61r/145 вопль их пред б҃гмъ. и пусти ны г҃ь б҃гъ потребити ꙗ. видите ꙗко мужа два здѣ ѿ трех имену а. ихже авраам видѣ. и посем г҃лет писание поне по щадѣ и г҃ь б҃гъ. видите и двою сею агг҃лу г҃а б҃га писание ѿкрывает. понеже тѣмаже мужема лотъ г҃ле. г҃и єлма ѡбрѣте рабъ твои бл҃гть пред тобою. пакы сею агг҃лу писание сказует єдинственое ѿвѣщание к лоту г҃лꙗ. и рече єму. се чюдохса лицу твоему и слову. потщися оубо да са сп҃сеши ту. не могу сотворити дѣтели. донде внидеши тамо. видите ꙗко сїа. и мужа и агг҃ла два что ѿкрывает писание равны б҃гу. пред нимъже єще стоꙗше авраам. два оубо г҃лет писание агг҃ла. и мужа таꙗже. во єдино г҃ьство ѡба лица полагаа. внегда г҃лати писанию. и рече лотъ к нима молю тꙗ г҃и. се же рещи и рече к нима. два лица показует. заже рещи к нима. а не рещи и рече shows that those two angels were "Lord" and were "God", given that the Scripture first called them "men" and "angels", but subsequently, it showed them to be both "Lord" and "God".

31.7. And as to those of whom the Scriptures spoke as "the Lord God" during their (visit with) Lot, it is clear that Scriptures were not referring to the one before whom Abraham was still standing, but to the "two men" who came (to Sodom) separately from the third man, who was seen earlier.[303] For the Scripture says, "And having risen up from there, the men turned their face toward Sodom. And Abraham went with them to see them off. And the Lord said, 'I will not hide from Abraham, my servant'" (Gen. 18:16–17). Likewise, it says,[304] "And the men, having departed from there, came to Sodom; and Abraham was still standing before the Lord God" (Gen. 19:22). It also says that "the men stretched forth their hands and pulled Lot into the house" (Gen. 19:10). And then, it says, "And the men said to Lot, 'Do you have anyone else here—sons-in-law, or sons, or anyone else in the city that belongs to you? Bring them out of this place, because we are going to destroy this place. For their outcry has been raised up | 61r/145
before God, and the Lord God has sent us to destroy it'" (Gen. 19:12–13).

31.8. Do you see how he calls them "two men" here as he did those "three", whom Abraham saw? And then, when the Scriptures say, "for the Lord God spared him" (Gen. 19:16), do you see how the Scripture[305] reveals these two angels to be the Lord God? For it is to the same men, that Lot says, "Lord, if I have found grace in your sight" (Gen. 19:19). Next, the Scripture speaks of these angels as replying to Lot in the singular person, stating, "And he said to him, 'Behold, I found your face and word delightful. Hurry, therefore, to get rescued there, I cannot do anything until you enter there'" (Gen. 19:21–22). You see how the Scripture clearly reveals these two as being both "men" and "angels", equal with God, before whom Abraham "was still standing".

31.9. Thus, the Scripture speaks of two angels,[306] and it presents the same men as persons who share common lordship,[307] when the Scripture states, "And Lot[308] said to them, 'I pray, Lord'" (Gen. 19:18). By stating (in the dual), "And he said to them", it shows two persons because he[309] said (in the dual),

303 (to Sodom) separately from the third man, who was seen earlier.] (to Sodom), calling them "men" just as the other "three", whom Abraham saw.
304 Likewise,] Later,
305 Scripture] it
306 angels,] angels that came to Sodom,
307 lordship] statehood
308 Lot] he
309 he] Lot

лотъ к немꙋ. но рⷱ҇е лотъ к нима. еже есть
чⷭ҇то къ двѣма. еже глⷮ҇е молю тꙗ гⷭ҇и. еди
но гⷭ҇ьство показоуⷮе. не рⷱ҇е к нима молю ваю
гⷭ҇на. но рⷱ҇е к нима молю та гⷭ҇и. показа ѡбою
61v/146 едино гⷭ҇ьство. ꙗко ѡба агг҃ла единъ есть гⷭ҇ь.
ꙗкⷤо прⷤе три состава единⷢ҇о бг҃а. единого гⷭ҇а
именова при авраамѣ. такⷤо и здѣ при
лотѣ. двою въ единⷢ҇о гⷭ҇а именова. молю
та гⷭ҇и рⷱ҇е. и понⷤе пощадѣ и гⷭ҇ь бг҃ъ. и ѿвѣще
ваше се чⷣю̈хса лицꙋ твоемꙋ. и не могꙋ
сотворити дѣтели дондⷤе внидеши тамо.
тⷤа болши ѿкрываⷮе писание въ трⷪ҇цы бг҃а
гл҃еть. взыдⷤе слⷩ҇це на землю. лотⷤъ вни
де в сигоръ. гⷭ҇ь же надожди в содомъ и гомⷪ҇
камыки горащїи. и ѡгнь ѿ гⷭ҇а посла и рⷥа
сыпа грады. Смотрите писанїа добрѣ
и видите ꙗко ꙗвленно показа писание гⷭ҇а
ѡгнь ѿ гⷭ҇а. пославша на содⷨо и гоморъ. гⷭ҇ь ѿ гⷭ҇а
посылаⷮе ѡгнь. се гⷭ҇ь се ѿ гⷭ҇а писание рече.
ѿ гⷭ҇а рⷱ҇е ѡдожди ѡгнь. нѣсть ли се ѿ бг҃а ѿца.
гⷭ҇ь надожди в содⷨо и гоморъ камыки горащїи.
двою мꙋжꙋ глⷮ҇е единъ гⷭ҇ь. нѣсть ли се слово
сн҃ъ бж҃їи. и дх҃ъ ст҃ыи гⷭ҇ь. вшедыи в содѡмъ
ꙗⷤ преже мꙋжи именова писание. потⷨо
гⷭ҇ь. еже слово и дх҃ъ ст҃ыи. ѡгнь ѿ бг҃а посла
на содомы. к ним же рⷱ҇е бг҃ъ. сотворимъ
62r/147 чл҃ка по ѡбразоу нш҃емꙋ и по пⷣ҇ⷪбию. и придѣте
сшⷣ҇еше смѣсⷨ҇и и. понⷤе авраамꙋ ꙗвⷭ҇и треми моу
жми. и в содомѣ гⷭ҇ь ѿ гⷭ҇а ѡдожди. иⷤ прⷤе имено

"to them", instead of saying (in the singular), "And Lot said to him". Rather, (the dual form in),[310] "Lot said to them" makes it clear that they are two, while (the singular form in), "I pray, Lord"[311] shows one lordship. For he did not say to them, "I pray to both of you, lords". Instead, he said (first in the dual for "them", and then in the singular for "Lord"), "he said to *them*, 'I pray, *Lord*'", showing that the two | share one lordship and that both angels are one Lord.[312] Just as 61v/146
before, in the case of Abraham, it referred to the three subsistences of the one God, as well as of the one Lord, so here, too, in the case of Lot, it refers to the two as one Lord, (when it says) "I pray, Lord". It is said, "for the Lord God spared him", and (God) answered, "I found your face delightful and cannot do anything until you enter there" (Gen. 19:21–22).[313]

31.10. Similarly, the Scripture gives an even greater revelation when it speaks of God as Trinity, (stating), "And the sun had risen over the earth when Lot entered into Sigor. And the Lord rained down burning sulfur on Sodom and Gomorrah and sent fire—from the Lord, and he overthrew the cities" (Gen. 19:23–24). Consider the Scriptures carefully and recognize that the Scripture clearly shows the "Lord", who sends fire on Sodom and Gomorrah "from the Lord". The Lord sends fire "from the Lord". Indeed, the Scripture spoke of the "Lord", who was "from the Lord" and said that fire was sent "from the Lord". Is this not from God the Father, that burning sulfur was rained down on Sodom and Gomorrah? (And as for) the two men who are referred to in the singular as "Lord", isn't it the Word, who is the Son of God, and the Holy Spirit—both of them being "Lord"—who came to Sodom and whom the Scripture previously called "men", and then "Lord"? It was the Word and the Holy Spirit, who sent down fire from God on Sodom and to whom God said, "Let us make | man in 62r/147
our image and likeness", and "Come, and having gone down, let us confuse him". For they appeared to Abraham as three men, and in Sodom, the Lord rained

310 in),] in) the phrase,

311 "I pray, Lord"] "Lord"

312 lords". Instead, he said (first in the dual for "them", and then in the singular for "Lord"), "he said to them, 'I pray, Lord'", showing that the two share one lordship and that both angels are one Lord.] lords", as he formerly said (in the dual) when he met them, "Behold, lords, turn in to the house of your servant, so that you may rest" (Gen. 19:2). And instead of saying here, "lords", he says (first in the dual for "them", and then in the singular for "Lord"), "he said to them, 'I pray, Lord'", showing that the two share one statehood (and) that both angels, represented as men, are one Lord.

313 It is said, "for the Lord God spared him", and (God) answered, "I found your face delightful and cannot do anything until you enter there"] It is to the two as well, that the (Scripture) said, "for the Lord God spared him", and when it presented (God's) answer, "I found your face delightful and cannot do anything until you enter there"

ваніи мѹжи и агг҃ли. потоⷨ же ѿкрышаⷭ҇ тіиⷤ и бг҃ъ и гⷭ҇ь. Пакы глⷮ҇е писание. при авраамѣ и исацѣ. И бысть по гл҃аніи сⷨе бг҃ъ искоуша[314]ше авраама. и рⷱ҇е к немѹ. аврааме. аврааме. сейⷤ рече се аⷥ. и рече поими сн҃а своⷢ҇е возлюбленнаго егоⷤ возлюби исаⷶка. и иди на землю высокѹ. и возвⷣе его въ требоу на единѹ ѿ горъ юⷤти рекѹ. воставⷤъ заѹтра аврааⷨ ѡсѣдла ѡсла свое. и поꙗ с собою два раба. и исаака сн҃а своⷢ҇е. и исцѣпѣвъ дрова требѣ. воставъ поиде на мѣсто. на нⷤе бѣ емѹ реклъ бг҃ъ. приидоста на мѣсто на нⷤе реклъ емѹ бг҃ъ. и созда тѹ аврааⷨ требникъ. и возложи дрова и сваза исаака сн҃а своⷢ҇е. и възложи на требникъ верхѹ дровъ. и сⷤа аврааⷨ рѹкою своею. и вза

314 *In the margin*: глаⷡ҇ иі҃.

down fire "from the Lord". Those who were first called "men" and "angels", and afterward, the same ones revealed themselves as both God and Lord.[315]

32. CHAPTER 18.[316]

32.1. And next,[317] the Scripture reports at the time of Abraham and Isaac, "And after these words came to pass, God tested Abraham and said to him, 'Abraham, Abraham'. And he said, 'Here I am'. And he said, 'Take your beloved son, whom you have loved—Isaac, and go into the high land, and offer him as a burnt offering on one of the mountains, of which I will tell you'. And Abraham rose up in the morning[318] and saddled his ass, and he took with him two servants, and Isaac, his son, and having chopped wood[319] for a burnt offering, he arose and went to the place of which God had spoken to him"[320] (Gen. 22:1–3).

32.2. "And there Abraham built an altar, and laid down the wood, and bound Isaac, his son, and laid him on the altar, on top of the wood.[321] And Abraham

315 The Lord sends fire "from the Lord". Indeed, the Scripture spoke of the "Lord", who was "from the Lord" and said that fire was sent "from the Lord". Is this not from God the Father, that burning sulfur was rained down on Sodom and Gomorrah? (And as for) the two men who are referred to in the singular as "Lord", isn't it the Word, who is the Son of God, and the Holy Spirit—both of them being "Lord"—who came to Sodom and whom the Scripture previously called "men", and then "Lord"? It was the Word and the Holy Spirit, who sent down fire from God on Sodom and to whom God said, "Let us make man in our image and likeness", and "Come, and having gone down, let us confuse him". For they appeared to Abraham as three men, and in Sodom, the Lord rained down fire "from the Lord". Those who were first called "men" and "angels", and afterward, the same ones revealed themselves as both God and Lord.] Indeed, the Lord sent fire "from the Lord", as the Scripture said. Is this not really (showing), then, that the Lord sent God's Word and the Spirit "from the Lord"—from God the Father—to overthrow the cities? It is to two men, that he says, "Lord". Is this not "Lord" the Word, the Son of God, and the Holy Spirit, to whom God also said before, "Let us make man in our image and likeness", and "Come, and having gone down, let us confuse him"? They appeared to Abraham as three men, of whom two went to Sodom, (and) in Sodom, they rained down fire "from the Lord". Those who were first called "men", were also (called) "angels", and afterward, the same ones revealed themselves as both God and Lord.

316 CHAPTER 18.] **On God's glory manifested in the divinely inspired Scripture at the time of great Abraham when he was commanded to offer his son Isaac as a sacrifice to God.** CHAPTER 18.

317 next,] also

318 in the morning] *omitted*

319 chopped wood] split wood

320 him"] him". And somewhat later, it says, "(Both of them) came to the place of which God spoke to him".

321 and laid down the wood, and bound Isaac, his son, and laid him on the altar, on top of the wood.] *omitted*

ножь да заколеⷮ с҃на своего. и возва и агг҃лъ г҃нь с н҃бсе. и реⷱ ему. аврааме. аврааме. сейⷤ реⷱ се аⷥ г҃и. и реⷱ не возложи руки своеꙗ на ѡтрочищь. ни сотвори ему ничтоⷤ. н҃нѣ разумеⷯ 62v/149 ꙗко боишиⷭ ты б҃га. и не пощадѣ с҃на своеⷢ любимаⷢ мене раⷣ. Ꙗко возвавыи с н҃бсе агг҃лъ г҃нь авраама равенъ сыи по писанию. г҃ь бо еⷭ. и тойⷤ саⷨ искушааше авраама ѿ исаацѣ б҃гъ.

Видите пакы писание б҃га именующа агг҃ла. гл҃еⷮ бо агг҃ла возвавша авраама. к нему же начинаа беседовати. не аки агг҃лъ но аки б҃гъ реⷱ. н҃нѣ разумеⷯ. ꙗвлꙗеⷮ же са ꙗко тойⷤ и в началѣ повелѣвыи аврааму с҃на своего на требу себѣ вознести. егоⷤ тамо б҃га и менова. тойⷤ и здѣ возвавыи авраама. повелѣваа заклати с҃на своеⷢ. егоⷤ агг҃ломъ именова. посему. понеⷤ не реⷱ н҃нѣ разоумѣ б҃гъ ꙗко боишиⷭ ты еⷭ. но реⷱ ꙗко самъ возвавыи разумѣ. и аще бы единъ ѿ служебныⷯ агг҃лъ г҃нь былъ гл҃аи ко аврааму. не бы смѣⷧ продерзовати. равеⷩствомъ и властию и честию къ б҃гу подобеⷩ быти. и гл҃ати тако. н҃нѣ разоумѣⷯ. и не пощадѣ с҃на своеⷢ любимаⷢ мене ради. а не гл҃ати сице. ꙗко н҃нѣ разоу

stretched forth his hand and took the knife to pierce his son. And an angel of the Lord called him out of heaven and said to him, 'Abraham, Abraham'. And he said, 'Here I am, Lord'. And he said, 'Do not lay your hand on the child, or do anything to him. Now I know | that you fear God, and for my sake, you have not 62v/149
spared your beloved son'" (Gen. 22:9–13).

33. Showing that the angel of the Lord, who called Abraham out of heaven, was not a servant, according to the Scriptures, but equal (with God), given that he is Lord and the same God who tested Abraham concerning Isaac.[322]

33.1. Do you see, again,[323] how Scripture calls God an angel? For it says that the "angel of the Lord" called out Abraham, and when he began to speak with him, he spoke not as an angel but as God, saying, "Now I know". And it is clear that the same one, who (commanded) Abraham to offer his son as a burnt offering, him ⟨the Scripture⟩ also named God here; and he also calls Abraham and commands him here to not slaughter his son,[324] and he is called an angel. Hence, it did not say,[325] "Now God knows that you fear him", but said ⟨"Now I know"⟩, (showing) that it was the one who called, he himself knew. And if he had been one of the ministering angels of the Lord, (sent) to speak to Abraham, he would not have dared to liken himself to God, in his audacity, with respect to the equal power and honor, and say such things as, "Now I know", and "for my sake, you have not spared your beloved son". It was not befitting for him to say, "Now[326]

---

322 **Showing that the angel of the Lord, who called Abraham out of heaven was not a servant, according to the Scriptures, but equal (with God), given that he is Lord and the same God who tested Abraham concerning Isaac.] Showing that the one who called Abraham out of heaven is not a servant, according to the Scriptures, but equal with God, given that it calls him "the angel of the Lord".**

323 Do you see, again,] Don't you see here, again,

324 clear that the same one, who (commanded) Abraham to offer his son as a burnt offering, him ⟨the Scripture⟩ also names God here; and he also calls Abraham and commands him here to not slaughter his son,] clear from this that the same one who in the beginning commanded Abraham to offer his son as a burnt offering, him the Scripture also names as God here. For it says this way, "And after these words came to pass, God tested Abraham, and said to him, 'Take your beloved son, whom you have loved—Isaac, and go into the high land, and offer him as a burnt offering'" (Cf. Gen. 22:1–2). And when Abraham was fulfilling the command, the same one was revealed here, too, by calling Abraham and commanding him to not slaughter his own son.

325 it did not say,] there was a reason why it did not say,

326 It was not befitting for him to say, "Now] Instead, he would have spoken as it befits the one in a ministering rank, that "Now

мѣ бг҃ъ ꙗко боишⷭи ты ег҃. не пощадѣ сн҃а своег҃
любимаг҃ бг҃а радⷷ. посемꙋ разꙋмѣваетса. са
мого
63r/150 бг҃а видѣти возвавша авраама. а не прⷣѣстоꙗ
щаг҃ бг҃ꙋ аггл҃а. заж҃е гл҃ати. нн҃ѣ разꙋмѣх ꙗко бо
ишⷭи ты бг҃а. и не пощадѣ сн҃а своег҃ любимаго
мене радⷷ. а не гл҃ати нн҃ѣ разоумѣ бг҃ъ. ꙗко бо
ишиса ты ег҃. и не пощадѣ сн҃а своег҃ любимаг҃
его радⷷ. тѣмже разꙋмѣвша себе гл҃ет возва
выи авраама. и не пощадѣтиж҃ сн҃а своег҃ авра
амꙋ его радⷷ. самог҃ сего возвавшаго ради не по
щадѣ авраам сн҃а своег҃. гл҃ет же нн҃ѣ разꙋмѣхъ
ꙗко боишⷭи ты бг҃а. а не гл҃ет нн҃ѣ разꙋмѣхъ
ꙗко боишⷭи ты мене. сим показа писание ꙗк
аггл҃ъ гн҃сь сеи. слово бж҃ие бг҃ъ есть. разꙋмѣ
слово бж҃ие сн҃ъ бж҃їи авраама. ꙗко боитса
авраам бг҃а ѿца его. единославное и едино
чтс҃ное бг҃ꙋ и словꙋ его сими гл҃ы ѿкры писа
ние. ꙗкож҃ и при лотѣ в содомѣхъ. едино гс҃ь
ственое показа писание слова и дх҃а бг҃ꙋ
ѿцꙋ. внегда гл҃ати тамо сице. гс҃ь же надо
жди в содомъ и гоморъ камыкы горащїи. и
ѡгнь ѿ гс҃а посла. сегож҃ гс҃а пре ж҃ именова писан҃е
двою мꙋжꙋ и двою аггл҃ꙋ. ѿ гс҃а же надожди
вша камыкы горащїи. пославша ѡгнь в содом
63v/151 и гоморъ. гс҃а ѿ гс҃а гл҃ꙗ. едино гс҃ьственое ꙗви бг҃оу
слова его и дх҃а ег҃ ст҃го. сице и здѣ равное бж҃тсва
показꙋет писание бг҃а ѿца и слова ег҃ гл҃ꙗ. и рече
нн҃ѣ разꙋмѣх ꙗко боишⷭи ты бг҃а и не пощадѣ
сн҃а своег҃ любимаг҃ мене радⷷ. тѣмже нѣсть ег҃
нъ ѿ слꙋжебных аггл҃ъ возвавыи съ нб҃си авра

God knows that you fear him, and for God's sake, you have not spared your beloved[327] son".

33.2. Therefore, we must understand | and see[328] that the one who called out 63r/150
Abraham was God himself, and not an angel (from among those who) stand before God. For it is said, "Now I know that you fear God, and for my sake, you have not spared your beloved son", as opposed to saying, "Now God knows that you fear him, and for his sake, you have not spared your beloved son". Hence, the one who called out Abraham says of himself that he "knows", and (as to the fact that) Abraham "did not spare his own son for his sake", it is for the sake of this one who called him out, that Abraham did not spare his own son.[329] And he says, "Now I know that you fear God", instead of saying, "Now I know that you fear me". With this, the Scripture showed that this "angel of the Lord" was the divine Word of God, and[330] the Word of God, who is God's Son, knew Abraham, that he feared his God the Father.

33.3. With these words, the Scripture reveals the common glory and honor of God and his Word, just as the Scripture also showed the common lordship that the Word and Spirit shared with God at the time of Lot in Sodom, when it said the following there, "And the Lord rained down burning sulfur on Sodom and Gomorrah and sent fire—from the Lord" (Gen. 19:26). Earlier, the Scripture referred to the same "Lord" as "two men" and "two angels", and this Lord rained down burning sulfur and sent fire on Sodom | and Gomorrah. In saying that 63v/151
the "Lord" (sent fire) "from the Lord", it shows the common lordship that God shares with his Word and his Holy Spirit.

33.4. Thus, here, too, the passage of Scripture that says, "Now I know that you fear God, and for my sake, you have not spared your beloved son" (Gen. 22:13), shows the equal divinity of God the Father and the Word, who is the Son. Therefore, the one who called out of heaven, when God was previously testing

---

327 beloved] *omitted*

328 and see] *omitted*

329 as opposed to saying, "Now God knows that you fear him, and for his sake, you have not spared your beloved son". Hence, the one who called out Abraham says of himself that he "knows", and (as to the fact that) Abraham "did not spare his own son for his sake", it is for the sake of this one who called him out, that Abraham did not spare his own son.] *omitted. MS 61 adds*: **Showing that God, who tested Abraham concerning Isaac, is the same as the "angel of the Lord", who promptly called him; and he is also the Lord.**

330 and] and that

ама агг҃лъ гⷭ҇нь. но тоиⷤ есть и возвавыи с нб҃сѣ иⷤ прⷤе искꙋшаше авраама бг҃ъ. гл҃ⷮе бо писание. и бысть по гл҃анїи семъ бг҃ъ искꙋшааше авраама и рⷱ҇е к немꙋ. аврааме аврааме. сеиⷤ рече се аⷥ. и рече поими сн҃а своⷢ҇е возлюбленнаго егоⷤ

Abraham, is not one of the ministering (spirits), for the Scripture says,[331] "And after these words came to pass, God tested Abraham, and said to him, 'Abraham, Abraham'. And he said, 'Here I am'. And he said, 'Take your beloved son, whom

---

331 With these words, the Scripture reveals the common glory and honor of God and his Word, just as the Scripture also showed the common lordship that the Word and Spirit shared with God at the time of Lot in Sodom, when it said the following there, "And the Lord rained down burning sulfur on Sodom and Gomorrah and sent fire—from the Lord" (Gen. 19:26). Earlier, the Scripture referred to the same "Lord" as "two men" and "two angels", and this Lord rained down burning sulfur and sent fire on Sodom and Gomorrah. In saying that the "Lord" (sent fire) "from the Lord", it shows the common lordship that God shares with his Word and his Holy Spirit. Thus, here, too, the passage of Scripture that says, "Now I know that you fear God, and for my sake, you have not spared your beloved son" (Gen. 22:13), shows equal divinity of God the Father and the Word, who is the Son. Therefore, the one who called out of heaven, when God was previously testing Abraham, is not one of the ministering (spirits), for the Scripture says,] And the fact that he speaks to himself, (when he says), "Now I know", shows that he himself is the one who tested Abraham. And the phrase that follows, "that you fear God", shows that the Word of God, the Son, shares with God the Father one desire and one will, and that, with equal honor and the same glory. And as for the words, "and for my sake, you have not spared your beloved son", they show that (the speaker) is the same one who commanded Abraham to take his beloved son Isaac and offer him as a burnt offering. With these words, the Scripture expressly reveals the Son of God, the Word, as a singular subject with the Father, just as earlier, at the time of Lot in Sodom, the Scripture showed the Word and Spirit as sharing with God one lordship, and one will, and one desire, when it said there this, "And the Lord rained down burning sulfur on Sodom and Gomorrah and sent fire—from the Lord, and he overthrew the cities" (Gen. 19:26). And above, the Scripture states, "The Lord said to Abraham, 'The outcry of Sodom and Gomorrah has increased, and their sins are enormously great. I will, therefore, go down to see if they correspond with the outcry that comes to me, and if not, that I may know'. And the men, having departed from there, came to Sodom; and Abraham was still standing before the Lord God" (Gen. 18:20–22). Just as above, where the Scripture described God as "three men", so here, it speaks of the "two men" from those three, (the two) who "came to Sodom" when "Abraham was still standing before the Lord God". And in Sodom, it says, "And the Lord rained down burning sulfur on Sodom and Gomorrah and sent fire—from the Lord". With these words, the Scripture shows that the "three men" are God. And the three share one will, and one desire, and one power in this act. It was them (acting) together, when the Lord said to Abraham, "I will, therefore, go down to see"—which clearly means Sodom—"if they correspond with the outcry that comes to me". And the two went there, while the Lord that was "from the Lord", and before whom Abraham "was standing", "rained down burning sulfur on Sodom and Gomorrah and sent fire—from the Lord". What else would explain better the common will, the common desire, and the common lordship of the three? Thus, here, too, this passage that says, "Now I know that you fear God, and for my sake, you have not spared your beloved son" (Gen. 22:13), shows equal divinity, and the same will, and the same desire of God the Father and the Word, who is the Son. And let us, again, consider what is written and truly understand that the "angel of the Lord" is not one of the ministering (spirits),

возлюби исаака. и иди на землю высокꙋ. и возведи ⷢ҇е тамо в требꙋ. на единꙋ ѿ горъ юⷤ ти рекꙋ. въставъ заⷤꙋтра авраⷨа ѡсѣдла ѡслѧ свое. и поѧ с собою два раба. и исаака сн҃а своⷢ҇е и прочее. таⷤ и приидоста реⷱ҇ на мѣсто. на неⷤ бѣ реклъ емꙋ бг҃ъ. и созда тꙋ авраⷨа требниⷦ҇. и возложи дрова. и свѧза исаака сн҃а своего и возложи на требникъ верхꙋ дровъ. и сѧже авраⷨа рꙋкою своею. и взѧ ноⷤ да заколеⷮ сн҃а своⷢ҇е. и возва и агг҃лъ гн҃ь съ нб҃сѣ и рече емꙋ. аврааме аврааме. сеⷤи рече се ⷠа гⷭи. и реⷱ҇ не возлоⷤ [64r/153] рꙋки своеѧ на ѡтрочищь. ни сотвори емꙋ ничтоⷤ. нн҃ѣ разоумѣⷯ ꙗко боишⷭи ты бг҃а. и не пощадѣ сн҃а своⷢ҇е любимаⷢ мене дѣлѧ. ѿкровенно показа писание. ꙗко едиⷩ и тоⷤи бг҃ъ иⷤ повелѣвыи на требꙋ исаака возвести. и паки не возложи рꙋки своеѧ реⷱ҇ авраамꙋ на ѡтрочищь. внегда гл҃ати емꙋ. нн҃ѣ разꙋмѣⷯ ꙗко боишⷭи ты бг҃а и не пощадѣ сн҃а своⷢ҇е любимаⷢ мене раⷣ. а ⷤе глⷮе писание. и возва и агг҃лъ гн҃ь съ нб҃сѣ. показꙋⷮе не самоⷢ бг҃а ѿца возвавша авраама. но сн҃ъ слово бж҃ие возвавыи есть авраама. сеⷢ ради и агг҃ла гн҃а именоваⷢе писание. показаⷤ писание. ꙗко слово бж҃їе истовыи бг҃ъ есть внегда гл҃ати писанию ꙗко бг҃ъ искꙋшаше авраама. и гл҃ати приидоста на мѣсто на неⷤ гл҃а емꙋ бг҃ъ. и внегда гл҃ати нн҃ѣ разоумѣⷯ. гл҃атиⷤ и не пощади сн҃а своⷢе мене дѣлѧ. ѿкровенно в сеⷨ бг҃а сꙋща гл҃юща писанию. внегдаⷤ гл҃ати писанию. возва и агг҃лъ гн҃ь съ нб҃сѣ. и гл҃атиⷤ ꙗко боишⷭи ты бг҃а. ѿкровенно показа сн҃а бж҃иѧ и меноваⷡ его агг҃ла гн҃а. а не ѿ прⷣстоѧщихъ

you have loved—Isaac, and go into the high land, and offer him there[332] as a burnt offering on one of the mountains, of which I will tell you'. And Abraham rose up in the morning and saddled his ass, and he took with him two servants and Isaac, his son", etc. (Gen. 22:1–2). And it is also said, "(Both of them) came to the place of which God spoke to him. And there, Abraham built the altar, and laid the wood, and bound Isaac, his son, and laid him on the altar, on top of the wood. And Abraham stretched forth his hand and took the knife to pierce his son. And an angel of the Lord called him out of heaven and said to him, 'Abraham, Abraham'. And he said, "'Here I am, Lord'. And he said, 'Do not lay | your 64r/153
hand on the child,[333] or do anything to him. Now I know that you fear God, and for my sake, you have not spared your beloved son'" (Gen. 22:9–13).

33.5. The Scripture explicitly showed that it was one and the same God, who (first) commanded (Abraham) to sacrifice Isaac as a burnt offering, and then told Abraham not to lay his hand on the child, when he said to him,[334] "Now I know that you fear God, and for my sake, you have not spared your beloved son" (Gen. 22:13). And when the Scripture says, "the angel of the Lord called him out of heaven", it shows not God the Father himself as the one who called Abraham, but the Son, the Word of God, as calling Abraham. That is why the Scripture called him the "angel of the Lord". And the Scripture showed that the Word of God was the true God when the Scripture said that God tested Abraham, stating, "(Both of them) came to the place of which God spoke to him", and saying, "Now I know", and saying, "because of me you have not spared your beloved son".

33.6. In all of this, the Scripture explicitly speaks of God.[335] And when the Scripture says, "and the angel of the Lord called him out of heaven", and when it says, "that you fear God", it[336] explicitly shows the Son of God and calls him the "angel of the Lord". Instead of naming him as one of the angels that surround

332 there] *omitted*

333 'Do not lay your hand on the child,] 'Do not lay a hand on your child,

334 and then told Abraham not to lay his hand on the child, when he said to him,] and then commanded him to not lay his hand on the child, for he said to Abraham,

335 And the Scripture showed that the Word of God was the true God when the Scripture said that God tested Abraham, stating, "(Both of them) came to the place of which God spoke to him", and saying, "Now I know", and saying, "because of me you have not spared your beloved son". In all of this, the Scripture explicitly speaks of God.] The Word of God is the true God, because when the Scripture said that God tested Abraham and said, "(Both of them) came to the place of which God spoke to him", and said, "Now I know", and said, "because of me you have not spared your beloved son", the Scripture showed the divine Word of God, through that.

336 it] Scripture

64v/154 аг҃гловъ единоⷢ. нарекова писание аг҃гла гнⷭ҇а но поⷣбнаго и соѡбразнаⷢ сопрⷭ҇тльнаⷢ. и единоволнаго. и единосꙋщнаⷢ аг҃гла гнⷭ҇а гⷭ҇ꙋ бг҃ꙋ. не возможно бо слꙋжебномꙋ аг҃глꙋ бж҃ие имѧ и лице возложити на сѧ. бꙋдеⷮ бо противниⷦ бг҃ꙋ. но сопрⷭ҇тльствꙋющемꙋ и подобномꙋ и соѡбразномꙋ бг҃ꙋ. возлагати на сѧ имѧ и лице бж҃ие томꙋ есть. да покажет сѧ еⷣ новолное и единочⷭ҇тное. Ꙗко в ветхоⷨ бг҃одх҃новеннⷨо писанїи тонцѣ ѿкрываемъ еⷭ сн҃ъ бж҃їи бг҃ъ[337]

Прїидемъ паки на ино мѣсто писаниа. и видиⷨ[338] сн҃а бж҃їа. показꙋющꙋ писанию бг҃а съ бг҃мъ съ ѿцемъ сꙋща. а не ѿнюⷣ оуединена бг҃а. не в треⷯ составеⷯ бг҃а. пишеⷮ бо въ сщ҃енныхъ книгаⷯ.

Изыде иѧковъ ѿ стꙋденца клѧтвенаго. ѡбрѣ теⷤ мѣсто и оуспе тꙋ. сл҃нцⷺ заиде. и взѧ ѿ ка менїа мѣста тоⷢ и положи возглавие себѣ и ꙋспе на мѣстѣ тоⷨ. и видѣ сонъ. и се лѣствица оу твержена на землѣ. еѧⷤ конецъ досѧзаше до нбⷭ҇ѣ. и аг҃гли бж҃їи восхожахꙋ. и ниⷥхожа хꙋ по неи. г҃ь же. восланѧшеⷭ на неи. и реⷱ азъ бг҃ъ авраамль ѿца твоеⷢ. и бг҃ъ исаакоⷡ. не бои. 65r/156 землѧ идѣⷤ ты спиши на неи. тебѣ даⷨ ю и племени твоемꙋ. и бꙋдеⷮ племѧ твое ѩко пѣсоⷦ земныи. и раⷥширитсѧ до морѧ и до въстокъ и запаⷣ. и до сѣвера. бл҃гословѧтсѧ ѡ тебѣ вси

337 *Text continues in the margin*: сꙋщь со ѿцемъ бг҃оⷨ.

338 *In the margin*: глⷡ҇а ф҃і.

(God), | the Scripture called him[339] the "angel of the Lord", and that "angel of the Lord" is one who is rather like the Lord God and who shares the same image, and the same throne, and one will, and consubstantiality. For it is impossible[340] for a ministering angel to put on himself the name and appearance of God because it would make him an enemy to God.[341] But for the one who shares the same throne with God as well as the same likeness and image[342] with him, it is proper to put on himself the name and appearance of God in order to show one will and one honor. 64v/154

34. Showing that the divinely inspired Scripture of the Old Testament specifically reveals the divinity of God's Son together with the Father. CHAPTER 19.[343]

34.1. Let us next[344] come to another place of Scripture and see how the Scripture shows the Son of God to be God with God the Father and in no way estranged from God, but rather God in three subsistences.[345] For here is what is written in the sacred Scriptures, "And Jacob went forth from the well of the oath. And found a certain place and slept there, for the sun had gone down.[346] And he took one of the stones from that place, and put it at his head, and lay down to sleep in that place. And he dreamed, and behold, a ladder was fixed on the earth, whose top reached to heaven, and the angels of God ascended and descended on it. And the Lord was ascending on it[347] and said, 'I am the God of your father Abraham, and the God of Isaac. Do not fear, | the land on which 65r/156
you sleep, to you will I give it, and to your offspring. And your offspring will be as the sand of the earth; and it will spread abroad to the sea, and to the East, and to the West, and to the North; and in you and in your offspring will all the

339 him] him here

340 For it is impossible] For it does not befit, nor is it possible

341 to God,] to God, and will not be the "angel of the Lord".

342 likeness and image] image and likeness

343 **Showing that the divinely inspired Scripture of the Old Testament specifically reveals the divinity of God's Son together with the Father. CHAPTER 19.] Once again, on the glory of the Godhead, shown in the holy book of Genesis, and on how to understand the episode where Jacob saw a ladder and worshiped the Lord on it, and on (the question) of whom it is that Jacob fought with a man at night. CHAPTER 19.**

344 next] *omitted*

345 with God the Father and in no way estranged from God, but rather God in three subsistences.] with God; where it clearly shows the Son with the Father and that he is in no way estranged from God, but rather God in three hypostases.

346 for the sun had gone down.] *omitted*

347 Lord was ascending on it] Lord stood upon it firmly

ꙗзыцы земнїи въ племени твоеⷨ. сеⷤ азъ с тобою. сохраняа тя на всеⷨ пꙋти. амоⷤ идеши. и вовращꙋ тя в землю сию. ꙗко не ѡставлю тебе. дондеⷤ сотворю все еⷤ гл҃аⷯ тебѣ.

По сеⷨ гл҃етъ писание. внегда пꙋсти иꙗковъ слы преⷣ собою ко исавꙋ братꙋ своемꙋ. и возвратишаⷭ слы ко иꙗковꙋ гл҃юще. ходихоⷨ къ братꙋ твоемꙋ исавꙋ. и саⷨ идеⷮ противꙋ тебе. и четыреста моужь с нимъ. оубояжеⷭ иꙗкоⷡ ѕѣло. и возне оумѣ. и разлꙋчи челяⷣ свою. рече же иꙗковъ. бг҃ъ ѿца моеⷢ авраама. и бг҃ъ ѿца моеⷢ исаака. бг҃ъ гл҃авыи мнѣ. иди в землю рожеⷩ҇ꙗ твоеⷢ. и бл҃га тя сотворю. довлѣеⷮ ми ѿ всея правды и ѿ всея истинны. юⷤ сотвори рабꙋ своемꙋ. съ жезлоⷨ бо сиⷨ преидоⷯ иерданъ. нн҃ѣ бы в два поⷧка. избави мя ѿ рꙋкꙋ брата моеⷢ исава. ꙗко боюⷭ его. еда пришеⷣ оубиеⷮ мя и м҃три с чады. а ты реⷱ добрѣ бл҃га тя сотворю. 65v/157 и поставлю племя твое ꙗко пѣсоⷦ морьскїи. иже ся не изочтеть ѿ мноⷤства. и лежа тꙋ тои нощи. Таⷤ гл҃етъ писание. въставъ тои нощы поꙗ ѡбѣ женѣ. и ѡбѣ женимїи. и первыꙗ дѣтеи свойⷯ. и минꙋ то шествие иꙗковъ. и поиⷨꙗ минꙋ водотеⷱ. и преведе все свое. ѡстаⷤ иꙗкоⷡ единъ. и боряшеⷭ с ниⷨ моу до ꙋтрїа. видѣвъⷤ ꙗко не може емꙋ противꙋ емꙋ. и преяⷭ въ стегна его. пречеса стегна иꙗковля. внегда боряшеⷭ с нимъ. реⷱ емꙋ пꙋсти мя взыде бо свѣтъ. сеи реⷱ не пꙋщоу тебе аще не бл҃виши мене. и реⷱ емꙋ како ти имя есть. сеиⷤ рече иꙗковъ. сеиⷤ рече емꙋ. николиⷤ не прозовется имя твое иꙗковъ. но їил҃ь бꙋдеⷮ имя твое. ꙗко крѣпи съ бг҃мъ и с чл҃ки силенъ. вопрашаⷤ иꙗковъ и реⷱ повѣж ми имя твое. и рече се въскꙋю вопрашаеши имени моеⷢ. чюⷣно бо се есть. бл҃виⷭ тоу. и прозва їаковъ има мѣстꙋ томꙋ ѡбразъ бж҃їи. видѣⷯ бо бг҃а лицемъ к лицꙋ. и сп҃се ми ся nations of the earth be blessed. And behold, I am with you, I will keep you on every path where you go; and I will bring you back to this land; for I will not leave you until I have done all that I told you'" (Gen. 28:10–15).

34.2. After this, the Scripture talks about the time when Jacob "sent his messengers ahead of him to his brother Esau" (Gen. 32:3),[348] and "when the messengers returned to Jacob, they said, 'We came to your brother Esau, and he himself is coming toward you, and four hundred men with him'. And Jacob was taken by great fear and was perplexed;[349] and he divided up his slaves. And Jacob said, 'God of my father Abraham, and God of my father Isaac, God who told me, 'Go to the land of your birth, and I will do you good'. 'It is sufficient for me to have all the justice and all the truth that you have done for your servant; for with this staff, I crossed the Jordan, and now I have become two camps. Deliver me from the hands of my brother Esau, for I am afraid of him, lest he come and kill me, and the mothers along with the children. But you said it well, I will do you good | and will make your offspring as the sand of the sea, which cannot be 65v/157
numbered for multitude'. And he lodged there that night" (Gen. 32:6–7, 9–13).

34.3. Also,[350] the Scripture says, "And he rose up that night and took his two wives, and two maidservants, and his older children,[351] and Jacob crossed over that ford. And taking them, he passed over the brook and brought over all he had. And Jacob was left alone; and a man wrestled with him until morning. And he saw that he could not overpower him; and he touched his hip and dislocated the socket of Jacob's hip when he wrestled with him. He[352] said to him, 'Let me go, for the dawn has arisen'. (But) he said, 'I will not let you go unless you bless me'. And he said to him,[353] 'What is your name'? And he replied, 'Jacob'. And he said to him, 'Your name will no longer be called Jacob, but Israel will be your name; for you have become strong with God and will be powerful with men'. And Jacob asked and said, 'Tell me your name'. And he said, 'Well, why do you ask my name? For it is wondrous'. (And) he blessed him there. And Jacob called that place by the name of 'Image of God', for (he said), 'I saw God face to face,

---

348 After this, the Scripture talks about the time when Jacob "sent his messengers ahead of him to his brother Esau" (Gen. 32:3),] And after this, the Scripture says, following the time when Jacob returned from Laban, his father-in-law, that Jacob was afraid of his brother Esau and "sent his messengers ahead of him to his brother Esau" (Gen. 32:3), and at the time when Jacob's messengers were with Esau, his brother, it is written,

349 was perplexed] aspired in his mind

350 Also,] And somewhat later,

351 older children] cf. "eleven children" *in the 1581 edition of the* Ostrog Bible *in Острозька Біблія* [*Ostrog Bible*], (Львів: Українське Біблійне Товариство, 2006), p. 71.

352 He] And he

353 to him,] *omitted*

дша. и взыде емꙋ слнце егда ѿиде ѡбраⷥ бжїи.
Пакй глⷮе писание. простреⷤ иꙗковъ десницꙋ
66r/158 и възложи на главꙋ ефремлю. сеⷤй бѣꙗше мнїи.
а лѣвицꙋ на главꙋ манасиинꙋ. премѣнивъ
рꙋцы. и блⷭви а и реⷱ. бгъ емꙋ оугодиша ѿцы
мои преⷣ нимъ. авраⷨ и исакъ. бгъ ⷤи мѧ коⷬми
ⷥи млада и до днешнѧⷢ дни. и агглъ ⷤи мѧ изба
влѧеⷮ ѿ всеⷭ ѕла блⷭви дѣтища сїа. Пакы глюⷮ
книги. Моисеⷤй бѣꙗше пасыи ѡвца ра
гꙋила тестѧ своеⷢ сщенника мадиⷨаска.
и гнаше ѡвца в пꙋстыню. и прїиде в горꙋ бжию
хоривъ. ꙗви же сѧ емꙋ агглъ гⷭнь. въ пламени
ѡгненѣ ис кꙋпины. и видѣ ꙗко кꙋпина го
рꙗше и не сгараше. рецеⷤ моисеи. мимо
шеⷣ вижю что видѣние великое се. ꙗко не
съгараше кꙋпина. и ꙗко видѣ гⷭь. ꙗко при
стꙋпаеⷮ видѣти. и возва его агглъ гⷭнь и
с кꙋпины глѧ. моисеи моисеи. ѡнⷤъ рече
се аⷥ. рецеⷤ гⷭь. не приближаисѧ сѣмо. изꙋи
сапогъ ѿ ногъ твоⷯй. ибо мѣсто на немⷤъ
ты стоиши землѧ стаⷭ есть. и реⷱ емꙋ. аⷥ
есмь бгъ ѿца твоеⷢ. бгъ авраамовъ. бгъ иса
аковъ. бгъ иꙗковль. ѿвратиⷤ лице свое
моисеи. говѣꙗше бо зрѣти преⷣ бга. рецеⷤ гⷭь
66v/174 к моисѣеви. видѧ видеⷯ бѣдꙋ людеи моихъ.
ⷤи во египтѣ. и вопль ⷯи оуслышаⷯ. ѿ дѣлъ при
ставникъ видеⷯ болѣзнь ⷯи. и снидоⷯ изатї ⷯи
ѿ рꙋкꙋ египеⷮскꙋ. извести а ⷥи землѧ тоа.
таⷤ пишеⷮ. рецеⷤ бгъ к моисею глѧ. боудꙋ с то
бою. сеⷤ ти знамение ꙗко аⷥ тѧ пꙋщаю извести
людеи моⷯй изъ египта. да сѧ помолѧⷮ бгꙋ в го
рѣ сеи. Пакы глеⷮ писание. Рецеⷤ моисеи ко
гꙋ. се ты мнѣ реⷱ извести люди сиа. и ты
не повѣда мнѣ кого пꙋщаеши со мною. тыⷤ
мнѣ реⷱ. вѣм тѧ паⷣ всеⷯ. и блгⷣть имаши ѿ
мене. и реⷱ моисеи аще есмь ѡбрѣлъ блгⷣть
преⷣ тобою. ꙗви ми саⷭм ꙗвѣ да вижю тѧ.

and my soul was spared'. And the sun rose upon him when he passed by the 'Image of God'" (Gen. 32.22–31).

34.4. And the Scripture says again,[354] "And Jacob stretched out his right
hand | and laid it on the head of Ephraim, and he was the younger one;[355] and 66r/158
his left hand on the head of Manasseh, changing his hands. And having blessed them, he said, 'The God in whose sight my fathers, Abraham and Isaac, were well pleasing, the God who has fed me from my youth and until this day; and the angel who delivers me from all evil, bless these boys'" (Gen. 48:14–16).

34.5. And again, the Scriptures say, "And Moses was shepherding the sheep of Raguel, his father-in-law, the priest of Midian; and he drove the sheep to the wilderness and came to Horeb, the mountain of God. And the angel of the Lord appeared to him in flaming fire out of the bush, and he saw that the bush burned with fire, but did not burn up. And Moses said, 'I will go near and see what this great sight is that the bush does not burn up'. And when the Lord saw that he approaches to see it, the angel of the Lord called him out of the bush, saying, 'Moses, Moses'! And he said, 'Here I am'. And the Lord said, 'Do not come near here. Take the boots off your feet, for the place on which you are standing is holy ground'. And he said to him, 'I am the God of your father, the God of Abraham, the God of Isaac, the God of Jacob'. And Moses turned away
his face, for he was afraid to look at God. And the Lord said | to Moses, 'I have 66v/174
surely seen the trouble of my people that is in Egypt, and I have heard their cry caused by their taskmasters. I have seen their affliction and have come down to deliver them out of the hands of the Egyptians, to bring them out of that land'" (Ex. 3:1–8). It is also written,[356] "And God spoke to Moses, saying, 'I will be with you, and this will be the sign to you that I am sending[357] you to bring my people out of Egypt: you will pray to God on this mountain'" (Ex. 3:12).

34.6. Next, the Scripture says,[358] "And Moses said to the Lord, 'See, you said to me', 'Lead this people out', 'but you did not tell me whom you will send with me. And you said to me, 'I know you better than all others, and you have found grace from me'. And Moses said, 'If then, I have found grace before you, reveal

354 again,] furthermore,
355 and he was the younger one;] *omitted*
356 It is also written,] And somewhat later, it says,
357 I am sending] I will send
358 says,] says, addressing the sons of Levi,

ꙗкоⷤ ѡбрѣлъ блг҃ть прⷣе тобою. да ѹвѣдꙗть
ꙗко людие твои сїи ꙗзыкъ великъ. и реⷱ емѹ
гⷭ҇ь аⷥ самъ поидѹ прⷣе тобою. и оуставлю та.
и реⷱ к немѹ моисѣи. аще саⷨ ты не идеши с наⷨ
да не изведеши насъ ѿ сюдѣ. или како ꙗвѣ
боуⷣте истинною. ꙗко ѡбрѣтоⷯ блг҃ть прⷣе то
бою. азъⷤ и людие твои паⷣ всѣⷯ ꙗзыкъ. елика
на земли есть. речеⷤ гⷭ҇ь к моисѣю. сети слово
еже вѣща приꙗти сотворю. ѡбрⷮѣ еси
67ʳ/175 блг҃ть прⷣе мною. и видѣ тꙗ паⷣ всѣⷯ. и реⷱ мои
сѣи. покажи ми славѹ свою. речеⷤ гⷭ҇ь моисѣ
еви. аⷥ идѹ прⷣе тобою славою моею. и прозо
вѹ имꙗ свое прⷣе тобою гⷭ҇ь. и помилѹю егоⷤ
аще помилѹю. и оущⷣерю егоⷤ аще оущедрю.
и реⷱ не возможеши видѣти славы лица моеⷢ.
нѣⷭть бо аще видиⷮ члвкъ лице мое и живъ быⷮ
и реⷱ гⷭ҇ь се мѣсто ѹ мене и станеше ѹ камени
егдаⷤ придеⷮ слава моа. и поставлю тꙗ оу дѹ
плꙗ камыка. и покрыю рѹкою моею наⷣ то
бою. дондеⷤ минѹ. и ѿимѹ рѹку мою тогда
оузриши заⷣ мои. а лице мое не ꙗвиⷮ ти са. оу
рань моисѣи заѹтра. и взыде на горѹ сина
искую. ꙗкоⷤ заповѣда емѹ гⷭ҇ь. и взꙗ моисѣи
с собою двѣ дъсцѣ каменны. ꙗцѣⷤ первїи.
и сниде гⷭ҇ь во ѡблацѣ и ста прⷣе нимъ тѹ. и во
зва именеⷨ гⷭ҇нимъ. и минѹ гⷭ҇ь прⷣе лицеⷨ его. про
зва гⷭ҇а. гⷭ҇ь бг҃ъ щⷣръ и млⷭтвъ. дⷧготерпѣлиⷡ.
и истиненъ правдѹ сна бдꙗ. и творꙗ млⷭть
в тысꙗщаⷯ. ѿмщаа безакониа неправды.
и не потребитса вина еⷢ. возлагаа грѣхы ѿцъ
на чада. и внѹчата. и на четвертыи. и третїи
роⷣ.
67ᵛ/176 потщⷡаса моисѣи приведеⷭ и поклониⷭ бг҃ѹ. рече же
аще есмь ѡбрⷮѣ блг҃ть прⷣе тобою. дабы шеⷣ гⷭ҇и
прⷣе нами. и реⷱ гⷭ҇ь к моисѣю. се аⷥ полагаю ти за
вѣⷮ прⷣе всѣми лю҇ми своими. сотворю вели
каа и славнаа ꙗⷤ не бѣша по всеи земли. ни во
всѣⷯ странаⷯ. оузрꙗⷮ вси лю҇ⷣ в нихъⷤ ты еси дѣ
леса гⷭ҇на. ꙗко чю҇на соуⷮ. ꙗже сотворю аⷥ тебѣ.
вонми ты все елико аⷥ заповѣдаю тебѣ.

yourself to me visibly so that I may see you that I have found grace in your sight; that they may know that this great nation is your people'. And the Lord said to him, 'I myself will go before you and give you rest'. And Moses said to him, 'If you do not go with us yourself, do not bring us up from here. Or how will it be truly evident,[359] that your people and I have found grace before you above all nations that are on this earth'? And the Lord said to Moses, 'This very thing that you have spoken I will do. You have found | grace before me, and I know 67r/175
you better than all others'. And Moses said, 'Show me your glory'. And the Lord said to Moses, 'I will pass by before you with my glory, and I will call out my name, the 'Lord', before you. And I will have mercy on whom I will have mercy and will have compassion on whom I will have compassion'. And he said, 'You are not able to see the glory of my face,[360] for no man can see my face and live'. And the Lord said, 'Behold, there is a place by me, and you will stand on the rock. And when my glory passes by, I will put you into a cleft of the rock; and I will cover you with my hand until I have passed by. And I will take away my hand, and then, you will see my back; but my face will not appear to you'" (Ex. 33:12–23).

34.7. "Early in the morning, Moses rose and went up on Mount Sinai, as the Lord had commanded him; and Moses took the two stone tablets with him, as the first time. And the Lord descended in the cloud, and stood near him there, and called upon the name of the Lord. And the Lord passed by before his face, and[361] he called upon the Lord, 'The Lord God, compassionate and merciful, long-suffering and true, supplying with righteousness and conducting mercy for thousands, taking revenge for iniquity, unrighteousness,[362] and (the sinner's) guilt will not be discarded. He lays the sins of the fathers upon the children, and grandchildren, and to the third and fourth generation'. | Hav- 67v/176
ing hurried, Moses bowed to the ground and worshiped God. And he said, 'If I have found grace before you, let the Lord[363] go before us'. And the Lord said to Moses, 'Behold, I am establishing a covenant with you before all my people. I will do great and glorious things, which have not been done in all the earth nor among any of the nations. And all the people among whom you are will see the works of the Lord, that they are wonderful, which I will do for you. Observe

359 evident] *omitted*
360 the glory of my face,] my face,
361 and] *omitted*
362 unrighteousness,] unrighteousness, sins,
363 Lord] *omitted*

Паки пишⷮе в книгаⷯ. реⷱ҇ гⷭ҇ь к моисѣю. поими вса
головы лⷣюски и ѡбличи а гⷭ҇ꙋ прамо сл҃нцꙋ. и
ѿврати гнѣвъ ꙗрости гⷭ҇на ѿ ї҆ил҃ꙗ. Вижⷣь

---

364 Next, it is written in the Scriptures,] Next, the divinely inspired Scripture also states,

365 Lord] "And the Lord

366 And again, the Scriptures say, "And Moses was shepherding the sheep of Raguel, his father-in-law, the priest of Midian; and he drove the sheep to the wilderness and came to Horeb, the mountain of God. And the angel of the Lord appeared to him in flaming fire out of the bush, and he saw that the bush burned with fire, but did not burn up. And Moses said, 'I will go near and see what this great sight is that the bush does not burn up'. And when the Lord saw that he approached to see, the angel of the Lord called him out of the bush, saying, 'Moses, Moses'! And he said, 'Here I am'. And the Lord said, 'Do not come near here. Take the boots off your feet, for the place on which you are standing is holy ground'. And

everything I command you'" (Ex. 34:4–11). Next, it is written in the Scriptures,[364] "The Lord[365] said to Moses, 'Take all the leaders of the people and bring them out in the sun before the Lord, and the anger of the Lord will be turned away from Israel'" (Num. 25:4).[366]

---

he said to him, 'I am the God of your father, the God of Abraham, the God of Isaac, the God of Jacob'. And Moses turned away his face, for he was afraid to look at God. And the Lord said to Moses, 'I have surely seen the trouble of my people that is in Egypt, and I have heard their cry caused by their taskmasters. I have seen their affliction and have come down to deliver them out of the hands of the Egyptians, to bring them out of that land'" (Ex. 3:1–8). It is also written, "And God spoke to Moses, saying, 'I will be with you, and this will be the sign to you that I am sending you to bring my people out of Egypt: you will pray to God on this mountain'" (Ex. 3:12). Next, the Scripture says, "And Moses said to the Lord, 'See, you said to me', 'Lead this people out', 'but you did not tell me whom you will send with me'. And you said to me, 'I know you better than all others, and you have found grace from me'. And Moses said, 'If then, I have found grace before you, reveal yourself to me visibly so that I may see you that I have found grace in your sight; that they may know that this great nation is your people'. And the Lord said to him, 'I myself will go before you and give you rest'. And Moses said to him, 'If you do not go with us yourself, do not bring us up from here. Or how will it be truly evident, that your people and I have found grace before you above all nations that are on this earth'? And the Lord said to Moses, 'This very thing that you have spoken I will do. You have found grace before me, and I know you better than all others'. And Moses said, 'Show me your glory'. And the Lord said to Moses, 'I will pass by before you with my glory, and I will call out my name, the 'Lord', before you. And I will have mercy on whom I will have mercy and will have compassion on whom I will have compassion'. And he said, 'You are not able to see the glory of my face, for no man can see my face and live'. And the Lord said, 'Behold, there is a place by me, and you will stand on the rock. And when my glory passes by, I will put you into a cleft of the rock; and I will cover you with my hand until I have passed by. And I will take away my hand, and then, you will see my back; but my face will not appear to you'" (Ex. 33:12–23). "Early in the morning, Moses rose and went up on Mount Sinai, as the Lord had commanded him; and Moses took the two stone tablets with him, as the first time. And the Lord descended in the cloud, and stood near him there, and called upon the name of the Lord. And the Lord passed by before his face, and he called upon the Lord, 'The Lord God, compassionate and merciful, longsuffering and true, supplying with righteousness and conducting mercy for thousands, taking revenge for iniquity, unrighteousness, and (the sinner's) guilt will not be discarded. He lays the sins of the fathers upon the children, and grandchildren, and to the third and fourth generation'. Having hurried, Moses bowed to the ground and worshipped God. And he said, 'If I have found grace before you, let the Lord go before us'. And the Lord said to Moses, 'Behold, I am establishing a covenant with you before all my people. I will do great and glorious things, which have not been done in all the earth nor among any of the nations. And all the people among whom you are will see the works of the Lord, that they are wonderful, which I will do for you. Observe everything I command you'" (Ex. 34:4–11). Next, it is written in the Scriptures, "The Lord said to Moses, 'Take all the leaders of the people and bring them out in the sun before the Lord, and the anger of the Lord will be turned away from Israel'" (Num. 25:4).] *omitted* сщ҃енное писание. повелѣнныа книги ѿ б҃а моисѣю. всепремдⷬ҇ѣ сн҃а бж҃їа. егоⷤ множицею аггла гⷭ҇на именꙋюща. бг҃а истинна показоу юща тогоⷤ равна бг҃ꙋ ѿц҃ꙋ сꙋща. токмо про читаи сщ҃енное писание не лицемѣрне. и ра зꙋмѣваи правѣ. вса бо права писанїа ра зꙋмѣвающⷨ҇и. и права соуть ѡбрѣтающимъ разоумъ по соломонꙋ. Слыши оубо прочи таемаа въ книзѣ. їаковъ оуспе на мѣсте и соⷩ҇ видѣ. лѣствица оутвержена на земли еѧⷤ конецъ досазаше до нб҃си. и аггли бж҃їи [68r/159] въсхожахꙋ. и нⷥ҇исхожахꙋ по неи. гⷭ҇ь же въсланашеⷭ҇ на неи. и рече аⷥ҇ бг҃ъ авраамль ѿца твоеⷢ҇. и бг҃ъ исааковъ. не боиⷭ҇. земла иⷤ ты спиши на неи тебѣ даⷨ҇ ю и сѣмени твоемꙋ. и боудеⷮ҇ племѧ твое ꙗко пѣсокъ земныи. и раⷥ҇ширитса до мора и до въстокъ и запаⷣ҇. и до сѣвера. блвⷭ҇а тса ѡ тебѣ вси ꙗзыци земнїи въ племени твоеⷨ҇. сеⷤ азъ с тобою съхранѧа та на всѣхъ пꙋⷮеⷯ. амоⷤ идеши и возвращꙋ та на землю сию. и не ѡставлю тебе дондеⷤ сотворю все еⷤ глаⷯ тебѣ. Смотрите писанїа. реⷱ҇ бо ꙗко гⷭ҇ь оутвержашеса на лѣствицы. и рече аⷥ҇ бг҃ъ авраамль и проⷱ҇а. и по прочиⷯ ѡбѣтованїихъ їаковꙋ реⷱ҇. се же аⷥ҇ с тобою сохранѧа та на всѣⷯ пꙋⷮеⷯ амоⷤ идеши. Посеⷨ҇ глют҃ь книги. вне гда сказаша їаковꙋ послы его. хоⷣвшїи ѿ неⷢ҇. къ исавꙋ братꙋ его. ꙗко идеⷮ҇ исавъ противꙋ емꙋ и четыреста мꙋжь с нимъ. и глеⷮ҇ писаⷩ҇е. оубоажеⷭ҇ їаковъ ѕѣло. речеⷤ їаковъ бг҃ъ ѿца моеⷢ҇ авраама. и бг҃ъ ѿца моеⷢ҇ исаака. бг҃ъ гла выи мнѣ иди в землю роженїа твоеⷢ҇. и блг҃а та сотворю. избави ма ѿ рꙋкꙋ брата моеⷢ҇ [68v/160] исава. ꙗко боюⷭ҇ его. егⷣа пришеⷣ оубиеⷮ мѧ и мт҃ри

34.8. See how most wisely the sacred Scripture—the books with the commandments that Moses received from God—(shows) the Son of God, whom it often calls the "angel of the Lord", and whom it also reveals as the true God and of the equal essence with God the Father. Just read the sacred Scripture sincerely and perceive it correctly! For "all of the Scriptures are right to the discerning, and they are right to those who find knowledge", according to Solomon (Prov. 8:9). Now, listen to what was read in the Scripture, "Jacob slept there", "and dreamed" "a ladder was fixed on the earth, whose top reached to heaven, and the angels of God | ascended and descended on it. And the Lord stood on it 68r/159
firmly, and he said, 'I am the God of your father Abraham, and the God of Isaac. Do not fear, the land on which you sleep, to you will I give it, and to your seed. And your offspring will be as the sand of the earth; and it will spread abroad to the sea, and to the East, and to the West, and to the North; and in you and in your offspring will all the nations of the earth be blessed. And behold, I am with you, I will keep you in all the ways where you go, and I will bring you back to this land; for I will not leave you until I have done all that I told you'" (Gen. 28:11–15).[367]

34.9. Observe the Scriptures, for they said that the Lord "stood firm on a ladder", and they said, "I am the God of your father Abraham" and of others; and after some promises, it was said to Jacob, "And behold, I am with you, I will keep you in all the ways where you go" (Gen. 28:15). Then,[368] the Scriptures say that Jacob's messengers, who went to Esau, his brother, told him that Esau "was coming[369] toward him, and four hundred men with him" (Gen. 32:6). And the Scripture says, "And Jacob was taken by great fear. And Jacob said, 'God of my father Abraham, and God of my father Isaac, God, who told me, 'Go to the land of your birth, and I will do you good.' Deliver me from the hand of my brother | 68v/160
Esau, for I am afraid of him, lest he come and kill me, and the mothers along with the children'" (Gen. 32:7, 9, 11).

---

367 *MS 61 adds*: **Showing that it was one and the same Lord, who appeared to Jacob on the ladder and who, as a man, wrestled with Jacob. It is the same Lord, who is also (represented) as the "Image of God", which means the "Son of God".**

368 Then,] After these things,

369 "was coming] "himself was coming

с чады.

Ѥако единъ г҃ь иⷤ ꙗвиⷭ на лѣствицѣ ꙗковꙋ. той г҃ь и борꙗшеⷭ со ӏаковоⷨ мꙋжь еⷭ с҃нъ бж҃їи.

Тамо во снѣ видѣ г҃а на лѣствицѣ. ѡбѣщавающа емꙋ дати землю и ꙋмножити сѣмꙗ его. и бл҃вити всѣмъ ꙗзыкоⷨ въ племени еⷭ. и реⷱша емꙋ. се же аⷥ с тобою сохранꙗа та на всакомъ пꙋти. си҃ здѣ и молитса ӏаковъ бг҃ꙋ. преⷣлагаа самое ѡбѣщание бж҃ие бывшее к немꙋ. и се҃ раⷣ внегда ѡста ӏаковъ единъ реⷱ писание. ибо рашеⷭ с нимъ мꙋⷤ до ꙋтрїа. вопрошаⷤ его ӏакоⷡ и реⷱ повѣжь ми има твое. и реⷱ въскꙋю вопрашаеши имени мое҃. чюно бо се есть. бл҃ви тꙋ. и прозва ӏаковъ има мѣстꙋ томꙋ ѡбраⷥ бж҃їи. видѣⷯ бо бг҃а лицеⷨ к лицꙋ. и сп҃се миⷭ дш҃а. и взыде емꙋ сл҃нце. егда ѿиде ѡбраⷥ бж҃їи. Видите показꙋⷮе здѣ писание ѿкровенно сн҃а бж҃їа понеⷤ не реⷱ и взыде емꙋ сл҃нце егда ѿиде моужь. ниⷤ рече егда ѿиде аг҃глъ бж҃їи. или егда ѿиде г҃ь. но реⷱ писание егда ѿиде ѡбраⷥ бж҃їи. а ꙗко ѡбраⷥ бж҃їи сн҃ъ бж҃їи есть. а не слꙋжебныи аг҃глъ. но бг҃ъ есть саⷨ сн҃ъ бж҃їи. понеⷤ не рече 69r/162 ӏꙗковъ ꙗко видѣⷯ ѡбраⷥ бж҃їи лицеⷨ к лицꙋ и сп҃се миⷭ дш҃а. но реⷱ ӏаковъ видѣⷯ бг҃а лицеⷨ к лицꙋ и сп҃се миⷭ дш҃а. ниⷤ рече видѣⷯ аг҃гла лицемъ к лицꙋ. показоуⷮе писание. ꙗко тоиⷤ есть и на лѣствицы г҃ь гл҃авыи ӏаковꙋ. аⷥ бг҃ъ авраамль ѿца твоеⷢ.

35. Showing that it was one and the same Lord, who appeared to Jacob on the ladder and who, as a man, wrestled with Jacob. He is the Son of God.[370]

35.1. In his dream there, he saw the Lord on the ladder who promised to give him the land and multiply his seed, as well as bless all the nations through his offspring. And he said to him, "And behold, I am with you, I will keep you on every path" (Gen. 28:15). It is here that Jacob prays to God, setting forth the same divine promise in his prayer to God that was given to him. And in view of that, when Jacob "was left alone", as the Scripture said, "a man wrestled with him until morning" (Gen. 32:24). "And Jacob asked and said, 'Tell me your name'. And he said, 'Why do you ask my name? For it is wondrous'. And he blessed him there. And Jacob called that place with the name the 'Image of God', for (he said), 'I saw God face to face, and my soul was spared'. And the sun rose upon him when he passed by the 'Image of God'" (Gen. 32:24, 29–31).[371]

35.2. You see, the Scripture explicitly shows the Son of God here. For it[372] did not say, "And the sun rose upon him when the man left", nor did it say, "when the angel of God left", nor "when the Lord[373] left". Instead, the Scripture said,[374] "when he passed by the 'Image of God'". And in being the "Image of God", the Son has a divine status rather than one of a ministering angel. The Son of God is rather himself God, which is why Jacob did not say, | "I saw the 'image of God' 69r/162
face to face, and my soul was spared". Instead, Jacob said, "I saw God face to face, and my soul was spared" (Gen. 32:30). Nor did he say, "I saw an angel".[375] The Scripture shows that in being Lord, he was also the one who said to Jacob on the ladder, "I am the God of your father Abraham, and the God of Isaac" (Gen.

---

370 **Showing that it was one and the same Lord, who appeared to Jacob on the ladder and who, as a man, wrestled with Jacob. He is the Son of God.**] *omitted*

371 *MS 61 adds*: **Showing that we can perceive the Son of God in the Old Testament when the Scripture calls God the "Image of God". It is from the same (clue), that he is also recognized at the creation of man, when it says, "Let us make (man) in our image".**

372 it] Scripture

373 Lord] God

374 Instead, the Scripture said,] For while it said, "for I saw God face to face", the Scripture said,

375 "I saw the 'image of God' face to face, and my soul was spared". Instead, Jacob said, "I saw God face to face, and my soul was spared" (Gen. 32:30). Nor did he say, "I saw an angel".] "I saw the 'image of God' face to face, and my soul was spared", nor did he say, "I saw an angel". Instead, Jacob said, "I saw God face to face, and my soul was spared"

и бг҃ъ исаакоⷡ҇. реⷱ҇ бо ꙗко видѣⷯ бг҃а лицемъ к лицꙋ и сп҃се миⷭ҇ дш҃а. и поⷩ҇е на лѣствицы по всѣхъ ѡбѣтованїихъ ѡбѣтова їаковꙋ бг҃ъ и се. сⷤ҇е с тобою съхранаꙗ та на всеⷨ пꙋти амоⷤ пои деши. елма ꙋбоꙗⷭ҇ їаковъ исава брата своего ѕѣло. и помолиⷭ҇ къ бг҃ꙋ ѡбѣтованиⷨе бж҃їимъ ⷤе к немꙋ. сⷢ҇е ради ꙗвлꙗетса г҃ь. ꙗко мꙋⷤ борꙗⷭ҇ с нимъ. по ѡбѣтованию своемꙋ ⷤе на лѣстви цѣ. ꙗко с ниⷨ сыи г҃ь сохранꙗаⷭ҇ е на всꙗкомъ пꙋти. а ꙗко не чл҃къ бораше со їаковоⷨ моⷤꙋ. ниⷤ агг҃лъ. поⷩ҇е реⷱ҇ їаковꙋ борꙗиса с нимъ їил҃ь бꙋдеⷮ имꙗ твое. ꙗко ꙋкрѣпи съ бг҃омъ и съ чл҃ки силенъ. и ꙗко рекъ їаковъ видѣⷯ бо бг҃а лицемъ к лицꙋ и сп҃се миⷭ҇ дш҃а. и посемꙋ паки нѣсть бг҃ъ ѿц҃ъ ниⷤ агг҃лъ бораиⷭ҇ со їаковоⷨ. поⷩ҇е въпроси їаковъ имени его. и ѿвѣща емꙋ. се въскꙋю вопрашаеши имени моⷢ҇е. чюⷣно бо се есть. 69v/163 чюⷣно ꙋбо воистиннꙋ имꙗ сн҃а бж҃їа. егоⷤ҇ име ни не бѣ подобно времꙗ евреоⷨ слышати и наꙋчитиⷭ҇ ѡ немъ. не могꙋщеⷨ в разꙋмѣ своеⷨ

28:13), for he said, "I saw God face to face, and my soul was spared".[376] For in all his promises that God promised to Jacob on the ladder, God promised this, too,[377] "And behold, I am with you, I will keep you on every path, where you will go" (Gen. 28:15). For Jacob was greatly afraid of his brother Esau, and he[378] prayed to God (referring to) the very promise of God that he was given.[379] For that reason, too, the Lord appears as a man who wrestles with him, according to his promise given on the ladder, (showing) that the Lord is with him and keeps him on every path.

35.3. And as for the man, who wrestled with Jacob, he is not a human nor an angel, for after having wrestled with him, he said to Jacob, "Israel will be your name, for you have become strong with God and will be powerful with men" (Gen. 32:28).[380] And as I said regarding Jacob's (words),[381] "I saw God face to face, and my soul was spared", ⟨it was not God the Father, whom Jacob "saw face to face" and addressed as "God"⟩. Therefore, again, it was not God the Father nor an angel, who wrestled with God, for Jacob asked about his name, and he replied to him, "Why do you ask my name? For it is wondrous" (Gen. 32:29).[382] | 69ᵛ/163
For the name of the Son of God is indeed wondrous, and it was not the right time for the Jews to hear his name and to know about him.[383] They could not

376 shows that in being Lord, he was also the one who said to Jacob on the ladder, "I am the God of your father Abraham, and the God of Isaac" (Gen. 28:13), for he said, "I saw God face to face, and my soul was spared".] shows that it was the same Lord in both instances: he said to Jacob on the ladder, "I am the God of your father Abraham, and the God of Isaac" (Gen. 28:13), and it is to him, that Jacob also says after his wrestling, "I saw God face to face, and my soul was spared".

377 God promised this, too,] he promised this, too, saying,

378 he] Jacob

379 given.] given, when he saw him in his dream (standing) on the ladder.

380 And as for the man, who wrestled with Jacob, he is not a human nor an angel, for after having wrestled with him, he said to Jacob, "Israel will be your name, for you have become strong with God and will be powerful with men"] And as for the man, who wrestled with Jacob, he is not a human nor an angel, but God. It was him, who wrestled with Jacob, for he himself told Jacob during his struggle with him, that it was God, who wrestled with Jacob. (This took place) when he blessed Jacob, saying, "Israel will be your name, for you have become strong with God". Since Jacob prevailed in his wrestling with him, in view of that, it said that (Jacob) "became strong with God", and that it was "God" in the form of man, who wrestled with Jacob.

381 And as I said regarding Jacob's (statement),] And as for the words, which Jacob said,

382 Therefore, again, it was not God the Father nor an angel, who wrestled with God, for Jacob asked about his name, and he replied to him, "Why is it that you ask my name? For it is wondrous"] Therefore, when Jacob asked about his name, he replied to him, "Why is it that you ask my name? For it is wondrous" (Gen. 32:29).

383 and it was not the right time for the Jews to hear his name and to know about him.] and it was not yet the right time for the Jews to hear his name and know about him then.

прїати бг҃оначаⷧ҇ныѧ трⷪ҇ца единьство. бжⷭ҇тва. соѡбращающимсѧ еще во мноⷢ҇ бж҃їи. и ложныѧ бг҃и многи чтомы зраще. сеⷢ҇ ради и ѿцъ иⷯ҇ їиⷧ҇ь не сподоблѧетсѧ оуслы шати имени сн҃а бж҃їа. да не племѧ его во многобж҃ие возметсѧ. разоумѣвъⷤ҇ їиⷧ҇ь оумоⷨ҇ сн҃а бж҃їа. славѧше его и блвⷭ҇ѧше глѧ. видѣⷯ҇ бо бг҃а лицеⷨ҇ к лицꙋ и спⷭ҇е миⷭ҇ дш҃а. аще и слꙋхомъ не научеⷩ҇ їиⷧ҇ь но дхомъ просвѣщеⷩ҇. разꙋмѣ кто есть борѧисѧ с нимъ. и ꙋра зоумѣвъ не оумⷪ҇ча. но блвⷭ҇ѧ проповѣда. ѧко видѣ бг҃а лицеⷨ҇ к лицꙋ. и сеⷢ҇ ради спⷭ҇есѧ емꙋ дш҃а. а ѧко не ѿца бжⷭ҇твꙋ бг҃а пропо вѣдаше їаковъ глѧ. видѣⷯ҇ бо бг҃а лицемъ к ли цꙋ. понеⷤ҇ прозва имѧ мѣстꙋ томꙋ ѡразъ бж҃їи. а ѧко тоⷤ҇й прозванныи ѡбраⷥ҇ бж҃їи. и здѣ и на лѣствицѣ преⷤ҇ тоⷤ҇й гⷭ҇ь рекїи їако вꙋ. аⷥ҇ есмь бгъ авраамль ѿца твоеⷢ҇. понеже тогда на лѣствицѣ ѡбѣщаваа реⷱ҇ їаковꙋ.
70r/164 ѧко не ѡставлю тебе донⷣ҇ⷤ сотворю всеⷤ҇ е глаⷯ҇ тебѣ. и здѣ борашеⷭ҇ с нимъ ѧко моуⷤ҇. зане не ѡ ставлѧше їакова с ниⷨ҇ сыи. сохранѧаⷢ҇ е на всемъ пꙋти. понеⷤ҇ ѕѣло ꙋбоѧⷭ҇ їакоⷡ҇ брата своеⷢ҇ исава. емꙋⷤ҇ боѧзнь ѿемлѧ гⷭ҇ь борашеⷭ҇ ѧко мꙋⷤ҇ с нимъ. їа ковъⷤ҇ оусладивсѧ борбою со спⷭ҇ителеⷨ҇ своимъ. и боѧзни всеи избывъ. бл҃гословъствꙋѧ пропо вѣдаше своеⷢ҇ спⷭ҇а глѧ. видѣⷯ҇ бг҃а лицеⷨ҇ к лицоу

accept the one Godhead of the supremely divine Trinity in their minds; they were still living in the midst of polytheism and saw the worship of many false deities around them. For that reason, neither was their father Israel privileged to hear the name of God's Son, lest his offspring be taken into polytheism.

35.4. Yet Israel[384] did discern the Son of God with his mind, praising and blessing him, when he said, "I saw God[385] face to face, and my soul was spared". Even though Israel did not hear any verbal instruction, he was, nevertheless, enlightened by the Spirit to know who it was that wrestled with him. And having learned that, he did not remain silent, but blessed and proclaimed that he "saw God face to face", and despite that, his "soul was spared". And since he called that place the "Image of God", it was not God the Father, whom Jacob proclaimed as God, saying, "for I saw God face to face".[386]

35.5. And (it is clear) that the one who is called here the "Image of God" (Gen. 32:30) is the same Lord, who earlier said to Jacob on the ladder, "I am the God of your father Abraham"[387] (Gen. 28:13), because at that point on the ladder, he gave Jacob a promise, saying, | "I will not leave you until I have done all that 70r/164
I told you" (Gen. 28:15). And when he wrestled with him here as a man, he, therefore, did not leave him. He was with him, keeping him "on every path" (Gen. 28:15). While Jacob was greatly afraid of his brother Esau, his fear was taken away by the Lord, who wrestled with him as a man. After he was relieved from the wrestling with his High Priest (cf. Heb. 4:14–15) and free of all fear, he blessed and proclaimed his Savior, saying, "I saw God face to face, and my soul was spared" (Gen. 28:15).[388]

---

384 Yet Israel] Yet Jacob, Israel,

385 God] Lord

386 And since he called that place the "Image of God", it was not God the Father, whom Jacob proclaimed as God, saying, "for I saw God face to face".] And it was not God the Father, whom Jacob proclaimed as God, saying, "for I saw God face to face". Instead, it was God's Son, whom he proclaimed as God, after seeing him "face to face", which is why he called that place the "Image of God".

387 father Abraham"] father"

388 and my soul was spared"] and my soul was spared", and that "he did not leave him, keeping him on every path" (Gen. 28:15), as he promised to him on the ladder. **Showing that the Scripture speaks of the man, who was in actuality God and wrestled with Jacob, as a reminder of the three men whom Abraham saw when God appeared to him, and through that, it indicates that it was with them, that God spoke, saying, "Let us make man in our image and likeness".**

и сп҃се миⷭ҇ дш҃а. гл҃етъⷤ писание ꙗко ѿиде ѿ неⷢ҇
не бг҃ъ нйⷤ мѹжь. но ѡбраⷥ҇ бж҃їи. а борашеⷭ҇ с нимъ не
ѡбраⷥ҇ бж҃їи ни бг҃ъ. но мѹⷤ҇ борашеⷭ҇ с нимъ гл҃еⷮ писаⷩ҇е.
самъⷤ їаковъ видѣⷮ҇ емѹ гл҃еⷮ не ѡбраⷥ҇ бж҃їи ни мѹ
жа. но бг҃а. видѣⷯ бо бг҃а лицеⷨ к лицѹ и сп҃се ми са
дш҃а. всѣми сими ѿкрываеⷮ свѣтло сн҃а бж҃їа.
именѹа тогоⷤ мꙵѹжа. бравшаⷭ҇ съ їаковомъ.
и бг҃а сп҃сающа їакова. и ѡбраⷥ҇ бж҃їи ѿходѧⷲ҇
ѿ їакова. и гⷭ҇ь на лѣствицы ѡбѣщаⷡ҇са со їа
ковоⷨ быти вездѣ и не ѡставити еⷢ҇. Нари
цаетъⷤ его мѹжа бравшаⷭ҇ съ їаковоⷨ. посылаа
памѧть послѹшателеи. к первѣи бесѣдѣ
ѧⷤ при авраамѣ. ꙗкоⷤ тамо возрѣⷡ҇ авраамъ
и видѣ три мѹжи наⷣ нимъ. и в содоⷨ идоста мѹжа.
70v/166 и здѣ паки гл҃еⷮ. и борѧшеⷭ҇ со їаковоⷨ мѹⷤ҇ до ѹтрїа.
воспоминаа и нн҃ѣ мѹжа бравшаⷭ҇ со їаковомъ.
к разѹмѹ возводѧ ꙗко борѧшеⷭ҇ со їаковоⷨ мѹжь
тои йⷤ ѡбѣдавыи оу авраама единъ ѿ триеⷯ.
и в содомѣ надождивыи камыки горащїи.
и ѡгнь ѿ гⷭ҇а посла гⷭ҇ь сыи саⷨ. и со їаковоⷨ борѧиⷭ҇
мѹⷤ҇. проповѣдѹемыйⷤ бг҃ъ сп҃съ ѡбраⷥ҇ бж҃їи. к то
мѹ оубо бг҃ѹ сп҃сѹ ѡбразѹ бж҃їю и преⷤ реⷱ҇ бг҃ъ. сотво
рйⷨ чл҃ка по ѡбразѹ нш҃емѹ и по поⷣобию. Ꙗко

35.6. And the Scripture says that the one who departed from him was neither "God" nor "man",[389] but the "Image of God". And the one who wrestled with him was[390] neither the "Image of God" nor "God", but "man" that wrestled with him. Yet what Jacob himself saw, as the Scripture says, was neither the "Image of God" nor "man", but "God", for he said, "I saw God face to face, and my soul was spared" (Gen. 28:15). Through all of this, (the Scripture) clearly reveals the Son of God, calling him (with different names): a "man" who wrestled with Jacob, and "God" who spared Jacob, and the "Image of God" that departed from Jacob, and the "Lord" who gave Jacob a promise on the ladder to be with him everywhere and not leave him.

35.7. And it calls him "man" who wrestled with Jacob to remind the listeners of the first conversation that took place at the time of Abraham, as it ⟨says⟩ there, "And Abraham looked up and saw three men in front of him" (cf. Gen. 1:2). And[391] "men" also went to Sodom (Gen. 18:22), | just as here, again, it says,[392] 70v/166
"a man wrestled with Jacob until morning" (Gen. 32:24). Reminding us now of a "man" who wrestled with Jacob, it lifts our minds to (help us recognize) the fact that the "man" who wrestled with Jacob was the same one of those three, who ate with Abraham (Gen. 18:1–5), and who "rained down burning sulfur on Sodom", "and sent fire—from the Lord" (Gen. 19:26). It was the Lord himself, who, as man, wrestled with Jacob, and whom the latter proclaimed as "God", and "Savior", and the "Image of God". Now, it is to the same "God" and "Savior" and "Image of God", that God said previously, "Let us make man in our image and likeness" (Gen. 1:26).

389 from him was neither "God" nor "man",] from Jacob was neither "man" nor "God",

390 And the one who wrestled with him was] And of the one who wrestled with him, the Scripture says that it was

391 And] And likewise,

392 it says] it speaks of "men", saying,

писание б҃га г҃леть. иⷤ со ӏаковоⷨ борющагоⷭ҇ мꙋжа и памѧⷮ полагаа видѣнныⷯ авраамоⷨ треⷯ мꙋжеи. ꙗвльшагоⷭ҇ емꙋ б҃га. и тѣмъ оуказꙋа. ꙗко с тѣми[393]

Видете како премⷬ҇е и правѣ разꙋмꙋ наꙋчаеⷮ с҃щенное писание. посылаа к памѧти реченныⷨ треⷤ. понеⷤ оубо треⷤ реⷭ҇ писание. ꙗко реⷭ҇ б҃гъ сотворимъ ч҃лка по ѡбразꙋ н҃шемꙋ и по подⷪ҇бию. таⷤ показꙋа г҃леⷮ. ꙗко ꙗвиⷭ҇ б҃гъ авраамꙋ. бытиⷤ треⷨ мꙋжеⷨ ꙗвлѧюшемꙋса. гоⷭ҇ же единомꙋ паки треⷨ тѣмже мꙋжеⷨ быти. таⷤ при содомеⷯ г҃леть аг҃гла два. и паки таѧⷤ аг҃гла мꙋжа два г҃леⷮ. таⷤ паки сею двою гаⷭ҇ б҃га г҃леть при лотѣ. ꙗко пощадии реⷭ҇ гь б҃гъ. таⷤ г҃леть [71r/167] гаⷭ҇ пославша ѡгнь ѿ гаⷭ҇. таⷤ пакы б҃га. искꙋшати авраама г҃леⷮ при исацѣ. паки тогоⷤ аг҃гла г҃леⷮ возвавша авраама исповѣдавшаⷤ себе б҃га. понеⷤ разꙋмѣ возвавыи авраама боѧщаⷭ҇ б҃га. и не пощадѣвша с҃на возвавшаⷢ҇ раⷣ. таⷤ на лѣствицѣ видѣти ӏаковꙋ во снѣ гаⷭ҇ г҃летъ. таⷤ бравшаⷭ҇ с нимъ мꙋжа г҃леⷮ. видѣтиⷤ емꙋ лицеⷨ к лицꙋ б҃га с҃паса сеⷢ҇ мꙋжа тоⷤ ѡбраⷥ б҃жии нареⷭ҇. поновлаѧ памѧⷮ писаниа. къ комꙋ тогда реⷭ҇ б҃гъ сотвориⷨ ч҃лка по ѡбразꙋ н҃шемꙋ и по подⷪ҇бию. нн҃ѣ здѣ сие показа мꙋжа г҃лѧ б҃га с҃паса ѡбраⷥ б҃жии. посемꙋ ꙗвьствено ѿкры

393 *Text continues in the margin*: г҃ла б҃гъ. ⷭ҇ сотвориⷨ ч҃лка по ѡбразꙋ н҃шемꙋ и подⷪ҇бию.

36. Showing that the Scripture speaks of the man who came as God and wrestled with Jacob, as a way of reminding us of the three men whom Abraham saw when God appeared to him, and through that, it indicates that it was with them, that God spoke, saying, "Let us make man in our image and likeness".[394]

36.1. You see how the sacred Scripture[395] teaches us in supreme wisdom[396] and accurate knowledge, reminding us of what was said before. For indeed[397] in the earlier case, the Scripture stated that "God said, 'Let us make man in our image and likeness'", and (now), it shows the same thing, when it says that God appeared to Abraham as God revealed himself in the form of "three men", though, again, it was one Lord, who appeared in those "three men".[398] And likewise, speaking of "two angels" in Sodom, it describes the same angels again as "two men"; and (in what comes) next, it speaks of those two[399] as the "Lord God" at the time of Lot, when the "Lord God spared him", as it is said (Gen. 19:16).

36.2. Similarly, at the time of Isaac, it says | that God tested Abraham, and 71r/167
again, it speaks of the same angel, who called out Abraham, as God. And he professed himself as God because after calling out Abraham, he understood that the latter feared God and did not spare his son for the sake of the one who called him out (Gen. 22:13). In the same way, it says that Jacob saw the Lord on the ladder in his dream; and it also speaks of the man who wrestled with him and whom he "saw face to face" as God the Savior, calling this same man the "Image of God". The Scripture refreshes our memory as to whom it was, that God spoke at that point (with the words) "Let us make man in our image and likeness", showing that this time the man who is treated here as "the Image of God" is God the Savior.[400]

---

394 **Showing that the Scripture speaks of the man who came as God and wrestled with Jacob, to remind us of the three men whom Abraham saw when God appeared to him, and through that, it indicates that it was with them, that God spoke, saying, "Let us make man in our image and likeness".**] *omitted*

395 sacred Scripture] divinely inspired Scripture

396 supreme wisdom] highly supreme wisdom

397 indeed] *omitted*

398 it was one Lord, who appeared in those "three men".] it was one Lord, who spoke through those "three men".

399 two] two men

400 *MS 61 adds*: **Showing that in the Scripture, the name of the "angel of the Lord" is not given without reason, (for) a name goes together with a certain action. (The Scripture) speaks of the "angel of the Lord" on account of the counsel and obedience with respect to the Father, and it uses the name, "man" when it depicts him undertaking a journey and wrestling, while in other places, we can find a different situation.**

писание с҃на б҃жїа во ѡбразѣ б҃жїи. и д҃ха ст҃го съ б҃гомъ б҃га сꙋща. понⷤе сказа писаⷩе. сотворити иⷨ чл҃ка по ѡбразꙋ иⷯ и по подобию иⷯ. и быти треⷨ мꙋжемъ оу авраама. ꙗвившемⷭꙋ б҃гꙋ авраамꙋ. и со їаковомъ братиⷭ мꙋжꙋ б҃гꙋ сп҃сꙋ ѡбразꙋ б҃жїю.

Нѣсть оубо в писанїи скитатиⷭ внѣ истинны. любащиⷨ б҃га и не ѿстꙋпившимъ ѿ неⷢ. именꙋⷮе бо писание с҃на б҃жїа и д҃ха ст҃го и совѣтники б҃гꙋ. тѣхⷤъ и ѡбраⷥ б҃жїи. тѣхⷤъ
71v/168 и мꙋжа. тѣхⷤъ и аг҃гли. тѣхⷤъ и б҃га. тѣхⷤъ и гⷭа. приемлꙗ нарицаꙗ иⷨ има противꙋ дѣанию иⷯ подаваа разоумъ. ꙗко подобники б҃гꙋ с҃нъ и д҃хъ ст҃ыи. б҃ⷤъ и гⷭь есть за единосꙋществїе. и аг҃глы послꙋшанїа раⷣ ихъ къ б҃гꙋ ѿц҃ꙋ. ꙗко нѣсть сꙋпротивїа въ трⷪцы ко ѿц҃ꙋ с҃на и д҃ха ст҃го ни распра ни рати. ꙗкⷤо во лживыхъ еллиньскиⷯ многыⷯ б҃говъ. сꙋпротивие и распра и рати. но едина волꙗ едино хотѣние тремъ ѿц҃ꙋ и с҃нꙋ и ст҃мꙋ д҃хꙋ. и не по насилию ни не волею послꙋшающимъ с҃нꙋ и д҃хꙋ ст҃мꙋ б҃га ѿц҃а. Но волею[401] повинꙋющеⷭ б҃гоу ѿц҃ꙋ с҃нъ и д҃хъ ст҃ыи. по единомꙋ хотѣнию и по единои воли. равносиⷧны и единопрⷭтльны б҃гꙋ ѿц҃ꙋ сꙋща. за единосꙋщество бжⷭтва и вⷣчества. и сего раⷣ аг҃глы и совѣтникы с҃на и д҃ха ст҃го б҃гꙋ ѿц҃ꙋ именꙋа писание. понⷤе едина волꙗ едина мысль едино хотѣ

---

401 *In the margin*: но любовїю.

36.3. Therefore, the Scripture explicitly reveals the Son of God—in the form of the "Image of God"—and the Holy Spirit[402] as existing together with God. For that reason, the Scripture stated that they created man in their image and likeness. And at the time of Abraham, there were three[403] men when God appeared to Abraham, and the man who wrestled with Jacob was God the Savior, the "Image of God". Thus, with what we have in the Scripture, there is no need for those who love God and have not strayed from him to wander around outside of truth. For the Scripture[404] calls the Son of God and the Holy Spirit "divine counselors", and the same ones are the "Image of God", and they are | also "men",[405] and they are also "angels", and they are also "God", and they 71ᵛ/168
are also "Lord". It gives them a name according to what they do,[406] helping us understand that the Son and the Holy Spirit are alike with God.[407]

36.4. And they are "God" and "Lord" in view of their consubstantiality.[408] And (it calls them) "angels" on account of their[409] obedience toward God the Father, because[410] there is no contradiction within the Trinity,[411] among the Father and the Son[412] and the Holy Spirit; neither is there any disagreement nor competition, like the contradiction and disagreement and competition among the many false Hellenistic deities. Instead, the three[413]—Father, and Son, and Holy Spirit—have one will and one desire.

36.5. And it is not because of force nor of necessity that the Son and the Holy Spirit obey God the Father, but the Son and the Holy Spirit submit to God the Father, rather, out of love.[414] They do it according to the common desire and according to the common will, as those who have equal power and share the same throne with God the Father on account of consubstantial divinity and dominion. That is why the Scripture calls the Son and Holy Spirit "angels" and "counselors" with respect to God the Father, for the Son and Holy Spirit have a

402 and the Holy Spirit] *omitted*
403 three] *omitted*
404 Scripture] sacred Scripture
405 and they are also "men",] *omitted*
406 they do,] they presently do,
407 are alike with God.] share a common image with God.
408 And they are "God" and "Lord" in view of their consubstantiality.] And it calls them "God" and "Lord" in view of their consubstantiality with God the Father.
409 their] *omitted*
410 because] showing that
411 Trinity,] divine Trinity,
412 the Son] his Son
413 the three] the Trinity
414 out of love] *MS 337 places this reading in the margin, while the reading in the text says*: by will.

ние съ б҃омъ с҃на и д҃ха ст҃го. ѿкрываꙗ же едино бж҃ство едино г҃ьства. съ б҃омъ ѿцⷨе с҃на его и д҃ха ст҃го писание. именꙋⷮе б҃га и г҃а. тогⷪⷤ и три мꙋжи. ꙗвлꙗа съ б҃гомъ 72r/169 ѿцⷨе с҃на ⷭе и д҃ха ст҃го. Паки писание именꙋⷮе б҃га тогоⷤ агг҃ломъ нарицаа внегда пишеть. Простреⷤ иꙗкоⷡ десницꙋ и возложи на главꙋ ефрѣмлю. сеиⷤ бѣꙗше мнїи. а лѣвицꙋ на главꙋ манасиинꙋ премѣнивъ рꙋцѣ. и реⷱ. б҃гъ емꙋ оуг҃оша ѿц҃ы мои преⷣ нимъ. авраамⷣ и исаⷦкъ. б҃гъ иⷤ мꙗ корми из млада и до днешнꙗⷢ дне. и агг҃лъ иже мꙗ избавлꙗеⷮ ѿ всеⷭ ѕла. блⷭ҇ви дѣтища сїа. Ꙗко ïакоⷡ бл҃вꙗа вн꙯ки своꙗ б҃га трⷪцꙋ проповѣда. Видите здѣ б҃га и агг҃ломъ именова. нѣсть слꙋжебномоу агг҃лꙋ вкꙋпѣ съ б҃гомъ бл҃вати. невозможно бо агг҃лꙋ слꙋжебномꙋ быти равнꙋ б҃гꙋ. б҃га ꙋбо иꙗковъ агг҃ломъ нареⷱ. понеⷤ не агг҃лъ избавлꙗаи есть иакова ѿ всеⷭ ѕла. слышаⷧ еси писание г҃лющее. ꙗко на лѣствицѣ ко common will and common thought with God.[415] And revealing the one Godhead and one lordship of God the Father and his Son[416] and the Holy Spirit, the Scripture refers both to "God" and "Lord". And it displays the three men as God the Father alongside his Son and the Holy Spirit.[417] | 72r/169

36.6. Again, the Scripture applies (various) names to the Lord[418] ⟨not once, but frequently⟩, and it calls him an "angel" when it recounts,[419] "And Jacob stretched out his right hand and laid it on the head of Ephraim, and he was the younger one; and his left hand on the head of Manasseh, changing his hands. And he said, 'The God in whose sight my fathers, Abraham and Isaac, were well pleasing, the God who has fed me from my youth and until this day; and the angel who delivers me from all evil, bless these[420] boys'" (Gen. 48:14–16).

37. Showing that Jacob proclaimed the Trinity when he blessed his grandchildren.[421]

37.1. You see, it calls God an "angel" here, (but) a ministering angel cannot offer a blessing together with God.[422] For it is impossible for a ministering angel to be equal with God.[423] Thus, it must be recognized that Jacob called God an "angel" and that it was not the "angel", who was delivering Jacob from all evil, (but God).[424] You heard the Scripture saying that it[425] was not the ascending

415 common thought with God] common desire with God the Father.

416 Son] Son, the Word,

417 And it displays the three men as God the Father alongside his Son and the Holy Spirit. **Showing that Jacob proclaimed the Trinity when he blessed his grandchildren.**

418 Lord] God

419 recounts,] recounts that Joseph brought his sons before his father, Israel, in order to receive the blessing from him. And he put the older one next to Israel's right hand, and the younger son next to his left hand, but when Israel was blessing his grandchildren, it says,

420 these] your

421 **Showing that Jacob proclaimed the Trinity when he blessed his grandchildren.**] *omitted*

422 You see, it calls God an "angel" here, (but) a ministering angel cannot offer a blessing together with God.] You see, here, too, it calls God an "angel", for it is impossible for a ministering angel to offer a blessing together with God.

423 For it is impossible for a ministering angel to be equal with God.] For how is it possible for a ministering angel to be equal with God?

424 Thus, it must be recognized that Jacob called God an "angel" and that it was not the "angel", who was delivering Jacob from all evil, (but God).] And in this instance, too, it must be recognized that Jacob called God an "angel" because it was not an "angel", who was delivering Jacob from all evil, but the one who spoke on the ladder, the Lord, the God of Abraham and Isaac (Gen. 28:13); he was the one, who was delivering Jacob from all evil.

425 You heard the Scripture saying that it] You heard the Scripture saying that when Jacob had a dream in his sleep, it

иꙗковꙋ гл҃юща. не агг҃лы восходѧщаа и ниⷥходѧщаа по неи. но гⷭ҇а на лѣствицѣ восланающⷭ҇а рекша ко иꙗковꙋ. а҆ⷥ҇ бг҃ъ авраамль ѿц҃а твоеⷢ҇ бг҃ъ исааковъ сеⷤ҇ азъ с тобою сохранѧꙗ та на всѧкоⷨ҇ пꙋти ꙗможе поидеши. ꙗко не ѡставлю тебе.

72v/171 Видите ꙗко не агг҃лъ ѡбѣщⷭ҇а иꙗковꙋ избавлꙗⷮ҇ его ѿ всеⷢ҇ ѕла. но гⷭ҇ь егоⷤ҇ видѣвъ на лѣствицѣ бг҃ъ авраамль и исаковъ. того и здѣ иꙗковъ призываше бл҃вити дѣтища ї҆ѡсифлꙗ нарицаа его агг҃ла. наꙋчивса внегда мꙋжь бораше҃ с ниⷨ. ꙗко ѡбраⷥ҇ бж҃їи бг҃ъ есть. сегоⷤ҇ раⷣ҇ агг҃ла е҃ нареⷱ҇ здѣ ї҆аковъ. понеⷤ҇ не бысть наꙋчеⷩ҇ тогда имени сн҃а бж҃їа. дх҃омⷤ҇ оубо просвѣщенъ проповѣдаше бг҃а бравшⷭ҇а с ниⷨ егоⷤ҇ бл҃ва сп҃са дш҃и своеи позна. тоⷢ҇ здѣ агг҃лоⷨ҇ нареⷱ҇. емꙋ же и молꙗше҃ бл҃вити внꙋчата своꙗ. Аще хощеши не любопернѣ разꙋмѣти. и здѣ иꙗковъ трⷪ҇цꙋ показоваше гл҃ꙗ. бг҃ъ емꙋ же оугⷪ҇диша ѿц҃ы мои прⷣ҇е нимъ авраⷨ҇ и исаакъ. таⷤ҇ аки къ второмꙋ лицꙋ гл҃еⷮ. бг҃ъ иⷥ҇ мꙗ корми иⷥ҇ млада и до днешнаⷢ҇ дни. таⷤ҇ аки третие лице ꙗви гл҃ꙗ. и агг҃лъ иⷤ҇ мꙗ избавлꙗеⷮ҇ ѿ всеⷢ҇ ѕла. таⷤ҇ и паки три лица въ единоначаⷭ҇ство полагаа гл҃еⷮ. бл҃ви дѣтища сїа. не раздѣли бо агг҃ла ѿ бг҃а и бг҃а. но вкꙋпѣ молꙗшеса бг҃ꙋ и бг҃ꙋ и агг҃лꙋ бл҃вити дѣтища сиꙗ.

73r/172 по семꙋ показа не оуединеное бжⷭ҇тво. но въ треⷯ҇ ипостасеⷯ҇ бжⷭ҇тво ꙗви. понеⷤ҇ млтⷭ҇во ваше гл҃ꙗ. къ бг҃ꙋ и къ бг҃ꙋ и къ агг҃лꙋ бл҃вити дѣтища сиꙗ. аще бы ꙋединено бжⷭ҇тво and descending angels, who "firmly stood" on the ladder and who said, "I am the God of your father Abraham, and the God of Isaac", and "Behold, I am with you, I will keep you on every path where you go; and I will not leave you" (Gen. 28:13, 15). | 72v/171

37.2. You see, it was not the "angel", who promised Jacob to deliver him from all evil, but the Lord, whom he saw on the ladder, the God of Abraham and Isaac. It was the same one, whom Jacob called upon there when he was blessing Joseph's boys[426] and referred to him as an "angel". He learned (to discern) God in the "Image of God" at the time when a "man" wrestled with him (Gen. 32:24). And the reason Jacob called him "angel" here is that he was not yet taught at that point (to recognize) the name of the Son of God. But having, then, been enlightened by the Spirit, he proclaimed him, who wrestled with him, to be God, and him he blessed, and him he acknowledged to be the Savior of his soul. He whom he called here an "angel", to him he also prayed for the blessing upon his grandchildren.

37.3. And if you wish to understand without arguing, here, too, Jacob shows the Trinity when he says ⟨with reference to the first person⟩,[427] "The God in whose sight my fathers, Abraham and Isaac, were well pleasing"; and then, as if speaking to the second person, (he says), "the God who has fed me from my youth and until this day"; and finally, as if exhibiting the third person, he says, "and the angel who delivers me from all evil". And then, also referring to the three persons as having one headship,[428] he says, "bless these[429] boys". For he did not make a distinction between the angel who appeared as God and God himself, but prayed to God collectively, both to God and the angel, (asking him) to bless those[430] boys. | Therefore, he showed the Godhead, not in solitariness, 73r/172
but rather disclosed the Godhead in three hypostases, for he prayed for the blessing of those boys,[431] referring to God as both "God" and the "angel".

---

426 Joseph's boys] boys

427 says,] says by referring to the first person,

428 And then, also referring to the three persons as having one headship,] And also, referring to the three persons who have one lordship,

429 these] your

430 those] his

431 Therefore, he showed the Godhead, not in solitariness, but rather disclosed the Godhead in three hypostases, for he prayed for the blessing of those boys,] Therefore, the Godhead is shown not in solitariness, but rather the Godhead is disclosed in three hypostases, to whom he prayed for the blessing of the boys,

во едино[432] ипостаси показати хотѣлъ. до вон҃о бы единою бг҃а нарещи гл҃ѧ. бг҃ъ емꙋ оуго̑ша ѿцы мои преⷣ нимъ. авраⷨа и исаⷦа. йⷤ и корми йⷥмлада и до днеⷭ҇ избавлѧаи ма ѿ всеⷭ҇ ѕла. Но ꙗвлено три ипостаси нареⷱ҇ гл҃ѧ. бг҃ъ емоуⷤ оуго̑ша ѿцы мои преⷣ нимъ авраⷨа и исаакъ. бг҃ъ йⷤ мѧ корми йⷥ млада и до днешнѧⷭ҇ дне. и агг҃лъ йⷤ мѧ избавлѧеⷮ ѿ всеⷭ҇ ѕла. не агг҃лъ бо еⷭ҇ избавлѧше ѿ всеⷭ҇ зла ꙗкоⷤ и преⷤ рекоⷯ. но гл҃авыи на лѣствицѣ к немꙋ. авраамль. бг҃ъ и исааковъ. сеⷤ с тобою есмь сохранѧа та на всеⷨ пꙋти ꙗмоⷤ поидеши. ꙗко не ѡставлю тебе. Ꙗко моисѣю в кꙋпинѣ. ꙗвльшагоⷭ҇ нареⷱ҇ писание агг҃ла гн҃ѧ. сн҃ъ еⷭ҇ бж҃ïи. понеⷤ той агг҃лъ исповѣда себе моисѣю бг҃а авраамова. и исакова и ïаковлѧ. ~[433]

432 *Read*: во единои.

433 *In the margin*: глаⷡ҇ к҃.

37.4. And if he had wished to show a solitary Godhead in the form of one hypostasis, it would have been sufficient to refer to one God and say,[434] "The God in whose sight my fathers, Abraham and Isaac, were well pleasing, and who has also fed me from my youth and until this day, delivers me from all evil". Yet he explicitly referred to the three hypostases, saying, "The God in whose sight my fathers, Abraham and Isaac, were well pleasing, the God who has fed me from my youth and until this day; and the angel who delivers me from all evil". For it was not the angel,[435] who delivered him from all evil, as I said before, but the one who said to him on the ladder, "I am the God of Abraham and of Isaac.[436] Behold, I am with you, I will keep you on every path where you go; I will not leave you" (Gen. 28:13, 15).

38. Showing that the one whom the Scripture called the "angel of the Lord" that appeared to Moses out of the bush is the Son of God, for the same angel professed himself to Moses as the "God of Abraham, and of Isaac, and of Jacob". CHAPTER 20.[437]

434 sufficient to refer to one God and say,] sufficient, in my view, to use the name "God" and "one", and thus to say,

435 evil". For it was not the angel,] evil, bless these boys", proclaiming the one dominion shared by three divine persons, depicting them as both "God" an "angel", and as those who possessed equal power among themselves. And from this, too, it is evident that he called God an "angel", and in prayer to him, he treated him as God, who possessed common honor. Furthermore, it was not the angel,

436 who said to him on the ladder, "I am the God of Abraham and of Isaac.] who was at the top of the ladder and who said to him, "I am the God of your father Abraham, the God of Isaac.

437 **Showing that the one whom the Scripture called the "angel of the Lord" that appeared to Moses out of the bush is the Son of God, for the same angel professed himself to Moses as the "God of Abraham, and of Isaac, and of Jacob". CHAPTER 20.] On the divine glory that in the former times was brightly displayed in the divinely inspired Scripture, to Moses the Prophet at the bush found on (Mount) Horeb, and on how the glory of the Godhead was manifested to Moses on the mountain when his face shone forth with light. CHAPTER 20.**

Паки при кꙋпинѣ писание нарⷱ҇е агг҃ла. тогоⷤ
73v/173 и гⷭ҇а. тогоⷤ и бг҃а гл҃ꙗ. Моисѣиⷤ бѣꙗше па
сыи ѡвца. рагꙋила тестꙗ своеⷢ҇. сщ҃енни
ка мадиамьска. и гнаше ѡвца в пꙋсты
ню. и прїиде в горꙋ бж҃ию хоривъ. ꙗвижеⷭ҇
емꙋ агг҃лъ гⷭ҇нь в пламени ѡгненѣ ис кꙋпи
ны. и видѣ ꙗко кꙋпина гораше ѡгнемъ
и не съгараше. речеⷤ моисѣи. мимошⷣ҇е
вижꙋ что видѣние великое се. ꙗко не
согараше кꙋпина. и ꙗко видѣ гⷭ҇ь ꙗко
пристꙋпаеть видѣти. и возва его агг҃лъ
гⷭ҇нь ис кꙋпины гл҃ꙗ моисѣи моисѣи.
ѡнъⷤ рече се аⷥ. речеⷤ гⷭ҇ь не приближаиса сѣ
мо. изꙋи сапогъ ѿ ногъ твоиⷯ. ибо мѣ
сто на немъⷤ ты стоиши землꙗ ст҃а еⷭ҇.
и рⷱ҇е емꙋ аⷥ есмь бг҃ъ ѿц҃а твоеⷢ҇. бг҃ъ авраа
мовъ. бг҃ъ исааковъ. бг҃ъ иꙗковль.
ѿвратиⷤ лице свое моисеи. говѣꙗше бо
зрѣти прⷣ҇е бг҃а. Глⷮ҇е писание. ꙗко ꙗвиⷭ҇

---

438 Again, the one whom the Scripture called "angel" in the bush, is also described as "Lord" and "God", saying,] Let us next come to another place of the divinely inspired Scripture and see God in many ways, as both "God" and "Lord", and when the Lord is called an "angel". The same one becomes shown as God even more clearly to those who read without arguing, and rather seek to read in love of the truth, (or) to say it more precisely, to those who with all their soul love God (Deut. 6:5; Matt. 22:37) and seek "your just decrees" (Ps. 119:164) with all their heart. And thus, it is written, "And Moses was shepherding the sheep of Raguel his father-in-law, the priest of Midian; and he drove the sheep to the wilderness and came to Horeb, the mountain of God. And the angel of the Lord appeared to him in flaming fire out of the bush, and he saw that the bush burned with fire, but did not burn up. And Moses said, 'I will go near and see this great sight, why the bush does not burn up'. And when the Lord saw that he approaches to see, the angel of the Lord called him out of the bush, saying, 'Moses, Moses'! And he said, 'Here I am'. And he said, 'Do not come near here. Take the boots off your feet, for the place on which you are standing is holy ground'. And he said to him, 'I am the God of your father, the God of Abraham, the God of Isaac, the God of Jacob'. And Moses turned away his face, for he was afraid to look at God. And the Lord said to Moses, 'I have surely seen the trouble of my people that is in Egypt, and I have heard their cry (caused) by their taskmasters. I have seen their affliction and have come down to deliver them out of the hand of the Egyptians, to bring them out of that land'" (Ex. 3:1–8). And somewhat later, he says, "And God spoke to Moses, saying, 'I will be with you, and this will be the sign to you that I will send you to bring my people out of Egypt: you will pray to God on this mountain'" (Ex. 3:12). Furthermore, the Scripture says, addressing the sons of Levi, "And Moses said to the Lord, 'See, you said to me', 'Lead this people out', 'but you did not tell me whom you will send with me. And you said to

38.1. Again, the one whom the Scripture called "angel" in the bush, is also | 73^{v}/173 described as "Lord" and "God", saying,[438] "And Moses was shepherding the sheep of Raguel his father-in-law, the priest of Midian; and he drove the sheep to the wilderness and came to Horeb, the mountain of God. And the angel of the Lord appeared to him in flaming fire out of the bush, and he saw that the bush burned with fire, but did not burn up. And Moses said, 'I will go near and see this great sight, why the bush does not burn up'. And when the Lord saw that he approached (the bush) to see, the angel of the Lord called him out of the bush, saying, 'Moses, Moses'! And he said, 'Here I am'. And the Lord said, 'Do not come near here. Take the boots off your feet, for the place on which you are standing is holy ground'. And he said to him, 'I am the God of your father, the God of Abraham, the God of Isaac, the God of Jacob'. And Moses turned away his face, for he was afraid to look at God" (Ex. 3:1–6).

---

me, 'I know you better than all (others), and you have found grace from me''. And Moses said, 'If then, I have found grace before you, reveal yourself to me visibly so that I may see you (and know) that I have found grace in your sight; that they may know that this great nation is your people'. And the Lord said to him, 'I myself will go before you and give you rest'. And Moses said to him, 'If you do not go with us yourself, do not bring us up from here. Or how will it be truly evident, that your people and I have found grace before you above all nations that are on this earth'? And the Lord said to Moses, 'This very thing that you have spoken I will do. You have found grace before me, and I know you better than all (others)'. And Moses said, 'Show me your glory'. And the Lord said to Moses, 'I will pass by before you with my glory, and I will call out my name, the 'Lord', before you. And I will have mercy on whom I will have mercy and will have compassion on whom I will have compassion'. And he said, 'You are not able to see my face, for no man can see my face and live'. And the Lord said, 'Behold, there is a place by me, and you will stand on the rock. And when my glory passes by, I will put you into a cleft of the rock; and I will cover you with my hand until I have passed by. And I will take away my hand, (and) then, you will see my back; but my face will not appear (to you)'" (Ex. 33:12–23). "Early in the morning, Moses rose and went up on Mount Sinai, as the Lord had commanded him; and Moses took the two stone tablets with him, as the first time. And the Lord descended in the cloud, and stood near him there, and called upon the name of the Lord. And the Lord passed by before his face, and he called upon the Lord, 'The Lord God, compassionate and merciful, longsuffering and true, supplying with righteousness and conducting mercy for thousands, taking revenge for iniquity, unrighteousness, (and) sins, and (the sinner's) guilt will not be discarded. He lays the sins of the fathers upon the children, and grandchildren, and to the third and fourth generation'. Having hurried, Moses bowed to the ground and worshipped God. And he said, 'If I have found grace before you, let the Lord go before us'. And the Lord said to Moses, 'Behold, I am establishing a covenant with you before all my people. I will do great and glorious things, which have not been done in all the earth, nor among any of the nations. And all the people among whom you are will see the works of the Lord, that they are wonderful, which I will do for you. Observe everything I command you'" (Ex. 34:4–11). Next, the divinely inspired Scripture also states, "And the Lord said to Moses, 'Take all the leaders of the people and bring them out in the sun before the Lord, and the anger of the Lord will be turned away from Israel'" (Num. 25:4).

моисѣю агглъ гнь в пламени ѡгненѣ ис купины. и видѣ моисѣи ꙗко купина гораше и не согараше. приступаше видѣти. и ꙗко видѣ гь ꙗко приступае видѣти. [74r/177] ꙗвити убо агглу ре в купинѣ. видѣти гу приступающа моисѣа купину видѣти. нѣсть ли оубо се ꙗко его рече аггла ꙗвльша в купинѣ. того ре и га видѣти приступающа моисѣа. се аггла ре писание. того ре га. ꙗви ре агглъ гнь в купинѣ. видѣ гь ꙗко приступае моисѣи. та паки повторꙗе писание. глꙗ аггла бга исповѣдавша себе. ре бо писание. и возва его агглъ гнь ис купины. глꙗ моисеи моисеи. ѡнъ рече се азъ. рече гь не приближай сѣмо. и ре ему. азъ бгъ авраамовъ. бгъ исааковъ. бгъ иꙗковль. ѿврати лице свое моисеи. говѣꙗше бо зрѣти пре бга. Видите писание возвати ре агглу гню ис купины моисѣа. внегда ѡзвати моисѣю ко агглу. и рещи ему се азъ. тогда моисѣю глте. рече гь не приближаися сѣмо. гдѣ не приближати повелѣвае моисѣю гь. не ꙗвѣ ли ꙗк к купинѣ. поне моисе ре. мимошедъ вижу что видѣние великое се. ꙗко купина не съгараше. [74v/179] и ис купины моисѣа возва агглъ гнь. к ней повелѣвае не приближати моисею гь. не ꙗвѣ ли есть ꙗко в коупинѣ гь. его пре именова аггла гна. послѣди того аггла га именова. поне моисѣи приближаше купину видѣти. палꙗщу. и возванъ бѣꙗше моисеи ис коупины. и къ купинѣ моисѣи не приближати повелѣнъ. поне рече моисею гь не при

38.2. The Scripture says that "the angel of the Lord appeared to Moses in flaming fire out of the bush, and Moses saw that the bush burned in flame,[439] but did not burn up". And he went near to see, "and when the Lord saw that Moses approaches | the bush to see", it is said that "the angel, then, appeared 74^{r}/177
out of the bush", though it was the Lord who saw Moses as the latter approached to see the bush (Ex. 3:3–4).

38.3. Now, is this not speaking of the same one, (first) as the "angel" appearing out of the bush, and (then), as the "Lord" who saw that Moses was approaching?[440] Indeed, the one of whom the Scripture spoke as an "angel", it also described as the "Lord", saying, "the angel of the Lord appeared out of the bush", and "when the Lord saw that Moses approached".[441] The Scripture repeats the same thing over again, when it speaks of the angel who professes himself as God. For the Scripture said, "And the angel of the Lord called him out of the bush, saying, 'Moses, Moses'! And he said, 'Here I am'. And the Lord said, 'Do not come near here'. And he said to him, 'I am the God of Abraham, the God of Isaac, the God of Jacob'. And Moses turned away his face, for he was afraid to look at God" (Ex. 3:4–6).[442]

38.4. You see, the Scripture[443] ⟨shows⟩ that it was the "angel of the Lord", who spoke to Moses out of the bush, but when Moses responded to the angel and said to him, "Here I am", then it was said to Moses, "And the Lord said, 'Do not come near here' ". But what place is the Lord commanding Moses not to approach? Is it not evident that it is the bush? For Moses said, "I will go near and see this great sight, why the bush | does not burn up"; and while "the angel 74^{v}/179
of the Lord called Moses out of the bush", it was the Lord, who commanded Moses to not approach it (Ex. 3:4–5).

38.5. Is it not obvious that it was the Lord, (who appeared) in the bush, and that he is first called the "angel of the Lord", and afterward, the same angel is called "Lord"? (This is clear from the sequence of events): for Moses (first) approached to see the burning bush, and Moses was called out of the bush, and he was commanded not to come near the bush because the Lord said to

---

439 burned in flame] burned

440 approaching?] approaching the bush?

441 Indeed, the one of whom the Scripture spoke as an "angel", it also described as the "Lord", saying, "the angel of the Lord appeared out of the bush", and "when the Lord saw that Moses approached".] It said, "the angel of the Lord appeared out of the bush" and "when the Lord saw that Moses approaches to see".

442 *MS 61 adds*: **Showing that the one whom the Scripture called the "angel of the Lord" when he appeared to Moses out of the bush, is the Son of God, for the same angel professed himself to Moses as the God of Abraham, and of Isaac, and of Jacob.**

443 You see, the Scripture] You see how well the Scripture

ближаⷭи сѣмо. си̏ реⷱ кꙋпинꙋ видѣти не прихоⷣ҇. таⷤ тогоⷤ гаⷭ гл҃юща. ис кꙋпины показа гл҃ꙗ. и реⷱ емꙋ азъ бг҃ъ авраамовъ. бг҃ъ исааковъ. бг҃ъ иꙗковль. моисѣи же стыдꙗшеⷭ смотрѣти преⷣ бг҃а. нѣстьⷧ҇ иⷤ в кꙋпинѣ того же агг҃ла гⷭна бг҃а самоⷢ показа писание. понеⷤ возвавыи его преⷤ гл҃ꙗи емꙋ ис кꙋпины не приближаⷭи сѣмо. и реⷱ азъ бг҃ъ ѿц҃а твоего. аще бы слꙋже

444 but when Moses responded to the angel and said to him, "Here I am", then it was said to Moses, "And the Lord said, 'Do not come near here'". But what place is the Lord commanding Moses not to approach? Is it not evident that it is the bush? For Moses said, "I will go near and see this great sight, why the bush does not burn up"; and while "the angel of the Lord called Moses out of the bush", it was the Lord, who commanded Moses to not approach it (Ex. 3:4–5). Is it not obvious that it was the Lord, (who appeared) in the bush, and that he is first called the "angel of the Lord", and afterward, the same angel is called "Lord"? (This is clear from the sequence of events): for Moses (first) approached to see the burning bush, and Moses was called out of the bush, and he was commanded not to come near the bush because the Lord said to Moses "Do not come near here" (Ex. 3:5), which means "do not come to see the bush". Then, it shows the same Lord speaking out of the bush, saying, "I am the God of Abraham, the God of Isaac, the God of Jacob", and Moses hesitated to look at God. Isn't the Scripture showing this angel of the Lord, who (appeared) in the bush, to be God? For the one who first called him out of the bush and said, "Do not come near here" (Ex. 3:5), also said, "I am the God of your father" (Ex. 3:6).] But when Moses responded to the angel and said to him, "Here I am", then it is written that the Lord spoke to Moses out of the bush. For Moses said, "I will go near and see this great sight, why the bush does not burn up"; and while "the angel of the Lord called Moses out of the bush", it was the Lord, who commanded Moses to not approach it (Ex. 3:4–5). Is it not obvious that it was the Lord, (who appeared) in the bush, even though he is first called the "angel of the Lord"? For if it had not been the Lord in the bush, but rather the angel that had been in the bush, he would not have said, "when the Lord saw that Moses

Moses "Do not come near here" (Ex. 3:5), which means "do not come to see the bush". Then, it shows the same Lord speaking out of the bush, saying, "I am the God of Abraham, the God of Isaac, the God of Jacob", and Moses hesitated to look at God. Isn't the Scripture showing this angel of the Lord, who (appeared) in the bush, to be God? For the one who first called him out of the bush and said, "Do not come near here" (Ex. 3:5), also said, "I am the God of your father" (Ex. 3:6).[444]

---

approaches to see" (Ex. 3:4). And if I had said that it was not out of the bush, that the Lord saw Moses approaching to see the bush, I could have signified any place for the Lord, from which the Lord saw that Moses was approaching. But the Scripture does not indicate a different place. Instead, it talks about (the events) in a certain order: that the angel of the Lord appeared in flaming fire, and that the Lord saw approaching Moses, and that the angel of the Lord called Moses out of the bush. And when Moses responded, the Scripture says, "And he said, 'Do not come near'" (Ex. 3:5), and the Scripture does not show any other place besides the bush, from which the angel of the Lord appeared. And it is evident that it was from it, that the Lord spoke, and no other place is indicated for the Lord by the Scripture, only the bush. But someone could say that the Scripture refers to the angel once again, (when it says), "and the angel of the Lord called him out of the bush" (Ex. 3:5), (suggesting) that the Scripture shows the *angel* speaking out of the bush, and not the *Lord*; and that by calling him the "angel" who spoke out of the bush, it indicates this even more clearly. But even though it calls him the "angel of the Lord" repeatedly, it, nevertheless, shows very plainly that it was the Lord, who spoke out of the bush, despite the fact that it calls him the "angel of the Lord" and and again. For it says, "And the angel of the Lord called him out of the bush, saying, 'Moses, Moses'! And he said, 'Here I am'. And Lord said, 'Do not come near here. Take the boots off your feet, for the place on which you are standing is holy ground'. And he said to him, 'I am the God of your father, the God of Abraham, the God of Isaac, the God of Jacob'. And Moses turned away his face, for he was afraid to look at God" (Ex. 3:4–6). In my opinion, the scriptural indication that the angel who called Moses out of the bush was the Lord is said far more plainly than (what is said) of the angel out of the bush, because the angel, who called Moses out of the bush, professed himself as God. For the Scripture explicitly says that Moses responded to the one who called him out of the bush, "Here I am", and the one who called him out, also commanded him not to come near the bush. And the same one who called Moses out of the bush presents himself to Moses as God, saying, "I am the God of your father, the God of Abraham, the God of Isaac, the God of Jacob". And likewise, the Scripture reveals God speaking out of the bush even more clearly in the words that say, "And Moses turned away his face, for he was afraid to look at God". And no longer does the Scripture speak of the "angel of the Lord", but rather what it says to Moses in the remaining part of the passage is that it was the Lord and the "God of Abraham, the God of Isaac, the God of Jacob", who spoke to him. And it speaks of Moses being afraid to look at God, and not at the angel. Thus, the Scripture speaks of no other place but the bush, from which the Lord professed himself as God on the mountain. Therefore, the Scripture says that it was the angel of the Lord who appeared to Moses, and the angel also called him out of the bush, but when the Lord speaks out of the bush, it shows God himself.

бныи агг҃лъ ꙗвиⷭ҇ѧ моисѣю в кꙋпинѣ. не бы смѣлъ гл҃ати себе. аⷥ бг҃ъ авраамовъ. бг҃ъ исааковъ. бг҃ъ иꙗковль. не возмоⷤ҇но бо агг҃лꙋ бг҃омъ нарещи себе. Ибо егда ви дѣ

75r/181 і҃съ навгиⷩ҇ ꙗвльшаⷭ҇ емꙋ агг҃ла. вопросивъ реⷱ҇ кто еси. нашь ли еси или ѿ сꙋпостатъ. тогда не реⷱ҇ емꙋ агг҃лъ. аⷥ есмь бг҃ъ авраамовъ и бг҃ъ исааковъ и бг҃ъ иꙗковль. но реⷱ҇. азъ есмь архистратигъ силы гⷭ҇на исповѣда ꙋбо себе агг҃лъ і҃сꙋ навгинꙋ кто есть. ꙗко архистратигъ силы гⷭ҇на есть а не бг҃ъ. здѣ же ис кꙋпины гл҃ꙗ и агг҃лъ исповѣда себе бг҃а а не агг҃ла. гл҃ꙗ. аⷥ бг҃ъ авраамовъ. бг҃ъ исааковъ бг҃ъ иꙗковль. и писание реⷱ҇ моисѣи стыдꙗшеся зрѣти преⷣ бг҃а. а не реⷱ҇ писание ꙗко мӧсеи стыдꙗшеⷭ҇ зрѣти преⷣ агг҃ла. сими оубо всѣми оуказꙋⷮ҇е писание сн҃а бж҃їа быти. именовавъ агг҃ломъ. и авраама возвавша съ нбⷭ҇ѣ прї исаацѣ. и в содомеⷯ вшеⷣша. и огнь ѿ гⷭ҇а пославша. и со иаковоⷨ бравшаⷭ҇. и їаковоⷨ призываемы блⷭ҇вити внꙋки. и моисѣю в кꙋпинѣ ꙗвле

38.6. And if the one who appeared to Moses out of the bush had been a ministering angel,[445] he would not have dared to say of himself, "I am the God of Abraham, the God of Isaac, the God of Jacob". For an angel cannot call himself God,[446] as when | Joshua, son of Nun, saw an angel that appeared to him,[447] 75r/181 the latter asked him, saying, "Are you one of ours or of our enemies"? (Josh. 5:13). And at that moment, the angel did not say to him, "I am the God of Abraham, the God of Isaac, the God of Jacob" (Ex. 3:6). Instead, he said, "I am the commander of the host of the Lord" (Josh. 5:14). Thus, the angel professed who he was before Joshua, the son of Nun,[448]—"the commander of the host of the Lord", and not God.[449]

38.7. And the angel who spoke out of the bush here also professed himself as God, and not as an angel, saying,[450] "I am the God of Abraham, the God of Isaac, and God of Jacob". And the Scripture said that Moses "hesitated[451] to look at God" (Ex. 3:6), and the Scripture did not say that he hesitated[452] to look at the angel. In all of this, then, the Scripture indicates[453] the Son of God, calling him[454] an "angel". The same thing applies to the angel who called Abraham out of heaven at the time of Isaac, and who came to Sodom, and who sent fire "from the Lord", and who wrestled with Jacob, and whom Jacob called upon when he was blessing his grandchildren, and who appeared to Moses out of the bush.[455]

---

445 had been a ministering angel,] had been one of the angels that stand before the Lord,

446 For an angel cannot call himself God,] For in as much as he is an angel that stands before the Lord, he cannot call himself God. Everyone knows this!

447 For when Joshua, son of Nun, saw an angel that appeared to him,] Thus, on seeing an angel, who appeared to Joshua, the son of Nun,

448 Thus, the angel professed who he was before Joshua, the son of Nun,] Thus, the angel that appeared to Joshua, the son of Nun, professed who he was

449 God.] the "God of Abraham".

450 And the angel who spoke out of the bush here also professed himself as God, and not as an angel, saying,] And here, the angel that appeared to Moses out of the bush professed himself as God, and not as an angel, for he said,

451 hesitated] was afraid

452 he hesitated] Moses was afraid

453 In all of this, then, the Scripture indicates] In all of this, the Scripture shows

454 him] God

455 The same thing applies to the angel who called Abraham out of heaven at the time of Isaac, and who came to Sodom, and who sent fire "from the Lord", and who wrestled with Jacob, and whom Jacob called upon when he was blessing his grandchildren, and who appeared to Moses out of the bush.] This is also the case when the angel called Abraham out of heaven but showed himself to be God when Isaac was about to be sacrificed; and when the angels came to Sodom and showed themselves as "God" and "Lord", sending fire "from the Lord". And the one who wrestled with Jacob with the name the "Image of God", him, too, Jacob addressed as the "angel" and "God"; and the God who blessed (Jacob's) grandchildren, (then) appeared to Moses out of the bush.

иса. понеⷤ сн҃ъ бж҃їи совѣтникъ сыи бг҃у
ѿц҃у своему. единоволенъ и послушанъ.
сеⷢ҇ раⷣ и аггл҃оⷨ его именуⷮе писание. бг҃аⷤ
75v/182 ѿц҃а неⷭ҇ видѣти в писанїи аггл҃оⷨ именуема.
но вездѣ разумѣваетсѧ сн҃ъ бж҃їи. аггл҃оⷨ
гⷭ҇нимъ именуемъ в писанїи бг҃ъ сыи. и дх҃ъ
ст҃ыи. ꙗкоⷤ ꙗви писание при лотѣ в содо
мѣ двою аггл҃у пришеⷣшу ю. еюⷤ рече послѣ
ди гⷭ҇а бг҃а пощадѣвша лота. и гⷭ҇ь ѿ гⷭ҇а ѡгнь
посла в содоⷨ. такоⷤ и при исацѣ аггл҃а реⷱ҇
бг҃аⷤ показа. и ꙗко при їѡсифѣ аггл҃а реⷱ҇.
бг҃а съ бг҃омъ показа. и здѣ при купинѣ
аггл҃а реⷱ҇. показаⷤ бг҃а авраамлѧ. бг҃а иса
акова. бг҃а иꙗковлѧ. по сеⷨ глⷭ҇еть пи
сание. речеⷤ гⷭ҇ь к моисеѡви. видѧ видѣⷯ
бѣду людеи моиⷯ иже въ египтѣ. и вопль
иⷯ оуслышаⷯ. ѿ дѣлъ приставникъ болѣ
знь иⷯ. и снидоⷯ и зѧти иⷯ ѿ руку египеⷮску
известїа иⷯ земли тоѧ. в землю бл҃гу
и многу. Ꙗко писание бг҃а и аггл҃ы не едино еⷭ҇
ствены глⷭ҇еть. не раⷥньственѣ ѿ бг҃а аггл҃ы
полагаеⷮ. бг҃а сходѧща. аггл҃ыⷤ восходѧща и по
сему оуказоуеⷮ разумѣти сн҃а бж҃їа гⷭ҇а. внегда еⷭ҇
нарицаеⷮ аггл҃а гⷭ҇на.

38.8. For the Son of God is a counselor to his God the Father; he has one will with him and renders obedience.[456] For that reason, the Scripture calls him an "angel".[457] But as for God | the Father, we see no place in the Scripture,[458] 75v/182 where he is called an "angel".[459] Instead, the name of the "angel of the Lord" in the Scripture is always understood in reference to the Son of God and the Holy Spirit as being divine. The Scripture showed it at the time of Lot when the two angels came to Sodom—and whom it described afterward as the "Lord God" who spared Lot—and when the Lord sent fire[460] on Sodom "from the Lord".

38.9. Likewise, at the time of Isaac, it spoke of an angel[461] but showed him to be God. And at the time of Joseph, it spoke of an angel but showed God with God.[462] And here at the bush, it spoke of an angel in this way, but showed him to be the "God of Abraham, the God of Isaac, the God of Jacob". Later the Scripture says,[463] "And the Lord said to Moses, 'I have surely seen the trouble of my people that is in Egypt, and I have heard their cry caused by their taskmasters. I have seen their affliction and have come down to deliver them out of the hand of the Egyptians, to bring them out of that land into a good and spacious land'" (Ex. 3:7–8).

39. Showing that the Scripture does not speak of God and the angels on par with one another but treats the angels differently than God. Thus, (it speaks of) God as the one who descends, and of the angels as the ones who ascend, and thus, suggests acknowledging the "Son of God" as "Lord", while calling him the "angel of the Lord".[464]

---

456 obedience.] obedience to him.

457 "angel".] "angel of God".

458 in the Scripture,] *omitted*

459 "angel".] "angel of the Lord".

460 fire] *omitted*

461 angel] angel calling Abraham out of heaven,

462 And at the time of Joseph, it spoke of the angel but showed God with God.] Jacob, at the time of Joseph, referred to the angel when he was blessing his grandchildren, but acknowledged him as God.

463 *MS 61 adds*: **Showing that the Scripture does not speak of God and the angels on par with one another but treats the angels differently than God. Thus, it speaks of God as the one who comes in descent (as opposed to ascending), and thus, allows us to recognize the "Son of God" as the "Lord God", while calling him the "angel of the Lord".**

464 **Showing that the Scripture does not speak of God and the angels on par with one another but treats the angels differently than God. Thus, (it speaks of) God as the one who descends, and of the angels as the ones who ascend, and thus, suggests acknowledging the "Son of God" as "Lord", while calling him the "angel of the Lord".**] *omitted*

Видитеⷤ писание и всеⷨ. како разлꙋчаеⷮ весѣ
дою
76r/184 слꙋжебныⷯ аггл҃ъ ѿ гⷭ҇аⷯ. ѡ аггл҃еⷯ иже на лѣстви
цѣ гл҃еⷮ писание. ꙗко по лѣствицѣ аггли
восхожахꙋ и ниⷥхожахꙋ. и ко іс҃ꙋ навгинꙋ
реⷱ҇ аггл҃ъ. аⷥ есмъ архистратигъ силы гⷭ҇на
нн҃ѣ пріидоⷯ а не рече нн҃ѣ снидоⷯ. но рече
нн҃ѣ пріидоⷯ. и на лѣствицѣ аггли бж҃їи
не реⷱ҇ ꙗко ниⷥхожахꙋ и восхажахꙋ по неи.
но реⷱ҇ ꙗко восхожахꙋ аггли бж҃їи и ниⷥхожа
хꙋ по неи. гⷭ҇ь же реⷱ҇ видѣⷯ болѣзнь иⷯ и снидоⷯ
изатї ихъ. ꙗкоⷤ и при стоⷬ҇пѣ сшеⷣше смѣ
сиⷨ а реⷱ҇. такоⷤ и при авраамѣ ѡ содомѣ.
сшеⷣ реⷱ҇ да вижꙋ. тако и здѣ ис кꙋпины гл҃ѧ.
и снидоⷯ рече и зꙗтї иⷯ. Ꙗко свѣтло писание
ѿкрываеⷮ бг҃а въ тⷪ҇рцы. а не оуединена бж҃твоⷨ.
Тⷤа гл҃еⷮ писание. реⷱ҇ бг҃ъ к моисѣю гл҃ѧ бꙋдꙋ
с тобою. сеⷤ ти знамение ꙗко аⷥ та пꙋщаю
извести люди мои иⷯ египта. да сѧ по
молѧⷮ бг҃ꙋ в горѣ сеи. видите бг҃а повелѣ
вающа помолитиⷭ бг҃ꙋ. рече бо бг҃ъ к моисѣю
ꙗко аⷥ та пꙋщаю извести лю҃ моꙗ иⷥ египта.

39.1. You see how in this passage, too, Scripture distinguishes between the description | of the ministering angels and their Lord.[465] Regarding the angels 76r/184
on the ladder,[466] the Scripture says that "the angels of God ascended and descended" on the ladder (Gen. 28:12). And to Joshua, the son of Nun, the angel said, "I am the commander of the host of the Lord; I have now come"[467] (Josh. 5:14). ⟨Instead of saying⟩, "I have now *come down*", he said, "I have now *come*".[468] And concerning the angels of God on the ladder, it was not said[469] that they descended and ascended on it, but rather it was said (in the opposite order) that the "angels of God ascended and descended on it".[470]

39.2. But as for the Lord, he said, "I have seen their affliction[471] and have *come down* to deliver them", as also at the Tower of Babylon, he said, "Having *gone down*, let us confuse them" (Gen. 11:7). And (speaking) of Sodom at the time of Abraham, he said, "I will *go down*, that I may see" (Gen. 18:21), just as here, too, he speaks[472] out of the bush, saying, "I have *come down* to deliver them" (Ex. 3:8).

40. Showing that the Scripture plainly reveals God to be the Trinity rather than a solitary deity.[473]

40.1. The Scripture also states,[474] "God spoke to Moses, saying, 'I will be with you, and this will be the sign to you that I am sending you to bring my people out of Egypt: you will pray to God on this mountain'" (Ex. 3:12). You see,[475] God commands us to pray to God, for God said to Moses, "I am sending you to

---

465 You see how in this passage, too, Scripture distinguishes between the description of the ministering angels and their Lord.] You see the difference that the Scripture draws in this passage, too, distinguishing between the description of God and that of his angels that serve him.

466 Regarding the angels on the ladder,] For when it comes to the angels, whom Jacob saw on the ladder,

467 come"] come to help you"

468 ⟨Instead of saying⟩, "I have now *come down*", he said, "I have now *come*".] Instead of saying, "I have now *come down*", the commander of the Lord's host said, "I have now *come*".

469 said] said about them

470 but rather it was said (in opposite order) that the "angels of God ascended and descended on it".] *omitted*

471 affliction] affliction caused by their taskmasters

472 speaks] speaks to Moses

473 **solitary deity.] solitary being. Thus, God is one but in three hypostases on account of consubstantiality and the persons (that share it).**

474 The Scripture also says,] After this, the Scripture says,

475 You see,] Observe and see what is well written: the Scripture reveals God with God;

да са помолꙗт҇ бгу҃ в горѣ сеи. а не реч҇ бгъ҃ ꙗко
аз҇ та пущаю извести люд҇и моꙗ да са помолꙗт҇
76ᵛ/185 мнѣ в горѣ сеи. но реч҇ да са помолꙗт҇ бгу҃ в горѣ
сеи. бгъ҃ повелѣваѥт҇ паки бгоу҃ж помолитис҇
в горѣ тои. на неж҇и к моисею гл҃ет҇. бгъ҃ оубо
бга҃ проповѣдаѥт҇. колико ꙗвно книги бга҃
и бга҃ показаша. а не оуединено бжс҇тво.
во единм҇о ипостаси бга҃ сказаша. понеж҇ ем҇у сам҇
бгъ҃ пущаѥт҇ моисѣа извести люд҇и своꙗ из҇ еги
пта. да са помолꙗт҇ бгу҃ в горѣ. а не гл҃а бгъ҃
да сꙗ помолꙗт҇ ему в горѣ люд҇и его. но бгу҃ па
ки да са помолꙗт҇ рече. кїи же оубо бгъ҃ пу
щаѥт҇ моисеа извести люд҇и своа да са помо
лꙗт҇ бгоу҃ж в горѣ. нѣсть ли се бгъ҃ снъ҃ пущаѥт҇
моисѣа извести люд҇и своꙗ из҇ египта. да
са помолꙗт҇ бгу҃ ѡ҇тцу҃ в горѣ. понеж҇ снъ҃ славит҇
ѡ҇тца своѥг҇. сице и единение присньства
бга҃ ѡ҇тца и бга҃ сна҃ едину и волю едино и хо
тѣние. показоваху книги. а не ꙗкоже
еллиньстїи ложнїи бз҃и. свирѣпьству
ющес҇ сами на са ратующес҇ кождо другго
му завидуа. ꙗкож҇е бгъ҃ кронъ своа дѣти
пожирающе. да не боудет҇ кто ѿ сновъ҃ его по
мн҇е бгъ. и мнимыи бгъ зевесь снъ҃ кронов҇
77ʳ/187 оукраденыи ѿ пожренїа ѿ҇ча. крона ѡ҇тца своѥг҇
уби. и растезавъ ег҇ на уды погрузи в тинѣ
ї інїи инако убивающес҇ погибоша ложнїи
бз҃и еллиньстїи. сщ҃еннаꙗж҇ книга ѕѣло пре
мдрѣ научаѥт҇. единого бга҃ в трцу҃ познават҇и
всѣмъ. едину волю и едино хотѣние иму
ща. ѿводꙗ чл҃ки ѿ многих҇ скверных҇ бговъ.
показуа единого прс҇тг҇а бга҃ с сномъ҃ его и

bring my people out of Egypt: you will pray to God on this mountain". And God
did not say, "I am sending you to bring my people: you will pray | *to me* on this 76v/185
mountain". Instead, he said, "you will pray *to God* on this mountain".[476] Again,
the God to whom they were to pray on that mountain, also speaks to Moses on
it.[477] God, therefore, proclaims God.

40.2. That is how the Scriptures explicitly revealed God with God, rather than speaking of a solitary Godhead in one divine hypostasis. For God himself sends Moses to bring his people out of Egypt that they may pray to God on the mountain, and God did not say, "his people will pray *to him* on that mountain", but rather, he said, "you will pray *to God* on this mountain".[478] Who, then, is this God, who sends Moses to bring his people out of Egypt so that they may pray to God on the mountain?[479] Is this not the Son of God, who sends Moses to bring his people out of Egypt so that they may pray to God the Father on the mountain? Since the Son glorifies his Father,[480] the Scriptures show the eternal unity between God the Father and God the Son, their common will, and common desire (which is the case in this passage, too).

40.3. And this is different from the false Hellenistic deities, who rage among
themselves in violence and fight[481] in envy to one another, as their god Cronus
did by eating his own children, lest any of his sons become god after him; and
as did also the fictional god Zeus, the son of Cronus, | who was kidnapped from 77r/187
being devoured by his father, and who killed his own father Cronus, and after
cutting him into pieces, thrust him into the mire;[482] and all the other Hellenis-
tic deities, who murdered one another, defeating whomever they could.

40.4. But the sacred Scripture most wisely teaches everyone to recognize one God in Trinity, who has one will and one desire, turning men away from the many outrageous deities, showing the one most holy[483] God, with his Son and

476 say, "I am sending you to bring my people: you will pray *to me* on this mountain". Instead, he said, "you will pray *to God* on this mountain".] *omitted*

477 Again, the God to whom they were to pray on that mountain, also speaks to Moses on it.] God commands them to pray to God on that mountain, and on it, he speaks to Moses out of the bush.

478 For God himself sends Moses to bring his people out of Egypt that they may pray to God on the mountain, and God did not say, "his people will pray to him on that mountain", but rather, he said, "you will pray to God on this mountain".] Since God himself sends Moses to bring his people out of Egypt that they may pray to God on the mountain, so God also says to Moses, "you will pray to God on the mountain".

479 mountain?] To what God are they to pray on that mountain?

480 Since the Son glorifies his Father,] God the Son glorifies his God the Father,

481 fight] fight one another

482 and after cutting him into pieces, thrust him into the mire;] *omitted*

483 most holy] most pure, most holy

со ст҃ымъ дх҃омъ. нераздѣлнꙋ трⷪ҇цꙋ едино
гⷭ҇ьственꙋ. единосилнꙋ единовⷭ҇онꙋ. понеⷤ
рѣша книги ꙗко рⷱ҇е к моисѣю бꙋдꙋ с тобою
сеⷤ ти знамение. ꙗко аⷥ та пꙋщаю извести
люди моиⷯ изъ египта да са помолꙗⷮ бг҃ꙋ
в горѣ сеи. сиⷨ ꙗвиша книги единꙋ волю и
едино хотѣние. бг҃а ѿц҃а. и бг҃а сн҃а. ꙗко
славиⷮ сн҃ъ ѿц҃а своего. Паки гл҃ю книги.
речеⷤ моисѣи ко гⷭ҇ꙋ се ты мнѣ рⷱ҇е извеⷣ люди сїа
а ты не повѣда мнѣ коⷢ҇ пꙋщаеши со мною.
тыⷤ мнѣ рⷱ҇е вѣдꙗ та паⷱ҇ всѣⷯ. и блг҃ть имаши
ѿ мене. и рⷱ҇е моисеⷣ аще есмь ѡбрѣⷮ блг҃ть преⷣ
тобою ꙗви миⷭ҇ самъ. ꙗвѣ да вижю та и
рⷱ҇е емꙋ гⷭ҇ь аⷥ самъ поидꙋ преⷣ тобою и оуставлю тꙗ.
77ᵛ/187 и рⷱ҇е к немꙋ моисѣи. аще не ты шествꙋеши с наⷨ
то не изведеши наⷭ ѿсюдꙋ. и како ꙗвѣ боудеⷮ
истиною. ꙗко ѡбрѣтоⷯ блⷣть преⷣ тобою.
азъⷤ и люⷣе твои паⷱ҇ всѣⷯ ꙗзыкъ елико на земли
есть. речеⷤ гⷭ҇ь к моисею се ти слово еже вѣ
ща приꙗти сотворю. ѡбрѣⷮ еси блг҃ть преⷣ
мною. и вѣдѣ та паⷱ҇ всѣⷯ. и рⷱ҇е моисеи пока
жи ми славꙋ свою. речеⷤ гⷭ҇ь к моисеѡви. аⷥ
идꙋ преⷣ тобою славою моею. и прозовꙋ има
свое преⷣ тобою гⷭ҇ь. и помилꙋю егоⷤ аще поми
лꙋю. и оущедрю егоⷤ аще ꙋщедрю. и рⷱ҇е не во
зможеши видѣти славы лица моего. нѣⷭ
бо аще видиⷮ чл҃къ лице мое и живъ быти. и
рⷱ҇е гⷭ҇ь се мѣсто ꙋ мене. и станеши оу камени
егдаⷤ придеⷮ слава моꙗ. и поставлю та оу дꙋ
плꙗ камыка. и покрыю рꙋкою моею наⷣ та.
доньдеⷤ минꙋ. и ѿимꙋ рꙋкꙋ мою тогда оузри
ши заднꙗа моа. а лице мое не ꙗвиⷮ ти са.
оураниⷤ моисеи заꙋтра и взыде на горꙋ сина
искꙋю ꙗкоⷤ заповѣда емꙋ гⷭ҇ь. и взꙗ моисѣи
с собою двѣ дъсцѣ каменїи ацѣ же первїи.
и сниде гⷭ҇ь во ѡблацѣ и ста преⷣ нимъ тоу.
78ʳ/188 и возва именеⷨ гⷭ҇нимъ. и минꙋ гⷭ҇ь преⷣ лицеⷨ его
и призва гⷭ҇а. гⷭ҇ь бг҃ъ црⷭ҇ъ и мл҃тивъ. долго
терпѣливъ и истиненъ правдꙋ снабдꙗ.
и творꙗ млⷭ҇ть в тысаща. ѿмщаа беза

with the Holy Spirit, the undivided Trinity, in which there is one lordship, one power, one will. In view of what the Scriptures have stated, that "He[484] said to Moses, 'I will be with you, and this will be the sign to you that I am sending you to bring my people out of Egypt: you will pray to God on this mountain'" (Ex. 3:12), the Scriptures reveal in this the one will and one desire of God the Father and God the Son—in the fact that the Son glorifies his Father.

40.5. Again, the Scriptures state, "And Moses said to the Lord, 'See, you said to me', 'Lead this people out', 'but you did not tell me whom you will send with me'. And you said to me, 'I know you better than all (others), and you have found grace from me'. And Moses said, 'If I have found grace before you, reveal yourself to me openly[485] so that I may see you'. And the Lord said to him, 'I myself will go before you and give you rest'. | And Moses said to him, 'If you do not go 77ᵛ/187
with us yourself, do not bring us up from here. And how will it be truly evident, that your people and I have found grace before you above all nations that are on the earth'? And the Lord said to Moses, 'This very thing that you have spoken, I will do. You have found grace before me, and I know you better than all (others)'.

40.6. And Moses said, 'Show me your glory'. And the Lord said to Moses, 'I will pass by before you with my glory, and I will call out my name, the 'Lord', before you. And I will have mercy on whom I will have mercy and will have compassion on whom I will have compassion'. And he said, 'You are not able to see the glory of my face, for no man can see my face and live'. And the Lord said, 'Behold, there is a place by me, and you will stand on the rock. And when my glory passes by, I will put you into a cleft of the rock; and I will cover you with my hand until I have passed by. And I will take away my hand,[486] and then, you will see my back; but my face will not appear to you'" (Ex. 33:12–23).

40.7. And "early in the morning, Moses went up on Mount Sinai, as the Lord had commanded him; and Moses took the two stone tablets with him, as the first time. And the Lord descended in the cloud, and stood near him there, | 78ʳ/188
and called upon the name of the Lord. And the Lord passed by before his face, and he called upon the Lord, 'The Lord God, compassionate and merciful, long-suffering and true, supplying with righteousness and conducting mercy

484 he] God
485 openly] recognizably
486 my hand] hand

конїа неправды грѣхи. и не потребитсѧ
вина его. возлагаѧ грѣхи ѿц҃ъ на чада и внꙋ
чата. на четвертыи и третїи рⷣо. по
тщавсѧ моисеи приведⷭе и поклонⷭи бг҃оу.
речⷤе аще есмь ѡбрⷭѣ блг҃ть прⷣе тобою да
бы шⷭе гⷭи прⷣе нами. и рⷱе гⷭь к моисѣю. се аⷥ
полагаю тебѣ завⷮѣ прⷣе всѣми лⷣюми сво
ими. сотворю великаѧ и славнаѧ. ꙗкоⷤ
не бѣша по всеи земли. ни во всⷯѣ странаⷯ.
и оузрꙗⷮ вси лⷣюе в нихⷤъ ты еси дѣлеса гⷭнѧ
ꙗко чⷣюна сꙋть. ꙗⷤ сотворю аⷥ тебѣ. вⷩоми
ты все елико аⷥ заповѣдаю тебѣ. Видите
ꙗко в кꙋпинѣ рⷱе бг҃ъ моисею гл҃ꙗ боудꙋ с то
бою. сⷤе ти знамение. ꙗко аⷥ тѧ пꙋщаю иⷥ
вести людеи моⷯи изъ египта да сѧ помо
лꙗⷮ бг҃ꙋ в горѣ сеи. и понⷤе изведе моисеи иⷥ е
гипта лⷣю с чюдесы страшными в горꙋ сию.
молꙗшⷭе моисеи видѣти славꙋ пославшаⷢ его
78v/189 извести лⷣю изъ египта. прⷣелагаѧ емꙋ в мл҃твꙋ.
на оумоление самое посланїа его гл҃ꙗ. се ты мнѣ
рⷱе извⷣе люди сїа а ты не повѣда мнѣ коⷢ пꙋ
щаеши со мною. тыⷤ мнѣ рⷱе вѣм тѧ паче
всⷯѣ и блг҃ть имаши ѿ мене. аще есмь ѡбрⷭѣ
блг҃ть прⷣе тобою ꙗви миⷭ самъ ꙗвѣ да вижюⷮⷽ
~~прⷣе~~. ꙗкоⷤ ѡбрѣтоⷯ блг҃ть прⷣе тобою. да ꙋвѣ
дꙗⷮ ꙗко лⷣюе твои сїи ꙗзыкъ великъ. и рече
емꙋ гⷭь. аⷥ самъ поидꙋ прⷣе тобою и оуставлю
тѧ. тои оубо гⷭь ꙗвиⷭ и в кꙋпинѣ моисею.
тои повелѣ и лⷣю своꙗ извести иⷥ египта.
да сѧ помолꙗⷮ бг҃ꙋ в горѣ. томꙋ и молꙗшесѧ
моисеи показати славꙋ его. и оубо в кꙋпи

for thousands, taking revenge for iniquity, unrighteousness, sins, and not allowing (the sinner's) guilt to go unpunished. He lays the sins of the fathers upon the children, and grandchildren, and to the third and fourth generation'.

40.8. Having hurried, Moses bowed to the ground and worshiped God. And he said, 'If I have found grace before you, may the Lord go before us'. And the Lord said to Moses, 'Behold, I am establishing a covenant for you before all my people. I will do great and glorious things, which have not been done in all the earth nor among any of the nations. And all the people among whom you are will see the works of the Lord, that they are wonderful, which I will do for you. Observe everything I command you'" (Ex. 34:4–11).[487]

40.9. You see how God spoke to Moses in the bush,[488] saying, "I will be with you, and this will be the sign to you that I am sending you to bring my people out of Egypt: you will pray to God on this mountain" (Ex. 3:12). And now that Moses was bringing people out of Egypt to this mountain, accompanied with awesome miracles (Ex. 7:1–11:10), Moses prayed to see the glory of the one who sent him | to bring the people out of Egypt, with the very words that he 78v/189
received for his mission,[489] saying, "See, you said to me, 'Lead this people out', but you did not tell me whom you will send with me. And you said to me, 'I know you better than all (others), and you have found grace from me'. If then, I have found grace before you, reveal yourself to me visibly so that I may see you (and know) that I have found grace in your sight;[490] that they may know that this great nation is your people. And the Lord said to him, 'I myself will go before you and give you rest'" (Ex. 33:12–14).

40.10. The same Lord, then, who appeared to Moses in the bush, also commanded him to bring his people out of Egypt so that they might pray to God[491] on the mountain, and to him also, Moses prayed, (asking him) to show his

487 *MS 61 adds*: **Showing that here, too, the Scripture revealed the Son of God most clearly, along with one divinity and lordship on account of the common will and common desire.**

488 You see how God spoke to Moses in the bush,] Remember how God spoke to Moses out of the bush

489 And now that Moses brought people out of Egypt to this mountain, accompanied with awesome miracles (Ex. 7:1–11:10), Moses prayed to see the glory of the one who sent him to bring the people out of Egypt, with the very words that he received for his mission,] And now that Moses brought the people out of Egypt with awesome miracles (Ex. 7–12), according to the words of the Lord, and Moses wished to see the glory of the one, who sent him to bring the people out of Egypt, he, therefore, prayed and pleaded with him in his prayer with the very words that he received for his mission,

490 reveal yourself to me visibly so that I may see you (and know) that I have found grace in your sight;] *omitted*

491 to God] *omitted*

нѣ бг҃ъ авраамовъ ї исааковъ и ꙗковль. по молитⷭ҇и бг҃ꙋ людⷨе повелѣваⷮе. показꙋѧ бг҃ъ бг҃а. и нн҃ѣ паки тоⷤи гⷭ҇ь показꙋⷮе паки гⷭ҇а. за нⷤе рече ко иꙗковꙋ не ѡставлю тебе. доⷩ҇де же сотворю всꙗ елика гл҃аⷯ тебѣ. сего раⷣ҇ и здѣ реⷱ҇ моисею. азъ саⷨ поидꙋ преⷣ тобою и оуставлю тꙗ. но моисеи молꙗшеⷭ҇ паки ви дѣти славꙋ бж҃ию гл҃ꙗ. покажи ми славꙋ свою. речеⷤ гⷭ҇ь моисеѡви. аⷥ идꙋ преⷣ тобою.
79r/190 славою моею. и реⷱ҇ не возможеши видѣти сла вы лица моⷢ҇е. не можеⷮ бо чл҃къ видѣти лице мое и живъ быти. и реⷱ҇ гⷭ҇ь се мѣсто ꙋ мене и станеши оу камени. и оурани моисё заꙋ тра реⷱ҇ писание. и прїиде на горꙋ синаискꙋю ꙗкоⷤ заповѣда емꙋ гⷭ҇ь. и сниде гⷭ҇ь во ѡблацѣ и ста преⷣ нимъ тꙋ. и возва именеⷨ гⷭ҇нимъ и минꙋ гⷭ҇ь преⷣ лицеⷨ его и призва гⷭ҇а. нѣсть ли ꙋбо се ꙗко гⷭ҇ь призва гⷭ҇а. кїⷤи гⷭ҇ь призываⷮе аще не тои. к немоⷤу речено преⷤ. сотворимъ чл҃ка по ѡбразоу н҃шемꙋ и по пⷣоⷪбию. и в содоⷨ ѡгнь ѿ гⷭ҇а посла. и лю̈ⷣ своꙗ иⷥ египта изве сти повелѣ да са помолꙗⷮ бг҃ꙋ. не то или оубо гⷭ҇ь призываⷮе гаⷭ тоⷢ҇. емоⷤу помолитⷭ҇и в горѣ людⷨе заповѣда. иⷤ и в началѣ гл҃а сотворимъ

glory. And thus, the God of Abraham, and of Isaac, and of Jacob[492] commanded the people out of the bush to pray to God, and this became the way that God showed God.[493] And so, then, the same Lord (who appeared) ⟨in the bush⟩, also showed the Lord anew (in the cleft of the rock). Just as he said to Jacob,[494] "I will not leave you until I have done all that I told you" (Gen. 28:15), so here, too, he said to Moses, "I myself will go before you and give you rest" (Ex. 33:14). But Moses prayed once again[495] to see the divine glory, saying, "'Show me your glory'; and the Lord said to Moses, 'I myself will go before you | in my glory'. And 79r/190
he said, 'You are not able to see the glory of my face, for no man can see my face and live'. And the Lord said, 'Behold, there is a place by me, and you will stand on the rock'" (Ex. 33:13–14, 21).

40.11. And the Scripture said that "early in the morning, Moses went up on Mount Sinai, as the Lord had commanded him. And the Lord descended in the cloud, and stood near him there, and called upon the name of the Lord. And the Lord passed by before his face, and he called upon the Lord" (Ex. 34:4–6). Is this not, then, where the Lord called upon the Lord? Who is this Lord that does the calling, if not the same Lord, to whom belong the words spoken earlier, "Let us make man in our image and likeness" (Gen. 1:26); and who sent fire when in Sodom; and who commanded (Moses) to bring the people out of Egypt that they may pray to God?[496] Indeed, is this not where the Lord called upon the very Lord, to whom he commanded people to "pray on that mountain" (Ex.

492 God of Abraham, and of Isaac, and of Jacob] God of Abraham, the God of Isaac, the God of Jacob

493 God] God at that moment.

494 Just as he said to Jacob,] Just as in his appearance to Jacob on the ladder, the Lord said to him,

495 But Moses prayed once again,] And Moses, burning in his desire toward God, prayed once again,

496 Who is this Lord that does the calling, if not the same Lord, to whom belong the words spoken earlier, "Let us make man in our image and likeness" (Gen. 1:26); and who sent fire when in Sodom; and who commanded (Moses) to bring the people out of Egypt that they may pray to God?] Who is this Lord that calls upon the Lord, if not the same Lord, who called the one to whom it was said in the beginning, "Let us make man in our image and likeness" (Gen. 1:26); and to whom the Lord said at the Tower of Babel, "Having gone down, let us confuse him" (Gen. 11:7); and who sent fire when in Sodom; and who called Moses out of the bush (revealing himself) as the Lord and commanding him to not approach the bush; and who commanded (Moses) to bring the people out of Egypt?

чл҃ка по ѡбразоу нⷲемꙋ и по пⷪ҇бию. Пока
зꙋа оубо писание г҃а и г҃а. показаⷤ и нераздво
еное г҃а и г҃а. реⷱ бо аⷥ идꙋ преⷣ тобою славою
моею. и прозовꙋ имꙗ мое преⷣ тобою г҃ь. и
помилꙋю егоⷤ аще помилꙋю. и ꙋщедрю его же
аще оущедрю. единьственое воли и хотениꙗ
и вл҃чества. показаа г҃а и г҃а. а не ꙗко краденыи
79v/192 растесоваа ѿц҃а своⷢ. или кроⷩ своа дети по
жираа. и проⷱа ложныⷯ бг҃овъ злаа побеженїа.
но прⷭ҇ное бе соединение г҃а и г҃а показа гл҃ꙗ г҃ь.
и прозовꙋ имꙗ свое преⷣ тобою г҃ь. не бо ино
имꙗ бж҃ства ѿц҃ꙋ. и ино имꙗ бж҃ства сн҃оу
ⷤе быти бол҃шемꙋ и меншемꙋ бг҃ꙋ. но еди
но бж҃тво ѿц҃ꙋ и сн҃ꙋ показа. поне рече аⷥ
идꙋ преⷣ тобою славою моею. и прозовꙋ
има свое преⷣ тобою г҃ь. г҃а же и г҃а пока
за внегда пишеⷮ. и сниде г҃ь во ѡблаце и
ста преⷣ нимъ тꙋ. и возва имене г҃нимъ. и
миноу г҃ь преⷣ лицеⷨ его. и призва г҃а. вкꙋпе
г҃а и г҃а показа. вкꙋпе и единство хоте

3:12)? ⟨And is this not the same Lord⟩, who said in the very beginning,[497] "Let us make man in our image and likeness" (Gen. 2:26)?

40.12. The Scripture thus shows the Lord and the Lord, and in doing so, it shows the Lord indivisibly from the Lord. For it said, "I will go before you with my glory, and I will call out[498] my name, the 'Lord', before you. And I will have mercy on whom I will have mercy and will have compassion on whom I will have compassion" (Ex. 33:19), which shows that the Lord and the Lord have a single will, and desire, and dominion. And this is different from the cunning one,[499] | who split his father Cronus into pieces, and from Cronus himself 79v/192 who devoured his own children, and from other false deities with their evil schemes. But as for the Lord and the Lord, their eternal union is shown in the words of the Lord, "I will call out my name, the 'Lord', before you" (Ex. 33:19).

40.13. For the divinity of the Father is not named differently from the divinity of the Son, with no distinction between a "greater ⟨God⟩" and a "lesser God". Instead, it showed one divinity of the Father and the Son, for it is said,[500] "I will go before you with my glory, and I will call out my name, the 'Lord', before you" (Ex. 33:19). And the Lord showed the Lord also in writing, "And the Lord descended in the cloud, and stood near him there,[501] and called upon the name of the Lord. And the Lord passed by before his face, and he called upon the Lord" (Ex. 34:5–6). It showed the Lord collectively with the Lord, and also collectively, it showed the unity of desire and will as well as the undivided

497 Indeed, is this not where the Lord called upon the very Lord, to whom he commanded people to "pray on that mountain" (Ex. 3:12)? ⟨And is this not the same Lord⟩, who said in the very beginning,] Indeed, what Lord is this Lord calling upon? Isn't it evident, then, that he called upon the very Lord, to whom he commanded people to "pray (as) God on that mountain" (Ex. 3:12); and from whom he sent fire on Sodom, "from the Lord" (Gen. 19:26); and before whom, as God said, Abraham had fear when he did not spare his beloved son for (God's) sake (Gen. 22:13); and to whom he said at the Tower of Babel, "Having gone down, let us confuse him" (Gen. 11:7)? And is this not the same Lord whom the Lord called upon when he previously made that statement, saying to him,

498 call out] call upon

499 cunning one] the Hellenistic god, Deus,

500 for it is said,] of whom it is said,

501 there] *omitted*

нб҃а и воли. и нераздѣлное прⷭ҇ньства. гⷭ҇ь
ствⷤа и чести и бл҃гости. и бл҃говоленїа по
каза. гⷭ҇а и гⷭ҇а бг҃а и бг҃а. и напрⷣе идыи писа
ние паки согласное бл҃говоленїа. и бл҃гости
и хотѣнїа гⷭ҇а и гⷭ҇а бг҃а и бг҃а показа гл҃ѧ.
Потщавса моисеи привⷣе са поклониⷭ҇ бг҃оу
речⷤе аще ⷭ҇емь обрѣлъ бл҃гть прⷣе тобою да
бы шⷣе гⷭ҇и прⷣе нами. и рⷱ҇е гⷭ҇ь к моисею. се ⷥа
полагаюⷮ завⷮѣ прⷣе всѣми лⷣюми своими.
80r/194 сотворю великаа и славнаа ꙗкⷤо не бѣша по всеи
земли ни во всⷯѣ странⷯа. и оузрѧⷮ всѣ лⷣюⷷе дѣле
са гⷭ҇на ꙗко чⷣюна сꙋть. ꙗⷤ сотворю ⷥа тебѣ.
вонми ты все елика ⷥа заповѣдаю тебѣ.
Ѕѣло мнⷢо здѣ писание показа бг҃а ѿ бг҃а. глⷮѣ бо
ꙗко сниде бг҃ъ изати людеи свойⷯ. из рꙋки еги
пⷮески. оуслыша вопль и стенание йⷯ. бгⷤъ
исповѣдꙋемъ. бг҃ъ авраамⷡо. бг҃ъ исаакⷡо. бг҃ъ
їаковль. сниде избавити лⷣю своа. и тⷷо бг҃ъ
рⷱ҇е моисею гл҃ѧ. сⷤе ти знамение ꙗко ⷥа та пꙋ
щаю. извести людⷷе мойⷯ из египта. да са
помолѧⷮ бгⷤꙋ в горѣ сеи. бг҃ъ авраамⷡо бг҃ъ исаакⷡо
бг҃ъ иаковль. пꙋсти моисѣа извести людⷷе
свойⷯ из египта. помолитⷭ҇и бгⷤꙋ в горѣ хорѣ
вѣ. се бг҃ъ повелѣвⷮае молитиса бжⷭ҇и. нб҃ ли

eternality, and lordship, and honor, and goodness, and benevolence that belong to the Lord and Lord, God and God.[502]

40.14. And going onward, the Scripture once more showed the consent in benevolence, and goodness, and desire, which belong to the Lord and Lord, God and God, saying, "Having hurried, Moses bowed to the ground and worshiped God. And he said, 'If I have found grace before you, let the Lord go before us'. And the Lord said to Moses, 'Behold, I am establishing a covenant for you before all my people. | I will do great and glorious things, which have not been 80r/194
done in all the earth nor among any of the nations. And all the people among whom you are will see the works of the Lord, that they are wonderful, which I will do for you. Observe everything I command you'" (Ex. 34:8–11).

40.15. There are very many[503] ways here, in which the Scripture showed God from God. (To state the obvious), it says that God descended in order to deliver his people out of the hand of the Egyptians after hearing their outcry and moaning. And God, who is confessed as the God of Abraham, the God of Isaac, the God of Jacob, descended to deliver his people.[504] And the same God spoke to Moses, saying, "And this will be the sign to you that I will send you to bring my people out of Egypt: you will pray to God on that mountain" (Ex. 3:12). The God of Abraham, the God of Isaac, and the God of Jacob sent Moses to bring his people out of Egypt so that they may pray to God on Mount Horeb. Here, God

---

502 God and God.] God and God, according to his own words, in which the Lord says, "I will call out my name, the 'Lord', before you" (Ex. 33:19), and (when) it is said that "he descended in the cloud and stood near Moses, and the Lord called upon the name of the Lord" (Ex. 34:5). The same thing is also written, when the Lord said, "I will go before you with my glory, and I will call out my name, the 'Lord', before you" (Ex. 33:19). And when it is written, "And the Lord passed by before his face, and he called upon the Lord: 'The Lord God, compassionate and merciful'" (Ex. 34:6), it has a clear sense that the Lord did not call upon his own name, but rather called upon his Lord God, saying, "The Lord God, compassionate and merciful". This is the God, upon whom he called, and whom the Lord previously commanded to "pray to God on the mountain" (Ex. 3:12) when he spoke to Moses out of the bush. And once the Lord called upon his name at the time when the Lord "stood near Moses and called upon the name of the Lord" (Ex. 34:5), the Lord thus fulfilled his own words, in which he said, "I will call out my name, the 'Lord', before you" (Ex. 33:19). And in the fact that he called upon the Lord as "the Lord God, compassionate and merciful" (Ex. 34:6), the Scripture showed that the Lord called upon the Lord God. Thus, the Lord, who was there (as a distinct subject), called upon the Lord God. Is this not where the Scripture confesses the Lord from the Lord, and God from God?

503 very many] many

504 And God, who is confessed as the God of Abraham, the God of Isaac, the God of Jacob, descended to deliver his people.] *omitted*

се бг҃ъ ѿ бг҃а. паки тоиⷤ бг҃ъ бⷤ҇їи показавыи
славꙋ свою моисею в горѣ. и призва бг҃аⷤ и бг҃а.
пишеⷮ бо и сниде гⷭ҇ь во ѡблацѣ и ста преⷣ нимъ
тꙋ. и возва именеⷨ гⷭ҇нимъ. и минꙋ гⷭ҇ь преⷣ лицеⷨ
его. и призва гⷭ҇а. гⷭ҇ь бг҃ъ щⷣръ и млⷭ҇твъ. преⷤ оубо
реⷱ моисею гⷭ҇ь. аⷥ идꙋ преⷣ тобою славою моею.
и прозовꙋ имѧ свое преⷣ тобою гⷭ҇ь. ꙗкоⷤ реⷱ гⷭ҇ь.
80v/195 и прозовꙋ имѧ свое преⷣ тобою гⷭ҇ь. сие пишеⷮ.
и ста преⷣ нимъ тꙋ. и возва именеⷨ гⷭ҇нимъ. ска
зоуеⷮ писание ꙗⷦ ꙗⷤ реⷱ гⷭ҇ь. аⷥ идꙋ преⷣ тобою сла
вою моею. и прозовꙋ имѧ свое преⷣ тобою
гⷭ҇ь. се самое пишеⷮ. ꙗко сниде гⷭ҇ь во ѡбла
цѣ и ста преⷣ нимъ тꙋ. и возва именемъ
гⷭ҇нимъ. и минꙋ гⷭ҇ь преⷣ лицеⷨ его. се сказоуеⷮ
писание. ꙗко по гл҃ꙋ своемꙋ гⷭ҇ь гл҃ющемꙋ.
прозовꙋ имѧ свое преⷣ тобою гⷭ҇ь. возва
гⷭ҇ь именеⷨ гⷭ҇нимъ. ста преⷣ моисеѡⷨ. аⷤ е
пишеⷮ и минꙋ гⷭ҇ь преⷣ лицемъ еⷢ҇. и призва гⷭ҇а.
гⷭ҇ь бг҃ъ щⷣръ и млⷭ҇тивъ. сие не свое имѧ
прозываеⷮ гⷭ҇ь. но гⷭ҇а бг҃а призва гⷭ҇ь гл҃ѧ. гⷭ҇ь
бг҃ъ щⷣръ и млⷭ҇тивъ. тогда бо прозва имѧ
свое гⷭ҇ь. внегда ста преⷣ нимъ гⷭ҇ь. и возва
именеⷨ гⷭ҇нимъ. тꙋ сверши гⷭ҇ь гл҃ъ свои гл҃ю
щїи. прозовꙋ имѧ свое преⷣ тобою гⷭ҇ь. стаⷡ
бо преⷣ нимъ возва именеⷨ гⷭ҇нимъ. здѣⷤ ми
ноувь гⷭ҇ь преⷣ лицеⷨ его и призва гⷭ҇а. гⷭ҇ь бг҃ъ ще
дръ и млⷭ҇тивъ. показоуеⷮ писание гⷭ҇а при
зывающа гⷭ҇аⷤ бг҃а. гⷭ҇ь оубо сыи призва гⷭ҇а бг҃а.
нѣⷭ҇ ли се гⷭ҇а ѿ гⷭ҇а. и бг҃а ѿ бг҃а. исповѣдꙋющее
81r/195 писание. Паки пишеⷮ. реⷱ гⷭ҇ь к моисею. се аⷥ по

commands them to pray to God! Is this not (showing) God from God? Again,[505] the same God with God showed his glory to Moses on Sinai, and God called upon God. For it is written, "And the Lord descended in the cloud and stood near him there, and he called upon the name of the Lord, and the Lord passed by before his face, and he called upon the Lord: 'The Lord God, compassionate and merciful'" (Ex. 34:5–6).

40.16. Now, before the Lord said to Moses, "I will go before you with my glory, and I will call out my name, the 'Lord', before you" (Ex. 33:19), which is the statement spoken by the Lord, | the following is written, "and I will call out my name, 80v/195
the 'Lord', before you; and he stood near him there, and he called upon the name of the Lord" (Ex. 34:5). The Scripture states the same thing in both cases: when the Lord said, "I will go before you with my glory, and I will call out my name, the 'Lord', before you" (Ex. 33:19), and when it is written that "the Lord descended in the cloud and stood near him there, and he called upon the name of the Lord, and the Lord passed by before his face" (Ex. 34:5–6). Here, the Scripture speaks of one person as saying his own words (to another): "I will call out my name, the 'Lord', before you" (Ex. 33:19), and "the Lord called upon the name of the Lord as he stood before Moses" (Ex. 34:5). And when it is written, "And the Lord passed by before his face, and he called upon the Lord: 'The Lord God, compassionate and merciful'" (Ex. 34:6), the Lord was not calling upon his own name, but rather the Lord called upon the Lord God, saying, "The Lord God, compassionate and merciful" (Ex. 34:6). For the Lord called upon his name at the time when the Lord "stood near him and called upon the name of the Lord" (Ex. 34:5).

40.17. That is where the Lord fulfilled his own word, in which he said, "I will call out my name, the 'Lord', before you" (Ex. 33:19). For he did call upon the name of the Lord, when he stood before him. And here the "Lord passed by before his face and called upon the Lord: 'The Lord God, compassionate and merciful'" (Ex. 34:6). The Scripture shows that the Lord called upon the Lord God. Thus, the Lord, who was there (as a distinct subject), called upon the Lord God. Is this not where the Scripture confesses the Lord from the Lord, and God from God? | 81r/195

505 mountain" (Ex. 3:12). The God of Abraham, the God of Isaac, and the God of Jacob sent Moses to bring his people out of Egypt so that they may pray to God on Mount Horeb. Here, God commands to pray to God! Is this not (showing) God from God? Again,] you will pray to God on Mount Horeb" (Ex. 3:12). Again,

лагаю тебѣ завѣт прѣ всѣми лю̑ми своими. сотворю великаа и славнаа. ıакова̑ж не бѣша по всеи земли ни во всѣх странах. и оузрат вси лю̑е в ни̑х же ты еси дѣлеса г̑на ıако чю̑на соут. ıаж а̑з тебѣ. Гь оубо ѡбѣтова̑е сотворити великаа и славнаа. и оузрı̑ат ре̑ вси людие дѣлеса г̑на ıако чю̑на соут. ıаж азъ сотворю тебѣ. Видите̑ како ѿкры писание бга ѿ бга. сотворıа̑е бо гь дѣлеса г̑на̑. по семоу ѕѣло показа писание га̑ г̑на. поне̑ж не гла гь и оузрıа̑т вси лю̑е в нихъ ты еси дѣлеса моа. ıако чю̑на соут. ıаж сотворю а̑з тебѣ. но гла гь и оузрıат всѣ лю̑е в ни̑х же ты еси дѣлеса г̑на. ıако чю̑на соут. ıаж сотворю а̑з тебѣ. оубо гь сотворıа̑е дѣла не своа но г̑на. гь дѣлесъ чю̑ны сотворıа̑е своа дѣлеса чю̑наа не собою са̑м но гдемъ своа дѣлеса чю̑наа сотворıа̑е гь дѣлесъ чю̑ны. нѣ ли се и ѱалм̑ское писание ж̑е речено. словесе̑м г̑ним нбса оутвердиша. нѣ ли оубо се гь слово бжие единоро̑дное. сотвораюи дѣлеса бжїа. ѿча чю̑наа.

81v/196 истинно показа сщ̑нное писание. га̑ г̑на стго прчтаго. едино̑ бжтва и гьства. единоначалноую трцоу. премрѣ ѿводıа члки ѿ мн̑оначаственых скверных и ложных мртвых бгов. ѿкрываа неложна жива бга со прным с̑ном его и дхом его стым. многими глы. и извѣстоуа единачаственое. единогьственое. единохотѣнное. едино

40.18. Again, it is written, "The Lord said to Moses, 'Behold, I am establishing a covenant with you before all my people. I will do great and glorious things, which have not been done in all the earth nor among any of the nations. And all the people among whom you are will see the works of the Lord, that they are wonderful, which I will do for you'"[506] (Ex. 34:10). Thus,[507] the Lord promises to "do great and glorious things", saying that "all the people will see the works of the Lord, that they are wonderful, which I will do for you" (Ex. 34:10). Don't you see how the Scripture reveals God from God?[508] For the Lord was doing the works of the Lord, ⟨and not his own⟩.

40.19. Thus,[509] the Scripture effectively showed the Lord's Lord again, because the Lord did not say, "And all the people among whom you are will see *my* works, that they are wonderful, which I will do for you". Instead, the Lord said, "And all the people among whom you are will see the works of the Lord, that they are wonderful, which I will do for you" (Ex. 34:4–11). Therefore, the works[510] that the Lord does are not his but the Lord's. And the Lord of the wonderful works does his wonderful works, but not by himself. Instead, the Lord of the wonderful works does his wonderful works through the Lord. Is this not what is spoken in the words of the Psalm, "By the word of the Lord the heavens were established"[511] (Ps. 33:6). Is this not, then, the Lord, the only-begotten Word of God, that does the wonderful works of God the Father?[512] | 81v/196

40.20. The sacred Scripture truly shows the Lord of the Lord, the holy and all pure and single divinity and lordship of the supreme Trinity.[513] In its supreme wisdom, it steers men away from the deities of the Greeks that are oligarchic, evil, false, and dead.[514] In many of its words, it reveals the true[515] living God with his Son, who is proper to him, and[516] his Holy Spirit. It declares the monarchy, the common lordship, the common desire, the common will of the one divinity

506 Again, it is written, "The Lord said to Moses, 'Behold, I am establishing a covenant with you before all my people. I will do great and glorious things, which have not been done in all the earth nor among any of the nations. And all the people among whom you are will see the works of the Lord, that they are wonderful, which I will do for you'"] *omitted*

507 Thus,] Likewise,

508 Don't you see how the Scripture reveals God from God?] In what way did the Scripture reveal God with God?

509 Thus,] In this,

510 the works] the wonderful works

511 established"] established, and by the breath of his mouth all their host"

512 God the Father] Lord, the Father

513 supreme Trinity] consubstantial Trinity

514 false and dead] dead and false

515 true] only true

516 his Son, who is proper to him, and] his everlasting Son and

вⷭ҇ное. единоⷭ҇ бжⷭ҇тва. ѿца и сн҃а и ст҃го дх҃а. всесъвершено всемирно. всенераздѣлно всепрⷭ҇нено. ꙗко гⷭ҇ь единородныи сн҃ъ слово бж҃ие. сотвораⷮ бж҃їа ѿча гн҃а дѣлеса чюⷣнаа. Паки пишеⷮ в книгаⷯ. реⷱ҇ гⷭ҇ь к моисею. поими вса головы люⷣски. и ѡбличиа гⷭ҇у прамо сл҃нцу. и ѿврати гнѣвъ ꙗрости гн҃а ѿ їил҃ꙗ. Зрите ꙗко паки и паки писание возводить разоуⷨ к видѣнию бг҃а ѿ бг҃а. показуа га҃ ѡ гⷭ҇ѣ гл҃юща. прїими реⷱ҇ гⷭ҇ь моисею всꙗ головы люⷣски. и ѡбличиа гⷭ҇у. внемлите убо ꙗко не рече гⷭ҇ь моисею тако. поимⷨ вса головы люⷣски и ѡбличиа мнѣ прамо сл҃нцу. но реⷱ҇ гⷭ҇ь моисею сице. поими вса го-
82r/197 ловы люⷣски и ѡбличїа гⷭ҇у прамо сл҃нцу. нѣ ли оубо се ꙗко гⷭ҇ь повелѣваⷮ ко гⷭ҇у же главы люⷣски ѡбличиⷮ. паки не реⷱ҇ гⷭ҇ь ѿврати гнѣвъ ꙗрости моеа ѿ їил҃ꙗ. но реⷱ҇ гⷭ҇ь и ѿврати гнѣⷡ ꙗрости гн҃а ѿ їил҃ꙗ. И много и пресвѣтло ѕѣло ѿкры писание. бг҃а истинна ѿ бг҃а истинна. Разумѣитеⷤ и вѣдите колико противитса косои сщ҃нному писанию. пачеⷤ самому бв҃и съпротивлꙗетса. и ругаꙗⷭ҇ бг҃у. носиⷮ косои сщ҃енныа книги въ сквернꙋю руку свою. ѕлѣ развращаа писание. по своеи злобѣ. оуча оучение сотонино. проповѣдаа хⷭ҇а проста чл҃ка. велꙗ ѿступиⷮ ѿ бг҃а истиннаго. прославлꙗемаⷢ в треⷯ ипостасеⷯ бжⷭ҇твеныⷨ писаниеⷨ. бг҃а ѿца и единородна сн҃а его. и все ст҃го дх҃а его. Чю

of the Father and the Son and the Holy Spirit (who exist) in supreme perfection, supreme peace, supreme inseparability, supreme eternality. It shows the Lord to be the only-begotten Son, the Word of God, doing the wonderful works of the Lord, God the Father.

40.21. Again, it is written in the Scriptures,[517] "And the Lord said to Moses, 'Take all the leaders of the people and bring them out in the sun before the Lord, and the anger of the Lord will be turned away from Israel'" (Num. 25:4). See how over and over again,[518] the Scripture lifts up the mind to the vision of God from God,[519] showing the way the Lord speaks of the Lord, when the Lord says to Moses, "Take all the leaders of the people and bring them out before the Lord". Indeed, observe the fact that the Lord did not say to Moses the following, "Take all the leaders of the people and bring them out in the sun *before me*". Instead, here is what the Lord said to Moses,[520] "Take all | the leaders of the 82ʳ/197
people and bring them out in the sun *before the Lord*". Is this not, then, where the Lord commands the Lord to bring the leaders of the people? And again, the Lord did not say, "and *my anger* will be turned away from Israel", but said, "and *the anger of the Lord* will be turned away from Israel".[521]

40.22. The Scripture effectively revealed the true God with the true God in ways that are both plentiful and clear.[522] Recognize and see how resistant is Kosoy.[523] He objects to the sacred Scripture, and above all, to God[524] himself. And in his blasphemy against God, Kosoy carries the holy books in his nasty hands, distorting the sacred Scriptures in an evil way according to his wickedness, teaching the doctrine of Satan, preaching Christ as a mere man, instructing (men) to depart from the true God, whom the divine Scripture praises[525] in three hypostases: God the Father, and his only-begotten Son,[526]

517 Scriptures,] divinely inspired Scriptures. **On the fact that the Lord proclaims the Lord, meaning that the Son, the Word of God, glorifies his Father and God.**

518 See how over and over again,] Again,

519 vision of God from God,] knowledge of God with God,

520 "Take all the leaders of the people and bring them out in the sun before me". Instead, here is what the Lord said to Moses,] *omitted*

521 Israel".] Israel". The Lord himself commands Moses to bring the leaders of the people, while also revealing the Lord, when he says, "Take all the leaders of the people and bring them out before the Lord".

522 The Scripture effectively revealed the true God with true God in ways that are both plentiful and clear.] In its numerous and very clear ways, the Scripture effectively revealed the true God with true God. Instead of a secluded being, (it showed) the true God in unity.

523 how resistant is Kosoy.] how much Kosoy resists the Scripture.

524 God] Lord

525 praises] sets forth

526 Son,] Son, who is the Word,

жюⷭ҇ како таковїи въ чл҃цеⷯ ѡбрѣтошаⷭ҇. да послꙋшаюⷮ раба лꙋкава. тата. бѣглеца. прⷭ҇е стителя. клятвопрестꙋпника. законо престꙋпника. крива. безбожна. раⷥвра щающа чистыя книги. сїа гл҃авъ рекоⷯ крылошаноⷨ ѿити. яко мноⷢ҇ ꙋтрꙋдиⷯса.~

...

91v/216

Пришеⷭтвїе трееѕ крыло шанъ. Ѿ аки сказанїе яко ї҃съ х҃с сн҃ъ бж҃їи роженъ а не сотвореⷩ҇ есть.[527]

Паки съшеⷣшеса вопросиⷯ ихъ гл҃я. рекосте ми ꙋбо вчера гл҃юще. яко въскꙋю гл҃ю а҇ еже косои не при емлеⷮ ха҃. рцыте мни ꙋбо в чесоⷨ косои ха҃ приемлеⷮ. и како е҇ исповѣдываеⷮ. во всеⷨ бо косои съпроти вляетса хꙋ҃. и всемꙋ законꙋ гн҃ю. Решаⷤ ми крылошане ѡни. повѣдахоⷨ ти яко косои даеⷮ прочитаⷮ разгибая книги апⷭ҇льскїа писаное. яко реⷱ҇ петръ. твердо ꙋбо да разꙋмѣеⷮ весь доⷨ їилевъ. яко ї г҃а и х҃а е҇ бг҃ъ сотвориⷧ҇ есть сеⷢ҇ ї҃са. и паки апⷭ҇лово павлово. единъ бо е҇ бг҃ъ и единъ ходатаи бгꙋ҃ и чл҃комъ чл҃къ ї҃съ х҃ъ. Яко апⷭ҇ли

527 *In the margin*: глⷡ҇а кв҃.

and his supremely Holy Spirit. I am greatly amused over the fact that there are such people, who listen to the deceiving slave, thief, runaway, seducer, perjurer, law-breaker, squint-eyed, godless, distorter of the pure Scriptures.

40.23. Having said this, I told the kliros-chanters to leave, for I had become very tired.[528]

41. THIRD VISIT OF THE KLIROS-CHANTERS

42. An additional argument that Jesus Christ, the Son of God, is begotten, and not made. CHAPTER 22.[529] 91ᵛ/216

42.1. And on meeting again, I asked them[530] and said: Now, you told me yesterday[531] that you wondered why I said that Kosoy did not accept Christ. Tell me, then,[532] in what way does Kosoy accept Christ, and how does he confess him? For Kosoy entirely opposes Christ, as well as the Law of the Lord in all respects![533]

42.2. And those kliros-chanters said to me, "We told you how Kosoy opened the apostolic Scriptures and had us read the words that Peter said, 'Therefore, let all the house of Israel know for certain that God has made him both Lord and Christ, this Jesus' (Acts 2:36), and then, from the Apostle Paul, 'For there is one God, and there is one mediator between God and men, the man Jesus Christ'" (1 Tim. 2:5).

---

528 tired.] tired and had no strength.

529 **An additional argument that Jesus Christ, the Son of God, is begotten, and not made. CHAPTER 22.] Investigation of the words spoken in the Acts by the pre-eminent Peter that "God has made him both Lord and Christ, this Jesus whom you crucified" (Acts 2:36), and of the words spoken by the Apostle Paul that "there is one mediator between God and men, the man Christ Jesus" (1 Tim. 2:5), and of how the Apostles accepted Jesus Christ by speaking of him as both Lord and man in their writings. CHAPTER 22.**

530 And on meeting again, I asked them,] And when we met, I asked them again,

531 yesterday] before today's (meeting)

532 Tell me, then,] But tell me

533 as well as the Law of the Lord in all respects!] *omitted*

і҃са х҃а глаша ч҃лка с҃е ради понеⷤ воплотиⷭ҇ с҃нъ б҃їи и быⷭ҇ ч҃лкъ. а не привидѣниеⷨ на земли поживе б҃гъ сыи. Ѿвѣщавⷤ азъ гл҃аⷯ имъ. добрѣ оубо рⷯ҇ѣ ѥко бⷥ҇ебженъ е҃ косои. законꙋ бо оучиⷮ паⷨ хвы бл҃гти. и закоⷩ҇ престꙋпаⷮ҇ велиⷮ. ѥкоⷤ и саⷨ законопрестꙋпникъ. понеⷤ закоⷩ҇ пропо вѣда і҃са х҃а б҃га сꙋща. косоⷤ҇ реченаꙗ добрѣ ст҃ыⷨ
92r/217 ап҃лы гл҃е злѣ. проповѣдаеⷮ х҃а проста ч҃лка а не б҃га. и по рⷥ҇авращенномꙋ своемꙋ оумꙋ. ѥкоⷤ и арїи еретикъ. наго приеⷨ слово и рⷥ҇сꙋжаеⷮ ѕлѣ. глⷮ҇е бо ап҃ла петра гл҃юща. ѥко сотвори с҃е і҃са б҃гъ. к томꙋ приводꙗ и павлово ѡно е҃ⷤ единъ есть б҃гъ и единъ ходатаи б҃гꙋ и ч҃ломъ ч҃лкъ і҃съ х҃ъ. сими гл҃ы и сотворена х҃а и ч҃лка е҃ проста глⷮ҇е его косои а не б҃га х҃а. но нⷩ҇ѣ тако ѥкоⷤ хꙋлиⷮ косои на б҃га. гл҃ѥ на высотꙋ неправдꙋ. глⷮ҇е оубо ап҃лъ павеⷧ не токмо к тимоѳею пиша. воспоминаꙗ х҃а ч҃лка бывающа. но и к римлѥноⷨ пишеⷮ тоⷤ воспоминаꙗ. ѥко быⷭ҇ ч҃лкъ х҃съ. но не бжтво ѿ х҃а ѿемлеⷮ павеⷧ гл҃ѥ ч҃лка х҃а. на ипачеⷤ сими гл҃ы павеⷧ проповѣдаеⷮ х҃а. б҃га кꙋпно и ч҃лка. сказоуа ѥко х҃съ не нагъ б҃гъ но и ч҃лкъ е҃ х҃съ. и ч҃лкъ х҃съ не простъ паки но и б҃гъ е҃ х҃съ. едино бо еу҃лїе проповѣдаше со їѡаноⷨ бг҃ословоⷨ. и павеⷧ ѥкоⷤ їѡа глⷮ҇е. і҃са х҃а во плоти пришеⷣша. сїе самое и павеⷧ глⷮеть. ѥко х҃съ и б҃гъ и ч҃лкъ е҃. прочтемъⷤ оубо свыше ап҃лово писание. да разꙋмнѣе боудеⷮ. глⷮ҇е оубо павелъ тимоѳею пиша сице. Молю оубо преⷤ всего
92v/218 твориⷮ молитвы моленїа прошенїа бл҃годаренїа. за вса ч҃лки. за цр҃а и за всѧ иⷤ во власти сꙋщиⷯ. да тихо и бⷥ҇молъвно житие поживемъ. во всѧкоⷨ бл҃говѣрїи и ч҃тотѣ. себе добро и приѥтно преⷣ сп҃сителеⷨ н҃шимъ б҃гомъ. иⷤ всѣмъ ч҃ломъ хощеⷮ сп҃тиса и в разоуⷨ истинныи прїити. едиⷩ бо е҃ б҃гъ и единъ ходатаи б҃гꙋ и ч҃ломъ ч҃лкъ і҃съ х҃съ. давыи себе изба

43. Showing that the Apostles spoke of Jesus Christ as a man, because the Son of God became incarnate and lived as a man instead of dwelling on this earth as a divine phantom.

43.1. And in response, I said to them: It was right, then, for me to say that Kosoy was a godless man. For his teaching is more about the Law than about Christ's grace, and compels us to break the Law, himself being the law-breaker. For the Law proclaims Jesus Christ to be God.[534] But Kosoy takes what is spoken well by the holy | Apostles and states it in a distorted way, declaring that Christ is 92r/217 a mere man, and not God. And in his perverse mind, just like the heretic[535] Arius, he treats the Word lightly and reasons in an evil way when making reference to Peter's statement that says, "God made this Jesus" (Acts 2:36). And to this, he also adds Paul's words that "there is one God, and there is one mediator between God and men, the man Jesus Christ" (1Tim. 2:5). With these statements, Kosoy says that Christ is both "made" and a "mere man", and that Christ is not God. But though Kosoy blasphemes God by uttering lies against heaven, this is not how things are.[536]

43.2. Now, in speaking of (Christ), the Apostle Paul recalls the time when Christ existed as a man not only in writing to Timothy, but also in writing to the Romans, he likewise recalls the time when Christ existed as a man. Yet Paul does not deprive Christ of his divinity when he speaks of him as a human. Rather, Paul makes these statements in order to preach Christ as being simultaneously God and man. He says that Christ is not just God but that Christ is also man; and again, (he says) that Christ is not just man, but that Christ is God, too. For Paul preached the same Gospel that John the Theologian also preached. That is, John speaks of Christ as coming in the flesh, and so does Paul when he says that Christ is both God and man. So, let us read the words of the Apostle, taking into account the overall context, in order to understand them better.

43.3. Now, in writing to Timothy, Paul says this, "First of all, then, I urge | that 92v/218 prayers, supplications, intercessions, and thanksgiving be made for all people, for the king and all who are in power, that we may lead a godly and pure life in every way. This is good and pleasing in the sight of God our Savior, who desires all people to be saved and to come to the knowledge of the truth. For there is one God, and there is one mediator between God and men, the man Jesus

534 God.] God, and the Apostles, likewise, teach that our Lord Jesus Christ is God and man.

535 heretic] *omitted*

536 *MS 61 adds*: **Showing that Jesus Christ, the Son of God, is begotten, and not made.**

вление за всѣхъ. И внегда рⷱ҇е и единъ ходатаꙵ
бг҃ꙋ и чл҃комъ чл҃къ і҃съ х҃съ. и абие наведе ап҃лъ
давыꙵ себе рⷱ҇е избавление за всⷯ҇ѣ. не положи
просто ап҃лъ гл҃ꙗ чл҃къ і҃съ х҃съ но приложилъ є҃
и се. ⷤ҇є давыи себе избавление за всѣхъ. Ви
дите ꙗко не оукарꙗа гл҃ю косⷪ҇о бⷥ҇ебж҃ьна и за
конопрестꙋпна и грѣшна. но по послѣдова
нию бесѣды истинꙋ ѡ нⷨ҇е гл҃ю. слышасте бо
ап҃ла законъ полⷪ҇ⷤ҇оша мл҃твы творⷮ҇иꙵ прⷤ҇е всⷢ҇е
мл҃ніа прошеніа бл҃годареніа. за всꙗ чл҃ки.
за цр҃а и за вса ⷤ҇и во власти сꙋщⷯ҇и. и се гл҃еть
быти добро и приꙗтно прⷣ҇е сп҃сителⷨ҇е нш҃ⷨи
бг҃омъ. косⷤ҇ои гл҃еть не подобаⷮ҇е покланати҃
и молити҃. и моление непⷣⷪ҇обно именꙋⷮ҇е. съпро
93r/220 тивлꙗаⷭ҇а бг҃ꙋ престꙋпаⷮ҇е запоⷣⷦ҇ѣ косои. сице
и вса глⷮ҇е на рⷥ҇авращение ꙗⷤ҇ гл҃еть. и сⷨ҇а собе ꙗ
вленно показоуⷮ҇е во ж҃и и в законопрестꙋпле
ніи своⷨ҇е. хота во ѡнⷯ҇ѣ законоположеніихъ
в престꙋпаемыхъ ѿ него. х҃а чл҃ка проста ввѣ
рити. по семꙋ и безоумие его послѣднее ꙗвле
нно є҃. гл҃ꙗⷤ҇ ап҃лъ ꙗко ѡⷤ҇е преже всего мл҃твы
творити. моленіа бл҃годареніа за вса чл҃ки.
за цр҃а и за вса ⷤ҇и во власти сꙋщⷯ҇и. показа ꙗко
сⷢ҇е ради тихо и бⷥ҇емолъвно житие пожити є҃.
во всⷨ҇е бл҃говѣріи и чт҃отѣ. и се самое добро
и приатно прⷣ҇е сп҃сителⷨ҇е нш҃имъ бг҃омъ. на
казавъ оубо сие оуказоуетⷤ҇ъ ꙗко хотѣние
бж҃ие є҃ гл҃ꙗ. понⷤ҇е всѣмъ чл҃комъ хощⷮ҇е сп҃ти҃
и в разоуⷨ҇ истинныꙵ приити. тⷤ҇а сказоуⷮ҇е хо
тѣніа бж҃іа волю. ꙗко се х҃смъ есть. сего
рⷣ҇аꙵ глⷮ҇е по послѣдованию ꙗко единъ є҃ бг҃ъ и
едⷩ҇и ходатаꙵ сп҃сеніа нш҃его чл҃ческⷢ҇а къ бг҃оу
ѿцꙋ і҃са х҃а. и ѡбрⷥ҇а ходатаиства глⷮ҇е х҃ва. ꙗⷦ҇

Christ, who gave himself as a deliverance for all" (1 Tim. 2:1–6). And after saying,[537] "and there is one mediator between God and men, the man Jesus Christ", the Apostle immediately specified, "who gave himself", as he said, "as a deliverance for all". In this verse, the Apostle is not saying simply, "the man Jesus Christ", but has also added the phrase, "who gave himself as a deliverance for all".

43.4. You see, I do not misjudge Kosoy when I say that he is a godless man and law-breaker and sinful fellow. Instead, I am telling the truth about him based on what unfolds as the discourse develops.[538] For you heard how the Apostle commanded: "first of all" "to make prayers, supplications, intercessions, and thanksgiving for all people, for the king and all who are in power" (1 Tim. 2:1–2). And he says that it is "good and pleasing in the sight of God our Savior" (1 Tim. 2:3). But Kosoy says that we should not worship and pray, and he also calls supplication unacceptable. | In his opposition to God, Kosoy thus breaks commandments, and everything he says is spoken for the purpose of disruption. 93ʳ/220 And he himself clearly shows his own deception and law-breaking[539] when he wishes to use the very commandments that he breaks to convince people that Christ is presented in them as a mere man. That is why his extreme insanity is revealed that way.

43.5. But the Apostle Paul said that we must "first of all make prayers, supplications, and thanksgiving for all people, for the king and all who are in power", showing that on account of this, "we will lead a peaceful and quiet life, godly and pure in every way", and that "this is good and pleasing in the sight of God our Savior" (1 Tim. 2:1–3). Having given us this instruction,[540] then, he indicates that this is God's desire by saying that he "desires all people to be saved and to come to the knowledge of the truth" (1 Tim. 2:1–4). Likewise, speaking of God's desire and will, he relates it to Christ, for he follows by saying that[541] "there is one God, and there is one mediator" before God the Father, Jesus Christ, for our salvation[542] (1 Tim. 2:5–6). And regarding the nature of Christ's mediatory role,

537 And after saying, "And there is one mediator between God and men, the man Jesus Christ", the Apostle immediately specified,] Now, the Apostle consistently said, "And there is one mediator between God and men, the man Jesus Christ", and immediately specified,

538 *MS 61 adds*: **Showing that the Apostles spoke of Jesus Christ as a man, because the Son of God became incarnate and lived as a man. God did not live among men on this earth as a phantom. Instead, God truly became man.**

539 And he himself clearly shows his own deception and law-breaking] And he himself shows his own law-breaking and deception

540 instruction] instruction and commandment,

541 for he follows up, saying that] for after making this statement, he says that

542 for our salvation] for the salvation of men

далъ еⷭ҇ себе самого избавление за всѣⷯ. еже
есть распатие и смр҃ть пострадавъ за наⷭ҇
іⷭ҇ъ хⷭ҇ъ. и понеⷤ бг҃ꙋ пострадаⷮ҇ невозможно.
93v/221 сн҃ъ же бж҃іи бг҃ъ еⷭ҇. емꙋⷤ аще не въ плоⷮ ѡбоⷧ҇кшꙋⷭ҇
невозможно пострадати емꙋ бг҃ꙋ сꙋщꙋ. сеⷢ҇
раⷣ҇ быⷭ҇ слово плоⷮ іⷭ҇ъ хⷭ҇ъ пришеⷣ во плоти даде
себе избавление за всѣⷯ. крⷭ҇тъ и смр҃ть при
емъ избави насъ воскрⷭ҇ниемъ своимъ. ибо не
возможно простꙋ чл҃кꙋ избавиⷮ҇ всѣхъ ѿ грѣ
ха и ѿ смр҃ти. всѣ бо поⷣ грѣхоⷨ бѣша и пови
нни. единъ іⷭ҇ъ хⷭ҇ъ пришедыи во плоти тои
бо грѣха не сотвори ниⷤ ѡбрѣтеⷭ҇ леⷭ҇ во ꙋстѣⷯ
его. тои бо грѣха не сотвори. тои послꙋшлиⷡ҇
бг҃ꙋ ѿц҃ꙋ. смр҃тию и крⷭ҇томъ и всю волю бж҃ию
сотворивъ. избави насъ ѿ престꙋпленіа и
клꙗтвы. и смр҃ть попра. невозможно бо
чл҃кꙋ простꙋ дати себе во избавꙋ за всѣхъ.
всꙗⷦ҇ бо чл҃къ ложь по пррⷪ҇кꙋ. едиⷩ҇ неповиненъ
гⷭ҇ь іⷭ҇ъ хⷭ҇ъ. могіи избавити всѣⷯ собою даⷡ҇
себе за всѣхъ. беⷥгрѣшенъ сыи. Ꙗко хⷭ҇ъ и
скони бг҃ъ еⷭ҇ преⷤ вѣкъ сыи. и послѣⷣ воплотиⷭ҇.
заⷤе сп҃ти насъ. А ꙗко бг҃ъ еⷭ҇ искони іⷭ҇ъ хⷭ҇ъ
а не по восхищению быⷭ҇ бг҃ъ іⷭ҇ъ х҃с. но прнⷭ҇о бг҃ъ
сыи х҃с. и смири себе за млⷭ҇рдие во плоти. во
лею сниде. вⷧ҇ка сыи ѡбраⷥ рабіи приꙗти. ꙗкоⷤ
94r/222 и апⷭ҇лъ павеⷧ сказоуа пишеⷮ ѳилиписеѡⷨ гл҃ꙗ. сеⷤ

he says that he "gave himself as a deliverance for all" (1 Tim. 2:6), which is the crucifixion and death that Jesus Christ suffered for us.[543]

43.6. And since it is impossible for God to undergo suffering, | it was also 93^{v}/221
impossible for the divine Son of God to suffer other than by clothing himself in flesh, given that he is God by nature. For that reason, the "Word became flesh" (Jn. 1:14); Jesus Christ came in the flesh, "gave himself for the deliverance of all", accepted the cross and death, delivering us through his own resurrection. For it is impossible for a mere man to deliver all from sin and from death. For all men are under sin and guilty (Rom. 3:19, 23). Jesus Christ, who came in the flesh, alone "committed no sin, nor was any deceit found in his mouth" (1 Pet. 2:22). He "was obedient" to God the Father "to the point of death, even death on a cross" (Phil. 2:8). And having fulfilled the entire will of God, he delivered us from our transgressions and curse, and conquered death[544] (2 Tim. 1:10). For it is impossible for a mere man to give himself for the deliverance of all, because "everyone is a liar", according to the Prophet (Ps. 116:11). Jesus Christ alone, being without guilt, was able to deliver all men through himself;[545] and being without sin, he gave himself for all.

44. Showing that Christ was God in the very beginning, before all ages; and afterward, he became incarnate in order to save us.[546]

44.1. And we have it as a fact that Jesus Christ was God from the very beginning. Jesus Christ did not count divinity as something "to be grasped" (Phil. 2:6), but rather, Christ was always God.[547] And in his compassion, he "humbled himself" in the flesh (Phil. 2:8). Being sovereign Lord, he was willing to come down
in order to take the form of a servant. | The Apostle Paul teaches this when he 94^{r}/222

543 *MS 61 adds*: **Showing that Christ, the Son of God, was God before all ages; and afterward, he became incarnate in order to save us.**

544 conquered death] abolished death and sin

545 through himself] *omitted*

546 **Showing that Christ was God in the very beginning, before all ages; and afterward, he became incarnate in order to save us.**] *omitted*

547 And the fact is that Jesus Christ was God from the very beginning. Jesus Christ did not count divinity as something "to be grasped" (Phil. 2:6), but rather Christ was always God.] And being God from the very beginning, Jesus Christ did not become God in a new way, nor did he count divinity as something "to be grasped" (Phil. 2:6). And upon becoming man, Christ did not "empty" himself of divinity, but always remained God (Phil. 2:7).

да мⷣръствоуетсѧ в васъ ⷤе ѡ хⷭѣ іⷭѣ иже во зраць бж҃ии сыи. не восхищениⷨе непщева быти равенъ бг҃оу. но себе излїа зракъ раба приемъ в подобїи чл҃честѣ бывъ. и ѡбразоⷨ ѡбрѣтеⷭ ꙗко чл҃къ смири себе. бывъ послоушливъ до смр҃ти смр҃тиⷤ крⷭтоу. Видите ли истинноу гл҃ахъ. ꙗко сеⷢ ради хⷭа чл҃ка реⷱ апⷭлъ. плоти раⷣ. и понеⷤ даде себе избавление за всѣⷯ не проста чл҃ка назнаменано и бг҃а. ходатаиства раⷣ бг҃оу и чл҃комъ. ꙗко ст҃лꙗ нареⷱ чл҃ка іⷭа хⷭа. избавлениꙗⷤ ради всѣⷯ показа хⷭа бг҃а сꙋща. ⷭе оубо хⷭво имꙗ на бжⷭтво приемлемо апⷭлы. іⷭсово имѧ на чл҃чество. и понеⷤ гл҃ати апⷭлоу ст҃льство хⷭво еже ⷭе ходатаиство бг҃оу и чл҃комъ. чл҃ка реⷱ іⷭа. и хⷭа коупно именовавъ. раⷣ всѣхъ избавленїа ꙗви хⷭа бг҃а. ⷤе и бг҃ословъ іѡⷩа в посланїи своеⷨ сказоуѧ гл҃ꙗ. Ꙗко бг҃ъ любы ⷭе. ѡ семъ ꙗвиⷭ любы бж҃їа в насъ. ꙗко сн҃а своеⷢ единороⷣнаⷢ посла бг҃ъ в миръ. да живеⷨ ѡ немъ. ѡ семъ ⷭе любы. не ꙗко мы возлюбихоⷨ бг҃а но ꙗко тӧ возлюби насъ. и посла сн҃а своеⷢ ѡчищеⷩе ѡ грѣсеⷯ нш҃иⷯ.
94v/223 Такоⷤ и к римлꙗноⷨ пишеⷮ павелъ. не токмо тимоѳею чл҃ка нарицаѧ іⷭа хⷭа. но к римлꙗноⷨ пиша преⷤ ꙗви. іⷭа хⷭа сн҃а бж҃їа по плоти ѿ дв҃да пришеⷣша. таⷤ чл҃ка гл҃еⷮ хⷭа. таⷣ и наⷣ всѣми бг҃а гл҃еⷮ хⷭа. пишеⷮ бо в началѣ посланїа. Павеⷧ іⷭъ хⷭвъ зваⷩ апⷭлъ. избраⷩ въ бл҃говѣстие бж҃їе. ⷤе преже ѡбѣща прⷪрки своими. в писанїиⷯ ст҃ыⷯ ѡ сн҃ѣ своеⷨ. бывшемъ ѿ сѣмени дв҃дова по плоти. нареченаⷢ сн҃а бж҃їа в силѣ.

writes to the Philippians, saying,[548] "Let this mind be in you, which was also in Christ Jesus, who being in the form of God, did not count equality with God something to be grasped, but emptied himself by taking the form of a servant, being made in the likeness of men. And being found in human form, he humbled himself by becoming obedient to the point of death, even death on a cross" (Phil. 2:5–8).

44.2. Don't you see that I am telling the truth, that it was on account of Christ becoming man, and on account of the flesh, and because of his giving himself for the deliverance of all, that the Apostle said this, indicating that (Christ) was not a mere man, but also God? For on account of the mediating role between God and men, the Apostle calls the man Jesus Christ a "High Priest" (Cf. Heb. 3:2). And on account of the "deliverance for all", he showed Christ to be God. Thus, the Apostles[549] applied the name "Christ" for divinity, and the name "Jesus" for humanity. And since the Apostle needs to speak of Christ as a "High Priest", which is his mediating role between God and men, he speaks of him in human terms as "Jesus".[550] And when he simultaneously calls him "Christ", he does so in view of the "deliverance for all", revealing Christ as God.

44.3. And John the Theologian in his Epistle says the same when he states that "God is love. In this, the love of God was made manifest among us, that God sent his only Son into the world so that we may live through him. In this is love, not that we have loved God but that he loved us and sent his Son to be the cleansing of our sins" (1Jn. 4:8–10). | 94ᵛ/223

44.4. Paul writes similarly to the Romans, (as he shows) that he called Jesus Christ "man", not only in (writing) to Timothy but also in his writing to the Romans, revealing first of all that Jesus Christ, the Son of God, came "from David[551] according to the flesh" (Rom. 1:3). Just as he speaks of Christ as "man", so he also speaks of Christ as God, who is above all things. For he writes at the beginning of his Epistle, "Paul, ⟨a servant⟩ of Jesus Christ, called to be an Apostle, chosen for the good news of God, which he promised beforehand through his Prophets in the sacred Scriptures, concerning his Son, who was from the seed of David according to the flesh, and was named the Son of God in power

548 himself" in flesh (Phil. 2:8). Being sovereign Lord, he was willing to come down in order to take the form of a servant. The Apostle Paul teaches (this), when he writes to the Philippians, saying,] himself", with mercy (Phil. 2:8). Being willing to come down, he clothed himself in flesh. Being sovereign Lord, he took the form of a servant, as the Apostle Paul teaches in Philippians, when he writes as follows:

549 Thus, the Apostles] We can recognize, then, that the Apostles

550 he speaks of him in human terms as "Jesus".] he reveals him as a human, saying "Jesus".

551 David] the seed of David

по дх҃ꙋ ст҃на. и̑ воскр҃шенїа мртвыͯ. ї҃са х҃а
г҃а н҃шего. имж͛ приѧхо͛ блгть. и ап҃льство
в послꙋшание вѣры во всѣ ѧзыцѣͯ ѡ имени
его. в нихж͛ есте и вызвани ї҃сꙋ х҃ꙋ всѣмъ
сꙋщи͛ в римѣ. возлюблены͛ бг҃ꙋ. званы͛ ст҃ы.
блгть вамъ и миръ ѿ бг҃а ѿц҃а н҃шего и г҃а ї҃са х҃а.
Показоуе͛ павелъ х҃а многими глы бг҃а сꙋща.
блгть бо глѣ приѧ͛ посланїа в послꙋшание вѣ
ры. во всѣ ѧзыцѣͯ ѡ имени х҃вѣ. и аще не бѣ
бг҃ъ х҃съ како блгть послание в вѣрꙋ х҃вꙋ всѣ͛
ѧзыко͛ глеть. и аще ѡ имени ї҃съ х҃вѣ вѣра
проповѣдаетсѧ. оубо бг҃ъ е͛ х҃съ. не просто͛
проповѣдаетсѧ вѣра во имѧ ї҃съ х҃во. но прѣ͛
95r/224 ѡбѣщанны͛ благовѣстие͛ бж҃їимъ пррки е͛. в пи
санїи ст҃ы͛ ѡ сн҃ѣ бж҃ие͛ проповѣдаетсѧ. и блго
да͛ имъ дарꙋе͛ и миръ ѿ бг҃а ѿц҃а и г҃а ї҃са х҃а. кꙋпно
и нераздѣлно. сказꙋа и̑ ї҃са х҃а равна бг҃ꙋ ѿц҃ꙋ.
еди͛ бо миръ и единꙋ блгть. и вкꙋпѣ ѿ бг҃а ѿц҃а.
и ѿ г҃а ї҃са х҃а подавъ. не главъ ѿ бг҃а бо͛ша и ѿ бг҃а
ме͛ша. но то͛ и едино бг҃а ѿц҃а и г҃а ї҃са х҃а. блгть
и миръ. И паки глѣ. нн҃ѣ кромѣ закона пра
вда бж҃їа ѧви͛. свидѣтествꙋема ѿ закона
и пррк. правда͛ бж҃їа вѣрою ї҃съ х҃вою во всѧ
и на всѧ вѣрꙋющаѧ. нѣ͛ бо разньствїа. всѣ
бо согрѣшиша и лишаютсѧ славы бж҃їа. ѡ пра
вдающе͛ тꙋне. того блгтию избавлениемъ
е͛ ѡ х҃ѣ ї҃сѣ. его͛ прѣположи бг҃ъ ѡчищение вѣ
рою и кровию е͛. въ ѧвление правды е͛. за ѿ
пꙋщение прѣ͛ бывши͛ грѣховъ. Ѩко никто͛

according to the Spirit of holiness by his resurrection from the dead, Jesus Christ our Lord, through whom we received grace and apostleship[552] to bring about the obedience of faith for the sake of his name among all the nations; and this includes you, who are called to belong to Jesus Christ. (Indeed), to all those in Rome, who are loved by God and called to be saints: Grace to you and peace from God our Father and the Lord Jesus Christ" (Rom. 1:1–7).

44.5. Paul shows Christ to be God in numerous statements. For he says that "we received" "the mission to bring about the obedience of faith for the sake of his name among all the nations" (Rom. 1:5). And if Christ were not God, how would ⟨Paul⟩ speak of "grace and[553] mission to bring" "all the nations" to "faith" in Christ? And if faith is preached through the name of Jesus Christ, then Christ is God. And not only is faith preached in the name of Jesus Christ. But | also, the 95ʳ/224
Son of God is preached, "who is promised beforehand through his Prophets in the sacred Scriptures" (Rom. 1:2). And he sends them "grace" and "peace" from God the Father and the Lord Jesus Christ, simultaneously and without separation, speaking to them about the Lord Jesus Christ as being equal to God the Father. For he greeted[554] them speaking of one single "peace" and one single "grace" coming simultaneously from God the Father and from the Lord Jesus Christ. He did not say that "grace" and "peace" from "God" were greater, while from the ⟨"Lord"⟩[555] they were lesser, but that they were one and the same from God the Father and from the Lord Jesus Christ.

44.6. And, again, he says,[556] "But now apart from the Law, the righteousness of God has been manifested, (as a righteousness) to which the Law and the Prophets testify, the righteousness of God through faith in Jesus Christ for all and upon all who believe. For there is no distinction, because all have sinned and fall short of the glory of God, and are justified by his grace as a gift, through the deliverance that is in Christ Jesus, whom God put forward as a cleansing by his blood, and[557] through faith. This was to show his righteousness because of the forgiveness of sins that were formerly committed" (Rom. 3:21–25).

552 apostleship] mission of being sent

553 "grace and] *omitted*

554 greeted] *omitted*

555 ⟨"Lord"⟩] *the reading in* MS *337 is* "God"

556 *MS 61 adds*: **Showing that no one can justify sinful humanity, except for the one who is himself sinless.**

557 and] *omitted*

бе̑грѣшенъ. токмо бг҃ъ единъ. Видитеⷭ҇
апⷭ҇ла проповѣдающа хⷭ҇а бг҃а вочл҃чьшаⷭ҇. гл҃еⷮ бо
правдꙋ бж҃ию быти вѣрою іⷭ҇съ хⷭ҇вою. вѣраⷤ
къ бг҃ꙋ а не къ чл҃кꙋ гл҃еть писание. сꙋетно спⷭ҇се
ние чл҃ческо ѡ бз҃ѣ сотвориⷨ силꙋ. се самое
апⷭ҇лъ гл҃еть бг҃а хⷭ҇а сказꙋа. правда бж҃їа реⷱ
вѣрою іⷭ҇съ хⷭ҇вою. и ѡправдаемса тꙋне тоⷢ
95v/226 бл҃гтию. избавлениемъ еⷤ ѡ хⷭ҇ѣ іⷭ҇сѣ. ѡпра
вдатиⷤ и избавлıати бж҃ие еⷭ҇ а не чл҃ческо. по
неⷤ ѡ чл҃коⷯ гл҃еⷮ. нѣⷭ҇ бо раньствїа. вси бо согрѣ
шиша. и лишаются славы бж҃їа. согрѣши
вшимиⷤ и лишеными славы бж҃иа ѡправда
тиⷭ҇ невозможно. ниⷤ избавлению быти+[558] ѿ
согрѣшившаⷢ. но бе̑грѣшномꙋ дати са еⷭ҇. за
всѣⷯ избавление. бе̑грѣшенъⷤ никтоⷤ точию
единъ бг҃ъ. к немоⷤу ни едина мꙋка прикоснꙋ
тиⷭ҇ може҄ⷮ. **Ӕко невозможно чл҃чество со
грѣшившее ѡправдаⷮ никомꙋ. токмо еди
номꙋ самомꙋ бе̑грѣшномꙋ. П**редатиⷤ
себе за избавление повинныⷯ. неповинно
мꙋ подобаеⷮ. ктоⷤ ꙋбо неповиненъ развѣ бг҃ъ
единъ. преданиеⷤ во избавꙋ нѣⷭ҇ инако аще
мꙋкꙋ токмо претерпѣти. неповинномꙋ
за повинныа. тогда бо повинныⷯ всѣⷯ ѿ
вины избавиⷮ мꙋченїа. егда неповинномꙋ
мꙋки за всѣⷯ приıати бꙋдеⷮ. ıако праведеⷩ
гьⷭ҇ и правдꙋ возлюби. сеⷢ раⷣ приде во плоти
іⷭ҇съ хⷭ҇съ. да не повинныи своею смртию всѣⷯ
96r/227 повинныⷯ избавиⷮ. понеⷤ къ бг҃ꙋ мꙋка и смрть при
ближитиⷭ҇ не можеⷮ. тѣмже посла бг҃ъ сн҃а своеⷢ
ражающаⷭ҇ въ чл҃чествѣ. да по чл҃чествꙋ пострa
давъ мꙋкꙋ и смрть неповинныи сн҃ъ бж҃їи.
и сн҃ъ чл҃ческїи. всѣⷯ избавиⷮ повинныⷯ. **П**аки гл҃еⷮ

558 *In the margin*: + возможно всѣⷯ.

45. Showing that no one is without sin, except for God alone.[559]

45.1. Don't you see that the Apostle is proclaiming Christ as God who became man? For he speaks of "the righteousness of God through faith in Jesus Christ". And the subject of faith is God, not man, ⟨for⟩ the Scripture says, "human salvation is worthless, in God we will gain strength" (Ps. 60:11–12). The Apostle says the same thing when he speaks of Christ as God: "the righteousness of God", he
said, | (is manifested) "through faith in Jesus Christ", and "we are justified by his 95^{v}/226
grace as a gift, through the deliverance that is in Christ Jesus" (Rom. 3:22, 24).

45.2. But "justifying" and "bringing deliverance" belong to God, and not man. For that reason, he says about humans, "there is no distinction: for all have sinned and fall short of the glory of God" (Rom. 3:23). And it is impossible to become "justified" through those who "have sinned and fallen short of the glory of God", nor is it possible to have "deliverance for all"[560] from the one who sinned.[561] Instead, the "deliverance for all" must be done by one who is sinless. And no one is without sin except for God alone, whom no affliction can touch.

46. Showing that no one can justify sinful humanity, except for the one who is himself sinless.[562]

46.1. And to deliver those who are guilty, one must be without any guilt. But who, then, is without guilt but God alone? And there is no other way to give oneself "for the deliverance (of all)", but to undergo the punishment for those who are guilty, by the one who is without guilt. When the one who is without guilt takes the punishment for all, then all those who are guilty will be delivered from the punishment of guilt. On that account, Jesus Christ, who is the righteous Lord and who loved righteousness, comes in the flesh so that through
his death, he who is without guilt, | may deliver all those who are guilty. And 96^{r}/227
because affliction and death cannot approach God, therefore, God sent his own Son to be born as a man so that he may suffer affliction and death according to humanity, and being[563] without guilt, the Son of God and Son of man, may deliver all who are under guilt.

---

559 **Showing that no one is without sin, except for God alone.**] *omitted*

560 "deliverance for all"] *MS 337 places this reading in the margin.*

561 *MS 61 adds*: **Showing that no one is without sin, except for God alone.**

562 **Showing that no one can justify the sinful humanity, except for the one who is himself sinless.**] *omitted*

563 being] alone being

апⷭ҇лъ. составлıаетⷤ҇+[564] любовь в насъ бг҃ъ. ıако и еще грѣшникоⷨ҇ сꙋщимъ наⷨ҇ хⷭ҇ъ за ны оумре много ꙋбо паⷱ҇ ѡправдившеⷭ҇ нн҃ѣ кровию еⷢ҇. сп҃семса имъ ѿ гнѣва. аще бо врази сꙋще примирихомса къ бг҃ꙋ смр҃тию сн҃а еⷢ҇. мноⷢ҇ паче премѣⷩ҇шеса сп҃семса в животѣ его не точиюⷨ҇ но и хвалимса ѡ бз҃ѣ. гⷭ҇ѣ нш҃емъ ıс҃ъ хм҃ъ. им же нн҃ѣ измѣнение приıахоⷨ҇ сеⷢ҇ ради ıакоⷤ҇ единѣмъ чл҃комъ грѣⷯ҇ в миръ вниде. и грѣхомъ смр҃ть. и тако во вса чл҃ки смр҃ть вниде. ѡ немⷤ҇ вси согрѣшиша. до закона бо грѣⷯ҇ бѣ в мирѣ. грѣхⷤ҇ не вмѣ нашеⷭ҇ не сꙋщꙋ законꙋ. но црⷭ҇твова смр҃ть ѿ адама даⷤ҇ и до моисеа. и на несогрѣшшиⷯ҇. по подобию престꙋпленıа адамова. иⷤ҇ есть ѡбраⷥ҇ градꙋщаⷢ҇. но не ıакоⷤ҇ престꙋпление такои даръ. аще бо единоⷢ҇ прегрѣшениⷨ҇ 96^{v}/228 мнози оумроша. много паⷱ҇ бл҃гть бж҃ıа и даръ. бл҃гтию единоⷢ҇ чл҃ка ıс҃ъ хⷭ҇а. во многиⷯ҇ избысть. видисте ли апⷭ҇лъ преⷤ҇ бг҃а показавъ хⷭ҇а гл҃ıа. но и хвалимса ѡ бз҃ѣ гм҃ъ нш҃имъ ıс҃ъ хм҃ъ. имⷤ҇ нн҃ѣ измѣнение приıахоⷨ҇. таⷤ҇ потомъ чл҃ка еⷢ҇ рече. гл҃ıа аще ꙋбо единоⷢ҇ прегрѣшениⷨ҇ мнози оумроша. много паⷱ҇ бл҃гть бж҃иа и даръ бл҃гтию единоⷢ҇ чл҃ка ıс҃а хⷭ҇а. во многиⷯ҇ избыса. по послѣдованию слова. и имıа емꙋ примаа во всеⷨ҇ проповѣдаеⷮ҇ его бг҃а вочл҃чьшаⷭ҇. и томꙋ единомꙋ избавити всѣⷯ҇. понеже ѿ адама црⷭ҇твова смр҃ть и на несогрѣшьшиⷯ҇. по пⷣобию престꙋпленıа адамова. хⷭ҇ъⷤ҇ правдꙋ сотворивъ ѡсꙋжение послꙋшаниⷨ҇ оупразнивъ. реⷱ҇ бо апⷭ҇лъ по сиⷯ҇. да ıакоⷤ҇ црⷭ҇твова грѣⷯ҇ смр҃тию тако и бл҃гть воцр҃итса правдою в жизнь вѣчнꙋю. исоуⷭ҇ хм҃ъ гм҃ъ нш҃имъ. Смотритеⷤ҇ и паки апⷭ҇ла проповѣдающа бг҃а во плоти хⷭ҇а. гл҃еть оубо по сиⷯ҇. молıаⷯ҇ бо сıа самъ аⷥ҇ ѿлꙋченъ быти ѿ хⷭ҇а по братıи моеи срⷣ҇никъ моиⷯ҇ по плоⷮ҇ иⷤ҇ сꙋть ıильте. им же вс҃нение слова и завѣⷮ҇

564 *In the margin*: + свою.

46.2. Again, the Apostle says, "but God shows his[565] love for us in that while we were still sinners, Christ died for us. Having thus been justified by his blood, how much more will we be saved by him from the wrath (of God)? For if, while we were enemies, we were reconciled[566] to God by the death of his Son, much more, having been restored, will we be saved by his life. Not only that, but we also boast in God through our Lord Jesus Christ, through whom we have now received transformation. Therefore, just as sin entered the world through one man, and death through sin, and thus death came to all men, because in him all sinned—for sin was in the world before the Law, but[567] sin is not counted where there is no Law. Yet death reigned from Adam to Moses, even over those who did not sin with a transgression like that of Adam, who was a type of the one who was to come. But the gift is not like the trespass. For if many died by the trespass | of the one man, the grace of God and the gift by the grace of that 96ᵛ/228
one man, Jesus Christ, has abounded far more for many" (Roman 5:8–15).

46.3. Didn't you see[568] that the Apostle first showed Christ to be God, saying, "but we also boast in God through our Lord Jesus Christ, through whom we have now received transformation" (Rom. 5:11), and afterward, he also spoke of him as man, saying, "For if many died by the trespass of the one man, much more have the grace of God and the gift by the grace of that one man, Jesus Christ, abounded for many" (Roman 5:15)? Depending on what he speaks about, he assigns the (appropriate) name, always proclaiming him to be God incarnate and the one who delivered all men. Since "death reigned from Adam to Moses, even over those who did not sin with a transgression like that of Adam" (Rom. 5:14), Christ accomplished the righteous act, abolishing the condemnation through his obedience[569] (Cf. Roman 5:19). For after this, the Apostle said, "Just as sin reigned in death, so also grace may reign through righteousness leading to eternal life through Jesus Christ, our Lord" (Rom. 5:21).

46.4. See how the Apostle repeatedly proclaims Christ as God in the flesh! Now, after this, he says:[570] "For I pleaded that I myself might be accursed and cut off from Christ for the sake of my brothers, my kinsmen according to the flesh. They are Israelites, and to them belong the adoption, and the glory, and

---

565 his] *MS 337 places this reading in the margin.*

566 reconciled] restored

567 but] for

568 Didn't you see] Don't you see

569 abolishing the condemnation through his obedience] abolishing the condemnation for disobedience through his obedience

570 *MS 61 adds*: **Showing that the Son of God became man in order to justify humankind, for he alone is without sin, while no man is sinless.**

и законоположенїа. и слоуженїа ѡбѣтоваⷩа҇.
97r/229 имⷤ ѿцы и ѿ нихⷤ хⷭ҇ъ по плоти сыи наⷣ всѣми
бг҃ъ блⷭвенъ во вѣки амиⷩ. Оубо познастеⷭ҇
косоⷣ беⷥбжествие. ꙗко прочитаⷮе апⷭла павла
ре҇ние ѡноⷤ е едиⷩ бо е бг҃ъ и едиⷩ ходатаи бг҃оу и чл҃коⷨ
чл҃къ іс҃ъ хс҃. почтоⷤ не прочитаⷮе сего. ⷤе ѿцы
ѿ нихⷤ по плоти сыи наⷣ всѣми бг҃ъ блⷭвенъ
въ вѣки аминь. ꙗкоⷤ бо к тимоѳѣю апⷭлово
послание ѡно. такоⷤ тогоⷤ апⷭла и к римлꙗноⷨ
сїе писание. Паки апⷭлъ пишеⷮ к нимⷤ. мо
гоущемоу васъ оутвердити по бл҃говѣство
ванию моемоу. и проповѣданию іс҃ъ хв҃оу. по
ѿкровению таины. лѣты вѣчными оумоⷧ҇
чаннѣи. ꙗвльшиⷤся нн҃ѣ писанми прⷪ҇рческиⷨ.
по повелѣнию вѣчнаⷢ бг҃а. в послоушание вѣры.
во всѣⷯ ꙗзыцѣⷯ познавшися. единѣмъ пре
мⷣрымъ бг҃омъ іс҃ъ хм҃ъ. емоуⷤ слава во вѣки
амиⷩ. Видите бг҃а сказоуⷮе хⷭ҇а несотворе
на ѿкровено апⷭлъ. невозможноⷤ сотворе
номоу наⷣ всѣми бг҃оу быти. и единомоу премⷣро
моу бг҃оу быти. аще не ествоⷨ бг҃ъ боудеⷮ. хⷭ҇а же
апⷭлъ наⷣ всѣми бг҃а проповѣдаⷮе. и единоⷢ его
премⷣраго бг҃а. тѣмже хⷭ҇ъ бг҃ъ ествомъ е.
97v/231 а не сотвореⷩ бг҃ъ хⷭ҇ъ. Пишетⷭ и к коринѳоⷨ.

the covenants, and the giving of the Law, and the worship, and the promises. | To 97r/229
them belong the patriarchs, and from them, according to the flesh, is the Christ, who is God over all, blessed forever. Amen" (Rom. 9:3–5). Don't you recognize, then, the godlessness of Kosoy? In reading this statement from the Apostle Paul, "For there is one God, and there is one mediator between God and men, the man Jesus Christ" (1 Tim. 2:5), why does he not read this other passage that "from them, according to the flesh, is the Christ, who is God over all, blessed forever. Amen" (Rom. 9:5)? For the Apostle's Epistle to Timothy belongs to the same Apostle who wrote these words in Romans.[571]

46.5. Again, the Apostle writes to the same recipient,[572] "And to him who is able to establish you according to my Good News and the preaching of Jesus Christ, according to the revelation of the mystery, which has been kept secret through the ages of time, but now is revealed, and by the Scriptures of the Prophets, according to the commandment of the eternal God, is made known for the obedience of faith to all the nations; to the only supremely wise God, through Jesus Christ, to whom be the glory to the ages.[573] Amen" (Rom. 14:24–26). You see how the Apostle Paul is openly speaking[574] of Christ as God uncreated?

46.6. And it is impossible[575] for God, who is "over all" (Rom. 9:5), to be created; and he cannot be the "only supremely wise God" if he is not God by nature (Rom. 14:26). But the Apostle is preaching Christ as God, who is "over all" and the "only supremely wise God" (Rom. 9:5; 14:26). Therefore, Christ is God by nature, | and being God, Christ is not created.[576] And to the Corinthians, he 97v/231

571 In reading this statement from the Apostle Paul, "For there is one God, and there is one mediator between God and men, the man Jesus Christ" (1 Tim. 2:5), why does he not read this other passage that "from them, according to the flesh, is the Christ, who is God over all, blessed forever. Amen" (Rom. 9:5)? For the Apostle's Epistle to Timothy belongs to the same Apostle who wrote these words in Romans.] And just as the words, "there is one mediator between God and men, the man Jesus Christ" (1 Tim. 2:5) come from the Apostle's Epistle to Timothy, so do the words in Romans belong to the same Apostle, "They are Israelites, and to them belong the adoption, and the glory, and the covenants, and the giving of the Law, and the worship, and the promises. To them belong the patriarchs, and from them, according to the flesh, is the Christ, who is God over all, blessed forever. Amen" (Rom. 9:4–5).

572 *MS 61 adds*: **Showing that Jesus Christ is not made, but begotten from God the Father before all ages, and his flesh was created in the Virgin's womb.**

573 to the ages,] to the ages of ages,

574 You see how the Apostle Paul is openly speaking] Don't you see here, then, that the Apostle Paul is proclaiming the blessings and speaking

575 And it is impossible] For how is it possible

576 and being God, Christ is not created.] Christ is not created, but is God.

гл҃емъ премⷬ҇ость бж҃ию в таинѣ съкровеⷩ҇нꙋ. ꙗⷤ҇ пронарⷭ҇е бг҃ъ прⷤ҇е вѣкъ в славꙋ нш҃ꙋ. еꙗⷤ҇ ни ктоже ѿ кн҃зь вѣка сⷭ҇е разоумѣ. аще бо быша разꙋмѣли не быша гⷭ҇а славѣ распали. ктⷤ҇о ꙋбо можⷭ҇е сотворенъ гⷭ҇ь славѣ быти. аще не ⷭ҇естⷨ҇во истинныи бг҃ъ точию. Паки к нимⷤ҇ъ пишⷮ҇е. Вѣмы ꙗко ни единъ идолъ в мирѣ. и ꙗко никтⷤ҇о бг҃ъ инъ. токмо едⷩ҇и. ибо аще и сꙋть гл҃емїи бз҃и. ли на нб҃си ли на земли. ꙗкⷤ҇о сꙋть бози мнози и гдⷭ҇їе мнози. но намъ единъ бг҃ъ ѿц҃ъ. из негⷤ҇о вса и мы оу нⷭ҇е едⷩ҇и гⷭ҇ь ї҃съ х҃с. имⷤ҇ъ вса и мы тѣмъ. Слышасте апⷭ҇ла проповѣдающа единⷭ҇о бг҃а ѿц҃а. из негⷤ҇о вса. и единⷭ҇о гⷭ҇а ї҃са хⷭ҇а им же вса. тѣмже нⷭ҇ѣ сотворенъ бг҃ъ гⷭ҇ь ї҃съ хⷭ҇ъ. понⷤ҇е вса тѣмъ быша тои вса сотвори имⷤ҇ъ вса быша рⷭ҇е. то ꙋⷡ҇ по безꙋмию косⷭ҇о аще сотворенъ хⷭ҇ъ. сⷨ҇а себе сотворⷩ҇и ⷭ҇е хⷭ҇съ. глⷮ҇е бо бг҃ословъ їⷩ҇ѡа въ еѵⷭ҇алїи вса тⷨ҇ѣ быша. и без нⷭ҇е ничтⷤ҇о бⷭ҇ы еже бⷭ҇ы. сие и павⷭ҇е глⷮ҇е единъ гⷭ҇ь ї҃съ хⷭ҇съ иⷨ҇ же вса и мы тѣмъ. творца оубо всемꙋ хⷭ҇а апⷭ҇ли проповѣдаша. 98ʳ/232 а не самⷭ҇о хⷭ҇а сотворена. аще и рекоша гдѣ хⷭ҇а чл҃ка истинⷩ҇ою въчл҃чение ⷭ҇е проповѣдаша. а не мнинⷨ҇е ни привидⷨ҇ѣние чл҃ка бывша. и понⷤ҇е часта крⷭ҇тъ и кровь и смрⷭ҇ть ⷭ҇е проповѣдахꙋ. тогда и чл҃ка его глахꙋ. понⷤ҇е пострадати ⷭ҇е чл҃кꙋ а не бгꙋ. внегдаⷤ҇ кромѣ крⷭ҇та writes, too, "We declare God's wisdom, hidden in mystery, which God decreed before the ages for our glory. None of the rulers of this age understood this, for if they had understood, they would not have crucified the Lord of glory" (1 Cor. 2:7–8). Who of the created beings can, then, be the "Lord of glory", except for the true God alone who is such by nature? Again, he[577] writes to them, "We know that 'an idol is nothing at all in the world' and that 'there is no God but one'. For even if there are so-called gods, whether in heaven or on earth—as indeed there are many 'gods' and many 'lords'—yet for us, there is but one God, the Father, from whom are all things and with whom we are; and there is but one Lord, Jesus Christ, through whom are all things and through whom we are" (1 Cor. 8:4–6).

46.7. Did you hear[578] how the Apostle Paul preached "one God, the Father, from whom are all things", and "one Lord, Jesus Christ, through whom are all things" (1 Cor. 8:6)? Therefore, the Lord, Jesus Christ, being God,[579] is not created. If all things come into being "through" him, then he also made all of them, as it is said, "through him, all things were made" (Jn. 1:3). Consequently, if Christ is made, according to the insanity of Kosoy, then Christ had to make his own being through himself. For John the Theologian says[580] in the Gospel, "All things were made through him, and without him, nothing was made that was made" (Jn. 1:3). And Paul says the same thing, "there is but one Lord, Jesus Christ, through whom are all things and through whom we are" (1 Cor. 8:6). The Apostles, then, preached that Christ was Maker of all things, | and not that 98r/232
Christ himself was made.

46.8. And when they did say in some places that Christ was man, they preached that he truly became human, and not that Christ was made man (simply) in thought, or as an illusion.[581] And since they often preached about the cross and blood and his death, they naturally spoke of him in human terms.[582] For suffering is proper to man, and not to God.[583] And when they[584] did not

577 he] Apostle
578 Did you hear] Didn't you hear
579 being God] being Lord and God
580 says] says, too
581 illusion.] illusion, as those lost Manichees are falsely saying against Christ.
582 And since they often preached about the cross and blood and his death, they naturally spoke of him in human terms.] And since the Apostles often preached about the cross and blood and his death—through which Christ accomplished for us salvation—and since the Apostles speak about the Savior's passion, so they spoke of Christ in human terms.
583 For suffering is proper to man, and not to God.] Since it is man, and not God, who is capable of suffering, God, that is Christ, truly became human.
584 they] the Apostles

и смⷬ҇ти гл҃ати иⷨ҇ ѡ х҃ѣ. тогда бг҃а истинн҃а проповѣдоваху его. сеⷢ҇ ради и петръ верховныи. їюдѣа наказываа реⷱ҇ ꙗко ї га҃ и ха҃ еⷭ҇ бг҃ъ сотвори се ї҃са его вы распꙗсте. подобаеⷮ҇ бо июдѣа научити первие ѡно. ꙗко пострадавыи ѿ ниⷯ҇ распатие тои еⷭ҇ пронареченныи гь҃ їс҃ и хс҃. рече сотвори еⷭ҇ бг҃ъ и г҃а и х҃а. поне слышати тꙗко июдѣѡⷨ҇ вчера видѣвшимъ на кр҃тѣ оумеша. днесь слышати еⷭ҇ бг҃а в. н. тыи бо дн҃ь по воскрⷭ҇нїи гн҃и гл҃аше сїа петръ июдѣѡмъ. и гл҃аше иⷨ҇ муку и смⷬ҇ть хв҃у. еже чл҃ка дѣло еⷭ҇ а не бг҃а. се ради возводиⷮ҇ ихъ не мнити ї҃са точию мч҃ена и распата оумерша. но и воскрша еⷭ҇ вѣдати. и то еⷭ҇ ѿ бг҃а иⷥ҇ воскрⷭ҇нїа мртвыⷯ҇ сотворенъ и гь҃ и хс҃. а не в клꙗтву ѡставлеⷩ҇. аще и смⷬ҇ть претерпѣ на древѣ.

98v/234 гл҃аше бо петръ. се пронарекованныⷨ҇ совѣтоⷨ҇ и проразумѣниеⷨ҇ бж҃їемъ. продана приемше руками безаконныⷯ҇. пригвоꙁьше оубисте. сиⷯ҇ ради словесъ реⷱ҇ и ѡно. еⷤ҇ и сотвори тоⷢ҇ распатаго ї҃са и г҃а и х҃а. ꙗкоⷤ҇ и преⷤ҇ гл҃ахъ. ꙗко страдати чл҃ку еⷭ҇ а не бг҃у. тѣмже и петръ ѡ страданїи еⷢ҇ чл҃ку вса гл҃еть х҃у. понеⷤ҇ и еще времꙗ ѡно таковыⷯ҇ гл҃ъ требоваше кр҃та раⷣ҇ и смⷬ҇ти.

speak of the cross and death, they preached Christ in terms that showed him to be the true God. That was[585] done by the pre-eminent Peter, who admonished the Jews, saying that "God made this Jesus, whom you crucified, both Lord and Christ" (Acts 2:36). For it befits us to teach the Jews about this first: that he[586] who suffered the crucifixion from them is the one who was prophesied to be "both Lord and Christ", as he said, "God made this Jesus both Lord and Christ"[587] (Acts 2:36). For while the Jews saw him dying on the cross one day, the next day, they heard that he was God.[588] For Peter told the Jews this on the fiftieth day of the resurrection[589] of the Lord. And Peter told them[590] of the affliction and death suffered by Christ, done by the humans, and not by God.[591]

46.9. For that very reason, he guides them not only to think of Christ's affliction and death in crucifixion, but also to be aware of his resurrection, accomplished by God, who raised him from the dead and made him "both Lord and Christ" (Acts 2:36), rather than leaving him as a "curse", even though he endured death on a tree[592] (Gal. 3:13). | For Peter said, "This man, handed over to you 98ᵛ/234
according to the predetermined plan and foreknowledge of God, you killed by nailing him (to the cross) by the hands of lawless men" (Gal. 2:23). It is in light of these words that Peter also said, "He made this Jesus", who was crucified, "both Lord and Christ" (Acts 2:36), just as he mentioned earlier that it belongs to man to suffer, and not to God.

46.10. Therefore, when Peter speaks of the suffering that belongs to man, he ascribes to Christ everything (that he experienced), for it was necessary to say such things regarding the cross and death at the right time, because these

---

585 That was] that was also

586 he] Jesus

587 as he said, "God made this Jesus both Lord and Christ"] For he said, "God made this Jesus both Lord and Christ" (Acts 2:36), because the latter assumed humanity, through which Jesus truly became man and endured the cross and death.

588 For while the Jews saw him dying on the cross one day, the next day, they heard that he was God.] It was hard for the Jews first to hear that (just) one day before they saw someone dying on the cross, and then, the next day, to hear that it was God. For they were expecting a human Christ, who was supposed to be an earthly king and rule only from them, and now they are seeing that the one who was (not supposed) to die, did die.

589 resurrection] crucifixion and resurrection

590 them] Jews

591 And Peter told them of the affliction and death suffered by Christ, done by the humans, and not by God.] And Peter told the Jews of Christ's affliction and death, which belong to man, and not God, for the divinity is impassible, but humanity is passible.

592 "curse", even though he endured death on a tree] "curse", "hanging on a tree" (Gal. 3:13) like all others sentenced to death, even though he endured the cross as a man.

ꙗко блⷥи бывшⷨи и тꙋ сꙋщⷨи и еще. егдаⷤ на во скр҃ние е҃ приде гл҃ѧ петръ. тогда и бж҃тва і҃сова не оумо҃ча. но проповѣда бг҃а х҃а аще и чл҃къ бы. гл҃аше бо се і҃са воскр҃си бг҃ъ. емꙋⷨ вси мы свидѣтеле. десницею ꙋбо бж҃иею возне се҃. ѡбѣтованиⷨе стг҃о дх҃а приемъ ѿ ѿц҃а. и злѣѩ. се еⷤ нн҃ѣ вы видите и слышите. не бо дв҃дъ взыде на нб҃са. гл҃е бо самъ. р҃е г҃ь гв҃и мо емꙋ сѣди ѡдеснꙋю мене дондⷤе положꙋ враги твоа по҃ножие ногама твоима. Видитеⷣ петра. ѡ нⷨе же р҃е. ꙗко и г҃а и х҃а сотвори҃ есть бг҃ъ. сего і҃са егⷤо вы распасте. того прⷤе несо творенное е҃ бж҃тво. показа ѿ пр҃рка приⷨе гл҃ѧ. р҃е г҃ь гв҃и моемꙋ сѣди ѡдеснꙋю мене. сотворе 99r/235 номꙋ же десное сопрт҃льство бж҃ие. како возмо жно приѧти. сие и паве҃ гл҃еть. не восхищениⷨе непщева быти равенъ бг҃ꙋ. но себе излїа. ѡ ба проповѣдаста несотвореное бж҃тво х҃во. и чл҃чества ра҃ не прело҃шаса ѿ бж҃тва. распа таⷤ сꙋща и ꙋбита. воскресиⷡ аки чл҃ка бг҃ъ сотво ри е҃ и г҃а и х҃а. пр҃но бо при ср҃ти его чл҃чества дѣиство гл҃е ѡ немъ. тоⷤ и паве҃ гл҃ѧ р҃е ѡ немъ бывъ послꙋшливъ до см҃рти. см҃ртиⷤ кр҃тꙋ. наве҃ абие. тѣмже и бг҃ъ то҃ превознесе. и дарова емꙋ има еⷤ паче всако҃ имени. да ѡ имени і҃совѣ всѩко колѣно поклонитса нб҃ныхъ и земныⷯ и преиспо҃нихъ. пр҃е гл҃авъ ꙗко не по восхищению равенъ бг҃ꙋ прⷤе вѣкъ сыи. рекше по родꙋ превѣчное бж҃тво имѣа things[593] preceded what was yet to come. But when Peter moves to speak of his resurrection, then he is no longer silent about Jesus' deity, but preaches that Christ is God, even though he became man. For he said, "God raised up this Jesus, and we all are witnesses of that. Being, therefore, exalted at the right hand of God, and having received from the Father the promise of the Holy Spirit, he has poured out what you now see and hear. For David did not ascend into the heavens, because he himself[594] says, 'The Lord said to my Lord, 'Sit at my right hand, until I make your enemies your footstool''" (Acts 2:32–35).

46.11. Don't you see how Peter, who said of him, "God has made this Jesus, whom you crucified, both Lord and Christ" (Acts 2:36), also showed his uncreated divinity as something preceding, when he took the quote from the Prophet, "The Lord said to my Lord, 'Sit at my right hand'" (Ps. 110:1; Acts 2:35). | 99r/235
But how is it possible for a created being to share the throne of God at his right hand? Paul affirms the same when he says that "he did not count equality with God something to be grasped, but emptied himself" (Phil. 2:6). Both of them preached the uncreated divinity of Christ, and the fact that his divinity did not change because of his humanity.[595] And after being crucified and killed, he was resurrected as a man and "made" "both Lord and Christ" by God (Acts 2:36).[596] For in (Paul's) description, the actions (of Christ) always go along with the passions of his humanity.

46.12. Likewise, Paul also described him, saying, "He was obedient to the point of death, even death on a cross" (Phil. 2:8), and at once specified, "Therefore, God exalted him and gave him the name that is above every name so that at the name of Jesus every knee should bow, in heaven and on earth and under the earth" (Phil. 2:8–10). Earlier, he said that (Christ) "did not count equality with God something to be grasped", and that he existed before the ages, which means that he possessed pre-eternal divinity by nature from the beginning, but

593 these things] cross and death

594 himself] *omitted*

595 Both of them preached the uncreated divinity of Christ and the fact that his divinity did not change because of his humanity.] Both of them preached the uncreated divinity of Christ. And his divinity did not change because of his humanity, but even in humanity, Christ (retained his) lordship, not according to their own expectations—either making a claim for a human throne on this earth or having them think that by killing Jesus on a tree on the basis of their own power they would be able to take away his lordship—but in order to have them understand that Jesus suffered "according to the predetermined plan and God's foreknowledge", directing them to the prophecies (Gal. 2:23).

596 by God (Acts 2:36).] by God (Acts 2:36). It is on account of (assumed) humanity, that he speaks of him as "made".

искони. послꙋшаниꙗⷤ ради ко ѿцꙋ смиривъ себе излиа. приꙗти послѣди зракъ рабии. и петръ тоⷮ глеть гл҃авъ. воскрⷭние реⷱ и возне сение хв҃о. вкꙋпѣ и ѡдеснꙋю бг҃а ѿц҃а сидѣние еⷭ. тꙋ и послание к нимъ ст҃го дх҃а ѿ ѿц҃а реⷱ. хотѧⷤ паки крⷭтъ и смрⷮь хвꙋ глати. реⷱ паки члⷱе ское смиреное по гл҃анию оуⷤ высоты бж҃тва хв҃а.
99v/236 ꙗко и г҃а и х҃а сотвориⷧ есть бг҃ сеⷢ і҃са. егоⷤ вы реⷱ распасте. сие и павеⷧ ст҃льство гл҃а. еже чл҃чествꙋ достоино хвꙋ. и единъ ходатаи бгꙋ и чл҃комъ члкъ і҃съ хс. давыи себе избавле ние за всѣхъ.+[597] Слыши потоⷨ еже пишеⷮ к тимо ѳеюⷤ. Велика еⷭ блгочестию таина. бгъ ꙗвиⷭ во плоти. ѡправдаⷭ в дсѣ. ꙗвиⷭ аггломъ про повѣданъ быⷭ въ ꙗзыцѣⷯ вѣрова жеⷭ в мирѣ. во знесеⷭ въ славѣ. И к титꙋ пишеⷮ. просвѣ ти бо сѧ блгть бж҃іа спситенаа всѣмъ члкѡⷨ. наказающи наⷭ. да ѿвергшеⷭ нечтиа и мирь скиⷯ похотеи. цѣломрено и правено и блговѣ рно поживеⷨ в нынешнеⷨ вѣцѣ. чающе блже ннаⷢ ꙋпованіа. и просвѣщеніа славы вели каⷢ бга и спса ншего іса ха. иⷤ дасть себе за ны. да избавиⷮ ны ѿ всакого безакониа. и ѡчи стиⷮ себѣ люⷣ избраны. ревнителѧ добрыⷨ дѣ

---

597 *In the margin:* ⟨...⟩ ... єⷭто и сѣгрѣшиⷲ. а члкъ ни единъ сѣгрѣшенъ єⷭ.

(then, he added that) for the sake of showing obedience to the Father,[598] he afterward, humbled and emptied himself by assuming the form of a servant (Phil. 2:5–8).

46.13. And in Peter's speech, too, after speaking of the "resurrection", he spoke of the "exaltation" of Christ along with his "sitting" at the right hand of God the Father; and he also mentioned here the "sending" of the Holy Spirit upon them from the Father (Acts 2:32–35). Wishing[599] next to speak of the cross and death of Christ, he went on to talk, then, about human "humbling" in light of what he had already said about the supreme divinity[600] of Christ, | namely, that "God 99ᵛ/236
made this Jesus, whom you crucified, both Lord and Christ" (Acts 2:36).

46.14. And Paul does the same thing when he speaks of Christ's high priesthood, belonging to Christ on account of his humanity, that "there is one mediator between God and men, the man Jesus Christ, who gave himself as a deliverance for all" (1Tim. 2:5–6).

47. Showing that the Son of God became man to justify humanity, for he alone is without sin, while no man is sinless.[601]

47.1. Listen to what he (Paul) writes to Timothy afterward, "Great is the mystery of godliness: God appeared in the flesh, was vindicated in the Spirit, appeared to angels, was preached among the nations, was believed on in the world, was taken up in glory" (1Tim. 3:16).

47.2. And to Titus, he writes, "For the grace of God has shone forth, bringing salvation to all people. It teaches us to renounce ungodliness and worldly passions so that we may live chaste, upright, and godly lives in the present age, anticipating the blessed[602] hope and the shining forth of the glory of our great God and Savior, Jesus Christ, who gave himself for us in order to deliver us from all lawlessness and to purify for himself a special people, who are zealous for good works"[603] (Tit. 2:11–14).

598 obedience to the Father] obedience that is to the Father
599 Wishing] On finishing this statement and wishing
600 supreme divinity] divinity
601 **Showing that the Son of God became man to justify humanity, for he alone is without sin, while no man is sinless.**] *omitted*
602 blessed] divine
603 and to purify for himself a special people, who are zealous for good works] *omitted*

ломъ. Ꙗко і҃съ х҃с б҃гъ и ч҃лкъ е҃. поне҃ единъ тои е҃
ч҃лкъ и б҃гъ. по бж҃твꙋ ѿч҃ю и по воплощению
ч҃лчества. Видите ли ап҃ла проповѣдающа
х҃а. не точию ч҃лка но б҃га во плоти. и б҃га вели
ка и сп҃са і҃са х҃а. чесо҃ ра҃ косои се҃ писанїа ап҃льска҃
100r/238 не разгибае҃ и не дае҃ прочита҃ аще не безбж҃енъ
бы бы҃ косои. почто҃ оубо и писанаа добрѣ и ст҃ы҃
ап҃лы косо҃ злѣ прочитае҃. слышите҃ и прочꙋю
ап҃льскꙋю пропове҃. х҃а несотворена б҃га. пи
ше҃ оубо к коринѳомъ павелъ. и х҃съ за всѣ оумре
да живꙋщїи не себѣ живоу҃. но ꙋмершемꙋ за ни҃
и вскр҃шемꙋ ре҃. и помалѣ аще ли҃ и разꙋмѣхо҃
по плоти х҃а. но н҃нѣ оу҃ не разꙋмѣе҃. и потомъ
пише҃ к нимъ. Вѣсте бо бл҃гть г҃а н҃шего і҃са х҃а.
ꙗко васъ ра҃ ѡбница бога҃ сыи. И къ еѳесѡ҃
пише҃. поминание ва҃ твора в мл҃тва҃ мои҃.
да б҃гъ г҃а н҃шего і҃са х҃а. ѿц҃ъ славы да҃ вамъ д҃хъ
премд҃рости и ѿкровенїа в познание е҃. про
свѣщенѣ ѡчи ср҃ца ваше҃. оувѣдѣти ва҃. что е҃
оупование званїа е҃. и что бога҃ство славы
достоꙗниа е҃ во ст҃ы҃. и что преспѣющее ве
личествие силы е҃ в насъ вѣрꙋющи҃. по дѣи
ствꙋ державы крѣпости е҃. ꙗ҃ содѣа ѡ х҃ѣ. во
скр҃шь его из мертвы҃. и посажь ѡдеснꙋю себе.

48. Showing that while Jesus Christ is both divine and human, he is one and the same person: God according to the Father's divinity and man according to the assumed humanity.[604]

48.1. Don't you see that the Apostle is preaching Christ not only in human terms, but also as God in the flesh and the great God and Savior, Jesus Christ?[605] Why does Kosoy not open these apostolic[606] passages of Scripture | and give them to 100r/238
us to read, unless it is because Kosoy is a godless man? Why, then, does Kosoy misread what is written well by the holy Apostles?

48.2. And listen also to other things[607] found in the apostolic preaching of Christ as the uncreated God![608] Thus, Paul writes to the Corinthians, saying, "And Christ died for all, that those who live may no longer live for themselves, but for him who for their sake died and was raised" (2 Cor. 5:15). And somewhat later,[609] "Even though we once regarded Christ according to the flesh, we no longer regard him as such" (2 Cor. 5:16). And afterward, he writes to them, "For you know the grace of our Lord Jesus Christ, that though he was rich, yet for your sake he became poor" (2 Cor. 8:9).

48.3. And to the Ephesians, he writes, "I keep remembering you in my prayers, that the God of our Lord Jesus Christ, the Father of glory, may give you the Spirit of wisdom and of revelation in the knowledge of him, having the eyes of your hearts enlightened, that you may know what is the hope of his calling, and what are the riches of his glorious inheritance in the saints, and what is the enormous greatness of his power toward us who believe, according to the working of his great might, that he worked in Christ when he raised him from the dead and

---

604 **Showing that while Jesus Christ is both divine and human, he is one and the same person: God according to the Father's divinity and man according to the assumed humanity.**] *omitted*

605 Christ?] Christ? And just as with Timothy, the Apostle also preached the great God and Savior, Jesus Christ, in the flesh. It is account of this that he speaks of him in human terms, preaching God's immense grace and immeasurable goodness that God became incarnate in order to "give himself" as a "deliverance" for us (1 Tim. 2:6). Being a deliverer and great God, he carried out a ministry of the High Priest with his own blood, as the Apostle writes (about this) to Timothy and Titus, namely, "God appeared in the flesh, was vindicated by the Spirit" (1 Tim. 3:16), and "For the grace of God has shone forth, bringing salvation to all people" (Tit. 3:11), and "waiting for the blessed hope and the shining forth of the glory of our great God and Savior, Jesus Christ, who gave himself for us to deliver us from all lawlessness" (Tit. 2:13–14).

606 apostolic] *omitted*

607 other things] more things

608 God!] Lord!

609 later] later, he says,

на нбⷭны. превыше всакоа власти и влⷣче
ства и силы и гⷭ҇ства. и всакⷢ҇ имени име
нꙋюща҇. не точию в вѣцѣ сеⷨ҇ но и в градꙋщеⷨ.
100ᵛ/239 И помалѣ пишеⷮ. бгъ богаⷮ сыи въ мⷭ҇ти за мно
гꙋю любовь свою. еюⷤ възлюби наⷭ҇. и сꙋщаа ны пре
грѣшенми ѡживи хмⷭ҇ъ. Пишеⷮ же и пакы
к нимⷨ. Мнѣ меншемꙋ всѣⷯ стыⷯх. даⷣ са блгⷭ҇ть
сиа въ ıазыцеⷯ. блговѣстиⷮ не ислѣⷣдованное
богаⷮство хⷭ҇во. и просвѣтиⷮ вса. что еⷭ҇ смо
трение таины съкровенныа ѿ вѣкъ в бз҃ѣ
создавшеⷨ всıаческаа исⷭ҇ хмⷭ҇ъ. И пакы
пишеⷮ. Се бо да есте вѣдꙋще. ıако всıакъ
блꙋⷣникъ или нечⷭ҇тъ или лихоимецъ еже еⷭ҇
идолослꙋжитеⷭ҇. не имаⷮ достоıанїа въ цⷭ҇ртвїи
хⷭ҇а бга. никтоⷤ васъ да льстиⷮ сꙋетными сло
весы. сиⷯ бо раⷣ градеⷮ гнѣвъ бжїи на снⷭ҇ы про
тивленїа. Пишетⷤ къ каласаеⷨ. Снемшеⷭ҇
в любвѣ и во всıакоⷨ богаⷭ҇ствѣ. извѣщенїа
разꙋмꙋ. в познание таины бга ѿца и хⷭ҇а.
в немⷤ сꙋть вса сокровища премⷣрости и
разꙋма ꙋтаена. Ї помалѣ пишеⷮ. братие
блюдитеⷭ҇ егда кто вы еⷭ҇ крадоводıахи тростию
и тщетною лестию. по преданию чл҃ческо
мꙋ. по составлениеⷨ мира сеⷢ҇. а не по хⷭ҇ѣ.
ıако в тоⷨ живеⷮ всако исполнение бжⷭ҇тва
101ʳ/240 телеснѣ. И паки глⷭ҇еть. аще ꙋбо воскрⷭ҇нꙋсте
со хмⷭ҇ъ вышниⷯ ищите. идѣⷤ есть хⷭ҇съ ѡде
снꙋю бга сѣдıа. Пишетⷤ и к селꙋнаномъ.
братие. стоите держите преданїа имⷤ
наоучистеⷭ҇. аще словоⷨ аще посланиемъ ншⷨи.
самⷤ гⷭ҇ь ншь їсⷭ҇ъ хⷭ҇с и бгъ ѿцъ ншь. возлю
бивыи насъ. и давыи оутѣшение вѣчно.
и оупование блгⷭ҇о въ блгⷣти. да оутѣшиⷮ ва
ша срⷣца. и да ꙋтвердиⷮ вы во всакоⷨ словѣ

seated him at his right hand in the heavenly places, far above all authority and dominion and power and lordship, and above every name that is named, not only in this age but also in the one to come" (Eph. 1:16–21). | 100v/239

48.4. And somewhat later, he writes,[610] "But God, being rich in mercy, because of his great love with which he loved us, even when we were dead in our trespasses, made us alive through Christ" (Eph. 2:4–5). And again, he writes to them, "To me, though I am the very least of all the saints, this grace was given, to preach to the Gentiles the unsearchable riches of Christ, and to bring to light for everyone what is the economy of the mystery hidden for ages in God, who created all things—Jesus Christ" (Eph. 3:8–9). And next, he writes,[611] "For you should know this, that everyone who is sexually immoral or impure, or who is covetous, that is, an idolater, has no inheritance in the kingdom of Christ and God. Let no one deceive you with empty words, for because of these things the wrath of God comes upon the sons of disobedience" (Eph. 5:5–6).

48.5. And to the Colossians, too,[612] he writes, "being knit together in love (to reach) all the riches of complete understanding in order that they may know the mystery of God the Father and Christ, in whom are hidden all the treasures of supreme wisdom and knowledge" (Col. 2:2–3). And somewhat later,[613] he writes, "Brothers, see to it that no one takes you captive by trickery and empty deceit, according to human tradition, according to the elements of this world, and not according to Christ. For in him, the whole fullness of divinity dwells | 101r/240 bodily" (Col. 2:8–9). And again, he writes, "If then, you have been raised with Christ, seek the things that are above, where Christ is, seated at the right hand of God" (Col. 3:1).

48.6. And to the Thessalonians, he also writes, "Brothers, stand firm, hold to the traditions that you were taught, either by our words or letters. And may our Lord Jesus Christ himself, and God and our Father, who loved us and gave us eternal comfort and good hope through grace, comfort your hearts and establish you in every good word and deed" (2 Thess. 2:15–17).

610 he writes,] *omitted*
611 writes] writes to them
612 too,] *omitted*
613 And somewhat later,] And to the same recipient somewhat later,

и дѣле блазѣ. Ѩко іⷭ҇ъ хⷭ҇ не сотворенъ ⷭ҇е. но роженъ ѿ б҃га б҃гъ сыи. Слышасте ап҃ла пишꙋща. самъⷤ҇ рече гⷭ҇ь н҃шь іⷭ҇ъ хⷭ҇ и б҃гъ и ѿ҃цъ н҃шь. возлюбивыи наⷭ҇ и давыи оутѣшение вѣчно. и оупование бл҃го въ блⷣ҇ти. аще оубо сотворенъ бы бы҇ гⷭ҇ь н҃шь іⷭ҇ъ хⷭ҇ъ. и не ѿ҃чее равносⷭ҇ное бжⷭ҇тво имⷭ҇ѣ бы. не бы апⷭ҇лъ прⷣ҇ерещи дерзнꙋлъ гⷭ҇а іⷭ҇са хⷭ҇а б҃га ѿ҃ца. и гл҃ати его великое дѣло б҃га единоⷢ҇ со ѿцеⷨ҇ бгⷨ҇ъ творити. ѿкꙋдꙋ проповѣдꙋⷮ҇е косои сотворена хⷭ҇а. сопротивлаюⷭ҇ сⷮмꙋ дхⷭ҇ꙋ. иⷤ гл҃а апⷭ҇лы и прⷪ҇ркы ѡ хⷭ҇ѣ несотворена б҃га. не можеⷮ оубо сотвореное прⷣ҇ерещиса несотворенomꙋ.

101v/241 не можеⷮ сотвореныи даⷮ оутѣшение вѣчно. не можеⷮ сотвореныи даⷮ оупование бл҃го въ бл҃годаⷮ. аще сотворенъ бы бы҇ гⷭ҇ь. не бы гл҃алъ ⷢ҇е павелъ и къ коласаемъ. седѣти емꙋ ѡдеснꙋю б҃га. ниⷤ гл҃а҇ бы ѡ неⷨ ѩко в тоⷨ живеⷮ все исполнение бжⷭ҇тва телеснѣ. понеⷤ б҃гъ хⷭ҇ъ гⷭ҇ь бы члⷭ҇къ іⷭ҇ъ. не премениⷭ҇ бжⷭ҇твоⷨ ѿ приатїа плоти. сеⷢ҇ раⷣ проповѣдаеⷮ апⷭ҇лъ не ѿчасти ни ѡсїанием имѣюща бжⷭ҇тво хⷭ҇а аки сотворенъ. но ѩко несотворенъ хⷭ҇ъ воплотиⷭ҇ и быⷭ҇ члⷭ҇къ. живеⷮ в тоⷨ рече все исполнение бжⷭ҇тва телеснѣ. показавъⷤ и преⷤ имъ сн҃а бжиѩ не сотворена но рожена гл҃ѩ. Бл҃года раще б҃га и ѿ҃ца призвавшаⷢ҇ ваⷭ҇ в причастие наслѣдїа ст҃ыхъ въ свѣⷮ иже избави насъ ѿ власти темныѧ. и престави въ црⷭ҇тво сн҃а любвѣ своеѧ. ѡ нем же имамы избавление кровию его ѡставление грѣховъ. иⷤ есть ѡбраⷥ б҃га невидимаго. перворожеⷩ҇ всакои твари. ѩко ѡ неⷨ создана быша всаческаа ѩⷤ на нбⷭ҇ѣⷯ и ѩⷤ на земли видимаа и невидимаа. Показаⷤ и ефесѩноⷨ.

49. Showing that Jesus Christ is not made, but begotten from God, and is God.[614]

49.1. You heard how the Apostle wrote, "our Lord Jesus Christ himself", (and then) he said, "and God and our Father, who loved us and gave us eternal comfort and good hope through grace" (2 Thess. 2:16). If then, our Lord Jesus Christ had been made, and not been equally divine with the Father, the Apostle would not have dared to say what he did above, namely, speaking of the Lord Jesus Christ on par with God the Father and describing him[615] as doing the great work of one God together with God the Father.

49.2. What inspired Kosoy to preach Christ as a created being and oppose the Holy Spirit, considering that the Apostles and Prophets spoke of Christ as the uncreated God?[616] Of course, no created being can be prophesied as uncreated, | and the one who is created cannot "give" "eternal comfort", nor can this 101v/241
created being "give" "good hope through grace" (2 Thess. 2:16).

49.3. If the Lord had been made, Paul would not have spoken of him in Colossians as sitting at the right hand of God, nor would he have said in his regard that "in him, the whole fullness of deity dwells bodily" (Col. 2:9). And even though Christ, being God and Lord, became the man Jesus, his divinity did not change because of his taking on flesh. For that reason, the Apostle does not say in his preaching that Christ is divine only partially, or as a result of special enlightening like the created being, but that uncreated Christ was incarnated and became man. He said that "in him, the whole fullness of deity dwells bodily" (Col. 2:9).

49.4. And to show them that the Son of God was not created but begotten, he says,[617] "giving thanks to God and Father, who has called you to share in the inheritance of the saints in light. He delivered us from the dark powers and transferred us to the kingdom of his beloved Son, in whom we have deliverance through his blood, the forgiveness of sins. He is the image of the invisible God, the firstborn of all creation. For through him, all things were created, things in heaven and things on earth, visible and invisible" (Col. 1:12–16).

---

614 **Showing that Jesus Christ is not made, but begotten from God, and is God.**] *omitted*

615 him] *omitted*

616 as the uncreated God?] as the uncreated and true God?

617 was not created but begotten, he says,] was uncreated before (he was made man), he writes,

102r/242 несотворена хⷭа. писавъ иⷨ гл҃ꙗ. Что еⷭ смотре
ние таины сокровенныꙗ ѿ вѣкъ в б҃зѣ созда
вшиⷨ всаческаа і҃ⷭсъ хмⷭъ. Аще вса созда
і҃ⷭсъ х҃с. ꙗвно саⷨ несозданъ еⷭ. понеⷤ вса тои
сотвори. ꙗкоⷤ и бг҃ословъ їѡⷩа проповѣда
гл҃ꙗ. Вса тѣмъ быша. и без неⷢ ничтоⷤ быⷭ
еⷤ быть. преⷤ гл҃авъ. ꙗко искони бѣ слово
и слово бѣ къ бг҃ꙋ. и бг҃ъ бѣ слово. и помалѣ
гл҃ⷮе. и слово плоⷮ быⷭ. и вселиⷭ в ны и видѣхомъ
славꙋ его. славꙋ ꙗко единороⷣнаго ѿ ѡца.
исполнь блⷢ҃ти и истинны. бг҃а никтоⷤ
видѣ нигдѣⷤ. единороⷣныи сн҃ъ сыи в лонѣ
ѿч҃и. тои исповѣда. Не гл҃ⷮе бг҃ословъ со
творена хⷭа. но в началѣ слово ꙋ бг҃а и саⷨ
бг҃ъ бѣ слово. и послѣди слово плоⷮ быⷭ. и видѣ
ша славꙋ его. не аки сотворенаго славꙋ.
но ꙗко единороⷣнаго ѿ ѡца славꙋ видѣша.
посемꙋ не повреⷣса славою единороⷣныи сн҃ъ
бж҃їи бывъ плоть. но и во плоти тꙋюⷤ славꙋ
бжтⷭва прнⷭѣ имаⷮ. понеⷤ единороⷣныи сн҃ъ
бж҃їи сыи. ꙗкоⷤ и саⷨ рече. азъ и ѿц҃ъ едино
есвѣ. Тѣмже оубо апⷭлъ павеⷧ в посланїиⷯ своиⷯ
102v/243 ꙗⷤ воспомꙗнꙋхоⷨ. не сотворена сн҃а бж҃їа и
истинна проповѣда. И петръ апⷭлъ ни
чтоⷤ странно реⷱ крⷭта ради и смр҃ти. ꙗко
и гⷭа и хⷭа сотвори бг҃ъ сего іⷭса. понеⷤ и при
реⷱ егоⷤ вы распасте. внегдаⷤ воскрⷭнїа раⷣ
высотꙋ бжтⷭва хвⷭа. преⷤ проповѣдаⷡ оуⷤ
ꙗвиⷭ вознесенїа раⷣ его на нб҃са. и сидѣниеⷨ
его ѡдеснꙋю ѿц҃а. и посланїа раⷣ дх҃а стг҃о к ниⷨ.
еⷤ краинее величество бжтⷭва не сотво
реннаⷢ показа. тогда и смиреное крⷭта раⷣ

49.5. And to the Ephesians, he also showed | Christ as uncreated, when he wrote to them, saying,[618] "(To bring to light) what is the economy of the mystery which for ages has been hidden in God, who created all things by Jesus Christ" (Eph. 3:9). And if Christ "created all things", it is clear that he himself is not created. For he is the one who created all things, as John the Theologian proclaimed, saying, "All things were made through him, and without him, nothing was made that was made" (Jn. 1:3). And prior to that, he said, "In the beginning was the Word, and the Word was with God, and the Word was God" (Jn. 1:1); and somewhat later, he stated, "The Word became flesh and was dwelling among us, and we saw his glory, the glory as of the only-begotten (Son) from the Father, full of grace and truth"; "no one has ever seen God; the only-begotten Son who is in the bosom of the Father, he declared him" (Jn. 1:14, 18). The Theologian[619] is not saying that Christ is made. Instead, "In the beginning was the Word, and he was with God, and the Word himself was God"[620] (Jn. 1:1). 102r/242

49.6. And then, "The Word became flesh, and we saw his glory" (Jn. 1:14). And the glory they saw was not the glory of a created being but one of "the only-begotten (Son) from the Father" (Jn. 1:14). Therefore, the only-begotten Son of God did not impair the glory of the Godhead, even after becoming flesh. Instead, he (retained) in the flesh the glory of his deity that he eternally possessed.[621] For the Son of God is the only-begotten, as he himself said,[622] "I and the Father are one" (Jn. 10:30).

49.7. Hence, the Apostle Paul in his epistles, | as we recalled, preached the Son of God to be uncreated and true God. And the Apostle Peter did not declare anything strange concerning the cross and death,[623] that "God made him both Lord and Christ,[624] this Jesus", for he also added, "whom you crucified" (Acts 2:36). After he had clearly expressed the exalted divinity of Christ, through what he had already preached concerning his resurrection, and after he had shown the ultimate greatness of the uncreated divinity, due to his ascension to the heavens and his seating at the right hand of God and his sending of the Holy Spirit to them, he went on to speak of his humiliation through the cross and 102v/243

618 to them, saying,] to them the following,

619 The Theologian] See, the Theologian

620 and he was with God, and the Word himself was God"] and the Word was with God, and the Word was God"

621 possessed.] possessed by nature.

622 himself said,] himself taught, saying,

623 did not declare anything strange concerning the cross and death,] did nothing strange when he spoke of the cross and death,

624 both Lord and Christ,] Lord Christ,

и смрти рⷱ҇е. за сѹщее еⷭ҇ приатие плоти
нш҇еа. ꙗко ї гⷭ҇а и хⷭ҇а сотвори бгⷭ҇ъ сеⷭ҇ ӏⷭ҇са. По
казаⷠ҇ пав҇е къ каласаⷨ҇ пиша. ѡбоꙗ въ хⷭ҇ѣ
бжⷭ҇тво и чл҇чество. внегда гл҇аше в посла
нїи к нⷨ҇. блгодаряще бг҇а и ѿц҇а призвавшаⷭ҇
ваⷭ҇ в причастие. наслѣдїа стⷯ҇ы въ свѣтѣ.
иⷤ҇ избави наⷭ҇ ѿ власти темныа. и преста
вивъ цртⷭ҇во сн҇а любвѣ своеа. ѡ нем же
имамы избавление кровию его ѡставле
ние грѣхомъ. Ѡбщѹ показа блгⷣ҇ть чл҇комъ
ѿ бг҇а ѿц҇а и сн҇а. сн҇а ѹбо рⷦ҇е показа несо
творенаа хⷭ҇ва. и ѡ немⷤ҇ имамы избаⷡ҇е
103r/244 ние рⷦ҇е. показа ѿцⷭ҇ѹ единосѹщна сн҇а. кровию еⷭ҇
ѡставление грѣхомъ рекъ. показа бг҇а и чл҇ка
вкѹпѣ. да не мнⷮ҇и кто быти всемѹ ѿчю. но
паⷭ҇ да помышляеⷮ҇ ѡбщѹ блгⷣ҇ть. ѡ нем же рⷱ҇е
снѹ҇. рекше ѡ нем же имамы избавление. ꙗⷦ҇
ѿцъ ѹбо прелоⷤ҇и. снъ дасть винѹ кровию еⷭ҇
ѡставление грѣхоⷨ҇ содѣлавъ. аще бо быша
грѣси не ѡставлени. не быхоⷨ҇ преставлени
были въ цртⷭ҇вие сн҇а бжиа возлюблен҇а.Речеⷤ҇
апл҇ъ иⷤ҇ есть ѡбраⷥ҇ бг҇а не видимаⷭ҇ первенецъ
всеи твари. непремѣннаго и по всемѹ равна.
и пⷣ҇обна ѡбразоⷨ҇ ѿцѹ сн҇а нарицаеⷮ҇. первенецъ
рⷱ҇е всеи твари видимеⷤ҇ и невидимеⷯ҇. еже еⷭ҇
преⷤ҇ твари первенецъ. и единочаⷣ҇ рожьⷭ҇а ѿ
ѿц҇а. бывъ сопрⷭ҇носѹщенъ первенецъ всеи тва

death, that he suffered because he assumed our flesh when "God made him both Lord and Christ, this Jesus" (Acts 2:36).[625]

49.8. For in writing to the Colossians, Paul showed both the divinity and humanity of Christ, when he said in his epistle the following, "giving thanks to God and Father, who has called you to share in the inheritance of the saints (who abide) in light. He delivered us from the dark powers and transferred us to the kingdom of his beloved Son, in whom we have deliverance through his blood, the forgiveness of sins" (Col. 1:12–14). He showed to humankind the common grace that comes from God the Father and Son. Thus, as it is said, he showed the Son to be the uncreated Christ.[626]

49.9. And in saying, "in whom we have deliverance" (Col. 1:14), | he showed 103r/244
that the Son was consubstantial with the Father, ⟨for it is in the nature of God alone to be the deliverer⟩. In saying, "through his blood is the forgiveness of sins" (Col. 1:14), he showed him to be simultaneously God and man so that[627] no one may think that everything was done by the Father (alone), but rather, acknowledge the common grace. In speaking of the Son, or more specifically, "in whom we have deliverance", he implied that the Father offered the sacrifice, while the Son dealt with the main problem (of men)—bringing about the "forgiveness of sins" "through his blood" (Col. 1:14). For if the sins had not been forgiven, we would not have been transferred to the "kingdom" of the "beloved Son" of God (Col. 1:13).

49.10. And[628] the Apostle said, "He is the image of the invisible God, the firstborn of all creation" (Col. 1:15). He[629] treats the Son as unchanging, calling him the "image" of the Father, equal and alike in everything. He says that he is "the firstborn of all creation", "visible and invisible"; he is[630] before the creation, firstborn and only-begotten, begotten from the Father, eternally existing with

625 *MS 61 adds*: **And according to Moses and David and all the others, as well as according to the Apostles John and Peter and Paul, Jesus Christ is not made but begotten from God. He remained God when he took on flesh that was created and made after his incarnation.**

626 uncreated Christ.] uncreated, to whom, by virtue of being Son, it is proper to be begotten, and not made, for the Father, too, begets him rather than makes him, which is why he is "Father". And the Son is not made by him as Son. Instead, he is begotten by him, which is why he is "Son".

627 God and man so that] God and man. Indeed, "to forgive sins" is proper to God, whereas "blood" is what relates to humanity, through which the God-man suffered the cross and had his flesh pierced through, so that

628 And] Likewise,

629 He] Apostle

630 he is] who is

ри. ꙗвѣ оубо апⷭ҇лъ хⷭ҇а равна ѿцꙋ҃ и рекъ еⷭ҇ и силꙋ.
гл҃етⷤ и чл҃колюбие его. ꙗко всѣⷯ сыи гⷭ҇ь и влⷣка.
сꙋщаа долѣ чл҃кы счета себѣ. прⷤ҇ первовѣ
чное его рекъ гл҃ꙗ. Всяческаа тѣмъ и ѡ неⷨ
создашаⷭ҇. и тои еⷭ҇ преже всѣⷯ. и всяческаа
ѡ немъ состоꙗтся. и тои еⷭ҇ глава цр҃кви.
иⷤ есть начало перворожень иⷥ мр҃твыⷯ. ꙗко
103ᵛ/245 да бꙋдеⷮ во всѣⷯ тои первеⷩствꙋꙗ. ꙗко ѡ немъ
бл҃гоизволи всяко исполнение вселитиⷭ҇. и
тѣмъ смириⷮ всяческаа. к себѣ смири кро
вию распятия своеⷢ собою. ащеⷤ земнаа
аще лиⷤ нб҃наа. Начало рекъ воскрⷭ҇ниꙗ и ви
ны бывыи. да боудеть реⷱ во всѣⷯ первеньствꙋ
ꙗи. понеⷤ прⷤ всѣⷯ вѣкъ ражается ѿ ѿца.
и прⷤ всѣⷯ чл҃къ воскресе ѿ мр҃твыⷯ. воскрⷭ҇нїе
к томꙋ неоумирающимъ. и бл҃говоление реⷱ
но быⷭ ѡ немъ. се же еⷭ҇ хⷭ҇ви все исполнение все
литиⷭ бж҃твꙋ. не частнѣ но сꙋщественѣ
всели слово в плⷮо. и тѣмъ смириⷮ всячеⷭкаа
реⷱ. реⷱ тѣмъ еⷤ есть саⷨ себѣ же и ѿцꙋ чл҃кы
примири. древнюю враждꙋ разрꙋшивъ. къ
бг҃ꙋ и агглоⷨ и чл҃коⷨ миръ сотвори. к себѣ смиⷬ
реⷱ кровию распятия своеⷢ собою. да не
мниши еⷢ слꙋги чиноⷨ се сотворити. Виждь
же реⷱнныⷯ извѣщение примири реⷱ и смири
наⷭ имъ. еⷤ есть не глю повелѣвъ но плоⷮски
дѣиствовавъ. не простоⷤ его раⷣ но крове его
раⷣ излиянныꙗ. заклания поносныꙗ ради
смр҃ти распятиеⷨ. ѡбраⷥ примиренїа полагаа.
104ʳ/246 вѣдыи бж҃твеное еⷭ сꙋщество. ꙗко тѣла его
раⷣ рече примири. ꙗко не токмо ꙋранень и за
ꙋшень но и оумеⷬ поносною смр҃тию. помалѣ
бо реⷱ апⷭлъ. нн҃ѣ смири. в тѣле плоти еⷢ смр҃тию.
Такоⷤ и къ ефесоⷨ хⷭа бг҃а чл҃ка сказоуеⷮ еже ꙋ и помя
нꙋⷯоⷨ прⷤ. глетⷤ и бл҃гть ѡно. еⷤ въ ꙗзыцеⷯ

him, "firstborn of all creation". It is clear,[631] then, that the Apostle also speaks of Christ's equality with the Father in terms of power. And he also speaks of his love toward humankind, (showing) that even as Lord and sovereign of all, he united himself with humanity that is below his stature.

49.11. Before that, he spoke of his eternal pre-existence, saying, "all things were created through him and in him. And he is before all things, and in him all things hold together. And he is the head of the church. He is the beginning, the firstborn from the dead, that | in everything he might be preeminent. For in 103ᵛ/245 him all the fullness (of God) was pleased to dwell, and through him, to reconcile to himself all things, whether things on earth or things in heaven, making peace by the blood of his crucifixion" (Col. 1:16–20). (The Apostle) said that he is the "beginning" of resurrection; and being the cause (of all things), as it is stated, he must be "preeminent in everything" (Col. 1:18).

49.12. Since he was begotten from the Father before all ages, and rose[632] from the dead before all other men, his resurrection is what finally will end death for others. And (the Apostle) said[633] that (God's) good pleasure dwelled in him (Christ), which refers to the indwelling of "all the fullness of God" in Christ; the Word was dwelling in the flesh not in some limited way, but with his entire being (Col. 1:19). And in the statement, "through him, to reconcile to himself all things" (Col. 1:20), he said, "through him", meaning that he reconciled men to himself and the Father, "putting to death" the old "hostility" (Eph. 2:15–16), and reconciling God with men and angels. He "reconciled to himself (all things)", it is said, through himself and "by the blood of his crucifixion" so that you may not think that this action was done to create servants for him (Col. 1:20). Rather, give heed to the words of those statements that claim, "making peace" and "through him, he reconciled" us.

49.13. These words that I am quoting are not about his command, but about his acting according to the flesh. They are not about anything done purely for him, but about his doing it (for others): his shedding blood, becoming a sacrifice, establishing reconciliation by dying a shameful death through crucifixion, | while knowing his divine nature.[634] It is said "reconciled" in view of 104ʳ/246 his flesh, that he was not only wounded and mocked, but also died a shameful death. For somewhat later, the Apostle said, "he has now reconciled in his body of flesh by his death" (Col. 1:22). In the same way, he also speaks to the Ephesians of Christ as both God and man, as I have already mentioned earlier.

631 It is clear,] It shows,

632 Since he was begotten from the Father before all ages, and rose] Because he rose

633 he said] it is said

634 while knowing his divine nature.] knowing that his divine nature could not be touched.

благовѣстиⷮ емꙋ. неисⷥлѣдованное богаⷮство
х҃во. и просвѣтиⷮ вса. аще богаⷮство е҃ неисⷥлѣ
дованно. что ꙋ҃ ѡ сꙋществѣ его любовеще
стоваⷮ. како не хощете приати косого
ꙗко безⷥбж҃ьна. и лжива и лꙋкава. иⷤ вовсе б҃е
ственое писание лжꙋща и ѕлѣ раⷥвраща
юща. и б҃га хꙋлꙗща безмѣрно. правдꙋ бо
бж҃ию косои ѿати хощеⷮ. законныѧ книги
носа. и оуча законⷪⷨ сп҃сати. еѵ҃алїю ꙋбо
проповѣдающꙋ пр҃но. ꙗко законъ моисеⷨ҃
данъ бы҃. блг҃тⷭь и истинна і҃съ хⷭмъ бы҃.
самомꙋ г҃ꙋ ѿвѣщавшꙋ. ꙗко законъ и прⷪ҃рцы
до їѡанна. ѿ днїⷨ їѡанна кр҃тлѧ цр҃твие
нб҃ное нꙋдитса. и нꙋжницы восхищаюⷮ е.
посемꙋ и в самыи закоⷩ҃ солга косои. престꙋ
повавъ то҃. раⷥвращаа лꙋкавнѣ. ратꙋа
104^{v}/247 на г҃а і҃са х҃а и б҃га. и гл҃ете в чесоⷨ безⷥбж҃енъ косоⷷ.
Рѣшаⷤ ми крылошане. в чесоⷨ разварщаеⷮ косоⷷ
законъ престꙋпова въ то҃. саⷨ крѣпцѣ де
ржиⷮ всегда законныѧ книги. и прочитаеⷮ
иⷯ. Ѿвѣщавъ азъ к ним и рекоⷯ. законъ
ꙋбо и прⷪ҃рцы х҃во пришествие провозвѣ
стиша. косоиⷤ престꙋпаеⷮ закона посе
мꙋ. понеⷤ не приимаеⷮ і҃са х҃а во плоти б҃га
пришеⷣша. и ꙗко законъ и прⷪ҃рцы до їѡаⷩ
нна кр҃тлѧ по гн҃ю гл҃сꙋ. посемꙋ закоⷩ пра
зденъ бы҃ ѿ дни їѡанна кр҃тлѧ. ꙗко егоⷤ
преⷤ законъ проѡбразоваше х҃а, тои при
иде. и пришеⷣ сверши того. тѣмже не
к томꙋ проⷪ҃е законꙋ мощи на преⷣ ити.
х҃ꙋ і҃сꙋ во плоти пришеⷣшꙋ и скончa того
своимъ пришествиеⷨ і҃съ х҃съ. нѣ҃ бо за
конъ ничтоⷤ. точию пѣстꙋствоⷩꙋа люⷣ.
ко х҃вꙋ і҃совꙋ во плоти пришествию. ꙗкоⷤ
ап҃лъ павеⷧ сказоуеⷮ во всеⷯ свои посланиїⷯ.
пришеⷣшꙋ і҃сꙋ х҃ꙋ во плоти. комꙋ прочее и
еще имаⷮ законъ пѣстꙋствоваⷮ. х҃ꙋ при
емшꙋ оуⷤ кр҃тъ и погребение по писанию.
105^{r}/248 и воскрⷭшꙋ и на нб҃са вошеⷣшꙋ. и д҃ха ст҃го ѿ ѿц҃а
излиавшаⷢ на вѣрныѧ. тѣмже косои аще еще

And at one point there, he also speaks of grace, which he was to "preach to the Gentiles" as the good news of "the unsearchable riches of Christ", and "to bring to light for everyone" (what it was) (Eph. 3:8–9).

49.14. If his "riches" are "unsearchable", then what can be said about his very essence? How[635] is it that you do not want to recognize Kosoy as a godless and deceitful and cunning man, who lies against divine Scripture in everything, and badly distorts it, and seriously blasphemes God? For Kosoy wishes to take away God's truth. He carries the books of the Law and teaches a salvation that depends on keeping the Law, whereas the Gospel persistently preaches that the "Law was given through Moses, but grace and truth came through Jesus Christ" (Jn. 1:17). And the Lord himself responded that "the Law and the Prophets remained until John; (and) since the days" of John the Baptist, "the kingdom of God" is to be taken by force, and (only) those who "force their way" (into it) will see it (Lk. 16:16). For that reason, Kosoy lied against the very Law (that he pretended to keep), breaking it, distorting it with cunning, fighting | against the 104ᵛ/247
Lord Jesus Christ and against God. And you still ask,[636] "In what way is Kosoy godless"?

49.15. Nevertheless, the kliros-chanters said to me, "In what way does Kosoy distort the Law by breaking it? He always carefully keeps (what is written in) the books of the Law and reads them". But I responded to them and said: Now, the Law and the Prophets proclaimed the coming of Christ, but Kosoy breaks the Law precisely because he does not accept Jesus Christ as God coming in the flesh. And since, according to the words of the Lord, the Law and the Prophets remained until John the Baptist, the Law, therefore, has been invalid from the days of John the Baptist. For the one whom it formerly prefigured—Christ—has come and fulfilled it with his advent. Hence, from that point on, the Law could no longer go forward.

49.16. Jesus Christ came in the flesh, and this Jesus Christ fulfilled it (the Law) by his coming. For the Law is meant for no other purpose than to guide people to the coming of Christ Jesus in the flesh, just as the Apostle Paul claims it in all his epistles. And now that Jesus Christ has come in the flesh, who else should the Law keep guiding, for Christ already became incarnate and Christ already suffered on the cross and was buried and was resurrected, according to the Scriptures, | and he ascended to the heavens and poured out the Holy Spirit 105ʳ/248
from the Father to the faithful?

---

635 How] And how
636 still ask,] ask,

ѿ закона ꙋчиⷮ престꙋпаеⷮ законъ. коⷢ҇ бо иноⷢ҇ хо
щеⷮ проповѣдати законоⷨ. ꙗко законныꙗ кни
ги носиⷮ и оучиⷯ в ниⷯ. аще лиⷤ точию заповѣⷣ ꙋчиⷮ
ѿ закона. почтоⷤ ꙋбо по законꙋ ничтоⷤ твориⷮ
самъ. престꙋпаа всꙗ в законѣ. не постиса
бо. и не ѡчищаетсѧ. ни жрътвы жреⷮ ни ѡ
брѣзꙋетсѧ. ни пасхꙋ законнꙋю твориⷮ. ѡ сеⷨ
же аще боꙗсѧ ѡбличенїа косои. златаустаⷢ҇
иⷤ в маргаритеⷯ. речеⷮ всꙗко. ꙗко въ ї҆ерⷭ҇лимеⷯ
жрети пасхꙋ подобаеⷮ. егоⷤ нн҃ѣ ꙗзыцы соде
ржаⷮ а не июдее. пасхи ꙋбо и жертвѣ внѣ ї҆ерⷭ҇лма
жидовоⷨ невозможно творити. поⷩже и ѡбрѣ
зание и кромѣ ї҆ерⷭ҇лима сотворашеⷭ҇. не то
чию в данилѣ видѣти и во иныⷯ прⷪ҇рцеⷯ. но и саⷨ
павеⷧ҇ во антиѡхїи и в корабли в римъ пловыи
оузникъ постиⷭ҇. и тимоѳеа ѡбрѣза. вса сїа
сотвори павеⷧ҇ кромѣ ї҆ерⷭ҇лма. почто ꙋбо и косӧ
кромѣ ї҆ерⷭ҇лима не поститсѧ. ни ѡбрѣзꙋетсѧ.
оуча и еще ѿ ветхаⷢ҇ закона в моисѣѡвыⷯ книгаⷯ.
всемꙋ писанию ветхомꙋ скончаннꙋ оуⷤ сꙋщꙋ.
105v/249 и съвершившꙋсѧ хⷭ҇выⷨ пришествиеⷨ. еже и мно
гаⷤды оуⷤ рекоⷯ. ꙗко все ветхое сщ҃енное писа
ние. прознаменаше хⷭ҇во пришествие. сн҃а
бж҃иѧ во плоти быти. к немꙋⷤ в вѣрꙋ вса
чл҃ки пѣстуньствоваше. наказоваа к со
вершенномꙋ блⷢ҇ти бж҃иꙗ. пребл҃гиꙗ намъ

49.17. Therefore, if Kosoy continues his teaching based on the Law, he breaks the Law. For to whom else does he want to preach by means of the Law, as he carries the books of the Law and gives them for instruction? And even if he does accurately teach the commands of the Law, why, then, is he himself not doing everything according to the Law, and is breaking all that is in the Law? For he does not fast, and does not perform the rituals of purification, and does not offer sacrifices, and does not circumcise, and does not keep the Passover according to the Law.

49.18. Moreover, even if Kosoy[637] constantly cites Chrysostom[638] from the *Pearls*,[639] in fear of being reproached, then (his teaching implies that) the Passover must still be celebrated in Jerusalem. But it is presently in the hands of the Gentiles, and not of the Jews. Thus, because it is impossible for the Jews to celebrate the Passover and make sacrifices outside of Jerusalem,[640] they fast and circumcise in places other than Jerusalem. This is seen not only in Daniel and other Prophets, but even in Paul himself, who fasted in Antioch (Acts 13:1–3) and in Rome, (when he came) there, after sailing as a prisoner (Acts 27:9), and who circumcised Timothy (Acts 16:1–5). Paul did all that outside of Jerusalem. Why, then, does Kosoy not fast and not circumcise while he is himself outside of Jerusalem, and is also teaching from the Mosaic books of the Old Testament Law?[641]

49.19. Meanwhile, all the writings of the Old Testament | have already been 105ᵛ/249
completed and fulfilled by Christ's advent. I[642] have already discussed this repeatedly: that all the sacred writings of the Old Testament prophesied the coming of Christ and the fact that the Son of God had to appear in the flesh.

637 Kosoy] he

638 Chrysostom] according to Chrysostom

639 Pearls *is an Old Russian miscellany, containing a set of homilies by John Chrysostom. It was one of the very few patristic writings that Kosoy used to support his arguments. For more details, see* Е.Т. Казенина, "'Маргарит' и Историко-культурная ситуация на Руси XV–XVI в." [E.T. Kazenina, "'*The Pearl*' and the Historical-Cultural Situation in Rus' during the XV–XVI centuries], *Древняя Русь. Вопросы медиевистики*, 4/10 (2002): pp. 57–66.

640 Thus, because it is impossible for the Jews to celebrate the Passover and make sacrifices outside of Jerusalem,] *omitted*

641 Why, then, does Kosoy not fast and not circumcise while he is himself outside of Jerusalem, and is also teaching from the Mosaic books of the Old Testament Law?] Why, then, does Kosoy break the Law, abusing it in all respects: not fasting and not circumcising outside of Jerusalem, and teaching from the Mosaic books of the Old Testament Law?

642 I] We

с҃номъ еⷢ҇ истинныⷨ бг҃мъ і҃съ хⷭ҇мъ. сїа гл҃авъ ѿити рекоⷯ крылошаномъ. ~

ПРИШЕⷭ҇ТВЇЕ ЧЕТВЕРТОⷷ КРЫЛОⷩ҇ША.

Во ѹтрїиⷤ крылошане ѡба мниха ї иконниⷦ҇. пришеⷣше рѣша ми. гдѣ оубо в законѣ проповѣдано сн҃ѹ бж҃ию воплотиⷮ҇сѧ. како в вѣрѹ хⷭ҇вѹ пѣстⷩ҇ѹствова закоⷩ҇. и како стѣневно ѕнаменаше хⷭ҇вѹ блⷣ҃ть чл҃коⷨ закоⷩ҇. не единого ли точию бг҃а законъ проповѣда. и всѧ иныꙗ боги крѣпко ѹничижи.

Взыскание аще еⷭ҇ прописание в законѣ воплощение сн҃а бж҃їа. ~ ѿвѣщавъ оубо аⷥ и рекоⷯ к ниⷨ. вопрошение ваше сие показоуⷮе самⷢ҇о косⷢ҇о. и ѿ оученїа еⷢ҇ быⷮ гл҃омъ симъ. не мню бо жидовоⷨ сихъ вѣщати гл҃ъ. 106r/250 аще бо и мнѧтсѧ жидоⷡ҇скиѧ гл҃ы быⷮ. ибо жидове законоⷨ наказани чаюⷮ хⷭ҇ва пришествиѧ. и беⷥсмⷬ҇тнаⷢ҇ его цⷭ҇ртвїа. аще и за бесчисленое иⷯ непокоⷬ҇ство къ бг҃ѹ. самⷢ҇о пришествїа хⷭ҇ва ѿвергошаⷭ҇. и ѡнѣⷯ противленїа ради призвание быⷭ҇ всѣмъ ꙗзыкоⷨ къ бг҃ѹ вѣрою і҃съ хⷭ҇вою. жидовеⷤ прⷧ҇ѣстившеⷭ҇ ѿ истины на лжѹ. правды бж҃їа не познаша. ждѹть антихриста. сїиⷤ гл҃и иⷯⷤ рекосте ко мнѣ ꙗвлꙗютсѧ ꙗко беⷥбж҃ьныⷯ сѹть гл҃и. ꙗко выⷤ. косого раⷥвращенїа. ѡбачеⷤ есть и не

And all men are guided into faith in him, being admonished toward perfection by God's supremely good grace (given) to us through his Son, true God, Jesus Christ.[643]

49.20. Having said this, I told the kliros-chanters to leave.

50. FOURTH VISIT OF THE KLIROS-CHANTERS

50.1. And in the morning, the kliros-chanters—two monks and the icon-painter—came[644] and said to me, "Now, where in the Law is there preached that the Son of God must be incarnated? In what way did the Law guide (men) to faith in Christ[645] (Gal. 3:24), and how did the Law foreshadow the grace of Christ to humankind (Heb. 10:1)? Does the Law not preach only one God and decisively denounce all other deities"?

51. Investigation as to whether the Law foretells the incarnation of the Son of God.[646]

51.1. Then, in response, I said to them: This inquiry of yours exhibits Kosoy himself, and these words derive from his own doctrine. For I do not think that these words are appropriate for the Jews, | even though they do resemble Jewish state- 106r/250
ments. For the Jews, who are condemned by the Law, await the coming of Christ and his immortal kingdom, while in view of their never-ending disobedience to God—which led them to reject[647] the very coming of Christ[648]—and on account of their resistance, all other nations have been called to God through faith in Jesus Christ. But the Jews, having been seduced from truth into falsehood, did not acknowledge[649] the righteousness of God. They await[650] the anti-Christ.

51.2. And these words that you told me resemble words that belong to the godless,[651] which is what Kosoy's distortions are. And it actually befits unbe-

643 Jesus Christ.] our Lord Jesus Christ.
644 And in the morning, the kliros-chanters—two monks and the icon-painter—came] And there, again, those kliros-chanters came
645 Law guide (men) to faith in Christ] Law guide faith in Christ
646 **Investigation as to whether the Law foretells the incarnation of the Son of God.**] *omitted*
647 to reject] *omitted*
648 Christ] *omitted*
649 did not acknowledge] did not want to know
650 They await] They set forth their own righteousness and therefore, await
651 that you told me resemble words that belong to the godless,] *omitted*

вѣдѹщимъ вопрашати ѡ сеⷨ. ѡ немⷤъ реко сте ми. тѣмже и аⷥ. аще и выше наⷭ҇ еже ѡ сеⷨ вѣщати. и тажко ѕило. ѡбаче аще сама истинна посоⷠствѹеⷮ поистиннѣ. подасть и нⷲемѹ неможению. всеⷭ҇тго бл҃гаго бг҃а. дх҃а бл҃гть. даде бо иногда и валамовѣ истинѹ вѣщаⷮ и не достоинѹ сѹщию емѹ. оуповающеⷤ на силѹ живоⷮворащаго дх҃а вѣрою хвⷭ҇ою и выше нⷲеа немощи дерзнѹвъ ѿвѣщаю ваⷨ. ꙗко истиⷩною единою пещиⷭ҇ проѹставивше сами в себѣ в началѣ. се и нн҃ѣ точию 106v/252 твораще а не коварне. Понеⷤ преⷤ ѿ закона взыскающе единоⷢ бг҃а. и ѡбрѣтохомъ ѹбо единоⷢ бг҃а в треⷯ ипостасеⷯ. еже єⷭ҇ в треⷯ лицеⷯ. ѿц҃а и сн҃а и ст҃го дх҃а. а не мнее. ниⷤ множае. ꙗⷦ внегда создати чл҃ка восхотѣ бг҃ъ рече. сотвориⷨ чл҃ка по ѡбразѹ нⷲемѹ и по подобию. ѿ сеⷢ познахоⷨ равносилныⷯ бг҃ѹ. беспредѣлныⷯ единопрⷭ҇тльныⷯ. нераздѣлныⷯ сѹщиⷯ. тоⷤ сотворающихъ съ бг҃омъ. ꙗⷤ бг҃ъ сотвораⷮе. сихⷤ познахоⷨ кто сѹть в созданноⷨ ими по ѡбразоу иⷯ и по подобию. иⷤ въ чл҃цѣ. по ѹмнои и словеснои дш҃и. и познахомъ ꙗко сеⷢ ради бг҃ъ ꙗви себе съвершена в треⷯ лицеⷯ в чл҃чи зданїи. понеⷤ чл҃кѹ бг҃а славити ѹсты. и пѣти ꙗзыкоⷨ и оустнами єⷢ. въ нбⷭ҇номⷤъ и земномъ творенїи. бг҃ъ не ꙗви себе в треⷯ лицеⷯ. понеⷤ нбⷭ҇а добротою своею славѹ бж҃ию возвѣщають. а не словесы ꙗкоже и чл҃къ. разоумѣхоⷨ бг҃а в треⷯ ипостасеⷯ единочⷭ҇тна единосѹщна единогⷭ҇ьстве lievers to pose the kind of questions that you have asked me. Therefore, even though answering them[652] goes beyond our ability and is very difficult, still, if the truth itself genuinely helps us, it will supply our incompetence with the grace[653] of the supremely holy and good Spirit of God. For it once allowed even Balaam, an unworthy man, to prophesy the truth (Num. 22:24). And placing my trust in the power of the life-giving Spirit, through faith in Christ, I venture to answer you beyond our ability,[654] being determined from the very beginning to be concerned only with the truth, | and not with deception.[655] 106v/252

51.3. Based on our earlier search of the one God in the Law, we thus found God to be one in three hypostases, which means in three persons—the Father and the Son and the Holy Spirit—neither more nor fewer. When God wished to create man, he said, "Let us make man in our image and likeness" (Gen. 1:26), from which we learned that God has those who have power that is equal to his, who are limitless, who share the same throne with him, who are indivisible,[656] who fashion with God the same things that God fashions.

51.4. And we learned about them—who they are—(by looking) at man, whom they created according to their image and likeness, with respect to his intelligent and rational soul. And we acknowledged that by virtue of that fact, God offered a perfect revelation of himself in three persons through the creation of humanity, for it belongs to man to glorify God with his mouth and sing about him with his[657] mouth and tongue. God did not reveal himself in three persons through celestial and earthly works, because the heavens proclaim God's glory through their goodness, and not[658] through their words, as man does. And we acknowledged God in three hypostases sharing one honor,

652 them] us

653 with the grace] making us capable through the grace

654 ability,] ability in regard to what you asked me,

655 *MS 61 adds*: **Showing that it is easy to recognize God as Trinity in the book of Genesis, and from the common image and identical likeness (to recognize) the consubstantial Trinity.**

656 God has those who have equal power with him, who are limitless, who share the same throne with him, who are indivisible,] God has those who share with him the same image and are like him in divinity, who have equal power with God, who are limitless, indivisible beings,

657 his] *omitted*

658 heavens proclaim God's glory through their goodness, and not] heavens and the earth proclaim God's glory silently—through their goodness—and not

на. внегда ꙗви҃ бг҃ъ авраамꙋ и возрѣвъ авраа҃. видѣ три мꙋжи верхꙋ его. Оувѣ 107r/253 дахомъ ѿца и сн҃а и стг҃о дх҃а. единꙋ власть и силꙋ. единꙋ волю и едино хотѣние. при чл҃чи созданїи. и при размѣшенїи ꙗзыкъ. и при содоме. идоста бо в содо҃ мꙋжа два сама а не послана. лотꙋ рекоста ꙗко пꙋсти ны гь҃ погꙋби҃ содомъ. ѡдожди҃ гь҃ ѡгнь в содо҃ ѿ г҃а. и по ни҃ рече бг҃ъ авраамꙋ. съше҃ рече да вижꙋ. и не иде. но идоша два мꙋжа в содомъ. тако҃ и при кꙋпинѣ внегда ре҃ бг҃ъ моисѣю. ꙗко а҃ тѧ пꙋщаю извести люде҃ мои҃ и҃ египта. да сѧ помолѧ҃ бгꙋ в горѣ сеи. и призва гь҃ имене҃ гн҃имъ г҃а. Расꙋдихомъ посемꙋ самомꙋ писанию трц҃ꙋ бг҃а. в заповѣди ѡнои. е҃ слыши їил҃ю гь҃ бг҃ъ твои гь҃ единъ есть. Ꙗко аще кто истинно вѣрꙋе ветхомꙋ законꙋ. тои може҃ познати воистинꙋ хв҃о во плоти пришествие. на спс҃ение всемꙋ мирꙋ. Помолимсѧ про҃ видѣти в законѣ ꙗвлѧемо воплощение слова еже е҃ сн҃а бж҃иѧ. в началѣ оубо прочитахо҃ книгꙋ ѡ сотворенїи нб҃си и земли и всѣмъ и҃ в нихъ. тамо ꙋбо тогда гл҃ахо҃ 107v/254 зае҃ вѣда҃ не ложна҃ бг҃а. бг҃ъ истинныи в тре҃ one substance,[659] one lordship when (we read that) God appeared to Abraham, "And Abraham looked up and saw three men that stood in front of him"[660] (Gen. 18:2). | 107ʳ/253

51.5. And we learned of one dominion and power, and of one will, and of one desire[661] of the Father and Son and Holy Spirit from the accounts of man's creation and of the confusion of tongues and of Sodom.[662] For the two men who came to Sodom, did it on their own initiative instead of being sent (Gen. 19:1). And they said to Lot that the "Lord sent us to destroy" Sodom[663] (Gen. 19:13), and "the Lord rained down fire on Sodom—from the Lord" (Gen. 19:24). Accordingly,[664] God said to Abraham, "I will go down to see" (Gen. 18:21), but after saying it, did not go; and instead, there were two men that went to Sodom[665] (Gen. 19:1).

51.6. Likewise, at the bush, God said to Moses, "I am sending you to bring my people out of Egypt so that they may pray to God on this mountain" (Ex. 3:12), and the Lord called upon the Lord by the name of the Lord. And according to the same Scripture, we considered the divine Trinity also in that command that says, "Hear, O Israel: The Lord your God, the Lord is one" (Deut. 6:4).

52. Showing that he who truly believes in the Law of the Old Testament can truly recognize the bodily coming of Christ for the salvation of the whole world.[666]

52.1. Let us pray that we may see the incarnation of the Word, who is the Son of God, in the rest of the Law.[667] Thus, we began by reading the holy book (of Genesis) about the creation of the heavens and the earth, and everything that is in them. At that point, then, our discussion | led us to acknowledge the true 107ᵛ/254

---

659 one substance,] one substance, one throne,

660 him".] him", and the rest of the things after this

661 desire] desire, and of one divinity

662 of the confusion of tongues and of Sodom.] of Abraham and of Sodom.

663 Sodom] this place

664 Accordingly,] Since

665 went to Sodom] went for him to Sodom

666 **Showing that he who truly believes in the Law of the Old Testament can truly recognize the bodily coming of Christ for the salvation of the whole world.**] *omitted*

667 *MS 61 adds*: **Investigation in the holy book of Genesis as to how we should understand the statement spoken by God, "Let us make man in our image and likeness"; and when the image grew weak and broke down in its fallenness, how, then, it was renewed and restored back to the likeness it had in the creation of Adam and Eve; and when God makes anything, how he envisions it; and on how God knows all future things even before they come to be; and on how highly man must be esteemed. CHAPTER 23.**

ипостасеⷯ. ꙗвленъ е҃ ѿц҃ъ и сн҃ъ и ст҃ыи дх҃ъ.
нн҃ѣⷤ паки тꙋю сщ҃еннꙋю книгꙋ восприѧⷮ
заⷤ оувѣдати бг҃ꙋ словꙋ. в законѣ воѡбра
жено воплощение. Ꙗко бг҃ъ в началѣ не
просто совѣтова сотворити чл҃ка. но во
площенїа раⷣ слова е҃. заⷤ поновиⷮ паки ѡбраⷥ
свои.[668] Взыдемо и паки на бг҃одх҃новенное
писание. глⷮе ꙋбо тамо. ꙗко искони сотво
ри бг҃ъ нб҃о и землю. таⷤ глⷮе и реⷱ҇ бг҃ъ да бꙋдеⷮ свѣⷮ.
и реⷱ҇ бг҃ъ да бꙋдеⷮ твердь разлꙋчающе посреди
воды и воды. и проⷱ҇ твари вса творенїа.
и по сиⷯ всѣⷯ реⷱ҇ бг҃ъ. сотвориⷨ чл҃ка по ѡбра
зꙋ нш҃емꙋ и по поⷣобию. что раⷣ бг҃ъ многаа
и великаа твориⷮ начинаа и твора. не во
сприѧⷮ совѣтовати тогда. послѣдиⷤ оуже
всеа твари создаⷣ единоⷢ҇ чл҃ка восхотѣ. то
гда совѣтовавъ созда чл҃ка. не оубо боⷣши
нбсѣ чл҃къ. ниⷤ тѧжчаиши землѧ и воды.
да примеⷮ бг҃ъ спомагающиⷯ емꙋ на созда
ние чл҃ка. реⷱ҇ бо бг҃ъ сотвориⷨ чл҃ка по ѡбразꙋ
нш҃емꙋ и по поⷣобию. глⷮе сщ҃енное писание.
108r/255 не сегоⷣ ради совѣтова бг҃ъ вкꙋпѣ съ словоⷨ своимъ
и дх҃мъ своиⷨ сотвориⷮ чл҃ка ꙗко чт҃нѣишее зда
ние хоташе сотвориⷮ паⷱ҇ всеа твари. по ѡ
бразꙋ своемꙋ и по поⷣобию сотвори чл҃ка. да
ѡбладаеⷮ рече рыбами морьскими. и птицаⷨ
нбⷭ҇ными. и звѣрми и скоты. и всею землею.
и всѣми гады пресмыкающимиⷭ҇ по земли.

---

668 *In the margin*: глаⷡ҇ кг҃.

God,[669] and the fact that the true God is revealed in three hypostases, the Father and the Son and the Holy Spirit. This time, we will once more consider the same sacred[670] book (of Scripture) in order to learn how the incarnation of God's Word is presented in the Law.

53. Showing that in the beginning, God took counsel not only because of the creation of man, but because of the incarnation of his Word, in order to renew his image and likeness (in man). CHAPTER 23.[671]

53.1. Let us go back to the divinely inspired Scripture[672] again. For it says there that "In the beginning, God made the heaven and the earth" (Gen. 1:1). And it also says, "And God said, 'Let there be a vault in the midst of the waters, and let it separate the waters from the waters'" (Gen. 1:6). And the same thing happened with respect to all the other creatures of the world.[673] And after all of those things, God said, "Let us make man in our image and likeness" (Gen. 1:26). Why is it that God did not take counsel at the time when he began to create all the numerous and great things, but then, following the creation of all the works, he wished to create man, and did take counsel at that point?

53.2. Man is certainly not greater than the heavens, nor is he weightier than the earth and water, that God should call upon his helpers in order to create man. For the sacred Scripture says, "God said, 'Let us make man in our image and likeness'" (Gen. 1:26). | Isn't the reason for which God took counsel—"Let 108r/255
us make man"[674]—with his Word and his Holy Spirit, related to the fact that he wished to make the most honorable creature above all the other works? He[675] made man "in his image and likeness" so that the latter may subdue, as he said, "the fish of the sea, and the birds of the heavens, and the beasts, and the livestock, and all the earth, and every creeping thing that creeps on the earth" (Gen.

669 discussion led us to acknowledge the true God,] discussion was aimed at describing the true God

670 sacred] divinely inspired

671 **Showing that in the beginning, God took counsel not only because of the creation of man, but because of the incarnation of his Word, in order to renew his image and likeness (in man). CHAPTER 23.] Showing that he who truly believes in the Law of the Old Testament, can truly recognize the bodily coming of Christ for the salvation of the world.**

672 divinely inspired Scripture] first book of the sacred Scripture

673 And the same thing happened with respect to all the other creatures of the world.] And concerning all the other creatures, God spoke, and they came to be.

674 "Let us make man"] *omitted*

675 He] For he

понеⷤ ѡбраⷥ бж҃їи аки и бг҃ъ самовластие имѣѧ. и аки подⷪбенъ бг҃ꙋ бл҃гїа дѣтели да твориⷮ. по подⷪбию бл҃гаго бг҃а создавшаго еⷢ. не то кмⷪⷤ сего раⷣ еже чтⷭнѣишее здание паче всеѧ твари. но понеⷤ хоташе чл҃къ ѿ самовластиѧ своеⷢ сокрꙋшити и истлѣти поѡбразное и подобное бж҃ие в себѣ. и ꙗко словесное живое сего раⷣ хоташе послаⷮ бг҃ъ въⷤ е спⷭти погибшаⷢ чл҃ка. ѡбновити в неⷨ престꙋплениеⷨ и истлѣвшїи свои ѡбраⷥ и подобное наздаⷮ паки иⷤ сокрꙋшившеесѧ прегрѣшенми. не инакоⷤ сего поновити есть аще тоюⷤ плотию не ѡдѣетсѧ. само то слово бж҃ие. и сего раⷣ совѣтꙋѧ реⷱ бг҃ъ к нимъ. сотвориⷨ чл҃ка по ѡбразꙋ нш҃емꙋ и по подⷪбию.
108v/257 понеⷤ самоⷢ того бг҃а ѿц҃а бл҃говоление словꙋ плотию быти. и дхⷪмъ ст҃ымъ ѿ чтⷭыѧ крови въ чреви составитиⷭ беⷥсѣменно плоти словꙋ. и се самое ꙗвлѧѧ бг҃ъ ѿц҃ъ. словꙋ своемꙋ и дх҃ꙋ своемꙋ ст҃мꙋ. ꙗко быти посланꙋ словꙋ во плотитиⷭ на исцѣление чл҃ка. пишеⷮ бо в законѣ. посла слово свое и исцѣли иⷯ. посланꙋ быти и дх҃ꙋ ст҃мꙋ. на беⷥсѣменное плоти зачатїа. тѣмже к ниⷨ и реⷱ бг҃ъ сотвориⷨ чл҃ка по ѡбразꙋ нш҃емꙋ и по подⷪбию. паки бы гл҃алъ сїа бг҃ъ ѿц҃ъ къ сн҃ꙋ своемꙋ единороⷣномꙋ. и къ дх҃ꙋ своемꙋ ст҃мꙋ. созидаемꙋ ѡбразꙋ семꙋ нш҃емꙋ и подⷪбию. внегда емꙋ ѡбетшавшꙋ съкрꙋшитиⷭ. тогда тебѣ сн҃оу поновити его воплощениемъ своимъ. и тебѣ дх҃ꙋ нашествиемъ содѣистоваⷮ. моеи силѣ ѡсѣнающи. того раⷣ сотвориⷨ

1:26). For the image of God, just as God himself, is self-governing and made like God in order to do good acts, in imitation of the good God who created him.[676]

53.3. And the reason why God took counsel during the creation of man was not just because he (intended) to make man into the most honorable creature, above all other works, but because man wanted to use his capacity for self-governing to demolish the prototype and corrupt the likeness of God in himself. That[677] is the reason why God was willing to send the One who was rational and living[678] in order to save the man who was perishing, to renew in him the image that was corrupted by transgression, and recreate the likeness that was broken by sins.[679] And there was no other way to accomplish this renewal other than by means of the very flesh into which the Word of God clothed himself. That is why God[680] took counsel and said to them, "Let us make man in our image and likeness". | 108v/257

53.4. For it was by the good pleasure of the same God the Father, that the Word became flesh, and it was through the Holy Spirit, that the Word was formed into flesh within the womb, (and formed) of pure blood and without a male seed. And to reveal this very thing, God the Father ⟨said⟩ to his Word and his Holy Spirit,[681] ⟨"Let us make man in our image and likeness"⟩, so that (in due time), the Word may become incarnate in order to heal man, for[682] it is written in the Law, "He sent out his Word and healed them" (Ps. 107:20), and that the Holy Spirit may be sent in order for the ⟨Word⟩ to be conceived in the flesh without a male seed.

53.5. Therefore, God said to both of them together, "Let us make man in our image and likeness", as if God the Father were saying the following to his only-begotten Son and his Holy Spirit, "Now that this image and likeness of ours that we created has grown weak and become broken, it remains for you, Son, then, to renew it through the incarnation, and it remains for you, Holy Spirit, to descend and advance my illuminating power. Therefore, 'let us make man

676 *MS 61 adds*: **Showing that in the beginning, God took counsel not only because of the creation of man, but because of the incarnation of his Word, in order to renew his image and likeness (in man).**

677 That] And that

678 the One who was rational and living] his living Word

679 in him his image that was corrupted by transgression, and recreate the likeness that was broken by sins.] in him the likeness and that which was corrupted, as well as to recreate his broken image.

680 That is why God] That is the reason, therefore, why we understand that God

681 and his Holy Spirit] *omitted*

682 heal man, for] heal man—their image and likeness—for

чл҃ка по ѡбразꙋ н҃шемꙋ и по пⷣⷪбию. понеⷤ
совокꙋпитиⷭ҇ емꙋ в нашꙋ бл҃гть. прибли
жениⷨ ѡбраза раⷣ н҃шего и пⷣⷪбиа. тѣмⷤ
в сотворенїи нбⷭ҇ѣ и землꙗ. и всѣⷯ иже
в ниⷯ. не совѣтова ѡ ниⷯ ѿц҃ъ бг҃ъ со словоⷨ
109r/258 своиⷨ сн҃омъ. и со ст҃ымъ дⷯомъ. ꙗко не приати
словꙋ сн҃ꙋ бж҃ию нбⷭ҇ныа плоⷮ ни агг҃льскиа. но
приати чл҃чю плоⷮ словꙋ бж҃ию дⷯомъ ст҃ымъ.
заⷤе поновиⷮ ѡбраⷥ свои и пⷣⷪбие. сего раⷣ на созда
нїи реⷱ҇ бг҃ъ къ сн҃ꙋ своемꙋ и дⷯꙋ. сотвориⷨ чл҃ка
по ѡбразꙋ н҃шемꙋ и по пⷣⷪбию. Ꙗко вса вѣⷭ҇
бг҃ъ. и не невѣⷭ҇ ничесоⷤ преⷤ бытїа коегождо.
Вѣⷭ҇ бо бг҃ъ вса хотащаа быти преⷤ бытиа иⷯ.
вѣсть и адомово престꙋпление. вѣⷭ҇ и ѡбра
за своеⷢ҇ и подобиа в чл҃цѣ сокрꙋшение. тѣ
мⷤъ восхотѣ помиловати еⷢ҇. свободити
ѿ престꙋплениа. и исправиⷮ свои ѡбраⷥ и пⷣⷪ
бие. ибо гл҃а к моисею гⷭ҇ь. помилꙋю егоⷤ аще
помилꙋю. и оущⷣрю егоⷤ аще оущⷣрю. И ты
оубоⷤ е аще что начинаеши творити. вѣси
что хощеши сотворити. и кꙋзнецъ бо при
емлеⷮ желѣзо раⷥжигати. преⷤ оубо вѣсть что
хощеⷮ из неⷢ҇ ковати. или ролїи потребꙋ. или
секирꙋ. или серпъ. или ино что. бг҃ꙋⷤ ли зижю
щꙋ чл҃ка не хощеши даⷮ вѣдати ѡ чл҃цѣ. что
бꙋдеⷮ в чл҃цѣ. аще бо кꙋзнецъ имѣа в рꙋкꙋ свою
желѣзо. вѣⷭ҇ что еⷤ из неⷢ҇ сотворити. бг҃ъ ли
109v/259 не оувѣⷭ҇ зижа чл҃ка ꙗⷤ въ чл҃цѣ. Слышиⷨ бг҃а гл҃ю
ща къ їеремїи прⷪ҇ркꙋ. преⷤ даже не создаⷯ та

in our image and likeness' that he may[683] be linked to our grace in imitation of our image and likeness".[684]

53.6. Thus, God the Father did not take counsel about them with his Word, | 109r/258
the Son,[685] nor with the Holy Spirit, in creating the heavens and the earth and everything that is in them. And the Word, the Son of God,[686] took a body that was neither celestial nor the body of angels.[687] Instead, the Word of God assumed human flesh through the Holy Spirit in order to renew his image and likeness (in man). For that reason, when creating ⟨man⟩, it was to his Word and to the Spirit, that God said, "Let us make man in our image and likeness".

54. Showing that God knows everything, and there is nothing that he does not know about any single thing prior to the existence of each one of them.[688]

54.1. For God knows all things that are to come before[689] their existence. He also knows that Adam was to transgress. He knows that his image and likeness in man was to be broken;[690] which is why he also wished to have mercy on him, liberate him from transgression, and mend his image and likeness. For the Lord said to Moses, "I will have mercy on whom I will have mercy and will have compassion on whom I will have compassion" (Ex. 33:19).

54.2. Now, you, too, know what you want to make when you actually begin to make something. For in preparing to heat the iron, even the blacksmith knows beforehand what he actually wants to forge from it—either something needed for plowing, or an ax, or a sickle,[691] or some other thing. And do you want to deny the fact that God, who fashions man, knows man and (knows) what is going to be in man? For if the blacksmith knows what he will make out of the iron when he has it in his hand,[692] would not ⟨God⟩ | know what is to be found 109v/259
in man when creating man? Thus, we hear God saying to the Prophet Jeremiah,

---

683 that he may] by which he may

684 *MS 61 adds*: **Showing that God knows everything, and there is nothing that he does not know about any single thing prior to the existence of each one of them.**

685 Son,] and the Son,

686 Word, the Son of God,] Word of God

687 angels.] angels, and none of them were made in the image of God and (his) likeness.

688 **Showing that God knows everything, and there is nothing that he does not know about any single thing prior to the existence of each one of them.**] *omitted*

689 before] even before

690 broken;] broken and corrupted

691 or a sickle,] or some kind of weapon,

692 has it in his hand,] takes it into his hand,

въ чревѣ свѣм тѧ. и ко иеву рⷱ҇е. кто щадѧ
гл҃ъ в срⷣцѣ своеⷨ непщуеⷮ же мене таити.
и внегдаⷤ созидаⷮ чл҃ка бг҃у. непщуеши ли ему
не вѣдаⷮ вса. что хоташе быⷮ ѡ чл҃чествѣ
до скончанїа. ты не вѣдыи воздушныⷯ вре
меⷩ. аще буⷣеⷮ студень многа или не буⷣеⷮ. ѡбаⷱ
чаеши зимы по прежнему года ѡⷝхожению.
сего раⷣ и пещь въ храминѣ своеи созидаеши.
и дрова готовиши. и шюбы стажаваⷮ тщи
шиса. ища согрѣтиⷭ еще не пришеⷭши зимѣ.
такоⷤ и покровъ храминѣ твердо покрыва
еши. не вѣдыи или буⷣеⷮ дождь или не будеть.
точию чаа дожда покровъ оутвержаеши.
бг҃у ли хощеши даⷮ вѣдати. преⷣ ниⷯ толико.
елико ты чааниеⷨ вѣси приходащаа. и ка
ко въ їевѣ рⷱ҇ено. капла дождевныа в число
проливаа на землю бг҃ъ. и аще вѣⷭ бг҃ъ числиⷮ
каплıа дождевныа елико каплеи когда подо
баеⷮ ему дати на землю. вѣсть и чл҃чество
како хощеⷮ жити. или чѣмъ истлѣтиса.
110r/260 тѣмъⷤ преже даⷤ создаⷮ его. поможение худости
его уготовлıаеⷮ. совѣтуа къ сн҃у своему еди
нороⷣному и дх҃у своему ст҃му рⷱ҇е бг҃ъ. сотвориⷨ
чл҃ка по ѡбразу нⷲ҇ему и по поⷣбию. и аще не сие
проѡбразуа бг҃ъ совѣтуа ѕижа чл҃ка. еⷤ послаⷮ
ему слово свое воплотитиⷭ и спⷭти чл҃ка содѣи
ствующу и ст҃му дх҃у. можаше и чл҃ка сотво
рити бг҃ъ беⷥ совѣта. ıако иⷤ и преⷤ чл҃ка сотво
реную твⷭа. не совѣтовавъ сотвори. колика
убо нб҃са. каковаⷤ земла и море. слн҃це и луна.
и вса звѣзды. воздуⷯ ѡблацы. горы и хоⷧми.
древеса и злакъ травныи. источницы же
и рѣки. рыби и киты и птица. звѣриⷤ и ско
ты. и гады. бесчисленыа роды сотвораа. ни
гдѣⷤ не глⷮе писание ıако совѣтова ѡ ниⷯ бг҃ъ.
и не рⷱ҇е сотвориⷨ нб҃са или землю. или елико в ниⷯ.
но токмо ѡ единоⷨ чл҃цѣ сказоуеⷮ ст҃енное пи
сание. ıако рⷱ҇е бг҃ъ сотворимъ чл҃ка по ѡбразу
нⷲ҇ему и по поⷣбию. не оубо просто мимохоⷣ

"Even before I formed you in the womb, I knew you" (Jer. 1:5). And to Job, he asked, "Who is it that spares the words in his heart, thinking to hide them from me"? (Job 38:2). And with regard to God's creation of man, do you think he did not know everything that he wanted to do with humankind until the very end?

54.3. You do not know the changing conditions of the air—whether it will be very cold or not—yet you expect the winter to come by the end of the passing year, and in view of that, you build a furnace in the house, and prepare firewood, and seek to acquire fur coats, trying to keep yourself warm during the coming winter. Likewise, you also tightly seal the roof of the house, without knowing whether the rain will come or not; you build the roof only in expectation of the rain. And do you deny that God knows things ahead of time when you yourselves rely on the knowledge of things you expect to happen? And what about the statement from Job, "The drops of rain that God[693] poured on the earth are numbered" (Job 26:27)? And if God knows the number of raindrops—how many drops, and when he needs to distribute them on the earth—he also knows how humanity will live and what will cause its corruption. | 110r/260

54.4. Thus, even before creating him, God established help for (man's) weakness, taking counsel with his only-begotten Son and his Holy Spirit, saying, "Let us make man in our image and likeness". And if God had taken counsel at the time of creation for something other than to prefigure the fact that he would send his own Word to become incarnate, and save humanity through the assisting work of the Holy Spirit, then God could have made man without counsel, just as he made all other created works that were before man, without taking counsel.

54.5. Now, how great are the heavens, and how great are the earth, and the sea, and also the sun and the moon, and all the stars, the air, the clouds, the mountains and the hills, the woods and the green plants, and also the springs and the rivers, the fish, including the big ones, and the birds, and also the beasts and the livestock, and the creeping things! (And yet), there is no place in Scripture where it says that in making an infinite number of different things, God took counsel about them. And it did not say, "Let us make the heavens, or the earth, or[694] all that is in them". Rather, only of man alone does the sacred Scripture states that God said, "Let us make man in our image and likeness".[695]

---

693 God] *omitted*

694 or] and

695 *MS 61 adds*: **Showing that we should not treat the divine words in simplicity, for it is a grave sin. Instead, we should consider every divine word with great fear. Even if something insignificant is spoken, we must be in much tremble before it.**

бж҃ию бесѣдꙋ. аще цр҃ви такомꙋ чл҃кꙋ сꙋщꙋ
ꙗковⷤ и ты бесѣдꙋющꙋ что. не смѣеши пре
wбидѣ. то бж҃июⷮ бесѣдꙋ смѣеши преwбидѣ.
110v/261 и гдѣ wбращеши толико дерзовавъ. бг҃ъ оубо
созда чл҃ка на бесмртиеⷤ бꙑти чл҃кꙋ безъ
смртнꙋ. ꙗко wбраⷥ бж҃ии и подобие ⷭ҇. чл҃кꙋ бꙑⷭ
попознꙋтиⷭ волею своею въ смрть. подобаⷮ
бг҃ꙋ не презрѣти чл҃ка смртию wбладаема.
wбраⷥ его и подобие ⷭ҇ сꙋще. тѣмже не изгото
вить ли изначала зданиꙗ. wбразꙋ своемꙋ
и подобию помощь. въⷤ ⷭ҇ wбновити паки wбраⷥ
свои и подобие. ꙗвѣ ꙗко сего раⷣ и гл҃е бг҃ъ совѣ
тꙋꙗ хотꙗ созда чл҃ка. къ единороⷣномꙋ си сн҃ꙋ
и ст҃мꙋ дх҃ꙋ своемꙋ. сотвориⷨ рⷪ҇ чл҃ка по wбра
зꙋ нш҃емꙋ и по подобию. ꙗко сн҃ꙋ его единороⷣно
мꙋ воплотитиⷭ. и собою воскрⷭ҇ти оумръ
швенаⷭ чл҃ка. ст҃мꙋ дх҃ꙋ его содѣиствꙋющꙋ
в сиꙗ. Рѣшаⷤ ми крылошане. что ꙋбо ты
гл҃еши. ꙗко созидаа чл҃ка бг҃ъ. в началѣ и по
можение попознꙋти ю ⷭ҇ изготова. что
ꙋбо чл҃къ или что ⷭ҇ сие ⷭ҇ оумреⷤ чл҃къ. не ꙋми
раюⷮ ли рꙑбꙑ великиꙗ в мори. и гадꙑ и китꙑ.
такоⷤ и птицꙑ нбⷭ҇нꙑꙗ и звѣри и лвꙑ. и слонꙑ
великиꙗ на земли. вса та создание бж҃ие
ꙗкоⷤ и чл҃къ. бꙋ оубо ꙗко и восхотѣ бг҃ъ чл҃кꙋ.
111r/263 помощь изготоваⷮ. да чесо ꙋбо раⷣ сн҃ꙋ его воплоти
тиⷭ. а не послаⷮ бг҃ꙋ иного коⷢ на помоⷱ хꙋдости чл҃чи.

54.6. Now, do not disregard the words of God by simply bypassing them. If you do not dare to neglect the things announced by a king, who is a man like you,[696] then would you dare to neglect the words of God? | And if you do, what will be result of such audacity? Now, God created man for immortality so that man, representing God's image and likeness, could be immortal.[697] But man slipped into death by his own will,[698] and it was fitting for God to not neglect man—his image and likeness—after he was overtaken by death. 110v/261

54.7. Therefore,[699] would he not have devised help for that which was his image and likeness even from the beginning of creation in order to renew his image and likeness? It is evident[700] that this was the reason why God spoke in such a way when he wanted to create man,[701] taking counsel with the only-begotten Son and his Holy Spirit. In saying, "Let us make man[702] in our image and likeness", (he implied) that his only-begotten Son would become incarnate and bring the dead man back to life through himself, and that the Holy Spirit would work together in all of this.[703]

54.8. But the kliros-chanters said to me,[704] "Now, what do you mean when you say that in creating man, God devised help for his fall from the beginning? Indeed, what is man or what is this (help for) if man dies? Does not death reign over the great fish in the sea, and the things that creep, and the monstrous animals in large waters, and also the birds of the heavens, and the beasts, and the lions, and the huge elephants on the earth? All these works of God are like man. And if God really wanted to prepare help for man, | why should God have his Son become incarnate rather than sending someone else to help human weakness"?[705] 111r/263

696 you,] you, with the nature of similar kind,

697 immortal.] immortal, as the Scriptures say.

698 will,] will, after being deceived by the snake

699 Therefore,] And then,

700 evident,] evident, then,

701 when he wanted to create man,] at the creation of man

702 man] *omitted*

703 this.] this. If a human king were to walk by and see his portrait—(originally designed with) gold or silver, or gilded and decorated with paint—and if he were to see it collapsed and broken, he would not have bypassed it in disdain. Instead, he would have repaired it and brought it back to its initial state of royal likeness. And if a human king does that, then how much more so would God not neglect his image (in man) but rather renew and restore it?

704 to me,] *omitted*

705 weakness"?] weakness, just as the human king (would entrust) his portrait to the artists for repair or renovation"?

Ѿвѣщавъ азъ к ниⷨ глѧ. чл҃къ оубо прⷭ҇тное бж҃ие здание паⷭ҇ всеѧ твари. поне́ⷤ по ѡбразꙋ бж҃ию и по пⷣобию е҆ⷭ҇ сотворенъ. ꙗкоⷤ гл҃еⷮ бг҃одхⷩ҇овенное писание. И сотвори бг҃ъ чл҃ка по ѡбразꙋ бж҃ию сотвори его. и здѣ есть видѣти паки бг҃а и бг҃а. бг҃ъ бо сотвори чл҃ка по бж҃июⷤ ѡбразꙋ. а не реⷱ҇ писание. и сотвори бг҃ъ чл҃ка по ѡбразꙋ своемꙋ сотвори е҆ⷭ҇. но реⷱ҇ сщ҃нное писание. и сотвори бг҃ъ чл҃ка по ѡбразꙋ бж҃ию сотвори е҆ⷭ҇. по ѡбразꙋ оубо бж҃ию чл҃къ. ꙗко дш҃ꙋ имѣа оумнꙋ словеⷭ҇нꙋ. и ꙗко самовластенъ е҆ⷭ҇ чл҃къ. понеⷤ вса тварь по е҆ⷭ҇ствꙋ своемꙋ нꙋжею дви жение имаⷮ. единъ чл҃къ волю имаⷮ. избрати е҆ⷤ хощеⷮ. или к добрыⷨ двизатиⷭ҇ или къ злымъ. и владѣеⷮ землею и рыбами морьскими. и пти цами и скоты. по ѡбразꙋ бж҃ию. аще и пре слꙋшанием чл҃къ сию власть свою погꙋби но е҆ⷭ҇ и нн҃ѣ истинна самовластиа чл҃ча видѣⷯ. елицы бо бж҃ию повелѣнию повинꙋвшеⷭ҇. прпⷣбно и правеⷣно ѡправданиа бж҃иа сотвориша. 111v/264 и стрⷭ҇ти своа ѡдолѣша. тїи ѡбладахꙋ на земⷧ҇и не токмо скоты и птицами и рыбами. но и на нбⷭ҇и слнцемъ и лꙋною. ꙗцыⷤ ап҃ли и прⷪ҇рцы и мч҃нцы. и ѿцы прпⷣбнїи. ꙗкоⷤ видѣти мои сѣа твораща. и навгина і҆ⷭ҇са. и илию. и ели сѣа и три ѡтроки и данила в ветхомъ. по хвⷭ҇ѣⷤ воплощении бесчисленое мноⷤство стыⷯ. сотвориша ꙗкоⷤ и древнїи в ветхоⷨ многаа чюдеса. и посемꙋ видѣти чл҃ка ѿ бг҃а создана лꙋчша всеѧ видимыѧ твари. вса бо тварь видимаа чл҃кꙋ потребꙋ при носиⷮ. и аки цр҃а зрѣⷯ коеⷢ҇ чл҃ка во всеи твари

54.9. And in response to them, I said: Well, man is the most honorable work of God, above all works, for he was made in God's image and likeness, as[706] the divinely inspired Scripture says, "And God made man, in the image of God he made him" (Gen. 1:27). And here again, we can see God and God, for God made man according to the image of God. And the Scripture did not say, "And God made man, in *his image*[707] he made him". Instead, the sacred Scripture said, "And God made man, in the *image of God* he made him".[708]

54.10. Now, for man to be in the image of God means to have an intelligent and rational soul; and it means that man is self-governing. In view of this, while all other works need to move according to their nature, man alone has the will to choose in what direction he wants to move—toward good things or toward things that are evil; and he subdues the earth, and the fish of the sea, and the birds, and the livestock, (as being made) in the image of God. Even though man destroyed this power of his through disobedience, yet the human ability to remain self-governed is truly seen with him even now.[709]

54.11. For all those who obeyed God's command, carried out the righteousness of God in a way that was honorable and holy, | and overcame their passions; and these came to possess not only the livestock, and the birds, and the fish on this earth, but also the sun and the moon in the heavens. Such were the Apostles and the Prophets,[710] the martyrs and the holy fathers. And we see this in what was done by Moses, and Joshua, son of Nun, and Elijah, and Elisha, and the three young men with Daniel in the Old Testament. And after the incarnation of Christ, a great multitude of saints performed many miracles like those that were performed through[711] men of ancient times. 111v/264

54.12. That is why we must view man as being created by God to be better than all other visible works, for all the visible works are there to serve the needs of man. And we can view man as some sort of a king made (to rule) over all the

706 God, above all works, for he was made in God's image and likeness, as] God, and God made man with his own hand above all works, which is not how the human king did it by making his portrait through the artist and (not how) he also renovated it through the same artist. But man was made by the hand of God himself in view of the image and likeness of God, as

707 And the Scripture did not say, "And God made man, in *his image*] *omitted*

708 him".] him". And it is evident that the Son, the divine Word of God, makes him in the image of God the Father.

709 now] now, and all creatures fear him.

710 the Apostles and the Prophets,] the Prophets, the Apostles,

711 a great multitude of saints performed many miracles like those that were performed through] the multitude of saints performed miracles that were far greater than those performed through

бжиеи создана. аще и создаⷭ҇ чл҃къ ѿ пе҇сти малы и хѹ҆ды вещи. но высотою чести болши всеа видимыа твари вознесена. самовластие по ѡбразѹ бж҃ию имѣа. и по по҃бию бж҃ию. ꙗкоⷤ҇ бг҃ъ бесплотныи сн҃а бесплотна роди. беⷥ҇ женьства бес предѣла. собезнача҃на. такоⷤ҇ и чл҃кѹ. оумъ раждаеⷮ҇ слово бесплотно беⷥ҇ женьства. и добродѣтелию и мдрⷭ҇ием блг҃омѹ бг҃ѹ подобитиⷭ҇ могии. и посемѹ видѣти чл҃ка ѕѣло присвоена бг҃ѹ. паⷱ҇ всеа

112r/265 твари в самоⷨ҇ зданїи чл҃чи. и ѿ сего мноⷢ҇ подаеⷮ҇ разѹмѣти. ꙗко еⷭ҇ бл҃говоление бж҃ие въчлчитиⷭ҇ словѹ его ѿ дх҃а ст҃го. елма приближнѣиши всеа твари присвоити къ своемѹ бж҃твѹ чл҃ка. аще бо нб҃са и земля и всеⷤ҇ е в ниⷯ҇. аще агг҃ли и архагг҃или. и пр҃тли. ничтоⷤ҇ по ѡбразѹ бж҃ию и по по҃бию. токмо единъ чл҃къ по ѡбразѹ бж҃ию и по по҃бию. и еⷭ҇ из начала сотворениа присвоенъ чл҃къ бж҃твѹ ѡбразоⷨ҇ и подобиеⷨ҇. и нѣⷭ҇ли в сеⷨ҇ в нача҃номъ закона писанїи воображено. сн҃а бж҃иа воплощение. аще кто хощеⷮ҇ не коварне ни любопривѣ послѣдоваⷮ҇ бж҃ию ѡправданию. **Ꙗко во всеи твари бж҃їи чтн҃ѣиши еⷭ҇ чл҃къ. и къ б҃ви ѹсвоенъ ближае всеа твари.** Ещеⷤ҇ гл҃еⷮ҇ бг҃одхⷩ҇овенное писание. и созда бг҃ъ чл҃ка перьсть вземъ ѿ земля. и вдѹнѹ на лице еⷭ҇ дыхание жизни. и быⷭ҇ чл҃къ в дш҃ѹ живѹ. колико твари сотвори бг҃ъ и колико животныⷯ҇ родовъ. и нигдѣⷤ҇ ни ѡ которомъ не реⷱ҇ писание. ꙗко взеⷨ҇ сотвори бг҃ъ. но реⷱ҇ бг҃ъ и быⷭ҇ тако. ѡ чл҃цѣⷤ҇ гл҃еⷮ҇. созда бг҃ъ чл҃ка пеⷭ҇сть вземъ ѿ земля создаеⷮ҇. и ѹбо зижемое works of God. Even though human hands produce only small and insignificant things, yet in his high honor, (man) is exalted above all the visible works, possessing the ability to be self-governed, according to the image and likeness of God.[712]

54.13. Just as God, being incorporeal, begot the incorporeal Son without a female partner—in a way that is infinite and without beginning—so[713] does the human mind generate the incorporeal word without a female partner; and it is able to imitate the good God in (producing) virtue and mercy. And this is why we can view man as being exceptionally close to God above all other | 112r/265
works, by virtue of how man was actually fashioned. And from this, we must recognize multiple things, (in particular), the fact that it was God's good pleasure to have the Word become human by means of the Holy Spirit, drawing man—the closest to him of all the works—to his own divinity. For neither the heavens and the earth and everything that is in them, nor the angels and archangels and thrones[714] are made in the image and likeness of God. Only man alone is in the image and likeness of God, and from the beginning of creation man is set close to the Godhead through the image and likeness. And can we not find the incarnation of God's Son prefigured in these first books of the Law,[715] if we seek to follow God's truth without deceiving or arguing?

55. Showing that among all the works of God, man is the most honorable being, and he is also the closest to God of all the works.[716]

55.1. And the divinely inspired Scripture also says, "And God formed man by taking the dust of the ground, and he breathed into his face the breath of life, and the man became a living soul" (Gen. 2:7). What a great number of works that God framed and what a numerous variety of living creatures, and yet there is no place in the Scripture where it is said of anything that God took (the dust of the ground) to fashion it. Instead, ⟨the Scripture states⟩, "God said, and it was so", but of man it says, "God formed man; by taking the dust of the ground, he made him".

712 *MS 61 adds*: **Showing that man is both the most honorable of all the works and the closest to God of all the works.**

713 Son without a female partner—in a way that is infinite and without beginning—so] Son—infinite and limitless—so

714 and thrones] and seraphim and cherubim

715 books of the Law,] books,

716 **Showing that among all the works of God, man is the most honorable being, and he is also the closest to God of all the works.**] *omitted*

112v/266 рꙋками зижетсѧ. тѣмже рꙋкою своею бг҃ъ созда чл҃ка. сие самое дв҃дъ исповѣдаеⷮ гл҃ѧ. рꙋцѣ твои сотвористе мѧ и создасте мѧ. внегда созидаⷮ҇ чл҃ка совѣтꙋеⷮ бг҃ъ гл҃ѧ. сотворимъ чл҃ка по ѡбразꙋ нш҃емꙋ и по пⷣобию. и внегда зижеⷮ чл҃ка. рꙋкою своею вземъ пеⷭ҇ть ѿ землѧ и созидаеⷮ чл҃ка. или не возмоⷤ бг҃ъ словоⷨ сотвориⷮ҇ чл҃ка ꙗкоⷤ и всю твⷬ҇ прⷭ҇е его словоⷨ сотвори. аще ѿ небытиѧ возмоⷤ всѧ сотворити словоⷨ. и ѿ несꙋщиⷯ в сꙋщество привести всѧ. множае паⷱ҇ возмоглъ бы ѿ бывшаⷢ҇ и ѿ сꙋщиѧ оуⷤ персти словоⷨ чл҃ка сотвориⷮ҇. аще не проѡбраженние кое показꙋѧ таковыⷨ дѣиствомъ бг҃ъ. бⷧ҇шиѧ и лꙋчшиѧ дѣтеⷮ҇ премлⷭ҇тиваⷢ҇ смотрѣниѧ еⷭ҇ на чл҃цѣ. ꙗко соединити и ѡбжити чл҃ка своимъ сꙋшествиеⷨ. и в началѣ оубо видѣти еⷭ҇ ꙗко ближаише паⷱ҇ всеѧ твари присвоение чл҃кꙋ къ бг҃ꙋ. понеⷤ ꙗко возлюбленѣиша тварь паче всѣⷯ твареⷯ еⷭ҇ чл҃къ. ꙗко преⷤ зданїа чл҃ча совѣтꙋеⷮ бг҃ъ еⷤ по ѡбразꙋ своемꙋ и по пⷣобию зижемое сотворити. и твора чл҃ка рꙋкою своею. зижеⷮ бг҃ъ чл҃ка.

113r/267 еⷤ ѕѣло ꙋсвоитеⷧ҇на твⷬ҇. и многовозлюбленѣишаа бг҃ꙋ чл҃къ. ѡбо ѡбраза раⷣ҇ и подобиа. ѡбоⷤ рꙋкꙋ его раⷣ҇ созиданиѧ. тѣмже ꙗко ꙋсвоение мноⷢ҇ имаⷮ къ бжⷭ҇твꙋ чл҃къ. по ѡбразꙋ еⷭ҇ и по подобию бывъ. ꙗко и возлюбленое ѕило бг҃ꙋ здание чл҃къ. содѣланиа раⷣ҇ рꙋки еⷭ҇. ѿ сеⷢ҇ готово даеⷮ разꙋмѣтиⷭ҇ ѡправдание бж҃ие. ꙗко не имаⷮ ѡставиⷮ҇ или презрѣти бг҃ъ. внегда ѡветшати ѡбразꙋ его и пⷣобию. и пасти любимомꙋ созданию рꙋкꙋ его. но бл҃головиⷮ и паⷦ҇ поновити ѡбраⷥ свои и пⷣобие. и исправиⷮ҇ рꙋкꙋ свою создание любимое. исправитиⷤ дѣло бж҃ию рꙋкꙋ. и ѡбновиⷮ҇ ѡбраⷥ свои и пⷣобие. комꙋ иномꙋ возмощи аще не ходатаеⷨ нѣкиⷨ. ходатаюⷤ подобаеⷮ быти ѡ чл҃цѣ к бг҃ꙋ таковомꙋ. иⷤ бꙋдеⷮ ближаиши чл҃ка къ бг҃ꙋ. и мноⷢ҇чтнѣиши чл҃ка ѡбраза бж҃иа и пⷣобиа. сщ҃нноеⷤ писание не показа приближнѣиши присвоениеⷨ

55.2. And, indeed, | we use hands to manufacture things. Hence, God formed man with his own hand. This very thing is professed by David, when he says, "Your hands made me and formed me" (Ps. 119:73). And in creating man, God takes counsel, saying, "Let us make man in our image and likeness"; and when he frames man with his own hand, he takes the dust of the ground and forms man. But was God not capable of making man with his word, as he made all the works that came before him—through his word? If God was able to make everything out of nothing through his word, and bring into being all the things that did not exist, all the more would he be able to make man—who had already come into being and had his existence out of the ground—through his word. But it was to prefigure something else—the greater and better deeds of his supremely merciful economy toward man, which is to unite and deify man through his descent—that God displayed such an action. 112ᵛ/266

55.3. And from the very beginning,[717] it could be seen that, of all his works, man was supposed to come near to God the most closely. Since man is the greatest and most beloved of his creatures, above all works, God takes counsel concerning him before creating man, as he forms his work according to his image and likeness. And in making man, God forms man with his own hand, | making man, the creature closest to God and most beloved by him, both on account of the image[718] and likeness, and because of his creating hand. Therefore, man is especially close to God, because he was made in his image and likeness, and because as the most beloved work of God, man was made by his hand. 113ʳ/267

55.4. From this, we can understand the justice of God—that God did not have to abandon or despise his image and likeness (in man), when it grew weak[719] and when the beloved creature of his hand fell. Instead, in his goodness he was willing to renew his image and likeness (in man) and mend his beloved creature with his own hand. And who else is able to mend the work of God's hand and renew his image and likeness,[720] if not a certain mediator? And the mediator for man must be in such a relation to God that he is closer to God[721] than man and more honorable compared to man's[722] image and likeness. But the sacred Scripture showed no other work that had a position closer

717 from the very beginning] from everything in the beginning
718 the image] his image
719 grew weak] became impoverished
720 his image and likeness,] the image and likeness of God,
721 to God] *omitted*
722 and more honorable compared to man's] *omitted*

чл҃ка къ бж҃твꙋ. ни единои ѿ твари иныѧ нⷤ҇и возлюбленѣиши бж҃твꙋ кою тварь инꙋю показа. да возможеⷮ ходатаиствоваⷮ҇ къ бг҃ꙋ ѡ ѡ[723] чл҃чествѣ. и сп҃ти чл҃ка. но е҆ видѣти въ ст҃ыⷨ писаніи.
113ᵛ/268 ꙗко всеѧ твари ближаиши присвоение имаⷮ҇ бж҃твꙋ чл҃къ. совѣта раⷣ҇ бж҃твенаⷢ ѡ неⷨ паⷱ҇ всеѧ твари. внегда созидаⷮ҇ чл҃ка. и ꙗⷦ҇ созданъ чл҃къ по ѡбразꙋ бж҃ию и по подо҃бию, таⷦ҇ кⷭ҇о и возлюбленѣиши паⷱ҇ всеѧ твари чл҃къ бж҃твꙋ. ꙗко рꙋкою бж҃иею созданъ чл҃къ бы҃. еⷤ҇ инои твари ни которои не бы҃ таковое бытие. ꙗко созданѣеи быⷮ҇ рꙋкою бж҃иею. и созидати҃ по ѡбразꙋ бж҃ию и по подо҃бию. егоⷤ҇ ради и приближнѣишее оусвоение чл҃къ къ бж҃твꙋ имаⷮ҇. сего раⷣ҇ и возлюбленъ ѕѣло бг҃мъ чл҃къ. ꙗко к бо҃шемꙋ ѡ меншеⷨ҇ хꙋжшемꙋ ходатаⷮ҇ствовати невозмоⷤ҇но. но лꙋчшемꙋ ѡ хꙋжшеⷨ҇ ходатаиствоваⷮ҇. И понеⷤ҇ не бы҃ ина тварь ни единаⷭ҇ возлюбленѣиши. и чт҃нѣиши бж҃твꙋ чл҃ка. то ѿ не самомꙋ ли бг҃ꙋ создание свое паⷣ҇шее исправиⷮ҇. и ѡбраⷥ҇ свои истлѣвшіи поновиⷮ҇. понеⷤ҇ и в началѣ саⷨ҇ бг҃ъ созда рꙋкою своею чл҃ка. и послѣⷣ҇ погибшаго е҆ самомоуⷤ҇ взыскавъ и сп҃ти. нѣⷭ҇ бо иноⷢ҇ в твари иⷤ҇ паⷱ҇ чл҃ка. да возможеⷮ҇ коимъ ходатаиствоⷨ҇ къ бг҃ꙋ чл҃ка сп҃ти. каꙗⷤ҇ бо и бꙋдеⷮ҇ тварь
114ʳ/269 бж҃твꙋ приближнѣиши своиствоⷨ҇ чл҃ка. не сꙋщи ни едина. рꙋкою божиею создана. нⷤ҇и по ѡбразꙋ бж҃ию и по подо҃бию сотворена. ни звѣзды ни лꙋна ни слн҃це ни нб҃са ни нб҃наѧ силы. ни аг҃гли. тѣмже и невозможно твари чл҃ка сп҃ти. меⷩ҇ши сꙋщи чл҃ка достоинъствомъ. ѿ бо҃шагоⷤ҇ меншее спасаетсѧ. ѿ хꙋжшаго же бо҃шемꙋ невозможно спасатисѧ. Ꙗко ра

723 ѡѡ (*sic*).

to God than man, nor did it show any work more greatly loved by God that it could mediate on behalf of humankind before God and save man.

55.5. And we can see in the sacred | Scripture that out of all these works, 113v/268
man has the position closest to the Godhead, above all works, on account of the divine counsel that took place about him when man was created. And just as man is created in the image and likeness of God, so he is also most beloved by God, above all other works. For man was formed by the hand of God, whereas no other work was made in such a way, that is, to be framed by the hand of God, and be made in God's image and likeness. For that reason, man has the position closest to the Godhead and for that reason, man[724] is also greatly loved by God.

56. Showing that it is impossible for him who is inferior to mediate on behalf of the one that is lower before him who is superior. Instead, he who is better must mediate on behalf of him who is worse.

56.1. And since there is no other work that is more beloved and honorable by God than man, should not God himself mend his fallen creature and renew his corrupted image (in man)? Since God himself formed man by his own hand[725] in the beginning, he himself had to seek, afterward, what was perishing and save it. For among the works there is no one else who is above man, that they would somehow be able to mediate before God so as to save man. For which of the works | possesses the characteristics that would bring it closer to God 114r/269
than man, given that not one of them is formed by the hand of God, nor is anything else made in God's image and likeness: neither the stars, nor the moon, nor the sun, nor the heavens, nor the heavenly hosts, nor the angels. Therefore, it is also not possible for a work with a lower position of dignity to save man. For that which is inferior is saved by that which is superior, and that which is better cannot be saved by that which is worse.

724 on that account] *omitted*

725 by his own hand,] by nothing else but his own hand,

вночⷭ҇тныи точию возможеⷮ избавити мⷩ҇е
шаⷢ҇ ѿ вины тажки. И посемꙋ точию бг҃ꙋ са
момꙋ своею рꙋкꙋ созданныи ѡбраⷥ свои и пⷣоⷪбие
сп҃ⷭти. иномꙋⷤ никомꙋ нⷭ҇ѣ возможно чл҃чествꙋ
помоци. сего раⷣ҇ ꙗкоⷤ и в началѣ самъ бг҃ъ своею
рꙋкою изволи создати чл҃ка. такоⷤ и послⷣ҇ѣ
истлѣвшее чл҃чество создание рꙋкꙋ его сꙋ
ще и ѡбраⷥ и пⷣоⷪбие бжⷭ҇тва его. бл҃говоли паⷦ҇
саⷨ бг҃ъ слово. исправиⷮ҇ плотию рꙋкꙋ свою соⷣза
ние. и ѡбраⷥ свои и пⷣоⷪбие ѡбновити. позна
тиⷤ моци и ѿсюдꙋ ꙗко ѕѣло возлюбленъ быⷭ҇.
бг҃мъ чл҃къ. по внегда бо создаⷮ҇ емꙋ чл҃ка. то
гда приведе к немꙋ вся животная. видⷮ҇ѣ
что наречеⷮ та. иⷤ е нареⷱ҇ адаⷨ. се и имя емꙋ
114v/271 оустави бг҃ъ. ꙗкоⷤ сказꙋⷮе писание. пакиⷤ прибли
жное присвоение видѣти къ бг҃ꙋ чл҃ка. паче
всея твари ѿ самыя бесѣды бж҃ия. внегда
хотяше изгнаⷮ҇ его из рая. реⷱ҇ бо бг҃ъ. се адаⷨ быⷭ҇
ꙗко единъ ѿ насъ. ⷤе разꙋмѣти добро и лꙋкаво.
и нн҃ѣ да некако простреⷮ рꙋкꙋ и возметь ѿ дре
ва жизни и снѣсть и живъ боудеть во вѣки.
мню гл҃ъ бж҃їи сеи. ⷤе бысть адаⷨ ꙗко единъ ѿ
наⷭ҇. неⷤ е по престꙋпленїи прибыⷮ҇ емꙋ разꙋ
мꙋ. снѣдию ѿ древа ѡнⷢ҇о еже разꙋмѣти до
бро и лꙋкаво. понеⷤ и преⷤ вкꙋшения древа
ѡнⷢ҇о многъ разꙋⷨмⷪъ адамъ. и премⷣръ бысть
ѕѣло. Аще бо бы ѿ древа разꙋмнаго приⷮ҇я
разꙋмъ адамꙋ. какоⷤ преⷤ древа имена на
реⷱ҇ животныⷨ всѣмъ комꙋⷣжо по коегоⷣжо
еⷭ҇ствꙋ. ⷤе ѕѣло премногаⷢ҇ разꙋма еⷭ҇. вижⷣь

57. Showing that one can deliver another person with a lower status from heavy guilt only if one possesses a position of equal honor.[726]

57.1. And for that reason,[727] only God himself, by his own hand, can save his created image and likeness. There is no one else who is able to help humankind.[728] And therefore, just as God himself wished to form man by his own hand in the beginning, so also later, when humanity—the work of his own hand, and the image and likeness of his Godhead—became corrupted, God the Word himself, in his goodness and through his flesh, was willing to mend and renew the work of his own hand and his image and likeness (in man).[729]

57.2. And here is how we can know that man is greatly beloved by God. For when he created man, he, then, brought to him all the animals "to see what he would name them; and whatever Adam called them", that name | God assigned 114v/271
to each of them, as the Scripture says (Gen. 2:19). And again, man's position of being close to God, above all his works, can be seen from the very words of God when he wished to expel him from paradise, for "God said, 'Behold, Adam has become as one of us, knowing good and evil, and now, lest he somehow reach out his hand and take of the tree of life, and eat, and live forever'" (Gen. 3:22). I think that this statement of God—"Adam has become as one of us"[730]—does not mean that, after breaking the command by eating from a certain tree, he gained more knowledge for understanding good and evil. For Adam had much knowledge and was very wise even before he ate from that tree.[731] If Adam were to receive knowledge from the tree of knowledge, how did he name all the individual animals, according to their natural characteristics, even before (seeing) the tree; for this required a great abundance of knowledge?[732]

---

726 **Showing that one can deliver another person with a lower status from heavy guilt only if one possesses a position of equal honor.**] *omitted*

727 And for that reason,] Therefore, and for that very reason,

728 humankind.] humankind. Indeed, human kings make portraits of themselves not by their own hands, but through artists. For that reason, the ones who repair and renovate the deteriorating portraits are not the kings themselves, but the artists.

729 *MS 61 adds*: **Showing that indeed one's ability to deliver someone requires a possession of equal honor with him, and it is entirely impossible for him who is lower to deliver him from heavy guilt.**

730 us"] us, knowing"

731 that tree] the tree of transgression

732 knowledge, how did he name all the individual animals according to their natural characteristics even before (seeing) the tree; for this required a great abundance of knowledge?] knowledge from the tree of knowledge, he would not foreknow by any means which names to give to all the individual animals according to each of their natural characteristics, until the time he was to eat from the tree of which he was commanded (not to eat) and obtain greatly abounding knowledge.

же и премр҇ость емꙋ великꙋ. оубꙋжьшꙋ бо҇
адамꙋ видѣвъ помоцника по немꙋ. приве
дена к немꙋ бг҃омъ. разꙋмѣеа быти. ко
сть ѿ его кости. и плоть ѿ его плоти. и на
ре҇ еа женꙋ. ꙗко ѿ мꙋжа еа взатꙋ. а не ви
дѣвъ созданиа еа. спаше бо внегда изꙗ бг҃ъ
86r/272[733] ѿ него ребро и созда емꙋ женꙋ. и толикаа премно
гаа премр҇сти и разꙋмѣ ада҇. пре҇ даже и еще не асти
емꙋ ѿ древа разꙋмна҇. и по вкꙋшенїи древа ра
зꙋмна҇. гл҃а бг҃ъ. се адамъ бы҇ ꙗко единъ ѿ насъ.
е҇ разꙋмѣвати добро и лꙋкаво. всако ꙋбо бг҃ъ
показꙋе҇ гл҃омъ симъ приближное присвоение
чл҃ка къ бж҃твꙋ своемꙋ. и тр҇цꙋ въ бж҃твѣ ѿ
кры бг҃ъ гл҃омъ симъ. ре҇ бо се адамъ бы҇ ꙗко еди҇
ѿ насъ. е҇ три назнамена ꙗко единъ ѿ насъ
рекъ. ꙗко҇ пре҇ рече. сотвори҇ чл҃ка по wбразꙋ
нш҃емꙋ и по по҇бию. сице и нн҃ѣ ре҇ бг҃ъ. се бысть
ада҇ ꙗко единъ ѿ на҇. а не ре҇ бг҃ъ се бы҇ адамъ
ꙗко҇ азъ. е҇ бы едино назнаменало. но ре҇ бг҃ъ
се бы҇ адамъ ꙗко единъ ѿ насъ. е҇ тре҇ въ бж҃твѣ
ꙗвивъ а не единого. пре҇сти евгꙋ ѕмїа гл҃ꙗ.
аще сн҃ѣсте ре҇ ѿ древа бꙋдете аки бози. ра
зꙋмѣюще добро и зло. вожелѣста҇ быти
аки бози евга и ада҇. сего ра҇ ꙗдоста ѿ дре
ва наводꙗщаго смр҇ть. иже ѿ хꙋды вещи
в бытие ѿ небытиа пришеше. ѿ пе҇сти бо
создани быша. вравнити҇ к создателю во
схотѣста. и непоко҇ство и противление
86v/273 к создателю показаста. wбличае҇ ихъ низъ
па҇шихъ ѿ разꙋма бж҃їа. бывши҇ бли҇ сотво
ршаго и҇ возлюбленїа ра҇. и оусвоены҇ к немꙋ
wбраза ра҇ и подобиа. е҇ самое ꙗвлꙗе҇ гл҃ъ бж҃їи
гл҃ꙗ имъ. се бы҇ ада҇ ꙗко единъ ѿ насъ. ꙗвѣ ꙗко
wбраза ра҇ и по҇биа а е҇ разꙋмѣти добро и лꙋ

733 *The leaves 86–87 are displaced in the manuscript.*

57.3. And observe also his great and exceptional wisdom (evidenced) in that when Adam woke up, he saw a helper for himself, whom God brought to him. And he learned that she was bone of his bone and flesh of his flesh, and he called her "woman", because she was taken out of man (Gen. 2:23). And this was without him seeing how she was created, for he was asleep, when God took | 86ʳ/272 <[734]*one of his ribs and created the woman for him. And Adam had such great wisdom in his mind*[735] *even before eating from the tree of the knowledge. And after he ate from the tree of knowledge, God said to him, "Behold, Adam has become as one of us, knowing good and evil". With all of this, then, God in this statement shows man's position of closeness to his Godhead.*

57.4. *And God also revealed the triune Godhead in these words, for he said,*[736] *"Behold, Adam has become as one of us", whereby he signified the "three" in saying "as one of us". As he said once before, "Let us make man in our image and likeness", so also this time, God said, "Behold, Adam has become as one of us". God did not say, "Behold, Adam has become as I am", which would have signified a single person. Instead, God said, "Behold, Adam has become as one of us", which revealed the "three" in the Godhead, and not "one".*

57.5. *And the serpent deceived Eve when it spoke to her and said, "If you eat from the tree,*[737] *you will be as gods, knowing good and evil" (Gen. 3:5). And because Adam and Eve craved becoming as gods, they ate from the tree that caused death. Those who came into being from deficiency and non-being—for*[738] *they were created by the hand (of God)—wished to become equal with the Creator, showing both disobedience and opposition* | *toward the Creator. In their fall* 86ᵛ/273 *from the knowledge of God, they are reproached by the fact that they were close to the one who made them on account of his love, and were tied to him on account of their image and likeness. This very thing is evident from the divine statement that says to them,*[739] *"Behold, Adam has become as one of us", which clearly refers to the image and likeness.*

---

734 *The italicized text in the angle brackets is displaced in the codex and found on ff. 114ᵛ–115ʳ.*

735 in his mind] *omitted*

736 for he said] *omitted*

737 the tree] this tree

738 for] and

739 the divine statement that says,] that divine statement,

каво. мню сие ⷤе да не како простреⷮ рꙋкꙋ и возмеⷮ ѿ древа животнаⷢ҇ и снѣсть и живъ бꙋдеⷮ во вѣки. да не како не оумреⷮ адаⷨ. лꙋка вновавъ противитиⷭ҇ бгꙋ҇. ⷤе восхотѣ быⷮ ꙗко и бгꙋ҇. и цѣло боудеⷮ злоба грѣха. ꙗко не возмощи исцѣлити ѿ грѣха. живꙋ сꙋщꙋ адамꙋ снѣшꙋ ѿ древа животнаⷢ҇. и посемꙋ внегда оумершꙋ адамꙋ и истлѣвшꙋ. и грѣⷯ его в неⷨ истлѣⷮ. и истлѣвшꙋ грѣхꙋ его с плотию его. слово бж҇ие воплотиⷭ҇ новыи адаⷨ быⷭ҇. ѡбнови пришеⷣ истлѣвшаⷢ҇ древнаго адама грѣха раⷣ҇. не сотвори бо грѣха новы҇ адамъ. сего раⷣ҇ и плоⷮ его не видѣ истлѣниꙗ. по двдꙋ прркꙋ. сице бо пишеⷮ в законѣ. и со грѣшившаꙗ дш҇а истрытиеⷨ истрыетсꙗ. и грѣⷯ еꙗ в неⷨ. показꙋющꙋ словꙋ. ꙗко аще 87r/274 согрѣшившаꙗ дш҇а не истрыетсꙗ до конца истрытиеⷨ ни грѣⷯ еꙗ не истрыетсꙗ. но цѣло ѕлое грѣха пребываеⷮ. внегдаⷤ согрѣшившаꙗ дш҇а истрытиеⷨ истрыетсꙗ. тогда съ дш҇ею и грѣⷯ еꙗ истрыетсꙗ в неи. ꙗко погибнꙋти грѣхꙋ въ дш҇и. и не пребꙋдеⷮ ѕлое цѣло грѣха. истрывшꙋⷭ҇ емꙋ истрытиеⷨ в неи. сего раⷣ҇ рече бгъ҇ ѡ адамѣ. да не како нн҇ѣ простеръ рꙋкꙋ возметь ѿ древа жизни. и снѣсть и живъ бꙋдеⷮ во вѣки. понеⷤ адамꙋ согрѣшившꙋ. подобаеⷮ емꙋ смр҇тию грѣⷯ премѣнити. и истрытиⷭ҇ грѣхꙋ тлѣниеⷨ въ плоти. да новыи адаⷨ беⷥ грѣшныи пришеⷣ воздвигнеⷮ ветхаⷢ҇ адама. первомꙋ грѣхꙋ в перьсти истлѣвшꙋ веⷮхаго адама. новыи адаⷨ смр҇ть приеⷨ бес тлꙗ воскреси на себѣ ветхаго адама. ѡмывъ грѣхи кровию своею. ѡставление прегрѣшению давъ. Рѣшаⷤ ми крылошане. гл҇еши ꙗко бгъ҇ рꙋкою своею созда адама. ѡбновитиⷤ прииде адама сн҇ъ бж҇ии. воплотиⷮсꙗ. и исправиⷮ создание свое. почто ꙋбо саⷨ приходить въ плоⷮ. можаше бо рꙋкою своею и паки поновиⷮ

57.6. *And concerning the "good and evil"—I mean the phrase, "lest*[740] *he somehow reach out his hand and take of the tree of life and eat, and live forever"* (*Gen.* 3:22)*—there was no way for Adam not to die after his evil rebellion against God, lest having desired to become like God and having completed the wicked sin, he may not be able to be healed from sin, for Adam would have remained alive by eating from the tree of life. And therefore,*[741] *after Adam died, and the corruption of sin consumed his flesh, the Word of God was incarnated and became the new Adam, so that, through his coming, he might renew the old Adam, corrupted because of sin.*

57.7. *For the new Adam did not commit sin, which is why his flesh did not come to see*[742] *corruption, according to Prophet David* (*Ps.* 15:10). *For in the Law,* ⟨*too*⟩, *such a thing is described, and "the soul that sins will perish in destruction"* (*Ezek.* 20:18), *and its sin* (*will perish*) *with it. This statement*[743] *shows that if*[744] | *the soul* 87^{r}/274
that sins does not perish in its total destruction, and if its sin is not destroyed, then all the evil of its sin will remain; but when the soul that sins perishes in its destruction, then its sin will perish together with the soul. With sin being destroyed together with the soul, all the evil of sin would not remain either, having perished in the destruction together with (*the soul*). *On this account, God said concerning Adam, "lest he somehow reach out his hand and take of the tree of life, and eat, and live forever"* (*Gen.* 3:22). *And because Adam sinned, his sin inevitably led to death, and sin had to perish together with the flesh in the destruction so that the new sinless Adam could restore*[745] *the old Adam by his coming. While the first sin was corrupted in dust, the new Adam took death, and raised the old Adam in himself for incorruption, by cleansing*[746] *the sins through his own blood for the forgiveness of transgression.*

57.8. *And*[747] *the kliros-chanters said to me, "You are saying that God formed Adam by his own hand, and the Son of God came in the flesh to renew Adam and mend his creation. Why, then, does he himself need to come in the flesh? For he*

---

740 "lest] "and now lest

741 And therefore, after Adam died, and] Therefore, we can recognize that after Adam died in his corruption, and his sin was corrupting him, and

742 see] know

743 This statement] it

744 If] *omitted*

745 restore] re-establish

746 new sinless Adam could restore old Adam by his coming. While the first sin was corrupted in dust, the new Adam took death, and raised the old Adam in himself for incorruption, by cleansing] sinless Adam could re-establish old Adam by coming and cleansing

747 And] *omitted*

87^{v}/275 ѡбраⷥ свои ~~и поⷣⷪбие~~. и не воплотивса. Ꙗкоⷤ
созда чл҃ка саⷨ бг҃ъ. такоⷤ и поновиⷮ҇ самомоу
бг҃ꙋ собою поⷣⷪбаⷮе. Ѿвѣщавⷤъ азъ и рⷯѣ к ниⷨ
понеⷤ в началѣ ѿ небытїа на бытие приво
да чл҃ка бг҃ъ. чⷭтнѣиши паⷱ всеа твари
хота создаⷮ҇. потребова рꙋкою своею соⷣза
ти чл҃ка. паⷣшⷤꙋ чл҃кꙋ ѿ небытиа проⷱе в бы
тие привести чл҃ка. да рꙋкою паки испра
виⷮ созданное. и ѡбраⷥ свои и подобие поновиⷮ.
елма оуⷤ и не единъ чл҃къ бысть. но мноⷢ мно
жное чл҃чество возрасте. и ꙋмножиса.
и испоⷧни всю землю по бл҃вению бж҃ию. тѣ
мⷤъ и не рꙋки здѣ потребова на поновление
ѡбраза. и на исправление созданїа. не ѿ
небытїа бо в бытие здѣ привести еⷭ чл҃че
ство ꙗкоⷤ и преⷤ. еⷤ и гл҃ахъ оуже. но сꙋщее
оубо и еⷭ чл҃чество напоⷧнившее землю. па
даниемⷤъ истлѣвшее. поновиⷮ҇ исправле
ниеⷨ. того раⷣ҇ самъ бг҃ъ приходиⷮ. на сво҇ ѡ
браⷥ. и всеⷢ чл҃ка создание и подобие на са во
сприеⷨ. ѡблекса чл҃чествоⷨ. ѡбразоⷨ своиⷨ
и поⷣⷪбиемъ. и тако саⷨ собою исправи паⷣшее
115^{r}/276 создание свое. поновивъ ѡбетшавшїи ѡбраⷥ
свои и поⷣⷪбие. еⷤ и достоино бл҃гомꙋ бг҃ꙋ. поми
ловати и ꙋщедриⷮ҇ рꙋкꙋ своею создание паⷣше
сꙋще. ѡбразⷤъ и поⷣⷪбие бжⷭтва еⷢ. и помиловаⷡ
снити на неⷢ. и оущеⷣрити. и ѡбоⷧкъса в него
ꙋдобриⷮ҇ его и сⷭпти. Рѣша ми крылошане.
гл҃еши чисто поновити ѡбетщавшїи
ѡбраⷥ свои бг҃ꙋ. и создание паⷣшее возⷣвигнꙋ
ти емꙋ. и исправиⷮ҇. не гл҃ешиⷤ что ѡбетша

could have renewed his | image and likeness (in man) by his own hand, without being incarnated". 87v/275

58. *Showing that since God himself created man the way he did, it was also right for God himself, through his own person, to perform the renewal.*[748]

58.1. *And in response, I said to them:*[749] *Since God, in the beginning, brought man from non-being into being, wishing to make him the most honorable (creature), above all his works, he had to form man by his own hand. But when man fell, there was no longer any need to bring man from non-being into being, only to mend his creation and renew his image and likeness (in man) by his own hand again. For there was no longer one man, but rather, humanity had greatly increased, and multiplied, and filled all the earth according to God's blessing. Therefore, in this case, there was no need for the hand (of God) to either renew the image, or to mend the creature. By then, there was no need to bring humanity from non-being into being, as was the case in the beginning, of which I have already spoken. Rather, there was a need to renew and mend the humanity*[750] *that actually existed, that had filled the earth and become corrupted through the fall.*

58.2. *For that reason, God himself comes (to renew) his image and assumes the entirety of created man and likeness into himself. He clothed himself with humanity—his image and likeness—and*[751] *in that way, through his own person, he himself, mended his fallen>* | creation by renewing his own image and 115r/276
likeness, (since) that had grown weak (in man). And it befitted the good God to use his hand as a means of mercy and generosity toward his creation; but when the image and likeness of his Godhead (that was in man) fell, he came down to him in mercy, and by having clothed himself with (humanity), he mended and saved him in his generosity.

58.3. And the kliros-chanters said to me, "You make it clear that God had to renew his image because it grew weak, and to restore and mend his fallen creature, but you do not say what it means for the image to grow weak, and what it

748 **himself created man the way he did, it was also right for God himself, through his own person, to perform the renewal.] himself, in his own person, created man the way he did, it was also right for God himself to renew the corrupted man in his own person.**

749 And in response, I said to them:] Then, I responded to them:

750 of which I have already spoken. Rather, there was a need to renew and mend the humanity] *omitted*

751 He clothed himself with humanity—his image and likeness—and] By clothing himself with humanity—his image and likeness—he truly became man, and

ние ѡбразꙋ. чтоⷤ ли зданию падение. Азⷤъ рекоⷯ к нимъ. еда єⷭ҇ кто не вѣдыи сеⷢ҇. всꙗкъ прочитаа и бг҃одхⷯновеннаа писанїа. ꙗко бжⷭ҇твеныи ѡбраⷥ въ чл҃чествѣ истлѣ. Крылошанеⷤ рѣша ми. да како ѡбраⷥ бж҃їи въ чл҃чествѣ истлѣ. чл҃комъ живꙋщимъ единако и пребывающимъ ꙗкоⷤ ѿ начала. такоⷤ и по хв҃ѣ пришествїи. тоⷤ чл҃комъ пребывающимъ и живꙋщимъ. ражающимса и оумирающиⷨ. елицы здрави бывахꙋ чл҃цы. зⷣравии пребываюⷮ. елицыⷤ в недꙋги впадаюⷮ чл҃цы тїи истлѣваюⷮ различно. которое ꙋбо томꙋ поновление или возⷣвижение єⷭ҇. всѣмъ такоⷤ пребывающиⷨ

115^{v}/277 чл҃комъ. ꙗкоⷤ до пришествиа хв҃а. такоⷤ и по пришествїи егѡ. Ꙗко преслꙋшаниⷨ съкрꙋшиⷭ҇ ѡбраⷥ и пѡⷣбие бж҃ие. падеⷤ ѿ бесмⷬ҇тїа въ смⷬ҇ть. и истлѣ заблꙋжениемъ ѿ бг҃а ко идолоⷨ. Ѿвѣщавъ азъ и рекоⷯ имъ. оубо крылошане есте ꙗкоⷤ повѣдасте себе. гл҃етеⷤ гл҃ы иⷤ не сꙋⷭ крылошаⷩ. ниⷤ хрⷭ҇тїаньскиа гл҃ы. но по всемꙋ невѣрны во хⷭ҇а ваши гл҃ы. кто бо не вѣⷢ елицы прочитаюⷮ или послꙋшаюⷮ сщⷭ҇нна писанїа. ꙗко чл҃къ по ѡбразꙋ бж҃ию и по подобию есть. не ꙗко ꙋдеса в телесѣ имаⷮ. главꙋ ѻⷱ҇ оуши ноздри. оуста шею. рꙋцѣ перси. чрево нози. иⷤ и звѣри тыаⷤ оудеса имѣюⷮ. но паⷱ звѣреи дш҃ꙋ имаⷮ чл҃къ живꙋ словеснꙋ. понеⷤ ѡбраⷥ и пѡⷣбие бж҃ие єⷭ҇ чл҃къ. и по неи ꙋбо ѡбраⷥ бж҃їи истлѣ. и паде созданное бж҃ие оукрашение. єⷤ и въ смⷬ҇ть впаде. какоⷤ ꙋбо истлѣ и паде means for the work to fall".[752] And I said to them: Is there anyone who does not know this? Everyone who reads the divinely inspired Scriptures (knows) that the divine image in man became corrupted.

58.4. Yet the kliros-chanters said to me,[753] "But how did the image of God in humanity become corrupted, if men still continued to live and remain the way they were from the beginning? And likewise, after Christ's coming, men continue to remain[754] and live, to be born and die. The men who are healthy,[755] remain healthy until their death; and the men who fall into illnesses, fade away in various ways. What kind of renewal or restoration is there for those who have remained the very same | both before the coming of Christ and after his coming"? 115v/277

59. Showing that the image and likeness of God became broken because of disobedience, and it fell from immortality to death and became corrupted on account of falsehood (when it turned) from God to idols.

59.1. And in response, I said to them: Now, you are the kliros-chanters, as you profess yourselves, but the words you say do not befit the kliros-chanters, nor do these words have any Christian sense. Instead, these words of yours are entirely against the faith in Christ.[756]

59.2. For what man among those who read and listen to the sacred Scripture does not know that man is (made) in God's image and likeness? It is not because he has certain parts of the body, namely, the head, the eyes, the ears, the nostrils, the mouth, the neck, the hands, the fingers, the stomach, and the legs. The beasts have the same parts of the body, but man has the rational living soul that places him above the beasts,[757] for man is the image and likeness of God, and therefore, the image of God became corrupted together with (the soul), and the created beauty fell, and that fall led to death.

---

752 said to me, "You make definite claims that God had to renew his image because it grew weak, and to restore and mend his fallen creature, but you do not say what it means for the image to grow weak, and what it means for the work to fall".] said, "Now, why are you repeatedly saying that God had to renew his image because grew weak, and to restore and mend his fallen creature, without saying what it means for the image to grow weak, what it means for the work to fall, and how his renewal and restoration and mending happened"?

753 to me,] *omitted*

754 from the beginning? And likewise, after Christ's coming, men continue to remain] *omitted*

755 healthy,] healthy in their bodies,

756 Instead, these words of yours are entirely against the faith in Christ.] *omitted*

757 but man has the rational living soul that places him above the beasts,] but what man has above the beasts is the rational living soul,

чл҃къ. слышиши сщ҃нное писание. ꙗко бг҃ъ созда чл҃ка. почтивъ тⷢ҇о своимъ ѡбразомъ и пⷣобиемъ. и рꙋкою своею сотвори тⷢ҇о. еꙗⷤ҇ почтⷭ҇и ни едина тваⷬ҇ спⷣобиса. и вл҃кꙋ его земли постави. покори емꙋ пⷣо нозѣ ѡвца 116r/278 и волы̑ вса скоты. и звѣра и птица нбⷭ҇ныа. и рыбы моⷬ҇скиа. ѿ сего разꙋмѣвается. ꙗко и нбо и землю и слнце и лꙋнꙋ и звѣзды. море и рѣки и древеса. и злакъ травныи чл҃ка раⷣ҇ бг҃ъ сотвори. чл҃къ въ чⷭ҇ти толицеи пребыⷭ҇ не бл҃го даренъ на мнозѣ. к создателю своемꙋ непо корьство показа. единꙋ бо заповѣⷣ создатеⷧ҇ чл҃кꙋ положи на сохранение живота его. да не снѣсть и оумреⷮ ѿ единоⷢ҇ древа токмо. всаⷤ҇ древа в раю ꙗсти повелѣнъ. не восхотѣ по слꙋшливъ быти. создателю своемꙋ не по коривса. заповѣⷣ престꙋпи. ꙗде ѿ древа смртнаго. противиⷭ҇ бгꙋ вмѣсто покореⷩ҇а чл҃къ. бг҃ъ бо на живоⷮ беⷥсмртныи созда чл҃ка. и древо жизни насаⷣ҇ в раю его раⷣ҇. и ѿ смртнаⷢ҇ древа заповѣда емꙋ не ꙗсти. да не ꙋмреть. ѿ древа животнаⷢ҇ и возбранивъ емꙋ ꙗсти. да живъ бꙋдеⷮ во вѣки. чл҃къⷤ҇ не послꙋшавъ бг҃а создавшаго ⷢе по ѡбразꙋ своемꙋ и по пⷣобию. вземъ ѿ древа смртнаⷢ҇ и аде. ї истлѣ проти влениⷨ своиⷨ къ бгꙋⷤ҇ е в неⷨ по ѡбразꙋ бжию и по пⷣобию. ѿ беⷥсмртиа смрть паⷱ҇ возлюбиⷡ҇. 116v/279 малы раⷣ҇ красоты плода. ѿпаде ѿ бга. тѣмъⷤ҇ бгъ ⷢе призываше гла. адаме гдѣ бѣ. понеⷤ҇ па де ѕлѣ ѿ бга преслꙋшавъ заповѣ. сокрꙋши по ѡбразꙋⷤ҇ е в немъ и по пⷣобию бжию. въ смрть волею попоⷧзса. егоⷤ҇ ради и бгъ ѿвѣща емꙋ. ꙗко земла еси и в землю поидеши. аки бы глалъ. понеⷤ҇ возлюбиⷧ҇ еси паⷱ҇ живота смрть. сего раⷣ҇ и ꙋмреши. сице падеⷭ҇ возлюбленное бжие здание въ смрть. и ѿ непослꙋшанїа противлениⷨ къ бгꙋ. сокрꙋши ѡбраⷥ и пⷣобие.

59.3. Now, as for the question of how man became corrupted and fell, you heard the sacred Scripture, that God created man, honoring him with his image and likeness and forming him with his own hand, which was an honor that no other creature was privileged to receive. And he made him master of the earth, subjecting under his feet[758] the sheep, | and the oxen, and all the livestock, and 116r/278
the beasts, and the birds of the heavens, and the fish of the sea. From this, we recognize that the heaven and the earth, the sun and the moon, and the stars, and the sea, and the rivers, and the trees, and the green plants were made by God for the sake of man. Although he was endowed with such honor, man did not remain grateful for long and demonstrated disobedience to his Creator.

59.4. For the Creator gave a single command for the preservation of his life, that there was only one tree[759] from which he should not eat in order not to die. Although he was allowed to eat from all the trees that were in paradise, he did not wish to be obedient and did not submit to his Creator. He broke[760] the command and ate from the death-giving tree. Instead of submitting to God, man opposed him. For God created man for immortal life, and it was for his sake that (God) planted the tree of life in paradise. And the reason he gave the command not to eat of the death-giving tree was to keep him from dying. He did [not][761] prohibit him from eating from the tree of life ⟨before his breaking the command⟩ to have him live for ages. But man did not obey God, who created him according to his image and likeness. Instead, he took from the death-giving tree and ate.

59.5. And in his opposition to God, whose divine image and likeness he bore, he became corrupted. He came to love[762] death more than immortality. | For 116v/279
the sake of the fleeting enjoyment of the fruit, he fell away from God. Hence, God called him out, saying, "Adam, Adam, where were you"? Since he gravely fell away from God by violating the command, he experienced the brokenness of that which was in him according to God's image and likeness. Of his own will, he slipped into death, and on account of that, God responded to him, "You are dust, and to dust you will return" (Gen. 3:19), as if to say, "Since you have loved death more than life, you will die because of it". This was the way God's beloved work fell into death; and as a result of disobedience, in opposition to God, man experienced the brokenness of God's image and likeness in himself.

---

758 subjecting under his feet] subjecting to him

759 tree] tree that would force him into death.

760 obedient and did not submit to his Creator. He broke] obedient to his Creator. Instead, he submitted to his enemy, who deceived him. He obeyed him, broke

761 not] *emended*

762 He came to love] He preferred

бж҃ие в себѣ чл҃къ. и несе едино ѕло. но и забы чл҃чество сотворшаго его. и ѿстꙋпи ѿ гⷭ҇а бг҃а сп҃са своⷢ҇. содѣла сⷨ҇ собѣ идолы. и покло нⷭ҇и своⷯ҇ рꙋкъ дѣлесемъ. и нарⷱ҇е идолы боги собѣ. вмѣсто бг҃а истиннⷢ҇а. и жрътвы со твори старомꙋ враг~~ꙋмꙋ~~ своемꙋ. и дѣти своа томꙋ закла. вѣровавъ прелестникꙋ чл҃къ ѿстꙋпи ѿ создателꙗ своⷢ҇. по немⷤ҇ꙋ древнїи врагъ ѡблада чл҃ки. и во всако согрѣшение поринꙋ иⷯ. и старыи врагъ дьавⷧ҇о не могїи со творⷮ҇и своⷢ҇ зданїа. бж҃їимъ зданиⷨ҇е чл҃чествⷨ҇о совладе еⷤ҇го не сотвори. и чл҃чество гꙋбителꙗ [117r/280] вмѣсто сп҃са своⷢ҇ почте. колико ꙋбо ѕло падеⷩ҇е чл҃чествꙋ. каⷦ҇о не истлѣ в нⷨ҇е поѡбразное бж҃ие и пⷣ҇обное. и г҃лете како истлѣ. или ка ко паде здание бж҃ие. и приносите ꙗⷤ҇ кромѣ поѡбразнⷢ҇а и пⷣ҇обнаго. стⷭ҇рѣтьми недꙋжныⷨ҇ тлѣние чл҃чествꙋ. дⷧ҇жное сꙋщи истлѣнию. грѣха раⷣ҇ преслꙋшнⷢ҇а и смⷬ҇ти. Ꙗко хⷭ҇ воскре сением свои понови ѡбраⷥ҇ свои дарова вⷭ҇ѣ воскрⷭ҇нꙋти в послѣⷣ҇нїи дн҃ь. в бꙋдꙋщїи вѣкъ бесконеⷱ҇нꙋю жизнь. Прїидеⷤ҇ хⷭ҇ во плоти бывъ послꙋшливъ бгⷹ҇ ѿцꙋ толико елико и смⷬ҇ть приати. и послꙋшаниⷨ҇е свои новыи адамъ

59.6. And this was not the only evil that occurred, for humankind also forgot[763] its Maker and departed from the Lord God, its Savior. Man fashioned idols for himself and worshiped the work of his own hands. And he called idols his gods in place of the true God, and made[764] sacrifices to his old enemy. And his children, made in the image and likeness of God, he offered as burnt offerings. Having trusted the deceiver of men, he departed from his Creator.[765] Since then, the old enemy has held men in his possession and pushed them into all kinds of sin. And being unable to frame his own creation, the old enemy, the devil, came to possess God's work, humanity, (although) he did not make it. And humankind honored the murderer | instead of its Savior.[766] 117r/280

59.7. How bad, then, was the effect of humanity's fall? How would that which is according to the divine image[767] and likeness in him not become corrupted? And you ask how the work of God became corrupted or fallen; and what you offer in response fails to account for humanity's corruption in the sense of evil passions that affect the image and likeness, binding it to corruption because of the sin of disobedience and death.[768]

60. Showing that Christ renewed his image (in man) through his resurrection, by granting that everyone be raised on the last day and have endless life in the ages to come.[769]

60.1. And when Christ came in the flesh, he was obedient to God[770] the Father to such an extent that he even accepted death. By his obedience, the new Adam

763 And this was not the only evil that occurred. Humankind also forgot] And this lapse into evil was not the only thing that occurred. There was an even worse lapse in that humankind forgot

764 made] offered

765 trusted the deceiver of men, he departed from his Creator.] trusted his enemy that deceived him, he departed from God who made him.

766 sin. And being unable to frame his own creation, the old enemy, the devil, came to possess God's work, the humanity, (although) he did not make it. And humankind honored the murderer instead of its Savior.] sin, for humankind honored the murderer instead of its Savior.

767 image] prototype

768 sin of disobedience and death.] sin, disobedience, and death.

769 **image (in man) through his resurrection, by granting that everyone be raised on the last day and have endless life in the ages to come.] image and likeness (in man) through his resurrection, by letting everyone be raised on the last day and have endless life. And he mended the disobedience with obedience, and the falsehood with the divine knowledge from God to make us alive by washing away the sin with his blood.**

770 God] *omitted*

древнее преслꙋшание адамово исправи. и смр҃тию своею хс҃ъ. ѿ послꙋшанїа ко ѿцꙋ смрьⷤю ѿ преслꙋшанїа прибывшꙋю чл҃кꙋ оупразни. воскрⷭ҇ъ из мр҃твыⷯ хс. и чл҃комъ воскрⷭ҇нию пꙋⷮ сотвори. поновивъ свои ѡбраⷥ и побⷣие воздвиⷤ создание свое на своеⷨ чл҃ческомъ составѣ. егоⷤ раⷣ в последнїи дн҃ь всемꙋ чл҃чествꙋ воскрⷭ҇ние постави. а не ⷤе нн҃ѣ по хв҃ѣ пришествїи не страдаⷮ недꙋгоⷨ и болѣзньми чл҃чествꙋ. ниⷤ не оумирати. 117ᵛ/282 еще бо чл҃коⷨ ражающимса по хв҃ѣ пришествїи тѣмже и недꙋговаⷮ. и страдати и ꙋмирати чл҃коⷨ. понеⷤ и самъ хс и стрⷭ҇ть и смр҃ть приꙗⷮ. преⷤ роⷣ вса плотию. и потоⷨ воскрсе ѿ мр҃твыⷯ тогда. такоⷤ и чл҃чество нн҃ѣ ражаетса. и стражеⷮ и ꙋмираеⷮ. в последнийⷤ дн҃ь воскрⷭ҇неть. во второе хв҃о пришествие. сꙋⷣ приати по дѣлоⷨ своимъ. коⷤо ꙗⷤ содѣла. И рекосте вы ꙗⷦ глеⷮ косои за негоⷤ хстꙋ не оумреⷮ. чесо раⷣ восхотѣти бг҃ꙋ плоⷮ приати. и во ꙋтробѣ женьстѣи како бг҃ꙋви тати. и проходы таковыⷨ бг҃ꙋ проити. да покажеⷮ косои инꙋ тварь ближаишꙋ и любезнѣишю бв҃и чл҃ка. иⷤ возможеⷮ примѣриⷮ чл҃ка согрѣшивша къ бг҃ꙋ. но нѣⷭ҇ иныа твари ближаиши своиствоⷨ къ бг҃ꙋ паⷭ҇ чл҃ка. ꙗкоⷤ и преⷤ реⷱ҇. вса тварь словомъ бж҃їимъ ѿ небытїа бы. и не по ѡбразꙋⷩ ни по mended the old disobedience of Adam. And by the death that came with his obedience, Christ abolished the death that was caused by disobedience and persisted over man.[771] And Christ rose from the dead and granted men the way to resurrection. Having renewed his image and likeness (in man), he restored his work within his own human body, and because of him, all of humankind was offered the possibility of being raised on the last day.

60.2. But this does not mean that now,[772] after Christ's coming, humankind would no longer suffer affliction or disease, or would stop dying. | For men who 117v/282
are born after Christ's coming, still continue to experience affliction, and men still suffer and die.[773] For even Christ himself was first born in the flesh and experienced passion and death, and then, later rose from the dead.[774] Likewise, in the present time, humanity also experiences birth and suffers and dies, but on the last day, at Christ's second coming, it will be raised in order to receive judgment, each one according to one's own actions.

60.3. And you reported Kosoy's claim that Christ did not die for him, (asking) why God would want to assume flesh, and how God dwelled in the woman's womb, and how God came through all the bodily passages.[775] Let Kosoy show another creature that is so close to God and beloved by him, that it may be able to reconcile the sinful man to God. However, there is no such creature that has a position closer to God than man.[776] As I said before, the entire creation began to exist out of non-being by the word of God, and it was made neither in the

---

771 that was caused by disobedience and persisted over man.] that persisted over man.

772 now,] *omitted*

773 still continue to experience affliction, and men still suffer and die.] *omitted*

774 from the dead.] from the dead in order to renew his image (in man).

775 And you reported Kosoy's claim that Christ did not die for him, (asking) why God would want to assume flesh, and how God dwelled in the woman's womb, and how God came through all the bodily passages.] You reported Kosoy's claim: "Supposedly, Christ did die for him in the past, but why did God want to assume flesh"?

776 God. However, there is no such creature that has a position closer to God than man.] God. And we see that a human king has a set procedure in place so that when his army commander commits an offense against him, a soldier cannot mediate on his behalf before the king, nor can any common person be a mediator on behalf of the royal counselor. Is it not even more appropriate for the Son to mediate before God on behalf of the man who sinned against God, unless man had someone else among the works with a closer position to God than himself, with a position of closeness above man, as I often said?

по҇до҇бию б҃жию. и поне҇ж нѣсть в твари хода
таа межи б҃га и ч҃лка. сего ра҇д с҃нъ б҃жїи во
плотивса ходатаиствова къ б҃гꙋ и ч҃лко҇м.

image nor in the likeness of God.[777] And since there is no mediator between God and man among the creatures, the Son of God was incarnated and (took on the task of) mediating on behalf of men before God the Father.[778]

777 As I said before, the entire work began to exist out of non-being by the word of God, and it was made neither in the image nor in the likeness of God.] For the entire work began to exist out of non-being by the word of God, and nothing (but man) was made in the image and likeness of God, nor was anything formed by the divine hand. But man was both formed by God's hand and made in the image and likeness of God. And we also see, then, that man's image is the most honorable one and supersedes all those who submit to him. For when the portrait of the king is brought into the capital cities, then it is not only the simple folks—peasants and craftsmen—who greet it with great honor and bow before the portrait of the human king as if it were the king himself, but also the king's soldiers, and the city elders, and the respected officials, and even the royal counselors themselves, and the army commanders, and the eparchs. And the portrait of the king is more honorable than those of all his royal counselors, and army commanders, and eparchs, and patricians. For all of them bow before the portrait of the king and greet it with great honor, as if it were the king himself, demonstrating in that way their submission to the king and their affection for him. From this, we can recognize that all the noble and great ranks of honor—the eparchs, and the army commanders, and the royal counselors—are inferior compared to the portrait of the king. And the human portrait of the king, decorated with gold and paint, is more honorable and superior than all of theirs. And if no rank of honor is equal to the portrait of the human king that is brought into each of the eparchies, then much more so is it with all the good works of God of which no one is equal in honor to the divine image and likeness. Rather, in comparison with all the works of God, his divine image and likeness is more honorable and superior, just as the portrait of the human king is more honorable than all the high ranks that are under him. And since the parallel between the human image of the king and the divine image and likeness clarifies well the idea of dignity, (it should be evident that) the honor of the divine image supersedes that of all works. And it is impossible for someone with a lower status to accomplish reconciliation or adequately mediate before a human king on behalf of him who rejected him, and committed offense, and caused him trouble. But someone who could do this is the king's son; (he could) reconcile his father, the king, with the one who rejected the king and caused him trouble. (The king) would forgive the offense of the one who rejected him on account of the natural (kinship) and love toward his son. The same thing applies to the image and likeness of God, (namely) the man who departed from God in that he worshiped and served idols, as well as committed offenses and caused trouble to God who made him. No created work can mediate before God on behalf of man—(the representative of) God's image and likeness—who sinned so greatly.

778 And since there is no mediator between God and man among the creatures, the Son of God incarnated and (took on the task of) mediating on behalf of men before God the Father.] And since there is no mediator between God and man in the whole creation of God, the Son of God became incarnated and (took on the task of) mediating before God the Father, to reconcile man by giving him mercy, and in compassion to him to renew the image and likeness through his incarnation as Son.

Рекоша крылошане ѡни. понеⷤ вса хⷭ҇мъ быша вса словоⷨ сотворена. почто и ѡбраⷥ и поⷣⷪбие [118r/285] словоⷨ не понови. и кромѣ вочлⷱ҇енїа вса мо гїи. Рѣхⷤъ имъ и аⷥ. вса оубо могїи бг҃ъ хⷭ҇. но и в началѣ зданїа не словоⷨ сотвори чл҃ка. но рꙋкою своею взеⷨ персть ѿ землꙗ. созда чл҃ка по ѡбразꙋ своемꙋ и по поⷣⷪбию. и аще не сице бы поⷣⷪбало бж҃їи премⷣрости. еⷤ свои ѡбраⷥ и поⷣⷪбие рꙋкою своею создати и словомъ со твориⷧ҇ бы чл҃ка иⷤ вса могїи. но понеⷤ сице бж҃їи премⷣрости поⷣⷪбно. ꙗко рꙋкою своею создати чл҃ка по ѡбразꙋ своемꙋ и по поⷣⷪбию. сицеⷤ по добно премⷣрости бж҃иеи самомꙋ и вопло тиⷮ҇са хⷭ҇ꙋ. да в плоти и саⷨ преслꙋшание а дамовоⷤе къ бг҃ꙋ свои послꙋшаниⷨе къ бг҃ꙋ ѿцꙋ исправивъ хⷭ҇. избавиⷮ всероⷣнаго адама ѿ грѣха и ѿ смрⷮ҇и. самое се крⷭ҇та раⷣ павеⷧ҇ глаше. понеⷤ премⷣростию бг҃а не разꙋмѣ миⷬ҇. блг҃оволи бг҃ъ бꙋиствоⷨ проповѣданїа спⷭ҇ти вѣ рꙋющаа. Рѣшаⷤ крылошане. странно и та жко слышати. ꙗко бг҃ъ вмѣсте кⷧ҇ане пре быть во чревѣ. и проходы женьскими про ити бг҃ꙋ. нечисто ѿ всѣ непщꙋемо.

60.4. Those kliros-chanters said:[779] "Since everything came into being through Christ, and all things were made by means of his word, why would he not also renew the image and likeness | through his word, without incarnation, 118r/285 given that he can do everything"?[780]

60.5. And I, too, said to them:[781] Being God, Christ can indeed do everything. However, in the beginning (God) made man not by means of his word, but by his hand. He took the dust of the ground and formed man in his image and likeness. And if creating his image and likeness by his hand was not suitable in accordance with God's wisdom, then he who is able to do everything, could have made man by his word. But just as it was appropriate for the wisdom of God to form man by his hand according to his image and likeness, so it was also appropriate for the wisdom of God to have Christ himself become incarnate[782] so that in the flesh and through his obedience to God the Father, God's Son could mend Adam's disobedience toward God and deliver Adam, as common ancestor, from sin and death.[783] That is precisely what Paul said with respect to the cross: "Since the world did not know God through wisdom, it pleased God by the foolishness of preaching to save those who believe" (1 Cor. 1:21).

60.6. But the kliros-chanters said, "It is strange and difficult to hear that God dwelled in such an impure place as the womb, and anyone would think that it is impure for God to go through female passages".[784]

---

779 Those kliros-chanters said:] And those kliros-chanters said to me:

780 "Since everything came into being through Christ, and all things were made by means of his word, why would he not also renew the image and likeness through his word, without incarnation, given that he can do everything"?] "If everything came into being through Christ, and (God) made all things by means of the word, why would he not also renew the image and likeness through the word, without incarnation, given that he can do everything as God"?

781 And I, too, said to them:] And I answered them that

782 But just as it befitted the wisdom of God to form man by his hand according to his image and likeness, so it also befitted the wisdom of God to have Christ himself become incarnate] But it did befit the wisdom of God to do it that way, and Christ became incarnate

783 sin and death] the judgment of both sin and death.

784 dwelled in such an impure place as the womb, and anyone would think that it is impure for God to go through the female passages".] in the woman's womb, and anyone would think that it is impure for God to go through its passages".

Ꙗкоⷤе рꙋкама и пⷬ҇есты проходиⷮ҇ составы и ꙋтробꙋ
118v/286 тꙋдꙋ и самомꙋ проити. єдино и тоⷤ есть.
Ѿвѣщавъ ꙋбо аⷥ к ниⷨ гл҃ꙗ. рекосте ꙋбо ꙗко книⷢ҇
ветхиа поⷣбаⷪеⷮ прочитаⷮ҇ точию. ихъ и стоⷬ
повыми нарицаете. книгъ ли не слышите.
гл҃ⷮе бо сщ҃ное писание. и влоⷤ бг҃ъ сонъ во адама
и оуспе. и взѧⷮ єдино ѿ ребръ его. испоⷧни плоⷮ
в него мѣсто. и созда гⷭь бг҃ъ ребро ⷤе взѧⷮ ѿ ада
ма женꙋ. и приведе ю ко адамꙋ. и реⷱ адамъ.
се нн҃ѣ кость ѿ костеи моиⷯ. и плоть ѿ плоⷮ
моѧ. сїа наречетсѧ жена. ꙗко ѿ мꙋжа
своеⷢ взѧта быⷭ си. сего раⷣ ѡставлѧеⷮ чл҃къ
ѿц҃а своеⷢ и мт҃рь и прилѣпитсѧ к женѣ свое
и бꙋдета ѡба в плоⷮ единꙋ. Слышасте ꙋбо
писание ꙗко созда гⷭь бг҃ъ ребро ⷤе взѧⷮ ѿ ада
ма женꙋ. взѧⷮ бг҃ъ ребро. рꙋкою своею взѧⷮ
ребро. и созидаше ребро в женꙋ бг҃ъ. оубо рꙋ
кою созидаше женꙋ бг҃ъ. ꙗкоⷤ и адама самоⷢ.
и аще созидаше бг҃ъ рꙋкою адама и женꙋ еⷢ.
созидаше имъ чревеса и ꙋтробꙋ рꙋкама сво
има бг҃ъ. такоⷤ рꙋкама своима созидаше
има бг҃ъ и проходы всѧ. ащеⷤ рꙋкама свои
ма зижеⷮ бг҃ъ всѧ оуды в телесѣ адамꙋ и женѣ еⷢ.
119r/288 тѣмже пⷬ҇есты бж҃їа проидоша всѣⷯ оудовъ соста

61. Showing that going through the body and womb with one's hands and fingers | is the same thing as going through them by oneself.[785] 118v/286

61.1. And then, in response to them, I said: Now, you claimed that we must read only the books of the Old Testament, and you call them foundational. But don't you hear what the books (say)? For the sacred Scripture states:[786] "And God brought a deep sleep upon Adam, and he slept, and he took one of his ribs, and filled up its place with flesh. And the Lord God formed the rib, which he took from Adam into a woman, and brought her to Adam. And Adam said, 'This now is bone of my bones, and flesh of my flesh; she will be called woman, because she was taken out of her husband'. That is why a man leaves his father and mother, and he will cleave to his wife, and they will be one flesh" (Gen. 2:21–24).

61.2. Now, you heard the Scripture (saying) that "the Lord God formed the rib which he took from Adam into a woman". When God was taking the rib, he took the rib with his own hand, and God formed the rib into a woman. Therefore, God formed woman with his own hand, just as he did Adam himself.[787] And if God formed Adam and his wife with his own hand, then God also formed their wombs and inner parts with his own hands. Likewise, God also formed all their passages with his own hands. And if God forms all the bodily parts of Adam and his wife with his own hands, | then God's fingers reached into all the ligaments 119r/288

785 **Showing that going through the body and womb with one's hands and fingers is the same thing as going through them by oneself.**] *omitted*

786 And then, in response to them, I said: Now, you claimed that we must read only the books of the Old Testament, and you call them foundational. But don't you hear what the books (say)? For sacred Scripture states:] And I said to them: the immeasurable greatness of God's goodness and infinite mercy poured upon humankind sets the voluptuous souls, who do not fear God, to unbelief; but those souls who love God, they burn with the most fervent faith in their insatiable desire toward the (divine) goodness. Now, you told me earlier that we must read the books of the Old Testament, and you call them foundational. But do you not listen to the books, to what this sacred Scripture says? And listen carefully to what is said: **Showing that God formed Adam and his wife with his own hands, and God's fingers reached into their wombs, and the inlets and the outlets, and all the parts of their bodies. And there is no difference between his reaching out with his hands and his entering there himself.**

787 When God was taking the rib, he took the rib with his own hand, and God formed the rib into a woman. Therefore, God formed woman with his own hand, just as he did Adam himself.] It is said that God took the rib. Therefore, he took the rib with his own hand. And God formed the rib into a woman. Therefore, he formed woman with his own hand, just as he did Adam himself earlier.

вы. и чревеса оутробы и проходы вся. мнащаꙗⷭ҇ка҇ныа и нечистыа. сего раⷣ нѣсть ничтоⷤ ка҇но ниⷤ не чиⷭто ниⷤ хꙋдо сотвореное бг҃мъ. глⷮе бо бг҃о дхⷯовенное писание. И видѣ бг҃ъ вся ꙗⷤ сотвори. и се вса добра ѕѣло. Ꙗко бж҃їа тварь добра ѕѣло вса и нѣⷭ не ѕѣло добра. аще и оутроба. аще и ложесна вса. Видиши ли ꙗко раⷥсмотри бг҃ъ сотворение свое. а не просто ѡстави сотворивъ тварь. но раⷥсмотри еа сотворивъ. и не ѡбрѣте въ творенїи своеⷨ порока никоегоⷤ бг҃ъ. и нѣⷭ ѡво добро сотворение. ѡвоⷤ не добро. или се ѕѣло добро сотворение. сеⷤ не ѕѣло добро сотворение. но затвори всꙗко ѿмышление таковое гл҃омъ симъ. еⷤ рече. и видѣ бг҃ъ вса ꙗⷤ сотвори. и се вса добра ѕѣло. аще саⷨ бг҃ъ раⷥсмотрѣ и видѣ ꙗⷤ сотвори. ꙗко вса добра ѕѣло. и нѣⷭ не ѕѣло добро в твари бжїи. но вса добра ѕѣло ꙗⷤ сотвори бг҃ъ. по семꙋ оубо во всеи твари бжїи. и оутроба и ло of their bodies, and the wombs, and all the passages that are considered[788] to be unclean and impure. For that reason, there is nothing unclean or impure or bad in the things made by God, for the divinely inspired Scripture says,[789] "And God saw all that he made, and it was all very good" (Gen. 1:31).

62. Showing that every work of God is very good, and there is no work that is not very good,[790] including the womb and all the inner parts.

62.1. Don't you see that God reflected on his creation?[791] Instead of simply leaving the work alone after creating it, he reflected on it. Having created it, God[792] did not find any single fault in his creation. And it cannot be that one part of God's creation is good, and another is not good, or that this part of creation[793] is very good, and that part of creation is not very good. Rather, judge every such[794] thought by the words that said, "And God saw all that he made, and it was all very good" (Gen. 1:31).[795] And if God himself reflected and saw that everything he made was very good, and there was nothing in God's creation that was not very good—instead, everything that God made was very good—for that reason, then, both the womb and the inner parts in all the creatures are very good.[796]

---

788 wombs, and all the passages that are considered] wombs, and the inner parts, and the inlets and the outlets, including all the passages that some consider

789 there is nothing unclean or impure or bad in the things made by God, for the divinely inspired Scripture says,] there is no thing that is unclean or impure or bad, for it is God's work! And you did hear all the things that the divinely inspired Scripture said about this and about the entire creation in the Old Testament? And if not, listen to this carefully, for it says this,

790 **very good,] very good. Rather, all things are very good: both the womb and the belly, and whatever else there is.**

791 about his creation?] about that which God made, about his entire creation?

792 Having created it, God] And he looked at everything that he made, and all those things were very good! Consider carefully the fact that God

793 creation] God's creation

794 such] *omitted*

795 good" (Gen. 1:31).] good" (Gen. 1:31). Since God's creation is the product of the supremely wise and supremely good wisdom, therefore, the entire work is very good because the supremely holy God makes all things supremely pure.

796 himself reflected and saw that everything he made was very good, and there was nothing in God's creation that was not very good—instead, everything that God made was very good—for that reason, then, both the womb and the inner parts in all the creatures are very good.] himself, supremely wise and supremely holy, reflected on his creation and saw that it was very good, then indeed all the things in God's creation are very good—the womb, and the inner parts, and all the inlets and the outlets. And there is nothing in God's creation that is not very good. Instead, everything is very good!

жесна добра ѕѣло. Ꙗко саⷨ бг҃ъ и нн҃ѣ сози
даеⷮ млⷣнца во Ѹтробаⷯ. Слышастеⷤ всако
119ᵛ/289 в писанїи бг҃а гл҃юща ко авраамѹ. ѡбращьса
прїидѹ к тебѣ по времени сеⷨ в часѣ. и родиⷮ сн҃ъ
жена твоа. и второе паки реⷱ҇ гь҃. все времѧ
возращѹса в часѣ и бѹдеⷮ саррѣ сн҃ъ. показѹ
ющѹ словѹ. ꙗко бг҃ъ зижеⷮ млⷣнца во Ѹтро
бѣ. чесо бо раⷣⷣ ѡбѣщавается возвратиⷮⷭа
бг҃ъ в часѣ. и сказѹеⷮ ꙗко тогда бѹдеⷮ саррѣ
сн҃ъ. егда возвращьса придеⷮ бг҃ъ в часѣ. и аще
не самъ бг҃ъ созидаеⷮ во Ѹтробѣ млⷣнца. не бы
гл҃алъ авраамѹ. ѡбращьса придѹ к тебѣ по
времени сеⷨ в часѣ. и родиⷮ сн҃ъ жена твоа.
Сицеⷤ и къ еремїи реⷱ҇ бг҃ъ преⷤ даⷤ не создаⷯ та въ
чревѣ свѣм та. и аще самъ бг҃ъ созидаеⷮ во
Ѹтробаⷯ млⷣнца. ꙗкоⷤ авраамѹ возвѣсти
бг҃ъ. и иеремїи реⷱ҇. и селико спо҇ѡблꙗетса
бг҃ъ. ꙗко во Ѹтробѣ мѹжнимъ женаⷨ созидаⷮⷭ
дѣти. тѣмже ничтоже ѿ сего мнееⷤ е
и самомѹ бг҃ѹ во Ѹтробѣ чистѣ беⷥмѹжныꙗ
дв҃ы вочлчитиⷭ. на зданїа раⷣⷣ и поновленїа
ѡбраза своеⷢ и поⷣбиа любимаⷢ. се оубо и нн҃ѣ
созидаеⷮ бг҃ъ млⷣнца во Ѹтробаⷯ. и како смѣеⷮ
косои хѹлиⷮⷭ оутробѹ прнⷭодвыꙗ. иⷤ и жеⷩскаа
120ʳ/291 оутроба добра ѕѣло преⷣ бг҃мъ. аще оутроба по
знавшїа оуⷤ мѹжа добра ѕило. какоⷤ не боудеⷮ ѕило
добра двча Ѹтроба не познавшїа мѹжа. и ка

63. Showing that even now, God himself continues to form the infants within the womb.[797]

63.1. And you surely[798] heard | how God spoke to Abraham in the Scripture,[799] "I will return and come to you at the right season, and your wife will give birth to a son" (Gen. 18:10). And the second time, again, the Lord said, "At this time, I will return to you at the right season, and Sarah will have a son" (Gen. 18:14). These words show that God[800] forms infants in the womb. For why is it promised that God would come at the right season and claimed that Sarah[801] would have a son at the time when God "returns and comes" "at the right season"? And if God himself had not formed infants in the womb, he[802] would not have said to Abraham, "I will return and come to you at the right season, and your wife will give birth to a son" (Gen. 18:14). And[803] in the same way, God also said to Jeremiah, "Before I formed you in the womb, I knew you" (Jer. 1:5). 119v/289

63.2. And if God himself forms infants in the womb, as God declared in his words to Abraham and Jeremiah, then God can also form children in women's wombs through husbands. Therefore, it is just as much a fact that,[804] for the sake of restoring and renewing his beloved image and likeness, God himself became incarnate in the womb of the pure Virgin who did not have a husband. Indeed, even now, God continues to form infants in the womb![805] And how does Kosoy dare to blaspheme the womb of the Ever-Virgin, if women's | wombs, too, are very good before God?[806] And if a womb that has already come to know its husband is very good,[807] then how would not the Virgin's womb, 120r/291

797 **Showing that even now, God himself continues to form the infants within the womb.] Showing that just as in the beginning, God himself created Adam and Eve, so now, too, God himself continues to form infants within the women's wombs.**

798 surely] *omitted*

799 in the Scripture,] in the Scripture specifically that

800 God] he himself

801 is it promised that God would come at the right season and claimed that Sarah] is God promising to Abraham that he will come at the right season? It clearly says that Sarah

802 he] God

803 And] For

804 Therefore, it is just as much a fact that] Therefore, it is no different, even though it marvelously transcends the nature, that

805 womb] women's wombs

806 *MS 61 adds*: **Showing that it is one and the same thing, and there is no difference between the way God first passes through (the body) with his hands and fingers, and the way he himself passes through there afterward.**

807 very good,] very good in God's eyes,

ко возможно таковꙋю хꙋлꙋ на бг҃а помышлаⷮ нⷤели и гл҃ати. Ꙗко нѣсть раⷥньства идѣⷤ рꙋ кама и пⷬ҇есты бг҃ꙋ прошеⷣшꙋ. и самомꙋ бг҃ꙋ тꙋ деⷤ проити. И что скверно или что нечтⷭ҇о. токмо грѣⷯ. грѣхъⷤ ничтоⷤ ино токмо пре зрѣние заповѣди бж҃їа. бг҃ꙋⷤ нѣⷭ҇ не чтоⷭ҇ ни чтоⷤ идѣⷤ ѡсѣниⷮ силою своею. и оубо нечтоⷭ҇ ли ѡстанеⷮ идѣⷤ персты и рꙋцы его проидꙋⷮ. сего раⷣ и ꙗкоⷤ егда созидаше адама и женꙋ еⷢ҇. сподобиⷭ҇ самъ своею блгⷭ҇тию рꙋкою своею и пⷬ҇есты своими созидати а. по ѡбразꙋ своемꙋ и по поⷣбию. и ꙋтробы има и ложесна. такоⷤ и внегда поновити ѡбраⷥ свои престꙋ плениеⷨ истлѣвшїи. блгⷭ҇тию своею сподо биⷭ҇ самъ в тѣхъⷤ оудесеⷯ вмѣститиⷭ҇. и во злещи. ҃ѳ. мцⷭ҇ъ. и тѣмиⷤ проходы послѣⷣ that has not come to know its husband,[808] be even more supreme in its goodness? And how is it possible to think[809] of such blasphemy against God, not to mention saying it out loud?[810]

64. Showing that there is no difference between the way God passes through (the body) with his hands and fingers, and the way God himself passes through there.[811]

64.1. And what is unclean, or what is impure? Only sin! And sin is nothing else than disregarding God's commands. But for God, nothing that has been permeated by God's power is unclean. And would a thing actually remain unclean, if his fingers and hands go through it?[812] That is why, also,[813] when the Lord was creating Adam and his wife according to his image and likeness, he was gracious to form them[814] with his own hands and his own fingers—their wombs and the inner parts.[815] Likewise, when he went about renewing his image (in man) that was corrupted because of transgression, he was gracious to accommodate himself in those bodily parts, and after spending nine months (in the

808 husband] husband, according to those holy words,

809 possible to think] possible for anyone who has the mind to think

810 out loud?] out loud? Thus, Kosoy committed a grave and very serious sin when he asked that question with bad intention, "Can God fit in the womb and go through the belly"? Instead of giving thanks to and blessing the great and unspeakable grace of God, he blasphemed it. Wishing to rule over God, Kosoy made himself doomed for eternal fire, from which the Lord will deliver all those who love his truth.

811 **Showing that there is no difference between the way God passes through (the body) with his hands and fingers, and the way God himself passes through there.**] *omitted*

812 And what is unclean, or what is impure? Only sin! And sin is nothing else but the disregard of God's commands. But for God, nothing is unclean that has been permeated by God's power. And would a thing actually remain unclean, if his fingers and hands go through it?] But what, then, is unclean, or what is impure? It is nothing else but sin, caused by the demons and men, but not by God. And sin is nothing else but the transgression of what God mandates, which is the opposition to the divine commands. And there is nothing unclean for God, for since God is the Lord God, therefore, he sanctifies all things. And wherever his power is allowed to rest, there it brings cleansing; and wherever his hands and fingers pass through, how would those areas remain unclean?

813 That is why, also,] Thus, indeed,

814 them] *omitted*

815 their wombs and the inner parts.] to create their wombs, and the inner parts, and all the parts of the body.

проити. юдꙋ̑ прⷤе рꙋцы его и перьсти рꙋ
кꙋ его прохожаста. похоженїⷨе созида
нїа. сего раⷣ наꙋчаⷮе та бг҇ъ. и заповѣдию
120v/293 в законѣ. пр҇твѣи чистотѣ сн҇а бж҇їа. во чре
вѣ и ложеснаⷯ пр҇нодв҇ыа гл҇ѧ. Всѧко wтро
ча развѣрзаа ложесна ст҇о бви҇. Ꙗко закоⷩ
извѣсто проповѣда. слова ст҇ое воплощение бж҇їа сн҇а.
Єдинъ бо іс҇ъ сн҇ъ бж҇їи. бракꙋ не искꙋснаа ло
жесна проиде токмо. сиⷤе самое пока
зꙋа во псалмѣ҇ беⷥ сѣменнаго зачатиа.
рж҇тво гл҇ѧ. ѩко ты еси исторгии ма
иⷥ чрева. к тебѣ приверженъ есмъ из ло
жеснъ. женамъ бо мꙋжие развѣрзаюⷮ ложе
сна иⷯ. подающе сѣма зачатию в ложеснаⷯ.
ихⷤъ wтрочата не развѣрзаюⷮ имъ ложеснъ.
понеже ѿцы иⷯ ѿверзоша ложесна испꙋща
юще сѣмѧ иⷯ. и исходѧⷮ оубо ѿрочата развѣ҇
стыми ложеснами. тѣмиⷤ имиⷤ прⷤе сѣме
немъ внидоша. Сн҇ъⷤ бж҇їи единъ беⷥ сѣме
нно воплоти҇ іс҇ъ х҇с. тѣмже токмо то
единъ воистиннꙋ по писаноⷨ заповѣⷣ в за
конѣ развѣрзаа не ѿвѣстаа прⷤе мꙋжⷨе
ложесна дв҇ыа. и воистинⷩꙋ ст҇ое бви іс҇ъ

womb), to pass through the same parts through which he first went with his own hands and his hands' fingers[816] at creation.[817]

64.2. That is why God teaches you concerning the supreme purity of God's Son, (who dwelled) in the womb and the inner parts of the Ever-Virgin, through the command | in the Law where he says, "Every child that opens the womb is consecrated to God" (Ex. 13:2, 12, 15). 120v/293

65. Showing that the Law clearly proclaimed the Word and his holy incarnation as God's Son.[818]

65.1. For the Son of God ⟨and the Son of Man⟩ is one Jesus, and it was precisely him, who passed through the womb[819] that did not know marriage. And showing this same thing in the Psalms—the birth that was conceived without a male seed—he says, "You are the one who forced me out of the womb; I lean on you from (my mother's) belly" (Ps. 21:10). For men[820] open the wombs of their wives when they dispense seed for conception in their bellies, and it is not their children, who open their (mothers') wombs, because their fathers open the wombs when they transmit their seed.[821] And then, children[822] come out of the wombs that are already open, going through the same path that the seed came in earlier. But the Son of God, Jesus Christ, is the only one who became incarnate without a male seed. Therefore, according to the command written in the Law, there is truly only one person who opens the Virgin's womb that was not opened by a husband earlier. He is Jesus Christ, who is truly consecrated to God.

---

816 his hands' fingers] the fingers

817 *MS 61 adds*: **Showing that the Law clearly proclaimed the Word and his holy incarnation as God's Son, which took place without a male seed from the All-pure Virgin, who did not know man.**

818 **Showing that the Law clearly proclaimed the Word and his holy incarnation as God's Son.**] *omitted*

819 passed through the womb] opened the womb

820 For men] And it is evident that such words are addressed from Jesus to his divine Father, though they were declared by David through the Holy Spirit. For men

821 open the wombs when they transmit their seed.] opened them first upon transmitting their seed into their (wives') bellies.

822 children] the first-born children

х҃с. гл҃ⷮе и еще писание. Прїидостаⷤ два[823]
аг҃гла в содоⷨ вечеⷬ. лотъⷤ сѣдаше преⷣ вра
ты
121r/294 содоⷨскими. видѣвъⷤ лотъ и срѣте ѧ и покло
ниⷭ лицеⷭ до земли. и реⷱ се г҃на ѡбратитаⷭ в доⷨ
раба ваю. да почиета и ѡмыета нози. ѡ
свѣтша изыдета на пꙋть свои с негоⷤ совра
тистаⷭ к рабꙋ своемꙋ. рѣшаⷤ ни оубо на сто
г҃наⷯ почиевѣ и нꙋжашеѧ. и совратистасѧ
в доⷨ его. и сотвори има пиръ и ѡприснoки
испече иⷨ. и ꙗдоста преⷣ спаниеⷨ. мꙋжиⷤ гра
да содоⷨска ѡбыдоша домъ ѿ юноты и до
старецъ. веⷭ нароⷣ вкꙋпѣ иⷥзывахꙋ лота.
и г҃люще к немꙋ гдѣ еста мꙋжа ꙗⷤ прїидо
ста к тебѣ нощию. изведи ѧ к наⷨ да боудеⷨ
с ними. и сшⷣе лотъ преⷣ двери к нимъ. две
риⷤ затвори за собою и рече имъ. никако же
братие не зазрите. еста бо ми дщери двѣ
иⷤ не знаета мꙋжа изведꙋ ѧ к вамъ. и сотво
рита с нима ꙗкоⷤ есть гоⷣно вамъ. точию
мꙋжема сима не сотворита ѕла. понеⷤ
прїидоста в завѣтие домꙋ моего. рѣшаⷤ
емꙋ. пришеⷣ еси сѣмо ꙋ наⷭ ѡбитаⷮ а не сꙋда
сꙋдиⷮ. н҃нѣ оубо ѧ оубиеⷨ не г҃ли ѡ наⷭ. и бѣ
дꙋ творѧхꙋ лотꙋ ѕило. и приступиша
121v/295 да разбиюⷮ двери. И сѧгшаⷤ мꙋжи рꙋкама вдеⷬ
нꙋста лота к себѣ в храминꙋ. и двери храмꙋ
заключиста. мꙋжаⷤ сꙋщаⷣ преⷣ дверми поби
ста невидимо. ѿ мала до велика. и погибо
ша ищꙋщеи дверё. рѣстаⷤ мꙋжа к лотꙋ. еⷭ ли
кто здѣ. или зѧⷮ или с҃нове или дщери. или кто
инъ или кто ти во градѣ. изведи ѧ ѿ мѣста

823 *In the margin*: гл҃аⷡ к҃.

66. CHAPTER 24.[824]

66.1. The Scripture also says:[825] "And the two angels came to Sodom at evening. And Lot sat by the gate | of Sodom, and having seen them, Lot met them, and 121r/294
he worshiped with his face to the ground, and said, 'Behold, lords, turn in to the house of your servant so that you may rest and wash your feet; and having risen early in the morning, you may depart on your journey, from which you turned aside to your servant'. And they said, 'No, we will lodge in the street'. And he constrained them, and they turned aside to his house. And he made a feast for them and baked unleavened cakes for them, and they ate before going to sleep.[826]

66.2. And the men of the city of Sodom, both young and old, all the people together, surrounded the house. They called out Lot and said to him, 'Where are the men who came to you tonight? Bring them out to us so that we may be with them'. And Lot went out to them at the doorway, and he shut the door after him and said to them, 'By no means, brothers, do not act wickedly. Since I have two daughters, who have not known a man, I will bring them out to you; do with them as it pleases you, only do no evil to these men, for they came under the roof of my house'. And they said to him, 'You have come to dwell here, and not to act like a judge. Now, therefore, we will kill you; do not argue with us'. And they caused Lot a great deal of trouble, and they drew near | to break the door. 121v/295

66.3. And the men reached out their hands and pulled Lot into the house with them, and shut the door of the house. And they struck the men who were at the door with blindness, both small and great, and they died seeking the door. And the men said to Lot, 'Do you have anyone here—sons-in-law, or sons, or daughters, or anyone else, or anyone in the city that belongs to you? Bring them

---

824 CHAPTER 24.] **Investigation in the divinely inspired Scripture concerning the coming of the two angels to Sodom. How should we understand that? And when something holy comes upon that which is impure, how are we to view it? And can the impure things persist in those places where holiness comes in? And when the Lord God called Adam, how should we understand that? CHAPTER 24. Showing that holiness is more supreme and greater than all impurity. Wherever holiness comes in, it destroys impurity, while holiness is not affected by anything impure.**

825 But the Son of God, Jesus Christ, is the only one who became incarnate without a male seed. Therefore, there is truly only one person, according to the written command in the Law, who opens the Virgin's womb that was not opened by a husband earlier. He is Jesus Christ, who is truly consecrated to God. The Scripture also says:] And there is truly only one person, according to the written command in the Law, who opens the womb of the Virgin. He is Jesus Christ, who is truly consecrated to God, and he is the only one who was conceived without a seed in the Virgin, who did not know marriage.

826 before going to sleep.] before rescuing.

сеⷢ҇. ıако погоублıаеⷨ мѣсто се. понеⷤ возвысиⷭ҇ вопль иⷯ преⷣ бгмъ. и поусти ны гⷭь бгъ потребити а. Ꙗко с҇тость аггльскаа множае еⷭ҇ всакїа скверны. не повреждаеⷮ бо са с҇тость нечⷭ҇тотою. пачеⷤ гдѣ настанеⷮ с҇тость. тамо[827]
Видите ли содома ıако скверн҇ѣиши соуⷮ всакиа нечⷭ҇тоты. и всеа скверны исполнена. како ѡⷠ҇ноцьствовахоу аггли с҇ти соуще в таковоⷨ мѣсте нечиⷭ҇тѣ. скверн҇ѣишиⷨ паⷣ всеа землıа. и како в жилище скверныⷯ людеи. иⷤ чреⷥ҇ еⷭство сквернащиⷯса. скверною скверненишею всакиа нечистоты. прїидоша аггли и не ѡскверневахоуса. въшеⷣшимъ аггломъ в содомы не прикасашеса к ниⷨ нечⷭ҇тота скверны содоⷨскиа почто.
122r/296 понеⷤ с҇тость аггльскаа бⷭ҇ши сквеⷬ҇ны содоⷨскиа. и ты не смѣеши глати. ıако внидоша аггли въ скверненшее мѣсто. и ѡбноцьствоваша в нечистѣ жилищи. пострадаша ли ѡскверниⷭ҇ти. проходаше и ѡбноцьствоующе в нечистыⷯ содомеⷯ. бгоⷨ ли дерзаеши глаⷮ иⷤ превыше и с҇тѣиши всакиа чⷭ҇тоты. како во оутробѣ калоⷨ ѡбьатоу быти. и проходы немощными проити. колика оубо деⷬзость беⷥбжьного ıазыка косоⷢ. в каковоу хоудость бга своди. въ аковоⷨ хоудость и ааггловъ невозможеⷮ привести. ѡ небл҇годарныи и хоулныи и лоукавыи чл҇че да оубо ли с҇тость аггльскоу не возмогаеⷮ нечⷭ҇тота содоⷨскаа ѡсквернити. бжиюⷤ ли с҇тость дв҇ича оутроба чиста возможеⷮ повредити. иⷤ самоую оутробоу еввы и входы и проходы. саⷨ бгъ в началѣ своима роукама проклепа. и пеⷬсты роукоу его проидоша в соⷥданїи вса оуды и члѣны. и селико спⷪбиса любвѣ раⷣ ѡбраза своеⷢ и поⷣобиа преклонитиⷭ преⷤ. и послѣ

827 *Text continues in the margin*: всакоую скверноу истреблıаеⷮ.

out of this place, because we are going to destroy this place. For their cry has been raised up before God, and the Lord God sent us to destroy it'" (Gen. 19:1–13).

67. Showing that angelic holiness supersedes any impurity. Holiness does not get affected by impurity. Instead, wherever holiness comes in, it destroys impurity there.[828]

67.1. Don't you see that Sodom was filled with every impurity and every shame? How is it that the holy angels came to spend the night in such an impure place, the most unclean of all on the earth? And how did the angels, who came to the dwelling place of unclean people—those that became unclean by subjecting their nature to the unclean ways of every impure uncleanness—not become unclean themselves? Indeed, when the angels came to Sodom, the impurity of the Sodomite uncleanness did not touch them. Why? | Because the holiness of 122r/296 the angels is far greater than the uncleanness of the Sodomites. And you should not dare to say that, after coming into the most unclean place and spending the night at the most impure dwelling, the angels suffered by becoming unclean, because of passing through, and spending the night at Sodom.

67.2. Do you dare to speak against God, who is higher and more holy than all things pure (when you ask), how he was confined to the impure womb[829] and went through the soft passages (of the body)? What an audacity, indeed, in the godless language of Kosoy! He reduces God to nothing, bringing him down so low that even the angels cannot be placed at such a level. O, ungrateful, blasphemous, deceitful man! Indeed, can the impurity of the Sodomites make the holiness of the angels unclean? Can the pure womb of the Virgin affect the holiness of God? It is the same womb that Eve had, and God touched it—including all the inlets and the outlets—with his own hands, and the fingers of his hand passed through all the parts and places (of her body) at creation.[830]

67.3. And that is how much he was willing to stoop down in his love for the sake of his image and likeness (in man) from the beginning. And would he not

828 **Showing that angelic holiness supersedes any impurity. Holiness is not affected by impurity. Instead, wherever holiness comes in, it destroys impurity there.**] *omitted*

829 impure womb] womb

830 at creation.] at creation, when he formed them.

ѡбновиⷮ ѡбраⷥ свои и поⷣⷪбие. не споⷣⷪбит ли сѧ 122v/297 тыиⷤ оудовы и чл҃ены восприѩвъ тѣмиⷤ проити. ихⷤъ преⷤ рꙋцы и перъсты еⷭ҇ прохожаста. и не повредивъ своеⷢ бж҃ства. елма и аг͡гли не возмогоша с҃тости своеа повредити. вшеⷣше в нечистыи содоⷨ и ѡбнощьствовавше в неⷨ. И реⷱ҇ миранинъ икониⷦ. ꙗко в домꙋ лотовѣ моужа правеⷣна ѡбнощьствоваша аг͡гли. Ѿвѣщаⷯ же имъ аⷥ гл҃ю. но не внидоша ли в содомъ аг͡гли и не проидоша ли граⷣ к домꙋ лотовꙋ. и неⷭ҇ ли писано. ꙗко ѿвѣщаша аг͡гли лотꙋ зовꙋⷳ ихъ в доⷨ. ни рѣша. оубо на стогнаⷯ почиевѣ. видиши ли ꙗко аг͡гли хотаста на стогнаⷯ градꙋ ѡбнощьствовати в нечистоⷨ содомѣ. и домъⷤ лотовъ самыи не бѣꙗше ли в томъⷤ скверноⷨ содомѣ. не содомлꙗне ли прїидоша и къ дверемъ домꙋ лотова. безаконие свое показающи. аг͡гльскаа оубо с҃тость своеа чистоты крѣпость имаⷮ аще и в содомы входиⷮ. аще и ѡⷠнощьствꙋеⷮ тамо. множаеⷤ бж҃иа с҃тости чистота. в чистыⷯ ложеснаⷯ оутробы дв҃ыа свою крѣ 123r/298 пость имаⷮ. аще и. ф҃. мцⷭъ ѡбнощьствоваⷡ тамо. Ꙗко в началѣ совѣⷮ бж҃їи ѡ созданїи чл҃ка. Ї искание бж҃їе в раю адама. и съшествие к размѣшению ꙗзыкъ. проѡбражение еⷭ҇ воплощению[831]

Видитеⷤ и раⷥсмотрите колико законъ ѿкровено наꙋⷮчаеⷮ воплощение сн҃а бж҃їа. многиⷨ воѡбраженми проповѣдаа воплощение сн҃а бж҃иа ѿ чистыа дв҃ы. чтоⷤ оубо мнитсѧ ваⷨ писанию гл҃ющꙋ. И слышаста глаⷭ гⷭа

831 *Text continues in the margin*: слова бж҃їа и содѣиствование с҃того дх҃а.

be willing | to assume the parts and members (of the body) that are the same as those through which he had passed, so that he might[832] afterward renew his image and likeness (in man)? His hands and fingers had passed through them before with no effect on his divinity, just as the angels were not affected[833] when they entered the impure Sodom and stayed the night in it. 122v/297

67.4. And one layman, an icon-painter, said that the angels stayed the night at the house of Lot, who was actually a righteous person. And in response, I said to them, asking: But didn't the angels enter Sodom, and didn't the citizens come to Lot's house?[834] And[835] is it not written that the angels answered Lot, who invited them into the house,[836] saying, "No, we will lodge in the street" (Gen. 19:2)? Don't you see that the angels wanted to spend the night lodging in the street of the city, in impure Sodom? And regarding Lot's house itself, wasn't it located in the same unclean Sodom? Was it also not the Sodomites who came to the door of Lot's house and displayed their iniquity? Thus, angelic holiness is endowed with a firmness that comes from their purity, even though they entered Sodom and even though they stayed the night there. And the purity of God's holiness (that rested) within the pure womb and the inner parts of the Virgin[837] | has its firmness, even though it dwelled there nine months. 123r/298

68. Showing that God's counsel concerning the creation of man in the very beginning, and God's search for Adam in paradise, and the descent to confuse the tongues, prefigure the incarnation of God's Son and the co-working of the Holy Spirit.[838]

68.1. Do take a look and consider how explicitly the Law teaches about the incarnation of God's Son, proclaiming the incarnation of the Son of God from the pure Virgin with multiple images. Now, what do you envision when Scrip-

832 so that he might] when he had to
833 angels were not affected] angels did not have their holiness affected
834 didn't the citizens come to Lot's house?] didn't they say they would lodge in the street of the city, and didn't the citizens come to Lot's house?
835 And] *omitted*
836 invited them into the house,] pressed them to come into his house,
837 virgin] All-holy Virgin
838 **Showing that God's counsel concerning the creation of man in the very beginning, and God's search for Adam in paradise, and the descent to confuse the tongues, prefigure the incarnation of God's Son and the co-working of the Holy Spirit.**] *omitted*

бг҃а ходѧща в раюⷡ полѹдне. и скрыста сѧ
посредѣ древа раискаго адамⷤъ и жена его.
и призва г҃ь бг҃ъ адама. Нѣ҃ ли оубо се про
ѡбраженіе сшествиѧ сн҃ѹ бж҃ию съ нбсе.
на взыскание чл҃ка заблѹжьшаⷭ҇ ѿ бг҃а исти
ннаго. во многобж҃ие ложное. и призва
вшаⷭ҇ в пакибытие сп҃сеніа. можаше бо
бг҃ъ и съ нбс҃ѣ возвавъ ѡбличити адама.
и не сшⷣе съ нбс҃ѣ в раи. ꙗкоⷤ и каина ѡ оуби
ствѣ брата еⷭ҇. съ нбс҃ѣ возвавъ ѡбличи
не сшⷣе на землю. Пакиⷤ при стоⷧ҇потворе
нии гл҃еⷮ бг҃ъ. Сшⷣеше оубо смѣсиⷨ ѧ. Что
оубо еда не возмоⷤ бг҃ъ на нбс҃ѣ пребываа
123v/299 размѣсити иⷯ. аще не снидеⷮ. и како потопи
всю поⷭ҇нбн҃ѹю не сшⷣе на землю. единоⷭ҇ стоⷧ҇
па смѣсиⷮ сходиⷮ съ нбс҃ѣ. и не токмо сходиⷮ
но и призываеⷮ на помощь равносиⷧ҇ны своиⷯ.
приидѣте реⷱ҇ смѣсимъ иⷯ. нѣ҃ ли и здѣ проѡ
браженіе бг҃оначаⷧ҇ныѧ тр҃ца дѣтели. еⷤ
по хв҃ѣ воскрⷭ҇нїи в пѧⷮдесатницѹ сшестви
еⷨ единого ѿ тр҃ца ст҃го дх҃а. смѣсиⷮ много
бж҃ие в вѣрѹ во едино бжⷭ҇тво беⷥначаⷧ҇ныѧ
тр҃ца. и ꙗко и блг҃оволение еⷭ҇ бг҃а ѿц҃а. сни
тию воплотиⷮсѧ единородномѹ сн҃ѹ его.
съдѣиствѹющѹ ст҃мѹ дх҃ѹ. нѣ҃ ли оубо сие сше
ствие бж҃ие размѣшениѧ раⷣ. показание
сшествїа сн҃а бж҃їа. призванїа раⷣ ꙗзыкъ
въ единение вѣры бж҃иа. аки бы рекъ бг҃ъ
сиа сн҃ѹ своемѹ и дх҃ѹ своемѹ ст҃мѹ. придѣ
те нн҃ѣ сшⷣеше смѣсиⷨ и. поне тебѣ словоу
моемѹ снити воплотиⷮсѧ се самоⷭ҇ ради еже
блѹдащаа беⷥпѹтиⷨ беⷥбж҃иа чл҃ки. на пѹⷮ по
знанїа моеⷭ҇ бжⷭ҇тва и страха наставити.
и тебѣ ст҃мѹ дх҃ѹ снити. размѣшеныѧ нн҃ѣ
сїа ꙗзыки зломыслиа ради иⷯ совокѹпити
124r/300 паки в бг҃оразѹмие. воплощениеⷨ слова моего.

ture says,[839] "And they heard the voice of the Lord God walking in the garden in the afternoon; and both Adam and his wife hid in the midst of trees of the garden. And the Lord God called Adam" (Gen. 3:8–9)? Now, is this not a prefiguring of the descent of God's Son from the heavens in order to seek man, who strayed away[840] from the true God into false polytheism, and to call him to salvation through the second birth?

68.2. For God could just as well have called and rebuked Adam from the heavens, without coming down to paradise from the heavens, as he also called and rebuked Cain concerning the murder of his brother, without going down to the earth. And again, at the Tower of Babel, God says, "Having gone down, let us confuse them" (Gen. 11:7). What then? Was God not capable of confusing them while remaining in the heavens, | without going down? And how is it that he 123v/299
flooded the entire world without going down to the earth, but did come from the heavens specifically to bring confusion at the Tower of Babel? And he not only comes down, but also calls upon the helpers—the counselors who have power equal to his—saying, "Come! Having gone down, let us confuse them".

68.3. Don't we have here, too, the prefigured acts of the supremely divine Trinity, of which one person, the Holy Spirit, being part of the Trinity, came down after Christ's resurrection on the day of Pentecost in order to confuse polytheism, (replacing it) with faith in the one Godhead of the Trinity that is without beginning? And is it not the good pleasure of God the Father that his only-begotten Son came down to become incarnate, while the Holy Spirit worked together with him? Indeed, doesn't this descent of God to bring confusion reveal the descent of God's Son in order to call the nations to one faith in God?

68.4. It is as if God[841] said this to his Son and his Holy Spirit: "Come! Let us confuse him now. For you, my Word, will subsequently come down in order to become incarnate for the sake of this very thing—to guide back to the fear and knowledge of my Godhead the people who have become lost on the pathless road of atheism. And you, my Holy Spirit, are to descend for the sake of those who now, on account of their evil-scheming, are confused by these tongues, in order to reconnect them | to the mind of God through the incarnation of my 124r/300

839 *MS 61 adds*: **Showing that God's counsel concerning the creation of man, which took place in the beginning, when God (conversed) with those who were equally divine with him, and the search of God for Adam in paradise, and the descent to confuse the tongues, (all of this) prefigures the incarnation of God's Son and the co-working of the Holy Spirit.**

840 man, who strayed away] the whole humankind that strayed away

841 God] God the Father

примирившꙋ ми сиа крⷭ҇томъ на нⷨе возвы шенꙋ бывшꙋ емꙋ. враждꙋ престꙋпленіа в раю и зломыслиа на стⷭ҇пѣ ѿемъ. крⷭ҇тⷨо юже ѿ древа злобоу стеръ. и высотꙋ злоꙋмїа стⷭ҇опа сⷭ҇е. на крⷭ҇тѣ простⷭ҇е рꙋцѣ низложⷺи соберⷮе в мое познание паки чⷧ҇чество мнѣ блⷢ҇говолѧщꙋ. и аще не се проѡбражаⷮ҇ сщⷭ҇нно мꙋ писанию. призыванїⷨе бжⷭ҇иимъ равноси лныⷯ емꙋ на сшествие размѣшению стⷭ҇опа. возможно бы оубо бгⷭ҇ꙋ и не глⷢ҇авшꙋ сⷭ҇е и на вы сотѣ пребывающꙋ беⷥ шествиа смѣсиⷮ сиа. иⷤ не подвигнꙋса ѿ высоты прⷤ҇е ни съшеⷣ всю землю водою истлѣ. Паки глⷮ҇е сщⷭ҇нное пи сание. Ꙗви жⷭ҇е авраамꙋ бгъ оу дꙋба маⷨрїа[842] сѣдащꙋ емꙋ. прⷣ҇е двермі храмꙋ его полꙋдне. возрⷤ҇ѣвъ ѡчима своима и вѣдⷤ҇ѣ сⷭ҇е трие мꙋжи стоахꙋ верхꙋ его. и вѣдѣвъ притече въ срѣтение иⷨ ѿ двереи храмꙋ его. и покло нⷭ҇и до земла. и рⷭ҇е гⷭ҇и аще есмь ѡбрⷭ҇ѣ блⷣ҇ть прⷣ҇е тобою не мини раба своⷢ҇е. да са прине сⷮ҇е вода да са ѡмыюⷮ ноги ваша. и простꙋдитⷭ҇е пⷣ҇о дꙋбⷨо. и принесꙋ хлѣбы да асте. и по сⷨ҇е ми
124v/301 нете на пꙋть свои с негⷤ҇о совратистⷭ҇а сѣмо к рабꙋ своемꙋ. и рѣша тако сотвори ꙗкⷤ҇о гла. и потщавса авраⷨа к саррѣ рⷱ҇е еи. подви жи и вмѣси три спꙋды мꙋки чисты. и сотво ри потребники. и тⷱ҇е авраⷨа въ кравы и поа телецъ тꙋченъ и добръ. и дасть и рабꙋ. и ꙋско ри и приготовити е. и вза масло и мⷣ҇е и мле ко. и телецъⷤ҇е приготова и постави прⷣ҇е ними и адоша. самⷤ҇ъ стоаще прⷣ҇е ними пⷣ҇о

842 *In the margin*: глⷡ҇а ке

Word and reconciliation of the cross.[843] He is to be hung upon it, and through the cross take away the hostility of transgression (that occurred) in paradise and the evil-scheming (that occurred) at the Tower of Babel, wiping away the enmity that originated at the tree, and overthrowing the extreme evil-scheming at the Tower of Babel. By extending his hands on the cross, he will re-assemble humankind toward the knowledge of me, fulfilling my good pleasure".

68.5. And if this is not what the sacred Scripture[844] prefigures, ⟨then what is it⟩ when God calls upon ⟨the counselors⟩, who share power equal to his, to come and bring confusion at the Tower of Babel? Indeed, God could have refrained from saying this and could have remained in the heavens, without going down to confuse them, just as he did not make any such movement from the heavens when he destroyed the entire earth with the flood.

69. CHAPTER 25.[845]

69.1. And again, the sacred Scripture says, "And God appeared to him by the oak of Mamre, as he sat by the door of his tent at noon. And he lifted up his eyes, and having seen them,[846] he ran to meet them from the door of his tent and bowed himself to the ground. And he said, 'Lord, if I have found grace in your sight, do not pass by your servant. Let water be brought, and let them wash your feet, and refresh yourselves | under the oak. And I will bring bread, that you may eat, 124v/301
and afterward, you may depart on your journey, from which you turned aside to your servant'. And they said, 'Do as you said'.

69.2. And Abraham hastened to Sarah, saying to her, 'Hurry, knead three measures of fine flour, and make unleavened bread'. And Abraham ran to the herd, and took a young calf, fat and good, and gave it to his servant, and he hurried him to prepare it. And he took butter, and honey, and milk, and the calf which he prepared; and he set it before them, and they ate, and he stood by

843 Word and reconciliation of the cross.] Word, who will reconcile them to me by means of the cross.

844 sacred Scripture] divinely inspired Scripture

845 CHAPTER 25.] **Investigation in the holy book of Genesis concerning the event when the Lord God stayed at Abraham's tent with the two others. Why did that happen, and how is it to be understood? And did Sarah upset the (action) of grace when she laughed? CHAPTER 25. Showing that God's visit with Abraham in the tent and his solution for Sarah's inability to bear children because of her old age is an antecedent of the descent in which God's Word became man and a sign of the future virginal conception that happened without a male seed.**

846 and having seen them,] and saw: Behold, three men stood in front of him; and having seen them,

дꙋбомъ. речеⷤ҇ к немꙋ гдѣ сарра жена твоꙗ. сеⷤ ѿвѣщавъ реⷱ҇ емꙋ. се въ храминѣ. и реⷱ҇ ѡбращьсѧ придꙋ к тебѣ. по времени сеⷨ҇ в часѣ. и родиⷮ҇ сн҃ъ сарра жена твоꙗ. Ꙗко витание бж҃ие оу авраама в храминѣ. и разрѣшение неплодїа старицы саррѣ. прописание схожеⷩ҇ѧ слова бж҃їа въ чл҃чⷭ҇тво. и проначертание беⷥ҇[847]
Что оубо раⷣ҇ приходиⷮ҇ бг҃ъ въ храминꙋ авраамовꙋ. сего ли раⷣ҇ понеⷤ҇ дрꙋгъ бж҃ии авраⷨ҇. и что се аще единого точию сего раⷣ҇ вниде ко авраамꙋ въ храминꙋ. ꙗко дрꙋгъ бж҃їи наречесѧ. то ꙋбо не ꙗвисѧ ли бг҃ъ авраамꙋ множицею 125r/302 и преⷤ҇. не множицею ли бг҃ъ и бесѣдова ко авраамꙋ преⷤ҇. но чесо раⷣ҇ ꙗвиⷭ҇ бг҃ъ авраамꙋ. и вниде въ храминꙋ его. сеⷢ҇ ли раⷣ҇ ꙗко сн҃а авраамꙋ подати. и разрѣшиⷮ҇ неплⷪ҇ство саррѣ женѣ авраамови. старицы сꙋщи подаⷮ҇ плⷪ҇ паче еⷭ҇ства. добрѣ оубо ѡбоеⷢ҇ ради приходиⷮ҇ бг҃ъ ко авраамꙋ. зане и дрꙋгъ наречесѧ и чадо подаⷮ҇. и понеⷤ҇ никто же ѿ чл҃къ тогда бг҃а взыска. токмо авраⷨ҇ единъ. меⷧ҇хиседекъ бо родꙋ ѿ себе не имаⷮ҇ комꙋ предаⷮ҇ бл҃гочестие ѡ бз҃ѣ. добрѣ оубо сице разꙋмѣваетсѧ ѡ пришествїи бж҃їи ко авраамꙋ. ꙗко вѣрнꙋ къ своемꙋ рабꙋ и сн҃а даровати. но оубо что сие аще и не таина велика се и ѡбраⷥ҇ высочаишиⷨ҇ и бⷪ҇шимъ. и пррⷪ҇чество бꙋдꙋщаⷢ҇. написꙋⷮ҇

847 *Text continues in the margin*: сѣменнаⷢ҇ зачатїа еⷭ҇ во плоти.

them under the oak tree. And he said to him, 'Where is Sarah, your wife'? And he answered and said to him, 'There, in the tent'. And he said, 'I will return and come to you at the right season, and Sarah, your wife, will bear a son'".[848] (Gen. 18:1–10).

70. Showing that God's visit with Abraham in the tent and his solution for Sarah's inability to bear children because of her old age is an antecedent of the descent of God's Word to humanity and a sign of his future conception in the body that took place without a male seed.[849]

70.1. Now, why does God come to Abraham's tent? Is it because Abraham was a friend of God? But what is so special about that? If it was only for that reason, that the Lord God came to Abraham in the tent—because the latter was called the friend of God—then didn't God appear to Abraham many times | before as 125r/302
well? Didn't God speak with Abraham many times earlier? But then, what was the reason that God appeared[850] to Abraham and entered his tent this time? Or was it because he was to give Abraham a son and solve the problem of Abraham's wife, Sarah, who was barren, giving the old woman an offspring beyond her natural capacity? Actually, it may well be that God comes to Abraham in view of both things: because he was called God's friend, and because he was to give him a child. For at that time, aside from Abraham alone, there was no man who searched for God. For Melchizedek did not leave a descendant, to whom he could pass on the faith in God.[851]

70.2. It may well be understood, then, that God came to Abraham because the latter was his faithful servant and because he was to give him a son. But what is this, then, if not a great mystery and the image of something high and grand? And isn't the coming of God to Abraham's tent a clear prophetic descrip-

848 son'".] son'; and Sarah heard at the door of the tent, being behind him. And Abraham and Sarah were old, advanced in days, and the way of women ceased to be with Sarah. And Sarah laughed, saying to herself, 'Well, (this) thing has not as yet happened to me, even until now, and here, my husband is old'. And the Lord God said to Abraham, 'Why is it that Sarah laughed to herself, saying, 'Will I really bear (a child), now that I am old'? Is anything that God says impossible for him? At this time, I will return at the right season, and Sarah will have a son'" (Gen. 18:1–10).

849 **Showing that God's visit with Abraham in the tent and his solution for Sarah's inability to bear children because of her old age is an antecedent of the descent of God's Word to humanity and a sign of his future conception in the body that took place without a male seed.**] *omitted*

850 then didn't God appear to Abraham many times before as well? Didn't God speak with Abraham many times earlier? But then, what was the reason that God appeared] *omitted*

851 God.] true God.

ꙗвьствено пришествие бж҃ие въ храминꙋ авраамовꙋ. и аще не бы таина велика ни прⷪ҇рчество бꙋдꙋщемꙋ ни ѡбраⷥ҇ бо҃шемꙋ. пришествие бж҃ие в кꙋщꙋ авраамлю. можаше бг҃ъ сн҃а авраамꙋ даровати и не подвижа вса ѿ мѣста своⷢ҇. и не плⷪ҇дѣ сарре разрѣшити и съ нбⷭ҇е. поне и исаака молꙗщаⷭ҇ оуслыша бг҃ъ на нбⷭ҇е. и ѿ нбⷭ҇ныхъ крꙋгъ не сше разрѣши ревецы неплⷪ҇дство.
125v/304 даровав има два сн҃а а не единого токмо. саррѣ единого сн҃а сам подати приходит и въ храминꙋ входит. что ꙋбо се колико чюⷣны твари сотвори со мнозѣмъ оудоⷭ҇ствоⷨ. нбо и землю аки ничто. женѣ единои не плⷪ҇де разрѣшити сам приходит. рече бо ѡбращꙋса и на се время приидꙋ в часѣ и бꙋдет саррѣ сн҃ъ. како повелѣ точию и землꙗ изнесе былїа злака. и древеса абие. не бывше никогдаⷤ зелиа злака. и древеса плодовитаа на земли. рече точию. да израстит землꙗ. и абие прорастошаⷭ҇ вса. послѣди аки не могїи разрѣшити ꙋтробы неплодие. разверзыи земленаа бока не плⷪ҇наа. прежⷷ на прорастение. глет ѡбращꙋса и на се время придꙋ в часѣ и бꙋдет саррѣ сн҃ъ. великои чюⷣно воистиннꙋ таинъство. ибо велие дѣло самоⷢ҇ бжⷭ҇тва есть. не оубо просто приходит бг҃ъ в кꙋщꙋ авраамовꙋ. ни просто приходит бг҃ъ разрѣшити не плⷪ҇де саррѣ. не ꙗк сего ради поне состари сарра и ꙋмерша оу ложесна имѣа ѿ мноⷤства лѣтнаⷢ҇. и не плⷪ҇ствием иссохше и старостию. но свое бжⷭ҇твеное
126r/305 дѣло съдѣваа вышеестⷭ҇веное. и како слышаⷭ҇ еси всако сщ҃нное писание. ꙗко ѡбѣтова бг҃ъ авраамꙋ ѿ сѣмени его блвити вса ꙗзыки еже есть ѡ хⷭ҇ѣ. ꙗко ꙋбо есть бж҃ие блговоление посла сн҃а своего еди

tion of what was to take place in the future? And if God's coming to Abraham's tent had not been a great mystery, nor a prophecy of the future, nor an image of something grand, then God could have given a son to Abraham[852] without moving from his place; and he could also have solved the problem of Sarah's[853] inability to bear children while staying in the heavens. For God did hear Isaac's prayer from the heavens, and in solving the problem of Rebecca's inability to bear children, he did not go down from the dome of the heavens.[854] | He gave 125v/304
them two sons, and not just one. And as for Sarah, he gives her one son by coming to her in his own person and by entering the tent.

70.3. What does it mean, then? He accomplished so many wondrous[855] works without any difficulty—the heaven and the earth—as if they were nothing! But to solve the problem of childbearing for one woman, he comes in his own person! For he said,[856] "At this time, I will return and come at the right season, and Sarah will have a son" (Gen. 18:14). (At creation), he simply gave an order, and the earth produced the plants and the trees immediately after, and there was never a delay in time before green plants[857] and fruitful trees grew on the earth. He only said, "Let the earth bring forth", and all things at once began to grow. And given that he had earlier opened up[858] the barren parts of the earth to have them sprout with green things, was he not able afterward to solve the problem of (Sarah's inability) to conceive a child in her womb, as he said, "I will return and come at the right season, and Sarah will have a son"?[859]

70.4. It is a truly great and marvelous mystery, for God himself does his awesome work. Indeed, God does not simply come to Abraham's tent, nor does God come simply to solve Sarah's problem with childbearing. It is not because of this, (that he comes). For Sarah grew old, and her womb became dead because of her great age, and she was unable to give birth to children due to debility and old age. But God | did something beyond what was natural.[860] In what way? You 126r/305
have surely heard the sacred Scripture, how God promised Abraham to bless all the nations in his seed (Gen. 22:18), which means "in Christ". And is this, therefore, not the good pleasure of God—that he would send his only-begotten Son

852 Abraham] his friend Abraham
853 Sarah's] *omitted*
854 from the dome of the heavens.] from the heavens.
855 wondrous] wondrous and astonishing
856 For he said,] God said,
857 and the trees immediately after, and there was never a delay in time before green plants] *omitted*
858 given that he had earlier opened up] he who had earlier opened up
859 a son"?] a son"? Yet the Scripture did not say, "The Lord God will return to Abraham".
860 what was natural.] what was natural as if it was a matter of his special divine care.

нороⷣнаго наздаⷮ҇ ѡбраⷥ свои истлѣвшїи. ıако еⷭ҇
послꙋшаⷮ҇ сн҃ꙋ бж҃ию бг҃а ѿц҃а. и сшеⷣ на землю во
плотиⷮ҇са словꙋ и сп҃ти чл҃чество. ıако и еⷭ҇ ст҃о
мꙋ дх҃ꙋ содѣствоваⷮ҇ блг҃оволение бж҃ие. того
раⷣ҇ ıавлıаетса бг҃ъ авраамꙋ въ треⷯ составеⷯ.
три бо мꙋжа видѣ аврааⷨ возрѣвъ ѡчима сво
има. тѣмже и приходиⷮ бг҃ъ трⷪ҇ца в кꙋщꙋ а
враамовꙋ. прїимаеⷮ ѡсазание ногꙋ во ѡмы
ванїи. аки мꙋжие пꙋ҃шествꙋющїи. и ıаде
пищꙋ преⷣставленꙋю. и ѡбѣтоваеⷮ саррѣ сн҃а.
ѿ негоⷤ племени быти сѣмени ѡбѣтованно
мꙋ. ѡ нем же блⷭ҇ватса вси ıазыцы земнїи.
по пеⷬвомꙋ ѡбѣщанию бж҃ию авраамꙋ. да
ꙋвѣдавъ ты бг҃а витавша в кꙋщи авраамⷧи
преⷤ. и оуслышавъ послѣди сн҃а бж҃иа во чревѣ
дв҃чи. ѳ҃. мцⷭ҇ь витавша веⷬꙋеши. и да не ѡ
пытоваеши мнⷢ҇о. како ꙋтроба дв҃ча вмѣ
сти бг҃а. понеⷤ вмѣсти бг҃а оуⷤ по преⷣ҇ кꙋща
126v/305 авраамова. паки ꙋвѣдаⷡ не плодове и ѿ ста
рости имѣющꙋ оумеръшвеныа ложеⷭ҇на ѿ
роча ражающꙋ. не невѣрꙋеши слышавъ дв҃цꙋ
беⷥ мꙋжа ражающꙋ. ıакоⷤ бо тогда сн҃ъ бж҃їи
со ѿцеⷨ своимъ и со ст҃ымъ дх҃омъ. вмѣстиⷭ҇
в кꙋщꙋ авраамовꙋ. претерпѣ ѡсазатиⷭ҇
и ıасти восприаⷮ. тако тоиⷤ нн҃ѣ слово бо
жие бг҃ъ. ѡсѣнениеⷨ силы бг҃а ѿц҃а. нашествиеⷨ
ст҃го дх҃а. вмѣстиⷭ҇ во ꙋтробѣ дв҃ыа во плоти
тиⷭ҇. и претеⷬпѣ пеленами повиваⷮ҇са. и ѿ
сосцꙋ питатиⷭ҇. ıакоⷤ тогда не плⷪ҇неи ста
рицы роⷣ҇ти возмощи дарова паⷱ мртⷭ҇вости
ложесненыа. сице и нн҃ѣ нашествиемъ
ст҃го дх҃а. и ѡсѣнениеⷨ силы вышнаго. чтⷭ҇аа
дв҃ца беⷥсѣменно роⷣ҇ сн҃а бж҃иа. ıакоⷤ тогда
ıавиⷭ҇ бг҃ъ авраамꙋ треми мꙋжми пꙋ҃шествꙋ

to renew his image that grew weak (in man), and that the Son of God would obey God the Father, and that the Word would come down and become incarnate and save humanity, and that the Holy Spirit would work together (to fulfill) God's good pleasure?

70.5. It is[861] on this account, that God appears to Abraham in three subsistences, for when Abraham looked up with his eyes, he saw three men. Thus, God comes to Abraham's tent as the Trinity. They have their feet washed, as if they were travelers, and eat food that they were offered, and give Sarah the promise about the son. From him, the descendants would receive the promised seed, in whom all the nations of the earth would be blessed according to what God promised to Abraham in the beginning[862] so that they might see God, who in the past stayed at Abraham's tent, and then, may also hear that the Son of God dwelled in the womb of the Virgin for nine months. They would be able to believe without questioning, again and again, as to how the womb of the Virgin could embrace God, for Abraham's tent had already embraced God earlier. | 126ᵛ/305
They would recognize, then, (how this is related to) the one who bore the child, even though her womb was dead because of old age; and upon hearing about the Virgin, who bore (a child) without a husband, they would not remain in unbelief.[863]

70.6. For just as at that time, the Son of God, together with his Father and with the Holy Spirit, placed themselves within the tent of Abraham, undergoing the affection of senses when they received and ate food, so also now,[864] the divine Word, who is God, would place himself into the womb of the Virgin—when the Holy Spirit came on her, and God's power touched her[865]—to become incarnate and go through (such things as) being wrapped in the swaddling clothes and suckling the breast. Just as[866] at that time, he allowed the old woman, who was barren, to give birth despite the deadness of her womb, so also now, the pure Virgin would give birth[867] to God's Son without a male seed when the Holy Spirit comes upon her, and the power of the Most High overshadows her (Lk. 1:35). Just as at that time, God appeared to Abraham in the

861 It is] And it is

862 in the beginning] before

863 and on hearing about the Virgin, who bore (a child) without a husband, they would not remain in unbelief.] *omitted*

864 when they received and ate food, so also now,] when they had their feet washed with human hands and when they received and ate food, so also afterward,

865 God's power touched her] the Father overshadowed her

866 Just as] And just as

867 pure Virgin would give birth] All-pure Virgin would be able to give birth

юцими. сице и послѣⷣ аки пꙋⷮшествоваше прїиде бж҃иѧ блгⷣть спⷭти чл҃чество. сшеⷣ бо с нб҃се воплотиⷭ бг҃ъ слово. дх҃ꙋ стм҃ꙋ нашеⷣ шꙋ на дв҃ꙋ. воплощению слꙋжащꙋю. и сила вышнѧⷢ ѡсѣни возмогающꙋю беⷥ сѣмени зачаⷮ сн҃а. понеⷤ великое бжⷭтвꙋ дѣло содѣлаⷮ. 127ʳ/306 еⷤ бг҃ꙋ воплотиⷮсѧ. заеⷤ избавиⷮ чл҃чество ѿ на силїа вражиѧ и ѿ грѣха и ѿ смⷬти. по бл҃гово лению бг҃а ѿц҃а. и по дѣиствꙋ ст҃го дх҃а. понеⷤ триеⷯ едина волꙗ и едино хотѣние. не ѿстꙋ пльшꙋ бо словꙋ сн҃ꙋ ѿ ѡц҃а бг҃а сниде воплотиⷮ сѧ. но волею бг҃а ѿц҃а сниде сн҃ъ. взыскаⷮ ѡбраⷥ свои и пⷣобⷪие хс҃. и пострада не неволею стрⷭть и крⷭтъ. но послꙋшание ко ѿц҃ꙋ исполнꙗꙗ. волею претерпѣ всѧ ꙗко чл҃къ чл҃ка раⷣ. и дх҃ъ ст҃ыи содѣиствова. сего раⷣ кꙋпно три вкꙋ щꙋ авраамовꙋ ходꙗⷮ. и ногаⷨ оумываютсѧ. и брашно ꙗдаⷮ. бесплотныи бг҃ъ. триеⷯ мꙋ жеи составы. аки плоⷮски ко авраамꙋ при ходиⷮ. таина велика еⷭ. проѡбражение бж҃їа во плоти пришествїа. и дв҃ыѧ беⷥсѣменно мꙋ ржⷭтвꙋ. родившїа старица не плоды. оумр҃ъшвены имꙋщїа ложесна. Ꙗко саррино сꙋмнѣние ѡ роженїи сн҃а еи. показание есть невѣрованїа жидовъ и еретиковъ. во пло[868]

Невѣрно помыⷭлившїа сарра оумр҃ъшвеныⷨ ложесны своими. возмощи сѣмѧ ѡживиⷮ. назнамена лꙋкавое не вѣрꙋющиⷯ бж҃ию во 127ᵛ/308 площению. и многосꙋесловащиⷯ. и хꙋлꙗщиⷯ великꙋю бж҃ию блгⷣть. рекꙋщи даⷤ доселе не быⷭ ми чада нн҃ѣ ли рожю. но бг҃ъ невѣрова нїа раⷣ саррина блгⷣти своеѧ не ꙋдержа а

868 *Text continues in the margin*: щению слова бж҃їа.

form of three traveling men, so also afterward, as if taking a journey, the grace of God will come to save humanity.

70.7. For God the Word became incarnate by descending from the heavens, the Holy Spirit came upon the Virgin to be the agent of the incarnation, and the power of the Most High overshadowed her, making it possible for her to conceive the Son without a male seed.[869] For the Godhead was to accomplish a great work | when God[870] became incarnate—to deliver humankind from the 127r/306
violence of the enemy, and from sin, and from death, according to the blessing of God the Father and according to the action of the Holy Spirit. For[871] these three have one will and one desire.

70.8. Therefore, the Son, who is the Word,[872] was not estranged from God the Father when he came down in the incarnation. Instead, the Son[873] came down carrying out the will[874] of God the Father to look for his image and likeness (i.e., man). And in going through the passion and the cross, Christ suffered not unwillingly, but out of obedience to the Father, willingly enduring everything, as man, and for man's sake. And the Holy Spirit was his co-worker. That is why there were three who entered Abraham's tent, and they had their feet washed and ate food. Incorporeal God came to Abraham in the ⟨form⟩ of three male persons, as if he had flesh, which is a great mystery prefiguring the coming of God in the flesh. And (his) birth from the Virgin without a male seed[875] (was prefigured) by the old woman who was barren and had a dead womb.

71. Showing that Sarah's doubt concerning the birth of her son points to the unbelief of the Jews and heretics regarding the incarnation of the Word of God.[876]

71.1. Sarah, with her doubts, not believing that the seed would not be able to bring back to life her dead womb, signifies the deception of unbelievers about | 127v/308
the incarnation of God,[877] and of the many who speak empty and blasphemous words against the grace of God, saying (with Sarah), "I have not had a child even until now. Will I really give birth to it now"? But God did not withhold his grace

869 seed.] seed, and giving the right to all who receive him to become the children of God.
870 God] Word of God
871 For] And
872 Son, who is the Word,] Son of God
873 Son] Son of God
874 will] good pleasure
875 without a male seed] *MS 61 corrects this reading in the margin to*: without a husband
876 **Word of God.] Son of God, and that unbelief is not able to destroy faith.**
877 God,] God's Son,

враамѹ. даде емѹ сн҃а исаака. такоⷤ и не
оудеⷬжа всемирныѧ бл҃гти своеѧ бг҃ъ. раⷣ
беⷥбл҃гтныⷯ невѣрныⷯ. но излїа богаⷮно бл҃гть
сп҃сенїе іс҃ъ хм҃ъ всемѹ мирѹ. Видѣтиⷤ
е҇ въ бг҃одхновеннѡⷨ писанїи. идѣже аще е҇
воѡбражение воплощение сн҃а бж҃їа. тѹ и
ст҃ыѧ трⷪ҇ца ѿкровение и ѩвление е҇. тако
на созданїи чл҃чи. реⷱ бо бг҃ъ тамо. сотвориⷨ
чл҃ка по ѡбразѹ нш҃емѹ и по поⷣбию. показа
совѣта раⷣ равносилныⷯ и единосѹщныⷯ съ гс҃ь
ствѹющиⷯ. и бесѣдою за раⷣ ѡбраза и поⷣбиа
своеⷢ. воплощение проѡбразовавъ. такоⷤ
и при изгнанїи адама из раа ѿкры гл҃ѧ. се
адамъ бы҇ ѩко единъ ѿ насъ. именовавъ наⷭ
а не себе. знамениⷤ даⷭ изганиⷨ из раа. ѩⷦ
паки взыскавъ ѡбратиⷮ его. бѹдеⷮ. егоⷤ раⷣ
и херѹвима с пламенныⷨ ѡрѹжиемъ ѡбраща
ющаⷭ постави храниⷮ вхоⷣ раю. можаше бо
128[r]/309 бг҃ъ затвориⷮ вхоⷣ раискїи адамѹ. и бес пламе
нноⷢ ѡрѹжиа ѡбращающагоⷭ. ѩко вса могїи
аще не хотѣ҇ бы сниⷮ на взыскание е҇ бг҃ъ и ѡбра
тиⷮ его паки. такоⷤ и при стлⷪ҇потворенїи съ
шествиⷨ ѡбразова схожение въ чл҃чество
сн҃а бж҃їа. и призывание равномощныⷯ к ра
змѣшению трⷪ҇цѹ показа. и аще не сие бы
было. чесо раⷣ сходиⷮ размѣсити стлⷪ҇па. по
чтоⷤ и призываеⷮ равномощныⷯ к содѣиство
ванию. такоⷤ и при авраамѣ треми мѹжи
въ трⷪ҇цы ѩви себе бг҃ъ. и вхоженїа раⷣ в кѹщѹ
авраамовѹ и дарованиⷨ сн҃а саррѣ. исхо
жениⷨ в содоⷨ. показа сшествие сн҃а бж҃їа

for Abraham[878] despite the unbelief of Sarah, giving him a son, Isaac. Likewise, the Lord did not withhold his grace for the whole world despite the unbelief of ungrateful men. Instead, through Jesus Christ,[879] God abundantly poured out his grace for the salvation of the whole world.

71.2. And we must recognize that wherever there is a sign of the incarnation of God's Son in the divinely inspired Scripture, there we also have the revelation and manifestation of the Holy Trinity. This was the case in the creation of man,[880] for God said there, "Let us make man in our image and likeness". In taking that counsel, God revealed the ones who were consubstantial with him, possessing equal power and dominion; and in talking to others, he prefigured the incarnation[881] for the sake of his image and likeness (in man).

71.3. Similarly, upon expelling Adam from paradise, he said, "Behold, Adam has become like one of us" (Gen. 3:22), making the reference to "us", and not "me". Through that expulsion from paradise,[882] he gave the sign that he would return to search for him once again, and in the meantime, "he placed the cherubim with a flaming weapon that turned every way to guard the entrance to paradise" (Gen. 3:24). Since God can do all things, he could have | closed the 128r/309
way to paradise for Adam without the "flaming weapon that turned every way", had God not wished to come down in order to search for him and turn him back.[883]

71.4. In the same way, he also used the Tower of Babel as an image that describes the descent of God's Son to humanity. He showed the Trinity by calling upon those who possessed power equal to his, to bring confusion. And if this was not so, then why did he come down to bring confusion at the Tower of Babel?[884] ⟨Given that he is omnipotent⟩, why did he call upon those who possessed power equal to his, to work together with him?

71.5. Likewise, God revealed himself to Abraham as Triune in the form of three men, and by entering into Abraham's tent and by giving a son to Sarah and by coming down to Sodom,[885] he exemplified the descent of God's Son,

---

878 Abraham] faithful Abraham

879 through Jesus Christ] to those who believed in Jesus Christ

880 man,] Adam,

881 incarnation] incarnation of God's Son

882 from paradise,] *omitted*

883 had God not wished to come down in order to search for him and turn him back.] had his Son not wished to come down and search for (man) in order to get him back again into paradise.

884 why did he come down to bring confusion] why did he wish to come down to confuse the tongues

885 and by coming down to Sodom,] *omitted*

воплотисѧ. изволение бга ѿца. и поспѣ
шество стго дха. показа и бесѣменное
двы ржтво сна бжїа. и аще не бы сие было
чесо ра приходи бгъ ко авраамꙋ ꙗви вса
емꙋ треми мꙋжи и въ храминꙋ вниде.
поне и множицею оу пре ꙗви бгъ авраа
мꙋ. не прихода к немꙋ в храминꙋ. гле бо
писание. ꙗви гь авраамꙋ и ре емꙋ. пло
дꙋ твоемꙋ да землю сию. и созда тꙋ авраа
128v/310 требни бгꙋ ꙗвльшемꙋ емꙋ. и пото глеть.
ре гь ко авраамꙋ ꙗко разлꙋчи лотъ ѿ него. во
зрѣвъ же си ѡчима и виждь. ꙗко всю землю ты
видиши тебѣ да ю и племени твоемꙋ. и па
пише. по глѣ семъ бысть слово гнѣ ко авра
амꙋ глꙗ. не бои авраме а защищꙋ та мза
ти бꙋде ѕило многа. и паки пише. бы же
авраа лѣтъ. чѳ. ꙗви гь авраамꙋ и ре емꙋ
азъ есмь бгъ твои и ꙋгажаи пре мною и бꙋ
непороченъ. и не гле тамо ꙗко вниде бгъ
ко авраамꙋ въ храминꙋ. или ꙗко ꙗвиса
бгъ авраамꙋ и види авраа три мꙋжи. но
здѣ приходи ко авраамꙋ въ храминꙋ и три
мꙋжи. егда даде емꙋ сна. и разрѣши еже
нѣ его неплодие па времене. Тако что
ра приходи бгъ в содомы погꙋбити содо
мы. егда немоществоваше бгъ на нбсѣ
и высотѣ пребываа долѣ сꙋщаа грады по
гꙋбити. ꙗко далече стоꙗщихъ ѿ высо
ты нбныꙗ на земли. и сего ли ра вниде в со
домы са. да бли бываа и внꙋтрь града сы
возможе ѡдожди в него камыки горащїи
129r/311 и ѡгнь посла. како не сниде ни приближиса по
гꙋби воа асирїискїа. погꙋбивъ во единомъ
чсѣ. ҏ҃п҃е҃. претащи погꙋби їерлмъ. їерлма
избави не вше во гра самъ бгъ. кое оудобнѣе

who became incarnate by the good pleasure of God the Father and with the assistance of the Holy Spirit; and he also exemplified the birth of God's Son through the Virgin without a male seed. And if this was not so, then why did God come to Abraham, appearing to him in the form of three men and entering into the tent? For God already appeared to Abraham many times before, without coming to him in the tent.

71.6. For the Scripture states, "The Lord[886] appeared to Abraham and said to him, 'I will give this land to your offspring'. And there, Abraham built an altar | 128ᵛ/310
to God, who appeared to him" (Gen. 12:7). And later, it says, "After Lot was separated from him, the Lord God said to Abraham, 'Lift up your eyes and see! All the land that you see, I will give to you and your offspring'" (Gen. 13:14–15). And again, it is written, "After this message, the word of the Lord came to Abraham, saying, 'Do not be afraid, Abraham, I will protect you, and you will have a truly great reward'" (Gen. 15:1). And again, it is written, "And when Abraham was ninety-nine years old, the Lord appeared to Abraham[887] and said to him, 'I am your God, be well-pleasing before me and be blameless'" (Gen. 17:1). In these places, it is not said that the Lord entered Abraham's tent or that God appeared to Abraham in such a way that Abraham saw three men. But, here, he does come to Abraham's tent and (appears) in the form of three men[888] in order to give him a son and solve the problem of his barren wife, even though it was past the time for her.[889]

71.7. Likewise, why did God come[890] to Sodom in his intention to destroy Sodom (Gen. 19:15–26)? Is God, who abides high in the heavens, not able to destroy the cities that are below, even at a great distance from the heavenly height? And did he himself enter Sodom because he could rain down burning sulfur | and send fire (Gen. 19:23) only after coming closer and coming into the 129ʳ/311
city? But then, how is it that he did not come down, nor set himself at a close distance when, during one night, he destroyed one hundred and eighty-five thousand Assyrian soldiers who sought to destroy Jerusalem[891] (2 Kgs. 19:35)? And God delivered Jerusalem without entering the city himself.

886 states, "The Lord] states that "God

887 Abraham] him

888 he does come to Abraham's tent and (appears) in the form of three men] *omitted*

889 *MS 61 adds*: **Showing that God's descent to Sodom for the purpose of destroying it reveals that by his coming to this world in the flesh, the Lord will destroy the sins of the whole world and save humanity. Just as he saved Lot in acknowledgment of his good faith, so he would also (save) those who receive him in faith.**

890 come] come down

891 Jerusalem] Jerusalem, and when he flooded the entire world, both populated and unpopulated regions? (Gen. 6:9–8:22).

сотворит внутрь града пребываа. погубити ли град или защитит его. не удобнѣе избавит град и защитит его ѿ ратных внутрь града пребываа. погубитиж град не удобнѣе ли внѣ пребываа. но бг҃ъ входит внутрь града содома погубит его. ієрслмъ ж не вшед избави его ѿ асиріи. и во единъ чс҃ъ погуби толико темъ асиріи. в содомеж и ѿбноцьствоваше. не могіи погубит града. ꙗко рек к лоту потщиса. не могу сотворити дѣтели сеѧ. донелѣж внидеши тамо. что убо се ес и чесо рад вса могіи сам приходит в содом погубит его. проꙗвленно оубо ꙗко троцу ѿкрываа писание. повѣдаа гс҃а ѿ гс҃а в содомы огнь одождивша. да покажет гс҃а в содоме сущa. и гс҃а на нбсѣ ѿхца. огнь посылаа гс҃ь на земли сыи ѿ гс҃а съ нбсѣ. да и стѣе оувѣси троцу вида писаное. гс҃ь ѿ гс҃а посылает огнь. и три мужи оу авраама вѣдыи бг҃а.

129v/312 *Ꙗко бг҃ъ в содом скверныи приде потребит его. не просто ес се. но показание ес. ꙗко пришествием своим хс҃ во плоти вгрехи всего мира грехи потребить.*

И паки вѣдыи бг҃а в содомех пришедша и ѿбноцьствовавша. и не осквернившаса. сего рад да не оусумнишиса оувѣдавъ бг҃а. во утробѣ пребывша двцы чистыѧ. и всег мира грехи потребльша. ꙗкож и в содомех прежскверну слышав еси погубивша. також и послѣд во плоти вса чс҃тною своею кровию всег мира грехи

71.8. But what is easier to do when you are inside a city: to destroy it or to protect it? Is it not easier to deliver and protect the city from enemies if one is inside the city? And is it not easier to destroy the city if one is outside the city? Yet God comes into the city of Sodom to destroy it, but he stays outside of Jerusalem to deliver it from Assyria and, within a short time, destroys thousands of Assyrians.[892] However, in coming to Sodom, he spent the night there. Was it because he was not able to destroy the city, for he said to Lot, "Hurry, for I cannot do anything until you enter there (Sigor)" (Gen. 19:22)? What was it for, then? And why did he, who is omnipotent,[893] come to Sodom himself to destroy it?

71.9. The actual reason is that (through his coming), the Scripture reveals the Trinity, telling us of the "Lord who rained down[894] fire" on Sodom "from the Lord" (Gen. 19:23), to show us the "Lord in Sodom" and the "Lord in the heavens", the Father. The Lord, who was on the earth, sent fire from the Lord, who was in the heavens so that we may recognize the Trinity more clearly and learn about God when we see the Scripture describing the Lord who sends fire from the Lord and the three men with Abraham. | 129v/312

72. Showing that God came to unclean Sodom in order to destroy it. And this is not just a story, but a demonstration of the fact that upon his coming in the flesh, Christ would destroy the sins of the whole world.[895]

72.1. And then, after discerning God in the event when he came to Sodom and spent the night there without becoming defiled, we will undoubtedly recognize God when he dwelled in the womb of the pure[896] Virgin and destroyed the sins of the whole world. Just as you heard that he previously destroyed the impurity of the Sodomites, so also you should believe that he subsequently became incarnate to cleanse the sins of the whole world by his pure blood.

---

892 And God delivered Jerusalem without entering the city in his own person. But what is easier to do when you are inside the city: to destroy it or to protect it? Is it not easier to deliver and protect the city from enemies if one is inside the city? And is it not easier to destroy the city if one is outside the city? Yet God comes into the city of Sodom to destroy it, but stays outside of Jerusalem to deliver it from Assyria and, within a short time, destroys thousands of Assyrians.] *omitted*

893 omnipotent,] omnipotent and omnipresent,

894 rained down] sent

895 **Showing that God came to unclean Sodom in order to destroy it. And this is not just a story, but a demonstration of the fact that upon his coming in the flesh, Christ would destroy the sins of the whole world.**] *omitted*

896 pure] All-pure

ѿмывша вѣрꙋеши. да повинꙋ вса оубо б҃ви
не противишⷭ҇и писанию. да не помыслиⷲ҇
недостоино б҃гꙋ во чревѣ чⷭ҇тыа дв҃цы плⷮо
восприꙗⷮ҇. оудостоившаⷭ҇ б҃га прⷤ҇е и в содо
мы внити. и ѿⷠноцьствоваⷮ҇ в немъ и не ѡ
сквернитиса. но паⷪ҇ нечистотꙋ в немъ
с ниⷨ҇ погꙋбившаⷢ҇ ѡгнⷨ҇е. и да вѣрꙋеши ꙗко во
плоцьса вⷥ҇е скверны б҃гъ всего мира грѣхи
потопи. пришⷣ҇е в миръ. и всего мира сп҃се
ѿ всегꙋбитⷭ҇ества. ꙗкⷤ҇о и лота ѿ содⷨ҇оскїа
погибели. Паки гл҃е бг҃одⷮ҇хновенное писа
ние. Ѡстаⷤ҇ иꙗкоⷡ҇ единъ и бораше с ниⷨ҇ мꙋⷤ҇
130r/313 до ꙋтрїа. видѣвъⷤ ꙗко не моⷤ҇ противꙋ емꙋ. и
преꙗⷭ҇ въ стегна еⷢ҇. и ꙋтерпѣ. пречеса стегна
їаковлꙗ. егда бораше с нимъ. речⷤ҇е емꙋ поу
сти ма. взыде бо свⷮ҇ѣ. сеиⷤ҇ рⷪ҇е не пꙋщꙋ тебе
аще не блⷭ҇виши мене. и рⷪ҇е емꙋ како ти има
есть сеиⷤ҇ рече иꙗковъ. сеиⷤ҇ рече емꙋ. нико
лиже не прозоветса има твое иꙗковъ.
но їиль бꙋдеть има твое. ꙗко ꙋкрѣпи съ
бг҃омъ и съ чл҃ки силенъ. вопрашаⷤ҇ иꙗковъ
и рⷪ҇е повѣж ми има твое. и рⷪ҇е се въскꙋю во
прашаеши имени моⷢ҇е. чⷪ҇но бо се еⷭ҇. блⷭ҇ви
тꙋ. и прозва їаковъ има мѣстꙋ томꙋ. ѡ
браⷥ҇ бж҃їи. видⷯ҇ѣ бо б҃га лицⷨ҇е к лицꙋ и сп҃семиⷭ҇
дш҃а. и взыде емꙋ сл҃нце. егда ѿиде ѡбраⷥ҇

Thus, you must obey God instead of resisting the Scripture. Do not have unworthy thoughts about God, who assumed flesh in the womb of the pure Virgin. God first found it fitting to enter Sodom and spend the night there and, instead of becoming defiled, he destroyed the impurity together with (the city) by fire. And you should believe that God, who became incarnate without getting defiled,[897] did so to wipe away the sins of the whole world. He came to the world and saved the entire world from total destruction, just as he also saved Lot from the destruction of Sodom.[898]

72.2. Again, the divinely inspired Scripture says, "And Jacob was left alone; and a man wrestled with him | until morning. And he saw that he could not 130ʳ/313
overpower him; and he touched his hip and dislocated the socket of Jacob's hip when he wrestled with him. And he said to him, 'Let me go, for the dawn has arisen'. But he said, 'I will not let you go unless you bless me'. And he said to him, 'What is your name'? And he replied, 'Jacob'. And he said to him, 'Your name will no longer be called Jacob, but Israel will be your name; for you have become strong with God and will be powerful with men'. And Jacob asked and said, 'Tell me your name'. And he said, 'Why is it that you ask my name? For it is wondrous'. And he blessed him there. And Jacob called that place with the name the 'Image of God', for (he said), 'I saw God face to face, and my soul was spared'. And the sun rose upon him when he passed by the 'Image of God'" (Gen. 32.24–31).

---

897 without getting defiled] immaculately

898 Sodom.] Sodom. For in the same way, he also prefigured (such things) when he came down to Moses. And Gerasim said, "Where did he prefigure (such things) in coming down to Moses? He does not prefigure any such things to Moses". In response, I said to them: You should read the account about Moses if you want to find it. But do listen and learn:

бж҃їи. Паки гл҃е бг҃одх҃новенное писание. Моѵсеи ͯ бѣꙗше пасыи ѡвца рагѹила те[899] ста своⷢ҇е сщ҃нника мадиꙗмьска. и гнаше ѡвца в пѹстыню. и приде в хоривъ в горѹ бж҃ию. ꙗвиже ⷭ҇ емѹ агг҃лъ гн҃ь въ пламени ѡгненѣ ис кѹпины. и вѣдѣ ꙗко кѹпина гораше ѡгнⷨ҇е и не сгараше. речеⷤ҇ моисеⷷ҇. мимо шеⷣ҇ вижѹ что видѣние великое се. ꙗко не
130v/314 сгараше кѹпина. и ꙗко видѣ гⷭ҇ь ꙗко приступаеⷮ҇ видѣти. и возваⷭ҇е агг҃лъ гн҃ь ис кѹпины гл҃ꙗ. моисеⷷ҇ моисеⷷ҇. ѡнⷤ҇ъ рече се аⷥ҇. речеⷤ҇ гⷭ҇ь. не приближаиса сѣмо. изѹи сапогъ ѿ ногъ твоⷯ҇и ибо мѣсто на нем же ты стоиши землꙗ стаⷭ҇ е. и реⷱ҇ емѹ аⷥ҇ есмь бг҃ъ ѿц҃а твоеⷢ҇. бг҃ъ аврамовъ. бг҃ъ исааковъ. бг҃ъ иꙗковль. ѿвратиⷤ҇ лице свое моисеⷷ҇. говѣꙗше бо зрѣⷷ҇ преⷣ҇ бг҃а. речеⷤ҇ гⷭ҇ь к моисеѡви. вида видѣⷯ҇ бѣдѹ людеи моиⷯ҇ иже въ египте. и вопль иⷯ҇ оуслышаⷯ҇. ѿ дѣлъ приставникъ видѣⷯ҇ болѣзнь иⷯ҇. и снидоⷯ҇ изатїⷯ҇ иⷥ҇ ѿ рѹкѹ егиⷮпеⷮскѹ. иⷥ҇вести а иⷥ҇ землꙗ тоа. в землю благѹ и многѹ. Ї по сиⷯ҇ гл҃е писание. Речеⷤ҇ гⷭ҇ь к мосеюⷷ҇, гл҃ꙗ. бѹдѹ с тобою. сеⷤ҇ ти знамение. ꙗко аⷥ҇ та пѹщаю извести людеи моиⷯ҇ иⷥ҇ египта. да са помолиⷮ҇ бг҃ѹ в горѣ сеи. Ї по сиⷯ҇ пишеть бг҃одх҃новенное писание. Рече гⷭ҇ь к мосеюⷷ҇. се аⷥ҇ полагаю тебѣ завѣⷮ҇. преⷣ҇ всѣми лю҆ми

899 *In the margin*: гл҃а кѕ҃.

73. CHAPTER 26.[900]

73.1. Again, the Scripture says,[901] "And Moses was shepherding the sheep of Raguel his father-in-law, the priest of Midian; and he drove the sheep to the wilderness and came to Choreb, the mountain of God. And the angel of the Lord appeared to him in flaming fire out of the bush, and he saw that the bush burned with fire, but did not burn up. And Moses said, 'I will go near and see this great sight, why | the bush does not burn up'. And when the Lord saw that 130ᵛ/314
he approaches to see, the angel of the Lord called him out of the bush, saying, 'Moses, Moses'! And he said, 'Here I am'. And the Lord said, 'Do not come near here. Take the boots off your feet, for the place on which you are standing is holy ground'. And he said to him, 'I am the God of your father, the God of Abraham, the God of Isaac, the God of Jacob'. And Moses turned away his face, for he was afraid to look at God. And the Lord said to Moses, 'I have surely seen the trouble of my people that is in Egypt, and I have heard their outcry caused by their taskmasters. I have seen their affliction and have come down to deliver them out of the hand of the Egyptians, to bring them out of that land into a good and spacious land'" (Ex. 3:1–8).

73.2. And after this, the Scripture says,[902] "And the Lord spoke to Moses, saying, 'I will be with you, and this will be the sign to you that I will send you to bring my people out of Egypt: you will pray to God on this mountain'" (Ex. 3:12). And, following this, the divinely inspired Scripture records:[903] "And the Lord said to Moses, 'Behold, I am establishing a covenant with you in the presence

---

900 CHAPTER 26.] **Investigation in the holy book of Genesis concerning the revelation of the angel of the Lord to Moses in flaming fire out of the bush. How should we understand it? And regarding the covenant, which the Lord made with Moses after giving him the written Law, what kind of covenant is it? CHAPTER 26.**

901 "And Jacob was left alone; and a man wrestled with him until morning. And he saw that he could not overpower him; and he touched his hip and dislocated the socket of Jacob's hip when he wrestled with him. And he said to him, 'Let me go, for the dawn has arisen'. But he said, 'I will not let you go unless you bless me'. And he said to him, 'What is your name'? And he replied, 'Jacob'. And he said to him, 'Your name will no longer be called Jacob, but Israel will be your name; for you have become strong with God and will be powerful with men'. And Jacob asked and said, 'Tell me your name'. And he said, 'Why is it that you ask my name? For it is wondrous'. And he blessed him there. And Jacob called that place by the name of the 'Image of God', for (he said), 'I saw God face to face, and my soul was spared'. And the sun rose upon him when he passed by the 'Image of God'" (Gen. 32.24–31). Again, the divinely inspired Scripture says,] *omitted*

902 And after this, the Scripture says,] And somewhat later, it is written,

903 *MS 61 adds*: **Showing that the Lord made the covenant with Moses clearly to save the whole world at a certain point.**

своими. сотворю великаа и славнаа. ꙗкоⷤ не бѣша по всеи земли ни во всѣⷯ странахъ. и оузрѧⷮ вси лю̑дѐ в нихъ ты еси дѣлеса гⷭна 131r/315 ꙗко чю̑на сѹ. ꙗ̑ⷤ сотворю а̑ тебѣ. Ꙗко ѿкровено гⷭь завѣⷮ моисею завѣща воплощенїа своѐ. во е̑ спⷭти[904] Видиⷨ нн҃ѣ ꙗⷤ гⷭь ѡбѣщаѐ моисеѡви. сотвориⷮ дѣ ла чю̑наа гⷭнѧ. ꙗковаⷤ не быша по всѐ земли ни во всѣⷯ странаⷯ. чю̑твоца бⷢа велика дѣ ла вса и дивна. ꙗⷤ ни вса глⷢати возможно. ниⷤ вса разумѣти мощно. елика саⷨ подасть ра зумѣти ѿ чю̑ныⷯ дѣⷭ свои. ѡ сиⷯ блⷢгодарити и славиⷮ его. еликаⷤ разумꙋ непостижна ѡстаю дивнаа е̑ⷭ дѣла. ѡ сиⷯ покланатиⷭ премⷣрости его. и с похвалою мⷭчати пⷣобаѐ. каꙗⷤ оубо сїа дѣла чю̑наа гⷭнѧ. ꙗⷤ гⷭь сотвориⷧ моисеѡ ви реⷱ. аще елико возмоⷤно рⷭасмотрѣти бꙋ дѐⷮ рцемъ. поне кꙋпинꙋ ѡгненꙋю не сгараю щꙋ моисею показа гⷭь. преⷣ ѡбѣщаниа сего рꙋкꙋ и жезлъ измѣнаемыа такоⷤ показа. воды в кроⷡ. и мꙋⷯи свирѣпыа. и жабы и мши ца. и гꙋсиница и прꙋзи. и прыщи и грады. тма и побиение первенецъ. быша оуⷤ въ египтѣ ѿ гⷭа. и свѣⷮ нощию столпоⷨ ѡгненыⷨ. и водне ѡсѣнение ѿ паленїа слнⷰна стоⷧпоⷨ ѡблачныⷨ быⷭ ї̈ильтаноⷨ. и сквозѣ море пѣши

904 *Text continues in the margin*: вѐⷭ миръ.

of all my people. I will do great and glorious things, which have not been done in all the earth nor in any of the nations. And all the people, among whom you are, will see the works of the Lord, | that they are awesome, which I will do for 131r/315
you'" (Ex. 34:10).

74. Showing that the Lord made the covenant with Moses clearly to save the whole world through his incarnation.[905]

74.1. Let us now see[906] that the Lord promises to Moses to do the awesome works of the Lord that have never been done before in all the earth nor in any of the nations.[907] For all the works of God, the Miracle-maker, are indeed great and marvelous, and not all of them can be explained, nor can everything be grasped.[908] Thus, whatever he himself gives us to understand of his awesome deeds, for that, we must give thanks and glory to him. And whatever remains incomprehensible of his marvelous works, that must be approached with worship for his supreme wisdom; and we must give him praise in silence. Thus, we will consider the awesome work of the Lord, which the Lord would do, as he said to Moses,[909] and we will speak inasmuch as we are able to.[910]

74.2. Now, long before the Lord gave this promise, he had already shown himself to Moses in a flaming bush that did not burn up, and he also showed himself (in the miracle) of the transformed hand and staff (Ex. 4:1–7), and he changed water into blood[911] (Ex. 7:14–21). And there were terrifying flies (Ex. 8:20–30), and frogs (Ex. 8:1–15), and gnats (Ex. 8:16–19), and caterpillars and locusts[912] (Ex. 10:1–20), and boils (Ex. 9:8–12), and a hailstorm (Ex. 9:13–35), and darkness (Ex. 10:21–29). And the Lord struck the firstborn that were found at that time in Egypt (Ex. 11), and there was light from the pillar of fire in the night, and the pillar of cloud provided the Israelites with shade from the burning sun during

905 **Showing that the Lord made the covenant with Moses clearly to save the whole world through his incarnation.**] *omitted*

906 Let us now see] Let us consider now as before

907 nations.] nations. Let us begin with the way Moses saw the Lord and how the Lord spoke to Moses there, and then anticipate to what extent and in what way the Lord would grant us to truly understand the true things as we seek the truth.

908 explained, nor can everything be grasped.] explained—what they are and how they happened—nor can everything be easily understood.

909 Moses,] Moses, and which was not revealed at that time but was manifested later.

910 able to.] able to, or I should say, inasmuch as the Lord himself grants us to speak the truth, for he himself is the truth and enables (others) to understand the truth.

911 blood] blood and blood into water

912 caterpillars and locusts] caterpillars

131v/316 проидоша. манна съ нб҃сѣ ѡдождевашеса на вса нощи. иноплеменники побиша чю҃дною помощию. и красте падоша ѡкртъ ста на и҃. и водꙋ ис камени несѣкома пиахꙋ. сїа великаа гн҃а чю҃днаа дѣла вса оуж быша. каа и еще ѡбѣщаваше гь дѣлеса гн҃а чю҃днаа и славнаа сотвори моисеѡви. ıа ли. ѡ кореи. и авиронѣ и дафанѣ и ѡ сонмѣ и бывшее. ихъ земла живы пожре и ѡгнь пожже. но не боши первы чюдесъ и ѡ египтанѣ. и египтаны бо море потопи живы. е ли слн҃це и лꙋнꙋ постави навгинꙋ ıсꙋ. и езекїи возврати слн҃це въспать. но не боши ѡбаче стопа ѡгненаго. и стопа ѡблачнаго. и четыредесате лѣ. не ѡскꙋдѣша нощию и днию. или же їерданъ возврати въ спать. ѡба не боши мора ѡгꙋстѣвшаго. и раздѣлившагоса ѡба полы пꙋти ıако стѣна. каа оубо ѡбѣща великаа и славнаа дѣла гн҃а сотвори гь. ıако чю҃дна сꙋть. ıа не бѣша по все земли ни во всѣ странах. ıа бо ѡ ѡгни и ѡ расѣданїи земли и ѡ преложенїи воды и ѡ мꙋченїи. 132r/317 быша оуж въ египтѣ и в пꙋстыни славнаа и чю҃дна. и поне послѣ гла се гн҃а не быша моисею боши и славнѣиши чюдеса. прежни дѣлесъ чю҃дны. ıа быша въ египтѣ и в пꙋстыни. каа

the day (e.g., Ex. 13:21–22). And they crossed the sea by foot[913] (Ex. 13:17–14:31), | 131v/316
and manna rained down from the heavens throughout the night, and the foreign people were destroyed[914] by miraculous help (e.g., Ex. 17:8–15). And quail fell over their camp (Ex. 16:12–13), and they drank water from the rock that was impossible to cut (Ex. 17:1–7).

74.3. All of those great and awesome works of the Lord had already taken place long before. What other kinds of awesome and glorious works of the Lord were yet to happen, as promised by the Lord to Moses? Does this refer to Korah, Dathan, and Abiram, whom the earth devoured and the fire burned alive together with their households (Num. 16)? But this is not greater than the earlier miracles performed among the Egyptians, when the Egyptians were drowned alive in the sea.[915] Does this refer to the (miracle) when the sun and moon were caused to stand still for Joshua, the son of Nun (Josh. 10:12–14), and when the sun went backward for Hezekiah (2 Kgs. 20:1–11)? But this is not greater than the pillar of fire and the pillar of cloud, which never failed during the forty years, night and day. Or does it refer to the (miracle) when the water of Jordan stopped flowing (Josh. 3)? However, this is not greater than the (miracle) of the sea, when two watersheds formed a kind of wall and separated a path (on both sides).[916]

74.4. But then, what other kinds of great and glorious works of the Lord were yet to happen, as promised by the Lord; (works) "that are awesome" and "which have not been done in all the earth nor in any nation" (Ex. 34:10)? For there had already been fire, and breaking up of the ground, and the transformation of water, and the plagues | in Egypt, and there had been great and glorious things 132r/317
in the desert. And since, after these words of the Lord, there were no greater and more glorious works for Moses to follow them, compared to the awesome works that were done earlier in Egypt and in the desert, what might be the other

913 by foot] by foot on dry ground

914 destroyed] devastated

915 when the Egyptians were drowned alive in the sea.] when the ten plagues fell upon them.

916 when two watersheds formed a kind of wall and separated a path (on both sides).] when two watersheds formed a kind of wall.

великаа и славнаа дѣла гⷭна хощеⷮ сотвориⷮ
гⷭь. ихⷤъ оузриⷮа вси людие ꙗко чюⷣна соуⷮ. Аще
кто хощеⷮ не любопривѣ приꙗти. готово
разоумѣваетса сїе ѡ воплощенїи самоⷢ тоⷢ
гⷭа. сиⷯ бо чюдеⷭ нѣсть было по всеи земли ни
во всѣхъ странаⷯ. и чюⷣна воистинноу оузрѣ
ша вси люⷣе. великаа и славнаа дѣла гⷭна ꙗⷤ
гⷭь сотвори. двⷭцу без моужа ражающⷭу. и ра
жающїи бгъ во плоти ⷭе. и стрⷭти страже.
ко кртⷭоу пригвождаетса. и оумираеⷮ ꙗко
члкъ. тридневноⷤ воскрсе члкъ ꙗко бгъ. и дхъ
стыи низпославъ. сотвори дѣлеса гⷭна ѿчаа
снъ бжїи гⷭь ~~моисею~~. воплотиⷡ и пострадаⷡ
воскрсе. и совоскрси члка. дха стго излїа.
ꙗⷤ оузрѣвше вси люⷣе дѣлеса гⷭна ꙗко чюⷣна соуⷮ.
ѡставиша ꙗзыцы вси боги своа и вѣрова
ша моисеѡвоу бгу въ трⷪцы. поклонишаса
бгоначалнѣи трⷪцы. ѿцу бгу и сну ⷭе и дху стму.
132v/318 понеⷤ рече гⷭь се полагаю тебѣ завѣⷮ преⷣ всѣми
люⷣми своими сотворю великаа и славнаа. ꙗкоⷤ
не бѣша по всеи земли ни во всеⷯ странаⷯ. и оу
зриⷮ вси люⷣе в нихⷤ ты еси. дѣлеса гⷭна ꙗко

great and glorious works of the Lord that the Lord wants to do, which "all the people would see, that they are awesome" (Ex. 34:10)?[917]

74.5. If[918] one is willing to accept it without arguing,[919] one can easily understand this as the incarnation of the very same God. For there have been no miracles so great in all the earth, nor in any of the nations. And that which all the people saw was truly awesome—"the works of the Lord", "the great and glorious things", which the Lord[920] accomplished. It is about the Virgin,[921] who gives birth without a husband, and about God who gets born in the flesh, and who suffers affliction,[922] who is nailed to a cross and dies as man, but in three days is raised as God, while also remaining human, and who sends out the Holy Spirit. The Son of God, being Lord, did the works of the Lord from the Father: he became incarnate and suffered, he rose from the dead, and thereby raised up humanity, and he poured out the Holy Spirit.[923] All the people who saw the works of the Lord, that they were awesome, left their gods, believing the God of Moses, who exists as one in the Trinity. All the nations worshiped the supremely divine Trinity, God[924] the Father and Son and Holy Spirit. | 132v/318

74.6. For the Lord said to Moses, "Behold, I am establishing a covenant with you in the presence of all my people. I will do great and glorious things, which have not been done in all the earth nor in any nation. And all the people,

917 (works) "that are awesome" and "which have not been done in all the earth nor in any nation" (Ex. 34:10)? For there had already been fire, and breaking up of the ground, and the transformation of water, and the plagues in Egypt, and there had been great and glorious things in the desert. And since, after these words of the Lord, there were no greater and more glorious works for Moses to follow them, compared to the awesome works that were done earlier in Egypt and in the desert, what might be the other great and glorious works of the Lord that the Lord wants to do, which "all the people would see, that they are awesome" (Ex. 34:10)?] (works), "which have not been done in all the earth nor in any nation" (Ex. 34:10)? And what further covenant is the Lord establishing with Moses, given that the first covenant was already written. And what people is it (when it says), "in the presence of all my people", and what are these other "works of the Lord" that are awesome, which the Lord will do for Moses (Ex. 34:10)? And when is it going to be that "all the people among whom is Moses will see" (such works) (Ex. 34:10)?

918 If] And therefore, if

919 arguing] arguing, and instead, obey the truth,

920 Lord] *omitted*

921 Virgin,] pure Virgin,

922 affliction,] death,

923 God, while also remaining human, and who sends out the Holy Spirit. The Son of God, being Lord, did the works of the Lord from the Father: he became incarnate and suffered, he rose from the dead and raised humanity, and he poured out the Holy Spirit.] God, and as God-man, he ascends to heaven and sends out the Holy Spirit.

924 God] *omitted*

чⷣюна сꙋть. ꙗⷤ сотворю аⷥ тебѣ. по семꙋ разꙋ
мѣти ꙗко нѣсть таковаⷶ дѣлеса гⷭ҇на ꙗⷤ
прⷤе сотвори. ⷤе рꙋкꙋ оубѣли. жезлъ въ змию пре
ложи. и водꙋ въ кровь. и жабы и мꙋхи. и граⷣ
и жаратокъ. и мшица. и мꙋхи и прꙋги. и тмꙋ
наведе. и море раздѣли. и водꙋ ис камени изве
де. вся сїа самѣмъ моисеѡⷨ сотворисъ же
злоⷨ его. сиⷤе гл҃ⷮе ꙗко полагаⷮе моисею завⷮѣ
прⷣе всѣми лⷣюми своими. ⷤе велико гл҃емо ⷭе.
и бⷪ҇ши и ѡного ⷤе тварию чюⷣдⷪѣиствовати.
но ново и преславно завѣщание. и не ⷤе законъ
заповѣданныи на времѧ моисеѡⷨ. но славнѣ
иши и бⷪ҇ши. понⷤе гⷭ҇на сꙋть дѣлеса. и емꙋ са
момꙋ гⷭ҇ꙋ гⷭ҇ню точию таа сотвориⷮ великаа
и славнаа. а не прⷪркꙋ ниⷤ агг҃лꙋ таа твориⷮ
чⷣюнаа дѣла гⷭ҇на ~~твориⷮ.~~ ꙗко реⷱ ꙗже сотворю аⷥ
тебѣ. а не ты мои прⷪркъ ниⷤ агг҃лъ мои сотво
риⷮ дѣлеса гⷭ҇на. великаа и славнаа. но саⷨ реⷱ
133^{r}/320 аⷥ гⷭ҇ь сотворю великаа и славнаа дѣла гⷭ҇на. Видѣтиⷤ

among whom you are, will see the works of the Lord, that they are awesome, which I will do for you" (Ex. 34:10). Based on this, we must understand that (the promise) does not refer to the works of the Lord that had been done earlier: when he made a hand white as snow (Ex. 4:6–7); when he turned a staff into a snake (Ex. 4:2–4); and changed water into blood (Ex. 7:14–21); and sent frogs (Ex. 8:1–15), and flies (Ex. 8:20–30),[925] and boils that came out of soot from a furnace (Ex. 9:8–12), and gnats (Ex. 8:16–19), and flies (Ex. 8:20–30), and caterpillars (Ex. 10:1–20),[926] and darkness (Ex. 10:21–29);[927] and when he split the sea (Ex. 13:17–14:31); and made water come out of the rock (Ex. 17:1–7).[928]

74.7. All of this, he accomplished directly through Moses and his staff.[929] And now he[930] says that he establishes a covenant in the presence of all his people. What he says is great, and far beyond the things miraculously[931] done through creatures. It is, rather, a new and supremely glorious promise, and it is different from the one promised in the Law during Moses.[932] It is more glorious and far greater than ⟨the covenant of which Moses wrote earlier⟩. For these works[933] belong to the Lord, and it is only the Lord himself, who does such great and glorious things[934] of the Lord. Neither a Prophet nor an angel can do such awesome works of the Lord, as it is said,[935] "which I will do for you" (Ex. 34:10), rather than (saying) "you, my Prophet" or "my angel", will do the great and glorious works of the Lord. Instead, he himself said, | "I, the Lord, will do the great 133ʳ/320
and glorious works of the Lord"[936] (Ex. 34:10).

925 flies (Ex. 8:20–30),] flies (Ex. 8:20–30), and hail with cold (Ex. 9:13–35)

926 and gnats (Ex. 8:16–19), and flies (Ex. 8:20–30), and caterpillars (Ex. 10:1–20),] and gnats (Ex. 8:16–19), and caterpillars (Ex. 10:1–20)

927 darkness (Ex. 10:21–29);] darkness (Ex. 10:21–29); and when he struck the firstborn (Ex. 11)

928 rock (Ex. 17:1–7).] rock (Ex. 17:1–7); and gave manna from the heavens (e.g., Ex. 17:8–15); and fed (Israel) with quail (Ex. 16:12–13).

929 *MS 61 adds*: **Showing that the Lord's promise to Moses concerning his coming in the flesh to bring about his salvation does not relate to Israel alone. Instead, it concerns all people, for he made all the nations to hear Moses' prophecy, which means that people from all nations will believe in Christ, who came in the flesh, according to Moses' prophecy.**

930 he] Lord

931 miraculously] *omitted*

932 promise, and it is different from the one promised in the Law during Moses.] promise, and the covenant is different from the one promised in the Scripture during the time of the Law.

933 works] awesome works

934 things] works

935 as it is said,] as the Lord said,

936 On the contrary, he himself said, "I, the Lord, will do the great and glorious works of the Lord"] These great and glorious works of the Lord are done by the Lord himself.

е҃. ко авраамꙋ завѣⷮ бж҃їи. бл҃вити ѿ сѣмени его вси ꙗзыки. и к моисею видѣⷮ той завѣⷮ завѣщаеⷮ гь҃ свое воплощение. ꙗкоⷤ и авраамꙋ. но понеⷤ моисеⷷ не ѿ июды но ѿ леввїа. сего раⷣ емꙋ глⷮе гь҃ ꙗⷤ азъ сотворю тебѣ. дв҃дꙋ ꙗко ѿ июды сꙋщꙋ ѡбѣтоваⷮ емꙋ реⷱ. ѿ плода чрева твоеⷢ посажю на прⷭ҇тлѣ твоеⷨ. моисеюⷤ ꙗко ѿ леввїа а не ѿ июды тоиⷤ завѣⷮ не тако ꙁавѣщаваⷮ. ꙗкоⷤ авраамꙋ и дв҃дꙋ. ѿ нихⷤ по плоти быти емꙋ. и завѣщаваⷮ моисею гл҃ꙗ. се полагаю тебѣ завѣⷮ. неⷤ е ѡ твоеⷨ сѣмени бл҃гватса вси ꙗзыци. или ѿ плода чрева твоеⷢ посажꙋ на прⷭ҇тлѣ твоеⷨ. но прⷣе всѣми лю҃ми своими сотворю великаа и славнаа. ꙗковаⷤ не бѣша по всеⷤ земли ни во всѣⷯ странаⷯ. Многа оубо быша бж҃їа чюдеса моисеⷨ. прⷣе фараѡномъ и прⷣе египтаны. ~~видѣти~~ и прⷣе ї̈ильты. и никакоⷤ никогдаⷣ люⷣе возрѣша къ бг҃ꙋ. видѣти дѣлеса гн҃а ꙗко чю҃дна сꙋть. и вѣроваⷮ бв҃и не ѡбратно. но егда сотвори самъ гь҃ ꙗкоⷤ рече великаа и славнаа дѣла гн҃а. плоⷮ восприꙗⷡ. пострада и воскресе. и дх҃ъ ст҃ыи 133v/321 нⷥипославъ. болꙗщаа исцѣли прокаженныꙗ ѡчисти. раⷥслабленыꙗ стагноувъ. беⷥ ѡчесъ роженымъ ѡчеса дарова. мр҃твыꙗ возⷣвиже. прⷪ҇рки прорекошаⷭ ꙗзыки новыми воⷥглашаⷭ. тогда оузрѣша вси люⷣе дѣлеса гн҃а ꙗко чю҃дна сꙋⷮ. ꙗⷤ сотвори гь҃. ꙗко бгъ҃ посла сн҃а

74.8. And we can see from God's covenant with Abraham that he intends to bless all the nations in his seed (Gen. 22:18). And this we see with Moses, to whom the Lord promises the same covenant concerning his incarnation as he did to Abraham. But since Moses is a descendant of Levi, and not of Judah, therefore, the Lord says, "I will do for you" (Ex. 34:10); whereas to David, who comes from Judah, he gives a promise that says, "Of the fruit of your womb, I will set (a king) on your throne" (Ps. 132:11).[937] But as for Moses, (again), he comes from Levi, and not from Judah, and in his case, the covenant is different from the one given to Abraham and David. He does descend from them in terms of the flesh, but (God) gives Moses a different promise, saying, "Behold, I am establishing a covenant with you" instead of (saying), "In your seed, all the nations of the earth will be blessed" (Gen. 22:18) or "Of the fruit of your womb, I will set (a king) on your throne" (Ps. 132:11). Rather, (he says), "In the presence of all my people, I will do great and glorious things, which have not been done in all the earth nor in any of the nations"[938] (Ex. 34:10).

74.9. Now, there were many divine miracles that took place through Moses in the presence of Pharaoh and in the presence of the Egyptians and in the presence of all the Israelites; but it was not at that time, in any sense whatsoever, that people looked up to God, to recognize that the works of the Lord were awesome, and to believe in God unwaveringly. But when God himself did the great and glorious works of the Lord, as he said—when he assumed flesh, suffered and rose again, and when he sent out the Holy Spirit, | healed the sick, 133v/321
cleansed the leprous,[939] gave strength to the paralyzed, gave sight to those who were born blind, raised the dead, let the Prophets prophesy and new tongues be spoken[940]—then all the people saw that the works of the Lord, which the Lord did, were awesome. (They recognized) that God sent his Son to call to

937 And we can see from God's covenant with Abraham that he intends to bless all the nations in his seed (Gen. 22:18). And this we see with Moses, to whom the Lord promises the same covenant concerning his incarnation as he did to Abraham. But since Moses is a descendant of Levi, and not of Judah, therefore, the Lord says, "I will do for you" (Ex. 34:10); whereas to David, who comes from Judah, he gives a promise that says, "Of the fruit of your womb, I will set (a king) on your throne" (Ps. 132:11).] And we can see (the differences and similarities) concerning the covenants with Abraham, and with Jacob, and with Moses, and with David. For he gave Abraham a promise to bless all the nations in his seed (Gen. 22:18), and to David, he said, "Of the fruit of your womb, I will set (a king) on your throne" (Ps. 132:11), which refers to David, a descendant of Judah: "from a shoot, my son", and so forth (Gen. 49:9).

938 nations" (Ex. 34:10).] nations. And all the people, among whom you are, will see the works of the Lord, that they are awesome, which I will do for you" (Ex. 34:10).

939 Spirit, healed the sick, cleansed the leprous,] Spirit, ascended to heaven,

940 let the Prophets prophesy and new tongues be spoken] let new tongues be spoken

своⷢе призвати к себѣ люⷣ своꙗ ꙗⷤ созда. и гⷭь
сн҃ъ ѿцꙋ своемꙋ бывъ послꙋшливъ и на смⷬть
крⷭтнꙋю. такоⷤ тогда вѣроваша люⷣе невозъ
вратно ст҃ѣи троⷪцы въ единомъ бжⷭтвѣ.
Ꙗко завѣща гⷭь моисею сотвориⷮ спⷭение свое
всѣмъ ꙗзыкоⷨ в нихⷤъ моисеи. прⷪрчествꙋꙗ
бꙋдеⷮ писаниеⷨ своиⷨ. ѡ хвⷭѣ во плоⷮ пришествïи[941]
Аⷤе глаⷮе гⷭь ꙗко преⷣ всѣми люⷣми своими. и вси люⷣе
в нихⷤъ ты еси. вса бо саⷨ созда чл҃ки гⷭь. посемꙋ
и вси люⷣе его. аще и заблꙋⷣша ꙗзыцы въ слⷣѣ не
сꙋщиⷯ боговъ. и всиⷤ людие в ниⷯ же моисе глаⷮе гⷭь.
оузриⷮ дѣла гⷭна ꙗко чюⷣна сꙋть. моисе бо писа
ниемъ своиⷨ оувѣри хвⷭо во плоти пришествие.
всꙗкъ ꙗзыкъ иⷤ прочитаеⷮ моисеꙗ. и вси люⷣ
прочитаюⷮ и писанïа еⷢ. в ниⷯ еⷭ моисе. прочи
134r/322 танïа бо раⷣ книгъ еⷢ имꙋⷮ в себѣ моисеꙗ. на
ставлꙗюща иⷯ ко хⷭꙋ. ꙗко писанïа раⷣ моисеѡва
имоуⷮ вѣроваⷮ вси люⷣ въ троⷪцꙋ едино бжⷭтво.
сего раⷣ глаⷮе моисею гⷭь. и оузриⷮ вси люⷣе в нихⷤъ
ты еси дѣлеса гⷭна ꙗко чюⷣна сꙋть. ꙗже аⷥ
сотворю тебѣ. рекше ꙗⷤ азъ сотворю вопло

941 *Text continues in the margin*: а не токмо ïилътꙗноⷨ единѣмъ.

knowledge of himself his people, whom he created, and that the Son, being Lord, was obedient to his Father, even until death.[942] And it was through these means, then, that people unwaveringly believed in the Holy Trinity existing in one Godhead.

75. Showing that the Lord's promise to Moses concerning the work of his salvation does not refer to Israelites alone. Instead, it concerns all the peoples among whom Moses' writings would prophesy concerning Christ's coming in the flesh.[943]

75.1. And as for the phrases, where the Lord says, "in the presence of all my people" and "all the people, among whom you are" (Ex. 34:10), ⟨they are easy to understand⟩, for the Lord[944] created all men, and for that reason, all the nations are his, even though some people went astray after non-existing deities. And as for the words, where the Lord says that "all the people, among whom" was Moses, "will see the works of the Lord, that they are awesome" (Ex. 34:10), this has to do with the fact that in his books, Moses assures (the reader) of the coming of Christ in the flesh. Moses is present among all those nations that would read about Moses, and among all the people that read from his books, for thanks to their reading, people do have Moses in their midst, | and he directs 134r/322
them toward Christ. It shows that, thanks to what Moses wrote, all the people will believe in the one Godhead of the Trinity.[945] That is why the Lord says to Moses, "And all the people, among whom you are, will see the works of the Lord, that they are awesome, which I will do for you" (cf. Ex. 34:10), which

942 to knowledge of himself his people, whom he created, and that the Son, being Lord, was obedient to his Father, even until death.] to knowledge of himself the people, and that the Lord was obedient to his Father, as his beloved Son, in doing the works of the Lord and surrendering himself to death on the cross for the sake of all men.

943 **Showing that the Lord's promise to Moses concerning the work of his salvation does not refer to Israelites alone. Instead, it concerns all the peoples among whom Moses' writings would prophesy concerning Christ's coming in the flesh.**] *omitted*

944 Lord] he himself

945 read about Moses, and among all the people that read from his books, for thanks to their reading, people do have Moses in their midst, and he directs them toward Christ. It shows that thanks to what Moses wrote, all the people will believe in the one Godhead of the Trinity.] read what Moses wrote, for on account of their reading from the books of Moses, people do have Moses in their midst, and he directs them toward the Lord Jesus Christ, who did the awesome works of the Lord. It shows that thanks to what Moses wrote, all the people will believe in the triune God.

щенїа раⷣ. по твоемꙋ прⷪ҇рчествꙋ. и по проѡбраженїю закона. аціⷤ҇ ли не сїа гⷭ҇на дѣла. ихⷤ҇ ѡбѣща гⷭ҇ь сотвориⷮ҇ емꙋ. подобаше писанию сказаⷮ. каа дѣла моисею сотвориⷮ гⷭ҇ь послѣ беседы сеа и видѣнїа гⷭ҇на моисею. ꙗже оузрѧⷮ вси лⷣюе. Иконникъ миранинъ реⷱ҇. ꙗко реⷱ҇ гⷭ҇ь. и оузрѧть вси лⷣюе в нихⷤ ты еси. само сие слово повѣдаеⷮ всѣⷮ людеи. їил҃ьтѧⷩ единѣⷯ. заⷤе гл҃ати гⷭꙋ к моисею. и оузрѧⷮ вси лⷣюе в нихⷤ ты еси. се ꙗвьствено показа їил҃ь ти. понⷤе моисеи посреⷣ їил҃ѧ бѣꙗше водѧ и. Ѿвѣщавⷤ азъ рекоⷯ к нимъ. боⷹ и тако ꙗкоже рекосте. ꙗко ѡ їил҃ьтѧнⷯо реⷱ҇ гⷭ҇ь моисею. еⷤ и оузрѧⷮ вси лⷣюе в нихⷤ ты еси. то не поⷣбаше оубо писанию и показаⷮ сотвореныⷯ ѡнѣⷯ великиⷯ и славныⷯ дѣлъ гⷭниⷯ. ꙗцѣхⷤ нⷭѣ было по всеⷣ земли но[946] всѣхъ странаⷯ. [134v/323] ѧⷤ оузрѧⷮ вси лⷣюе їил҃ьтане в ниⷯ же моисеи. писаниеⷤ не показа великиⷯ и славныⷯ дѣⷣ гⷭниⷯ. сотвореныⷯ гмⷭ҇ъ моисею посреⷣ їил҃ѧ. послѣⷣ словесе сеⷢ гⷭна. токмо ѡ въставшиⷯ на арона. ихⷤ землѧ пожре и ѡгнь пожⷤе. но сїа дѣла ѧⷤ ѡ кореи и даѳанѣ и авиронѣ. ихⷤ землѧ пожре и ѡгнь пожже. нⷭѣ болши ѡнѣⷯ дѣлъ. ѧⷤ преⷤ сеⷢ завѣта сотвори. водꙋ в крⷡ҇о прелоⷤ и граⷣ и тмꙋ и первенцы поби. и стⷪ҇пъ ѡгненыи и ѡблачныи и маннꙋ и крастели и водꙋ ис камени

946 *Read*: во.

is the same thing as saying, "I will become incarnate,[947] according to what you prophesied and according to what is prefigured in the Law".

75.2. And if the works of the Lord, which the Lord promised to do for him,[948] stand for something else, then the Scripture must specify what kind of works the Lord would do for Moses, such that "all the people will see" when they follow the vision of the Lord and the conversation that Moses had with him. And the icon-painter from the laymen, said, "Regarding the words, where the Lord says, 'And all the people, among whom you are, will see' (Ex. 34:10), they actually describe only the people of Israel, and do not relate to other nations. The phrase in which the Lord says to Moses, 'And all the people, among whom you are, will see' clearly relates to the Israelites because Moses lived[949] in the midst of Israel and guided them".

75.3. And in response, I said to them: If it were the way you said it was—that the phrase, in which the Lord said to Moses, "And all the people, among whom you are, will see", refers to the Israelites—then should the Scripture not also specify what they were, those great and glorious works that the Lord would have done, what it was that has "not been done in all the earth nor in any of the nations" | and which "all the people" of Israel, among whom was Moses, would 134v/323 see? Yet the Scripture does not show the great and glorious works of the Lord, which the Lord would have done[950] for Moses in Israel after the Lord spoke to him, except for those in connection with the men who rose against Aaron and whom the earth devoured and the fire burned (Ex. 16).

75.4. But the works that are connected with Korah, Dathan, and Abiram—who were[951] devoured by the earth and burned by fire—are not greater than those done prior to the covenant: when he changed water into blood (Ex. 7:14–21);[952] (and sent) hail (Ex. 9:13–35), and darkness (Ex. 10:21–29); and when he struck the firstborn (Ex. 11);[953] and when he gave the pillars of fire and cloud[954] (e.g., Ex. 13:21–22), and manna (e.g., Ex. 17:8–15), and quail (Ex. 16:12–13), and

947 which I will do for you" (cf. Ex. 34:10), which is the same thing as to say, "I will become incarnate,] which I will do, (namely), the incarnation,

948 him,] Moses,

949 lived] *omitted*

950 those great and glorious works that the Lord would have done, what it was that has "not been done in all the earth nor in any of the nations" and which "all the people" of Israel, among whom was Moses, would see? Yet the Scripture does not show the great and glorious works of the Lord, which the Lord would have done] *omitted*

951 who were] even if we consider the fact that they were

952 blood (Ex. 7:14–21);] blood (Ex. 7:14–21); and sent boils (Ex. 9:8–12),

953 firstborn (Ex. 11);] firstborn (Ex. 11); and when he led (the Israelites) through the sea on dry ground but drowned the Egyptians (Ex. 13:17–14:31);

954 pillars of fire and cloud] pillar of fire

еⷤ въ египтѣ и в мори и в пꙋстыни. пачеⷤ повѣ даеⷮ писание. ꙗко послѣⷣ сего завѣта примо и сеи не бѣꙗше дѣла великаа и славнаа со творена гмⷭ҇ъ. но и плакашеⷭ҇ много моисеи. писание сказоуеⷮ. и молꙗше гаⷭ҇ глꙗ. въскꙋю зазли рабꙋ своемꙋ и нн҃ѣ побїи мꙗ ты. и нѣⷭ҇ в писанїи ꙗвленыⷯ дⷭ҇ѣ гⷭ҇нихъ. ни во исходѣ ни в левитицы ни в числаⷯ ни во второзаконїи. послѣ завѣта сеⷢ҇ точныⷯ первыⷨ дѣломъ. неⷤ ли и бⷭ҇оши или славнѣе сотворено. разꙋмѣ тиⷤ есть гⷭ҇нь глъ реченныи. еⷤ и оузриⷮ вси люⷣе в нихъⷤ ты еси. сие не ѡ единыⷯ ї҇ил҃ьтаноⷨ
[135r/325] но ѡ всеⷨ мире люⷣе. понеⷤ не реⷱ гⷭ҇ь и оузриⷮ вси люⷣе сїи в ниⷯ же ты нн҃ѣ. но рече гⷭ҇ь и оузриⷮ вси люⷣе в ниⷯ же ты еси. еⷤ показоуеⷮ еще на далечи сꙋ щее бываемое всеⷯ земли люⷣе. в послѣⷣ лѣ тїа. а не тогда ї҇ил҃ьтоⷨ. понеⷤ ї҇ил҃ьтане по слѣ завѣта сеⷢ҇ при моисеи. множицею ѡбра щахꙋса срⷣцемъ своиⷨ въ египеⷮ. и плакахꙋса не хотаще вхоⷣти в землю ѡбѣщаннꙋю ѿцеⷨ ихъ ѿ бг҃а. и нѣⷭ҇ нигдѣ в писанїи ѡ ї҇ил҃ьтꙗноⷯ ꙗко возрѣша къ бгꙋ всѣ срⷣцемъ когда дⷭ҇ѣ ради гⷭ҇ниⷯ. пачеⷤ воѻчию имꙋще гⷭ҇на чюⷣⷭ҇а. не вни махꙋ чюдесеⷨ гⷭ҇нимъ ꙗко чюⷣны и ѿвращахꙋса часто ѿ бг҃а ї҇ил҃ьтане ко идолоⷨ. и при моисеи и послеⷣ единаⷢ҇ никогдаⷤ воⷥрѣша к чюдесеⷨ гⷭ҇ниⷨ. но токмо егда воплотиⷭ҇ гⷭ҇ь и сотвори вели каа и славнаа иⷤ не быша никогдаⷤ по всеⷯ зе мли ни во всѣⷯ странаⷯ. ꙗко бгъ ꙗвиⷭ҇ во плоти болꙗщаа исцѣли бѣсы прогна. мрⷮвыа воскрⷭ҇и. и саⷨ стрⷭ҇ти претерпѣвъ. смрⷮь крⷭ҇томъ при

water[955] out of the rock (Ex. 17:1–7), (in short), the things that took place in Egypt, and in the sea, and in the wilderness. And even following this covenant, the Scripture does not speak of the great and glorious works done by the Lord either. Instead, the Scripture describes how Moses often cried and prayed to the Lord,[956] saying, "Why have you afflicted your servant"? and "kill me now"! (Num. 11:11, 15). And there is no place in the Scripture—not in Exodus, nor in Leviticus, nor in Numbers,[957] nor in Deuteronomy—where it shows works of the Lord, following the covenant, that are like those that were done earlier, and they are certainly not greater nor more glorious.

75.5. We must understand[958] the words where the Lord said, "And all the people, among whom you are, will see", as speaking of men from the whole world, and not of the Israelites alone. | For the Lord did not say, "And all the people, 135r/325 among whom you are *now*, will see". Instead, the Lord said, "And all the people, among whom you are, will see", which shows something that was to take place in the distant future and across the whole world, to people from the later centuries, and not to the Israelites who lived at that time.

75.6. ⟨And there is another reason why such an interpretation is plausible⟩. It has to do with the fact that, following the covenant, when Moses was already in their midst, the Israelites were often turning their hearts back toward Egypt and lamenting (their situation), having no desire to enter the land that God promised to their fathers. And wherever the Israelites are (described) in the Scripture ⟨during the lifetime of Moses⟩, the Israelites do not look up to God with all their heart in response to the works of the Lord. Rather, the Israelites[959] saw the miracles of the Lord with their own eyes, but did not perceive the Lord's signs as awesome, and often turned from God to idols both before and after Moses,[960] without remembering yet the Lord's miracles. (This changed) only when the Lord became incarnate and did[961] "great and glorious things, which have not been done in all the earth nor in any of the nations" (Ex. 34:10).

75.7. It was the time when God appeared in the flesh, healed the sick,[962] drove out demons,[963] raised the dead, and himself suffered affliction[964] upon

955 water] gave water
956 Lord,] Lord, following this covenant,
957 nor in Leviticus, nor in Numbers,] nor in Numbers, nor in Leviticus,
958 We must understand] It is closer to the truth if we understand
959 Rather, the Israelites] Rather, we should notice that the Israelites
960 before and after Moses] before Moses and after Moses,
961 and did] when he did
962 sick] sick by his word
963 demons,] demons out of men,
964 affliction] death

ꙗⷮ. и во гробѣ положисѧ. и воскрⷭ҇ъ из мр҃твⷯы. вознесⷭ҇е на нбⷭ҇а. и дх҃а ст҃го наставника и ѹтѣшителѧ мирꙋ ниⷥпславъ. ꙗⷤ и оузрѣша
135v/326 вси лю̑ⷣе делѣса гн҃а ꙗко чюⷣна сꙋ. а не їиⷣль едⷩи. но вси лю̑ⷣе рⷭ҇е в нихⷤ ты еси. еже ⷭ҇е ѡни оузрѧⷮ вси лю̑ⷣе в нихⷤ ты еси. рекше иже тѧ прие млю ради писанїа твоⷢ҇е. а не їиⷣльтане иⷤ тѧ камениⷨе побивахꙋ. и иноⷢ҇ начаⷣника и вожа наⷣ тобою поставлѧхꙋ. вести иⷯ паки въ египⷮе. ѿринꙋвшїи тѧ прⷤе въ е гиптѣ рекꙋще ти. кто тѧ постави кн҃зѧ наⷣ нами. и саⷨ гⷭ҇ь рⷭ҇е въ еуⷢ҇алїи своⷨе їиⷣлю. аще бысте вѣроваⷣ моисеѡви. вѣровали бысте и мнѣ. ѡ мнѣ бо тои писа. самое оубо се показа гⷭ҇ь глⷢ҇о свои̑ⷨ въ еуⷢ҇алїи ѡ себѣ. ꙗко прїиде гⷭ҇ь сотвориⷮ ѡбѣщаннаѧ иⷨ моисе ѡви дѣлеса гⷭ҇на по писанию моисеѡвꙋ. ве ликаа и славнаа. ꙗковаⷤ не бѣша по всеⷨ зе мли ни во всѣⷯ странаⷯ. И ꙗко тои ⷭ҇е самъ и в кꙋпинѣ главыи ⷨⷪⷨ҇и сею. аⷥ бг҃ъ авраамовъ. бг҃ъ исааковъ. бг҃ъ иꙗковль. понⷤе живи емꙋ и по смр҃ти авраⷨа исаⷦа иаковъ. ихⷤ и бг҃ъ нарицашⷭ҇е. такоⷤ и моисⷨе емꙋ живъ есть и во всѣⷯ ѡнѣⷯ людеⷯ есть моисеи. кои лю̑ⷣе вѣрꙋ имꙋ моисею по писанию ⷢ҇е. ꙗко тои ⷭ҇е саⷨ
136r/327 положивыи завⷮѣ моисею. внегда показа емꙋ сла вꙋ свою видѣти просившꙋ. и гл҃а емꙋ тогда самыи завⷮѣ воплоценїа своⷢ҇е. се полагаю тебѣ завⷮѣ прⷣе всѣми лю̑ⷣми своими. сотво рю великаа и славнаа ꙗкоⷤ не бѣша по всеи зе мли ни во всѣⷯ странаⷯ. и оузраⷮ вси лю̑ⷣе в ни хⷤъ ты еси дѣлеса гⷭ҇на ꙗко чюⷣна соуⷮ. и ꙗко тоⷨ есть саⷨ гл҃ꙗи їиⷣльтаноⷨ. аще бысте вѣроваⷣ моисеѡви. вѣровали бысте и мнѣ. ѡ мнѣ бо тои писа. Взыдⷨе же вѣдѣти и кꙋпи

accepting death on the cross, and was laid in the grave, and rose from the dead, ascended to the heavens, and when he sent out the Holy Spirit to teach and comfort[965] the world. And all the people saw | that the works of the Lord were 135v/326 awesome. It was not just Israel alone, but as it is said, "all the people, among whom you are, will see".[966] The phrase "all the people, among whom you are" is meant to say, "they are those who will receive you on account of what you wrote, and not the Israelites, who threw rocks at you and installed a different head and leader over you to lead them back to Egypt, and who actually rejected you earlier in Egypt, saying to you, 'Who made you ruler and judge over us'?" (Ex. 2:14). For that is what the Lord himself said to Israel in his Gospel,[967] "If you had believed Moses, you would have believed me, for he wrote about me" (Jn. 5:46).

75.8. Indeed, that is exactly what the Lord demonstrated in the Gospel when he spoke of himself—that the Lord has come to do the works of the Lord that were promised to him and to Moses,[968] "the great and glorious things, which have not been done in all the earth nor in any of the nations", according to what Moses wrote (Ex. 34:10). And he is the same one who said to Moses out of the bush, "I am the God of Abraham, the God of Isaac, the God of Jacob" (Ex. 3:6), because he continued to live even after Abraham, Isaac, and Jacob died, and he is called the God ⟨of the living, and not of the dead⟩ (Mk. 12:27). In the same way, Moses, too, is alive, and Moses is present among all the people who trust the books that Moses wrote.[969] And it was (God) himself, | who established the 136r/327 covenant with Moses when the latter asked him to see his glory, and he also said concerning the covenant of his incarnation later, "Behold, I am establishing a covenant with you in the presence of all my people. I will do great and glorious things, which have not been done in all the earth nor in any of the nations. And all the people, among whom you are, will see the works of the Lord, that they are awesome" (Ex. 34:10). And it was the same one, who said to the Israelites, "If you had believed Moses, you would have believed me, for he wrote about me" (Jn. 5:46).[970]

---

965 and comfort] *omitted*

966 see".] see" the works of the Lord.

967 to Israel in his Gospel,] to the Jews in the Gospel,

968 to him and to Moses] to Moses

969 wrote.] wrote, for in the eyes of the Lord, Moses is alive, just as Abraham and Isaac and Jacob are alive as well.

970 *MS 61 adds*: **Showing that God's descent to the mountain and his dwelling within the bush is a prophetic account about the descent of God's Son in the flesh to the earth in order to deliver all humankind from slavery to the devil, just as the Israelites (were delivered) from Egyptian slavery.**

нꙋ ѡгнⷨе горащꙋю и несъгараюцꙋю. пока заннꙋю моисею в тои горѣ. глⷮе оубо писание. ꙗко рⷪе ис кꙋпины моисею гⷭь. азъ есмь бг҃ъ авраамовъ. бг҃ъ исааковъ. бг҃ъ иꙗковль. и рⷪе вида видⷯѣ бѣдꙋ людеи моⷯи иже въ еги птѣ. и вопль иⷯ оуслышаⷯ. ѿ дѣлъ приста вникъ видⷯѣ болѣзнь иⷯ. и снидоⷯ изати иⷯ.

Ꙗко в кꙋпинѣ бж҃ие съшествие и вселение. проꙗвление еⷭ съшествїа сн҃а бж҃їа во плоти. избавиⷮ все чл҃ⷭчтво ѿ работы дїаволꙗ. ꙗкоⷤ[971]

Что ꙋбо чюⷣное се и великое бж҃ие дѣло. оуслыⷮ ша вопль. и видѣвъ бѣдꙋ людеи исходиⷮ изатїⷯ и. 136v/329 и в кꙋпинѣ хꙋдѣ травѣ ѿⷠемлетса весь. емꙋ нбⷭа в пдⷭ. и землю сотвори аки ничтоⷤ. сходиⷮ на горꙋ. и в малѣ травѣ ѡбиемлетса. и сниде избавиⷮ люде своⷯи. како ꙋбо сие. положивыи морю предѣлъ. и заповѣдавъ емꙋ доздѣ прїити. и не преити рекїи да боудеⷮ свⷠѣ и быⷭ светъ. людиⷤ видѣвъ в бѣдѣ саⷨ сходиⷮ изатї ихъ. видѣти сие великое бж҃ие и славно дѣло еⷭ. не едино точиюⷤ е изати печаⷭныа лю. но и таиньство велико. и проѡбражение боⷭши дѣлъ бж҃їи. и аще не бы сие было. возможно емꙋ избавиⷮ люди своа и не сшеⷣ на горꙋ. ниⷤ вшеⷣ в травꙋ малꙋ ѿⷠавитиⷭ. повелѣ бо преⷤ единѣмъ глⷨо быти тверди нбⷭнѣи. и водѣ взыⷮ на твердь. и быⷭ въ единъ днь. людиⷤ изати ѿ работы египеⷮскиа сходиⷮ самъ. и в кꙋпинѣ пламеннѣ ꙗвлꙗется прⷪркꙋ. не оубо и зраⷣнѣе нбⷭъ гора да бг҃ъ водворитса в неⷮ. ниⷤ пространнѣе нбⷭъ кꙋпина да вселитса в неи бг҃ъ. что ꙋбо еⷭ се. бг҃ъ великїи крѣпкїи

971 *Text continues in the margin*: їнⷣьтꙗнъ ѿ египта.

75.9. And let us arise to contemplate the bush that burned with fire, but did not burn up, and which was shown to Moses earlier on the same mountain. Now, the Scripture asserts that the Lord said to Moses out of the bush, "I am the God of Abraham, the God of Isaac, the God of Jacob". And he said, "I have surely seen the trouble of my people who are in Egypt, and I have heard their outcry caused by their taskmasters. I have seen their affliction and have come down to deliver them" (Ex. 3:6–8).

76. Showing that God's descent to dwell in the bush foreshows the descent of God's Son in the flesh to deliver all humankind from slavery to the devil, just as the Israelites (were delivered) out of Egypt.[972]

76.1. Now, what is so awesome and great about this work of God? Having heard the outcry and having seen the trouble of his people, he[973] comes down to deliver them, | and his entire being appears in the feeble plant of the bush. 136ᵛ/329
The one for whom heaven is like the "breadth of a hand" (cf. Is. 40:12), and who made the earth as if it was no big thing, descends to the mountain and appears in a tiny plant; and he comes down in order to deliver his people. Indeed, how can this be? He who "gave the sea its boundary" and commanded the water to reach its set limit, and not exceed it (Prov. 8:29); he who said, "'Let there be light', and there was light" (Gen. 1:3), who also saw the people in trouble and himself came down to deliver them.

76.2. You see, this great and glorious work of the Lord is not just about delivering the troubled people,[974] but also about prefiguring the grand mystery of God's great works. And if this had not been the case, he could have delivered his people without coming down to the mountain and without entering into the tiny plant[975] to appear ⟨before Moses in humble condescension⟩. For in earlier times, he simply commanded with a word to have the heavenly vault appear, and have the water gathered above the vault, and so it was within one single day (Gen. 1:6–8). But to deliver the people from Egyptian slavery, he comes down in his own person and appears to the Prophet in a flaming bush. Now, the mountain is not superior to the heavens, that God should come to dwell on it, nor is the bush greater than the heavens, that God should come to abide in it. What is

---

972 **Showing that God's descent to dwell in the bush foreshows the descent of God's Son in the flesh in order to deliver all humankind from slavery to the devil, just as the Israelites (were delivered) out of Egypt.**] *omitted*

973 he] he himself

974 the troubled people,] people in trouble,

975 tiny plant] plant

имѣа пⷡрⷭ҇тлъ нⷣбса землю пⷣножие ногама
своима. в горѣ вселıаетса. и в травѣ малѣ
$137^{r}/330$ ѡбитаеⷮ. нѣⷭ҇ ли оубо се ıавьствено наꙋ҇чаеⷮ та ве
ликомꙋ таиньствꙋ. и чюⷣнаго бжⷭ҇їа бⷣошаго со
дѣланїа. слышиши бга сшⷣеша избавиⷮ҇ люди своа.
могїи избавиⷮ҇ сїа и не сшⷣе. бгъ бо еⷭ҇ и всесилеⷩ҇.
возмогии оутвердиⷮ҇ нбⷭ҇а. и землю на водаⷯ.
и покрыⷮ҇ водами превыспренıаа. паⷣ возмо
глъ и не сшⷣе на горꙋ ни водворитиⷭ҇ в кꙋпи
нѣ. избавити ѿ работы ïильтаны. и не
изволи бгъ великїи и крѣпкїи инако како и
збавити люⷣ҇ своа. но саⷨ сниде и на горѣ ви
таеⷮ и в кꙋпинѣ вселıаетса. заⷤ҇ избавиⷮ҇
люⷣ҇ своа. и да вѣровавъ семꙋ. такоⷤ҇ вѣрꙋⷲ҇е
и егда оуслышиши бга сшⷣеша на землю самоⷢ҇.
и ако саⷨ изволи избавиⷮ҇ собою вса чл҇ки ѿ ра
боты дїаволıа. не бꙋдеши невѣренъ. слыша
всеⷤ҇ бга ıавльшаса преⷤ҇ в кꙋпинѣ в ничтоⷤ҇ сꙋ
щеи травѣ. и оуслышавъ бга послⷣѣ҇ во чревѣ
двчи воплощьшаⷭ҇ да вѣрꙋеши. слышавъ ꙋбо
кꙋпинꙋ ѡгнеⷨ горащꙋ и неѡполѣвшꙋ преже.
послⷣѣ҇ слышавъ чрево носившее бга воплоще
на невреⷣвше еⷭ҇ да не ѡпытоваеши. ниⷤ҇ да
оусꙋмнишиⷭ҇. тоиⷤ҇ бо бгъ иⷤ҇ преⷤ҇ сниде изати
$137^{v}/331$ людеи своиⷯ из работы египеⷮски. и кꙋпинꙋ не ѡ
пали. тоиⷤ҇ паки бгъ и послⷣѣ҇ сниде избавити
и вса люⷣ҇ ѿ работы дїаволıа. и чрево двⷭ҇че не ѡ
пали. И рѣша ми крылошане. нѣⷭ҇ ли оубо сеⷢ҇
раⷣ҇ бгъ в кꙋпинѣ ıавлıаетса. да не оустраши
тса прⷪркъ. видѣвъ бгъ внезапꙋ. Рехъⷤ҇ к ниⷨ
и аⷥ. бꙋдии по вашемꙋ речению. ıако сего раⷣ҇ ıавиⷭ҇

this, then? That God, who is great and strong, who has the heavens as his throne and the earth as his footstool (Is. 66:1), should come to dwell on the mountain and abide in the small plant? | 137r/330

76.3. Does this not clearly teach you, then, about the great mystery and the awesome and grand actions of God? As[976] you hear about God's descent to deliver his people, (you must recognize) that he could have delivered them even without coming down. For God is omnipotent: he was able to establish the heavens, and (set) the earth among the waters, and cover with water the things that were on top. He certainly could have delivered the Israelites from slavery without coming down to the mountain and without inhabiting the bush. But the great and strong God was not willing to deliver his people, except by coming down himself. And he comes to reside on the mountain and inhabits the bush in order to deliver his people so that you may believe this, and that you may also have faith when you hear that God himself came down to the earth, and that he was willing to deliver all men[977] from the devil's slavery in and through his own person. And you[978] will no longer remain in unbelief.

76.4. And on hearing that God at one point appeared in the bush, in a mere plant, and hearing also that God later became incarnate within the womb of the Virgin, have faith.[979] Thus,[980] when you have heard about the bush that burned with fire in earlier times, although it did not burn up, you will also hear about the God who later became incarnate and was carried in the womb of the Virgin without being affected (by passion), and you should not question it or have doubts. It is one and the same God, who first came down to free | his people 137v/331
from slavery in Egypt—in the bush that did not burn up—and who later also came down to deliver all people from slavery to the devil, and[981] who inhabited the womb of the Virgin without letting it "burn up".

76.5. And the kliros-chanters said, "Now, didn't God appear in the bush to avoid frightening the Prophet, had the latter seen him too suddenly"? And I said to them, too:[982] Let it be as you say, that God appeared in the bush to avoid

976 As] Therefore, as

977 all men] humanity

978 And you] And thanks to that, you

979 have faith.] have faith and do not remain in unbelief.

980 Thus,] And

981 came down to free his people from slavery in Egypt—in the bush that did not burn up—and who later also came down to deliver all people from slavery to the devil, and] came down to the mountain in order to free his people from slavery in Egypt, and who inhabited the bush—the bush that did not burn up—and who later also came down from the heavens to the earth in order to deliver his people from slavery to the devil, and

982 too:] *omitted*

бг҃ъ в кꙋпинѣ да не оустрашиⷮ прⷪ҇рка. нѣⷭ҇ ли самое се проѡбражение ꙗвлению сн҃а бж҃їа всемꙋ мирꙋ. аще бо прⷪ҇ркъ хоташе ꙋстрашитиⷭ҇ внезаапꙋ. аще видѣвъ бꙋдеⷮ бг҃а. чтоⷤ хотахꙋ пострадаⷮ҇ люⷣе невѣжи ꙋвѣдѣвши внезапꙋ бг҃а. сего раⷣ҇ бг҃ъ во плоти ꙗвиⷭ҇ всемꙋ мирꙋ. да возмогꙋть кроⷮцѣ прїати видѣⷣ бг҃а люⷣе вси и невѣжи сꙋщїи. ꙗкоⷤ и преⷤ моисею в кꙋпинѣ ꙗвиⷭ҇ да оустрашиⷮ моисеа. ѡбаче нѣⷭ҇ се едино точию. еⷤ ꙗвитиⷭ҇ бг҃ꙋ в кꙋпинѣ прⷪ҇ркꙋ да не ꙋстрашиⷮ прⷪ҇рка. понеⷤ и егда восхотѣ бг҃ъ извести авраама иⷥ земла халдѣскїа. не ꙋстраши еⷢ҇ а и внезаапꙋ возвавъ его. такоⷤ иноа не оустраши повелѣвъ емꙋ сотвориⷮ ковчегъ. но и каиⷩ҇ ѡбличаемъ ѿ бг҃а ѿвѣщаваше къ бг҃ꙋ а и съ нб҃сѣ бг҃ꙋ гл҃ющꙋ каинꙋ. [138r/332] здѣ же ꙗвлаетса бг҃ъ прⷪ҇ркꙋ на горѣ в кꙋпинѣ. оудоⷠ҇ палима вещь сѣно. ѡгнеⷨ гораше и не сгараше. чюдо зримое прⷪ҇ркꙋ бг҃ъ показоваше. таиньствоⷤ великое проѡбразоваше в неⷨ. всемꙋ мирꙋ. всако та сиⷨ наꙋчаеⷮ бг҃ъ. да слыша бг҃а авраамлꙗ бг҃а исаакова бг҃а иꙗковлꙗ съшеⷣша на горꙋ. и ꙗвлꙗющаⷭ҇ в хꙋдѣ садѣ. да егда потоⷨ ꙋслышиши сн҃а бж҃їа съшеⷣша съ нб҃съ и вочл҃чьшаⷭ҇. не оубоишиⷭ҇ но вѣрꙋеши. и не оусꙋмнишиⷭ҇. ꙗко и преⷤ бг҃ъ сниде на горꙋ и в кꙋпинѣ ꙗвиⷭ҇. тѣмже да не невѣрꙋеши ниⷤ да ѡпытоваеⷲ҇. како сниде сн҃ъ бж҃ии с нб҃сѣ и примѣсиⷭ҇ чл҃чествꙋ. или како плоⷮ возмоⷤ бг҃а прїати. понеⷤ и кꙋпина ѡгнеⷨ гораше и несъгараше. тако и дв҃аа сн҃а бж҃їа роⷣ без мꙋжа. сего раⷣ да хꙋдословиши но точию вѣровавъ блⷭ҇виши бг҃а великими и славными дѣлы спⷭ҇ающаго та. ꙗⷤ сн҃ъ бж҃ии сотвори тебѣ. ты ꙋбо не смѣеши ѡпытовати. ниⷤ безвѣрьствоваⷮ. како бг҃ъ сниде на горꙋ. изꙗⷮ ѿ рꙋкꙋ египеⷮскꙋ люⷣ свога. или како в кꙋпинѣ вмѣщаетса бг҃ъ. какоⷤ ли кꙋпина ѡгнеⷨ гораше frightening the Prophet. But isn't this (way of appearing) in itself a prefiguring of God's Son appearing to the whole world? For if the Prophet could be frightened by seeing God too suddenly, how[983] all the more would ignorant people not be frightened by seeing God too suddenly? That is why God appeared to the whole world in the flesh so that all humble people, as well as those who are ignorant, could see and accept God, just as when God appeared to Moses in the bush in earlier times, without frightening Moses at all.

76.6. However, to avoid frightening the Prophet is not the only reason why God appeared to the Prophet in the bush. For when God wished to bring Abraham out of the land of the Chaldeans, he did not cause any fear by suddenly calling out to him.[984] Nor did he frighten Noah when he commanded him to build the ark. Even Cain had no trouble responding to God when he was rebuked by God, | despite the fact that God spoke to Cain from heaven. And 138r/332
here, when God appears to the Prophet, on the mountain, out of the bush—a thing that easily catches fire, a dry plant that burned with fire, but did not burn up—God showed the Prophet a visible sign, and in this he prefigured a great mystery to the whole world.

76.7. Through all these various ways, God teaches you ⟨to be perceptive⟩[985] so that upon hearing that the God of Abraham, the God of Isaac, the God of Jacob came down to the mountain and appeared among the feeble plants, you may have no fear, but have faith, and not doubt when you hear of his later descent from the heavens, and the incarnation of God's Son. This is similar to the way God came down to the mountain and appeared in the bush.

76.8. Therefore, do not be unbelieving, or question how the Son of God came down from the heavens and became a partaker of humanity, or how it was possible for the flesh to take in[986] God. ⟨For even⟩ the bush ⟨was able to take in God⟩ because[987] it burned with fire, but did not burn up. In like manner, the Virgin, too, gave birth to the Son of God without a husband.

76.9. For this reason, do not say anything bad against God, but simply believe and bless God. He saved you through the great and glorious works which the Son of God[988] did for you. Do not be so audacious as not to believe, or to question how God came down to the mountain in order to deliver his people from the hand of the Egyptians, or how God was accommodated within the bush,

983 how] then how
984 calling out to him.] calling out to him from the height.
985 ⟨perceptive⟩] perceptive, as I said earlier,
986 to take in] to bear
987 because] even though
988 Son of God] Lord, God's Son,

138v/333 сѣно и не сгараше. но точию покланаешиⷭ҇ чюде си. и славиши еⷭ҇. какоⷤ҇ смѣеши мноⷭ҇вещество вати и ѡпытовати тогоⷤ҇ бг҃а. како сн҃ъ бж҃їи воплотиⷭ҇. и како плоⷮ понесе бжⷭ҇тво. и како ѿ дв҃ы беⷥ сѣмени рⷣоса. и которӧ мтⷭ҇и достоинъ бꙋдеши. Взыдеⷨ҇ и еще на вышшее[989] писание. еⷤ҇ ѡ иакѡвѣ глⷮе. да познаеⷨ҇ и ѿсю дꙋ бжїе бл҃говоление на чл҃чествѣ. еⷤ҇ едино рⷣоному сн҃у его вочл҃читиⷭ҇ и сптⷭ҇и чл҃чество. внегда видѣ їаковъ во снѣ нощию на лѣствицы гⷭ҇а. ꙗко реⷱ҇ гⷭ҇ь ко їаковꙋ сїе. азъ есмь бг҃ъ авраамль ѿца твоеⷢ҇. и бг҃ъ исааковъ. не бойⷭ҇. земля идеⷤ҇ ты спиши на неи. тебѣ даⷨ҇ ю и племени твоемꙋ. и бꙋдеⷮ҇ плема твое ꙗко пѣсокъ земныи. и расширится до моря. и до вьстокъ и запаⷣ и до сѣвера. и блⷭ҇ватся ѡ тебѣ вси ꙗзыцы земнїи въ племени твоеⷨ҇. сеⷤ҇ азъ с тобою сохраняя тя на всеⷨ҇ пꙋти амоⷤ҇ идеши. и возвращꙋ тя на землю сию. ꙗко не ѡставлю тебе. дондеⷤ҇ сотворю все еⷤ҇ глахъ тебѣ. Ѿ сеⷭ҇ разꙋмѣвается. ꙗко послѣ̈ⷣ тойⷤ҇ гⷭ҇ь бг҃ъ снаса со їаковомъ и браса
139r/334 и возмоⷤ҇ к немꙋ їаковъ. понеⷤ҇ рече преⷤ҇. се же аⷥ с тобою сохраняя тя на всякоⷨ҇ пꙋти. и не ѡставлю тя дондеⷤ҇ сотворю все еⷤ҇ глаⷯ тебѣ. ѿ сеⷭ҇ видѣти ꙗко и в кꙋпинѣ ꙗвиⷭ҇ моисею тойⷤ҇ бг҃ъ авраамовъ бг҃ъ исааковъ бг҃ъ їаковль.

---

989 *In the margin*: гл҃а кⷦз.

or how the bush burned with fire | and how that very plant did not burn up. Instead, simply bow before his miracles and praise him,[990] and do not be so bold as to interrogate and question this God on how the Son of God became incarnate, and how the Godhead bore flesh, and how he was born from the Virgin without a male seed. (Otherwise), what mercy will you be worthy of receiving? 138v/333

77. Chapter 27.[991]

77.1. And let us arise once more to the height of Scripture that speaks of Jacob—when Jacob saw the Lord on the ladder[992] in a dream at night—so that from this, too, we may know God's good pleasure for humanity:[993] that his only-begotten Son became man and saved humankind. ⟨At that point⟩, God said to Jacob as follows, "I am the God of your father Abraham, and the God of Isaac. Do not fear, the land on which you sleep, to you will I give it, and to your offspring. And your offspring will be as the sand of the earth; and it will spread abroad to the sea, and to the East, and to the West, and to the North; and in you and in your offspring will all the nations of the earth be blessed. And behold, I am with you, I will keep you on every path where you go; and I will bring you back to this land; for I will not leave you until I have done all that I told you" (Gen. 28:13–15).[994]

77.2. From this, we can recognize that it was the same God who later appeared to Jacob in a dream and wrestled with him. | And Jacob was strengthened by him, for he soon said to him, "And behold, I am with you, I will keep you on every path where you go; I[995] will not leave you until I have done all that I told you" (Gen. 28:15). And we can see from this that Moses saw the same God in the bush, (the God) who appeared as the God of Abraham, the God of Isaac, 139r/334

---

990 him.] *omitted*

991 Chapter 27.] **Investigation in the holy book of Genesis concerning the covenants of God and the story in which a man wrestled with Jacob until morning and overpowered him. What is it, and how should we understand it? CHAPTER 27.**

992 on the ladder] fixed on the ladder

993 for humanity] manifested for humanity

994 *MS 61 adds*: **Showing that the promise to bless Abraham and Jacob relates to Christ. In the case of Abraham, it has to do with (the words) "in your seed" (Gen. 22:18), which indicate one person. And as for Jacob, it has to do with the statement "in your offspring", which means that Christ—the seed of Abraham—will shine through his offspring, and in it, all the nations will be blessed.**

995 I] for I

тамо на верхꙋ лѣствицѣ їаковꙋ ꙗвиⷭ҇. рекъ сотвориⷮ ми все гл҃анное емꙋ. здѣⷤ моисею гл҃еⷮ. ꙗко снидоⷯ изати люде свойⷯ ѿ египтаⷩ. вѣдѣвъ болѣзнь иⷤ и оуслышавъ вопль иⷯ. пока зꙋеⷮ ꙗко поманꙋ бг҃ъ завѣⷮ свои ко авраамꙋ еⷤ рече. ꙗко блⷭ҇ватса ѡ сѣмени твоемъ вси ꙗзыци земнїи. и еⷤ иꙗковꙋ тойⷭ҇ завѣⷮ. блва тса рⷱ҇е вси ꙗзыци въ племени твоⷨ. и тве рдо ꙗко не ѡставлю та рⷱ҇е. дондеⷤ сотво рю всеⷤ е глаⷯ тебѣ. посемꙋ и моисею рⷱ҇е еже снидоⷯ изатї ихъ ѿ рꙋкꙋ египеⷮскꙋ. сего раⷣ с моисеѡⷨ їил҃ꙗ саⷨ вожаше. и самое то гл҃а ше моисею гⷭ҇ь. аⷥ самъ поидꙋ преⷣ тобою и оу ставлю та. и еⷤ. се аⷥ полагаю тебѣ завѣⷮ преⷣ всѣми лⷣюми своими сотворю великаа и славнаа. ꙗкоⷤ не бѣша по всеⷯ земли ни во всѣⷯ странаⷯ. и оузраⷮ вси лⷣюе в ниⷯ же ты еси
[139v/335] дѣлеса гн҃а ꙗко чⷭ҇на сꙋⷮ ꙗже аⷥ сотворю тебѣ.

Ꙗко бг҃ъ в законѣ повелѣ їил҃ю женитиⷭ҇ в бли жнеⷨ племени своеⷢ колѣна. сего раⷣ. да извѣ сто боудеⷮ ѿ июды хⷭ҇во воплощение. по пррⷱ҇чествꙋ[996]

Сїи вси завѣти бж҃їи показꙋеⷮ бгодⷯновенное писание. ꙗко снити гⷭ҇ꙋ и воплотиⷮса да блⷭ҇виⷮ вса плеⷨеⷩна земнаа. раⷥньствоваⷤ завѣⷮ гⷭ҇ь авраамꙋ їаковꙋ с моисеѡⷨ. авраамꙋ їаковꙋ завѣща блⷭ҇вение ѿ ниⷯ всѣмъ ꙗзыкоⷨ земныⷨ, моисеюⷤ тойⷤ завѣтъ а не тако. понеⷤ не ѿ левгїина племени прїити гⷭ҇ꙋ воплотитиⷭ҇. но ѿ иудина племени. еⷤ оуже и преⷣ глахоⷨ. левгїйⷤ сщ҃енно пишеⷮ токмо ст҃льство хⷭ҇во.

996 *Text continues in the margin*: їаковлю и моисеѡвꙋ.

the God of Jacob. In[997] the first case, when he appeared to Jacob on the ladder, he said that he would do everything he told him (Gen. 28:15); and in the case of Moses, here, he says that he came down to deliver his people from the Egyptians, after seeing their affliction and hearing their outcry (Ex. 3:7–8).

77.3. It shows[998] that God remembered his covenant with Abraham—in which he said, "In your seed, all the nations of the earth will be blessed" (Gen. 22:18)—and the same covenant (that he made) with Jacob—when he said, "in your offspring[999] all the nations will be blessed", and assured him, "I will not leave you until I have done all that I told you" (Gen. 28:14). That is why he also said to Moses, "I have come down to deliver them out of the hand of the Egyptians" (Ex. 3:8). For the same reason, he was himself guiding Israel together with Moses, just exactly as the Lord said to Moses, "I myself will go before you and give you rest" (Ex. 33:14), and "Behold, I am establishing a covenant with you before all my people. I will do great and glorious things, which have not been done in all the earth nor among any of the nations. And all the people, among whom you are, will see | the works of the Lord, that they are wonderful, which 139v/335
I will do for you" (Ex. 34:10).

78. Showing that in the Law, God commands Israel to marry those who come from the clans related to their own tribes, to make known, in fulfillment of the prophecy to Jacob and Moses, that Christ's coming in the flesh was through Judah.[1000]

78.1. Through all of these covenants (made by) God, the divinely inspired Scripture shows that the Lord must come down and become incarnate so that he may bless all the nations of the earth. But there is a way in which the covenant of the Lord with Abraham and Jacob differs from the one with Moses. To[1001] Abraham and Jacob, he promised that all the nations of the earth would be blessed from them. But to Moses, he gave the same covenant—yet differently, because the Lord came and became incarnate not from the tribe of Levi, but from the tribe of Judah, as I already said before. And matters that are written about Levi have an allegorical sense, referring only to the priesthood of Christ,

997 In] Thus, in

998 It shows] In this, it is shown

999 "in your offspring] "in you and in your offspring

1000 **Showing that in the Law, God commands Israel to marry those who come from the clans related to their own tribes, to make known, in fulfillment of the prophecy to Jacob and Moses, that Christ's coming in the flesh was from Judah.**] *omitted*

1001 To] Thus, to

понеⷤ і҆с҃ъ х҃с бг҃ъ и чл҃къ ходатаиствова бг҃ꙋ и
чл҃комъ. плоⷮ же чл҃чества прїати емꙋ ѿ ию
ды. сего раⷣ в законѣ заповѣда не смѣшати҃
племени с племенеⷨ. ꙗко не поимаⷮ племеⷩ
рꙋвимовꙋ жены в племени сїмеѡновѣ. но
поимаⷮ рꙋвимовꙋ племени жены себѣ въ сво
емъⷤ племени рꙋвимовѣ такоⷤ и всѣмъ пле
меноⷨ ї҆и҃левомъ комꙋжⷣо поимаⷮ себѣ жены
въ своеⷨ племени по законꙋ. гл҃ⷮе бо закоⷩ сице.
140r/337 І да не сматетса причастие сн҃овъ ї҆и҃левъ ѿ
племени въ плема. ꙗко кожⷣо въ причастїи
племени ѿчества своеⷢ да са женѧⷮ сн҃ове
ї҆и҃леви. Бы҃ бо и авраамꙋ сн҃ъ измаиⷧ ѿ ага
ры. и ѿ хеттꙋры множаишїи сн҃ове. но ѡ иса
ацѣ сѣма нареⷱ бг҃ъ завѣта. такоⷤ и исаакꙋ
бы҃ сн҃ъ исавъ и возлюⷠⷧⷷнъ ѿ него. но бл҃вение на
ї҆акова положи. такоⷤ иаковꙋ. в҃і. сн҃овъ бы҃
но ѿ июды бл҃вению быти. сего раⷣ законъ по
ложи имъ гл҃ѧ. ꙗко кожⷣо въ причастїи пле
мени ѿчества своеⷢ да са женѧⷮ сн҃ове ї҆и҃леви.

as a reference to Jesus Christ as God and man, the intercessor between God and men. But from the human point of view, when he came in the flesh, he proceeded from Judah.[1002]

78.2. For this reason, the Law commands that one tribe should not mingle with another tribe. Men from the tribe of Reuben should not marry women from the tribe of Simeon. Instead, men from the tribe of Reuben should marry women from their own tribe, that of Reuben. Likewise, according to the Law, men from all other tribes of Israel should also marry women only from their respective tribes.[1003] For the Law says this, | "And the inheritance of the sons of 140r/337
Israel should not be transferred from one tribe to another tribe, for everyone of the sons of Israel should marry from those that belong to the inheritance of their own tribe, that of their fathers" (Num. 36:7).

78.3. For Abraham had a son Ishmael from Hagar, and he also had many sons from Keturah,[1004] but it was Isaac whom God named with regard to the seed of the covenant. Similarly, Isaac also had a son[1005] Esau, whom he loved, but the blessing was laid on Jacob. And Jacob, likewise, had twelve sons, but the blessing came through Judah.[1006] That is why, with regard to them, the Law specified, stating that[1007] "everyone of the sons of Israel should marry from those that belong to the inheritance of their own tribe, that of their fathers",

---

1002 men. But from the human point of view, when he came in the flesh, he proceeded from Judah.] men, as it has been shown many times, while the incarnation takes place from the tribe of Judah. **Showing that in the Law, God commands the Israelite men to marry women from their own tribes, from among the clans related to their own tribes, to make known, in fulfillment of the prophecy to Jacob and Moses, that Christ's coming in the flesh was from Judah.**

1003 Men from the tribe of Reuben should not marry women from the tribe of Simeon. Instead, men from the tribe of Reuben should marry women from their own tribe, that of Reuben. Likewise, according to the Law, men from all other tribes of Israel should also marry women only from their respective tribes.] Men from the tribe of Simeon should not marry women from the tribe of Levi, or of Judah, or of other tribes. Thus, they should not marry women in any of these (tribes). Instead, they should marry women only in their own tribes. This means that men from the tribe of Reuben should marry women from the tribe of Reuben, and men from the tribe of Simeon should marry women from the tribe of Simeon. And likewise, men from the tribe of Levi should marry women from their own tribe of Levi, and men from the tribe of Judah should marry women from their own tribe of Judah. Accordingly, as (commanded) in the Law, men from all the twelve tribes should marry women only from their respective tribes.

1004 from Hagar, and he also] from Hagar before he had Isaac, and after Isaac, he also

1005 son] first-born son

1006 Judah.] Judah, the fourth son.

1007 Law specified, stating that] Law was established that

и да не смѧтетсѧ причастие сн҃овъ ї҆илевъ ѿ племени въ племѧ. ꙗко да извѣсто бꙋдет при шествие гсне в племени наречено и знаемо боудет прореченное ѡ иудѣ. е не ѡскꙋдѣет кнѧзь ѿ иуды ни игꙋменъ ѿ бедрꙋ его. дондеже прїидет емꙋ же щадимо и то чаание ꙗзыком. вса сїа проѡбраженїе воплощенїа бжїа. и всѣмъ симъ пѣстꙋньствова законъ. рꙋко вода люд ко хсꙋ. Пишетъже паки. Ї борашесѧ с нимъ мꙋжь до ꙋтрїа. видѣвъже ꙗко не може противꙋ емꙋ. преꙗс въ стегна его и оутерпѣ.
140v/338 и пречеса стегна ї҆аковлꙗ егда борашесѧ с нимъ. рече же емꙋ пꙋсти мѧ взыде бо свѣт. се рече емꙋ не пꙋщꙋ тебе аще не блгвиши мене+.[1008] И преже оуже разꙋмѣхом се. ꙗко бгъ есть борѧисѧ со ї҆аковом. понеже самъ мꙋжь борѧисѧ повѣдасѧ иꙗко вꙋ ꙗко бгъ есть. внегда блвити его. рече бо к немꙋ ꙗко ꙋкрѣпи съ бгомъ. ннѣ же прилежит разꙋмѣти сїе. чесо ради бгъ толико сниде ꙗко съ члкомъ снатисѧ рꙋкама. не сеже токмо но и брашесѧ с нимъ аки мꙋж. сего ли ради токмо да ї҆акова ѿ боазни свободит исавовы ѿ члка брата его. а не ли и таина велика и проѡбражение болших дѣлъ бжїихъ. и аще не бы таина

1008 *Text continues in the margin:* + Ꙗко снатие бжие со ї҆аковом братис. проѡбраженние вочлвѣченїа сна бжїа есть во спсние всего мира ѿ насианлїа дьаволꙗ. и ꙗком ї҆акова ѿ исава избави. такожде и всѣхъ хс избави ѿ дыꙗ ⟨...⟩

and "the inheritance of the sons of Israel should not be transferred from one tribe to another tribe" (Num. 36:7).

78.4. This was the case so that the coming of the Lord would be recognized in the tribe specified, and (men) would know what was prophesied of Judah, namely, "A ruler will not fail from Judah, nor an elder from his loins, until that which has been stored up for him comes to pass; and he is the expectation of nations" (Gen. 49:10). All of this prefigures the incarnation of God,[1009] and through all of this, the Law guided people, leading them to Christ.

78.5. And again, it is written,[1010] "And a man wrestled with him until morning. And he saw that he could not overpower him; and he touched his hip | and dislocated the socket of Jacob's hip when he wrestled with him. And he said to him, 'Let me go, for the dawn has arisen'. (But) he said, 'I will not let you go unless you bless me'" (Gen. 32:24–26). 140v/338

79. Showing that God's descent to wrestle with Jacob prefigures the incarnation of God's Son, that took place to save the whole world from the violence of the devil. And just as Jacob was freed from Esau, so would Christ deliver everyone from the devil's deceit.[1011]

79.1. Now, we have already learned that the man who wrestled with Jacob was God. For this man himself, after wrestling with Jacob, said to him that he was God; when he was blessing him, he said[1012] to (Jacob) that he "became strong with God" (Gen. 32:28). Now, it remains for us to understand[1013] why God came down to such an extent that he used hands to wrestle with a man, and not only that, but also that he wrestled with him as a man. Is it just because he wanted to free Jacob from the fear of Esau, his human brother? Or is there also[1014] a great mystery and prefiguring of God's grand works?

1009 God,] God's Son,

1010 *MS 61 adds*: **Showing that God's descent to wrestle with Jacob prefigures the incarnation of God's Son, that took place to save the whole world from the violence of the devil. And just as Jacob was freed from Esau, so does Christ deliver all men from the devil's deceit and the rage of idols.**

1011 **Showing that God's descent to wrestle with Jacob prefigures the incarnation of God's Son, that took place to save the whole world from the violence of the devil. And just as Jacob was freed from Esau, so would Christ deliver everyone from the devil's deceit.**] *omitted*

1012 For this man himself, after wrestling with Jacob, said to him that he was God; when he was blessing him, he said] He himself said to Jacob that he was God, for when he was blessing him, he said

1013 understand] consider

1014 also] *omitted*

великаа бываемое ниⷤ проѡбраженіе сла
вны болшиⷯ дѣ҃ бж҃їихъ. можаше бг҃ъ и ина
ко наꙋчити їакова како не ꙋбоатиⷭ҇ емоу
ч҃лка брата своеⷢ҇. понеⷤ егда видѣ їаковъ
лѣствицꙋ оутверженꙋ. ѿ землѧ до нб҃си до
сажющꙋ. и аг҃глы восходащаа и ниⷥсхода
щаа по неи. и самого тоⷢ҇ бг҃а восланающаса
на неи. толико страшно видимое бѣаше.
тогда словоⷨ единѣмъ всю боꙗзнь емꙋ ѿꙗтъ.
141r/339 рекъ емꙋ токмо не бойⷭ҇. нн҃ѣ їаковꙋ оубоавшꙋⷢ҇
ч҃лка брата своеⷢ҇. ꙗко изыде въ срѣтеніе емꙋ
имѣа с нимъ идꙋщиⷯ. у҃. людеи еⷭ҇. тойⷤ бг҃ъ
самъ приходиⷮ снатиⷭ҇ и братиⷭ҇ со їаковомъ.
боⷣ и со враждою градыи исавъ ко їаковꙋ. ѡ
баⷪ браⷮ емꙋ еⷭ҇. ѿ единого ѿца и единоꙗ мт҃ре.
и покараꙗⷭ҇ їаковъ преⷣ нимъ ѕѣло. и гд҃мъ
себѣ нарицаа исава. не оукротиⷮ ли лица своеⷢ҇
исавъ ко їаковꙋ. покореніе приемлѧ ѿ него.
боⷣ и силеⷩ не мноⷢ҇ исавъ множае їакова. и мноⷤ
ство мꙋжеи вода с собою. но нѣⷭ҇ множае аг҃глъ
ихъⷤ видѣ їаковъ ходащиⷯ по лѣствицы. со
исавоⷨ бо. у҃. мꙋжеи токмо. аг҃гловъⷤ нечи
сленое множество на лѣствицы. аще бы
постигло число восходащиⷯ и ниⷥходащихъ
на лѣствицы аг҃гловъ. всако не оумолчало
бы писаніе сказати число аг҃гльское ходащиⷯ
по лѣствицы. ащеⷤ и силеⷩ исавъ но нѣⷭ҇ мощию
ꙗкоⷤ и единъ аг҃гль. и тамо словоⷨ гь҃ могїи страⷯ
їаковꙋ ѿати. и коⷪ страшно еⷭ҇ бг҃а видѣти
ѿ нбсъ. и аг҃гловъ восходащиⷯ и ниⷥходащихъ
къ нб҃си и ѿ нб҃си. ѡбаⷪ реⷱ токмо не бойⷭ҇ и страⷯ ѿбѣже.
141v/341 и оубо нѣⷭ҇ ли возможно бг҃ꙋ и нн҃ѣ. ꙗкоⷤ и преⷤ гл҃а

79.2. If there had been no great mystery in what took place there, nor a prefiguring of God's glorious and great works, God could have used a different method to teach Jacob about not being afraid of his human brother. For when Jacob saw a fixed ladder, stretching from the earth to the heavens, and the angels of God who were ascending and descending on it, and God himself, who was established on it, that vision was extremely frightening. At that moment,[1015] (God) took away all his fear with one word. | He only said to 141r/339
him,[1016] "Do not fear" (Gen. 28:13). But now Jacob was afraid of his human brother—for the latter went out to meet him with the four hundred men, which went with him—and disregarded the fact that God himself came to battle and wrestle with Jacob.[1017]

79.3. (But consider this): even though Esau was approaching Jacob with enmity, he was still his brother, (born) of the same father and the same mother; and Jacob totally submitted himself to him and called Esau his master. Would Esau not soften his attitude toward Jacob and accept his submission? And even though Esau was far more powerful than Jacob and led a multitude of men with him, their number was not as great as that of the angels whom Jacob saw walking on the ladder. For there were only four hundred men with Esau, whereas the number of the angels on the ladder was countless. For if the number of[1018] angels ascending and descending on the ladder could be counted, the Scripture would have certainly not failed to report the number of the angels that walked on the ladder. And even though Esau was strong, he nevertheless could not compare even with one angel in terms of his strength.[1019]

79.4. And the Lord was able to take away Jacob's fear with only one word there. And while it was so frightening to see God from the heavens,[1020] together with the angels ascending to the heavens and descending from the heavens, he simply said, "Do not fear", and his fear[1021] was gone. | And was it not possible 141v/341
for God in that situation, as we previously mentioned, to free Jacob from the

1015 At that moment,] And at that moment,

1016 to him] to him, then,

1017 But now Jacob was afraid of his human brother—for the latter went out to meet him with the four hundred men, which went with him—and disregarded the fact that God himself came to battle and wrestle with Jacob.] But now Jacob was afraid of his human brother—for Esau went out to meet him with his four hundred men, who went with him—instead of actually being afraid of the host of the angels whom he saw, or of God, despite the fact that God himself came to wrestle with Jacob.

1018 the number of] *omitted*

1019 strength.] strength and a large number (of men).

1020 God from the heavens,] God speaking from the heavens,

1021 his fear] every fear

хмо. иꙗкова ѿ боазни премѣнит исавовы и мꙋже его. аще не таина ес. и аще не проѡбражение великих и славных дѣлъ гсниихъ. ꙗж сотворит самъ гсь. ихж оузрат вси люде ꙗко чюдна сꙋ. что ино ес аще не се токмо. воистиноуж и се чюдно слышати. и страшно видѣт дѣемое бга снавшас съ члком. и рꙋкама члкъ ѡбьемлет бесплотнаго. и возмогает члкъ съ бгмъ. и оудержавает дотолика елико и испрашиватиса ѿ него. реч бо к немꙋ пꙋсти ма взыде бо свѣт. и возмогает толико ꙗко рещи не пꙋщꙋ та аще не блсвиши ма. оудивлꙗет всꙗкъ оумъ смысленыи. ꙗко возлюби бгъ члка толико ꙗко и снатис с нимъ. снав жес возлюби и еще и пожидати всю нощь в рꙋкꙋ члчю. и пожидавъ возлюби терпѣти не ѿпꙋщает. велми ꙋбо дивно како бга храмина авраамова вмѣсти егож нбса вмѣстит не могꙋть. реч бо въ пррцѣ. нбо мнѣ прстлъ землаж подножие ногама моима. дивно ꙋбо како терпаше гсь и внечстыхъ 142r/342 содомех ѡбнощьствоват. чюднѣе же се како сподобис бгъ в рꙋкꙋ члка оудержатис. бесплотен сыи и в хꙋдѣ травѣ кꙋпиннѣи водворитис. всако проѡбразоваше ѡно. еж завѣт положи моисею. сотворити великаа и славнаа ꙗж не бѣша по всеи земли ни во всѣх странах. дѣлеса гна. ꙗж гь сотвори моисею во їили. сшед с нбсѣ безсѣменно воплотиса и вочлчитис бгꙋ. и во чревѣ двчи водворитис. и родтиса ѿ двы бракꙋ неискꙋсныꙗ. и рꙋкама мтрнима поноситис и млекомъ ѿ сосцꙋ питатис. и на земли походти. и оутрꙋдитис. и взалкат и вжадат. и воспотѣтис и прослезити. и оудержанꙋ быти рꙋкама оубїицъ. и ко крстꙋ пригвоздитиса. и оумрети и во гробѣ положитис. и воскрснꙋти и на нбса паки взыти. и дхъ стыи оутѣ fear of Esau and his men, ⟨simply⟩ by (saying) a word? But didn't it happen in this way, rather, on account of the mystery and prefiguring of the great and glorious works of the Lord, which the Lord himself would do and which all people would see, that they are awesome (Ex. 34:10). And if this is not so, then what is it?

79.5. But it is a truly awesome and frightening thing to hear and see what God does! He wrestles with man; and the one who does not have a body is embraced by human hands; and the man is strengthened by God and holds him until the moment he makes a request to him, for (God) said to him, "Let me go, for the dawn has arisen" (Gen. 32:26). And he gains so much strength that he even says, "I will not let you go unless you bless me" (Gen. 32:26). It astonishes every intelligent mind[1022] that God loved the man so much that he even wrestled with him; and after wrestling, he loved him and even waited the whole night in human hands, and after waiting, he was still patient about not being allowed to go. It is marvelous, indeed, how Abraham's tent was able to accommodate God, whom even the heavens cannot embrace. For he[1023] said in the Prophets, "Heaven is my throne, and the earth is my footstool" (Is. 66:1). And while it is indeed marvelous how the Lord endured the night in impure | Sodom, it is even more 142r/342
marvelous that God—who is without a body and who inhabited the bush, the feeble plant that it was—was willing to be held in human hands!

79.6. All of this prefigures something else: the covenant that (God) established with Moses to do the great and glorious things which have not been done in all the earth nor in any of the nations, the works of the Lord that the Lord would do for Moses in Israel (Ex. 34:10)—(these prefigure) his coming down from the heavens when he became incarnate without a male seed. (It prefigures the time) when God became man, and dwelled[1024] within the womb of the Virgin, and was born from a mother who did not know marriage, and was carried in the mother's hands, and was fed with breast milk. And he walked on the earth and experienced weariness and hunger and thirst and sweat, and he wept and was held by the hands of his murderers,[1025] and was nailed to the cross, and he died,[1026] and was laid in the grave, and he rose again,[1027] and ascended back

1022 mind] *omitted*

1023 he] Lord

1024 dwelled] was accommodated

1025 and he wept and was held by the hands of his murderers,] and was beaten by the hands of his murderers

1026 died,] died as man,

1027 rose again,] rose again as God,

шитⷭ҇е нⷥ҇ипослати. и вса страны в позна
ние ко ѿцⷰ҇ привести. того раⷣ҇ вса сїа прⷤ҇е
проwбрази. да не внезапꙋ чл҃цы видѣвше
вса сїа и вострепетавше абие возопиють
ꙗкⷪ҇ⷤ и маное к женѣ своеи иногда. рⷱ҇е бо по
гибохоⷨ҇ w жено ꙗко бг҃а видѣхоⷨ҇. но познавше
142v/343 по воwбраженїю прежнемꙋ чл҃цы и разꙋмѣвше
премⷬ҇ое паⷱ҇ оума и словесе. бж҃їа бл҃говоленїа.
страшное смотрѣние сн҃а бж҃їа w наⷭ҇. w сеⷨ҇ покло
нившеⷭ҇ блвⷭ҇иⷮ҇ бг҃а. ꙗко ѩковъ вопиюще. ви
дѣхоⷨ҇ бг҃а лицеⷨ҇ к лицꙋ и сп҃сеса наⷭ҇ дш҃а. быша оу
бо проwбраженїа бл҃гтию бж҃иею. бл҃говоле
нїа его чл҃чьскомꙋ сп҃сенїю. и написашаⷭ҇ вса
сего раⷣ҇. да ты оуслышавъ сїа. познаеши бе
змѣрное чл҃колюбие бл҃гости бж҃їа. и оувѣ
даеши млⷭ҇ти его великꙋю тебѣ бл҃гть. и ра
зоумѣеши ис҃а хⷭ҇а въ плоти пришеⷣ҇ша сп҃ти
та. и вѣрꙋеши его быⷮ҇ бг҃а истинна ѿ бг҃а
истинна. прⷣ҇е всѣⷯ҇ вѣковъ. аще и вочлчⷭ҇и
послѣди. Видѣвъ оубо писаное гл҃юща
бг҃а. сотворимъ чл҃ка по wбразꙋ нш҃емоу
и по поⷣⷪ҇бию. и паки се быⷭ҇ адамъ ꙗко единъ
ѿ насъ. иⷤ҇е придѣте сше҃дше смѣсимъ и. иⷤ҇е
ꙗвиⷭ҇ бг҃ъ авраамꙋ полꙋдне. возрѣвъ авра
амъ видѣ. се трие мꙋжи стоꙗхꙋ верхꙋ его
и въставъ тече въ срѣтение имъ. и покло
ниⷭ҇ до землꙗ. и рⷱ҇е гⷭ҇и аще wбрѣтоⷯ҇ бл҃гть прⷣ҇е
тобою. иⷤ҇е идоста мꙋжа в содоⷨ҇. надожⷭ҇и
143r/344 гⷭ҇ь в содоⷨ҇ камыки горацїи. и wгнь ѿ гⷭ҇а посла.
иⷤ҇е се аⷥ҇ посылаю та иⷥ҇вести люди моихъ
иⷥ҇ египта да са помолиⷮ҇ бг҃ꙋ в горѣ сеи. иⷤ҇е
призва гⷭ҇ь именеⷨ҇ гн҃имъ. гⷭ҇ь бг҃ъ цр҃ъ и млⷭ҇тиⷡ҇
иⷤ҇е рече гⷭ҇ь моисею. поими вса главы люⷣски
wбличїа гⷭ҇ꙋ прамо слн҃цꙋ. и ѿврати гнѣвъ
ꙗрости гн҃а ѿ їил҃а. Сїа видѣвъ писано

to the heavens, and sent down the comforter, the Holy Spirit, and led all the nations to the knowledge of the Father.

79.7. He prefigured all these things so that men may not be taken by surprise after seeing all of them, and may not immediately tremble, crying out like Manoah, who once said to his wife, "We will die, oh woman, for we have seen God" (Judg. 13:22). Instead, | men will use these images concerning that which is 142v/343
in the future, to grasp the supreme wisdom that transcends the mind; and they will (understand) the words about God's good pleasure regarding the shocking economy of God's Son for our sake. They will worship and bless God[1028] for that, crying out like Jacob, "I saw God face to face, and yet our[1029] soul was spared" (Gen. 32:30).

79.8. Now, the things that have prefigured the future took place by the grace[1030] of his good pleasure for the salvation of humanity. And all of this is written so that after hearing about these things,[1031] you may learn about the immeasurable grace of God's love toward men, and know the grace of his great mercy to you, and recognize Jesus Christ, who came in the flesh to save you; and that you may believe that he is true God from the true God, from before all ages, but he subsequently became man.

79.9. Thus, we have examined (the following passages) of Scripture: when God said, "Let us make man in our image and likeness" (Gen. 1:26); and then, "Behold, Adam has become like one of us" (Gen. 3:22); and "Come, and having gone down,[1032] let us confuse him" (Gen. 11:7); and "God appeared to Abraham at noon. Abraham looked up and saw: Behold, three men stood in front of him. And he rose and ran to meet them. And he bowed himself to the ground. And he said, 'Lord, if I have found grace in your sight'" (Gen. 18:1–3); and "The men went to Sodom" (Gen. 18:22); and "The Lord rained down | burning sulfur on Sodom 143r/344
and sent fire—from the Lord" (Gen. 19:24); and,[1033] "Behold, I am sending you to bring my people out of Egypt that they may pray to God on this mountain" (Ex. 3:12); and "The Lord called upon the name of the Lord, 'The Lord God, compassionate and merciful'" (Ex. 34:6); and "The Lord said to Moses, 'Take all the leaders of the people and bring them out in the sun before the Lord, and the anger of the Lord will be turned away from Israel'" (Num. 25:4). After having

1028 They will worship and bless God] And they will worship and bless the true God

1029 our] cf. "my" *in the 1581 edition of the* Ostrog Bible *in Острозька Біблія* [*Ostrog Bible*], (Львів: Українське Біблійне Товариство, 2006), p. 72.

1030 grace] divine grace

1031 these things,] all these things,

1032 "Come, and having gone down,] "Having gone down,

1033 and,] and to Moses in the mountain,

въ бг҃одх҃новенныⷯ книгахъ. вѣрꙋеши единого бг҃а быⷮ въ трⷪцы. единосꙋщна. самопоⷣбна. единогⷭьсвена единосиⷧна. единовоⷧна. единопрⷭтльна. единочⷭтна. единославна ѿца и сн҃а и ст҃го дх҃а. Видѣвъⷤ паки въ сщ҃енномъ писанїи гл҃юща бг҃а. не добро быⷮ чл҃кꙋ единомꙋ. сотвориⷨ емꙋ помощницꙋ по немꙋ. иⷤе постави гⷭь херꙋвима стрещи вхоⷣ раа. пламенное ѡрꙋжие ѡбращающееса. иⷤе внити бг҃ꙋ въ храминꙋ ко авраамꙋ и асти. иⷤе рече гⷭь ѡбращꙋса и на се время прїидꙋ и боудеⷮ саррѣ сн҃ъ. иⷤе внити гⷭꙋ в содоⷨ. и ѡбноцьствовати. иⷤе братиⷭ бг҃ꙋ

143v/345 со їаковоⷨ. иⷤе в кꙋпинѣ ıавитиⷭ бг҃ꙋ моисею вѣрꙋеши въ плоти пришеⷣша їⷭса хⷭа. иⷤ слово бж҃ие сый бг҃ъ. сн҃ъ бж҃ї есть. а не простъ чл҃къ роⷣвыиса. видѣвъ писаное. ıако бг҃ъ сотвори чл҃ка. по ѡбразꙋ бж҃ию сотвори ⷢе. мꙋжа и женꙋ сотвори а. такоⷤ саррꙋ паче ⷭества престарѣвшꙋса не плодове бышꙋ. ражающꙋ сн҃а ѿ оуⷨмръшвеныⷯ ложеснъ. вѣрꙋеши сего раⷣ и дв҃ꙋ чистꙋ беⷥ мꙋжа ражающꙋ. беⷥсѣменно воплощьшаса сн҃а бж҃їа. Ꙗко идѣⷤ бжⷭтво наⷭстанеⷮ. и ıамоⷤ проходить. тамо вс҃аски чⷭтое просвѣщаеⷮ. скверноⷤ всакꙋю[1034] Видѣвъ писаное. ıако ѡбноцьствова гⷭь в содомѣ грѣшныⷯ ѕѣло. и в кꙋпинѣ гⷭа. кꙋпинаⷤ ѡгнеⷨ гораше и не съгараше. вѣрꙋеши гⷭа во ꙋтробѣ дв҃ыа прⷭто. ѳ҃. мцъ растꙋща.

1034 *Text continues in the margin:* потреблıаеⷮ.

seen all of this in the divinely inspired Scriptures, you must believe that God is one in the Trinity:[1035] the Father and Son and Holy Spirit, who are consubstantial, and each in themselves alike to the other, possessing the same lordship, the same power, the same will, the same throne, the same honor, and the same glory.

79.10. And then, we considered other matters in the sacred Scripture spoken by God: "It is not good for the man to be alone, let us make for him a helper suitable to him" (Gen. 2:18); and "The Lord placed the cherubim with a flaming weapon that turned every way to guard the entrance to paradise" (Gen. 3:24); and how God entered Abraham's tent in order to eat with him (Gen. 18:1, 8); and how the Lord said, "At this time, I will return to you at the right season, and Sarah will have a son" (Gen. 18:14); and how the Lord entered Sodom and spent the night there (Gen. 19:1–2); and how God wrestled with Jacob (Gen. 32:24); and how God[1036] appeared to Moses out of the bush[1037] (Ex. 3:2). (After seeing all of this), you must believe that Jesus Christ came in the flesh, that the Word | 143v/345
of God is divine, that he is the Son of God, and not a mere human born (from another human).[1038]

79.11. Among other things written (in the Scripture), we looked at the way "God made man, in the image of God he made him; male and female he made them" (Gen. 1:27); and also how aged Sarah gave birth to a son beyond her natural ability, despite her womb being dead and barren. In consideration of this, you should also believe that the Son of God became incarnate through the pure Virgin, who bore him without a husband and without male seed.

80. Wherever God appears and wherever he comes, purity shines forth in full measure there, while all impurity is destroyed.

80.1. After seeing what was written on how the Lord spent the night among the extremely sinful Sodomites, and how the Lord[1039] ⟨dwelled⟩ in the bush—the bush that burned with fire, but did not burn up (Ex. 3:2)—you should believe that the Lord[1040] grew within the womb of the pure Virgin for nine months

---

1035 one in the Trinity] not single, but triune

1036 God] Lord

1037 bush] bush in the mountain

1038 that the Word of God is divine, that he is the Son of God, and not a mere human born (from another human).] that the Word of God is divine—and not merely human—born from a Virgin.

1039 Lord] God

1040 Lord] he

и оутробꙋ не пожигающа. разꙋмѣв же не чтⷭ҇а сꙋща содома. в негоⷤ вшеⷣ гⷭ҇ь попаливъ еⷭ҇ потреби. в кꙋпинꙋⷹ вшеⷭ҇ гⷭ҇ь чистꙋ сꙋщꙋ ѡгнемⷤ просвѣти еѧ а не попали. вѣрꙋ ешиⷤ и гⷭ҇а в миръ плотию пришеⷣша. прегрѣ шенїа всеⷭ҇ мира потребивша. ꙗкоⷤ преже и содома скверна погꙋби. дв҃цꙋ прчⷭ҇тꙋ сꙋ щꙋ просвѣти и спⷭ҇се. ꙗкоⷤ и кꙋпинꙋ древле
144r/346 не ѡпали. видѣвъ паки писаное. ꙗко борашеⷭ҇ бгъ со їаковоⷨ до ꙋтра. и видѣвъ ꙗко не моⷤ про тивꙋ емꙋ преꙗⷭ҇ въ стегна его. вѣрꙋеши ꙗⷦ бжⷭ҇тво снатиⷭ҇ имаⷮ съ чл҃чествоⷨ. и прїимеⷮ бгъ на сѧ плоⷮ. понеⷤ преꙗсѧ въ стегна его. и вѣ рꙋеши ꙗко единъ їⷭ҇съ хⷭ҇с. бгъ и члⷭ҇къ еⷭ҇. и не смѣ шаⷭ҇ бжⷭ҇тво с плотию слитиеⷨ. но ѡба еⷭ҇ства бжⷭ҇тво и чл҃чество цѣла. въ единоⷨ составѣ не слитно їⷭ҇съ хвⷭ҇ѣ. ни бжⷭ҇твꙋ на плоⷮ преложившꙋⷭ҇. в немъ. ни плоⷮ на бжⷭ҇тво. и слыши самоⷢ того їакова прⷪ҇рчествꙋюща ѡ семъ. не ѡскꙋдѣⷮе кн҃зь гл҃а ѿ июды ни вожⷣе ѿ бедрꙋ его. дондеⷤ прїидеⷮ емꙋⷹ щадимо еⷭ҇. и тои чаꙗние ꙗзыкоⷨ. вѣрꙋешиⷤ ꙗко не раздѣли бжⷭ҇тво ѿ плоти. по снатїи бжⷭ҇твꙋ съ чл҃чествоⷨ посемꙋ. понеⷤ бгъ бораⷭ҇ не возмоⷤ противꙋ їакова. вѣдѣⷡ писание. ꙗко ꙋдержаⷭ҇ бгъ рꙋкама їаковлима и глеⷮ к немꙋ пꙋсти мѧ. и слыша ѿ члⷭ҇ка не пꙋ щꙋ тебе аще не бл҃виши мѧ. посемꙋ разꙋмѣ еши ꙋдержана ї гⷭ҇а їⷭ҇са хⷭ҇а рꙋкама оубїицъ пре дана и поимана. и мч҃ена и на крⷭ҇тъ возⷣви жена. и во гробѣ затворѧема. преⷤ оутрꙋшаса

and did not cause the womb "to burn up". Having understood the fact that in the case of impure Sodom, the Lord entered it to burn and destroy, but in the case of the bush, a plain thing, the Lord entered it to illumine with fire and not let it burn up, you should also believe that the Lord came to the world in the flesh[1041] and destroyed the transgressions of the entire world, just as he earlier destroyed unclean Sodom. (Also, believe) that he illumined the All-pure Virgin and brought salvation, just as in ancient times he (lit) the bush | without letting 144r/346
it burn up. Again, having looked at what was written on how God wrestled with Jacob[1042] until morning, (and about the fact that) "on seeing that he could not overpower him, he touched his hip" (Gen. 32:24), you should believe that it was God, who wrestled with humanity, and that God took flesh[1043] on himself, for "he touched his hip".

80.2. And you should believe that Jesus Christ is a single person, divine and human. The divinity did not mingle with the flesh into a fusion (of the two), but both natures were intact: the divinity and humanity in one person, Jesus Christ, without confusion. In him, divinity did not turn into flesh, nor did the flesh turn into divinity.[1044] And now that you have heard Jacob himself prophesying about this, (when he said), "A ruler will not fail from Judah, nor a leader from his loins, until the things stored up for him come to pass; and he is the expectation of nations" (Gen. 49:10), you should believe that when the Godhead wrestled with humanity, his divinity was not separated from the flesh. And the basis for this is, that in wrestling with Jacob, God did not overpower him[1045] (Gen. 32:24).

80.3. You learned[1046] from the Scripture how God was held in Jacob's hands, and how the former said to him, "Let me go", and (in response), he[1047] heard from the human, "I will not let you go unless you bless me" (Gen. 32:26). From this, you will recognize the way the Lord Jesus Christ was held by the hands of his murderers, and was betrayed, and was seized, and was tortured, and was lifted up on the cross, and was shut in the grave. And before that, he experi-

1041 in the flesh] *omitted*
1042 with Jacob] with Jacob in the form of man
1043 flesh] humanity
1044 divinity.] divinity. Instead, the divine and human natures remained whole and unconfused in one person.
1045 him] him, and that is why you must believe that Jesus Christ is truly God and man.
1046 learned] saw
1047 he] God

144v/347 и въспот҄ѣвша. подвизающаⷭ҇. и прослезившаⷭ҇ и алкавша и вжадавша. вѣрꙋешиⷤ҇ ꙗко бг҃ъ еⷭ҇ во плоти і҃съ х҃с. аще и пострада ꙗко чл҃къ. понеⷤ҇ водꙋ в вино прелоⷤ҇. патию хлѣⷠ҇цы. ҂е҃. мꙋжеи напита кромѣ женъ и дѣтеи. женыⷤ҇ и дѣти такоⷤ҇ насытишаⷭ҇ ѿ пати ѡнѣⷯ҇ хлѣⷠ҇цоⷡ҇. и двою рыбоу. с патию тысащию мꙋжми. мощиⷤ҇ разꙋмѣти и по семꙋ величество хлѣⷠ҇цо въ. ꙗко ѡтрочищь. е҃. хлѣбовъ ношаше. ꙗкоⷤ҇ сказоуⷮе їѡⷩ҇а бг҃ословъ. хлѣбцыⷤ҇ нарекоⷯ҇ понеⷤ҇ тоа страны хлѣбцы. ꙗковыⷤ҇ в нашеⷯ҇ странѣ просфиры въ цр҃кваⷯ҇ величествоⷨ҇. прокаженныа и бѣсныа словомъ исцѣли. раⷥслабленыа и сꙋхїа рꙋки и слаченыа сло воⷨ҇ исправи. по морю аки по сꙋхꙋ хоⷣ҇. мр҃твыа словоⷨ҇ воставі. и истлѣвша смердащаса мр҃твеца иⷥ҇ гроба возвавъ ѡживи. и самъ въ третїи дн҃ь иⷥ҇ мр҃твыⷯ҇ воскр҃се. и на нб҃са взыде. выⷤ҇ рекосте ми. ꙗко в законѣ нѣⷭ҇ писано воплотитиⷭ҇ сн҃ꙋ бж҃ию. и нѣⷭ҇ писано enced tiredness, | and he sweated, and struggled, and had tears,[1048] and was hungry, and was thirsty. 144v/347

80.4. And you will believe that Jesus Christ is God in the flesh, even though he suffered as man. For he[1049] turned water into wine (Jn. 2:1–11) and fed five thousand men, not counting women and children (e.g., Matt. 14:13–21). Women[1050] and children were nourished with those five loaves of bread and two fish just as fully as the five thousand men. And the quality of that "khlebtsy"[1051] type of bread can be gathered from the fact that the five loaves of bread were carried by a child, as John the Theologian says (Jn. 6:9). And the reason I referred to the loaves of bread as "khlebtsy" is that in terms of quality, bread in those regions was like the "prosfora"[1052] that are brought to churches in our land.[1053]

80.5. With[1054] his word, he healed the men who were leprous and demon-possessed (e.g., Matt. 8:1–4; Mk. 5:1–20); and with the same word, he restored the paralyzed (e.g., Mk. 2:1–12), and those who had withered hands[1055] (e.g., Matt. 12:9–13), and the crippled (Lk. 13:10–17); and he walked on the sea as if it was dry ground (e.g., Matt. 14:22–33), and raised the dead by speaking a word (e.g., Lk. 7:11–17); and, by calling him out of the tomb, he brought back to life the dead man who was already stinking and decaying (e.g., Jn. 11:38–44); and he himself rose from the dead on the third day (e.g., Matt. 28:1–10) and ascended[1056] to the heavens (Acts 1:9–14).

80.6. But you said to me that[1057] there is no place in the Law where it describes the incarnation of God's Son, and there is no place in the Law where

1048 before that, he experienced tiredness, and sweated, and struggled, and had tears, and was hungry,] before that, as a man, he labored, and struggled, and was hungry,

1049 For he] He

1050 Women] And it is clear that in that situation, women

1051 *"Khlebtsy" is a Slavonic word for "ordinary" bread used for meals.*

1052 *"Prosfora" is a Slavonic word for "ordinary" bread used for communion.*

1053 And the quality of that "khlebtsy" type of bread can be gathered from the fact that the five loaves of bread were carried by a child, as John the Theologian says it (Jn. 6:9). And the reason I referred to the loaves of bread as "khlebtsy" is that in terms of quality, bread in those regions was like the "prosfora" that are brought to churches in our land.] And the reason I referred to the loaves of bread as "khlebtsy" is that it is small, and in terms of quality, bread in those regions was like "prosfora" that are brought to churches in our land. And the quality of that "khlebtsy" type of bread can be gathered from the fact that the five loaves of bread were carried by a child in that desert, as John the Theologian says (Jn. 6:9).

1054 With] And with

1055 hands] *omitted*

1056 ascended] was ascended

1057 said to me that] said that according to Kosoy's assertions,

в законѣ трⷪ҇цы развѣ единⷪ҇ бг҃а. бл҃гтиюⷤ
всесⷧ҇наго ст҃го дх҃а бг҃а. показано ваⷨ быть
145r/349 в законѣ. бг҃ъ едиⷩ҇ но в трⷪ҇цы оубо ѿц҃ъ и сн҃ъ и ст҃ыи
дх҃ъ. и прѡбраженіе свѣтло сшествїа и во
плоценїа сн҃а бж҃їа. Крылошанеⷤ рѣша ми
ты дерзо писание прилагаеши к семꙋ. васⷧ҇ие
великїи не писа сⷢ҇е ꙗже ты гл҃еши. ни григо
реи бг҃ословъ. ни златоустыи їѡⷩ҇а. Ѿвѣ
щавъⷤ азъ и рѣⷱ к ниⷨ. сꙋе и тще оукараете
ма. рцыте ми оубо гдѣ писание все васⷧ҇їа
великаго видѣсте. или бг҃словле. или злаⷮоу
стⷢ҇а. в нашеи странѣ великⷢ҇а василїа. ⷣе
на токмо постническаа книга. шестодне
вникⷤа его. ї иⷤ на еретики списанїа его.
и торжественыа и мч҃ническїа. и тⷧ҇око
ванїа его ветхомꙋ писанию. и прⷪ҇рчествⷨо
и псалмомъ. в нашиⷯ странⷯа не ѡбрѣтается.
токмо на рⷭ҇жтво хⷭ҇во едино ⷢ҇е слово. и ѡ четы

it describes the Trinity, only God as a single person. Yet by the grace of the almighty God, the Holy Spirit, these things have been demonstrated to you | in 145r/349 the Law. God is indeed one, but in Trinity: the Father and Son and Holy Spirit; and the descent and incarnation of God's Son is clearly prefigured.

80.7. But the kliros-chanters said to me: "You make bold applications of Scripture here, although Basil the Great did not write about such matters as you speak of, nor did Gregory the Theologian, nor John Chrysostom". And in response, I said to them: You make a fruitless and counterproductive charge![1058] Now, tell me where you have seen[1059] all the books of Basil the Great, or of the Theologian, or of Chrysostom. For the only (writing) of Basil the Great that is available in our land is the *Book on Fasting*.[1060] And as for his *Hexaemeron*,[1061] and his writing against the heretics,[1062] and the solemn homilies,[1063] and (treatises) on the martyrs,[1064] and the commentaries on the Old Testament—whether on the Prophets[1065] or on the Psalms[1066]—none of them are found in our lands.[1067] In our land, we only have[1068] his *Homily on the Birth*

1058 You make a fruitless and counterproductive charge!] You charge me unfairly!

1059 Now, tell me where you have seen] If I have said anything that goes against the truth, then rebuke me. But if you want to suggest a different meaning (for these passages) of Scripture, you must demonstrate it. And now that you are making a reference to these great men of the church, tell me where you have actually seen

1060 the only (writing) of Basil the Great that is available in our land is the *Book on Fasting*.] we only know of one (writing) by Basil the Great, his *Book on Fasting*. *This is a reference to* Asceticon Magnum siue Quaestiones (CPG 2875).

1061 *This is a reference to* Homiliae in Hexaemeron (CPG 2835).

1062 his writing against the heretics] the writing against the heresies *This might be either of the two following texts*: Contra Sabellianos et Arium et Anomaeos (CPG 2869) or Adversus Eunomium Libri V (CPG 2837).

1063 *This is a likely reference to* Homiliae (CPG 2845–2869).

1064 *This is a likely reference to one or more of the following texts*: Homilia in Martyrem Iulittam (CPG 2849; BHG 972); In Barlaam Martyrem (CPG 2861; BHG 223); In Gordium Martyrem (CPG 2862; BHG 703); In Mamantem Martyrem (CPG 2868; BHG 1020); In Martyres Omnes (*dubia*; CPG 2941; BHG 1191m).

1065 *This is a likely reference to* Enarratio in Prophetam Isaiam (CPG 2911).

1066 *This is a reference to* Homiliae in Psalmos (CPG 2836).

1067 And as for his *Hexaemeron*, and his writing against the heretics, and the solemn homilies, and on the martyrs, and the commentaries on the Old Testament—either on the Prophets or on the Psalms—none of them are found in our lands.] And I do not know where you can find his *Hexaemeron* in our lands, and the writing against the heresies, and the solemn homilies, and on the martyrs, and the commentaries on the Old Testament—either on the Psalms or on the Prophets.

1068 we only have] we are only familiar with

редесатиⷯ мч҃нкоⷯ есть в нашё странѣ.
такоⷤ и григорїевыⷯ б҃гослова книгъ всѣⷯ нѣⷭ҇
в нашё странѣ. едина токмо. ѕ҃і. словеⷭ҇
его торжественыⷯ в нашё странѣ есть.
и злаⷮустаⷢ҇ такоⷤ не вса еⷢ҇ книги в нашё стра
нѣ ѡбрѣтаютса. ѡбаⷹ҇ вса таꙗⷤ гл҃аⷯ гл҃аша
145v/350 и ї҃ѡⷩа и григорие и васиⷧ҇ё. и аще кто хощеⷮ и сꙋ
щаа в нашё странѣ книги иⷯ прочитати.
ѡбращеⷮ ма не кромѣ словесъ иⷯ гл҃юща ваⷨ.
ѿ ниⷯ бо словесъ наꙋчиⷯса и аⷥ. наипачеⷤ то
гда при велицеⷯ сихъ ѿц҃еⷯ не быⷭ҇ еще беⷥб҃жь
ныа ереси. в неиⷤ косӧ ꙋчиⷮ раⷥвращаа ст҃аа
писанїа. посемꙋ и не быⷭ҇ вина ст҃ымъ симъ
ѡ таковыⷯ писати. и пачеⷤ ꙗко сие разꙋмѣ
ние сщ҃еннаⷢ҇ писанїа моисеѡва. вси хⷭ҇ти
ꙗне тогда вѣдахꙋ. тѣмже ни едина ноу
жа писати иⷨ ѡ сиⷯ быⷭ҇. вса сїа всѣмъ хⷭ҇тїа
номъ вѣдꙋщиⷨ. нꙋжаⷤ быⷭ҇ имъ писати. на во
зрастъшїа тогда ереси. на македонїа.
на евномїа. на арїа. и на аполинарїа. и на
савелїа. и на маркиѡна. и на прочаа ереси
иⷤ быша тогда. прⷣ҇еложꙋ вамъ единого ѿц҃а
иже ѿ треюсоⷮи. ӥі. тиⷯ. вселеⷩ҇скаⷢ҇ ст҃го со
бора перваⷢ҇. ѿ ѡсминадесатиⷯ словесъ еⷢ҇
три слова. им же послѣдовахꙋ и сами тїи
ст҃їи. василие великїи. и григорїе б҃гослоⷡ҇.

of Christ[1069] and another *On the Forty Martyrs*.[1070] Nor do we have all the books by Gregory the Theologian in our land.[1071] In our land, we only know of his sixteen solemn *Orations*. And it is the same with John Chrysostom—not all of his books are available in our land.[1072]

80.8. But even so, | John, and Gregory, and Basil say the same things[1073] that I 145v/350 have said. And if anyone wants to read the books of theirs that are available in our land, they will find that I have not said anything to you that goes contrary to their words, for I myself learned these things from them.[1074] Furthermore, during the lifetime of these great fathers, there was not yet any heresy as godless as the one presently taught by Kosoy, who distorts the sacred Scripture. Therefore, there was no need for those saints[1075] to write of such things. Moreover, at that time, these interpretations of the holy books of Moses were known to all Christians.[1076] Therefore, there was no need for them[1077] to write about such things, as all Christians knew them. What was actually needed was for them to write against the heresies that arose at that time: against Macedonius, against Eunomius, against Arius, against Apollinarius, against Sabellius, against Marcion, and against other heresies of that time.[1078]

80.9. And I would recommend to you (to read) one particular church father, blessed Cyril, the archbishop of Jerusalem, from the First Holy Ecumenical Council of the Three Hundred and Eighteen.[1079] ⟨Read⟩ three lectures of his eighteen lectures.[1080] He was followed by these other saints: Basil the Great, and

---

1069 *This is a reference to* In Sanctam Christi Generationem (CPG 2913; BHG 1922).

1070 *This is a reference to* In Quadraginta Martyres Sebastenses (CPG 2863; BHG 1205).

1071 Nor do we have all the books by Gregory the Theologian in our land.] The same also applies to Gregory the Theologian. I do not know whether we have all his books in our land.

1072 available in our land.] available to us.

1073 But even so, John, and Gregory, and Basil say the same things] But even so, these saints—John, and Gregory, and Basil—say the same things

1074 for I myself learned these things from them.] for I, too, have learned a lot from their discourses.

1075 those saints] them

1076 Christians.] Christians. For they believed in the supremely divine Trinity not in simplicity or because they borrowed things from the Jews and the Greeks, but by carefully studying the divinely inspired Scriptures. For they did not come to faith in God by force. Instead, they came to faith freely.

1077 them] these saints

1078 Marcion.] Marcion, and against other heresies of that time.

1079 *Zinoviy mistakenly relates Cyril to the Council of Nicaea in 325. It should be the Council of Constantinople instead, which took place in 381.*

1080 *This is a likely reference to* Catecheses ad Illuminandos (CPG 3585). *It contains twenty-three lectures, though Zinoviy refers to eighteen.*

и їѡⷩа златаустыи. бл҃женнаⷢ҇ кирила а
рхїеп҇кпа їерⷭ҇лмьскаⷢ҇. А ⷤе в законѣ архїерѣ̈
146ʳ/351 ство и жⷬ҇тва. пронач҃ⷮртание ⷭе хⷭ҇ва ст҃льства.
ⷤе ходатаиствоⷨ хⷭ҇выимъ приведение чл҃комъ къ
бг҃ꙋ и примирение. и кровию хⷭ҇вою ѡчищение
прегрѣшениⷨе всеⷢ҇ мира. и сп҃сение всѣмъ позна
ниⷨе бг҃а ѿц҃а и единородⷩаго ⷭе сн҃а г҃а нш҃его ї҃са хⷭ҇а.
и ст҃го дх҃а. и мнѣ ѡ архїерѣ̈ствѣ и ѡ жертвѣ
гл҃ати лишше ⷭе. поⷤне ап҃лъ павеⷭ въ еврѣистё
епистолїи извѣстно писа. и григорие бг҃о
словъ написа въ словѣ. ⷤе на пасхⷭ҇ꙋ емꙋⷢ҇ начало.
на стражи моеи станꙋ. азъⷤ елико возмо
жно и всакомꙋ бл҃гочⷭ҇тивомꙋ разꙋмѣти.
ⷤе в законѣ показание трⷪ҇цы. и проѡбраже
ние воплощению сн҃а бж҃їа сїа вамъ повѣдаⷯ.
ꙗко много ѿкровено в законѣ писано. ѡ бж҃ѣ
единомъ в трⷪ҇цы. и ѡ сшествїи сн҃а бж҃їа къ
чл҃чествꙋ. и готово ⷭе разꙋмѣти всакомꙋ
вѣрꙋющемꙋ правѣ къ бг҃ꙋ. безбж҃ьномꙋ и не
вѣрномꙋ нѣ разꙋмѣти. поⷤне тма беⷥвѣ
рїа по ѕлобѣ его помрачаⷮе емꙋ разꙋмъ. да
не восиаⷮе емꙋ свѣⷮ еѵ҃алїа бж҃їа. Какоⷤ за
конъ пѣстꙋнъствова в вѣрꙋ хⷭ҇вꙋ ап҃лъ павеⷭ
во всѣⷯ свои посланїихъ ѡ семъ сказꙋеⷮ. и мнѣ
146ᵛ/352 ѡ семъⷤ не ино что сказоваⷮ вамъ. и наⷨ бо самѣⷨ
просвѣщение и разоумъ ѡ сиⷯ ѿ ст҃го писанїа
бж҃твеныⷯ ап҃лъ ⷭе. и вы тамоⷤ во ап҃льскихъ
писанїиⷯ наꙋчитеⷭ. и аще не недꙋгꙋете беⷥ
бж҃ьствоⷨ косоⷢ҇ всако разꙋмѣете. Бл҃гⷣтию
оубо бл҃гаⷢ҇ г҃а в писанїи единосꙋщныа трⷪ҇ца

Gregory the Theologian, and John Chrysostom.[1081] (He writes) that the high-priesthood | and the sacrifices of the Law prefigure the high-priesthood and the 146r/351 ⟨sacrifice⟩ of Christ; that on account of Christ's intercession men are brought back, and are reconciled to God; and that through the blood of Christ, the whole world is cleansed of its transgression; and that everyone can be saved by coming to know God the Father, and his only-begotten Son, the Lord God, our Savior Jesus Christ, and the Holy Spirit. As for me, I find no need to write about the high-priesthood and about the sacrificial system.[1082] For this is well described by the Apostle Paul in the Epistle to the Hebrews, and it is also described by Gregory the Theologian in the *Oration on Easter*,[1083] which begins with the words, "I will stand at my watch-post".

80.10. But for my part, to the extent that I could do so by the grace of the almighty God, and to the extent that every pious man can understand it, I did tell you of how the Law reveals one God in Trinity, and prefigures the incarnation of God's Son. (I showed) that the Law contains many things that explicitly describe one God in Trinity and the descent of God's Son to humanity; and anyone who holds to right beliefs in God can readily understand it. But the godless and unfaithful man cannot understand it; for the darkness of unbelief obscures his mind, in keeping with his evil, not allowing the light of the divine Gospel to shine forth on him.

80.11. And as for the question of how the Law[1084] guided men to faith in Christ, the Apostle Paul talks about this in all of his epistles, and I | have nothing 146v/352 more to add to this for you. For we, too, as we along, learn and gain understanding about such things from the sacred Scriptures of the divine Apostles. And if you do not become infected with the godlessness of Kosoy, you will learn from the same things in the apostolic writings and understand everything. Thus, by the grace of the good God,[1085] we will be allowed to recognize the Godhead of

---

1081 And I would recommend you (to read) one particular church father, blessed Cyril, the archbishop of Jerusalem, from the First Holy Ecumenical Council of the Three Hundred and Eighteen. ⟨Read⟩ the three lectures of his eighteen lectures. He was followed by these saints (whom I mentioned): Basil the Great, and Gregory the Theologian, and John Chrysostom.] And if you are not indifferent, read the Book by Cyril of Jerusalem. He is one of the holy fathers who participated in the Second Ecumenical Council of the One Hundred and Fifty, together with these saints—Basil the Great, Gregory the Theologian, John Chrysostom.

1082 system.] system found in the Law

1083 *This is a reference to* In Sanctum Pascha II (CPG 3010 [45]).

1084 the Law] *omitted*

1085 God,] Lord God,

бжⷭтво и гⷭьство и вола едина дароваⷭ познаⷮ и косоⷢ лицемѣрнаⷢ лꙋкавъства беⷥбжїе ѡбличено быⷭ вмалѣ. бг҃ъ бо ѿц҃ъ съ единороⷣнымъ еⷢ сн҃омъ со ст҃ыⷨ дх҃мъ в бг҃одх҃новенноⷨ ветхоⷨ писанїи проповѣдаетсѧ. такоⷤ в неⷨ воплощение сн҃а бж҃їа воѡбражение сказꙋетсѧ. такоⷤⷶ законъ ст҃ѣнно писа блгⷣть бж҃ию хⷭмъ всемꙋ мирꙋ. ꙗкоⷤ пишеⷮ апⷭлъ павеⷧ въ еврїистеи епистолїи. и во всѣхъ своиⷯ посланїиⷯ. и хⷭ в ниⷯ бг҃ъ съвершенъ и чл҃къ съвершенъ исповѣдаеⷨ есть. и ꙗко архїерѣи хⷭ нбⷭнымъ блгоⷨ беⷥсмртнымъ своею кровию ст҃льствова. саⷨ себе ꙗко агньца не пороⷱна волею принесе бг҃ꙋ ѿц҃ꙋ за всѣⷯ сп҃сение. лꙋкавыⷤꙗ косоⷢ гл҃ы праⷥны. понеⷤ апⷭли проповѣдаша хⷭа не нага бг҃а и чл҃ка не проста. единоⷢ іⷭса хⷭа 147ʳ/353 бг҃а и чл҃ка. тогоⷤ распѧта и погребена по писанию. и воскрⷭша тридневно иⷥ мртвыⷯ.

Рѣшаⷤ ми крылошане косӧ не повелѣваеⷮ прочитаⷮ посланїа павлова къ еврѣѡⷨ. понеⷤ мрⷣо и не апⷭлово павлово иноⷢ павла. Ꙗко искони извѣсто еⷭ. еⷤ седми соборныⷨ апⷭльскимъ посланиеⷨ истинныⷨ быти и апⷭльскимъ воистиннꙋ. и къ еврѣемъ павла апⷭла послание воистиннꙋ еⷭ. ꙗкоⷤ[1086] Ѿвѣщавъⷤ азъ и рѣхъ к ниⷨ. в лѣпотꙋ косӧ бѣгаеⷮ апⷭльскоⷢ ко евреѡⷨ посланїа. тамо бо

1086 *Text continues in the margin*: свидѣтеⷭствоваша. аѳанасие. и василеи велицыи. и григореи, и златаустъ.

the consubstantial Trinity, and one lordship and one will in the Scripture;[1087] and soon the deceitful godlessness of the hypocrite Kosoy[1088] will be exposed. For the divinely inspired writing of the Old Testament declares God the Father together with his only-begotten Son and the Holy Spirit. And it also prefigures the incarnation of God's Son.

80.12. Likewise, the Law is written in such a way that it anticipates God's grace in Christ[1089] for the whole world, just as Paul describes it in the Epistle to the Hebrews and in all of his epistles, where Christ is confessed as fully divine and fully human, and where Christ is (depicted) as the high-priest who offered his own blood to himself, as the immortal gift of heaven; as a spotless lamb, he offered himself to God the Father by his own will for the salvation of all men. But the deceitful words of Kosoy have no weight because the Apostles did not preach only the divinity, or just the humanity of Christ. Instead, (they preached) Jesus Christ as one and the same person, | God and man, who was 147r/353 crucified and buried, according to the Scripture, and rose again from the dead in three days.

80.13. And the kliros-chanters said to me,[1090] "Kosoy does not let us read Paul's Epistle to the Hebrews because there is reason ⟨to think⟩ that this epistle belongs not to the Apostle Paul, but to a different Paul".[1091]

81. Showing that seven Catholic Epistles are known to be true and genuinely apostolic from the beginning, and that the Epistle to the Hebrews truly belongs to the Apostle Paul, as was testified by Athanasius, and Basil the Great, and Gregory, and Chrysostom.[1092]

81.1. And in response, I said to them:[1093] There is a clear reason why Kosoy avoids the apostolic Epistle to the Hebrews. For in that Epistle to the Hebrews,

1087 one lordship and one will in the Scripture;] one lordship and one will in the Mosaic writing

1088 Kosoy] *omitted*

1089 Christ] Jesus Christ

1090 to me,] *omitted*

1091 a different Paul".] some other Paul".

1092 **Showing that seven Catholic Epistles are known to be true and genuinely apostolic from the beginning, and that the Epistle to the Hebrews truly belongs to the Apostle Paul, as was testified by Athanasius, and Basil the Great, and Gregory, and Chrysostom.] Showing that all the faithful, who believe in Christ, informed us from the beginning that seven Catholic Epistles are truly apostolic, and also that the Epistle to the Hebrews truly belongs to the Apostle Paul.**

1093 in response, I said to them:] in response to them, I said:

въ евр҃ѣискомъ посланїи извѣстно ѹказѹеⷮ прообразѹема законоⷨ х҃а. егоⷤ павеⷧ бг҃а х҃а проповѣдаеⷮ в неⷨ. преⷤ вѣкъ сѹща сн҃а бж҃їа. тоиⷤ во плоти пришеⷣ закоⷩ преложи. на новъ законъ лѹчшїи. ꙗко сн҃ъ бж҃їи и ст҃ль великїи во вѣки по чинѹ мелхиседековѹ. а не проста чл҃ка ї҃са х҃а проповѣдаеⷮ въ евр҃ѣискоⷨ посланїи павелъ. и сего раⷣ ѿстѹпаеⷮ косои ѿ ѹченїа посланїа евр҃ѣискаго. понеⷤ косӧ хѹлить ї҃са х҃а. сказѹа х҃а чл҃ка проста а не бг҃а. апл҃иⷤ и самыи законъ проповѣдаю ї҃са х҃а бг҃а сѹща. ѿкѹдѹⷮ оувѣда косӧ не быⷮ посланию павловѹ
147^{v}/355 евреискомѹ. тысяща и пѧⷮсотъ лѣⷮ преидоша по ѹсѣкновенїи ап҃ла павла. до косӧ раⷥвращенїа. и никтоⷤ не ѿрече евр҃ѣискаⷢ послаⷩа пачеⷤ вси велицїи свѣтила и ѹчители. приꙗша и исповѣдаша быти ап҃ла павла къ еврѣемъ посланию. с нимиⷤ и григорие бг҃слоⷡ. златаустыиⷤ їѡⷩа и тоⷧкование изложи посланию къ евр҃ѣемъ ап҃ла павла. извѣстние сказавъ ꙗко ап҃ла павла еⷭ послание къ евр҃ѣомь. аѳанасиеⷤ великїи преⷤ григорїа и їѡⷩа собра вся ап҃льскїа книги и совокѹпи въ единѹ книгѹ. наченъ ѿ дѣанїи стыⷯ ап҃лъ. к нимъ приложи. з҃. соборныⷯ посланїи ап҃льскиⷯ. Брата гн҃а їакова послание едино. верховна ап҃ла петра посланїа два. їѡⷩа бг҃ослова посланїа три. июдино послание едино.

Paul clearly points out[1094] how Christ is prefigured in the Law, and declares Christ[1095] to be God, who, as the Son of God, existed before the ages. The same one came in the flesh and changed the old Law to a new and better Law. He is the Son of God and the great priest[1096] in the order of Melchizedek, for all ages. Paul does not proclaim Jesus Christ to be a mere man in the Epistle to the Hebrews. This is why Kosoy departs from the teaching found in the Epistle[1097] to the Hebrews, for Kosoy blasphemes Jesus Christ[1098] by describing Christ as a mere man, and not God. But the Apostles and the Law itself proclaim Christ as God.

81.2. And where did Kosoy learn that the Epistle to the Hebrews does not belong to Paul?[1099] | Now, a thousand and five hundred years have passed 147v/355
between the time the Apostle Paul was beheaded and the distortions of Kosoy, and nobody has denied the Epistle to the Hebrews. Moreover, all the great luminaries and teachers[1100]—among whom is Gregory the Theologian—accepted and acknowledged the Epistle to the Hebrews as belonging to the Apostle Paul. And John Chrysostom actually wrote a commentary[1101] on the Apostle Paul's Epistle to the Hebrews, clearly showing[1102] that the Epistle to the Hebrews belongs to the Apostle Paul.

81.3. And even prior to John and Gregory, the great Athanasius[1103] collected all the apostolic writings and put them into one book,[1104] beginning with the Acts of the Holy Apostles. To them, he added seven Catholic Epistles of the Apostles: one Epistle of James, the brother of the Lord, two Epistles of the preeminent Apostle Peter, three Epistles of John the Theologian, one Epistle of

---

1094 points out] explains
1095 Christ] him
1096 great priest] high-priest
1097 Epistle] apostolic Epistle
1098 Jesus Christ] Lord
1099 Paul] Apostle Paul
1100 luminaries and teachers] teachers and fathers
1101 *This is a reference to* In Epistulam ad Hebraeos Argumentum et Homiliae 1–34 (CPG 4440).
1102 clearly showing] and clearly showed
1103 *This is a reference to* Epistula Festalis 39.15–21 (CPG 2102).
1104 book,] book of Euphalius the Deacon, *Concerning the book of Euphalius the Deacon, see* А.А. Алексеев, ред., *Славянская Библия в эпоху раннего книгопечатания. К 510-летию создания библейского сборника Матфея Десятого* [A.A. Alekseyev, ed., *Slavonic Bible in the Period of Early Book Printing. Dedicated to the 510 years of the Creation of the Biblical Miscellany of Matfey Desyaty*], (Санкт-Петербург: Изд-во Пушкинского Дома, 2017), p. 184.

к ним же приложи. д҃і. посланїи павла апⷭ҇ла.
почитаѧ грⷣа в первыⷯ положиⷤе к римлꙗ
номъ послание едино. к коринѳомъ посла
нїа два. к галатоⷨ послание едино. къ кала
саеⷨ послание едино. к селꙋнѧноⷨ посланѧ̈ два.
къ еврѣѡⷨ послание едино. к тимоѳею
148r/356 посланїа два. к титꙋ послание едино. к ѳили
монꙋ послание едино. извѣстнѣе испытаⷡ҇
коежⷣо послание. по коемъждо быⷭ҇ послано по
рѧдꙋ счинивъ. предаде алеѯандрьстеи цр҃кви.
в первомⷤъ ст҃омъ вселеⷩ҇скомъ соборѣ по всѣмъ
цр҃квамъ ст҃їи ѿцы предаша всѧ апⷭ҇льскїа
книги. въ едино совокꙋплены. по счинению
аѳанасїа великого. ⷤе и до днⷭ҇ь хрⷭ҇тїаньскїа
цр҃кви съдержаⷮ. и никтоⷤ не ѿвержесѧ
ѿ посланїаⷤе ко еврѣѡⷨ апⷭ҇ла павла. токмо
едини хꙋлницы ѿвергошаⷭ҇ иже в беⷥбж҃ьнꙋю
ересь впадають. и сїа гл҃авше ѿити иⷨ рекоⷯ.

Judah.[1105] To them, he added fourteen Epistles of Apostle Paul: one Epistle to the Romans, which he put first, in honor of the city (of Rome), two Epistles to the Corinthians, one Epistle to the Galatians, ⟨one Epistle to the Ephesians, one Epistle to the Philippians⟩, one Epistle to the Colossians, two Epistles to the Thessalonians, one Epistle to the Hebrews, two Epistles to Timothy, | one 148r/356
Epistle to Titus, one Epistle to Philemon.

81.4. Having carefully examined each of the Epistles according to those to whom it was sent and having arranged them accordingly, he transmitted (the complete list) to the Alexandrian Church. And at[1106] the first Holy Ecumenical Council, the holy fathers transmitted the collection of all the apostolic writings to every church according to the manner in which they were organized by the great Athanasius; and this is also the way they have been kept by the Christian Churches until today. And nobody has denied that the Epistle to the Hebrews was written by the Apostle Paul. It is only blasphemers who deny it,[1107] falling into godless heresy.

81.5. And having said these things, I asked them to leave.[1108]

1105 Judah.] Apostle Judah.

1106 at] after

1107 who deny it,] who deny that the Epistle to the Hebrews belongs to the holy Apostle Paul,

1108 leave.] leave, for I became so tired that I felt exhausted.

Bibliography

Primary Sources

Акты Археографической экспедиции [*The Acts of the Archeographic Expedition*]. Том 1, № 239. Санкт-Петербург: Императорская академия наук, 1836.

Библиографические материалы, собранные Андреем Поповым. VIII. Книга Еразма о Святой Троице [*Bibliographic Materials Collected by A. Popov. Erasm's Book on the Holy Trinity*]. Москва: Издание Общества истории и древностей российских при Московском университете, 1880.

Баранкова, Г.С. & В.В. Мильков. *Шестоднев Иоанна экзарха болгарского. Памятники древнерусской мысли: Исследования и тексты* [G.S. Barankova & V.V. Milkov. *Hexameron of John the Exarch of Bulgaria. Documents of Old Russian Thought: Research and Texts*]. Выпуск 2. Санкт-Петербург: Алетейя, 2001.

Бодянский, О. *Розыск или список о богохульных строках и сумнении святых честных икон диака Ивана Михайлова Висковатого в лето 7062* [O. Bodyanskiy, *Investigation or Material of Dyak Ivan Mikhaylovich Viskovaty on the Blasphemous Lines and Doubts Regarding the Holy Honorable Icons in the Year 7062*]. Москва: Издание Общества истории и древностей российских при Московском университете, 1858.

Великие Минеи Четии, собранные Всероссийским митрополитом Макарием. Ноябрь 13–15 [*Great Menaia Reader, Collected by the Metropolitan of All Rus' Makariy. November 13–15*]. Выпуск 8. Москва: Синодальная типография, 1899.

Великие Минеи Четии, собранные Всероссийским митрополитом Макарием. Декабрь 25–31 [*Great Minaia Reader, Collected by the Metropolitan of All Rus' Makariy. December 25–31*]. Выпуск 13. Москва: Синодальная типография, 1912.

Еремин, И.П. "Литературное наследие Кирилла Туровского" [I.P. Eremin, "Kirill Turovskiy's Literary Legacy"]. In *Труды Отдела древнерусской литературы*. Том 15, 343–348. Москва–Ленинград, 1958.

Истины показание къ вопросившимъ о новом учении. Сочинение инока Зиновия [*Demonstration of Truth to Those Who Inquired about the New Teaching. The Book of Monk Zinoviy*]. Казань: Университетская типография, 1863.

Истрин, В.М. *Хроника Георгия Амартола в древнем славянском переводе. Текст, исследование и словарь. Текст* [V.M. Istrin, *Chronicle of George Hamartolos in Old Slavonic Translation. Text, Analysis, and Glossary*]. Том 1 (Slavonic Text), том 2 (Greek text). Петроград: Российская Государственная Академическая Типография, 1920.

Казакова, Н.А. & Я.С. Лурье. *Антифеодальные еретические движения на Руси XIV–начала XVI века* [N.A. Kazakova & Ya. S. Lurie. *Anti-Feudal Heretical Movements in Rus'*]. Москва–Ленинград: Изд-во Академии наук СССР, 1955.

Клибанов, А.И. & В.И. Корецкий. “Послание Зиновия Отенскому дьяку Я.В. Шишкину” [A.I. Klibanov & V.I. Koretskiy. “Zinoviy’s Letter to the Otenskiy Dyak Ya.V. Shishkin”]. In

Труды Отдела древнерусской литературы. Том 17, 201–224. Москва–Ленинград: Академия наук СССР, 1961.

Корецкий, В.И. “Новые послания Зиновия Отенского” [V.I. Koretskiy, “New Letters of Zinoviy Otenskiy”]. In *Труды Отдела древнерусской литературы*. Том 25, 120–134. Москва–Ленинград: Академия наук СССР, 1970.

Корецкий, В.И. “Вновь найденное противоеретическое произведение Зиновия Отенского” [V.I. Koretskiy, “Newly Found Anti-Heretical Writing of Zinoviy Otenskiy”]. In *Труды отдела древнерусской литературы*. Том 21, 166–182. Москва–Ленинград: Академия наук СССР, 1965.

Мильков В.В. *Древнерусские апокрифы* [V. Milkov, *The Old Russian Apocrypha*]. Санкт-Петербург: Изд-во РХГИ, 1999.

Острозька Біблія [*Ostrog Bible*]. Львів: Українське Біблійне Товариство, 2006.

Палея толковая [*Explanatory Paleya*]. Москва: Согласие, 2002.

Пенкова, П. *Св. Атанасий Александрийский. Трето Слово против арианите* [Athanasius of Alexandria. *Third Oration against the Arians*]. Том 2. София: Изд-во “Валентин Траянов”, 2016.

Полное собрание русских летописей: Летописный сборник, именуемый Патриаршей или Никоновской летописью [*Complete Collection of Russian Chronicles: The Chronicle Miscellany Known as the Chronicle of Patriarch or Nikon Chronicle*]. Том 13. Москва: Языки русской культуры, 2000.

Полное собрание русских летописей. Русский хронограф редакции 1512 года [*Complete Collection of Russian Chronicles. Russian Chronicle of the Year 1512*]. Том 22, часть 1. Санкт-Петербург: Типография М.А. Александрова, 1911.

Попов А. *Послание многословное. Сочинение инока Зиновия по рукописи XVI века (с приложением двух снимков)* [A. Popov, *Protracted Letter. The Work of Monk Zinoviy according to the Sixteenth-Century Manuscript with Two Photographs in the Appendix*]. Москва: Издание Общества истории и древностей российских при Московском университете, 1880.

Прокопенко, Л.В. *Славяно-русский Пролог по древнейшим рукописям. Тесты, источники, комментарии. Проект 2016–2020* [*The Slavonic Prologue of Russian Origin According to the Oldest Manuscripts. 2016–2020 Project*]. (http://prolog-manuscript.org/content_pr.php?page=t133d. Accessed 10.2.2023).

Просветитель или обличение ереси жидовствующихъ. Творение преподобного Отца нашего Иосифа, Игумена Волоцкаго [*Enlightener or Refutation of the Heresy of the Judaizers. The Writing of our Revered Father, Iosif, Hegumen of the Volotskiy Monastery*]. Изд. третье. Казань: Типо-литография Императорскаго Университета, 1896.

Русская историческая библиотека издаваемая Археографическою комиссиею [*Russian Historical Library Edited by the Archeographic Commission*]. Том 4. Сакт-Петербург: Типография и Хромолитография А. Траншеля, 1878.

Славова, Т. *Славянският превод на посланието на патриарх Фотий до княз Борис-Михаил* [T. Slavova, *Slavonic Translation of Patriarch Photius' Epistle to Khagan Boris-Mikhail*]. София: Университетско издателство "Св. Климент Охридски", 2013.

Тихонравов, Н.С. *Памятники отреченной русской литературы* [N.S. Tikhonravov, *Historical Texts of Recantation in Russian Literature*]. Том 2. Москва: Типография товарищества "Общественная польза", 1863.

Analecta Hymnica Graeca. Canones Martii, edited by I. Schiro. Vol. 7. Roma: Università di Roma, 1971.

Bibliotheca Hagiographica Graeca, edited by F. Halkin. Third edn. 1–3. Subsidia Hagiographica 8a. Bruxelles, 1957 (reprinted 1986).

Clavis Patrum Graecorsm: Qua Optimae Quaeque Scriptorum Patrum Graecorum Recensiones a Primaevis Saeculis Usque ad Octavum Commode Recluduntur, edited by M. Geerard. Turnhout: Brepols, 1974–1979.

Lytvynenko, V.V. *Athanasius of Alexandria, Oratio II contra Arianos: Old Slavonic Version* and *English Translation*. Patrologia Orientalis 248 (56.3). Turnhout: Brepols, 2019.

Lytvynenko, V.V. "Arius' *Thalia Fragments*: Old Slavonic Version of Athanasius' *Orations Against the Arians* 1:5–6", *Parresia. Revue pro vychodni krest'anstvi* 9–10 (2015–2016): 31–52.

Metzler, K. & K. Savvidis. *Orationes III contra Arianos*. Athanasius Werke. Die dogmatischen schriften, Band I, Teil 3, Lieferung 2. Berlin–New York: De Gryuter, 2000.

Metzler, K. & K. Savvidis. *Orationes I et II contra Arianos*, Athanasius Werke, Die dogmatischen schriften, Band II, Teil 1, Lieferung 2. Berlin–New York: De Gryuter, 1998.

Metzler, K. & K. Savvidis. *Epistula ad episcopos Aegypti et Libyae*, Athanasius Werke, Die dogmatischen schriften, Band I, Fascicle 1. Berlin–New York: De Gryuter, 1996.

Patrologiae cursus completus, edited by J.P. Migne. Series graeca. Paris, 1847–1866.

Vaillant, A. *Discours contre les Ariens de Saint Athanase. Version slave et traduction en français* Sofia: Académie des sciences de Bulgarie, 1954.

Weiher, E. & al. *Die Grossen Lesemenäen des Metropoliten Makarij: Uspenskij spisok*, Mai. Band 1: 1.–8. Mai, MLSDV 51. Freiburg i. Br.: Weiher, 2007.

Zhivova, M.V. "La ricezione del culto dei pontefici romani nella tradizione liturgico-letteraria medievale della Slavia Orthodoxa", Ph.D. Diss. Pisa: Università di Pisa, 2016 (the study includes our primary source on pp. 193–201).

Studies

Алексеев, А.А., ред. *Славянская Библия в эпоху раннего книгопечатания. К 510-летию создания библейского сборника Матфея Десятого* [A.A. Alekseyev, ed., *Slavonic Bible in the Period of Early Book Printing. Dedicated to the 510 years of the Creation of the Biblical Miscellany of Matfey Desyaty*]. Санкт-Петербург: Изд-во Пушкинского Дома, 2017.

Алексеев, А.И. *Религиозные движения на Руси последней трети XIV–начала XVI в.: стригольники и жидовствующие* [A.I. Alekseyev, *Religious Movements in Rus' During the Last Third of the XIV–early XVI Centuries: Strigolniki and Judaizers*]. Москва: Индрик, 2012.

Алексеев, А.И. *Сочинения Иосифа Волоцкого в контексте полемики 1480–1510* [A.I. Alekseyev, *The Writings of Iosif Volotskiy in the Context of the 1480–1510 Polemic*]. Санкт-Петербург: Российская национальная библиотека, 2010.

Анисимова, Т.В. "В поисках автографа Зиновия Отенского" [T.V. Anisimova, "In Search of the Autograph of Zinoviy Otenskiy"], *Обсерватория культуры*, том 13, № 6 (2016): 736–745.

Барсуков, Н.П. Источники русской агиографии [N.P. Barsukov, *Sources of Russian Hagiography*]. Том 81. Санкт-Петербург: Типография М.М. Стасюлевича, 1882.

Батунский, М.А. *Россия и ислам* [*Russia and Islam*], том 1 (Москва: Прогресс-Традиция, 2012).

Буланин, Д.М. "Зиновий Отенский" [D.M. Bulanin, "Zinoviy Otenskiy"]. In *Словарь книжников и книжности Древней Руси.* Выпуск 2 (вторая половина XIV–XVI в.), часть 1: А–К, 354–358. Ленинград: Наука, 1988.

Буланин, Д.М. "Кодикологические наблюдения над рукописью 'Послания многословного'" [D.M. Bulanin, "Codicological Observations concerning the Manuscript with the 'Letter of Many Words'"]. In *Festschrift für Fairy von Lilienfeld zum 65. Geburtstag*, edited by H.A. Rexheuser & K.H. Ruffmann, 153–164. Erlangen: Universität Erlangen–Nürnberg, 1982.

Гаврюшин, Н.К. "Первая русская энциклопедия" [N.K. Gavryushin, "First Russian Encyclopedia"]. In *Памятники науки и техники*, 119–130. Москва: Наука, 1982–1983.

Григоренко, А.Ю. "Иосифляне и нестяжатели—истоки противостояния" [A.Yu. Grigorenko, "The Josephites and the Non-Possessors"], *Вестник Русского христианского гуманитарного института* № 3 (2000): 89–95.

Дворкин, А. *Иван Грозный как религиозный тип. Статьи и материалы* [A. Dvorkin, *Ivan Grozny as a Religious Type. Articles and Essays*]. Нижний Новгород: Изд-во братства во имя Св. Александра Невского, 2005.

Дмитриев, М.В. *Православие и Реформация: Реформационные движения в восточнославянских землях Речи Посполитой во второй половине XVI в.* [M.V. Dmitriev,

Orthodoxy and Reformation: Reformational Movements in the East-Slav Lands of the Polish-Lithuanian Commonwealth in the Second Half of the XVI Century]. Москва: Изд-во Московского университета, 1990.

Емельянов, И. "Учение Феодосия Косого" [I. Yemel'yanov, "The Teaching of Feodosiy Kosoy"], *Труды Киевской духовной академии* 6 (1862): 176–215.

Емельянов, И. "Полемика против учения Косого" [I. Yemel'yanov, "Polemic with the Teaching of Kosoy"], *Труды Киевской духовной академии* 9 (1862): 88–120.

Зимин, А.А. *И.С. Пересветов и его современник. Очерки по истории русской общественно-политической мысли середины XVI века* [A.A. Zimin, *I.S. Peresvetov and his Contemporaries. Essays on the History of Russian Social and Political Thought in the mid-XVI Century*]. Москва: Изд-во Академии наук СССР, 1958.

Золотухина, Н.М. *Зиновий Отенский о власти, праве и правосудии* [N.M. Zolotukhina, *Zinoviy Otenskiy on Power, Law, and Administration of Justice*]. Москва: Норма Инфра-М, 2013.

Золотухина, Н.М. "Зиновий Отенский и Феодосий Косой: религиозно-философские, социальные и государственно-правовые воззрения" [N.M. Zolotukhina, "Zinoviy Otenskiy and Feodosiy Kosoy: Religious-Philosophical, Social, and State-Legal Beliefs"], *Историко-правовые проблемы: Новый ракурс* № 4/1 (2011): 113–141.

Казенина, Е.Т. "'Маргарит' и Историко-культурная ситуация на Руси XV–XVI в." [E.T. Kazenina, "'*The Pearl*' and the Historical-Cultural Situation in Rus' During the XV–XVI Centuries"], *Древняя Русь. Вопросы медиевистики* 4/10 (2002): 57–66.

Каравашкина, М.В. *Сочинения Зиновия Отенского в истории русского литературного языка XVI века* [M.V. Karavashkina, *The Writings of Zinoviy Otenskiy in the History of Russian Literary Language of the XVI Century*]. Диссертация. Москва: Московский педагогический государственный университет, 2000.

Калугин, Ф. *Зиновий, инокъ Отенский, и его богословско-полемические и церковно-учительные произведения. Исследование* [F. Kalugin, *Zinoviy, the Monk of the Otenskiy Monastery, and his Theological-Polemical and Church-Didactic Writings. A Study*]. Санкт-Петербург: Типография А. Катанскаго, 1894.

Клибанов, А.И. *Реформационные движения в России в XIV–первой половине XVI вв.* [A.I. Klibanov, *Reformational Movements in Russia in the XIV–first half of the XVI Centuries*]. Москва: Изд-во Академии наук, 1960.

Корецкий, В.И. "Христологические споры в России (середина XVI в.)" [V.I. Koretskiy, "Christological Controversies in Russia (mid-XVI Century)"]. In *Вопросы истории Религии и атеизма.* Том 11, 334–360. Москва: Изд-во Академии наук СССР, 1963.

Корогодина, М.В. "Переводы с греческого языка в Кормчей Вассиана Патрикеева" [M.V. Korogodina, "Texts Translated from Greek in the *Nomokanon* of Vassian Patrikeyev"], *Древняя Русь. Вопросы медиевистики* № 1/75 (2019): 161–166.

Костомаров, Н. *Исторические монографии и исследования* [*Historical Monographs and Studies*]. Том 12. Санкт-Петербург: Типография А. Траншеля, 1872.

Крюкова, А.Н. & et. Е.Е. Макаров, & Э.В. Шевченко, & И.А. Орецкая. "Ипатий" [A.N. Kryukova. & E.E. Makarov, & E.V. Shevchenko, & I.A. Oretskaya. "Hypatius"]. In *Православная Энциклопедия.* Том 26, 162–168. Москва: Церковно-научный центр "Православная энциклопедия", 2011.

Курбский, А.М. "Послание пану Кодиаку Чаплину" ["Letter to Kodiak Chaplin"]. In *Библиотека литературы Древней Руси.* Том 11, 535–537. Санкт-Петербург: Наука, 2001.

Макарий, Архимандрит (Веретенников). "Зиновий" [Makariy, Archimandrite (Veretennikov), "Zinoviy"]. In *Православная Энциклопедия.* Том 20, 149–154. Москва: Церковно-научный центр "Православная энциклопедия", 2009.

Макарий, Архимандрит (Веретенников). "Инок Зиновий Отенский—новгородский богослов XVI в." [Makariy, Archimandrite (Veretennikov), "Monk Zinoviy Otenskiy—Novgorodian Theologian of the XVI Century"], *Альфа и Омега* № 1/12 (1997): 134–156.

Морозов, С.А. *Описание собрания рукописей А.П. Голубцова (Ф. 596). Единица Хранения 46. XVII–XIX вв.* [S.A. Morozov, *Description of the Manuscript Collection of A.P. Golubtsov (F. 596). Shelf Number 46. XVII–XIX Centuries*]. Москва: Государственная Библиотека им. В.И. Ленина, 1974 (typeset description).

Морозова, Л.Е. "Тема праведного суда в сочинениях церковного публициста XVI в. Зиновия Отенского" [L.E. Morozova, "The Theme of Executing Justice in the Writings of Church Publicist of the XVI Century, Zinoviy Otenskiy"], *Палеоросия. Древняя Русь: во времени, в личностях, в идеях* № 2/10 (2018): 180–184.

Морозова, Л.Е. *Сочинения Зиновия Отенского* [L.E. Morozova, *Works of Zinoviy Otenskiy*]. Москва: Институт истории СССР, 1990.

Морозова, Л.Е. "Вопросы атрибуции 'Послания многословного'", полемического произведения XVI в. [L.E. Morozova, "Issues of Attribution of Protracted Letter, Sixteenth-Century Polemical Writing"], *История СССР* № 1 (1975): 101–109.

Петрова, В.Д. "Проблемы исихазма и древнеславянского 'плетение словес' в современной филологии" [V.D. Petrova, "Problems of Hesychasm and Old Slavonic 'Word-weaving' in Contemporary Philology"], *Вестник Чувашского университета* 1 (2011): 251–257.

Плигузов, А.И. *Полемика в Русской церкви первой трети XVI столетия* [*The Polemic in the Russian Church in the First Third of the Sixteenth Century*]. Москва: Квадрига, 2017.

Рыков, Ю.Д. "Утраченный и вновь обретенный солодовниковский список 'Истины показания' Зиновия Отенского" (историко-археографические заметки) [Yu.D. Rykov, "The Lost and Newly Found Manuscript of Solodovnikov with the *Demonstration of Truth* by Zinoviy Otenskiy (Historical Archeographical Notes)"],

144–186. In *От Средневековья к Новому времени. Сборник статей в честь Ольги Андреевны Белобровой*. Москва: Индрик, 2006.

Словарь русского языка XI–XVIII вв. [*Dictionary of the Russian Language of the XI–XVII Centuries*]. Выпуск 1 (А–В). Москва: Издательства Наука, 1975.

Словарь русского языка XI–XVII вв. [*Dictionary of the Russian Language of the XI–XVII Centuries*]. Выпуск 16 (Поднавесъ—Поманути). Москва: Наука, 1990.

Словарь русского языка XI–XVIII вв. [*Dictionary of the Russian Language of the XI–XVII Centuries*]. Выпуск 20 (Присвоение–Прочнутися). Москва: Наука, 1995.

Ткачев, Е.В. "Канонизация" [E.V. Tkachov, "Canonization"]. In *Православная Энциклопедия*, том 30, 269–359. Москва: Церковно-научный центр "Православная энциклопедия", 2012.

Фроянов, И.Я. *Драма русской истории. На путях к опричнине* [I.Ya. Froyanov, *Drama of Russian History. On the Ways to Oprichnina*]. Москва: Парад, 2007.

Шпаковский, М.В. "Естественная теология Зиновия Отенского в контексте древнерусской философской книжности" [M.V. Shpakovskiy, "Natural Theology of Zinovy Otensky in Light of the Philosophical Tradition of Medieval Russia"], *Вестник Православного Свято-Тихоновского гуманитарного университета. Серия I: Богословие. Философия. Религоведение*, том 92 (2020): 35–56.

Ульянов, О.Г. "О времени зарождения на Руси концепции 'Москва—Третий Рим' ('Donatio Constantini Magni' и 'Повесть о белом клобуке')" [O.G. Ul'yanov, "On the Origin of the Concept of 'Moscow—Third Rome' in Rus ('Donatio Constantini Magni' and 'The Legend of the White Cowl')"], 196–214. In *Терминология исторической науки. Историописание*. Москва: Институт всеобщей истории Российской академии наук, 2010.

Behr, J. *The Nicene Faith: Formation of Christian Theology*. Vol. 2, Part 1. New York: St. Vladimir's Seminary Press, 2004.

Bushkovitch, P. *Religion and Society in Russia: The Sixteenth and Seventeenth Centuries*. New York–Oxford: Oxford University Press, 1992.

Fairbairn, D. "Context, Context, Context: Athanasius' Biblical Interpretation in *Contra Arianos*", *Perichoresis* 12/2 (2014): 119–135.

Gregg, R.C. & D.E. Groh. *Early Arianism: A View of Salvation*. London: SCM Press, 1981.

Grillmeier, A. *Christ in Christian Tradition*: *From the Apostolic Age to Chalcedon (451)*. Vol. 1. Atlanta: John Knox Press, 1975.

Hanson, R.P.C. *The Search for the Christian Doctrine of God: The Arian Controversy 318–381*. Edinburgh: T&T Clark, 1993.

Lytvynenko, V.V. "Athanasius' *Orations Against the Arians*: Theological Glosses in Two Slavonic Manuscripts". In Сборникът "Преславска книжовна школа". Том 19, 77–101. Шумен: Научен център "Преславска книжовна школа", 2019.

Lytvynenko, V.V. "Joseph von Wolokolamsk". In *Biographisch-bibliographische Kirchenlexikon*. Band XL. Nordhausen: Verlag Traugott Bautz GmbH, 2019.

Lytvynenko, V.V. "Anti-Arian Arguments in Iosif Volotskij's Polemic against the Judaizers", *Parresia. Revue pro východní křesťanství* 9–10 (2015): 53–75.

Lytvynenko, V.V. & I.M. Gritsevskaya. "Athanasius in Slavonic". In *Studia Patristica.* Vol. CXXVII, 67–80. Papers presented at the Eighteenth International Conference on Patristic Studies held in Oxford 2019. Vol. 24: The First Half of the Fourth Century; Lactantius. Ed. M. Vinzent, O. Nicholson. Peeters: Leuven, 2021.

Madariaga, I. *Ivan the Terrible. First Tsar of Russia.* New Haven: Yale University Press, 2005.

Mainka, R.M. *Zinovij von Oten'. Ein russischer Polemiker und Theologe der Mitte des 16. Jahrhunderts.* Roma: Pontificium Institutum Orientalium Studiorum, 1961.

Martin, J. *Medieval Russia 980–1584.* Sec. edn. Cambridge: Cambridge University Press, 2007.

Wiles, M. *Archetypal Heresy: Arianism Through the Centuries.* Repr. Oxford: Oxford University Press, 2004.

Williams, R. *Arius.* Third edn. London: SCM Press, 2005.

Yanoshak, N. "The Author of *Poslanie Mnogoslovnoe*: A Fontological Inquiry", *Slavic Review* vol. 50, no. 3 (1991): 621–636.

Yanoshak, N. "A Fontological Analysis of the Major Works Attributed to Zinovii Otenskii", Ph.D. Diss. Georgetown: Georgetown University, 1981.

Index of Names

The figures refer to the paragraph numbers with their divisions

Panegyric to St. Hypatius of Gangra

Demonstration of Truth

Index of Biblical Quotations

The figures refer to the paragraph numbers with their divisions

Panegyric to St. Hypatius of Gangra

Demonstration of Truth